JOURNEYS IN THE WILDERNESS

JOURNEYS IN THE WILDERNESS

A John Muir Reader

Introduced by Graham White

BIRLINN

DEDICATION

For William F. Kimes (1907–1986) and Maymie B. Kimes (1909–2002) authors of *John Muir – A Reading Bibliography* (1986) – who did so much to bring John Muir's work to a wider audience in America and Scotland

and

Frank Tindall (1919–1998) – East Lothian's first Planning Officer from 1950–1975, who restored John Muir's Dunbar birthplace, established John Muir Country Park, organised the first UK exhibition on the life of John Muir and arranged the first publication of Muir's autobiographical books in Scotland.

This collection first published in 2009 by
Birlinn Limited
West Newington House
10 Newington Road
Edinburgh
EH9 1QS

www.birlinn.co.uk

ISBN: 978 1 84158 697 7

British Library Cataloguing-in-Publication Data
A catalogue record for this book is available from the British Library

Typeset by Iolaire Typesetting, Newtonmore
Printed and bound by Cox & Wyman Ltd, Reading

CONTENTS

OUR NATIONAL PARKS
(*Selection*)

THE YOSEMITE
(*Selection*)

STICKEEN
(*Complete*)

STEEP TRAILS
(*Selection*)

INTRODUCTION

This selection of John Muir's writings provides a broad introduction to the epic story of his life and achievements as mountaineer, explorer, botanist, glaciologist, conservationist, campaigner and nature-philosopher. It is not intended as a comprehensive reference library but as a collection of seminal books and essays, which will strike a chord with any reader who is interested in mountaineering, wildlife, nature conservation and environmental issues. At a deeper level, these works reveal the ethical fountainhead from which so many streams of the modern conservation movement flow.

I am grateful to Birlinn Press for allowing me to 'cherry-pick' some of Muir's finest story-telling and writing, in the hope of welcoming a new generation of readers into familiarity with John Muir as a great Scottish-American.

The current selection includes two of Muir's best-loved books in their entirety: *The Story of My Boyhood and Youth* (1913) and *My First Summer in the Sierra* (1911); many regard these as Muir's most 'complete' works in terms of style, story-telling and artistic fulfillment. The additional five sections of this volume consist of selected chapters from: *The Mountains of California* (1894), *Our National Parks* (1901), *The Yosemite* (1912), *Stickeen* (1909) *and Steep Trails* (1918).

The sequence in which these are presented does not follow the precise chronology of their publication but rather tracks the narrative arc of Muir's life, from childhood in Scotland and emigration to the United States; pioneer farming in Wisconsin; arrival in California and his 'discovery' of the 'Range of Light'. They also record Muir's witness to: the destruction of wilderness areas; his campaigns for the creation of national parks and his eventual emergence as the herald of the American conservation movement.

This book succeeds the Canongate Classics volume *John*

Muir – The Wilderness Journeys (1996) which enjoyed several editions before lapsing from print. It also reprises the earlier editions of *The Story of My Boyhood and Youth* and *My First Summer in the Sierra*, first published as Canongate Classics in 1987.

WHO WAS JOHN MUIR?

John Muir was born in Dunbar, Scotland, on 21 April 1838 and, at the age of eleven, he emigrated to the United States with his father, in February 1849. His early schooling at Dunbar Grammar gave him a grounding in English, Latin, Arithmetic and Geography; but from the time he left Scotland, he was entirely self-taught. Before he entered university at the age of twenty-two, he epitomised the pioneer-farmer, carving a home from the wilderness. His teenage years were spent in dawn to dusk labour: clearing the land, felling trees to make room for crops, with season after season of ploughing, planting, weeding and harvesting.

There were few signs during those teenage years that the Scottish farm-boy would go on to blaze the trail for an entirely new field of human endeavour – an ethical attitude to our stewardship of Nature which we now label 'Conservation'. Indeed, the talents which emerged during Muir's adolescence were largely mechanical; he seemed destined to become a great inventor and industrial entrepreneur, like his fellow Scot Andrew Carnegie. However, despite his obsession with the invention of water-clocks, barometers, thermometers, hygrometers, lathes and table-saws, Muir's ruling passion was his communion with the natural world that surrounded him in Dunbar and Wisconsin.

His later role in the birth of the American conservation movement evolved from his explorations of the mountain wildernesses of California, Oregon, Washington and Nevada. He remains the undisputed 'genius loci' of much of California, and especially of Yosemite National Park, but his wider influence persists in the dozens of national parks and nature reserves that span the American continent: from the maple forests of Appalachia to the sun-bleached canyons of Arizona; from the glaciers of Alaska to the bayous of the Florida Everglades.

Millions of Americans harbour a deep sense of gratitude

to John Muir as the founder of their national conservation movement; the first person to publicly campaign for the preservation and protection of wilderness and wildlife on a national scale. By the time of his death, on Christmas Eve 1914, he had been elevated to near-mythic status in the nation's environmental Pantheon, where he remains ensconced, along with Emerson, Thoreau and Audubon, as 'Father of the National Parks'.

Americans have named hundreds of sites in John Muir's honour, including: Muir Glacier and Mount Muir in Alaska, Muir Woods and Muir Beach near San Francisco, and the John Muir Wilderness and John Muir Trail, which follow the spine of the High Sierra. Moreover, across the length and breadth of America, hundreds of nature reserves, elementary schools, colleges, university departments and even hospitals bear his name. In Scotland, the tally of Muir-honorifics is largely confined to the single county of East Lothian and his birth-place, Dunbar.

In 1964, Congress designated his Martinez home The John Muir National Historic Site, in acknowledgement of the campaigns he fought to preserve the natural heritage of the United States. The Muir mansion is just one of 340 national historic sites and parks, comprising 80 million acres of wild land, cared for by the National Park Service, which Muir himself helped to create. Back East, in Marquette County Wisconsin, the John Muir Memorial Park overlooks the original Muir homestead at Fountain Lake. A granite memorial among the wildflowers, proclaims his epitaph:

JOHN MUIR, Foster son of Wisconsin, born in Scotland April 21st 1838.

He came to America as a lad of eleven, spent his teen years in hard work clearing the farm across this lake, carving out a home in the wilderness.

In the: 'sunny woods, overlooking a flowery glacial meadow and a lake rimmed with water lilies', he found an environment that fanned the fire of his zeal and love for all Nature, which as a man, drove him to study, afoot, alone and unafraid, the forests, mountains and glaciers of the West to become the most rugged, fervent naturalist America has produced, and the Father of the National Parks of our country.

Muir was already thirty when he arrived in California in 1868 and found work as a shepherd in Yosemite Valley, as recounted in *My First Summer in the Sierra*. However, within a few years he witnessed environmental degradation in many parts of the high country: the flower-filled alpine meadows were grazed and trampled by sheep; primeval mountain redwoods were being felled in their thousands, even blasted-down with dynamite; entire mountainsides were scoured away by gold miners using hydraulic water-jets. The erosion that resulted from the destruction of forests, meadows and mountain slopes, buried valleys, rivers and salmon beneath a shroud of rocks and mud. Moreover, the thousands of miners, loggers and herders who invaded the high country had to live-off the land; they fished, trapped, snared and shot every living creature that could be eaten: salmon, deer, bears, beaver, rabbits, birds – in a vast extermination of wildlife. The California population of grizzly bears, once more than 10,000 strong, was reduced to near-extinction during the 1880s; California finally declared the grizzly extinct in 1922; ironically, it only survives today as the iconic symbol of the 'bear-flag state'.

As a witness to the 'closing of the Western frontier', Muir felt such rapacious exploitation would soon destroy the country's remaining natural heritage, inexhaustible though it had once seemed. However, he was not eager to take on the public role of 'defender of the wilderness' and had to be persuaded by his friends that this was indeed the challenge he was made for. In 1889, encouraged by Robert Underwood Johnson, the influential editor of *Century Magazine*, Muir began to campaign for Yosemite to be rescued from the exploitative care of the State of California, and brought under the aegis of federal protection. This eventually led to a much-expanded Yosemite National Park, whose boundaries were largely proposed by Muir himself. The 1200 square miles of the new Yosemite National Park were established by Congress in 1890; the very first national park, Yellowstone, had been created in 1871.

However, Muir's seminal victory in Yosemite would not ensure protection of the nation's wider landscapes and ecosystems; political influence and legislation by Congress seemed the only way forward. In 1893 Muir played a leading role in the creation of the Sierra Club, to lobby for the protection of other wilderness areas as national parks; he served as the Club's founding president and national figurehead until his death in 1914.

After Muir's death, Robert Underwood Johnson sounded the paean for his friend:

> Muir's public services were not merely scientific and literary. His countrymen owe him gratitude as the pioneer of our system of national parks. Before 1889 we had but one of any importance, the Yellowstone. Out of the fight which he led for the better care of Yosemite by the state government grew the demand for extension of the system. To this many persons and organisations contributed, but Muir's writings and enthusiasm were the chief forces that inspired the movement. All the other torches were lighted from his . . . John Muir was not a 'dreamer', but a practical man, a faithful citizen, a scientific observer, a writer of enduring power, with vision, poetry, courage in a contest, a heart of gold and a spirit pure and fine . . .

President Theodore Roosevelt also wrote a heartfelt eulogy:

> His was a dauntless soul. Not only are his books delightful, not only is he the author to whom all men turn when they think of the Sierras and Northern glaciers, and the giant trees of the California slope, but he was also – what few nature-lovers are – a man able to influence contemporary thought and action on the subjects to which he had devoted his life. He was a great factor in influencing the thought of California and the thought of the entire country so as to secure the preservation of those great natural phenomena – wonderful canyons, giant trees, slopes of flower-spangled hillsides . . . our generation owes much to John Muir.

The scale of the legacy which Muir and the Sierra Club bequeathed to posterity is evident in America's National Parks, National Monuments and National Historic Sites: 376 protected zones ranging from Hawaii to Florida and Arizona to Alaska. More than 80 million acres of wild land are conserved within the fifty-four national parks; one single area, the Wrangell-St. Elias National Park in Alaska, extends to 13 million acres. The US Forest Service, whose earliest reserves were surveyed and recommended for protection by Muir, is responsible for 191 million acres, while the Fish and Wildlife Service manages a further 91 million acres of wild ecosystems. Arguably, more than 360 million acres of America are managed and protected, to varying degrees, as a result of the national movement for which John Muir carried the banner. America's national parks encompass an area four times greater than Scotland's entire land-area of 19.5 million acres.

Awareness of that historic debt remains undimmed in the national consciousness; on the 150th anniversary of Muir's birth, 21 April 1988, it was resolved that:

> . . . by the Senate and House of Representatives of the United States of America: that April 21, 1988, is designated as 'John Muir Day', and the President is authorized and requested to issue a proclamation calling upon the people of the United States to observe such day with appropriate ceremonies and activities.

*

The Story of My Boyhood and Youth (1912) was written when Muir was over seventy years of age, but he paints a colourful picture of his Dunbar childhood with clarity, insight and a wry Scottish humour. The opening paragraph is one of the most vivid evocations of a childhood experience of Nature:

> When I was a boy in Scotland, I was fond of everything that was wild, and all my life I've been growing fonder and fonder of wild places and wild creatures. Fortunately, around my native town of Dunbar, by the stormy North Sea, there was no lack of wildness . . . with red blooded playmates, wild as myself, I loved to wander in the fields, to hear the birds sing, and along the seashore to gaze and wonder at the shells and seaweeds, eels and crabs in the pools among the rocks when the tide was low.

In this book Muir allows us a glimpse of the childhood Eden, from which most of us are excluded as adults, but to which, somehow, he always found the way back.

It evokes Wordsworth's 'Intimations of Immortality in Recollections of Early Childhood', Blake's 'Auguries of Innocence' and Burns's poems; all books with which Muir had a deep familiarity.

John was sent to school at three, and at seven he entered Dunbar Grammar School to study English, Latin, French, Maths and Geography. Here he absorbed Scottish culture and history, from Bannockburn and Flodden to Burns and the Border Ballads. Muir's school-book heroes were William Wallace and Robert the Bruce, and with eager school-mates he often re-enacted the Wars of Independence among the ruins of Dunbar Castle, where Bruce and Wallace had once skirmished. To the end of his days, Muir remained a passionate devotee of all things Scottish; he was a fervent nationalist and supporter of James Bryce's Home Rule Bill at Westminster, and even after sixty years in America he still spoke with friends and family in vernacular Scots. For many years in California he paid a newspaper clippings service to send him the national press reports of every Burns Night celebration held throughout Scotland.

In the 1840s, letters and newspapers from America filtered back to Dunbar from Scots emigrants, encouraging relatives to join them in the promised land. John Muir's imagination was sparked by fireside tales of vast prairies and endless forests, filled with grizzly bears, wolves, mountain lions and war-bonneted indians; of maple trees dripping with syrup, and creeks sparkling with gold-dust. America was a country where eagles perched on every branch, and passenger pigeons darkened the sky from horizon to horizon, in uncountable myriads. Emigration offered the boundless possibilities of this young nation to millions of poor Scots and Irish, who had survived the potato famine of 1846.

In February 1849, encouraged by fellow Scottish 'Disciples of Christ' already in Wisconsin, Daniel Muir set sail in search of religious freedom, with the promise of cheap land and a better life for his family. Thus, at the age of eleven, with his sister Sarah and brother David, John Muir 'sailed away from Glasgow, carefree as thistle seeds on the wings of the winds, toward the glorious paradise over the sea'. The family endured a six-week winter voyage across the North Atlantic, on an unpowered, square-rigged vessel, crowded with emigrants; some fleeing the potato famine, others seeking land, or hoping to reach the California goldrush of that year.

On arrival in New York, the Muir family faced a long journey by train and boat to Chicago, thence by steamer Westward across the Great Lakes and onward by train and covered-wagon to Kingston, Wisconsin, where Daniel Muir purchased a section of unploughed prairie and woodland.

Near the end of his life, Muir recalled his first impression of the untouched wilderness at Fountain Lake:

> This sudden splash into pure wildness – baptism in Nature's warm heart – how utterly happy it made us! Nature streaming into us, wooingly teaching her wonderful glowing lessons, so unlike the dismal grammar ashes and cinders so long thrashed into us. Here, without knowing it, we were still at school; every wild lesson a love lesson, not whipped but charmed into us. Oh, that glorious Wisconsin wilderness!

But it was endless manual work which dominated Muir's first decade in Wisconsin, where he slaved as unpaid 'ploughboy, well-digger and lumberjack' under his father's Calvinist discipline. Daniel Muir often beat his sons for the smallest infraction, and refused to call a doctor, or allow time from work when John contracted mumps, and later pneumonia. As the boys grew into young men, their father increasingly left the physical work to them while he pursued his vocation as an evangelical preacher. Somehow, John Muir survived the hardships; he escaped to the solitude of the woods and the pristine lake fringed with water lilies; he immersed himself in books borrowed from Scottish neighbours and devoured Shakespeare, Wordsworth, Burns and Euclid. His literary heroes were Robert Burns and the explorer of South America, Alexander von Humboldt, whose adventures he hoped to emulate. Self-taught from the age of eleven, Muir showed signs of innate genius in his early teens, by the construction of a series of original, hand-made machines. Clocks, barometers, thermometers, semi-automatic table saws, an 'early-rising machine' all flowed from his fertile brain, whittled from hickory or with metal scavenged from farm implements. It was the fame of these inventions among the farming community, which eventually gained him admission to the University of Wisconsin at Madison in 1861. It was here, aged 23, that he first encountered minds like his own, and set his course for the future.

At Madison he came under the influence of 'Geology' Professor Ezra Carr, who was creating a revolution in university education at that time – insisting that students derive their facts from direct observation and testing of Nature in the field, rather than from theological textbooks, classical authorities and metaphysics. Jeanne Carr, the professor's wife, became Muir's lifelong friend and literary mentor, opening doors to the higher strata of American society and winning social influence for him through her extensive connections with luminaries such as Emerson.

My First Summer in the Sierra, published in June 1911, was assembled by Muir from his Yosemite journals of the 1870s. Muir's bibliographers, William and Maymie Kimes wrote of this book:

> Muir was seventy-two years old when he began to prepare his journal of his first summer in the Sierra for publication. With the skilful editing of his mature years, he retains the refreshing spontaneity of his youthful experience and observations, interspersed with his lyrical and oft-times mystical reflections. This book, published near the apex of his career, reaps the competence of age while capturing the essence of youth, and becomes, we believe, his finest book.
>
> (*John Muir, A Reading Bibliography*, section 299, p85)

*

The *First Summer* recounts Muir's arrival in California via the Panama Canal, following his thousand-mile walk from Indianapolis to the Gulf of Mexico. Disembarking at San Francisco in March 1868, he was repelled by the noise, poverty and crude materialism which he found in this burgeoning metropolis. Asking for 'the quickest way out of town' he hiked across the Central Valley to find work as a shepherd in the Yosemite high country. For the next seven years he based himself in and around Yosemite, exploring the High Sierra, developing his skills in botany, geology, ecology and climbing.

Self-taught as always, he declared he would 'read from the great book of Nature', trusting only his own observations and measurements, verifying every fact with his own eyes.

The book has been described as 'the journal of a soul on fire', and certainly Muir's first encounters with the glories of the High Sierra peaks, the flower-filled alpine meadows and the dashing waterfalls and streams seem filled with rapture; he experienced this paradaisical landscape as both a scientific revelation and a mystical epiphany. A deeply evangelical Christian, though not a church-goer, Muir was steeped in Scripture from his earliest days. He had been forced to memorise the entire New Testament before the age of eleven, and wrote that he 'had much of the Old Testament by heart as well'. But standing on the pinnacles of the High Sierra, bathed in the alpen-glow of the 'Range of Light', he forsook the gloomy Calvinism of his father's preaching for a more Romantic, environmental creed, whose prophets were Thoreau, Emerson, Wordsworth, Blake and Burns. A famous epigram which he wrote in the Sierras captures his beliefs in a single line:

My Altars are the Mountains, Oceans, Earth and Sky.

John Muir remained a Christian all his life, but a profound nature-mysticism pervades his writing from this period. After years alone in the mountains, studying the plants, the rocks, the glaciers and the wild creatures, Muir experienced a transcendental vision of Nature in which every rock, stream, plant and animal in the landscape seemed transfigured; each a divine manifestation, a unique thread in the intricately woven tapestry of life, from which no fibre could be teased without unravelling the fabric. Muir sensed a divine presence behind all created things, shining through them, imbuing them with profound meaning and infinite beauty. It is clear from the following passages that Muir was exploring the boundaries of a new area of Science, which today we call Ecology, though that term had only been coined by Haeckel in 1868.

He wrote:

Everything is flowing – going somewhere; animals and so-called lifeless rocks, as well as water. Thus the snow flows fast or slow in grand beauty-making glaciers and avalanches;

the air in majestic floods carrying minerals, plant leaves, seeds, spores, with streams of music and fragrance; water streams carrying rocks . . . While the stars go streaming through space pulsed on and on forever like blood . . . in Nature's warm heart.

and

When we contemplate the whole globe as one great dew-drop, striped and dotted with continents and islands, flying through space with all the other stars, all singing and shining together as one, the whole universe appears as an infinite storm of beauty. This grand show is eternal. It is always sunrise somewhere; the dew is never all dried at once; a shower is forever falling; vapor ever rising. Eternal sunrise, eternal sunset, eternal dawn and gloaming, on seas and continents and islands, each in its turn, as the round earth rolls.

THE REDISCOVERY OF JOHN MUIR IN SCOTLAND

In marked contrast with Muir's historic status in America, he was almost completely forgotten in Scotland until the late 1960s; none of his books were published in the UK until 1987, when Stephanie Wolfe Murray of Canongate Press published the first British editions of *The Story of My Boyhood and Youth* and *My First Summer in the Sierra*.

The event which catalysed the 'rediscovery' of Muir in Scotland occurred when Bill and Maymie Kimes, eminent Californian bibliographers of Muir, undertook a literary pilgrimage to Dunbar in 1967. They wrote in advance to the town's Lady Provost asking if some local historian could guide them around Dunbar Castle, Muir's High Street birthplace and the beaches of Belhaven, where he had first encountered wild nature in the 1840s. On receipt of this letter, the Provost was somewhat non-plussed and began an urgent search for background material on Muir, of whom she knew little. To her chagrin, neither Dunbar library nor the county library in Haddington had a single copy of any book by John Muir; the National Library in Edinburgh drew a similar blank. Eventually, some Muir books were borrowed from a library in Plymouth on the south coast of England, 500 miles to the south, and some information was gleaned.

Bill and Maymie Kimes were fêted with civic hospitality in Dunbar; on their return to California they wrote and suggested the ancient Burgh might acknowledge its most famous son by a plaque on the house in which he was born – at that time a shop. The Provost replied to say that a plaque had been agreed upon by the town council; it was installed on the building in 1969 with the inscription: 'Birthplace of John Muir, American Naturalist, 1838–1914'.

The 600th anniversary of the founding of the Royal Burgh of Dunbar followed in 1970 and, stimulated by the Kimes's visit, a modest exhibition of Muir books and photographs was arranged by the East Lothian Planning Department. The exhibition organiser was Frank Tindall, the first County Planning Officer employed in Scotland; but until the Kimes visit, he had heard nothing of John Muir. In 1974 Tindall began negotiations with the Earl of Haddington to lease part of the Tyninghame coastline, now designated as John Muir Country Park and officially opened in 1976. The name was actually proposed by Tindall's assistant, Ian Fullerton. This 1660-acre nature reserve ranges eight miles from the ruins of Dunbar Castle to Tyninghame sands in the west and overlooks the distant colonies of gannets, kittiwakes and guillemots on the Bass Rock. For many thousands of subsequent visitors, the park at Belhaven has been an introduction to the Scottish origin of Muir's story.

In 1977, Tindall planned a family holiday to California, determined to track-down the full story of Dunbar's most famous emigrant. Tindall's son was then studying architecture at Pennsylvania University and they hiked together in Yosemite National Park and visited Muir Woods and Muir Beach, north of the Golden Gate. To celebrate 'John Muir Day' on April 21st, the Tindall family were guests of honour at a Sierra Club barbecue in the grounds of Muir's Martinez mansion and later they stayed with Bill and Maymie Kimes at their Mariposa ranch. On returning to Scotland, Tindall was convinced that Scots should be made aware of the global stature which their kinsman had achieved, but he discovered that Muir's Dunbar birthplace was now threatened with redevelopment as a fish and chip shop! Fortunately, Tindall had few difficulties agreeing with Daisy Hawryluk, the owner of the building, that the upper floor should be converted into a Muir-birthplace museum while a photographic studio should be created on the ground floor.

The restoration of the historic house by East Lothian Council went ahead and in 1980 John Muir House was opened to the public; thousands of tourists and school-children visited over the next twenty years, with the Hawryluk family serving as unpaid, honourary curators.

Tindall was surprised to discover that in 1978 the National Library of Scotland still did not hold a single copy of any Muir book, nor any of the various biographies and literary analyses produced since 1924. He met with Professor Denis Roberts, the Director of the National Library and with Alexia Howe, the Assistant Keeper, who gladly agreed to collaborate on the first Scottish exhibition of Muir's life: 'A Man of the Wilderness: John Muir (1838–1914)', which was held at the library in July 1979. The annual report of the library for that year states:

> A private view of the exhibition was held at the National Library on 13th July and the exhibition was opened by The Right Hon. The Earl of Haddington. Sequoia seeds procured from the United States by Mr Frank Tindall, from whom came much of the enthusiasm for the Muir exhibition, were successfully germinated in Fochabers, and Sequoia seedlings were distributed to guests attending the private view.

For thousands of Scots this event was the portal to an awareness of the true scale of Muir's international legacy and status. With advice from the Kimeses in California, Alexia Howe began a comprehensive collection of Muir books and manuscripts from America for the National Library, which culminated in the acquisition of the complete microfilm edition of the entire collected John Muir Papers, in manuscript format. The microfilm edition was created in 1986 by the staff of the John Muir Center, of the Holt Atherton Institute, at the University of the Pacific in Stockton, California, where the John Muir Papers are preserved.

More recently, the Holt Atherton Institute has digitised the entire John Muir Papers and made them freely available online at: http://library.pacific.edu/ha/muir/content.asp.

This digital archive comprises: 7000 original letters; 485 original manuscripts, including book drafts, magazine articles and notebooks; 84 of Muir's surviving field-journals and the sketchbooks from his expeditions, spanning the period 1867–1913; 3000 photographs collected by Muir; and over 350 items of memorabilia, including his passport, herbarium lists, poems, a lock of his father's hair etc.

The donation of the earlier microfilm archive to the National Library was arranged by Bill and Maymie Kimes from California in 1986. However, there was still the issue that, for people in the UK, Muir's books remained difficult to obtain except by import from the USA.

In the light of this, Frank Tindall approached Stephanie Wolfe Murray at Canongate Publishing in Edinburgh with the aim of creating the first Scottish editions of Muir's works. This led to the publication of *The Story of My Boyhood and Youth* in 1987, followed a year later by *My First Summer in the Sierra*, both issued as Canongate Classics with the support of the Scottish Arts Council. These were later re-issued in 1996 as part of a five-volume omnibus, compiled by the present writer, entitled *John Muir, The Wilderness Journeys*. This compilation included three other books: *The Thousand Mile Walk to the Gulf*, *Travels in Alaska* and *Stickeen*.

In 1999 I was privileged to serve as the educational curator of a major international exhibition on the life of John Muir, 'An Infinite Storm of Beauty', which was created and hosted by the Edinburgh City Art Centre as part of its contribution to the Edinburgh International Festival. The US National Parks Service generously allowed the transatlantic loan of over 200 Muir artefacts from the Muir National Historic Site and other NPS museums; the Muir-Hanna family loaned priceless oil-paintings by William Keith, along with many other personal possessions of John Muir, which were allowed to leave the country for the very first time. The Festival exhibition was a great success, with over 30,000 people attending during its six-week run.

The repatriation of Muir's ideas and ethos to Scotland has involved action as well as ideas. In 1983, four years after the exhibition at the National Library, the John Muir Trust was founded in Scotland, to purchase and conserve wild land for future generations and to foster Muir's conservation ethos in Scotland and the UK, see (http://www.jmt.org/home.asp). To date the Trust has raised funds to purchase a number of areas of wild land in the Highlands and Islands, totalling over 50,000 acres: Li and Coire Dhorrcail in Knoydart (1987); Torrin on the Isle of Skye (1991); Sandwood Bay in Sutherland (1993); Strathaird and Bla Bheinn in the Skye Cuillin (1994); part of Shiehallion (1999); and Ben Nevis (2000). None of these areas is untouched 'wilderness' in the American sense; they all have crofting communities and people have lived there for hundreds of years, possibly thousands. Whatever the label, these wild landscapes, the haunt of the golden eagle, red deer and otter, are among the most beautiful and unspoiled in Britain. The John Muir Trust aims to demonstrate exemplary management of these areas, sharing responsibility with local communities for the sustainable use of the landscape, wildlife and natural resources. It aims to foster a wider knowledge of Muir's life and work among the Trust members as well as the general public.

THE JOHN MUIR AWARD

In 1994 I proposed to the John Muir Trust that it should foster an award for environmental endeavour, to be called the John Muir Award. This was intended to address the fact that, at that time, very few young Scots were involved in conservation, from a potential youth membership of over 1.3 million. Initially, the JMT trustees were not enthusiastic and the Award was only created due to the leadership of the Director of the Trust, Terry Isles, and the energetic advocacy of trustee Ben Tindall. The award scheme was launched in February 1997 with support from Scottish Natural Heritage and now has programmes and staff in Scotland, England and Wales. Students from Yosemite Valley Elementary School in California have also completed the Award as a transatlantic venture. The Award is non-competitive, open to all, makes no financial charge, and is offered in partnership with a wide range of schools, universities and youth organisations. It welcomes people of all ages to lifelong involvement with the environmental movement, with the emphasis on direct experience of conservation via personal action and outdoor adventure. At the time of writing, more than 100,000 people have completed the John Muir Award in the UK; it is widely regarded as being the most successful of the John Muir Trust's educational initiatives.

*

As long ago as 1888, John Muir wrote, in 'Essay on Mt Shasta':

> The great wilds of our country, once held to be boundless and inexhaustible, are being rapidly invaded, and everything destructible in them is being destroyed. Every landscape, low and high, seems doomed to be trampled and harried. The wedges of development are being driven hard and none of the obstacles or defences of nature can long withstand the onset of this immeasurable industry.

The environmental issues which Muir confronted during the 1880s contained the seeds of the current crisis faced by every nation in the twenty-first century: where do we draw the line in the exploitation of natural resources? How much development should be allowed in the wider countryside? What level of agricultural and industrial development, of roads, housing and power generation is sustainable, and for how large a population should we plan?

Muir's writings evoke a deep resonance with the issues which have dominated the public agenda in America and Europe throughout 2009. International financial and banking ruin, global warming fears, the collapse of fish-stocks in every ocean, the continued burning of the rain-forests, the extinction of species, the depletion of fossil-fuel reserves, the threat of 'dangerous climate change' and uncontrolled sea-rise. Other disturbing issues involve the continuing decline in British wildlife, the deaths of millions of honeybee colonies in America and Europe – all remind us that the issues which Muir confronted persist today; but they have proliferated to a global scale with labyrinthine complexity.

Currently, the UK faces the issue of whether it can support an officially forecast increase of ten million in population by the year 2030, overwhelmingly through economic migration. This would mean an unprecedented 14% increase in UK population within twenty years, and would require the infra-structure equivalent of seven new cities the size of Birmingham. This raises critical questions of where the houses, roads, power stations and schools required to cope with such a huge population increase could possibly be built. Where would the food, water, energy and recreational space be found to give such a populace a decent standard of living? At the time of writing not one environmental NGO in America or the United Kingdom seems willing to question the sustainability of such population increase or migration policies, even though these issues lie at the very heart of any nation's future social, economic and environmental wellbeing.

The UK government has similarly announced its intention to approve 8,000 new wind turbines to meet its renewable energy targets. If this programme goes ahead, virtually every mountain ridge and moorland in the UK will have a chain of 150 metres high industrial structures imposed upon it, linked by a web of new electricity pylons. It had been widely assumed that the National Parks would escape this industrialisation but at the time of writing, it has just been announced that even these wildest of landscapes must 'bear their share' of the march of the wind machines. The argument is, that to preserve the wild and beautiful landscapes of Snowdonia, Dartmoor, the Lake District and the Scottish Highlands from 'dangerous climate change' we must destroy their very wildness by erecting wind turbines on every mountain, ridge and moor. The logic echoes that of an American general during the Vietnam War who, after bombing and shelling the former Vietnamese imperial capital of Hue into a heap of charred ruins beside the Perfume River, said: 'in order to save it (from Communism), we had to destroy it'.

The catastrophe triggered by the globalisation of finance, markets, labour and resources which brought the world economy to the brink of total collapse in 2009 was foreseen by Muir in the 1880s. The environmental issues in his time pivoted on the 'robber barons' desire to convert every natural asset into a 'dollarable commodity' for sale to the highest bidder in distant markets, regardless of the human or environmental cost. Consider this, written in 1889:

> If possible, and profitable, every tree, bush and leaf, with the soil they are growing on . . . would be cut, blasted, scraped, shovelled and shipped away, to any market, home or foreign. Everything, without exception, even to Souls and Geography, would be sold for money, could a market be found for such articles.
>
> (*San Francisco Daily Evening Bulletin* – 29 June 1889)

In the UK, the corruption and greed of our political and business elites in parliament, the banks and a host of other public agencies has dominated public discourse throughout 2009. Muir had bitter experience of politicians and lawyers who were willing to sacrifice any public asset to feed their own greed. He wrote:

> If only one of our grand trees on the Sierra were preserved as an example . . . of all that is most noble and glorious in mountain trees, it would not be long before you would find a lumberman and a lawyer at the foot of it, eagerly proving, by every law terrestrial and celestial, that that tree must come down . . . The battle we have fought, and are still fighting, is a part of the eternal conflict between right and wrong, and we cannot expect to ever see the end of it.
>
> (Sierra Club Bulletin, January 1896)

There was no end to the environmental struggle:

> I often wonder what Man will do with the mountains? Will he cut down all the trees to make ships and houses? If so, what will be the final and far upshot? Will human destructions, like those of Nature – fire, flood and avalanche – work out a higher good, a greater beauty? Will a better civilisation come . . . ? What is the human part of the mountain's destiny?

In bringing this new collection of John Muir's writings to the public, it is hoped that readers will find inspiration in confronting current environmental and economic issues, from the vision and example of John Muir in the nineteenth century.

AFTERWORD

The Scottish Parliament established its first national parks at Loch Lomond and the Trossachs in 2002, and the Cairngorms in 2003. It is ironic that the land of Muir's birth waited more than a century after his creation of Yosemite National Park in 1890 before it followed his example. A great opportunity was missed – in that no attempt was made to link the establishment of Scotland's first national parks to Muir's historic role in the creation of America's parks. Indeed, apart from East Lothian Council's designation of 'John Muir Country Park' no other reserve has been named for Muir in Scotland or the entire UK.

Perhaps some future government will eventually name a national park or coastal reserve in honour of John Muir, to acknowledge his seminal influence in global nature conservation. The 2014 centenary of his death gives us a five-year time window to consider such a visionary act. The efforts to repatriate Muir's conservation ethos and to establish his ideas in Scotland's education system and institutions have mostly sprung from East Lothian Council, the John Muir Trust, and the enthusiasm of individuals. With few honourable exceptions, Muir's life and achievements remain unknown and unreflected in the curricula of Scotland's schools, colleges and universities, and unacknowledged in the work of any department of Scottish and UK government, or their various quangos. It would be timely if this educational and cultural vacuum were to be addressed in time for Muir's centenary, in honour of this great Scottish-American.

Graham White
Coldstream, July 2009

THE STORY OF MY BOYHOOD AND YOUTH

(1913)

Chapter 1

A BOYHOOD IN SCOTLAND

When I was a boy in Scotland I was fond of everything that was wild, and all my life I've been growing fonder and fonder of wild places and wild creatures. Fortunately around my native town of Dunbar, by the stormy North Sea, there was no lack of wildness, though most of the land lay in smooth cultivation. With red-blooded playmates, wild as myself, I loved to wander in the fields to hear the birds sing, and along the seashore to gaze and wonder at the shells and seaweeds, eels and crabs in the pools among the rocks when the tide was low; and best of all to watch the waves in awful storms thundering on the black headlands and craggy ruins of the old Dunbar Castle when the sea and the sky, the waves and the clouds, were mingled together as one. We never thought of playing truant, but after I was five or six years old I ran away to the seashore or the fields most every Saturday, and every day in the school vacations except Sundays, though solemnly warned that I must play at home in the garden and back yard, lest I should learn to think bad thoughts and say bad words. All in vain. In spite of the sure sore punishments that followed like shadows, the natural inherited wildness in our blood ran true on its glorious course as invincible and unstoppable as stars.

My earliest recollections of the country were gained on short walks with my grandfather when I was perhaps not over three years old. On one of these walks Grandfather took me to Lord Lauderdale's gardens, where I saw figs growing against a sunny wall and tasted some of them, and got as many apples to eat as I wished. On another memorable walk in a hayfield, when we sat down to rest on one of the haycocks I heard a sharp, prickly, stinging cry, and, jumping up eagerly, called Grandfather's attention to it. He said he heard only the wind, but I insisted on digging into the hay and turning it over until we discovered the source of the strange exciting sound – a mother field mouse with half a dozen naked young hanging to her teats. This to me was a wonderful discovery. No hunter could have been more excited on discovering a bear and her cubs in a wilderness den.

I was sent to school before I had completed my third year. The first schoolday was doubtless full of wonders, but I am not able to recall any of them. I remember the servant washing my face and getting soap in my eyes, and Mother hanging a little green bag with my first book in it around my neck so I would not lose it, and its blowing back in the sea-wind like a flag. But before I was sent to school my grandfather, as I was told, had taught me my letters from shop signs across the street. I can remember distinctly how proud I was when I had spelled my way through the little first book into the second, which seemed large and important, and so on to the third. Going from one book to another formed a grand triumphal advancement, the memories of which still stand out in clear relief.

The third book contained interesting stories as well as plain reading and spelling lessons. To me the best story of all was 'Llewellyn's Dog,' the first animal that comes to mind after the needle-voiced field mouse. It so deeply interested and touched me and some of my classmates that we read it over and over with aching hearts, both in and out of school, and shed bitter tears over the brave faithful dog, Gelert, slain by his own master, who imagined that he had devoured his son because he came to him all bloody when the boy was lost, though he had saved the child's life by killing a big wolf. We have to look far back to learn how great may be the capacity of a child's heart for sorrow and sympathy with animals as well as with human friends and neighbors. This auld-lang-syne story stands out in the throng of old schoolday memories as clearly as if I had myself been one of that Welsh hunting-party – heard the bugles blowing, seen Gelert slain, joined in the search for the lost child, discovered it at last happy and smiling among the grass and bushes beside the dead, angled wolf, and wept with Llewellyn over the sad fate of his noble, faithful dog friend.

Another favorite in this book was Southey's poem 'The Inchcape Bell,' a story of a priest and a pirate. A good priest in order to warn seamen in dark stormy weather hung a big bell on the dangerous Inchcape Rock. The greater the storm and higher the waves, the louder rang the warning bell, until it was cut off and sunk by wicked Ralph the Rover. One fine day, as the story goes, when the bell was raging gently, the pirate put out to the rock, saying, 'I'll Sink that bell and plague the Abbot of Aberbrothok.' So he cut the rope, and down went the bell 'with a gurgling sound; the bubbles rose and burst around,' etc. Then 'Ralph the Rover sailed away; he scoured the seas for many a day; and now, grown rich with plundered store, he steers his course for Scotland's shore.' Then came a terrible storm with cloud darkness and night darkness and high roaring waves. 'Now where we are,' cried the pirate, 'I cannot tell, but I wish I could hear the Inchcape bell.' And the story goes on to tell how the wretched rover 'tore his hair,' and curst himself in his despair,' when 'with a shivering shock' the stout ship struck on the Inchcape Rock, and went down with Ralph and his plunder beside the good priest's bell. The story appealed to our love of kind deeds and of wildness and fair play.

A lot of terrifying experiences connected with these first schooldays grew out of crimes committed by the keeper of a low lodging-house in Edinburgh, who allowed poor homeless wretches to sleep on benches or the floor for a penny or so a night, and, when kind Death came to their relief, sold the bodies for dissection to Dr Hare of the medical school. None of us children ever heard anything like the original story. The servant girls told us that 'Dandy Doctors,' clad in long black cloaks and supplied with a store of sticking-plaster of wondrous adhesiveness, prowled at night about the country lanes and even the tow streets, watching for children to choke and sell. The Dandy Doctor's business method, as the servants explained it, was with lightning quickness to clap a sticking-plaster on the face of a scholar, covering mouth and nose, preventing breathing or crying for help, then pop us under his long black cloak and carry us to Edinburgh to be sold and sliced into small pieces for folk to learn how we were made. We always mentioned the name 'Dandy Doctor' in a fearful whisper, and never dared venture out of doors after dark. In the short winter days it got dark before school closed, and in cloudy weather we sometimes had difficulty in finding our way home unless a servant with a lantern was sent for us; but during the Dandy Doctor period the school was closed earlier, for if detained until the usual hour the teacher could not get us to leave the schoolroom. We would rather stay all night supperless than dare the mysterious doctors supposed to be lying in wait for us. We had to go up a hill called the Davel Brae that lay between the schoolhouse and the main street. One evening just before dark, as we were running up the hill, one of the boys shouted, 'A Dandy Doctor! A Dandy Doctor!' and we all fled pellmell back into the school-house to the astonishment of Mungo Siddons, the teacher. I can remember to this day the amused look on the good dominie's face as he stared and tried to guess what had got into us, until one of the older boys breathlessly explained that there was an awful big Dandy Doctor on the Brae and we couldna gang hame. Others corroborated the dreadful news. 'Yes! We saw him, plain as onything, with his lang black cloak to hide us in, and some of us thought we saw a sticken-plaister ready in his hand.' We were in such a state of fear and trembling that the teacher saw he wasn't going to get rid of us without going himself as leader. He went only a short distance, however, and turned us over to the care of the two biggest scholars, who led us to the top of the Brae and then left us to scurry home and dash into the door like pursued squirrels diving into their holes.

Just before school skaled (closed), we all arose and sang the fine hymn 'Lord, dismiss us with Thy blessing.' In the spring when the swallows were coming back from their winter homes we sang –

> Welcome, welcome, little stranger,
> Welcome from a foreign shore:
> Safe escaped from many a danger . . .

– and while singing we all swayed in rhythm with the music. 'The Cuckoo,' that always told his none in the spring of the year, was another favorite song, and when there was nothing in particular to call to mind any special bird or animal, the songs we sang were widely varied, such as –

> The whale, the beast for me,
> Plunging along through the deep, deep sea.

But the best of all was 'Lord, dismiss us with Thy blessing,' though at that time the most significant part I fear was the first three words.

With my school lessons Father made me learn hymns and Bible verses. For learning 'Rock of Ages' he gave me a penny, and I thus became suddenly rich. Scotch boys are seldom spoiled with money. We thought more of a penny those economical days than the poorest American schoolboy thinks of a dollar. To decide what to do with that first penny was an extravagantly serious affair. I ran in great excitement up and down the street, examining the tempting goodies in the shop windows before venturing on so important an investment. My playmates also became excited when the wonderful news got abroad that Johnnie Muir had a penny, hoping to obtain a taste of the orange, apple, or candy it was likely to bring forth.

At this time infants were baptized and vaccinated a few days after birth. I remember very well a fight with the doctor when my brother David was vaccinated. This happened, I think, before I was sent to school. I couldn't imagine what the doctor, a tall, severe-looking man in black, was doing to my brother, but as Mother, who was holding him in her arms, offered no objection, I looked on quietly while he scratched the arm until I saw blood. Then, unable to trust even my mother, I managed to spring up high enough to grab and bite the doctor's arm, yelling that I wasna gan to let him hurt my bonnie brither, while to my utter astonishment Mother and the doctor only laughed at me. So far from complete at times is sympathy between parents and children, and so much like wild beasts are baby boys, little fighting, biting, climbing pagans.

Father was proud of his garden and seemed always to be trying to make it as much like Eden as possible, and in a corner of it he gave each of us a little bit of ground for our very own, in which we planted what we best liked, wondering how the hard dry seeds could change into soft leaves and flowers and find their way out to the light; and, to see how they were coming on, we used to dig up the larger ones, such as peas and beans, every day. My aunt had a corner assigned to her in our garden, which she filled with lilies, and we all looked with the utmost respect and admiration at that precious lily-bed and wondered whether when we grew up we should ever be rich enough to own anything like so grand. We imagined that each lily was worth an enormous sum of money and never dared to touch a single leaf or petal of them. We really stood in awe

of them. Far, far was I then from the wild lily gardens of
California that I was destined to see in their glory.

When I was a little boy at Mungo Siddons's school a flower-
show was held in Dunbar, and I saw a number of the
exhibitors carrying large handfuls of dahlias, the first I had
ever seen. I thought them marvelous in size and beauty and, as
in the case of my aunt's lilies, wondered if I should ever be rich
enough to own some of them.

Although I never dared to touch my aunt's sacred lilies, I
have good cause to remember stealing some common flowers
from an apothecary, Peter Lawson, who also answered the
purpose of a regular physician to most of the poor people of
the town and adjacent country. He had a pony which was
considered very wild and dangerous, and when he was called
out of town he mounted this wonderful beast, which, after
standing long in the stable, was frisky and boisterous, and
often to our delight reared and jumped and danced about from
side to side of the street before he could be persuaded to go
ahead. We boys gazed in awful admiration and wondered how
the druggist could be so brave and able as to get on and stay on
that wild beast's back. This famous Peter loved flowers and
had a fine garden surrounded by an iron fence, through the
bars of which, when I thought no one saw me, I oftentimes
snatched a flower and took to my heels. One day Peter
discovered me in this mischief, dashed out into the street
and caught me. I screamed that I wouldna steal any more if
he would let me go. He didn't say anything but just dragged me
along to the stable where he kept the wild pony, pushed me in
right back of its heels, and shut the door. I was screaming, of
course, but as soon as I was imprisoned the fear of being
kicked quenched all noise. I hardly dared breathe. My only
hope was in motionless silence. Imagine the agony I endured! I
did not steal any more of his flowers. He was a good hard
judge of boy nature.

I was in Peter's hands some time before this, when I was
about two and a half years old. The servant girl bathed us
small folk before putting us to bed. The smarting soapy
scrubbings of the Saturday nights in preparation for the
Sabbath were particularly severe, and we all dreaded them.
My sister Sarah, the next older than me, wanted the long-
legged stool I was sitting on awaiting my turn, so she just

tipped me off. My chin struck on the edge of the bath-tub, and, as I was tallying at the time, my tongue happened to be in the way of my teeth when they were closed by the blow, and a deep gash was cut on the side of it, which bled profusely. Mother came running at the noise I made, wrapped me up, put me in the servant girl's arms and told her to run with me through the garden and out by a back way to Peter Lawson to have something done to stop the bleeding. He simply rubbed a wad of cotton into my mouth after soaking it in some brown astringent stuff, and told me to be sure to keep my mouth shut and all would soon be well. Mother put me to bed, calmed my fears, and told me to lie still and sleep like a gude bairn. But just as I was dropping of to sleep I swallowed the bulky wad of medicated cotton and with it, as I imagined, my tongue also. My scream over so great a loss brought Mother, and when she anxiously took me in her arms and inquired what was the matter, I told her that I had swallowed my tongue. She only laughed at me, much to my astonishment, when I expected that she would bewail the awful loss her boy had sustained. My sisters, who were older than I, oftentimes said when I happened to be talking too much, 'It's a pity you hadn't swallowed at least half of that long tongue of yours when you were little.'

It appears natural for children to be fond of water, although the Scotch method of making every duty dismal contrived to make necessary bathing for health terrible to us. I well remember among the awful experiences of childhood being taken by the servant to the seashore when I was between two and three years old, stripped at the side of a deep pool in the rocks, plunged into it among crawling crawfish and slippery wriggling snake-like eels, and drawn up gasping and shrieking only to be plunged down again and again. As the time approached for this terrible bathing, I used to hide in the darkest corners of the house, and oftentimes a long search was required to find me. But after we were a few years older, we enjoyed bathing with other boys as we wandered along the shore, careful, however, not to get into a pool that had an invisible boy-devouring monster at the bottom of it. Such pools, miniature maelstroms, were called 'sookin-in-goats' and were well known to most of us. Nevertheless we never ventured into any pool on strange parts of the coast before we had thrust a stick into it. If the stick were not pulled out of our hands, we boldly entered and enjoyed plashing and ducking long ere we had learned to swim.

One of our best playgrounds was the famous old Dunbar Castle, to which King Edward fled after his defeat at Bannockburn. It was built more than a thousand years ago, and though we knew little of its history, we had heard many mysterious stories of the battles fought about its walls, and firmly believed that every bone we found in the ruins belonged to an ancient warrior. We tried to see who could climb highest on the crumbling peaks and crags, and took chances that no cautious mountaineer would try. That I did not fall and finish my rock-scrambling in those adventurous boyhood days seems now a reasonable wonder.

Among our best games were running, jumping, wrestling, and scrambling. I was so proud of my skill as a climber that when I first heard of hell from a servant girl who loved to tell its horrors and warn us that if we did anything wrong we would be cast into it, I always insisted that I could climb out of it. I imagined it was only a sooty pit with stone walls like those of the castle, and I felt sure there must be chinks and cracks in the masonry for fingers and toes. Anyhow the terrors of the horrible place seldom lasted long beyond the telling; for natural faith casts out fear.

Most of the Scotch children believe in ghosts, and some under peculiar conditions continue to believe in them all through life. Grave ghosts are deemed particularly dangerous, and many of the most credulous will go far out of their way to avoid passing through or near a graveyard in the dark. After being instructed by the servants in the nature, looks, and habits of the various black and white ghosts, boowuzzies, and witches we often speculated as to whether they could run fast, and tried to believe that we had a good chance to get away from most of them. To improve our speed and wind, we often took long runs into the country. Tam o'Shanter's mare outran a lot of witches – at least until she reached a place of safety beyond the keystone of the bridge – and we thought perhaps we also might be able to out-run them.

Our house formerly belonged to a physician, and a servant girl told us that the ghost of the dead doctor haunted one of the unoccupied rooms in the second story that was kept dark on account of a heavy window-tax. Our bedroom was adjacent to the ghost room, which had in it a lot of chemical apparatus – glass tubing, glass and brass retorts, test-tubes, flasks, etc – and we thought that those strange articles were still used by the old dead doctor in compounding physic. In the long summer days David and I were put to bed several hours before sunset. Mother tucked us in carefully, drew the curtains of the big old-fashioned bed, and told us to lie still and sleep like gude bairns; but we were usually out of bed, playing games of daring called 'scootchers,' about as soon as our loving mother reached the foot of the stairs, for we couldn't lie still, however hard we might try. Going into the ghost room was regarded as a very great scootcher. After venturing in a few steps and rushing back in terror, I used to dare David to go as far without getting caught.

The roof of our house, as well as the crags and walls of the old castle, offered fine mountaineering exercise. Our bedroom was lighted by a dormer window. One night I opened it in search of good scootchers and hung myself out over the slates, holding on to the sill, while the wind was making a balloon of my nightgown. I then dared David to try the adventure, and he did. Then I went out again and hung by one hand, and David did the same. Then I hung by one finger, being careful not to slip, and he did that too. Then I stood on the sill and examined the edge of the left wall of the window, crept up the slates along its side by slight finger-holds, got astride of the roof, sat there a few minutes looking at the scenery over the garden wall while the wind was howling and threatening to blow me off, then managed to slip down, catch hold of the sill, and get safely back into the room. But before attempting this scootcher, recognizing its dangerous character, with commendable caution I warned David that in case I should happen to slip I would grip the rain-trough when I was going over the eaves and hang on, and that he must then run fast downstairs and tell Father to get a ladder for me, and tell him to be quick because I would soon be tired hanging dangling in the wind by my hands. After my return from this capital scootcher, David, not to be out-done, crawled up to the top of the window-roof, and got bravely astride of it; but in trying to return he lost courage and began to greet (to cry), 'I canna get doon. Oh, I canna get doon.' I leaned out of the window and shouted encouragingly,

'Dinna greet, Davie, dinna greet, I'll help ye doon. If you greet, fayther will hear, and gee us baith an awfu' skelping.' Then, standing on the sill and holding on by one hand to the window-casing, I directed him to slip his feet down within reach, and, after securing a good hold, I jumped inside and dragged him in by his heels. This finished scootcher-scrambling for the night and frightened us into bed.

In the short winter days, when it was dark even at our early bedtime, we usually spent the hours before going to sleep playing voyages around the world under the bed-clothing. After Mother had carefully covered us, bade us goodnight and gone downstairs, we set out on our travels. Burrowing like moles, we visited France, India, America, Australia, New Zealand, and all the places we had ever heard of; our travels never ending until we fell asleep. When Mother came to take a last look at us, before she went to bed, to see that we were covered, we were oftentimes covered so well that she had difficulty in finding us, for we were hidden in all sorts of positions where sleep happened to overtake us, but in the morning we always found ourselves in good order, lying straight like gude bairns, as she said.

Some fifty years later, when I visited Scotland, I got one of my Dunbar schoolmates to introduce me to the owners of our old home, from whom I obtained permission to go up-stairs to examine our bedroom window and judge what sort of ad-venture getting on its roof must have been, and with all my after experience in mountaineering, I found that what I had done in daring boyhood was now beyond my skill.

Boys are often at once cruel and merciful, thoughtlessly hard-hearted and tender-hearted, sympathetic, pitiful, and kind in ever-changing contrasts. Love of neighbors, human or animal, grows up amid savage traits, coarse and fine. When Father made out to get us securely locked up in the back yard to prevent our shore and field wanderings, we had to play away the comparatively dull time as best we could. One of our amusements was hunting cats without seriously hurting them. These sagacious animals knew, however that, though not very dangerous, boys were not to be trusted. One time in particular I remember, when we began throwing stones at an experienced old Tom, not wishing to hurt him much, though he was a tempting mark. He soon saw what we were up to, fled to the stable, and climbed to the top of the hay manger. He was still within range, however, and we kept the stones flying faster and faster, but he just blinked and played possum without wincing either at our best shots or at the noise we made. I happened to strike him pretty hard with a good-sized pebble, but he still blinked and sat still as if without feeling. 'He must be mortally wounded,' I said, 'and now we must kill him to put him out of pain,' the savage in us rapes idly growing with indulgence. All took heartily to this sort of cat mercy and began throwing the heaviest stones we could manage, but that old fellow knew what characters we were, and just as we imagined him mercifully dead he evidently thought the play was becoming too serious and that it was time to retreat; for suddenly with a wild whirr and gurr of energy he launched himself over our heads, rushed across the yard in a blur of speed, climbed to the roof of another building and over the garden wall, out of pain and bad company, with all his lives wide awake and in good working order.

After we had thus learned that Tom had at least nine lives, we tried to verify the common saying that no matter how far cats fell they always landed on their feet unhurt. We caught one in our back yard, not Tom but a smaller one of manageable size, and somehow got him smuggled up to the top story of the house. I don't know how in the world we managed to let go of him, for as soon as we opened the window and held him over the sill he knew his danger and made violent efforts to scratch and bite his way back into the room; but we determined to carry the thing through, and at last managed to drop him. I can remember to this day how the poor creature in danger of his life strained and balanced as he was falling and managed to alight on his feet. This was a cruel thing for even wild boys to do, and we never tried the experiment again, for we sincerely pitied the poor fellow when we saw him creeping slowly away, stunned and frightened, with it a swollen black and blue chin.

Again – showing the natural savagery of boys – we delighted in dog-fights, and even in the horrid red work of slaughter-houses, often running long distances and climbing over walls and roofs to see a pig killed, as soon as we heard the desperately earnest squealing. And if the butcher was good-natured, we begged him to let us get a near view of the mysterious insides and to give us a bladder to blow up for a foot-ball.

But here is an illustration of the better side of boy nature. In our back yard there were three elm trees and in the one nearest the house a pair of robin-redbreasts had their nest. When the young were almost able to fly, a troop of the celebrated 'Scottish Grays' visited Dunbar, and three or four of the fine horses were lodged in our stable. When the soldiers were polishing their swords and helmets, they happened to notice the nest, and just as they were leaving, one of them climbed the tree and robbed it. With sore sympathy we watched the young birds as the hard-hearted robber pushed them one by one beneath his jacket – all but two that jumped out of the nest and tried to fly, but they were easily caught as they fluttered on the ground, and were hidden away with the rest. The distress of the bereaved parents, as they hovered and screamed over the frightened crying children they so long had loved and sheltered and fed, was pitiful to see; but the shining soldier rode grandly away on his big gray horse, caring only for the few pennies the young songbirds would bring and the beer they would buy, while we all, sisters and brothers, were crying and sobbing. I remember, as if it happened this day, how my heart fairly ached and choked me. Mother put us to bed and tried to comfort us, telling us that the little birds would be well fed and grow big, and soon learn to sing in pretty cages; but again and again we rehearsed the sad story of the poor bereaved birds and their frightened children, and could not be comforted. Father came into the room when we were half asleep and still sobbing, and I heard Mother telling him that 'a' the bairns' hearts were broken over the robbing of the nest in the elm.'

After attaining the manly, belligerent age of five or fix years, very few of my schooldays passed without a fist fight, and half a dozen was no uncommon number. When any classmate of our own age questioned our rank and standing as fighters, we always made haste to settle the matter at a quiet place on the Davel Brae. To be a 'gude fechter' was our highest ambition, our dearest aim in life in or out of school. To be a good scholar was a secondary consideration, though we tried hard to hold high places in our classes and gloried in being Dux. We fairly reveled in the battle stories of glorious William Wallace and Robert the Bruce, with which every breath of Scotch air is saturated, and of course we were all going to be soldiers. On the Davel Brae battleground we often managed to bring on something like real war, greatly more exciting than personal combat. Choosing leaders, we divided into two armies. In winter damp snow furnished plenty of ammunition to make the thing serious, and in summer sand and grass sods. Cheering and shouting some battle-cry such as 'Bannockburn! Bannockburn! Scotland forever! The Last War in India!' we were led bravely on. For heavy battery work we stuffed our Scotch blue bonnets with snow and sand, sometimes mixed with gravel, and fired them at each other as cannon-balls.

Of course we always looked eagerly forward to vacation days and thought them slow in coming. Old Mungo Siddons gave us a lot of gooseberries or currants and wished us a happy time. Some sort of special closing-exercises – diggings, recitations, etc – celebrated the great day, but I remember only the berries, freedom from school work, and opportunities for runaway rambles in the fields and along the wave-beaten seashore.

An exciting time came when at the age of seven or eight years I left the auld Davel Brae school for the grammar school. Of course I had a terrible lot of fighting to do, because a new scholar had to meet every one of his age who dared to challenge him, this being the common introduction to a new school. It was very strenuous for the first month or so, establishing my fighting rank, taking up new studies, especially Latin and French, getting acquainted with new classmates and the master and his rules. In the first few Latin and French lessons the new teacher, Mr Lyon, blandly smiled at our comical blunders, but pedagogical weather of the severest kind quickly set in, when for every mistake, everything short of perfection, the taws was promptly applied. We had to get three lessons every day in Latin, three in French, and as many in English, besides spelling, history, arithmetic, and geography. Word lessons in particular, the wouldst-couldst-shouldst-have-loved kind, were kept up, with much warlike thrashing, until I had committed the whole of the French, Latin, and English grammars to memory, and in connection with reading-lessons we were called on to recite parts of them with the rules over and over again, as if all the regular and irregular incomprehensible verb stuff was poetry. In addition to all this, Father made me learn so many Bible verses every day that by the time I was eleven years of age I had about three fourths of the Old Testament and all of the New by heart and by sore flesh. I could recite the New Testament from the beginning of Matthew to the end of Revelation without a single stop. The dangers of cramming and of making scholars study at home instead of letting their little brains rest were never heard of in those days. We carried our school-books home in a strap every night and committed to memory our next day's lessons before we went to bed, and to do that we had to bend our attention as closely on our tasks as lawyers on great million-dollar cases. I can't conceive of anything that would now enable me to concentrate my attention more fully than when I was a mere stripling boy, and it was all done by whipping – thrashing in general. Old-fashioned Scotch teachers spent no time in seeking short roads to knowledge, or in trying any of the new-fangled psychological methods so much in vogue nowadays. There was nothing said about making the seats easy or the lessons easy. We were simply driven pointblank against our books like soldiers against the enemy, and sternly ordered, 'Up and at 'em. Commit your lessons to memory!' If we failed in any part, however slight, we were whipped; for the grand, simple, all-sufficing Scotch discovery had been made that there was a close connection between the skin and the memory, and that irritating the skin excited the memory to any required degree.

Fighting was carried on still more vigorously in the high school than in the common school. Whenever anyone was challenged, either the challenge was allowed or it was decided by a battle on the seashore, where with stubborn enthusiasm we battered each other as if we had not been sufficiently battered by the teacher. When we were so fortunate as to finish a fight without getting a black eye, we usually escaped a thrashing at home and another next morning at school, for other traces of the fray could be easily washed off at a well on the church brae, or concealed, or passed as results of play-ground accidents; but a black eye could never be explained away from downright fighting. A good double thrashing was the inevitable penalty, but without avail; fighting went on without the slightest abatement, like natural storms; for no punishment less than death could quench the ancient inherited belligerence burning in our pagan blood. Nor could we be made to believe it was fair that Father and teacher should thrash us so industriously for our good, while begrudging us the pleasure of thrashing each other for our good. All these various thrashings, however, were admirably influential in developing not only memory but fortitude as well. For if we did not endure our school punishments and fighting pains without flinching and making faces, we were mocked on the playground, and public opinion on a Scotch playground was a powerful agent in controlling behavior; therefore we at length managed to keep our features in smooth repose while enduring pain that would try anybody but an American Indian. Far from feeling that we were called on to endure too much pain, one of our playground games was thrashing each other with whips about two feet long made from the tough, wiry stems of a species of polygonum fastened together in a stiff, firm braid. One of us handing two of these whips to a companion to take his choice, we stood up close together and thrashed each other on the legs until one succumbed to the intolerable pain and thus lost the game. Nearly all of our playground games were strenuous – shin-battering shinny, wrestling, prisoners' base, and dogs and hares – all augmenting in no slight degree our lessons in fortitude. Moreover, we regarded our punishments and pains of every sort as training for war, since we were all going to be soldiers. Besides single combats we sometimes assembled on Saturdays to meet the scholars of another school and very little was required for the growth of strained relations, and war. The immediate cause might be nothing more than a saucy stare. Perhaps the scholar stared at would insolently inquire, 'What are ye glowerin' at, Bob?' Bob would reply, 'I'll look where I hae a mind and hinder me if ye daur.' 'Weel, Bob,' the outraged stared-at scholar would reply, 'I'll soon let ye see whether I daur or no,' and give Bob a blow on the face. This opened the battle, and every good scholar belonging to either school was drawn into it. After both sides were sore and weary, a strong lunged warrior would be heard above the din of battle shouting, 'I'll tell ye what we'll dae wi' ye. If ye'll let us alone we'll let ye alane!' and the school war ended as most wars between nations do; and some of them begin in much the same way.

Notwithstanding the great number of harshly enforced rules, not very good order was kept in school in my time.

There were two schools within a few roods of each other, one for mathematics, navigation, etc., the other, called the grammar school, that I attended. The masters lived in a big freestone house within eight or ten yards of the schools, so that they could easily step out for anything they wanted or send one of the scholars. The moment our master disappeared, perhaps for a book or a drink, every scholar left his seat and his lessons, jumped on top of the benches and desks or crawled beneath them, tugging, rolling, wrestling, accomplishing in a minute a depth of disorder and din unbelievable save by a Scottish scholar. We even carried on war, class against class, in those wild, precious minutes. A watcher gave the alarm when the master opened his house-door to return, and it was a great feat to get into our places before he entered, adorned in awful majestic authority shouting 'Silence!' and striking resounding blows with his cane on a desk or on some unfortunate scholar's back.

Forty-seven years after leaving this fighting school, I returned on a visit to Scotland, and a cousin in Dunbar introduced me to a minister who was acquainted with the history of the school, and obtained for me an invitation to dine with the new master. Of course I gladly accepted, for I wanted to see the old place of fun and pain, and the battleground on the sands. Mr Lyon, our able teacher and thrasher, I learned, had held his place as master of the school for twenty or thirty years after I left it, and had recently died in London, after preparing many young men for the English Universities. At the dinner-table, while I was recalling the amusements and fights of my old school-days, the minister remarked to the new master, 'Now, don't you wish that you had been teacher in those days, and gained the honor of walloping John Muir?' This pleasure so merrily suggested showed that the minister also had been a fighter in his youth. The old freestone school building was still perfectly sound, but the carved, ink-stained desks were almost whittled away.

The highest part of our playground back of the school commanded a view of the sea, and we loved to watch the passing ships and, judging by their rigging, make guesses as to the ports they had sailed from, those to which they were bound, what they were loaded with, their tonnage, etc. In stormy weather they were all smothered in clouds and spray, and showers of salt scud torn from the tops of the waves came flying over the playground wall. In those tremendous storms many a brave ship foundered or was tossed and smashed on the rocky shore. When a wreck occurred within a mile or two of the town, we often managed by running fast to reach it and pick up some of the spoils. In particular I remember visiting the battered fragments of an unfortunate brig or schooner that had been loaded with apples, and finding fine unpitiful sport in rushing into the spent waves and picking up the red-cheeked fruit from the frothy, seething foam.

All our school-books were extravagantly illustrated with drawings of every kind of sailing-vessel, and every boy owned some sort of craft whittled from a block of wood and trimmed with infinite pains – sloops, schooners, brigs, and full-rigged ships, with their sails and string ropes properly adjusted and named for us by some old sailor. These precious toy craft with lead keels we learned to sail on a pond near the town. With the sails set at the proper angle to the wind, they made fast straight voyages across the pond to boys on the other side, who readjusted the sails and started them back on the return voyages. Oftentimes fleets of half a dozen or more were started together in exciting races.

Our most exciting sport, however, was playing with gunpowder. We made guns out of gas-pipe, mounted them on sticks of any shape, clubbed our pennies together for powder, gleaned pieces of lead here and there and cut them into slugs, and, while one aimed, another applied a match to the touch-hole. With these awful weapons we wandered along the beach and fired at the gulls and solan-geese as they passed us. Fortunately we never hurt any of them that we knew of. We also dug holes in the ground, put in a handful or two of powder, tamped it well around a fuse made of a wheat-stalk, and, reaching cautiously forward, touched a match to the straw. This we called making earthquakes. Oftentimes we went home with singed hair and faces well peppered with powder-grains that could not be washed out. Then, of course, came a correspondingly severe punishment from both Father and teacher.

Another favorite sport was climbing trees and scaling garden-walls. Boys eight or ten years of age could get over almost any wall by standing on each other's shoulders, thus making living ladders. To make walls secure against marauders, many of them were finished on top with broken bottles imbedded in lime, leaving the cutting edges sticking up; but with bunches of grass and weeds we could sit or stand in comfort on top of the jaggedest of them.

Like squirrels that begin to eat nuts before they are ripe, we began to eat apples about as soon as they were formed, causing, of course, desperate gastric disturbances to be cured by castor oil. Serious were the risks we ran in climbing and squeezing through hedges, and, of course, among the country folk we were far from welcome. Farmers passing us on the roads often shouted by way of greeting: 'Oh, you vagabonds! Back to the toon wi' ye. Gang back where ye belang. You're up to mischief Ise warrant. I can see it. The gamekeeper'll catch ye, and maist like ye'll a' be hanged some day.'

Breakfast in those auld-lang-syne days was simple oatmeal porridge, usually with a little milk or treacle, served in wooden dishes called 'luggies,' formed of staves hooped together like miniature tubs about four or five inches in diameter. One of the staves, the lug or ear, a few inches longer than the others, served as a handle, while the number of luggies ranged in a row on a dresser indicated the size of the family. We never dreamed of anything to come after the porridge, or of asking for more. Our portions were consumed in about a couple of minutes; then off to school. At noon we came racing home ravenously hungry. The midday meal, called dinner, was usually vegetable broth, a small piece of boiled mutton, and barley-meal scone. None of us liked the barley scone bread, therefore we got all we wanted of it, and in desperation had to eat it, for we were always hungry, about as hungry after as before meals. The evening meal was called 'tea' and was served on our return from school. It consisted, as far as we children were concerned, of half a slice of white bread without butter, barley scone, and warm water with a little milk and sugar in it, a beverage called 'content,' which warmed but neither cheered nor inebriated. Immediately after tea we ran across the street with our books to Grandfather Gilrye, who took pleasure in seeing us and hearing us recite our next day's lessons. Then back home to supper, usually a boiled potato and piece of barley scone. Then family worship, and to bed.

Our amusements on Saturday afternoons and vacations

depended mostly on getting away from home into the country, especially in the spring when the birds were calling loudest. Father sternly forbade David and me from playing truant in the fields with plundering wanderers like ourselves, fearing we might go on from bad to worse, get hurt in climbing over walls, caught by gamekeepers, or lost by falling over a cliff into the sea. 'Play as much as you like in the back yard and garden,' he said, 'and mind what you'll get when you forget and disobey.' Thus he warned us with an awfully stern countenance, looking very hard-hearted, while naturally his heart was far from hard, though he devoutly believed in eternal punishment for bad boys both here and hereafter. Nevertheless, like devout martyrs of wildness, we stole away to the seashore or the green, sunny fields with almost religious regularity, taking advantage of opportunities when Father was very busy, to join our companions, oftenest to hear the birds sing and hunt their nests, glorying in the number we had discovered and called our own. A sample of our nest chatter was something like this: Willie Chisholm would proudly exclaim – 'I ken [know] seventeen nests, and you, Johnnie, ken only fifteen.'

'But I wouldna gie my fifteen for your seventeen, for five of mine are larks and mavises. You ken only three o' the best singers.'

'Yes, Johnnie, but I ken six goldies and you ken only one. Maist of yours are only sparrows and linties and robin-red-breasts.'

Then perhaps Bob Richardson would loudly declare that he 'kenned mair nests than onybody, for he kenned twenty-three, with about fifty eggs in them and mair than fifty young birds – maybe a hundred. Some of them naething but raw gorblings but lots of them as big as their mithers and ready to flee. And aboot fifty craw's nests and three fox dens.'

'Oh, yes, Bob, but that's no fair, for naebody counts craw's nests and fox holes, and then you live in the country at Belle-haven where ye have the best chance.'

'Yes, but I ken a lot of bumbee's nests, baith the red-legged and the yellow-legged kind.'

'Oh, wha cares for bumbee's nests!'

'Weel, but here's something! Ma father let me gang to a fox hunt, and man, it was grand to see the hounds and the lang-legged horses lowpin the dykes and burns and hedges!'

The nests, I fear, with the beautiful eggs and young birds, were prized quite as highly as the songs of the glad parents, but no Scotch boy that I know of ever failed to listen with enthusiasm to the songs of the skylarks. Oftentimes on a broad meadow near Dunbar we stood for hours enjoying their marvelous singing and soaring. From the grass where the nest was hidden the male would suddenly rise, as straight as if shot up, to a height of perhaps thirty or forty feet, and, sustaining himself with rapid wing-beats, pour down the most delicious melody, sweet and cleat and strong, overflowing all bounds, then suddenly he would soar higher again and again, ever higher and higher, soaring and singing until lost to sight even on perfectly clear days, and oftentimes in cloudy weather 'far in the downy cloud,' as the poet says.

To test our eyes we often watched a lark until he seemed a faint speck in the sky and finally passed beyond the keenest-sighted of us all. 'I see him yet!' we would cry, 'I see him yet!' 'I see him yet!' 'I see him yet!' as he soared. And finally only one of us would be left to claim that he still saw him. At last he, too, would have to admit that the singer had soared beyond his sight, and still the music came pouring down to us in glorious profusion, from a height far above our vision, requiring marvelous power of wing and marvelous power of voice, for that rich, delicious, soft, and yet clear music was distinctly heard long after the bird was out of sight. Then, suddenly ceasing, the glorious singer would appear, falling like a bolt straight down to his nest, where his mate was sitting on the eggs.

It was far too common a practice among us to carry off a young lark just before it could fly, place it in a cage, and fondly, laboriously feed it. Sometimes we succeeded in keeping one alive for a year or two, and when awakened by the spring weather it was pitiful to see the quivering imprisoned soarer of the heavens rapidly beating its wings and singing as though it were flying and hovering in the air like its parents. To keep it in health we were taught that we must supply it with a sod of grass the size of the bottom of the cage, to make the poor bird feel as though it were at home on its native meadow – a meadow perhaps a foot or at most two feet square. Again and again it would try to hover over that miniature meadow from its miniature sky just underneath the top of the cage. At last, conscience-stricken, we carried the beloved prisoner to the meadow west of Dunbar where it was born, and, blessing its sweet heart, bravely set it free, and our exceeding great reward was to see it fly and sing in the sky.

In the winter, when there was but little doing in the fields, we organized running-matches. A dozen or so of us would start out on races that were simply tests of endurance, running on and on along a public road over the breezy hills like hounds, without stopping or getting tired. The only serious trouble we ever felt in these long races was an occasional stitch in our sides. One of the boys started the story that sucking raw eggs was a sure cure for the stitches. We had hens in our back yard, and on the next Saturday we managed to swallow a couple of eggs apiece, a disgusting job, but we would do almost anything to mend our speed, and as soon as we could get away after taking the cure we set out on a ten or twenty mile run to prove its worth. We thought nothing of running right ahead ten or a dozen miles before turning back; for we knew nothing about taking time by the suns and none of us had a watch in those days. Indeed, we never cared about time until it began to get dark. Then we thought of home and the thrashing that awaited us. Late or early, the thrashing was sure, unless Father happened to be away. If he was expected to return soon, Mother made haste to get us to bed before his arrival. We escaped the thrashing next morning, for Father never felt like thrashing us in cold blood on the calm holy Sabbath. But no punishment, however sure and severe, was of any avail against the attraction of the fields and woods. It had other uses, developing memory, etc., but in keeping us at home it was of no use at all. Wildness was ever sounding in our ears, and Nature saw to it that besides school lessons and church lessons some of her own lessons should be learned, perhaps with a view to the time when we should be called to wander in wildness to our heart's content. Oh, the blessed enchantment of those Saturday runaways in the prime of the spring! How our young wondering eyes reveled in the sunny, breezy glory of the hills and the sky, every particle of us thrilling and tingling with the bees and glad birds and glad streams! Kings may be blessed; we were glorious, we were free – school cares and scoldings, heart thrashings and flesh thrashings alike, were forgotten in the fullness of Nature's glad wildness. These were my first excursions – the beginnings of lifelong wanderings.

Chapter 2

A NEW WORLD

Our grammar-school reader, called, I think, 'Maccoulough's Course of Reading', contained a few natural-history sketches that excited me very much and left a deep impression, especially a fine description of the fish hawk and the bald eagle by the Scotch ornithologist Wilson, who had the good fortune to wander for years in the American woods while the country was yet mostly wild. I read his description over and over again, till I got the vivid picture he drew by heart – the long-winged hawk circling over the heaving waves, every motion watched by the eagle perched on the top of a crag or dead tree; the fish hawk poising for a moment to take aim at a fish and plunging under the water; the eagle with kindling eye spreading his wings ready for instant flight in case the attack should prove successful; the hawk emerging with a struggling fish in his talons, and proud flight; the eagle launching himself in pursuit; the wonderful wing-work in the sky, the fish hawk, though encumbered with his prey, circling higher, higher, striving hard to keep above the robber eagle; the eagle at length soaring above him, compel him with a cry of despair to drop his hard-won prey; then the eagle steadying himself for a moment to take aim, descending swift as a lightning-bolt, and dog the falling fish before it reached the sea.

Not less exciting and memorable was Audubon's wonderful story of the passenger pigeon, a beautiful bird flying in vast flocks that darkened the sky like clouds, countless millions ambling to rest and sleep and rear their young in certain forests, miles in length and breadth, fifty or a hundred nests on a single tree; the overloaded branches bending low and often breaking; the farmers gathering from far and near, beating down countless thousands of the young and old birds from their nests and roosts with long poles at Bight, and in the morning driving their bands of hogs, some of them brought from farms a hundred miles distant, to fatten on the dead and wounded covering the ground.

In another of our reading-lessons some of the American forests were described. The most interesting of the trees to us boys was the sugar maple, and soon after we had learned this sweet story we heard everybody talking about the discovery of gold in the same wonder-filled country.

One night, when David and I were at Grandfather's fireside solemnly learning our lessons as usual, my father came in with news, the most wonderful, most glorious, that wild boys ever heard. 'Bairns,' he said, 'you needna learn your lessons the nicht, for we're gan to America the morn!' No more grammar, but boundless woods full of mysterious good things; trees full of sugar, growing in ground full of gold; hawks, eagles, pigeons, filling the sky; millions of birds' nests, and no game-keepers to stop us in all the wild, happy land. We were utterly, blindly glorious. After Father left the room, Grandfather gave David and me a gold coin apiece for a keepsake, and looked very serious, for he was about to be deserted in his lonely old age. And when we in fullness of young joy spoke of what we were going to do, of the wonderful birds and their nests that we should find, the sugar and gold, etc., and promised to send him a big box full of that tree sugar packed in gold from the glorious paradise over the sea, poor lonely Grandfather, about to be forsaken, looked with downcast eyes on the floor and said in a low, trembling, troubled voice, 'Ah, poor laddies, poor laddies, you'll find something else ower the sea forbye gold and sugar, birds' nests and freedom fra lessons and schools. You'll find plenty hard, hard work.' And so we did. But nothing he could say could cloud our joy or abate the fire of youthful, hopeful, fearless adventure. Nor could we in the midst of such measureless excitement see or feel the shadows and sorrows of his darkening old age. To my school-mates, met that night on the street, I shouted the glorious news, 'I'm gan to Amaraka the morn!' None could believe it. I said, 'Weel, just you see if I am at the skule the morn!'

Next morning we went by rail to Glasgow and thence joyfully sailed away from beloved Scotland, flying to our fortunes on the wings of the winds, carefree as thistle seeds.

We could not then know what we were leaving, what we were to encounter in the New World, nor what our gains were likely to be. We were too young and full of hope for fear or regret, but not too young to look forward with eager enthusiasm to the wonderful schoolless, bookless American wilderness. Even the natural heart-pain of parting from Grandfather and Grandmother Gilrye, who loved us so well, and from Mother and sisters and brother, was quickly quenched in young joy. Father took with him only my sister Sarah (thirteen years of age), myself (eleven), and brother David (nine), leaving my eldest sister, Margaret, and the three youngest of the family, Daniel, Mary, and Anna, with Mother, to join us after a farm had been found in the wilderness and a comfortable house made to receive them.

In crossing the Atlantic before the days of steamships, or even the American clippers, the voyages made in old-fashioned sailing-vessels were very long. Ours was six weeks and three days. But because we had no lessons to get, that long voyage had not a dull moment for us boys. Father and sister Sarah, with most of the old folk, stayed below in rough weather, groaning in the miseries of seasickness, many of the passengers wishing they had never ventured in 'the auld rockin' creel,' as they called our bluff-bowed, wave-beating ship, and, when the weather was moderately calm, singing songs in the evenings – 'The Youthful Sailor Frank and Bold,' 'Oh, why left I my hame, why did I cross the deep,' etc. But no matter how much the old tub tossed about and battered the waves, we were on deck every day, not in the least seasick, watching the sailors at their rope-hauling and climbing work; joining in their songs, learning the names of the ropes and sails, and helping them as far as they would let us; playing games with other boys in calm weather when the deck was dry, and in stormy weather rejoicing in sympathy with the big curly-topped waves.

The captain occasionally called David and me into his cabin and asked us about our schools, handed us books to read, and seemed surprised to find that Scotch boys could read and pronounce English with perfect accent and knew so much Latin and French. In Scotch schools only pure English was taught, although not a word of English was spoken out of school. All through life, however well-educated, the Scotch spoke Scotch among their own folk, except at times when

unduly excited on the only two subjects on which Scotchmen
get much excited, namely, religion and politics. So long as the
controversy went on with fairly level temper, only gude braid
Scots was used, but if one became angry, as was likely to
happen, then he immediately began speaking severely correct
English, while his antagonist, drawing himself up, would say:
'Weel, there's na use pursuing this subject ony further, for I see
ye hae gotten to your English.'

As we neared the shore of the great new land, with what
eager wonder we watched the whales and dolphins and
porpoises and seabirds, and made the good-natured sailors
teach us their names and tell us stories about them!'

There were quite a large number of emigrants aboard, many
of them newly married couples, and the advantages of the
different parts of the New World they expected to settle in
were often discussed. My father started with the intention of
going to the backwoods of Upper Canada. Before the end of
the voyage, however, he was persuaded that the States offered
superior advantages, especially Wisconsin and Michigan,
where the land was said to be as good as in Canada and
far more easily brought under cultivation; for in Canada the
woods were so close and heavy that a man might wear out his
life in getting a few acres cleared of trees and stumps. So he
changed his mind and concluded to go to one of the Western
States.

On our wavering westward way a grain-dealer in Buffalo
told Father that most of the wheat he handled came from
Wisconsin; and this influential information finally determined
my father's choice. At Milwaukee a farmer who had come in
from the country near Fort Winnebago with a load of wheat
agreed to haul us and our formidable load of stuff to a little
town called Kingston for thirty dollars. On that hundred-mile
journey, just after the spring thaw, the roads over the prairies
were heavy and miry, causing no end of lamentation, for we
often got stuck in the mud, and the poor farmer sadly declared
that never, never again would he be tempted to try to haul such
a cruel, heart-breaking, wagon-breaking, horse-killing load,
no, not for a hundred dollars. In leaving Scotland, Father, like
many other home-seekers, burdened himself with far too much
luggages as if all America were still a wilderness in which little
or nothing could be bought. One of his big iron-bound boxes

must have weighed about four hundred pounds, for it contained an old-fashioned beam-scales with a complete set of
cast-iron counterweights, two of them fifty-six pounds each, a
twenty-eight, and so on down to a single pound. Also a lot of
iron wedges, carpenter's tools, and so forth, and at Buffalo as if
on the very edge of the wilderness, he gladly added to his
burden a big cast-iron stove with pots and pans, provisions
enough for a long siege, and a scythe and cumbersome cradle
for cutting wheat, all of which he succeeded in landing in the
primeval Wisconsin woods.

A land-agent at Kingston gave Father a note to a farmer by
the name of Alexander Gray, who lived on the border of the
settled part of the country, knew the section-lines, and would
probably help him to find a good place for a farm. So Father
went away to spy out the land, and in the meantime left us
children in Kingston in a rented room. It took us less than an
hour to get acquainted with some of the boys in the village; we
challenged them to wrestle, run races, climb trees, etc., and in a
day or two we felt at home, carefree and happy, notwithstanding our family was so widely divided. When Father returned he
told us that he had found fine land for a farm in sunny open
woods on the side of a lake, and that a team of three yoke of
oxen with a big wagon was coming to haul us to Mr Gray's
place.

We enjoyed the strange ten-mile ride through the woods
very much, wondering how the great oxen could be so strong
and wise and tame as to pull so heavy a load with no other
harness than a chain and a crooked piece of wood on their
necks, and how they could sway so obediently to right and left
past roadside trees and stumps when the driver said *haw* and
gee. At Mr Gray's house, Father again left us for a few days to
build a shanty on the quarter-section he had selected four or
five miles to the westward. In the meanwhile we enjoyed our
freedom as usual, wandering in the fields and meadows,
looking at the trees and flowers, snakes and birds and squirrels. With the help of the nearest neighbors the little shanty was
built in less than a day after the rough bur-oak logs for the
walls and the white-oak boards for the floor and roof were got
together.

To this charming hut, in the sunny woods, overlooking a
flowery glacier meadow and a lake rimmed with white water-

lilies, we were hauled by an ox-team across trackless carex swamps and low rolling hills sparely dotted with round-headed oaks. Just as we arrived at the shanty, before we had time to look at it or the scenery about it, David and I jumped down in a hurry off the load of household goods, for we had discovered a blue jay's nest, and in a minute or so we were up the tree beside it, feasting our eyes on the beautiful green eggs and beautiful birds – our first memorable discovery. The handsome birds had not seen Scotch boys before and made a desperate screaming as if we were robbers like themselves, though we left the eggs untouched, feeling that we were already beginning to get rich, and wondering how many more nests we should find in the grand sunny woods. Then we ran along the brow of the hill that the shanty stood on, and down to the meadow, searching the trees and grass tufts and bushes, and soon discovered a bluebird's and a woodpecker's nest, and began an acquaintance with the frogs and snakes and turtles in the creeks and springs.

This sudden plash into pure wildness – baptism in Nature's warm heart – how utterly happy it made us! Nature streaming into us, wooingly teaching her wonderful glowing lessons, so unlike the dismal grammar ashes and cinders so long thrashed into us. Here without knowing it we still were at school; every wild lesson a love lesson, not whipped but charmed into us. Oh, that glorious Wisconsin wilderness! Everything new and pure in the very prime of the spring when Nature's pulses were beating highest and mysteriously keeping time with our own! Young hearts, young leaves, flowers, animals, the winds and the streams and the sparkling lake, all wildly, gladly rejoicing together!

Next morning, when we climbed to the precious jay nest to take another admiring look at the eggs, we found it empty. Not a shell-fragment was left, and we wondered how in the world the birds were able to carry off their thin-shelled eggs either in their bills or in their feet without breaking them, and how they could be kept warm while a new nest was being built. Well, I am still asking these questions. When I was on the Harriman Expedition I asked Robert Ridgway, the eminent ornithologist, how these sudden flittings were accomplished, and he frankly confessed that he didn't know, but guessed that jays and many other birds carried their eggs in their mouths; and when I objected that a jay's mouth seemed too small to hold its eggs, he replied that birds' mouths were larger than the narrowness of their bills indicated. Then I asked him what he thought they did with the eggs while a new nest was being prepared. He didn't know; neither do I to this day. A specimen of the many puzzling problems presented to the naturalist.

We soon found many more nests belonging to birds that were not half so suspicious. The handsome and notorious blue jay plunders the nests of other birds and of course he could not trust us. Almost all the others – brown thrushes, bluebirds, song sparrows, kingbirds, hen-hawks, nighthawks, whip-poor-wills, woodpeckers, etc – simply tried to avoid being seen, to draw or drive us away, or paid no attention to us.

We used to wonder how the woodpeckers could bore holes so perfectly round, true mathematical circles. We ourselves could not have done it even with gouges and chisels. We loved to watch them feeding their young, and wondered how they could glean food enough for so many clamorous, hungry, unsatisfiable babies, and how they managed to give each one its share; for after the young grew strong, one would get his head out of the door-hole and try to hold possession of it to meet the food-laden parents. How hard they worked to support their families, especially the red-headed and speckledy woodpeckers and flickers; digging, hammering on scaly bark and decaying trunks and branches from dawn to dark, coming and going at intervals of a few minutes all the live-long day!

We discovered a hen-hawk's nest on the top of a tall oak thirty or forty rods from the shanty and approached it cautiously. One of the pair always kept watch, soaring in wide circles high above the tree, and when we attempted to climb it, the big dangerous-looking bird came swooping down at us and drove us away.

We greatly admired the plucky kingbird. In Scotland our great ambition was to be good fighters, and we admired this quality in the handsome little chattering flycatcher that whips all the other birds. He was particularly angry when plundering jays and hawks came near his home, and took pains to thrash them not only away from the nest-tree but out of the neighborhood. The nest was usually built on a bur oak near a meadow where insects were abundant, and where no undesirable visitor could approach without being discovered. When a hen-hawk hove in sight, the male immediately set off after him, and it was ridiculous to see that great, strong bird hurrying away as fast as his clumsy wings would carry him, as soon as he saw the little, waspish kingbird coming. But the kingbird easily overtook him, flew just a few feet above him, and with a lot of chattering, scolding notes kept diving and striking him on the back of the head until tired; then he alighted to rest on the hawk's broad shoulders, still scolding and chattering as he rode along, like an angry boy pouring out vials of wrath. Then, up and at him again with his sharp bill; and after he had thus driven and ridden his big enemy a mile or so from the nest, he went home to his mate, chuckling and bragging as if trying to tell her what a wonderful fellow he was.

This first spring, while some of the birds were still building their nests and very few young ones had yet tried to fly, Father hired a Yankee to assist in clearing eight or ten acres of the best ground for a field. We found new wonders every day and often had to call on this Yankee to solve puzzling questions. We asked him one day if there was any bird in America that the kingbird couldn't whip. What about the sandhill crane? Could he whip that long-legged, long-billed fellow?

'A crane never goes near kingbirds' nests or notices so small a bird,' he said, 'and therefore there could be no fighting between them.' So we hastily concluded that our hero could whip every bird in the country except perhaps the sandhill crane.

We never tired listening to the wonderful whip-poor-will. One came every night about dusk and sat on a log about twenty or thirty feet from our cabin door and began shouting 'Whip poor Will! Whip poor Will!' with loud emphatic earnestness. 'What's that? What's that?' we cried when this startling visitor first announced himself. 'What do you call it?'

'Why, it's telling you its name,' said the Yankee. 'Don't you hear it and what he wants you to do? He says his name is "Poor Will" and he wants you to whip him, and you may if you are able to catch him.' Poor Will seemed the most wonderful of all the strange creatures we had seen. What a wild, strong, bold voice he had, unlike any other we had ever heard on sea or land!

A near relative, the bull-bat, or nighthawk, seemed hardly less wonderful. Towards evening scattered flocks kept the sky

lively as they circled around on their long wings a hundred feet
or more above the ground, hunting moths and beetles, inter-
rupting their rather slow but strong, regular wing-beats at
short intervals with quick quivering strokes while uttering
keen, squeaky cries something like *pfee*, *pfee*, and every
now and then diving nearly to the ground with a loud ripping,
bellowing sound, like bull-roaring, suggesting its name; then
turning and gliding swiftly up again. These fine wild gray
birds, about the size of a pigeon, lay their two eggs on bare
ground without anything like a nest or even a concealing bush
or grass-tuft. Nevertheless they are not easily seen, for they are
colored like the ground. While sitting on their eggs, they
depend so much upon not being noticed that if you are walking
rapidly ahead they allow you to step within an inch or two of
them without flinching. But if they see by your looks that you
have discovered them, they leave their eggs or young, and, like
a good many other birds, pretend that they are sorely
wounded, fluttering and rolling over on the ground and
gasping as if dying, to draw you away. When pursued we
were surprised to find that just when we were on the point of
overtaking them they were always able to flutter a few yards
farther, until they had led us about a quarter of a mile from the
nest; then, suddenly getting well, they quietly flew home by a
roundabout way to their precious babies or eggs o'er a' the ills
of life victorious, bad boys among the worst. The Yankee took
particular pleasure in encouraging us to pursue them.

Everything about us was so novel and wonderful that we
could hardly believe our senses except when hungry or while
Father was thrashing us. When we first saw Fountain Lake
Meadow, on a sultry evening, sprinkled with millions of
lightning-bugs throbbing with light, the effect was so strange
and beautiful that it seemed far too marvelous to be real.
Looking from our shanty on the hill, I thought that the whole
wonderful fairy show must be in my eyes; for only in fighting,
when my eyes were struck, had I ever seen anything in the least
like it. But when I asked my brother if he saw anything strange
in the meadow he said, 'Yes, it's all covered with shaky fire-
sparks.' Then I guessed that it might be something outside of
us, and applied to our all-knowing Yankee to explain it. 'Oh,
it's nothing but lightnin'-bugs,' he said, and kindly led us down
the hill to the edge of the fiery meadow, caught a few of the

wonderful bugs, dropped them into a cup, and carried them to the shanty, where we watched them throbbing and flashing out their mysterious light at regular intervals, as if each little passionate glow were caused by the beating of a heart. Once I saw a splendid display of glow-worm light in the foothills of the Himalayas, north of Calcutta, but glorious as it appeared in pure starry radiance, it was far less impressive than the extravagant abounding, quivering, dancing fire on our Wisconsin meadow.

Partridge drumming was another great marvel. When I first heard the low, soft, solemn sound I thought it must be made by some strange disturbance in my head or stomach, but as all seemed serene within, I asked David whether he heard anything queer. 'Yes,' he said, 'I hear something saying *boomp*, *boomp*, *boomp*, and I'm wondering at it.' Then I was half satisfied that the source of the mysterious sound must be in something outside of us, coming perhaps from the ground or from some ghost or bogie or woodland fairy. Only after long watching and listening did we at last discover it in the wings of the plump brown bird.

The love-song of the common jack snipe seemed not a whit less mysterious than partridge drumming. It was usually heard on cloudy evenings, a strange, unearthly, winnowing, spiritlike sound, yet easily heard at a distance of a third of a mile. Our sharp eyes soon detected the bird while making it, as it circled high in the air over the meadow with wonderfully strong and rapid wing-beats, suddenly descending and rising, again and again, in deep, wide loops; the tones being very low and smooth at the beginning of the descent, rapidly increasing to a curious little whirling storm-roar at the bottom, and gradually fading lower and lower until the top was reached. It was long, however, before we identified this mysterious wing-singer as the little brown jack snipe that we knew so well and had so often watched as he silently probed the mud around the edge of our meadow stream and spring-holes, and made short zigzag flights over the grass uttering only little short, crisp quacks and chucks.

The love-songs of the frogs seemed hardly less wonderful than those of the birds, their musical notes varying from the sweet, tranquil, soothing peeping and purring of the hylas to the awfully deep low-bass blunt bellowing of the bullfrogs.

Some of the smaller species have wonderfully clear, sharp voices and told us their good Bible names in musical tones about as plainly as the whip-poor-will. *Isaac, Isaac; Yacob, Yacob; Israel, Israel;* shouted in sharp, ringing, far-reaching tones, as if they had all been to school and severely drilled in elocution. In the still, warm evenings big bunchy bullfrogs bellowed, *Drunk! Drunk! Drunk! Jug o' rum! Jug o' rum!* and early in the spring, counts less thousands of the commonest species, up to the throat in cold water, sang in concert, making a mass of music, such as it was, loud enough to be heard at a distance of more than half a mile.

Far, far apart from this loud marsh music is that of the many species of hyla, a sort of soothing immortal melody filling the air like light.

We reveled in the glory of the sky scenery as well as that of the woods and meadows and rushy, lily-bordered lakes. The great thunder-storms in particular interested us, so unlike any seen in Scotland, exciting awful, wondering admiration. Gazing awe-stricken, we watched the upbuilding of the sublime cloud-mountains – glowing, sun-beaten pearl and alabaster cumuli, glorious in beauty and majesty and looking so firm and lasting that birds, we thought, might build their nests amid their downy bosses; the black-browed storm-clouds marching in awful grandeur across the landscape, trailing broad gray sheets of hail and rain like vast cataracts, and ever and anon gashing down vivid zigzag lightning followed by terrible crashing thunder. We saw several trees shattered, and one of them, a punky old oak, was set on fire, while we wondered why all the trees and everybody and everything did not share the same fate, for oftentimes the whole sky blazed. After sultry storm days, many of the nights were darkened by smooth black apparently structureless cloud-mantles which at short intervals were illumined with startling suddenness to a fiery glow by quick, quivering lightning-flashes, revealing the landscape in almost noonday brightness, to be instantly quenched in solid blackness.

But those first days and weeks of unmixed enjoyment and freedom, reveling in the wonderful wildness about us, were soon to be mingled with the hard work of making a farm. I was first put to burning brush in clearing land for the plough. Those magnificent brush fires with great white hearts and red flames, the first big, wild outdoor fires I had ever seen, were wonderful sights for young eyes. Again and again, when they were burning fiercest so that we could hardly approach near enough to throw on another branch, Father put them to awfully practical use as warning lessons, comparing their heat with that of hell, and the branches with bad boys. 'Now, John,' he would say – 'now, John, just think what an awful thing it would be to be thrown into that fire – and then think of hell-fire, that is so many times hotter. Into that fire all bad boys, with sinners of every sort who disobey God, will be cast as we are casting branches into this brush fire, and although suffering so much, their sufferings will never, never end, because neither the fire nor the sinners can die.' But those terrible fire lessons quickly faded away in the blithe wilderness air; for no fire can be hotter than the heavenly fire of faith and hope that burns in every healthy boy's heart.

Soon after our arrival in the woods someone added a cat and puppy to the animals Father had bought. The cat soon had kittens, and it was interesting to watch her feeding, protecting, and training them. After they were able to leave their nest and play, she went out hunting and brought in many kinds of birds and squirrels for them, mostly ground squirrels (spermophiles), called 'gophers' in Wisconsin. When she got within a dozen yards or so of the shanty, she announced her approach by a peculiar call, and the sleeping kittens immediately bounced up and ran to meet her, all racing for the first bite of they knew not what, and we too ran to see what she brought. She then lay down a few minutes to rest and enjoy the enjoyment of her feasting family, and again vanished in the grass and flowers, coming and going every half-hour or so. Sometimes she brought in birds that we had never seen before, and occasionally a flying squirrel, chipmunk, or big fox squirrel. We were just old enough, David and I, to regard all these creatures as wonders, the strange inhabitants of our new world.

The pup was a common cur, though very uncommon to us, a black and white short-haired mongrel that we named 'Watch.' We always gave him a pan of milk in the evening just before we knelt in family worship, while daylight still lingered in the shanty. And, instead of attending to the prayers, I too often studied the small wild creatures playing around us. Field mice scampered about the cabin as though it had been built for them alone, and their performances were very amusing. About dusk, on one of the calm, sultry nights so grateful to moths and beetles, when the puppy was lapping his milk, and we were on our knees, in through the door came a heavy broad-shouldered beetle about as big as a mouse, and after it had droned and boomed round the cabin two or three times, the pan of milk, showing white in the gloaming, caught its eyes, and, taking good aim, it alighted with a slanting, glinting plash in the middle of the pan like a duck alighting in a lake. Baby Watch, having never before seen anything like that beetle, started back, gazing in dumb astonishment and fear at the black sprawling monster trying to swim. Recovering somewhat from his fright, he began to bark at the creature, and ran round and round his milk pan, wouf-woufing, gurring, growling, like an old dog barking at a wild-cat or a bear. The natural astonishment and curiosity of that boy dog getting his first entomological lesson in this wonderful world was so immoderately funny that I had great difficulty in keeping from laughing out loud.

Snapping turtles were common throughout the woods, and we were delighted to find that they would snap at a stick and hang on like bull-dogs; and we amused ourselves by introducing Watch to them, enjoying his curious behavior and theirs in getting acquainted with each other. One day we assisted one of the smallest of the turtles to get a good grip of poor Watch's ear. Then away he rushed, holding his head sidewise, yelping and terror-stricken, with the strange buglike reptile biting hard and clinging fast – a shameful amusement even for wild boys.

As a playmate Watch was too serious, though he learned more than any stranger would judge him capable of, was a bold, faithful watch-dog, and in his prime a grand fighter, able to whip all the other dogs in the neighborhood. Comparing him with ourselves, we soon learned that although he could not read books he could read faces, was a good judge of character, always knew what was going on and what we were about to do, and liked to help us. We could run nearly as fast as he could, see about as far and perhaps hear as well, but in sense of smell his nose was incomparably better than ours. One sharp winter morning when the ground was covered with snow, I noticed that when he was yawning and stretching himself after leaving his bed he suddenly caught the scent of something that excited him, went round the corner of the house, and looked intently to the westward across a tongue of land that we called West Bank, eagerly questioning the air with quivering nostrils, and bristling up as though he felt sure that there was something dangerous in that direction and had actually caught sight of it. Then he ran toward the Bank, and I followed him, curious to see what his nose had discovered. The top of the Bank commanded a view of the north end of our lake and meadow, and when we got there we saw an Indian hunter with a long spear, going from one muskrat cabin to another, approaching cautiously, careful to make no noise, and then suddenly thrusting his spear down through the house. If well aimed, the spear went through the poor beaver rat as it lay cuddled up in the snug nest it had made for itself in the fall with so much far-seeing care, and when the hunter felt the spear quivering, he dug down the mossy hut with his tomahawk and secured his prey – the flesh for food, and the skin to sell for a dime or so. This was a clear object lesson on dogs' keenness of scent. That Indian was more than half a mile away across a wooded ridge. Had the hunter been a white man, I suppose Watch would not have noticed him.

When he was about six or seven years old, he not only became cross, so that he would do only what he liked, but he fell on evil ways, and was accused by the neighbors who had settled around us of catching and devouring whole broods of chickens, some of them only a day or two out of the shell. We never imagined he would do anything so grossly undoglike. He never did at home. But several of the neighbors declared over and over again that they had caught him in the act, and insisted that he must be shot. At last, in spite of tearful protests, he was condemned and executed. Father examined the poor fellow's stomach in search of sure evidence, and discovered the heads of eight chickens that he had devoured at his last meal. So poor Watch was killed simply because his taste for chickens was too much like our own. Think of the millions of squabs that preaching, praying men and women kill and eat, with all sorts of other animals great and small, young and old, while eloquently discoursing on the coming of the blessed peaceful, bloodless millennium! Think of the passenger pigeons that fifty or sixty years ago filled the woods and sky over half the continent, now exterminated by beating down the young from the nests together with the brooding parents, before they could try their wonderful wings; by trapping them in nets, feeding them to hogs, etc. None of our fellow mortals is safe who eats what we eat, who in any way interferes with our pleasures, or who may be used for work or food, clothing or ornament, or mere cruel, sportish amusement. Fortunately many are too small to be seen, and therefore enjoy life beyond our reach. And in looking through God's great stone books made up of records reaching back millions and millions of years, it is a great comfort to learn that vast multitudes of creatures, great and small and infinite in number, lived and had a good time in God's lose before man was created.

The old Scotch fashion of whipping for every act of disobedience or of simple, playful forgetfulness was still kept up in the wilderness, and of course many of those whippings fell upon me. Most of them were outrageously severe, and utterly barren of fun. But here is one that was nearly all fun.

Father was busy hauling lumber for the frame house that was to be got ready for the arrival of my mother, sisters, and brother, left behind in Scotland. One morning, when he was ready to start for another load, his ox-whip was not to be found. He asked me if I knew anything about it. I told him I didn't know where it was, but Scotch conscience compelled me to confess that when I was playing with it I had tied it to Watch's tail, and that he ran away, dragging it through the grass, and came back without it. 'It must have slipped off his tail,' I said, and so I didn't know where it was. This honest, straightforward little story made Father so angry that he exclaimed with heavy, foreboding emphasis: 'The very deevil's in that boy!' David, who had been playing with me and was perhaps about as responsible for the loss of the whip as I was, said never a word, for he was always prudent enough to hold his tongue when the parental weather was stormy, and so escaped nearly all punishment. And, strange to say, this time I also escaped, all except a terrible scolding, though the thrashing weather seemed darker than ever. As if unwilling to let the sun see the shameful job, Father took me into the cabin where the storm was to fall, and sent David to the woods for a switch. While he was out selecting the switch, Father put in the spare time sketching my play-wickedness in awful colors, and of course referred again and again to the place prepared for bad boys. In the midst of this terrible word-storm, dreading most the impending thrashing, I whimpered that I was only playing because I couldn't help it; didn't know I was doing wrong; wouldn't do it again, and so forth. After this miserable dialogue was about exhausted, Father became impatient at my brother for taking so long to find the switch; and so was I, for I wanted to have the thing over and done with. At last, in came David, a picture of open-hearted innocence, solemnly dragging a young bur-oak sapling, and handed the end of it to Father, saying it was the best switch he could find. It was an awfully heavy one, about two and a half inches thick at the butt and ten feet long, almost big enough for a fence-pole. There wasn't room enough in the cabin to swing it, and the moment I saw it I burst out laughing in the midst of my fears. But Father failed to see the fun and was very angry at David, heaved the bur-oak outside and passionately demanded his reason for fetching 'sic a muckle rail like that instead o' a switch? Do ye ca' that a switch? I have a gude mind to thrash you instead o' John.' David, with demure, downcast eyes, looked preternaturally righteous, but as usual prudently answered never a word.

It was a hard job in those days to bring up Scotch boys in the way they should go; and poor overworked Father was determined to do it if enough of the right kind of switches could be found. But this time, as the sun was getting high, he hitched up old Tom and Jerry and made haste to the Kingston lumberyard, leaving me unscathed and as innocently wicked as ever; for hardly had Father got fairly out of sight among the oaks and hickories, ere all our troubles, hell-threatenings, and exhortations were forgotten in the fun we had lassoing a stubborn old sow and laboriously trying to teach her to go reasonably steady in rope harness. She was the first hog that Father bought to stock the farm, and we boys regarded her as a very wonderful beast. In a few weeks she had a lot of pigs, and of all the queer, funny, animal children we had yet seen, none aroused us more. They were so comic in size and shape, in their gait and gestures, their merry sham fights, and the false alarms they got up for the fun of scampering back to their mother and begging her in most persuasive little squeals to lie down and give them a drink.

After her darling short-snouted babies were about a month old, she took them out to the woods and gradually roamed farther and farther from the shanty in search of acorns and roots. One afternoon we heard a rifle-shot, a very noticeable thing, as we had no near neighbors, as yet. We thought it must have been fired by an Indian on the trail that followed the right bank of the Fox River between Portage and Packwaukee Lake and passed our shanty at a distance of about three quarters of a mile. Just a few minutes after that shot was heard along came the poor mother rushing up to the shanty for protection, with her pigs, all out of breath and terror-stricken. One of them was missing, and we supposed of course that an Indian had shot it for food. Next day, I discovered a blood-puddle where the Indian trail crossed the outlet of our lake. One of Father's hired men told us that the Indians thought nothing of levying this sort of blackmail whenever they were hungry. The solemn awe and fear in the eyes of that old mother and those little pigs I never can forget; it was as unmistakable and deadly a fear as I ever saw expressed by any human eye, and corroborates in no uncertain way the oneness of all of us.

Chapter 3

LIFE ON A WISCONSIN FARM

Coming direct from school in Scotland while we were still hopefully ignorant and far from tame – notwithstanding the unnatural profusion of teaching and thrashing lavished upon us – getting acquainted with the animals about us was a never-failing source of wonder and delight. At first my father, like nearly all the backwoods settlers, bought a yoke of oxen to do the farm work, and as field after field was cleared, the number was gradually increased until we had five yoke. These wise, patient, plodding animals did all the ploughing, logging, hauling, and hard work of every sort for the first four or five years, and, never having seen oxen before, we looked at them with the same eager freshness of conception as we did at the wild animals. We worked with them, sympathized with them in their rest and toil and play, and thus learned to know them far better than we should hail we been only trained scientific naturalists. We soon learned that each ox and cow and calf had individual character. Old white-faced Buck, one of the second yoke of oxen we owned, was a notably sagacious fellow. He seemed to reason sometimes almost like ourselves. In the fall we fed the cattle lots of pumpkins and had to split them open so that mouthfuls could be readily broken off. But Buck never waited for us to come to his help. The others, when they were hungry and impatient, tried to break through the hard rind with their teeth, but seldom with success if the pumpkin was full grown. Buck never wasted time in this mumbling, slavering way, but crushed them with his head. He went to the pile, picked out a good one, like a boy choosing an orange or apple, rolled it down on to the open ground, deliberately kneeled in front of it, placed his broad, flat brow on top of it, brought his weight hard down and crushed it, then quietly arose and went on with his meal in comfort. Some would call this 'instinct,' as if so-called 'blind instinct' must necessarily make an ox stand on its head to break pumpkins when its teeth got sore, or when nobody came with an axe to split them. Another fine ox showed his skill when hungry by opening all the fences that stood in his way to the corn-fields.

The humanity we found in them came partly through the expression of their eyes when tired, their tones of voice when hungry and calling for food, their patient plodding and pulling in hot weather, their long-drawn-out sighing breath when exhausted and suffering like ourselves, and their enjoyment of rest with the same grateful looks as ours. We recognized their kinship also by their yawning like ourselves when sleepy and evidently enjoying the same peculiar pleasure at the roots of their jaws; by the way they stretched themselves in the morning after a good rest; by learning languages – Scotch, English, Irish, French, Dutch – a smattering of each as required in the faithful service they so willingly, wisely rendered; by their intelligent, alert curiosity, manifested in listening to strange sounds; their love of play; the attachments they made; and their mourning, long continued, when a companion was killed.

When we went to Portage, our nearest town, about ten or twelve miles from the farm, it would oftentimes be late before we got back, and in the summer-time, in sultry, rainy weather, the clouds were full of sheet lightning which every minute or two would suddenly illumine the landscape, revealing all its features, the hills and valleys, meadows and trees, about as fully and clearly as the noonday sunshine; then as suddenly the glorious light would be quenched, making the darkness seem denser than before. On such nights the cattle had to find the way home without any help from us, but they never got off the track, for they followed it by scent like dogs. Once, Father, returning late from Portage or Kingston, compelled Tom and Jerry, our first oxen, to leave the dim track, imagining they must be going wrong. At last they stopped and refused to go farther. Then Father unhitched them from the wagon, took hold of Tom's tail, and was thus led straight to the shanty. Next morning he set out to seek his wagon and found it on the brow of a steep hill above an impassable swamp. We learned less from the cows, because we did not enter so far into their lives, working with them, suffering heat and cold, hunger and thirst, and almost deadly weariness with them; but none with natural charity could fail to sympathize with them in their love for their calves, and to feel that it in no way differed from the divine mother-love of a woman in thoughtful, self-sacrificing care; for they would brave every danger, giving their lives for their off-spring. Nor could we fail to sympathize with their awkward, blunt-nosed baby calves, with such beautiful, wondering eyes looking out on the world and slowly getting acquainted with things, all so strange to them, and awkwardly learning to use their legs, and play and fight.

Before leaving Scotland, Father promised us a pony to ride when we got to America, and we saw to it that this promise was not forgotten. Only a week or two after our arrival in the woods he bought us a little Indian pony for thirteen dollars from a store-keeper in Kingston who had obtained him from a Winnebago or Menominee Indian in trade for goods. He was a stout handsome bay with long black mane and tail, and, though he was only two years old, the Indians had already taught him to carry all sorts of burdens, to stand without being tied, to go anywhere over all sorts of ground fast or slow, and to jump and swim and fear nothing – a truly wonderful creature, strangely different from shy, skittish, nervous, superstitious civilized beasts. We turned him loose, and, strange to say, he never ran away from us or refused to be caught, but behaved as if he had known Scotch boys all his life, probably because we were about as wild as young Indians.

One day when Father happened to have a little leisure, he said, 'Noo, bairns, rin doon the meadow and get your powny and learn to ride him.' So we led him out to a smooth place near an Indian mound back of the shanty, where Father directed us to begin. I mounted for the first memorable lesson, crossed the mound, and set out at a slow walk along the wagon-track made in hauling lumber; then Father shouted: 'Whup him up, John, whup him up! Make him gallop; gallopin' is easier and better than walkin' or trottin'.' Jack was willing, and away he sped at a good fast gallop. I managed to keep my balance fairly well by holding fast to the mane, but could not keep from bumping up and down, for I was plump and elastic and so was Jack; therefore about half of the time I was in the air.

After a quarter of a mile or so of this curious transportation, I cried, 'Whoa, Jack!' The wonderful creature seemed to understand Scotch, for he stopped so suddenly I flew over his head, but he stood perfectly still as if that flying method of dismounting were the regular way. Jumping on again, I bumped and bobbed back along the grassy, flowery track, over the Indian mound, cried, 'Whoa, Jack!' flew over his head, and alighted in Father's arms as gracefully as if it were all intended for circus work.

After going over the course five or six times in the same free, picturesque style, I gave place to brother David, whose performances were much like my own. In a few weeks, however, or a month, we were taking adventurous rides more than a mile long out to a big meadow frequented by sandhill cranes, and returning safely with wonderful stories of the great long-legged birds we had seen, and how on the whole journey away and back we had fallen off only five or six times. Gradually we learned to gallop through the woods without roads of any sort, bareback and without rope or bridle, guiding only by leaning from side to side or by slight knee pressure. In this free way we used to amuse ourselves, tilting at full speed across a big 'kettle' that was on our farm, without holding on by either mane or tail.

These so-called 'kettles' were formed by the melting of large detached blocks of ice that had been buried in moraine material thousands of years ago when the ice-sheet that covered all this region was receding. As the buried ice melted, of course the moraine material above and about it fell in, forming hopper-shaped hollows, while the grass growing on their sides and around them prevented the rain and wind from filling them up. The one we performed in was perhaps seventy or eighty feet wide and twenty or thirty feet deep; and without a saddle or hold of any kind it was not easy to keep from slipping over Jack's head in diving into it, or over his tail climbing out. This was fine sport on the long summer Sundays when we were able to steal away before meeting-time without being seen. We got very warm and red at it, and oftentimes poor Jack, dripping with sweat like his riders, seemed to have been boiled in that kettle.

In Scotland we had often been admonished to be bold, and this advice we passed on to Jack, who had already got many a

wild lesson from Indian boys. Once, when teaching him to
jump muddy streams, I made him try the creek in our meadow
at a place where it is about twelve feet wide. He jumped
bravely enough, but came down with a grand splash hardly
more than halfway over. The water was only about a foot in
depth, but the black vegetable mud half afloat was unfathom-
able I managed to wallow ashore, but poor Jack sank deeper
and deeper until only his head was visible in the black abyss,
and his Indian fortitude was desperately tried. His foundering
so suddenly in the treacherous gulf recalled the story of the
Abbot of Aberbrothok's bell, which went down with a gurgling sound while bubbles rose and burst around. I had to go to
Father for help. He tied a long hemp rope brought from
Scotland around Jack's neck, and Tom and Jerry seemed to
have all they could do to pull him out. After which I got a
solemn scolding for asking the 'puir beast to jump intil sic a
saft bottomless place.'

We moved into our frame house in the fall, when Mother
with the rest of the family arrived from Scotland, and, when
the winter snow began to fly, the bur-oak shanty was made
into a stable for Jack. Father told us that good meadow hay
was all he required, but we fed him corn, lots of it, and he grew
very frisky and fat. About the middle of winter his long hair
was full of dust and, as we thought, required washing. So,
without taking the frosty weather into account, we gave him a
thorough soap and water scouring, and as we failed to get him
rubbed dry, a row of icicles formed under his belly. Father
happened to see him in this condition and angrily asked what
we had been about. We said Jack was dirty and we had washed
him to make him healthy. He told us we ought to be ashamed
of ourselves, 'soaking the puir beast in cauld water at this time
o' year'; that when we wanted to clean him we should have
sense enough to use the brush and curry-comb.

In summer Dave or I had to ride after the cows every evening
about sundown, and Jack got so accustomed to bringing in the
drove that when we happened to be a few minutes late he used
to go off alone at the regular time and bring them home at a
gallop. It used to make Father very angry to see Jack chasing
the cows like a shepherd dog, running from one to the other
and giving each a bite on the rump to keep them on the run,
flying before him as if pursued by wolves. Father would

declare at times that the wicked beast had the deevil in him and would be the death of the cattle. The corral and barn were just at the foot of a hill, and he made a great display of the drove on the home stretch as they walloped down that hill with their tails on end.

One evening when the pell-mell Wild West show was at its wildest, it made Father so extravagantly mad that he ordered me to 'Shoot Jack!' I went to the house and brought the gun, suffering most horrible mental anguish, such as I suppose unhappy Abraham felt when commanded to slay Isaac. Jack's life was spared, however, though I can't tell what finally became of him. I wish I could. After Father bought a span of work horses he was sold to a man who said he was going to ride him across the plains to California. We had him, I think, some five or six years. He was the stoutest, gentlest, bravest little horse I ever saw. He never seemed tired, could canter all day with a man about as heavy as himself on his back, and feared nothing. Once fifty or sixty pounds of beef that was tied on his back slid over his shoulders along his neck and weighed down his head to the ground, fairly anchoring him; but he stood patient and still for half an hour or so without making the slightest struggle to free himself, while I was away getting help to untie the pack-rope and set the load back in its place.

As I was the eldest boy I had the care of our first span of work horses. Their names were Nob and Nell. Nob was very intelligent, and even affectionate, and could learn almost anything. Nell was entirely different; balky and stubborn, though we managed to teach her a good many circus tricks; but she never seemed to like to play with us in anything like an affectionate way as Nob did. We turned them out one day into the pasture, and an Indian, hiding in the brush that had sprung up after the grass fires had been kept out, managed to catch Nob, tied a rope to her jaw for a bridle, rode her to Green Lake, about thirty or forty miles away, and tried to sell her for fifteen dollars. All our hearts were sore, as if one of the family had been lost. We hunted everywhere and could not at first imagine what had become of her. We discovered her track where the fence was broken down, and, following it for a few miles, made sure the track was Nob's; and a neighbor told us he had seen an Indian riding fast through the woods on a horse that looked like Nob. But we could find no farther trace of her until a month or two after she was lost, and we had given up hope of ever seeing her again. Then we learned that she had been taken from an Indian by a farmer at Green Lake because he saw that she had been shod and had worked in harness. So when the Indian tried to sell her the farmer said: 'You are a thief. That is a white man's horse. You stole her.'

'No,' said the Indian, 'I brought her from Prairie du Chien and she has always been mine.'

The man, pointing to her feet and the marks of the harness, said: 'You are lying. I will take that horse away from you and put her in my pasture, and if you come near it I will set the dogs on you.' Then he advertized her. One of our neighbors happened to see the advertisement and brought us the glad news, and great was our rejoicing when Father brought her home. That Indian must have treated her with terrible cruelty, for when I was riding her through the pasture several years afterward, looking for another horse that we wanted to catch, as we approached the place where she had been captured she stood stock still gazing through the bushes, fearing the Indian might still be hiding there ready to spring; and she was so excited that she trembled, and her heartbeats were so loud that I could hear them distinctly as I sat on her back, *boomp*, *boomp*, *boomp*, like the drumming of a partridge. So vividly had she remembered her terrible experiences.

She was a great pet and favorite with the whole family, quickly learned playful tricks, came running when we called, seemed to know everything we said to her, and had the utmost confidence in our friendly kindness.

We used to cut and shock and husk the Indian corn in the fall, until a keen Yankee stopped overnight at our house and among other laborsaving notions convinced Father that it was better to let it stand, and husk it at his leisure during the winter, then turn in the cattle to eat the leaves and trample down the stalks, so that they could be ploughed under in the spring. In this winter method each of us took two rows and husked into baskets, and emptied the corn on the ground in piles of fifteen to twenty basketfuls, then loaded it into the wagon to be hauled to the crib. This was cold, painful work, the temperature being oftentimes far below zero and the ground covered with dry, frosty snow, giving rise to miserable crops of chilblains and frosted fingers – a sad change from the merry Indian-summer husking, when the big yellow pumpkins covered the cleared fields – golden corn, golden pumpkins, gathered in the hazy golden weather. Sad change, indeed, but we occasionally got some fun out of the nipping, shivery work from hungry prairie chickens, and squirrels and mice that came about us.

The piles of corn were often left in the field several days, and while loading them into the wagon we usually found field mice in them – big, blunt-nosed, strong-scented fellows that we were taught to kill just because they nibbled a few grains of corn. I used to hold one while it was still warm, up to Nob's nose for the fun of seeing her make faces and snort at the smell of it; and I would say: 'Here, Nob,' as if offering her a lump of sugar. One day I offered her an extra fine, fat, pomp specimen, something like a little woodchuck, or muskrat, and to my astonishment, after smelling it curiously and doubtfully, as if wondering what the gift might be, and rubbing it back and forth in the palm of my hand with her upper lip, she deliberately took it into her mouth, crunched and munched and chewed it fine and swallowed it, bones, teeth, head, tail, everything. Not a single hair of that mouse was wasted. When she was chewing it she nodded and grunted, as though critically tasting and relishing it.

My father was a steadfast enthusiast on religious matters, and, of course, attended almost every sort of church-meeting, especially revival meetings. They were occasionally held in summer, but mostly in winter when the sleighing was good and plenty of time available. One hot summer day Father drove Nob to Portage and back, twenty-four miles over a sandy road. It was a hot, hard, sultry day's work, and she had evidently been over driven in order to get home in time for one of these meetings. I shall never forget how tired and wilted she looked that evening when I unhitched her; how she drooped in her stall, too tired to eat or even to lie down. Next morning it was plain that her lungs were inflamed; all the dreadful symptoms were just the same as my own when I had pneumonia Father sent for a Methodist minister, a very energetic, resourceful man, who was a blacksmith, farmer, butcher, and horse-doctor as well as minister; but all his gifts and skill were of no avail. Nob was doomed. We bathed her head and tried to get her to eat something, but she couldn't eat, and in about a couple of weeks we turned her loose to let her come around the house and see us in the weary suffering and loneliness of the shadow of death. She tried to follow us children, so long her friends and workmates and playmates. It was awfully touching. She had several hemorrhages, and in the forenoon of her last day, after she had had one of her dreadful spells of bleeding and gasping for breath, she came to me trembling, with beseeching, heartbreaking looks, and after I had bathed her head and tried to soothe and pet her, she lay down and gasped and died. All the family gathered about her, weeping, with aching hearts. Then dust to dust.

She was the most faithful, intelligent, playful, affectionate, human-like horse I ever knew, and she won all our hearts. Of the many advantages of farm life for boys one of the greatest is the gaining a real knowledge of animals as fellow-mortals, learning to respect them and love them, and even to win some of their love. Thus Godlike sympathy grows and thrives and spreads far beyond the teachings of churches and schools, where too often the mean, blinding, loveless doctrine is taught that animals have neither mind nor soul, have no rights that we are bound to respect, and were made only for man, to be petted, spoiled, slaughtered, or enslaved.

At first we were afraid of snakes, but soon learned that most of them were harmless. The only venomous species seen on our farm were the rattlesnake and the copperhead, one of each. David saw the rattler, and we both saw the copperhead. One day, when my brother came in from his work, he reported that he had seen a snake that made a queer buzzy noise with its tail. This was the only rattlesnake seen on our farm, though we heard of them being common on limestone hills eight or ten miles distant. We discovered the copperhead when we were ploughing, and we saw and felt at the first long, fixed, half-charmed, admiring stare at him that he was an awfully dangerous fellow. Every fiber of his strong, lithe, quivering body, his burnished copper-colored head, and above all his fierce, able eyes, seemed to be overflowing full of deadly power, and bade us beware. And yet it is only fair to say that this terrible, beautiful reptile showed no disposition to hurt us until we threw clods at him and tried to head him off from a log fence into which he was trying to escape. We were barefooted and of course afraid to let him get very near, while we vainly battered him with the loose sandy clods of the freshly ploughed field to hold him back until we could get a stick. Looking us in the eyes after a moment's pause, he probably saw we were afraid, and he came right straight at us, snapping and looking terrible, drove us out of his way, and won his fight.

Out on the open sandy hills there were a good many thick burly blow snakes, the kind that puff themselves up and hiss. Our Yankee declared that their breath was very poisonous and that we must not go near them. A handsome ringed species common in damp, shady places was, he told us, the most wonderful of all the snakes, for if chopped into pieces, however small, the fragments would wriggle themselves together again, and the restored snake would go on about its business as if nothing had happened. The commonest kinds were the striped slender species of the meadows and streams, good swimmers, that lived mostly on frogs.

Once I observed one of the larger ones, about two feet long, pursuing a frog in our meadow, and it was wonderful to see how fast the legless, footless, wingless, finless hunter could run. The frog, of course, knew its enemy and was making desperate efforts to escape to the water and hide in the marsh mud. He was a fine, sleek yellow muscular fellow and was springing over the tall grass in wide-arching jumps. The green-striped snake, gliding swiftly and steadily, was keeping the frog in sight and, had I not interfered, would probably have tired out the poor jumper. Then, perhaps, while digesting and enjoying his meal, the happy snake would himself be swallowed, frog and all, by a hawk. Again, to our astonishment, the small specimens were attacked by our hens. They pursued and pecked away at them until they killed and devoured them, oftentimes quarreling over the division of the spoil, though it was not easily divided.

We watched the habits of the swift-darting dragonflies, wild bees, butterflies, wasps, beetles, etc., and soon learned to discriminate between those that might be safely handled and the pinching or stinging species. But of all our wild neighbors the mosquitoes were the first with which we became very intimately acquainted.

The beautiful in the spring meadow lying warm sunshine, outspread between our lily-rimmed lake and the hill-slope that our shanty stood on, sent forth thirsty swans of the little gray, speckledy, singing, stinging pests; and how tellingly they introduced themselves! Of little avail were the smudges that we made on muggy evenings to drive them away; and amid the many lessons which they insisted upon teaching us we wondered more and more at the extent of their knowledge, especially that in their tiny, flimsy bodies room could be found for such cunning palates. They would drink their fill from brown, smoky Indians, or from old white folk flavored with tobacco and whiskey, when no better could be had. But the surpassing fineness of their taste was best manifested by their enthusiastic appreciation of boys full of lively red blood, and of girls in full bloom fresh from cool Scotland or England. On these it was pleasant to witness their enjoyment as they feasted. Indians, we were told, believed that if they were brave fighters they would go after death to a happy country abounding in game, where there were no mosquitoes and no cowards. For cowards were driven away by themselves to a miserable country where there was no game fit to eat, and where the sky was always dark with huge gnats and mosquitoes as big as pigeons.

We were great admirers of the little black water-bugs. Their whole lives seemed to be play, skimming, swimming, swirling, and waltzing together in little groups on the edge of the lake and in the meadow springs, dancing to music we never could hear. The long-legged skaters, too, seemed wonderful fellows, shuffling about on top of the water, with air-bubbles like little bladders tangled under their hairy feet; and we often wished that we also might be shod in the same way to enable us to skate on the lake in summer as well as in icy winter. Not less wonderful were the boatmen, swimming on their backs, pulling themselves along with a pair of oar-like legs.

Great was the delight of brothers David and Daniel and myself when Father gave us a few pine boards for a boat, and it was a memorable day when we got that boat built and launched into the lake. Never shall I forget our first sail over the gradually deepening water, the sun-beams pouring through it revealing the strange plants covering the bottom, and the fishes coming about us, staring and wondering as if the boat were a monstrous strange fish.

The water was so clear that it was almost invisible, and when we floated slowly out over the plants and fishes, we seemed to be miraculously sustained in the air while silently exploring a veritable fairyland.

We always had to work hard, but if we worked still harder we were occasionally allowed a little spell in the long summer evenings about sundown to fish, and on Sundays an hour or two to sail quietly without fishing-rod or gun when the lake was calm. Therefore we gradually learned something about its inhabitants – pickerel, sunfish, black bass, perch, shiners, pumpkin-seeds, ducks, loons, turtles, muskrats, etc. We saw the sunfishes making their nests in little openings in the rushes where the water was only a few feet deep, ploughing up and shoving away the soft gray mud with their noses, like pigs, forming round bowls five or six inches in depth and about two feet in diameter, in which their eggs were deposited. And with what beautiful, unweariable devotion they watched and hovered over them and chased away prowling spawn-eating enemies that ventured within a rod or two of the precious nest!

The pickerel is a savage fish endowed with marvelous strength and speed. It lies in wait for its prey on the bottom, perfectly motionless like a waterlogged stick, watching everything that moves, with fierce, hungry eyes. Oftentimes when we were fishing for some other kinds over the edge of the boat, a pickerel that we had not noticed would come like a bolt of lightning and seize the fish we had caught before we could get it into the boat. The very first pickerel that I ever caught jumped into the air to seize a small fish dangling on my line, and, missing its aim, fell plump into the boat as if it had dropped from the sky.

Some of our neighbors fished for pickerel through the ice in midwinter. They usually drove a wagon out on the lake, set a large number of lines baited with live minnows, hung a loop of the lines over a small bush planted at the side of each hole, and watched to see the loops pulled off when a fish had taken the bait. Large quantities of pickerel were often caught in this cruel way.

Our beautiful lake, named Fountain Lake by Father, but Muir's Lake by the neighbors, is one of the many small glacier lakes that adorn the Wisconsin landscapes. It is fed by twenty or thirty meadow springs about half a mile long, half as wide, and surrounded by low finely modeled hills dotted with oak and hickory, and meadows full of grasses and sedges and many beautiful orchids and ferns. First there is a zone of green, shining rushes, and just beyond the rushes a zone of white and orange water-lilies fifty or sixty feet wide forming a magnificent border. On bright days, when the lake was rippled by a breeze, the lilies and sun-spangles danced together in radiant beauty, and it became difficult to discriminate between them.

On Sundays, after or before chores and sermons and Bible-lessons, we drifted about on the lake for hours, especially in lily time, getting finest lessons and sermons from the water and flowers, ducks, fishes, and muskrats. In particular we took Christ's advice and devoutly 'considered the lilies' – how they grow up in beauty out of gray lime mud, and ride gloriously among the breezy sun-spangles. On our way home we gathered grand bouquets of them to be kept fresh all the week. No flower was hailed with greater wonder and admiration by the European settlers in general – Scotch, English, and Irish – than this white water-lily (*Nymphoea odorata*). It is a magnificent plant, queen of the inland waters, pure white, three or four inches in diameter, the most beautiful, sumptuous and deliciously fragrant of all our Wisconsin flowers. No lily garden in civilization we had ever seen could compare with our lake garden.

The next most admirable flower in the estimation of settlers in this part of the new world was the pasque-flower or wind-flower (*Anemone Patens* var. *Nuttalliana*). It is the very first to appear in the spring, covering the cold gray-black ground with cheery blossoms. Before the axe or plough had touched the 'oak openings' of Wisconsin, they were swept by running fires almost every autumn after the grass became dry. If from any cause, such as early snowstorms or late rains, they happened to escape the autumn fire besom, they were likely to be burned in the spring after the snow melted. But whether burned in the spring or fall, ashes and bits of charred twigs and grass stems made the whole country look dismal. Then, before a single grass-blade had sprouted, a hopeful multitude of large hairy, silky buds about as thick as one's thumb came to light, pushing up through the black and gray ashes and cinders, and before these buds were fairly free from the ground they opened wide and displayed purple blossoms about two inches in diameter, giving beauty for ashes in glorious abundance. Instead of remaining in the ground waiting for warm weather and companions, this admirable plant seemed to be in haste to rise and cheer the desolate landscape. Then at its leisure, after other plants had come to its help, it spread its leaves and grew up to a height of about two or three feet. The spreading leaves formed a whorl on the ground, and another about the middle of the stem as an involucre, and on the top of the stem the silky, hairy long-tailed seeds formed a head like a second flower. A little church was established among the earlier settlers and the meetings at first were held in our house. After working hard all the week it was difficult for boys to sit still through long sermons without falling asleep, especially in warm weather. In this drowsy trouble the charming anemone came to our help. A pocketful of the pungent seeds industriously nibbled while the discourses were at their dullest kept us awake and filled our minds with flowers.

The next great flower wonders on which we lavished admiration, not only for beauty of color and size, but for their curious shapes, were the cypripediums, called 'lady's-slippers' or 'Indian moccasins.' They were so different from the familiar flowers of old Scotland. Several species grew in our meadow and on shady hillsides – yellow, rose-colored, and some nearly white, an inch or more in diameter, and shaped exactly like Indian moccasins. They caught the eye of all the European settlers and made them gaze and wonder like children. And so did calopogon, pogonia, spiranthes, and many other fine plant people that lived in our meadow. The beautiful Turk's-turban (*Lilium superbum*) growing on stream-banks was rare in our neighborhood, but the orange lily grew in abundance on dry ground beneath the bur-oaks and often brought Aunt Ray's lily-bed in Scotland to mind. The butterfly-weed, with its brilliant scarlet flowers, attracted flocks of butterflies and made fine masses of color. With autumn came a glorious abundance and variety of asters, those beautiful plant stars, together with goldenrods, sun-flowers, daisies, and liatris of different species while around the shady margin of the meadow many ferns in beds and vaselike groups spread their beautiful fronds, especially the osmundas (*O. claytoniana*, *regalis*, and *cinnamomea*) and the sensitive and ostrich ferns.

Early in summer we feasted on strawberries, that grew in rich beds beneath the meadow grasses and sedges as well as in the dry sunny woods. And in different bogs and marshes, and around their borders on our own farm and along the Fox River, we found dewberries and cranberries, and a glorious profusion of huckleberries, the fountain-heads of pies of wondrous taste and size, colored in the heart like sunsets. Nor were we slow to discover the value of the hickory trees yielding both sugar and nuts. We carefully counted the different kinds on our farm, and every morning when we could steal a few minutes before breakfast after doing the chores, we visited the trees that had been wounded by the axe, to scrape off and enjoy the thick white delicious syrup that exuded from them, and gathered the nuts as they fell in the mellow Indian summer, making haste to get a fair share with the sapsuckers and squirrels. The hickory makes fine masses of color in the fall, every leaf a flower, but it was the sweet sap and sweet nuts that first interested us. No harvest in the Wisconsin woods was ever gathered with more pleasure and care. Also, to our delight, we found plenty of hazelnuts, and in a few places abundance of wild apples. They were desperately sour, and we used to fill our pockets with them and dare each other to eat one without making a face – no easy feat.

One hot summer day Father told us that we ought to learn to swim. This was one of the most interesting suggestions he had ever offered, but precious little time was allowed for trips to the lake, and he seldom tried to show us how. 'Go to the frogs,' he said, 'and they will give you all the lessons you need. Watch their arms and legs and see how smoothly they kick themselves along and dive and come up. When you want to dive, keep your arms by your side or over your head, and kick, and when you want to come up, let your legs drag and paddle with your hands.'

We found a little basin among the rushes at the south end of the lake, about waist-deep and a rod or two wide, shaped like a sunfish's nest. Here we kicked and plashed for many a lesson, faithfully trying to imitate frogs; but the smooth, comfortable sliding gait of our amphibious teachers seemed hopelessly hard to learn. When we tried to kick frog-fashion, down went our heads as if weighted with lead the moment our feet left the ground. One day it occurred to me to hold my breath as long as I could and let my head sink as far as it liked without paying any attention to it, and try to swim under the water instead of on the surface. This method was a great success, for at the very first trial I managed to cross the basin without touching bottom, and soon learned the use of my limbs. Then, of course, swimming with my head above water soon became so easy that it seemed perfectly natural. David tried the plan with the same success. Then we began to count the number of times that we could swim around the basin without stopping to rest, and after twenty or thirty rounds failed to tire us, we proudly thought that a little more practice would make us about as amphibious as frogs.

On the fourth of July of this swimming year one of the Lawson boys came to visit us, and we went down to the lake to spend the great warm day with the fishes and ducks and turtles. After gliding about on the smooth mirror water, telling stories and enjoying the company of the happy creatures about us, we rowed to our bathing-pool, and David and I went in for a swim, while our companion fished from the boat a little way out beyond the rushes. After a few turns in the pool, it occurred to me that it was now about time to try deep water. Swimming through the thick growth of rushes and lilies was somewhat dangerous, especially for a beginner, because one's arms and legs might be entangled among the long, limber stems; nevertheless I ventured and struck out boldly enough for the boat, where the water was twenty or thirty feet deep. When I reached the end of the little skiff I raised my right hand to take hold of it to surprise Lawson, whose back was toward me and who was not aware of my approach; but I failed to reach high enough, and, of course, the weight of my arm and the stroke against the over-leaning stern of the boat shoved me down and I sank, struggling, frightened and confused. As soon as my feet touched the bottom, I slowly rose to the surface, but before I could get breath enough to call for help, sank back again and lost all control of myself. After sinking and rising I don't know how many times, some water got into my lungs and I began to drown. Then suddenly my mind seemed to clear. I remembered that I could swim under water, and, making a desperate struggle toward the shore, I reached a point where with my toes on the bottom I got my mouth above the surface, gasped for help, and was pulled into the boat.

This humiliating accident spoiled the day, and we all agreed to keep it a profound secret. My sister Sarah had heard my cry for help, and on our arrival at the house inquired what had happened. 'Were you drowning, John? I heard you cry you couldna get oot.' Lawson made haste to reply, 'Oh, no! He was joist haverin'.'

I was very much ashamed of myself, and at night, after calmly reviewing the affair, concluded that there had been no reasonable cause for the accident, and that I ought to punish myself for so nearly losing my life from unmanly fear. Accordingly at the very first opportunity I stole away to the lake by myself, got into my boat, and instead of going back to the old swimming-bowl for further practice, or to try to do sanely and well what I had so ignominiously failed to do in my first adventure, that is, to swim out through the rushes and lilies, I rowed directly out to the middle of the lake, stripped, stood up on the seat in the stern, and with grim deliberation took a header and dove straight down thirty or forty feet, turned easily, and, letting my feet drag, paddled straight to the surface with my hands as Father had at first directed me to do. I then swam round the boat, glorying in my suddenly acquired confidence and victory over myself, climbed into it, and dived again, with the same triumphant success. I think I went down four or five times, and each time as I made the dive-spring shouted aloud, 'Take that!' feeling that was getting most gloriously even with myself.

Never again from that day to this have I lost control of myself in water. If suddenly thrown overboard at sea in the dark, or even while asleep, I think I would immediately right myself in a way some would call 'instinct,' rise among the waves, catch my breath, and try to plan what would better be done. Never was victory over self more complete. I have been a good swimmer ever since. At a slow gait I think I could swim all day in smooth water moderate in temperature. When I was a student at Madison, I used to go on long swimming-journeys, called exploring expeditions, along the south shore of Lake Mendota, on Saturdays, sometimes alone, sometimes with another amphibious explorer by the name of Fuller.

My adventures in Fountain Lake call to mind the story of a boy who in climbing a tree to rob a crow's nest fell and broke his leg, but as soon as it healed compelled himself to climb to the top of the tree he had fallen from.

Like Scotch children in general we were taught grim self-denial, in season and out of season, to mortify the flesh, keep our bodies in subjection to Bible laws, and mercilessly punish ourselves for every fault imagined or committed. A little boy, while helping his sister to drive home the cows, happened to use a forbidden word. 'I'll have to tell Fayther on ye,' said the horrified sister. 'I'll tell him that ye said a bad word.' 'Weel,' said the boy, by way of excuse, 'I couldna help the word comin' into me, and it's na waur to speak it oot than to let it rin through ye.'

A Scotch fiddler playing at a wedding drank so much whiskey that on the way home he fell by the roadside. In the morning he was ashamed and angry and determined to punish himself. Making haste to the house of a friend, a gamekeeper, he called him out, and requested the loan of a gun. The alarmed gamekeeper, not liking the fiddler's looks and voice, anxiously inquired what he was going to do with it. 'Surely,' said he, 'you're no gan to shoot yourself.' 'No-o,' with characteristic candor replied the penitent fiddler, 'I dinna think that I'll juist exactly kill mysel, but I'm gaun to tak a dander doon the burn (brook) wi' the gull and gie mysel a deevil o' a fleg (fright)'.

One calm summer evening a red-headed woodpecker was drowned in our lake. The accident happened at the south end, opposite our memorable swimming-hole, a few rods from the place where I came so near being drowned years before. I had returned to the old home during a summer vacation of the State University, and, having made a beginning in botany, I was, of course, full of enthusiasm and ran eagerly to my beloved pogonia, calopogon, and cypripedium gardens, osmunda ferneries, and the lake lilies and pitcher-plants. A little before sundown the day-breeze died away, and the lake, reflecting the wooded hills like a mirror, was dimpled and dotted and streaked here and there where fishes and turtles were poking out their heads and muskrats were sculling themselves along with their flat tails making glittering tracks. After lingering awhile, dreamily recalling the old, hard, half-happy days, and watching my favorite red-headed woodpeckers pursuing moths like regular flycatchers, I swam out through the rushes and up the middle of the lake to the north end and back, gliding slowly, looking about me, enjoying the scenery as I would in a saunter along the shore, and studying

the habits of the animals as they were explained and recorded
on the smooth glassy water.

On the way back, when I was within a hundred rods or so of
the end of my voyage, I noticed a peculiar plashing disturbance
that could not, I thought, be made by a jumping fish or any
other inhabitant of the lake; for instead of low regular out-
circling ripples such as are made by the popping up of a head
or like those raised by the quick splash of a leaping fish, or
diving loon or muskrat, a continuous struggle was kept up for
several minutes ere the outspreading, interfering ring-waves
began to die away. Swimming hastily to the spot to try to
discover what had happened, I found one of my woodpeckers
floating motionless with outspread wings. All was over. Had I
been a minute or two earlier, I might have saved him. He had
glanced on the water I suppose in pursuit of a moth, was
unable to rise from it, and died struggling, as I nearly did at this
same spot. Like me he seemed to have lost his mind in blind
confusion and fear. The water was warm, and had he kept still
with his head a little above the surface, he would sooner or
later have been wafted ashore. The best aimed flights of birds
and man 'gang aft agley,' but this was the first case I had
witnessed of a bird losing its life by drowning.

Doubtless accidents to animals are far more common than is
generally known. I have seen quails killed by flying against our
house when suddenly startled. Some birds get entangled in
hairs of their own nests and die. Once I found a poor snipe in
our meadow that was unable to fly on account of difficult egg-
birth. Pitying the poor mother, I picked her up out of the grass
and helped her as gently as I could, and as soon as the egg was
born she flew gladly away. Oftentimes I have thought it
strange that one could walk through the woods and mountains
and plains for years without seeing a single blood-spot. Most
wild animals get into the world and out of it without being
noticed. Nevertheless we at last sadly learn that they are all
subject to the vicissitudes of fortune like ourselves. Many birds
lose their lives in storms. I remember a particularly severe
Wisconsin winter, when the temperature was many degrees
below zero and the snow was deep, preventing the quail, which
feed on the ground, from getting anything like enough of food,
as was pitifully shown by a flock I found on our farm frozen
solid in a thicket of oak sprouts. They were in a circle about a

foot wide, with their heads outward, packed close together for warmth. Yet all had died without a struggle, perhaps more from starvation than frost. Many small birds lose their lives in the storms of early spring, or even summer. One mild spring morning I picked up more than a score out of the grass and flowers, most of them darling singers that had perished in a sudden storm of sleety rain and hail.

In a hollow at the foot of an oak tree that I had chopped down one cold winter day, I found a poor ground squirrel frozen solid in its snug grassy nest, in the middle of a store of nearly a peck of wheat it had carefully gathered. I carried it home and gradually thawed and warmed it in the kitchen, hoping it would come to life like a pickerel I caught in our lake through a hole in the ice, which, after being frozen as hard as a bone and thawed at the fireside, squirmed itself out of the grasp of the cook when she began to scrape it, bounced off the table, and danced about on the floors making wonderful springy jumps as if trying to find its way back home to the lake. But for the poor spermophile nothing I could do in the way of revival was of any avail. Its life had passed away without the slightest struggle, as it lay asleep curled up like a ball, with its tail wrapped about it.

Chapter 4
A PARADISE OF BIRDS

The Wisconsin oak openings were a summer paradise for song birds, and a fine place to get acquainted with them; for the trees stood wide apart, allowing one to see the happy home-seekers as they arrived in the spring, their mating, nest-building, the brooding and feeding of the young, and, after they were full-fledged and strong, to see all the families of the neighborhood gathering and getting ready to leave in the fall. Excepting the geese and ducks and pigeons nearly all our summer birds arrived singly or in small draggled flocks, but when frost and falling leaves brought their winter homes to mind they assembled in large flocks on dead or leafless trees by the side of a meadow or field, perhaps to get acquainted and talk the thing over. Some species held regular daily meetings for several weeks before finally setting forth on their long southern journeys. Strange to say, we never saw them start. Some mornings we would find them gone. Doubtless they migrated in the night time. Comparatively few species remained all winter, the nuthatch, chickadee, owl, prairie chicken, quail, and a few stragglers from the main flocks of ducks, jays, hawks, and bluebirds. Only after the country was settled did either jays or bluebirds winter with us.

The brave, frost-defying chickadees and nuthatches stayed all the year wholly independent of farms and man's food and affairs.

With the first hints of spring came the brave little bluebirds, darling singers as blue as the best sky, and of course we all loved them. Their rich, crispy warbling is perfectly delightful, soothing and cheering, sweet and whisperingly low, Nature's fine love touches, every note going straight home into one's heart. And withal they are hardy and brave, fearless fighters in defense of home. When we boys approached their knot-hole nests, the bold little fellows kept scolding and diving at us and tried to strike us in the face, and oftentimes we were afraid they would prick our eyes. But the boldness of the little house-keepers only made us love them the more.

None of the bird people of Wisconsin welcomed us more heartily than the common robin. Far from showing alarm at the coming of settlers into their native woods, they reared their young around our gardens as if they liked us, and how heartily we admired the beauty and fine manners of these graceful birds and their loud cheery song of *Fear not, fear not, cheer up, cheer up*. It was easy to love them for they reminded us of the robin redbreast of Scotland. Like the bluebirds, they dared every danger in defense of home, and we often wondered that birds so gentle could be so bold and that sweet-voiced singers could so fiercely fight and scold.

Of all the great singers that sweeten Wisconsin one of the best known and best loved is the brown thrush or thrasher, strong and able without being familiar, and easily seen and heard. Rosy purple evenings after thunder-showers are the favorite song-times, when the winds have died away and the steaming ground and the leaves and flowers fill the air with fragrance. Then the male makes haste to the topmost spray of an oak tree and sings loud and clear with delightful enthusiasm until sundown, mostly I suppose for his mate sitting on the precious eggs in a brush heap. And how faithful and watchful and daring he is! Woe to the snake or squirrel that ventured to go nigh the nest! We often saw him diving on them, pecking them about the head and driving them away as bravely as the kingbird drives away hawks. Their rich and varied strains make the air fairly quiver. We boys often tried to interpret the wild ringing melody and put it into words.

After the arrival of the thrushes came the bobolinks, gush-ing, gurgling, inexhaustible fountains of song, pouring forth floods of sweet notes over the broad Fox River meadows in wonderful variety and volume, crowded and miffed beyond description, as they hovered on quivering wings above their hidden nests in the grass. It seemed marvelous to us that birds so moderate in size could hold so much of this wonderful song stuff. Each one of them poured forth music enough for a whole flock, singing as if its whole body, feathers and all, were made up of music, flowing, glowing, bubbling melody interpenetrated here and there with small scintillating prickles and spicules. We never became so intimately acquainted with the bobolinks as with the thrushes, for they lived far out on the broad Fox River meadows, while the thrushes sang on the tree-tops around every home. The bobolinks were among the first of our great singers to leave us in the fall, going apparently direct to the rice-fields of the Southern States, where they grew fat and were slaughtered in countless numbers for food. Sad fate for singers so purely divine.

One of the gayest of the singers is the redwing blackbird. In the spring, when his scarlet epaulets shine brightest, and his little modest gray wife is sitting on the nest, built on rushes in a swamp, he sits on a near-by oak and devotedly sings almost all day. His rich simple strain is *baumpalee, baumpalee,* or *bobalee* as interpreted by some. In summer, after nesting cares are over, they assemble in flocks of hundreds and thousands to feast on Indian corn when it is in the milk. Scattering over a field, each selects an ear, strips the husk down far enough to lay bare an inch or two of the end of it, enjoys an exhilarating feast, and after all are full they rise simultaneously with a quick birr of wings like an old-fashioned church congregation fluttering to their feet when the minister after giving out the hymn says, 'Let the congregation arise and sing.' Alighting on near-by trees, they sing with a hearty vengeance, bursting out without any puttering prelude in gloriously glad concert, hundreds or thousands of exulting voices with sweet gurgling *baumpalees* mingled with chippy vibrant and exploding globules of musical notes, making a most enthusiastic, indescribable joy-song, a combination unlike anything to be heard elsewhere in the bird kingdom; something like bagpipes, flutes, violins, pianos, and human-like voices all bursting and bubbling at once. Then suddenly someone of the joyful congregation shouts Chirr! Chirr! and all stop as if shot.

The sweet-voiced meadowlark with its placid, simple song of *peery-eery-odical* was another favorite, and we soon learned to admire the Baltimore oriole and its wonderful hanging nests, and the scarlet tanager glowing like fire amid the green leaves.

But no singer of them all got farther into our hearts than the little speckle-breasted song sparrow, one of the first to arrive and begin nest-building and singing. The richness, sweetness, and pathos of this small darling's song as he sat on a low bush often brought tears to our eyes.

The little cheery, modest chickadee midget, loved by every innocent boy and girl, man and woman, and by many not altogether innocent, was one of the first of the birds to attract our attention, drawing nearer and nearer to us as the winter advanced, bravely singing his faint silvery, lisping, tinkling notes ending with a bright *dee, dee, dee!* however frosty the weather.

The nuthatches, who also stayed all winter with us, were favorites with us boys. We loved to watch them as they traced the bark-furrows of the oaks and hickories head downward, deftly flicking off loose scales and splinters in search of insects, and braving the coldest weather as if their little sparks of life were as safely warm in winter as in summer, unquenchable by the severest frost. With the help of the chickadees they made a delightful stir in the solemn winter days, and when we were out chopping we never ceased to wonder how their slender flaked toes could be kept warm when our own were so painfully frosted though clad in thick socks and boots. And we wondered and admired the more when we thought of the little midgets sleeping in knot-holes when the temperature was far below zero, sometimes thirty-five degrees below, and in the morning, after a minute breakfast of a few frozen insects and hoarfrost crystals, playing and chatting in cheery tones as if food, weather, and everything was according to their own warm hearts. Our Yankee told us that the name of this darling was Devil-downhead.

Their big neighbors the owls also made good winter music, singing out loud in wild, gallant strains bespeaking brave comfort, let the frost bite as it might. The solemn hooting of the species with the widest throat seemed to us the very wildest of all the winter sounds.

Prairie chickens crane strolling in family flocks about the shanty, picking seeds and grasshoppers like domestic fowls, and they became still more abundant as wheat-and-corn-fields were multiplied, but also wilder, of course, when every shot-gun in the country was aimed at them. The booming of the males during the mating-season was one of the loudest and strangest of the early spring sounds being easily heard on calm mornings at a distance of a half or three fourths of a mile. As soon as the snow was off the ground, they assembled in flocks of a dozen or two on an open spot, usually on the side of a ploughed field, ruffled up their feathers, inflated the curious colored sacks on the sides of their necks, and strutted about with queer gestures something like turkey gobblers, uttering strange loud, rounded, drumming calls – *boom! boom! boom!* interrupted by choking sounds. My brother Daniel caught one while she was sitting on her nest in our corn-field. The young are just like domestic chicks, run with the mother as soon as hatched, and stay with her until autumn, feeding on the ground, never taking wing unless disturbed. In winter, when full-grown, they assemble in large flocks, fly about sundown to selected roosting-places on tall trees, and to feeding-places in the morning – unhusked corn-fields, if any are to be found in the neighborhood, or thickets of dwarf birch and willows, the buds of which furnish a considerable part of their food when snow covers the ground.

The wild rice-marshes along the Fox River and around Pucaway Lake were the summer homes of millions of ducks, and in the Indian summer, when the rice was ripe, they grew very fat. The magnificent mallards in particular afforded our Yankee neighbors royal feasts almost without price, for often as many as a half-dozen were killed at a shot, but we seldom were allowed a single hour for hunting and so got very few. The autumn duck season was a glad time for the Indians also, for they feasted and grew fat not only on the ducks but on the wild rice, large quantities of which they gathered as they glided through the midst of the generous crop in canoes, bending down handfuls over the sides, and beating out the grain with small paddles.

The warmth of the deep spring fountains of the creek in our meadow kept it open all the year, and a few pairs of wood ducks, the most beautiful, we thought, of all the ducks, wintered in it. I well remember the first specimen I ever saw. Father shot it in the creek during a snowstorm, brought it into the house, and called us around him, saying: 'Come, bairns, and admire the work of God displayed in this bonnie bird. Naebody but God could paint feathers like these. Juist look at the colors, hoo they shine, and hoo fine they overlap and blend thegether like the colors o' the rainbow.' And we all agreed that never, never before had we seen so awfu' bonnie a bird. A pair nested every year in the hollow top of an oak stump about fifteen feet high that stood on the side of the meadow, and we used to wonder how they got the fluffy young ones down from the nest and across the meadow to the lake when they were only helpless, featherless midgets; whether the mother carried them to the water on her back or in her mouth. I never saw the thing done or found anybody who had until this summer, when Mr Holabird, a keen observer, told me that he once saw the mother carry them from the nest tree in her mouth, quickly coming and going to a near-by stream, and in a few minutes get them all together and proudly sail away.

Sometimes a flock of swans was seen passing over at a great height on their long journeys, and we admired their clear bugle notes, but they seldom visited any of the lakes in our neighborhood, so seldom that when they did it was talked of for years. One was shot by a blacksmith on a millpond with a long-range Sharp's rifle, and many of the neighbors went far to see it.

The common gray goose, Canada honker, flying in regular harrow-shaped flocks, was one of the wildest and wariest of all the large birds that enlivened the spring and autumn. They seldom ventured to alight in our small lake, fearing, I suppose, that hunters might be concealed in the rushes; but on account of their fondness for the young leaves of winter wheat when they were a few inches high, they often alighted on our fields when passing on their way south, and occasionally even in our corn-fields when a snowstorm was blowing and they were hungry and wing-weary, with nearly an inch of snow on their backs. In such times of distress we used to pity them, even while trying to get a shot at them. They were exceedingly cautious and circumspect; usually flew several times round the adjacent thickets and fences to make sure that no enemy was near before settling down, and one always stood on guard, relieved from time to time, while the flock was feeding. Therefore there was no chance to creep up on them unobserved; you had to be well hidden before the flock arrived. It was the ambition of boys to be able to shoot these wary birds. I never got but two, both of them at one so-called lucky shot. When I ran to pick them up, one of them flew away, but as the poor fellow was sorely wounded he didn't fly far. When I caught him after a short chase, he uttered a piercing cry of terror and despair, which the leader of the flock heard at a distance of about a hundred rods. They had flown off in frightened disorder, of course, but had got into the regular harrow-shape order when the leader heard the cry, and I shall never forget how bravely he left his place at the head of the flock and hurried back screaming and struck at me in trying to save his companion. I dodged down and held my hands over my head, and thus escaped a blow of his elbows. Fortunately I had left my gun at the fence, and the life of this noble bird was spared after he had risked it in trying to save his wounded friend or neighbor or family relation. For so shy a bird boldly to attack a hunter showed wonderful sympathy and courage. This is one of my strangest hunting experiences. Never before had I regarded wild geese as dangerous, or capable of such noble, self-sacrificing devotion.

The loud, clear call of the handsome bob-whites was one of the pleasantest and most characteristic of our spring sounds, and we soon learned to imitate it so well that a bold cock often accepted our challenge and came flying to fight. The young run as soon as they are hatched and follow their parents until spring, roosting on the ground in a close bunch, heads out ready to scatter and fly. These fine birds were seldom seen when we first arrived in the wilderness, but when wheat-fields supplied abundance of food they multiplied very fast, although oftentimes sore pressed during hard winters when the snow reached a depth of two or three feet, covering their food, while the mercury fell to twenty or thirty degrees below zero. Occasionally, although shy on account of being persistently hunted, under pressure of extreme hunger in the very coldest weather when the snow was deepest they ventured into barn-yards and even approached the doorsteps of houses, searching for any sort of scraps and crumbs, as if piteously begging for food. One of our neighbors saw a flock come creeping up through the snow, unable to fly, hardly able to walk, and while approaching the door several of them actually fell down and died; showing that birds, usually so vigorous and apparently independent of fortune, suffer and lose their lives in extreme weather like the rest of us, frozen to death like settlers caught in blizzards. None of our neighbors perished in storms, though many had feet, ears, and fingers frost-nipped or solidly frozen.

As soon as the lake ice melted, we heard the lonely cry of the loon, one of the wildest and most striking of all the wilderness sounds, a strange, sad, mournful, unearthly cry, half laughing, half wailing. Nevertheless the great northern diver, as our species is called, is a brave, hardy, beautiful bird, able to fly under water about as well as above it, and to spear and capture the swiftest fishes for food. Those that haunted our lake were so wary none was shot for years, though every boy hunter in the neighborhood was ambitious to get one to prove his skill. On one of our bitter cold New Year holidays I was surprised to see a loon in the small open part of the lake at the mouth of the inlet that was kept from freezing by the warm spring water. I knew that it could not fly out of so small a place, for these heavy birds have to beat the water for half a mile or so before they can get fairly on the wing. Their narrow, finlike wings are very small as compared with the weight of the body and are evidently made for flying through water as well as through the air, and it is by means of their swift flight through the water and the swiftness of the blow they strike with their long, spear-like bills that they are able to capture the fishes on which they feed. I ran down the meadow with the gun, got into my boat, and pursued that poor winter-bound straggler. Of course he dived again and again, but had to come up to breathe, and I at length got a quick shot at his head and slightly wounded or stunned him, caught him, and ran proudly back to the house with my prize. I carried him in my arms; he didn't struggle to get away or offer to strike me, and when I put him on the floor in front of the kitchen stove, he just rested quietly on his belly as noiseless and motionless as if he were a stuffed specimen on a shelf, held his neck erect, gave no sign of suffering from any wound, and though he was motionless, his small black eyes seemed to be ever keenly watchful. His formidable bill, very sharp, three or three and a half inches long, and shaped like a pickaxe, was held perfectly level. But the wonder was that he did not struggle or make the slightest movement. We had a tortoiseshell cat, an old Tom of great experience, who was so fond of lying under the stove in frosty weather that it was difficult even to poke him out with a broom; but when he saw and smelled that strange big fishy, black and white, speckledy bird, the like of which he had never before seen, he rushed wildly to the farther corner of the kitchen, looked back cautiously and suspiciously, and began to make a careful study of the handsome but dangerous looking stranger. Becoming more and more curious and interested, he at length advanced a step or two for a nearer new and nearer smell; and as the wonderful bird kept absolutely motionless, he was encouraged to venture gradually nearer and nearer until within perhaps five or six feet of its breast. Then the wary loon, not liking Tom's looks in so near a view, which perhaps recalled to his mind the plundering minks and muskrats he had to fight when they approached his nest, prepared to defend himself by slowly, almost imperceptibly drawing back his long pickaxe bill, and without the slightest fuss or stir held it level and ready just over his tail. With that dangerous bill drawn so far back out of the way, Tom's confidence in the stranger's peaceful intentions seemed almost complete, and, thus encouraged, he at last ventured forward with wondering, questioning eyes and quivering nostrils until he was only eighteen or twenty inches from the loon's smooth white breast. When the beautiful bird, apparently as peaceful and inoffensive as a flower, saw that his hairy yellow enemy had arrived at the right distance, the loon, who evidently was a fine judge of the reach of his spear, shot it forward quick as a lightning-flash, in marvelous contrast to the wonderful slowness of the preparatory poising, backward motion. The aim was true to a hairbreadth. Tom was struck right in the centre of his forehead, between the eyes. I thought his skull was cracked. Perhaps it was. The sudden astonishment of that outraged cat, the virtuous indignation and wrath, terror, and pain, are far beyond description. His eyes and screams and desperate retreat told all that. When the blow was received, he made a noise that I never heard a cat make before or since; an awfully deep, condensed, screechy, explosive *Wuck!* as he bounced straight up in the air like a bucking bronco; and when he alighted after his spring, he rushed madly across the room and made frantic efforts to climb up the hard-finished plaster wall. Not satisfied to get the width of the kitchen away from his mysterious enemy, for the first time that cold winter he tried to get out of the house, anyhow, anywhere out of that loon-infested room. When he finally ventured to look back and saw that the barbarous bird was still there, tranquil and motionless in front of the stove, he regained command of some of his shattered senses and carefully commenced to examine his wound. Backed against the wall in the

farthest corner, and keeping his eye on the outrageous bird, he
tenderly touched and washed the sore spot, wetting his paw
with his tongue, pausing now and then as his courage increased to glare and stare and growl at his enemy with looks
and tones wonderfully human, as if saying: 'You confounded
fishy, unfair rascal! What did you do that for? What had I
done to you? Faithless, legless, long-nosed wretch!' Intense
experiences like the above bring out the humanity that is in
all animals. One touch of nature, even a cat-and-loon touch,
makes all the world kin.

It was a great memorable day when the first flock of
passenger pigeons came to our farm, calling to mind the story
we had read about them when we were at school in Scotland.
Of all God's feathered people that sailed the Wisconsin sky, no
other bird seemed to us so wonderful. The beautiful wanderers
flew like the winds in flocks of millions from climate to climate
in accord with the weather, finding their food – acorns,
beechnuts, pine-nuts, cranberries, strawberries, huckleberries,
juniper berries, hackberries, buckwheat, rice, wheat, oats, corn
– in fields and forests thousands of miles apart. I have seen
flocks streaming south in the fall so large that they were
flowing over from horizon to horizon in an almost continuous
stream all day long, at the rate of forty or fifty miles an hour,
like a mighty river in the sky, widening, contracting, descending like falls and cataracts, and rising suddenly here and there
in huge ragged masses like high-plashing spray. How wonderful the distances they flew in a day – in a year – in a lifetime!
They arrived in Wisconsin in the spring just after the sun had
cleared away the snow, and alighted in the woods to feed on
the fallen acorns that they had missed the previous autumn. A
comparatively small flock swept thousands of acres perfectly
clean of acorns in a few minutes, by moving straight ahead
with a broad front. All got their share, for the rear constantly
became the van by flying over the flock and alighting in front,
the entire flock constantly changing from rear to front, revol-
ving something like a wheel with a low buzzing wing roar that
could be heard a long way off. In summer they feasted on
wheat and oats and were easily approached as they rested on
the trees along the sides of the field after a good full meal,
displaying beautiful iridescent colors as they moved their necks
backward and forward when we went very near them. Every

shotgun was aimed at them and everybody feasted on pigeon pies, and not a few of the settlers feasted also on the beauty of the wonderful birds. The breast of the male is a fine rosy red, the lower part of the neck behind and along the sides changing from the red of the breast to gold, emerald green and rich crimson. The general color of the upper parts is grayish blue, the under parts white. The extreme length of the bird is about seventeen inches; the finely modeled slender tail about eight inches, and extent of wings twenty-four inches. The females are scarcely less beautiful. 'Oh, what bonnie, bonnie birds!' we exclaimed over the first that fell into our hands. 'Oh, what colors! Look at their breasts, bonnie as roses, and at their necks aglow wi' every color juist like the wonderfu' wood ducks. Oh, the bonnie, bonnie creatures, they beat a'! Where did they a' come fra, and where are they a' gan? It's awfu' like a sin to kill them!' To this some smug, practical old sinner would remark: 'Aye, it's a peety, as ye say, to kill the bonnie things, but they were made to be killed, and sent for us to eat as the quails were sent to God's chosen people, the Israelites, when they were starving in the desert ayont the Red Sea. And I must confess that meat was never put up in neater, handsomer-painted packages.'

In the New England and Canada woods beechnuts were their best and most abundant food, farther north, cranberries and huckleberries. After everything was cleaned up in the north and winter was coming on, they went south for rice, corn, acorns, haws, wild grapes, crab-apples, sparkle-berries, etc. They seemed to require more than half of the continent for feeding-grounds, moving from one table to another, field to field, forest to forest, finding something ripe and wholesome all the year round. In going south in the fine Indian-summer weather they flew high and followed one another, though the head of the flock might be hundreds of miles in advance. But against head winds they took advantage of the inequalities of the ground, flying comparatively low. All followed the leader's ups and downs over hill and dale though far out of sight, never hesitating at any turn of the way, vertical or horizontal that the leaders had taken, though the largest flocks stretched across several States, and belts of different kinds of weather.

There were no roosting- or breeding-places near our farm, and I never saw any of them until long after the great flocks were exterminated. I therefore quote, from Audubon's and Pokagon's vivid descriptions.

'Toward evening,' Audubon says, 'they depart for the roosting-place, which may be hundreds of miles distant. One on the banks of Green River, Kentucky, was over three miles wide and forty long.'

'My first view of it,' says the great naturalist, 'was about a fortnight after it had been chosen by the birds, and I arrived there nearly two hours before sunset. Few pigeons were then to be seen, but a great many persons with horses and wagons and armed with guns, long poles, sulphur pots, pine pitch torches, etc., had already established encampments on the borders. Two farmers had driven upwards of three hundred hogs a distance of more than a hundred miles to be fattened on slaughtered pigeons. Here and there the people employed in plucking and salting what had already been secured were sitting in the midst of piles of birds. Dung several inches thick covered the ground. Many trees two feet in diameter were broken off at no great distance from the ground, and the branches of many of the tallest and largest had given way, as if the forest had been swept by a tornado.

'Not a pigeon had arrived at sundown. Suddenly a general cry arose – ' Here they come!' The noise they made, though still distant, reminded me of a hard gale at sea passing through the rigging of a close-reefed ship. Thousands were soon knocked down by the pole-men. The birds continued to pour in. The fires were lighted and a magnificent as well as terrifying sight presented itself. The pigeons pouring in alighted everywhere, one above another, until solid masses were formed on the branches all around. Here and there the perches gave way with a crash, and falling destroyed hundreds beneath, forcing down the dense groups with which every stick was loaded; a scene of uproar and conflict. I found it useless to speak or even to shout to those persons nearest me. Even the reports of the guns were seldom heard, and I was made aware of the firing only by seeing the shooters reloading. None dared venture within the line of devastation. The hogs had been penned up in due time, the picking up of the dead and wounded being left for the next morning's employment. The pigeons were constantly coming in and it was after midnight before I perceived a decrease in the number of those that arrived. The uproar continued all night, and, anxious to know how far the sound reached I sent off a man who, returning two hours after, informed me that he had heard it distinctly three miles distant.

'Toward daylight the noise in some measure subsided; long before objects were distinguishable the pigeons began to move off in a direction quite different from that in which they had arrived the evening before, and at sunrise all that were able to fly had disappeared. The howling of the wolves now reached our ears, and the foxes, lynxes, cougars, bears, coons, opossums, and polecats were seen sneaking off, while eagles and hawks of different species, accompanied by a crowd of vultures, came to supplant them and enjoy a share of the spoil.

'Then the authors of all this devastation began their entry amongst the dead, the dying and mangled. The pigeons were picked up and piled in heaps until each had as many as they could possibly dispose of, when the hogs were let loose to feed on the remainder.

'The breeding-places are selected with reference to abundance of food, and countless myriads resort to them. At this period the note of the pigeon is *coo coo coo*, like that of the domestic species but much shorter. They caress by billing, and during incubation the male supplies the female with food. As the young grow, the tyrant of creation appears to disturb the peaceful scene, armed with axes to chop down the squab-laden trees, and the abomination of desolation and destruction produced far surpasses even that of the roosting places.'

Pokagon, an educated Indian writer, says: 'I saw one nesting-place in Wisconsin one hundred miles long and from three to ten miles wide. Every tree, some of them quite low and scrubby, had from one to fifty nests on each. Some of the nests overflow from the oaks to the hemlock and pine woods. When the pigeon hunters attack the breeding-places they sometimes cut the timber from thousands of acres. Millions are caught in nets with salt or grain for bait, and schooners, sometimes loaded down with the birds, are taken to New York, where they are sold for a cent apiece.'

Chapter 5

YOUNG HUNTERS

In the older eastern States it used to be considered great sport for an army of boys to assemble to hunt birds, squirrels, and every other unclaimed, unprotected live thing of shootable size. They divided into two squads, and, choosing leaders, scattered through the woods in different directions, and the party that killed the greatest number enjoyed a supper at the expense of the other. The whole neighborhood seemed to enjoy the shameful sport, especially the farmers afraid of their crops. With a great air of importance, laws were enacted to govern the gory business. For example, a gray squirrel must count four heads, a woodchuck six heads, common red squirrel two heads, black squirrel ten heads, a partridge five heads, the larger birds, such as whip-poor-wills and nighthawks two heads each, the wary crows three, and bob-whites three. But all the blessed company of mere songbirds, warblers, robins, thrushes, orioles, with nuthatches, chickadees, blue jays, woodpeckers, etc., counted only one head each. The heads of the birds were hastily wrung off and thrust into the game-bags to be counted, saving the bodies only of what were called game, the larger squirrels, bob-whites, partridges, etc. The blood-stained bags of the best slayers were soon bulging full. Then at a given hour all had to stop and repair to the town, empty their dripping sacks, count the heads, and go rejoicing to their dinner. Although, like other wild boys, I was fond of shooting, I never had anything to do with these abominable head-hunts. And now the farmers having learned that birds are their friends wholesale slaughter has been abolished.

We seldom saw deer, though their tracks were common. The Yankee explained that they traveled and fed mostly at night, and hid in tamarack swamps and brushy places in the daytime, and how the Indians knew all about them and could find them whenever they were hungry.

Indians belonging to the Menominee and Winnebago occasionally visited us at our cabin to get a piece of bread or some matches, or to sharpen their knives on our grindstone, and we boys watched them closely to see that they didn't steal Jack. We wondered at their knowledge of animals when we saw them go direct to trees on our farm, chop holes in them with their tomahawks and take out coons, of the existence of which we had never noticed the slightest trace. In winter, after the first snow, we frequently saw three or four Indians hunting deer in company, running like hounds on the fresh, exciting tracks. The escape of the deer from these noiseless, tireless hunters was said to be well-nigh impossible; they were followed to the death.

Most of our neighbors brought some sort of gun from the old country, but seldom took time to hunt, even after the first hard work of fencing and clearing was over, except to shoot a duck or prairie chicken now and then that happened to come in their way. It was only the less industrious American settlers who left their work to go far a-hunting. Two or three of our most enterprising American neighbors went off every fall with their teams to the pine regions and cranberry marshes in the northern part of the State to hunt and gather berries. I well remember seeing their wagons loaded with game when they returned from a successful hunt. Their loads consisted usually of half a dozen deer or more, one or two black bears, and fifteen or twenty bushels of cranberries; all solidly frozen. Part of both the berries and meat was usually sold in Portage; the balance furnished their families with abundance of venison, bear grease, and pies.

Winter wheat is sown in the fall, and when it is a month or so old the deer, like the wild geese, are very fond of it, especially since other kinds of food are then becoming scarce. One of our neighbors across the Fox River killed a large number, some thirty or forty, on a small patch of wheat, simply by lying in wait for them every night. Our wheat-field was the first that was sown in the neighborhood. The deer soon found it and came in every night to feast, but it was eight or nine years before we ever disturbed them. David then killed one deer, the only one killed by any of our family. He went out shortly after sundown at the time of full moon to one of our wheat-fields, carrying a double-barreled shotgun loaded with buck-shot. After lying in wait an hour or so, he saw a doe and her fawn jump the fence and come cautiously into the wheat. After they were within sixty or seventy yards of him, he was surprised when he tried to take aim that about half of the moon's disc was mysteriously darkened as if covered by the edge of a dense cloud. This proved to be an eclipse. Nevertheless, he fired at the mother, and she immediately ran off, jumped the fence, and took to the woods by the way she came. The fawn danced about bewildered, wondering what had become of its mother, but finally fled to the woods. David fired at the poor deserted thing as it ran past him but happily missed it. Hearing the shots, I joined David to learn his luck. He said he thought he must have wounded the mother, and when we were strolling about in the woods in search of her we saw three or four deer on their way to the wheat-field, led by a fine buck. They were walking rapidly, but cautiously halted at intervals of a few rods to listen and look ahead and scent the air. They failed to notice us, though by this time the moon was out of the eclipse shadow and we were standing only about fifty yards from them. I was carrying the gun. David had fired both barrels but when he was reloading one of them he happened to put the wad intended to cover the shot into the empty barrel, and so when we were climbing over the fence the buckshot had rolled out, and when I fired at the big buck I knew by the report that there was nothing but powder in the charge. The startled deer danced about in confusion for a few seconds, uncertain which way to run until they caught sight of us, when they bounded off through the woods. Next morning we found the poor mother lying about three hundred yards from the place where she was shot. She had run this distance and jumped a high fence after one of the buckshot had passed through her heart.

Excepting Sundays we boys had only two days of the year to ourselves, the 4th of July and the 1st of January. Sundays were less than half our own, on account of Bible lessons, Sunday-school lessons and church services; all the others were labor days, rain or shine, cold or warm. No wonder, then, that our two holidays were precious and that it was not easy to decide what to do with them. They were usually spent on the highest rocky hill in the neighborhood, called the Observatory; in visiting our boy friends on adjacent farms to hunt, fish, wrestle, and play games; in reading some new favorite book we had managed to borrow or buy; or in making models of machines I had invented.

One of our July days was spent with two Scotch boys of our own age hunting redwing blackbirds then busy in the corn-fields. Our party had only one single-barreled shotgun, which, as the oldest and perhaps because I was thought to be the best shot, I had the honor of carrying. We marched through the corn without getting sight of a single redwing, but just as we reached the far side of the field, a red-headed woodpecker flew up, and the Lawson boys cried: 'Shoot him! Shoot him! he is just as bad as a blackbird. He eats corn!' This memorable woodpecker alighted in the top of a white oak tree about fifty feet high. I fired from a position almost immediately beneath him, and he fell straight down at my feet. When I picked him up and was admiring his plumage, he moved his legs slightly, and I said, 'Poor bird, he's no deed yet and we'll hae to kill him to put him oot o' pain,' – sincerely pitying him, after we had taken pleasure in shooting him. I had seen servant girls wringing chicken necks, so with desperate humanity I took the limp unfortunate by the head, swung him around three or four times thinking I was wringing his neck, and then threw him hard on the ground to quench the last possible spark of life and make quick death doubly sure. But to our astonishment the moment he struck the ground he gave a cry of alarm and flew right straight up like a rejoicing lark into the top of the same tree, and perhaps to the same branch he had fallen from, and began to adjust his ruffled feathers, nodding and chirping and looking down at us as if wondering what in the bird world we had been doing to him. This of course banished all thought of killing, as far as that revived woodpecker was concerned, no matter how many ears of corn he might spoil, and we all heartily congratulated him on his wonderful, triumphant resurrection from three kinds of death – shooting, neck-wringing, and destructive concussion. I suppose only one pellet had touched him, glancing on his head.

Another extraordinary shooting-affair happened one summer morning shortly after daybreak. When I went to the stable to feed the horses I noticed a big white-breasted hawk on a tall

oak in front of the chicken-house, evidently waiting for a
chicken breakfast. I ran to the house for the gun, and when
I fired he fell about halfway down the tree, caught a branch
with his claws, hung back downward and fluttered a few
seconds, then managed to stand erect. I fired again to put
him out of pain, and to my surprise the second shot seemed to
restore his strength instead of killing him, for he flew out of the
tree and over the meadow with strong and regular wing-beats
for thirty or forty rods apparently as well as ever, but died
suddenly in the air and dropped like a stone.

We hunted muskrats whenever we had time to run down to
the lake. They are brown bunchy animals about twenty-three
inches long, the tail being about nine inches in length, black in
color and flattened vertically for sculling, and the hind feet are
half-webbed. They look like little beavers, usually have from
ten to a dozen young, are easily tamed and make interesting
pets. We liked to watch them at their work and at their meals.
In the spring when the snow vanishes and the lake ice begins to
melt, the first open spot is always used as a feeding-place,
where they dive from the edge of the ice and in a minute or less
reappear with a mussel or a mouthful of pontederia or water-
lily leaves, climb back on to the ice and sit up to nibble their
food, handling it very much like squirrels or marmots. It is then
that they are most easily shot, a solitary hunter oftentimes
shooting thirty or forty in a single day. Their nests on the rushy
margins of lakes and streams, far from being hidden like those
of most birds, are conspicuously large, and conical in shape
like Indian wigwams. They are built of plants – rushes, sedges,
mosses, etc – and ornamented around the base with mussel-
shells. It was always pleasant and interesting to see them in the
fall as soon as the nights began to be frosty, hard at work
cutting sedges on the edge of the meadow or swimming out
through the rushes, making long glittering ripples as they
sculled themselves along, diving where the water is perhaps
six or eight feet deep and reappearing in a minute or so with
large mouthfuls of the weedy tangled plants gathered from the
bottom, returning to their big wigwams climbing up and
depositing their loads where most needed to make them yet
larger and firmer and warmer, foreseeing the freezing weather
just like ourselves when we banked up our house to keep out
the frost.

They lie snug and invisible all winter but do not hibernate. Through a channel carefully kept open they swim out under the ice for mussels, and the roots and stems of water-lilies, etc., on which they feed just as they do in summer. Sometimes the oldest and most enterprising of them venture to orchards near the water in search of fallen apples; very seldom, however, do they interfere with anything belonging to their mortal enemy, man. Notwithstanding they are so well hidden and protected during the winter, many of them are killed by Indian hunters, who creep up softly and spear them through the thick walls of their cabins. Indians are fond of their flesh, and so are some of the wildest of the white trappers. They are easily caught in steel traps, and after vainly trying to drag their feet from the cruel crushing jaws, they sometimes in their agony gnaw them off. Even after having gnawed off a leg they are so guileless that they never seem to learn to know and fear traps, for some are occasionally found that have been caught twice and have gnawed off a second foot. Many other animals suffering excruciating pain in these cruel traps gnaw off their legs. Crabs and lobsters are so fortunate as to be able to shed their limbs when caught or merely frightened, apparently without suffering any pain, simply by giving themselves a little shivery shake.

The muskrat is one of the most notable and widely distributed of American animals, and millions of the gentle, industrious, beaver-like creatures are shot and trapped and speared every season for their skins, worth a dime or so – like shooting boys and girls for their garments.

Surely a better time must be drawing nigh when godlike human beings will become truly humane, and learn to put their animal fellow mortals in their hearts instead of on their backs or in their dinners. In the meantime we may just as well as not learn to live clean, innocent lives instead of slimy, bloody ones. All hale, red-blooded boys are savage, the best and boldest the savagest, fond of hunting and fishing. But when thoughtless childhood is past, the best rise the highest above all this bloody flesh and sport business, the wild foundational animal dying out day by day, as divine uplifting, transfiguring charity grows in.

Hares and rabbits were seldom seen when we first settled in the Wisconsin woods, but they multiplied rapidly after the animals that preyed upon them had been thinned out or exterminated, and food and shelter supplied in grain-fields and log fences and the thickets of young oaks that grew up in pastures after the annual grass fires were kept out. Catching hares in the winter-time, when they were hidden in hollow fence-logs, was a favorite pastime with many of the boys whose fathers allowed them time to enjoy the sport. Occasionally a stout, lithe hare was carried out into an open snow-covered field, set free, and given a chance for its life in a race with a dog. When the snow was not too soft and deep, it usually made good its escape, for our dogs were only fat, short-legged mongrels. We sometimes discovered hares in standing hollow trees, crouching on decayed punky wood at the bottom, as far back as possible from the opening, but when alarmed they managed to climb to a considerable height if the hollow was not too wide, by bracing themselves against the sides.

Foxes, though not uncommon, we boys held steadily to work seldom saw, and as they found plenty of prairie chickens for themselves and families, they did not often come near the farmer's hen-roosts. Nevertheless the discovery of their dens was considered important. No matter how deep the den might be, it was thoroughly explored with pick and shovel by sport-loving settlers at a time when they judged the fox was likely to be at home, but I cannot remember any case in our neighborhood where the fox was actually captured. In one of the dens a mile or two from our farm a lot of prairie chickens were found and some smaller birds.

Badger dens were far more common than fox dens. One of our fields was named Badger Hill from the number of badger holes in a hill at the end of it, but I cannot remember seeing a single one of the inhabitants.

On a stormy day in the middle of an unusually severe winter, a black bear, hungry, no doubt, and seeking something to eat, came strolling down through our neighborhood from the northern pine woods. None had been seen here before, and it caused no little excitement and alarm, for the European settlers imagined that these poor, timid, bashful bears were as dangerous as man-eating lions and tigers, and that they would pursue any human being that came in their way. This species is common in the north part of the State, and few of our enterprising Yankee hunters who went to the pineries in the fall failed to shoot at least one of them.

We saw very little of the owlish, serious looking coons, and no wonder, since they lie hidden nearly all day in hollow trees and we never had time to hunt them. We often heard their curious, quavering, whinnying cries on still evenings but only once succeeded in tracing an unfortunate family through our corn-field to their den in a big oak and catching them all. One of our neighbors, Mr McRath, a Highland Scotchman, caught one and made a pet of it. It became very tame and had perfect confidence in the good intentions of its kind friend and master. He always addressed it in speaking to it as a 'little man.' When it came running to him and jumped on his lap or climbed up his trousers, he would say, while patting its head as if it were a dog or a child, 'Coonie, ma mannie, Coonie, ma mannie, hoo are ye the day? I think you're hungry,' – as the comical pet began to examine his pockets for nuts and bits of bread – 'Na, na, there's nathing in my pooch for ye the day, my wee mannie, but I'll get ye something.' He would then fetch something it liked – bread, nuts, a carrot, or perhaps a piece of fresh meat. Anything scattered for it on the floor it felt with its paw instead of looking at it, judging of its worth more by touch than sight.

The outlet of our Fountain Lake flowed past Mr McRath's door, and the coon was very fond of swimming in it and searching for frogs and mussels. It seemed perfectly satisfied to stay about the house without being confined, occupied a comfortable bed in a section of a hollow tree, and never wandered far. How long it lived after the death of its kind master I don't know.

I suppose that almost any wild animal may be made a pet, simply by sympathizing with it and entering as much as possible into its life. In Alaska I saw one of the common gray mountain marmots kept as a pet in an Indian family. When its master entered the house it always seemed glad, almost like a dog, and when cold or tired it snuggled up in a fold of his blanket with the utmost confidence.

We have all heard of ferocious animals, lions and tigers, etc., that were fed and spoken to only by their masters, becoming perfectly tame; and, as is well known, the faithful dog that follows man and serves him, and looks up to him and loves him as if he were a god, is a descendant of the blood-thirsty wolf or jackal. Even frogs and toads and fishes may be tamed, provided they have the uniform sympathy of one person, with whom they become intimately acquainted without the distracting and varying attentions of strangers. And surely all God's people, however serious and savage, great or small, like to play. Whales and elephants, dancing, humming gnats, and invisibly small mischievous microbes – all are warm with divine radium and must have lots of fun in them.

As far as I know, all wild creatures keep themselves clean. Birds, it seems to me, take more pains to bathe and dress themselves than any other animals. Even ducks, though living so much in water, dip and scatter cleansing showers over their backs, and shake and preen their feathers as carefully as landbirds. Watching small singers taking their morning baths is very interesting, particularly when the weather is cold. Alighting in a shallow pool, they often-times show a sort of dread of dipping into it, like children hesitating about taking a plunge, as if they felt the same kind of shock, and this makes it easy for us to sympathize with the little feathered people.

Occasionally I have seen from my study-window red-headed linnets bathing in dew when water elsewhere was scarce. A large Monterey cypress with broad branches and innumerable leaves on which the dew lodges in still nights made favorite bathing-places. Alighting gently, as if afraid to waste the dew, they would pause and fidget as they do before beginning to plash in pools, then dip and scatter the drops in showers and get as thorough a bath as they would in a pool. I have also seen the same kind of baths taken by birds on the boughs of silver firs on the edge of a glacier meadow, but nowhere have I seen the dew-drops so abundant as on the Monterey cypress; and the picture made by the quivering wings and irised dew was memorably beautiful. Children, too, make fine pictures plashing and crowing in their little tubs. How widely different from wallowing pigs, bathing with great show of comfort and rubbing themselves dry against rough-barked trees!

Some of our own species seem fairly to dread the touch of water. When the necessity of absolute cleanliness by means of frequent baths was being preached by a friend who had been reading Combe's Physiology, in which he had learned something of the wonders of the skin with its millions of pores that had to be kept open for health, one of our neighbors remarked: 'Oh! that's unnatural. It's well enough to wash in a tub maybe once or twice a year, but not to be paddling in the water all the time like a frog in a spring-hole.' Another neighbor, who prided himself on his knowledge of big words, said with great solemnity: 'I never can believe that man is amphibious!'

Natives of tropic islands pass a large part of their lives in water, and seem as much at home in the sea as on the land; swim and dive, pursue fishes, play in the waves like surf-ducks and seals, and explore the coral gardens and groves and seaweed meadows as if truly amphibious. Even the natives of the far north bathe at times. I once saw a lot of Eskimo boys ducking and plashing right merrily in the Arctic Ocean.

It seemed very wonderful to us that the wild animals could keep themselves warm and strong in winter when the temperature was far below zero. Feeble-looking rabbits scud away over the snow, lithe and elastic, as if glorying in the frosty, sparkling weather and sure of their dinners. I have seen gray squirrels dragging ears of corn about as heavy as themselves out of our field through loose snow and up a tree, balancing them on limbs and eating in comfort with their dry, electric tails spread airily over their backs. Once I saw a fine hardy fellow go into a knot-hole. Thrusting in my hand I caught him and pulled him out. As soon as he guessed what I was up to, he took the end of my thumb in his mouth and sunk his teeth right through it, but I gripped him hard by the neck, carried him home, and shut him up in a box that contained about half a bushel of hazel- and hickory-nuts, hoping that he would not be too much frightened and discouraged to eat while thus imprisoned after the rough handling he had suffered. I soon learned, however, that sympathy in this direction was wasted, for no sooner did I pop him in than he fell to with right hearty appetite, gnawing and munching the nuts as if he had gathered them himself and was very hungry that day. Therefore, after allowing time enough for a good square meal, I made haste to get him out of the nut-box and shut him up in a spare bedroom, in which Father had hung a lot of selected ears of Indian corn for seed. They were hung up by the husks on cords stretched across from side to side of the room. The squirrel managed to jump from the top of one of the bed-posts to the cord, cut off an ear, and let it drop to the floor. He then jumped down, got a good grip of the heavy ear, carried it to the top of one of the slippery, polished bed-posts, seated himself comfortably, and, holding it well balanced, deliberately pried out one kernel at a time with his long chisel teeth, ate the soft, sweet germ, and dropped the hard part of the kernel. In this masterly way, working at high speed, he demolished several ears a day, and with a good warm bed in a box made himself at home and grew fat. Then naturally, I suppose, free romping in the snow and treetops with companions came to mind. Anyhow he began to look for a way of escape. Of course he first tried the window, but found that his teeth made no impression on the glass. Next he tried the sash and gnawed the wood off level with the glass; then Father happened to come upstairs and discovered the mischief that was being done to his seed corn and window and immediately ordered him out of the house.

The flying squirrel was one of the most interesting of the little animals we found in the woods, a beautiful brown creature, with fine eyes and smooth, soft fur like that of a mole or field mouse. He is about half as long as the gray squirrel, but his wide-spread tail and the folds of skin along his sides that form the wings make him look broad and flat, something like a kite. In the evenings our cat often brought them to her kittens at the shanty, and later we saw them fly during the day from the trees we were chopping. They jumped and glided off smoothly and apparently without effort, like birds, as soon as they heard and felt the breaking shock of the strained fibers at the stump, when the trees they were in began to totter and groan. They can fly, or rather glide, twenty or thirty yards from the top of a tree twenty or thirty feet high to the foot of another, gliding upward as they reach the trunk, or if the distance is too great they alight comfortably on the ground and make haste to the nearest tree, and climb just like the wingless squirrels.

Every boy and girl loves the little fairy, airy striped chipmunk, half squirrel, half spermophile. He is about the size of a field mouse, and often made us think of linnets and song sparrows as he frisked about gathering nuts and berries. He likes almost all kinds of grain, berries, and nuts – hazel-nuts, hickory-nuts, strawberries, huckleberries, wheat, oats, corn – he is fond of them all and thrives on them. Most of the hazel bushes on our farm grew along the fences as if they had been planted for the chipmunks alone, for the rail fences were their favorite highways. We never wearied watching them, especially when the hazel-nuts were ripe and the little fellows were sitting on the rails nibbling and handling them like tree-squirrels. We used to notice too that, although they are very neat animals, their lips and fingers were dyed red like our own, when the strawberries and huckleberries were ripe. We could always tell when the wheat and oats were in the milk by seeing the chipmunks feeding on the ears. They kept nibbling at the wheat until it was harvested and then gleaned in the stubble, keeping up a careful watch for their enemies – dogs, hawks, and shrikes. They are as widely distributed over the continent as the squirrels, various species inhabiting different regions on the mountains and lowlands, but all the different kinds have the same general characteristics of light, airy cheerfulness and good nature.

Before the arrival of farmers in the Wisconsin woods the small ground squirrels, called 'gophers,' lived chiefly on the seeds of wild grasses and weeds, but after the country was cleared and ploughed no feasting animal fell to more heartily on the farmer's wheat and corn. Increasing rapidly in numbers and knowledge, they became very destructive, especially in the spring when the corn was planted, for they learned to trace the rows and dig up and eat the three or four seeds in each hill about as fast as the poor farmers could cover them. And unless great pains were taken to diminish the numbers of the cunning little robbers, the fields had to be planted two or three times over, and even then large gaps in the rows would be found. The loss of the grain they consumed after it was ripe, together with the winter stores laid up in their burrows, amounted to little as compared with the loss of the seed on which the whole crop depended.

One evening about sundown, when my father sent me out with the shotgun to hunt them in a stubble field, I learned something curious and interesting in connection with these mischievous gophers, though just then they were doing no harm. As I strolled through the stubble watching for a chance for a shot, a shrike flew past me and alighted on an open spot at the mouth of a burrow about thirty yards ahead of me. Curious to see what he was up to, I stood still to watch him. He looked down the gopher hole in a listening attitude, then looked back at me to see if I was coming, looked down again and listened, and looked back at me. I stood perfectly still, and he kept twitching his tail, seeming uneasy and doubtful about venturing to do the savage job that I soon learned he had in his mind. Finally, encouraged by my keeping so still, to my astonishment he suddenly vanished in the gopher hole.

A bird going down a deep narrow hole in the ground like a ferret or a weasel seemed very strange, and I thought it would be a fine thing to run forward, clap my hand over the hole, and have the fun of imprisoning him and seeing what he would do when he tried to get out. So I ran forward but stopped when I got within a dozen or fifteen yards of the hole, thinking it might perhaps be more interesting to wait and see what would naturally happen without my interference. While I stood there looking and listening, I heard a great disturbance going on in the burrow, a mixed lot of keen squeaking shrieking, distressful cries, telling that down in the dark something terrible was being done. Then suddenly out popped a half-grown gopher, four and a half or five inches long, and, without stopping a single moment to choose a way of escape, ran screaming through the stubble straight away from its home, quickly followed by another and another, until some half-dozen were driven out, all of them crying and running in different directions as if at this dreadful time home, sweet home, was the most dangerous and least desirable of any place in the wide world. Then out came the shrike, flew above the run-away gopher children, and, diving on them, killed them one after another with blows at the back of the skull. He then seized one of them, dragged it to the top of a small clod so as to be able to get a start, and laboriously made out to fly with it about ten or fifteen yards, when he alighted to rest. Then he dragged it to the top of another clod and flew with it about the same distance, repeating this hard work over and over again until he managed to get one of the gophers on to the top of a log fence. How much he ate of his hard-won prey, or what he did with the others, I can't tell, for by this time the sun was down and I had to hurry home to my chores.

Chapter 6
THE PLOUGHBOY

At first, wheat, corn, and potatoes were the principal crops we raised; wheat especially. But in four or five years the soil was so exhausted that only five or six bushels an acre, even in the better fields, was obtained, although when first ploughed twenty and twenty-five bushels was about the ordinary yield. More attention was then paid to corn, but without fertilizers the corn-crop also became very meager. At last it was discovered that English clover would grow on even the exhausted fields, and that when ploughed under and planted with corn, or even wheat, wonderful crops were raised. This caused a complete change in farming methods; the farmers raised fertilizing clover, planted corn, and fed the crop to cattle and hogs.

But no crop raised in our wilderness was so surprisingly rich and sweet and purely generous to us boys and, indeed, to everybody as the watermelons and muskmelons. We planted a large patch on a sunny hill-slope the very first spring, and it seemed miraculous that a few handfuls of little fat seeds should in a few months send up a hundred wagon-loads of crisp, sumptuous, red-hearted and yellow-hearted fruits covering all the hill. We soon learned to know when they were in their prime, and when over-ripe and mealy. Also that if a second crop was taken from the same ground without fertilizing it, the melons would be small and what we called soapy; that is, soft and smooth, utterly uncrisp, and without a trace of the lively freshness and sweetness of those raised on virgin soil. Coming in from the farm work at noon, the half-dozen or so of melons we had placed in our cold spring were a glorious luxury that only weary barefooted farm boys can ever know.

Spring was not very trying as to temperature, and refreshing rains fell at short intervals. The work of ploughing commenced as soon as the frost was out of the ground. Corn- and potato-planting and the sowing of spring wheat was comparatively light work, while the nesting birds sang cheerily, grass and flowers covered the marshes and meadows and all the wild, uncleared parts of the farm, and the trees put forth their new leases, those of the oaks forming beautiful purple masses as if every leaf were a petal; and with all this we enjoyed the mild soothing winds, the hung of innumerable small insects and hylas, and the freshness and fragrance of everything. Then, too, came the wonderful passenger pigeons streaming from the south, and flocks of geese and cranes, filling all the sky with whistling wings.

The summer work, on the contrary, was deadly heavy, especially harvesting and corn-hoeing. All the ground had to be hoed over for the first few years, before Father bought cultivators or small weed-covering ploughs, and we were not allowed a moment's rest. The hoes had to be kept working up and down as steadily as if they were moved by machinery. Ploughing for winter wheat was comparatively easy, when we walked barefooted in the furrows, while the fine autumn tints kindled in the woods, and the hillsides were covered with golden pumpkins.

In summer the chores were grinding scythes, feeding the animals, chopping stove-wood, and carrying water up the hill from the spring on the edge of the meadow, etc. Then break-fast, and to the harvest or hay-field. I was foolishly ambitious to be first in mowing and cradling, and by the time I was sixteen led all the hired men. An hour was allowed at noon for dinner and more chores; we stayed in the field until dark, then supper, and still more chores, family worship, and to bed; making altogether a hard, sweaty day of about sixteen or seventeen hours. Think of that, ye blessed eight-hour-day laborers!

In winter Father came to the foot of the stairs and called us at six o'clock to feed the horses and cattle, grind axes, bring in wood, and do any other chores required, then breakfast, and out to work in the mealy, frosty snow by daybreak, chopping, fencing, etc. So in general our winter work was about as restless and trying as that of the long-day summer. No matter what the weather, there was always something to do. During heavy rains or snow-storms we worked in the barn, shelling corn, fanning wheat, thrashing with the flail, making axe-handles or ox-yokes, mending things, or sprouting and sorting potatoes in the cellar.

No pains were taken to diminish or in any way soften the natural hardships of this pioneer farm life; nor did any of the Europeans seem to know how to find reasonable ease and comfort if they would. The very best oak and hickory fuel was embarrassingly abundant and cost nothing but cutting and common sense; but instead of hauling great heart-cheering loads of it for wide, open, all-welcoming, climate-changing, beauty-making, Godlike ingle-fires, it was hauled with weary heart-breaking industry into fences and waste places to get it out of the way of the plough, and out of the way of doing good. The only fire for the whole house was the kitchen stove, with a fire-box about eighteen inches long and eight inches wide and deep – scant space for three or four small sticks, around which in hard zero weather all the family of ten persons shivered, and beneath which in the morning we found our socks and coarse, soggy boots frozen solid. We were not allowed to start even this despicable little fire in its black box to thaw them. No, we had to squeeze our throbbing, aching, chilblained feet into them, causing greater pain than toothache, and hurry out to chores. Fortunately the miserable chilblain pain began to abate as soon as the temperature of our feet approached the freezing-point, enabling us in spite of hard work and hard frost to enjoy the winter beauty – the wonderful radiance of the snow when it was starry with crystals, and the dawns and the sunsets and white noons, and the cheery, enlivening company of the brave chickadees and nuthatches.

The winter stars far surpassed those of our stormy Scotland in brightness, and we gazed and gazed as though we had never seen stars before. Oftentimes the heavens were made still more glorious by auroras, the long lance rays, called 'Merry Dancers' in Scotland, streaming with startling tremulous motion to the zenith. Usually the electric auroral light is white or pale yellow, but in the third or fourth of our Wisconsin winters there was a magnificently colored aurora that was seen and admired over nearly all the continent. The whole sky was draped in graceful purple and crimson folds glorious beyond description. Father called us out into the yard in front of the house where we had a wide view, crying, 'Come! Come,

Mother! Come, bairns! And see the glory of God. All the sky is clad in a robe of red light. Look straight up to the crown where the folds are gathered. Hush and wonder and adore, for surely this is the clothing of the Lord Himself, and perhaps He will even now appear looking down from his high heaven.' This celestial show was far more glorious than anything we had ever yet beheld, and throughout that wonderful winter hardly anything else was spoken of.

We even enjoyed the snowstorms, the thronging crystals, like daisies, coming down separate and distinct, were very different from the tufted flakes we enjoyed so much in Scotland, when we ran into the midst of the slow-falling feathery throng shouting with enthusiasm: 'Jennie's plucking her doos! Jennie's plucking her doos!' (doves).

Nature has many ways of thinning and pruning and trimming her forests – lightning-strokes, heavy snow, and storm-winds to shatter and blow down whole trees here and there or break off branches as required. The results of these methods I have observed in different forests, but only once have I seen pruning by rain. The rain froze on the trees as it fell and grew so thick and heavy that many of them lost a third or more of their branches. The view of the woods after the storm had passed and the sun shone forth was something never to be forgotten. Every twig and branch and rugged trunk was encased in pure crystal ice, and each oak and hickory and willow became a fairy crystal palace. Such dazzling brilliance, such effects of white light and irised light glowing and flashing I had never seen before, nor have I since. This sudden change of the leafless woods to glowing silver was, like the great aurora, spoken of for years, and is one of the most beautiful of the many pictures that enriches my life. And besides the great shows there were thousands of others even in the coldest weather manifesting the utmost fineness and tenderness of beauty and affording noble compensation for hardship and pain.

One of the most striking of the winter sounds was the loud roaring and rumbling of the ice on our lake, from its shrinking and expanding with the changes of the weather. The fishermen who were catching pickerel said that they had no luck when this roaring was going on above the fish. I remember how frightened we boys were when on one of our New Year holidays we were taking a walk on the ice and heard for the first time the sudden rumbling roar beneath our feet and running on ahead of us, creaking and whooping as if all the ice eighteen or twenty inches thick was breaking.

In the neighborhood of our Wisconsin farm there were extensive swamps consisting in great part of a thick sod of very tough carex roots covering thin, watery lakes of mud. They originated in glacier lakes that were gradually over-grown. This sod was so tough that oxen with loaded wagons could be driven over it without cutting down through it, although it was afloat. The carpenters who came to build our frame house, noticing how the sedges sunk beneath their feet, said that if they should break through, they would probably be well on their way to California before touching bottom. On the contrary, all these lake-basins are shallow as compared with their width. When we went into the Wisconsin woods there was not a single wheel-track or cattle-track. The only man-made road was an Indian trail along the Fox River between Portage and Packwauckee Lake. Of course the deer, foxes, badgers, coons, skunks, and even the squirrels had well-beaten tracks from their dens and hiding-places in thickets, hollow trees, and the ground, but they did not reach far, and but little noise was made by the soft-footed travelers in passing over them, only a slight rustling and swishing among fallen leaves and grass.

Corduroying the swamps formed the principal part of road-making among the early settlers for many a day. At these annual road-making gatherings opportunity was offered for discussion of the news, politics, religion, war, the state of the crops, comparative advantages of the new country over the old, and so forth, but the principal opportunities, recurring every week, were the hours after Sunday church services. I remember hearing long talks on the wonderful beauty of the Indian corn; the wonderful melons, so wondrous fine for 'sloken a body on hot days'; their contempt for tomatoes, so fine to look at with their sunny colors and so disappointing in taste; the miserable cucumbers the 'Yankee bodies' ate, though tasteless as rushes; the character of the Yankees, etcetera. Then there were long discussions about the Russian war, news of which was eagerly gleaned from Greeley's *New York Tribune*; the great battles of the Alma, the charges at

Balaklava and Inkerman; the siege of Sebastopol; the military genius of Todleben; the character of Nicholas; the character of the Russian soldier, his stubborn bravery, who for the first time in history withstood the British bayonet charges; the probable outcome of the terrible war; the fate of Turkey, and so forth.

Very few of our old-country neighbors gave much heed to what are called spirit-rappings. On the contrary, they were regarded as a sort of sleight-of-hand humbug. Some of these spirits seem to be stout able-bodied fellows, judging by the weights they lift and the heavy furniture they bang about. But they do no good work that I know of; never saw wood, grind corn, cook, feed the hungry, or go to the help of poor sinuous mothers at the bedsides of their sick children. I noticed when I was a boy that it was not the strongest characters who followed so-called mediums. When a rapping-storm was at its height in Wisconsin, one of our neighbors, an old Scotch-man, remarked, 'Thay puir silly medium-bodies may gang to the deil wi' their rappin' speerits, for they dae nae gude, and I think the deil's their fayther.'

Although in the spring of 1849 there was no other settler within a radius of four miles of our Fountain Luke farm, in three or four years almost every quarter-section of government land was taken up, mostly by enthusiastic home-seekers from Great Britain, with only here and there Yankee families from adjacent states, who had come drifting indefinitely westward in covered wagons, seeking their fortunes like winged seeds; all alike striking root and gripping the glacial drift soil as naturally as oak and hickory trees; happy and hopeful, establishing homes and making wider and wider fields in the hospitable wilderness. The axe and plough were kept very busy; cattle, horses, sheep, and pigs multiplied; barns and corn-cribs were filled up, and man and beast were well fed; a schoolhouse was built, which was used also for a church; and in a very short time the new country began to look like an old one.

Comparatively few of the first settlers suffered from serious accidents. One of our neighbors had a finger shot off, and on a bitter, frosty night had to be taken to a surgeon in Portage, in a sled drawn by slow, plodding oxen, to have the shattered stump dressed. Another fell from his wagon and was killed by the wheel passing over his body. An acre of ground was reserved and fenced for graves, and soon consumption came to fill it. One of the saddest instances was that of a Scotch family from Edinburgh, consisting of a father, son, and daughter, who settled on eighty acres of land within half a mile of our place. The daughter died of consumption the third year after their arrival, the son one or two years later, and at last the father followed his two children. Thus sadly ended bright hopes and dreams of a happy home in rich and free America.

Another neighbor, I remember, after a lingering illness died of the same disease in mid-winter, and his funeral was attended by the neighbors in sleighs during a driving snowstorm when the thermometer was fifteen or twenty degrees below zero. The great white plague carried off another of our near neighbors, a fine Scotchman, the father of eight promising boys, when he was only about forty-five years of age. Most of those who suffered from this disease seemed hopeful and cheerful up to a very short time before their death, but Mr Reid, I remember, on one of his last visits to our house, said with brave resignation: 'I know that never more in this world can I be well, but I must just submit. I must just submit.'

One of the saddest deaths from other causes than consumption was that of a poor feeble-minded man whose brother, a sturdy, devout, severe puritan, was a very hard taskmaster. Poor half-witted Charlie was kept steadily at work – although he was not able to do much, for his body was about as feeble as his mind. He never could be taught the right use of an axe, and when he was set to chopping down trees for firewood he feebly hacked and chipped round and round them, sometimes spending several days in nibbling down a tree that a beaver might have gnawed down in half the time. Occasionally when he had an extra large tree to chop, he would go home and report that the tree was too tough and strong for him and that he could never make it fall. Then his brother, calling him a useless creature, would fell it with a few well-directed strokes, and leave Charlie to nibble away at it for weeks trying to make it into stove-wood.

His guardian brother, delighting in hard work and able for anything, was as remarkable for strength of body and mind as poor Charlie for childishness. All the neighbors pitied Charlie, especially the women, who never missed an opportunity to give him kind words, cookies, and pie; above all, they bestowed

natural sympathy on the poor imbecile as if he were an unfortunate motherless child. In particular, his nearest neighbors,
Scotch Highlanders, warmly welcomed him to their home and
never wearied in doing everything that tender sympathy could
suggest. To those friends he ran gladly at every opportunity. But
after years of suffering from overwork and illness his feeble
health failed, and he told his Scotch friends one day that he was
not able to work any more or do anything that his brother
wanted him to do, that he was tired of life, and that he had come
to thank them for their kindness and to bid them goodbye, for
he was going to drown himself in Muir's lake. 'Oh, Charlie!
Charlie!' they cried, 'you mustn't talk that way. Cheer up! You
will soon be stronger. We all love you. Cheer up! Cheer up! And
always come here whenever you need anything.'

'Oh, no! my friends,' he pathetically replied, 'I know you
love me, but I can't cheer up any more. My heart's gone, and I
want to die.'

Next day, when Mr Anderson, a carpenter whose house was
on the west shore of our lake, was going to a spring he saw a
man wade out through the rushes and lily-pads and throw
himself forward into deep water. This was poor Charlie.
Fortunately, Mr Anderson had a skiff close by, and as the
distance was not great he reached the broken-hearted imbecile
in time to save his life, and after trying to cheer him took him
home to his brother. But even this terrible proof of despair
failed to soften his brother. He seemed to regard the attempt at
suicide simply as a crime calculated to bring harm to religion.
Though snatched from the lake to his bed, poor Charlie lived
only a few days longer. A physician who was called when his
health first became seriously impaired reported that he was
suffering from Bright's disease. After all was over, the stoical
brother walked over to the neighbor who had saved Charlie
from drowning, and, after talking on ordinary affairs, crops,
the weather, etc., said in a careless tone: 'I have a little job of
carpenter work for you, Mr Anderson.' 'What is it, Mr – – ?'
'I want you to make a coffin.' 'A coffin!' said the startled
carpenter. 'Who is dead?' 'Charlie,' he coolly replied. All the
neighbors were in tears over the poor child man's fate. But,
strange to say, the brother who had faithfully cared for him
controlled and concealed all his natural affection as incompa-
tible with sound faith.

The mixed lot of settlers around us offered a favorable field for observation of the different kinds of people of our own race. We were swift to note the way they behaved, the differences in their religion and morals, and in their ways of drawing a living from the same kind of soil under the same general conditions; how they protected themselves from the weather; how they were influenced by new doctrines and old ones seen in new lights in preaching, lecturing, debating, bringing up their children, etc., and how they regarded the Indians, those first settlers and owners of the ground that was being made into farms.

I well remember my father's discussing with a Scotch neighbor, a Mr George Mair, the Indian question as to the rightful ownership of the soil. Mr Mair remarked one day that it was pitiful to see how the unfortunate Indians, children of Nature, living on the natural products of the soil, hunting, fishing, and even cultivating small corn-fields on the most fertile spots, were now being robbed of their lands and pushed ruthlessly back into narrower and narrower limits by alien races who were cutting off their means of livelihood. Father replied that surely it could never have been the intention of God to allow Indians to rove and hunt over so fertile a country and hold it forever in unproductive wildness, while Scotch and Irish and English farmers could put it to so much better use. Where an Indian required thousands of acres for his family, these acres in the hands of industrious, God-fearing farmers would support ten or a hundred times more people in a far worthier manner, while at the same time helping to spread the gospel.

Mr Mair urged that such farming as our first immigrants were practicing was in many ways rude and full of the mistakes of ignorance, yet, rude as it was, and ill-tilled as were most of our Wisconsin farms by unskillful, inexperienced settlers who had been merchants and mechanics and servants in the old countries, how should we like to have specially trained and educated farmers drive us out of our homes and farms, such as they were, making use of the same argument, that God could never have intended such ignorant, unprofitable, devastating farmers as we were to occupy land upon which scientific farmers could raise five or ten times as much on each acre as we did? And I well remember thinking that Mr Mair had the better side of the argument. It then seemed to me that, whatever the final outcome might be, it was at this stage of the fight only an example of the rule of might with but little or no thought for the right or welfare of the other fellow if he were the weaker; that 'they should take who had the power, and they should keep who can,' as Wordsworth makes the marauding Scottish Highlanders say.

Many of our old neighbors toiled and sweated and grubbed themselves into their graves years before their natural dying days, in getting a living on a quarter-section of land and vaguely trying to get rich, while bread and raiment might have been serenely won on less than a fourth of this land, and time gained to get better acquainted with God.

I was put to the plough at the age of twelve, when my head reached but little above the handles, and for many years I had to do the greater part of the ploughing. It was hard work for so small a boy; nevertheless, as good ploughing was exacted from me as if I were a man, and very soon I had to become a good ploughman, or rather ploughboy. None could draw a straighter furrow. For the first few years the work was particularly hard on account of the tree-stumps that had to be dodged. Later the stumps were all dug and chopped out to make way for the McCormick reaper, and because I proved to be the best chopper and stump-digger I had nearly all of it to myself. It was dull, hard work leaning over on my knees all day, chopping out those tough oak and hickory stumps, deep down below the crowns of the big roots. Some, though fortunately not many, were two feet or more in diameter.

And as I was the eldest boy, the greater part of all the other hard work of the farm quite naturally fell on me. I had to split rails for long lines of zigzag fences. The trees that were tall enough and straight enough to afford one or two logs ten feet long were used for rails, the others, too knotty or cross-grained, were disposed of in log and cordwood fences. Making rails was hard work and required no little skill. I used to cut and split a hundred a day from our short, knotty oak timber, swinging the axe and heavy mallet, often with sore hands, from early morning to night. Father was not successful as a rail-splitter. After trying the work with me a day or two, he in despair left it all to me. I rather liked it, for I was proud of my skill, and tried to believe that I was as tough as the timber I mauled, though this and other heavy jobs stopped my growth and earned for me the title 'Runt of the family.'

In those early days, long before the great labor-saving machines came to our help, almost everything connected with wheat-raising abounded in trying work – cradling in the long, sweaty dog-days, raking and binding, stacking, thrashing – and it often seemed to me that our fierce, over-industrious way of getting the grain from the ground was too closely connected with grave-digging. The staff of life, naturally beautiful, often-times suggested the gravedigger's spade. Men and boys, and in those days even women and girls, were cut down while cutting the wheat. The fat folk grew lean and the lean leaner, while the rosy cheeks brought from Scotland and other cool countries across the sea faded to yellow like the wheat. We were all made slaves through the vice of over-industry. The same was in great part true in making hay to keep the cattle and horses through the long winters. We were called in the morning at four o'clock and seldom got to bed before nine, making a broiling, seething day seventeen hours long loaded with heavy work, while I was only a small stunted boy; and a few years later my brothers David and Daniel and my older sisters had to endure about as much as I did. In the harvest dog-days and dog-nights and dog-mornings, when we arose from our clammy beds, our cotton shirts clung to our backs as wet with sweat as the bathing-suits of swimmers, and remained so all the long, sweltering days. In mowing and cradling, the most exhausting of all the farm work, I made matters worse by foolish ambition in keeping ahead of the hired men. Never a warning word was spoken of the dangers of over-work. On the contrary, even when sick we were held to our tasks as long as we could stand. Once in harvest-time I had the mumps and was unable to swallow any food except milk, but this was not allowed to make any difference, while I staggered with weakness and sometimes fell headlong among the sheaves. Only once was I allowed to leave the harvest-field – when I was stricken down with pneumonia. I lay gasping for weeks, but the Scotch are hard to kill and I pulled through. No physician was called, for Father was an enthusiast, and always said and believed that God and hard work were by far the best doctors.

None of our neighbors were so excessively industrious as Father; though nearly all of the Scotch, English, and Irish worked too hard, trying to make good homes and to lay up money enough for comfortable independence. Excepting small garden-patches, few of them had owned land in the old country. Here their craving land-hunger was satisfied, and they were naturally proud of their farms and tried to keep them as neat and clean and well-tilled as gardens. To accomplish this without the means for hiring help was impossible. Flowers were planted about the neatly kept log or frame houses; barnyards, granaries, etc., were kept in about as neat order as the homes, and the fences and corn-rows were rigidly straight. But every uncut weed distressed them; so also did every ungathered ear of grain, and all that was lost by birds and gophers; and this overcarefulness bred endless work and worry.

As for money, for many a year there was precious little of it in the country for anybody. Eggs sold at six cents a dozen in trade, and five-cent calico was exchanged at twenty-five cents a yard. Wheat brought fifty cents a bushel in trade. To get cash for it before the Portage Railway was built, it had to be hauled to Milwaukee, a hundred miles away. On the other hand, food was abundant – eggs, chickens, pigs, cattle, wheat, corn, potatoes, garden vegetables of the best, and wonderful melons as luxuries. No other wild country I have ever known extended a kinder welcome to poor immigrants. On the arrival in the spring, a log house could be built, a few acres ploughed, the virgin sod planted with corn, potatoes, etc., and enough raised to keep a family comfortably the very first year; and wild hay for cows and oxen grew in abundance on the numerous meadows. The American settlers were wisely content with smaller fields and less of everything, kept indoors during excessively hot or cold weather, rested when tired, went off fishing and hunting at the most favorable times and seasons of the day and year, gathered nuts and berries, and in general tranquilly accepted all the good things the fertile wilderness offered.

After eight years of this dreary work of clearing the Fountain Lake farm, fencing it and getting it in perfect order, building a frame house and the necessary outbuildings for the cattle and horses – after all this had been victoriously accomplished, and we had made out to escape with life – Father bought a half-section of wild land about four or five miles to the eastward and began all over again to clear and fence and break up other fields for a new farm doubling all the stunting, heartbreaking chopping, grubbing, stump-digging, rail-splitting, fence-building, barn-building, house-building, and so forth.

By this time I had learned to run the breaking plough. Most of these ploughs were very large, turning furrows from eighteen inches to two feet wide, and were drawn by four or five yoke of oxen. They were used only for the first ploughing, in breaking up the wild sod woven into a tough mass, chiefly by the cordlike roots of perennial grasses, reinforced by the taproots of oak and hickory bushes, called 'grubs,' some of which were more than a century old and four or five inches in diameter. In the hardest ploughing on the most difficult ground, the grubs were said to be as thick as the hair on a dog's back. If in good trim, the plough cut through and turned over these grubs as if the century-old wood were soft like the flesh of carrots and turnips; but if not in good trim the grubs promptly tossed the plough out of the ground. A stout Highland Scot, our neighbor, whose plough was in bad order and who did not know how to trim it, was vainly trying to keep it in the ground by main strength, while his son, who was driving and merrily whipping up the cattle, would cry encouragingly, 'Haud her in, Fayther! Haud her in!'

'But hoo i' the deil can I haud her in when she'll no *stop* in?' his perspiring father would reply, gasping for breath between each word. On the contrary, with the share and coulter sharp and nicely adjusted, the plough, instead of shying at every grub and jumping out, ran straight ahead without need of steering or holding, and gripped the ground so firmly that it could hardly be thrown out at the end of the furrow.

Our breaker turned a furrow two feet wide, and on our best land, where the sod was toughest, held so firm a grip that at the end of the field my brother, who was driving the oxen, had to come to my assistance in throwing it over on its side to be drawn around the end of the landing; and it was all I could do to set it up again. But I learned to keep that plough in such trim that after I got started on a new furrow I used to ride on the crossbar between the handles with my feet resting comfortably on the beam, without having to steady or steer it in any way on the whole length of the field, unless we had to go round a stump, for it sawed through the biggest grubs without flinching.

The growth of these grubs was interesting to me. When an acorn or hickory-nut had sent up its first season's sprout, a few inches long, it was burned off in the autumn grass fires; but the root continued to hold on to life, formed a callus over the wound and sent up one or more shoots the next spring. Next autumn these new shoots were burned off, but the root and calloused head, about level with the surface of the ground, continued to grow and send up more new shoots; and so on, almost every year until very old, probably far more than a century, while the tops, which would naturally have become tall broad-headed trees, were only mere sprouts seldom more than two years old. Thus the ground was kept open like a prairie, with only five or six trees to the acre, which had escaped the fire by having the good fortune to grow on a bare spot at the door of a fox or badger den, or between straggling grass-tufts wide apart on the poorest sandy soil.

The uniformly rich soil of the Illinois and Wisconsin prairies produced so close and tall a growth of grasses for fires that no tree could live on it. Had there been no fires, these fine prairies, so marked a feature of the country, would have been covered by the heaviest forests. As soon as the oak openings in our neighborhood were settled, and the farmers had prevented running grass-fires, the grubs grew up into trees and formed tall thickets so dense that it was difficult to walk through them and every trace of the sunny 'openings' vanished.

We called our second farm Hickory Hill, from its many fine hickory trees and the long gentle slope leading up to it. Compared with Fountain Lake farm it lay high and dry. The land was better, but it had no living water, no spring or stream or meadow or lake. A well ninety feet deep had to be dug, all except the first ten feet or so in fine-grained sandstone. When the sandstone was struck, my father, on the advice of a man who had worked in mines, tried to blast the rock; but from lack of skill the blasting went on very slowly, and Father decided to have me do all the work with mason's chisels, a long, hard job, with a good deal of danger in it. I had to sit cramped in a space about three feet in diameter, and wearily chip, chip, with heavy hammer and chisels from early morning until dark, day after day, for weeks and months. In the morning, Father and David lowered me in a wooden bucket by a windlass, hauled up what chips were left from the night before, then went away to the farm work and left me until noon, when they hoisted me out for dinner. After dinner I was promptly lowered again, the forenoon's accumulation of chips hoisted out of the way, and I was left until night.

One morning, after the dreary bore was about eighty feet deep, my life was all but lost in deadly choke-damp – carbonic acid gas that had settled at the bottom during the night. Instead of clearing away the chips as usual when I was lowered to the bottom, I swayed back and forth and began to sink under the poison. Father, alarmed that I did not make any noise, shouted, 'What's keeping you so still?' to which he got no reply. Just as I was settling down against the side of the wall, I happened to catch a glimpse of a branch of a bur-oak tree which leaned out over the mouth of the shaft. This suddenly awakened me, and to Father's excited shouting I feebly murmured, 'Take me out.' But when he began to hoist he found I was not in the bucket and in wild alarm shouted, 'Get in! Get in the bucket and hold on! Hold on!' Somehow I managed to get into the bucket, and that is all I remembered until I was dragged out, violently gasping for breath.

One of our near neighbors, a stone mason and miner by the name of William Duncan, came to see me, and after hearing the particulars of the accident he solemnly said: 'Weel, Johnnie, it's God's mercy that you're alive. Many a companion of mine have I seen dead with choke-damp, but none that I ever saw or heard of was so near to death in it as you were and escaped without help.' Mr Duncan taught Father to throw water down the shaft to absorb the gas, and also to drop a bundle of brush or hay attached to a light rope, dropping it again and again to carry down pure air and stir up the poison. When, after a day or two, I had recovered from the shock, Father lowered me again to my work, after taking the precaution to test the air with a candle and stir it up well with a brush-and-hay bundle. The weary hammer-and-chisel-chipping went on as before, only more slowly, until ninety feet down, when at last I struck a fine, hearty gush of water. Constant dropping wears away stone. So does constant chipping, while at the same time wearing away the chipper. Father never spent an hour in that well. He trusted me to sink it straight and plumb, and I did, and built a fine covered top over it, and swung two iron-bound buckets in it from which we all drank for many a day.

The honey-bee arrived in America long before we boys did,

but several years passed ere we noticed any on our farm. The introduction of the honey-bee into flowery America formed a grand epoch in bee history. This sweet humming creature, companion and friend of the flowers, is now distributed over the greater part of the continent, filling countless hollows in rocks and trees with honey as well as the millions of hives prepared for them by honey-farmers, who keep and tend their flocks of sweet winged cattle, as shepherds keep sheep – a charming employment, 'like directing sunbeams,' as Thoreau says. The Indians call the honey-bee the white man's fly; and though they had long been acquainted with several species of bumblebees that yielded more or less honey, how gladly surprised they must have been when they discovered that, in the hollow trees where before they had found only coons or squirrels, they found swarms of brown flies with fifty or even a hundred pounds of honey sealed up in beautiful cells. With their keen hunting senses they of course were not slow to learn the habits of the little brown immigrants and the best methods of tracing them to their sweet homes, however well hidden. During the first few years none were seen on our farm, though we sometimes heard Father's hired men talking about 'lining bees.' None of us boys ever found a bee tree, or tried to find any until about ten years after our arrival in the woods. On the Hickory Hill farm there is a ridge of moraine material, rather dry, but flowery with goldenrods and asters of many species, upon which we saw bees feeding in the late autumn just when their hives were fullest of honey, and it occurred to me one day after I was of age and my own master that I must try to find a bee tree. I made a little box about six inches long and four inches deep and wide; bought half a pound of honey, went to the goldenrod hill, swept a bee into the box and closed it. The lid had a pane of glass in it so I could see when the bee had sucked its fill and was ready to go home. At first it groped around trying to get out, but, smelling the honey, it seemed to forget everything else, and while it was feasting I carried the box and a small sharp-pointed stake to an open spot, where I could see about me, fixed the stake in the ground, and placed the box on the flat top of it. When I thought that the little feaster must be about full, I opened the box, but it was in no hurry to fly. It slowly crawled up to the edge of the box, lingered a minute or two cleaning its legs that had become sticky with honey, and when it took wing, instead of making what is called a bee-line for home, it buzzed around the box and minutely examined it as if trying to fix a clear picture of it in its mind so as to be able to recognize it when it returned for another load, then circled around at a little distance as if looking for something to locate it by. I was the nearest object, and the thoughtful worker buzzed in front of my face and took a good stare at me, and then flew up on to the top of an oak on the side of the open spot in the centre of which the honey-box was. Keeping a keen watch, after a minute or two of rest or wing-cleaning, I saw it fly in wide circles round the tops of the trees nearest the honey-box, and, after apparently satisfying itself, make a bee-line for the hive. Looking endwise on the line of flight, I saw that what is called a bee-line is not an absolutely straight line, but a line in general straight made of many slight, wavering, lateral curves. After taking as true a bearing as I could, I waited and watched. In a few minutes, probably ten, I was surprised to see that bee arrive at the end of the outleaning limb of the oak mentioned above, as though that was the first point it had fixed in its memory to be depended on in retracing the way back to the honey-box. From the tree-top it came straight to my head, thence straight to the box, entered without the least hesitation, filled up and started off after the same preparatory dressing and taking of bearings as before. Then I took particular pains to lay down the exact course so I would be able to trace it to the hive. Before doing so, however, I made all experiment to test the worth of the impression I had that the little insect found the way back to the box by fixing telling points in its mind. While it was away, I picked up the honey-box and set it on the stake a few rods from the position it had thus far occupied, and stood there watching. In a few minutes I saw the bee arrive at its guide-mark, the overleaning branch on the tree-top, and thence come bouncing down right to the spaces in the air which had been occupied by my head and the honey-box, and when the cunning little honey-gleaner found nothing there but empty air it whirled round and round as if confused and lost; and although I was standing with the open honey-box within fifty or sixty feet of the former feasting-spot, it could not, or at least did not, find it.

Now that I had learned the general direction of the hive, I pushed on in search of it. I had gone perhaps a quarter of a mile when I caught another bee, which, after getting loaded, went through the same performance of circling round and round the honey-box, buzzing in front of me and staring me in the face to be able to recognize me; but as if the adjacent trees and bushes were sufficiently well known, it simply looked around at them and bolted off without much dressing, indicating, I thought, that the distance to the hive was not great. I followed on and very soon discovered it in the bottom log of a corn-field fence, but some lucky fellow had discovered it before me and robbed it. The robbers had chopped a large hole in the log, taken out most of the honey, and left the poor bees late in the fall, when winter was approaching, to make haste to gather all the honey they could from the latest flowers to avoid starvation in the winter.

Chapter 7
KNOWLEDGE AND INVENTIONS

I learned arithmetic in Scotland without understanding any of it, though I had the rules by heart. But when I was about fifteen or sixteen years of age, I began to grow hungry for real knowledge, and persuaded Father, who was willing enough to have me study provided my farm work was kept up, to buy me a higher arithmetic. Beginning at the beginning, in one summer I easily finished it without assistance in the short intervals between the end of dinner and the afternoon start for the harvest-and-hay-fields, accomplishing more without a teacher in a few scraps of time than in years in school before my mind was ready for such work. Then in succession I took up algebra, geometry, and trigonometry and made some little progress in each, and reviewed grammar. I was fond of reading, but Father had brought only a few religious books from Scotland. Fortunately, several of our neighbors had brought a dozen or two of all sorts of books, which I borrowed and read, keeping all of them except the religious ones carefully hidden from Father's eye. Among these were Scott's novels, which, like all other novels, were strictly forbidden, but devoured with glorious pleasure in secret. Father was easily persuaded to buy Josephus's 'Wars of the Jews,' and D'Aubigné's 'History of the Reformation,' and I tried hard to get him to buy Plutarch's Lives, which, as I told him, everybody, even religious people, praised as a grand good book; but he would have nothing to do with the old pagan until the graham bread and anti-flesh doctrines came suddenly into our backwoods neighborhood, making a stir something like phrenology and spirit-rappings, which were as mysterious in their attacks as influenza. He then thought it possible that Plutarch might be turned to account on the food question by revealing what those old Greeks and

Romans ate to make them strong; and so at last we gained our glorious Plutarch. Dick's 'Christian Philosopher,' which I borrowed from a neighbor, I thought I might venture to read in the open, trusting that the word 'Christian' would be proof against its cautious condemnation. But Father balked at the word 'Philosopher,' and quoted from the Bible a verse which spoke of 'philosophy falsely so-called.' I then ventured to speak in defense of the book, arguing that we could not do without at least a little of the most useful kinds of philosophy.

'Yes, we can,' he said with enthusiasm, 'the Bible is the only book human beings can possibly require throughout all the journey from earth to heaven.'

'But how,' I contended, 'can we find the way to heaven without the Bible, and how after we grow old can we read the Bible without a little helpful science? Just think, Father, you cannot read your Bible without spectacles, and millions of others are in the same fix; and spectacles cannot be made without some knowledge of the science of optics.'

'Oh!' he replied, perceiving the drift of the argument, 'there will always be plenty of worldly people to make spectacles.'

To this I stubbornly replied with a quotation from the Bible with reference to the time coming when 'all shall know the Lord from the least even to the greatest,' and then who will make the spectacles? But he still objected to my reading that book, called me a contumacious quibbler too fond of disputation, and ordered me to return it to the accommodating owner. I managed, however, to read it later.

On the food question Father insisted that those who argued for a vegetable diet were in the right, because our teeth showed plainly that they were made with reference to fruit and grain and not for flesh like those of dogs and wolves and tigers. He therefore promptly adopted a vegetable diet and requested Mother to make the bread from graham flour instead of bolted flour. Mother put both kinds on the table, and meat also, to let all the family take their choice, and while Father was insisting on the foolishness of eating flesh, I came to her help by calling Father's attention to the passage in the Bible which told the story of Elijah the prophet who, when he was pursued by enemies who wanted to take his life, was hidden by the Lord by the brook Cherith, and fed by ravens; and surely the Lord knew what was good to eat, whether bread or meat. And on

what, I asked, did the Lord feed Elijah? On vegetables
or graham bread? No, he directed the ravens to feed his
prophet on flesh. The Bible being the sole rule, Father at once
acknowledged that he was mistaken. The Lord never would
have sent flesh to Elijah by the ravens if graham bread were
better.

I remember as a great and sudden discovery that the poetry
of the Bible, Shakespeare, and Milton was a source of inspiring, exhilarating, uplifting pleasure; and I became anxious to
know all the poets, and saved up small sums to buy as many of
their books as possible. Within three or four years I was the
proud possessor of parts of Shakespeare's, Milton's, Cowper's,
Henry Kirke White's, Campbell's, and Akenside's works, and
quite a number of others seldom read nowadays. I think it was
in my fifteenth year that I began to relish good literature with
enthusiasm, and smack my lips over favorite lines, but there
was desperately little time for reading, even in the winter
evenings – only a few stolen minutes now and then. Father's
strict rule was, straight to bed immediately after family worship, which in winter was usually over by eight o'clock. I was
in the habit of lingering in the kitchen with a book and candle
after the rest of the family had retired, and considered myself
fortunate if I got five minutes' reading before Father noticed
the light and ordered me to bed; an order that of course I
immediately obeyed. But night after night I tried to steal
minutes in the same lingering way, and how keenly precious
those minutes were, few nowadays can know. Father failed
perhaps two or three times in a whole winter to notice my light
for nearly ten minutes, magnificent golden blocks of time, long
to be remembered like holidays or geological periods. One
evening when I was reading Church history Father was particularly irritable, and called out with hope-killing emphasis,
'*John, go to bed!* Must I give you a separate order every night
to get you to go to bed? Now, I will have no irregularity in the
family; you *must* go when the rest go, and without my having
to tell you.' Then, as an afterthought, as if judging that his
words and tone of voice were too severe for so pardonable an
offense as reading a religious book, he unwarily added: 'If you
will read, get up in the morning and read. You may get up in
the morning as early as you like.'

That night I went to bed wishing with all my heart and soul

that somebody or something might call me out of sleep to avail myself of this wonderful indulgence; and next morning to my joyful surprise I awoke before Father called me. A boy sleeps soundly after working all day in the snowy woods, but that frosty morning I sprang out of bed as if called by a trumpet blast, rushed downstairs, scarce feeling my chilblains, enormously eager to see how much time I had won; and when I held up my candle to a little clock that stood on a bracket in the kitchen I found that it was only one o'clock. I had gained five hours, almost half a day! 'Five hours to myself!' I said, 'five huge, solid hours!' I can hardly think of any other event in my life, any discovery I ever made that gave birth to joy so transportingly glorious as the possession of these five frosty hours.

In the glad, tumultuous excitement of so much suddenly acquired time-wealth, I hardly knew what to do with it. I first thought of going on with my reading, but the zero weather would make a fire necessary, and it occurred to me that Father might object to the cost of fire-wood that took time to chop. Therefore, I prudently decided to go down to the cellar, and begin work on a model of a self-setting sawmill I had invented. Next morning I managed to get up at the same gloriously early hour, and though the temperature of the cellar was a little below the freezing point, and my light was only a tallow candle, the mill work went joyfully on. There were a few tools in a corner of the cellar – a vise, files, a hammer, chisels, etc., that Father had brought from Scotland, but no saw excepting a coarse crooked one that was unfit for sawing dry hickory or oak. So I made a fine-tooth saw suitable for my work out of a strip of steel that had formed part of an old-fashioned corset, that cut the hardest wood smoothly. I also made my own bradawls, punches, and a pair of compasses, out of wire and old files.

My workshop was immediately under Father's bed, and the filing and tapping in making cogwheels, journals, cams, etc., must, no doubt, have annoyed him, but with the permission he had granted in his mind, and doubtless hoping that I would soon tire of getting up at one o'clock, he impatiently waited about two weeks before saying a word. I did not vary more than five minutes from one o'clock all winter, nor did I feel any bad effects whatever, nor did I think at all about the subject as to whether so little sleep might be in any way injurious; it was a grand triumph of will-power over cold and common comfort and work-weariness in abruptly cutting down my ten hours' allowance of sleep to five. I simply felt that I was rich beyond anything I could have dreamed of or hoped for. I was far more than happy. Like Tam o'Shanter I was 'glorious, O'er a' the ills o' life victorious.'

Father, as was customary in Scotland, gave thanks and asked a blessing before meals, not merely as a matter of form and decent Christian manners, for he regarded food as a gift derived directly from the hands of the Father in heaven. Therefore every meal to him was a sacrament requiring conduct and attitude of mind not unlike that befitting the Lord's Supper. No idle word was allowed to be spoken at our table, much less any laughing or fun or story-telling. When we were at the breakfast-table, about two weeks after the great golden time-discovery, Father cleared his throat preliminary, as we all knew, to saying something considered important. I feared that it was to be on the subject of my early rising, and dreaded the withdrawal of the permission he had granted on account of the noise I made, but still hoping that, as he had given his word that I might get up as early as I wished, he would as a Scotchman stand to it, even though it was given in an unguarded moment and taken in a sense unreasonably far-reaching. The solemn sacramental silence was broken by the dreaded question: –

'John, what time is it when you get up in the morning?'

'About one o'clock,' I replied in a low, meek, guilty tone of voice.

'And what kind of a time is that, getting up in the middle of the night and disturbing the whole family?'

I simply reminded him of the permission he had freely granted me to get up as early as I wished.

'I *know* it,' he said, in an almost agonized tone of voice, 'I *know* I gave you that miserable permission, but I never imagined that you would get up in the middle of the night.'

To this I cautiously made no reply, but continued to listen for the heavenly one-o'clock call, and it never failed.

After completing my self-setting sawmill I dammed one of the streams in the meadow and put the mill in operation. This invention was speedily followed by a lot of others – water-wheels, curious doorlocks and latches, thermometers, hygrometers, pyrometers, clocks, a barometer, an automatic contrivance for feeding the horses at any required hour, a lamp-lighter and fire-lighter, an early-or-late-rising machine, and so forth.

After the sawmill was proved and discharged from my mind, I happened to think it would be a fine thing to make a timekeeper which would tell the day of the week and the day of the month, as well as strike like a common clock and point out the hours; also to have an attachment whereby it could be connected with a bedstead to set me on my feet at any hour in the morning; also to start fires, light lamps, etc. I had learned the time laws of the pendulum from a book, but with this exception I knew nothing of timekeepers, for I had never seen the inside of any sort of clock or watch. After long brooding, the novel clock was at length completed in my mind, and was tried and found to be durable and to work well and look well before I had begun to build it in wood. I carried small parts of it in my pocket to whittle at when I was out at work on the farm using every spare or stolen moment within reach without Father's knowing anything about it. In the middle of summer, when harvesting was in progress, the novel time-machine was nearly completed. It was hidden upstairs in a spare bedroom where some tools were kept. I did the making and mending on the farm, but one day at noon, when I happened to be away, Father went upstairs for a hammer or something and discovered the mysterious machine back of the bedstead. My sister Margaret saw him on his knees examining it, and at the first opportunity whispered in my ear, 'John, Fayther saw that thing you're making upstairs.' None of the family knew what I was doing, but they knew very well that all such work was frowned on by Father, and kindly warned me of any danger that threatened my plans. The fine invention seemed doomed to destruction before its time-ticking commenced, though I thought it handsome, had so long carried it in my mind, and like the nest of Burns's wee mousie it had cost me mony a weary whittling nibble. When we were at dinner several days after the sad discovery, Father began to clear his throat to speak, and I feared the doom of martyrdom was about to be pronounced on my grand clock.

'John,' he inquired, 'what is that thing you are making upstairs?'

I replied in desperation that I didn't know what to call it.

'What! You mean to say you don't know what you are trying to do?'

'Oh, yes,' I said, 'I know very well what I am doing.'

'What, then, is the thing for?'

'It's for a lot of things,' I replied, 'but getting people up early in the morning is one of the main things it is intended for; therefore it might perhaps be called an early-rising machine.'

After getting up so extravagantly early all the last memorable winter, to make a machine for getting up perhaps still earlier seemed so ridiculous that he very nearly laughed. But after controlling himself and getting command of a sufficiently solemn face and voice he said severely, 'Do you not think it is very wrong to waste your time on such nonsense?'

'No,' I said meekly, 'I don't think I'm doing any wrong.'

'Well,' he replied, 'I assure you I do; and if you were only half as zealous in the study of religion as you are in contriving and whittling these useless, nonsensical things, it would be infinitely better for you. I want you to be like Paul, who said that he desired to know nothing among men but Christ and Him crucified.'

To this I made no reply, gloomily believing my fine machine was to be burned, but still taking what comfort I could in realizing that anyhow I had enjoyed inventing and making it.

After a few days, finding that nothing more was to be said, and that Father after all had not had the heart to destroy it, all necessity for secrecy being ended, I finished it in the half-hours that we had at noon and set it in the parlor between two chairs, hung moraine boulders that had come from the direction of Lake Superior on it for weights, and set it running. We were then hauling grain into the barn. Father at this period devoted himself entirely to the Bible and did no farm work whatever. The clock had a good loud tick, and when he heard it strike, one of my sisters told me that he left his study, went to the parlor, got down on his knees and carefully examined the machinery, which was all in plain sight, not being enclosed in a case. This he did repeatedly, and evidently seemed a little proud of my ability to invent and whittle such a thing, though careful to give no encouragement for anything more of the kind in future.

But somehow it seemed impossible to stop. Inventing and whittling faster than ever, I made another hickory clock, shaped like a scythe to symbolize the scythe of Father Time. The pendulum is a bunch of arrows symbolizing the flight of time. It hangs on a leafless mossy oak snag showing the effect of time, and on the snath is written, 'All flesh is grass.' This, especially the inscription, rather pleased Father, and, of course, Mother and all my sisters and brothers admired it. Like the first it indicates the days of the week and month, starts fires and beds at any given hour and minute, and, though made more than fifty years ago, is still a good timekeeper.

My mind still running on clocks, I invented a big one like a town clock with four dials, with the time-figures so large they could be read by all our immediate neighbors as well as ourselves when at work in the fields, and on the side next the house the days of the week and month were indicated. It was to be placed on the peak of the barn roof. But just as it was all but finished, Father stopped me, saying that it would bring too many people around the barn. I then asked permission to put it on the top of a black-oak tree near the house. Studying the larger main branches, I thought I could secure a sufficiently rigid foundation for it, while the trimmed sprays and leaves would conceal the angles of the cabin required to shelter the works from the weather, and the two-second pendulum, fourteen feet long, could be snugly encased on the side of the trunk. Nothing about the grand, useful timekeeper, I argued, would disfigure the tree, for it would look something like a big hawk's nest. 'But that,' he objected, 'would draw still bigger bothersome trampling crowds about the place, for whoever heard of anything so queer as a big clock on the top of a tree?' So I had to lay aside its big wheels and cams and rest content with the pleasure of inventing it, and looking at it in my mind and listening to the deep solemn throbbing of its long two-second pendulum with its two old axes back to back for the bob.

One of my inventions was a large thermometer made of an iron rod, about three feet long and five eighths of an inch in diameter, that had formed part of a wagon-box. The expansion and contraction of this rod was multiplied by a series of levers made of strips of hoop iron. The pressure of the rod against the levers was kept constant by a small counterweight, so that the slightest change in the length of the rod was instantly shown on a dial about three feet wide multiplied about thirty-two thousand times. The zero-point was gained by packing the rod in wet snow. The scale was so large that the big black hand on the white-painted dial could be seen distinctly and the temperature read while we were ploughing in the field below the house. The extremes of heat and cold caused the hand to make several revolutions. The number of these revolutions was indicated on a small dial marked on the larger one. This thermometer was fastened on the side of the house, and was so sensitive that when anyone approached it within four or five feet the heat radiated from the observer's body caused the hand of the dial to move so fast that the motion was plainly visible, and when he stepped back, the hand moved slowly back to its normal position. It was regarded as a great wonder by the neighbors and even by my own all-Bible father.

Boys are fond of the books of travelers, and I remember that one day, after I had been reading Mungo Park's travels in Africa, Mother said: 'Weel, John, maybe you will travel like Park and Humboldt some day.' Father overheard her and cried out in solemn deprecation, 'Oh, Anne! dinna put sic notions in the laddie's heed.' But at this time there was precious little need of such prayers. My brothers left the farm when they came of age, but I stayed a year longer, loath to leave home. Mother hoped I might be a minister some day; my sisters that I would be a great inventor. I often thought I should like to be a physician, but I saw no way of making money and getting the necessary education, excepting as an inventor. So, as a beginning, I decided to try to get into a big shop or factory and live awhile among machines. But I was naturally extremely shy and had been taught to have a poor opinion of myself, as of no account, though all our neighbors encouragingly called me a genius, sure to rise in the world. When I was talking over plans one day with a friendly neighbor, he said: 'Now, John, if you wish to get into a machine-shop, just take some of your inventions to the State Fair, and you may be sure that as soon as they are seen they will open the door of any shop in the country for you. You will be welcomed everywhere.' And when I doubtingly asked if people would care to look at things made of wood, he said, 'Made of wood! Made of wood! What does it matter what they're made of when they are so out-and-out original. There's nothing else like them in the world. That is what will attract attention, and besides they're mighty handsome things anyway to come from the backwoods.' So I was encouraged to leave home and go at his direction to the State Fair when it was being held in Madison.

Chapter 8

THE WORLD AND THE UNIVERSITY

When I told Father that I was about to leave home, and inquired whether, if I should happen to be in need of money, he would send me a little, he said, 'No; depend entirely on yourself.' Good advice, I suppose, but surely needlessly severe for a bashful, home-loving boy who had worked so hard. I had the gold sovereign that my grandfather had given me when I left Scotland, and a few dollars, perhaps ten, that I had made by raising a few bushels of grain on a little patch of sandy abandoned ground. So when I left home to try the world I had only about fifteen dollars in my pocket.

Strange to say, Father carefully taught us to consider ourselves very poor worms of the dust, conceived in sin, etc., and devoutly believed that quenching every spark of pride and self-confidence was a sacred duty, without realizing that in so doing he might at the same time be quenching everything else. Praise he considered most venomous, and tried to assure me that when I was fairly out in the wicked world making my own way I would soon learn that although I might have thought him a hard taskmaster at times, strangers were far harder. On the contrary, I found no lack of kindness and sympathy. All the baggage I carried was a package made up of the two clocks and a small thermometer made of a piece of old washboard, all three tied together, with no covering or case of any sort, the whole looking like one very complicated machine.

The aching parting from Mother and my sisters was, of course, hard to bear. Father let David drive me down to Pardeeville, a place I had never before seen, though it was only nine miles south of the Hickory Hill home. When we arrived at the village tavern, it seemed deserted. Not a single person was in sight. I set my clock baggage on the rickety platform. David said goodbye and started for home, leaving me alone in the world. The grinding noise made by the wagon in turning short brought out the landlord, and the first thing that caught his eye was my strange bundle. Then he looked at me and said, 'Hello, young man, what's this?'

'Machines,' I said, 'for keeping time and getting up in the morning, and so forth.'

'Well! Well! That's a mighty queer get-up. You must be a Down-East Yankee. Where did you get the pattern for such a thing?'

'In my head,' I said.

Someone down the street happened to notice the landlord looking intently at something and came up to see what it was. Three or four people in that little village formed an attractive crowd, and in fifteen or twenty minutes the greater part of the population of Pardeeville stood gazing in a circle around my strange hickory belongings. I kept outside of the circle to avoid being seen, and had the advantage of hearing the remarks without being embarrassed. Almost every one as he came up would say, 'What's that? What's it for? Who made it?' The landlord would answer them all alike, 'Why, a young man that lives out in the country somewhere made it, and he says it's a thing for keeping time, getting up in the morning, and something that I didn't understand. I don't know what he meant.' 'Oh, no!' one of the crowd would say, 'that can't be. It's for something else – something mysterious. Mark my words, you'll see all about it in the newspapers some of these days.' A curious little fellow came running up the street, joined the crowd, stood on tiptoe to get sight of the wonder, quickly made up his mind, and shouted in crisp, confident, cock-crowing style, 'I know what that contraption's for. It's a machine for taking the bones out of fish.'

This was in the time of the great popular phrenology craze, when the fences and barns along the roads throughout the country were plastered with big skull-bump posters, headed, 'Know Thyself,' and advising everybody to attend schoolhouse lectures to have their heads explained and be told what they were good for and whom they ought to marry. My mechanical bundle seemed to bring a good deal of this phrenology to mind, for many of the onlookers would say, 'I wish I could see that boy's head – he must have a tremendous bump of invention.'

Others complimented me by saying, 'I wish I had that fellow's head. I'd rather have it than the best farm in the State.'

I stayed overnight at this little tavern, waiting for a train. In the morning I went to the station, and set my bundle on the platform. Along came the thundering train, a glorious sight, the first train I had ever waited for. When the conductor saw my queer baggage, he cried, 'Hello! What have we here?'

'Inventions for keeping time, early rising, and so forth. May I take them into the car with me?'

'You can take them where you like,' he replied, 'but you had better give them to the baggage-master. If you take them into the car they will draw a crowd and might get broken.'

So I gave them to the baggage-master and made haste to ask the conductor whether I might ride on the engine. He good-naturedly said: 'Yes, it's the right place for you. Run ahead, and tell the engineer what I say.' But the engineer bluntly refused to let me on, saying: 'It don't matter what the conductor told you. I say you can't ride on my engine.'

By this time the conductor, standing ready to start his train, was watching to see what luck I had, and when he saw me returning came ahead to meet me.

'The engineer won't let me on,' I reported.

'Won't he?' said the kind conductor. 'Oh! I guess he will. You come down with me.' And so he actually took the time and patience to walk the length of that long train to get me on to the engine.

'Charlie,' said he, addressing the engineer, 'don't you ever take a passenger?'

'Very seldom,' he replied.

'Anyhow, I wish you would take this young man on. He has the strangest machines in the baggage-car I ever saw in my life. I believe he could make a locomotive. He wants to see the engine running. Let him on.' Then in a low whisper he told me to jump on, which I did gladly, the engineer offering neither encouragement nor objection.

As soon as the train was started, the engineer asked what the 'strange thing' the conductor spoke of really was.

'Only inventions for keeping time, getting folk up in the morning, and so forth,' I hastily replied, and before he could ask any more questions I asked permission to go outside of the cab to see the machinery. This he kindly granted, adding, 'Be careful not to fall off, and when you hear me whistling for a station you come back, because if it is reported against me to the superintendent that I allow boys to run all over my engine I might lose my job.'

Assuring him that I would come back promptly, I went out and walked along the foot-board on the side of the boiler, watching the magnificent machine rushing through the landscapes as if glorying in its strength like a living creature. While seated on the cow-catcher platform I seemed to be fairly flying, and the wonderful display of power and motion was enchanting. This was the first time I had ever been on a train, much less a locomotive, since I had left Scotland. When I got to Madison, I thanked the kind conductor and engineer for my glorious ride, inquired the way to the Fair, shouldered my inventions, and walked to the Fair Ground.

When I applied for an admission ticket at a window by the gate I told the agent that I had something to exhibit.

'What is it?' he inquired.

'Well, here it is. Look at it.'

When he craned his neck through the window and got a glimpse of my bundle, he cried excitely, 'Oh! You don't need a ticket – come right in.'

When I inquired of the agent where such things as mine should be exhibited, he said, 'You see that building up on the hill with a big flag on it? That's the Fine Arts Hall, and it's just the place for your wonderful invention.'

So I went up to the Fine Arts Hall and looked in, wondering if they would allow wooden things in so fine a place.

I was met at the door by a dignified gentleman, who greeted me kindly and said, 'Young man, what have we got here?'

'Two clocks and a thermometer,' I replied.

'Did you make these? They look wonderfully beautiful and novel and must, I think, prove the most interesting feature of the fair.'

'Where shall I place them?' I inquired.

'Just look around, young man, and choose the place you like best, whether it is occupied or not. You can have your pick of all the building, and a carpenter to make the necessary shelving and assist you every way possible!'

So I quickly had a shelf made large enough for all of them, went out on the hill and picked up some glacial boulders of the right size for weights, and in fifteen or twenty minutes the clocks were running. They seemed to attract more attention than anything else in the hall. I got lots of praise from the crowd and the newspaper reporters. The local press reports were copied into the Eastern papers. It was considered wonderful that a boy on a farm had been able to invent and make such things, and almost every spectator foretold good fortune. But I had been so lectured by my father above all things to avoid praise that I was afraid to read those kind newspaper notices, and never clipped out or preserved any of them, just glanced at them and turned away my eyes from beholding vanity. They gave me a prize of ten or fifteen dollars and a diploma for wonderful things not down in the list of exhibits.

Many years later, after I had written articles and books, I received a letter from the gentleman who had charge of the Fine Arts Hall. He proved to be the Professor of English Literature in the University of Wisconsin at this Fair time, and long afterward he sent me clippings of reports of his lectures. He had a lecture on me, discussing style, et cetera, and telling how well he remembered my arrival at the Hall in my shirt-sleeves with those mechanical wonders on my shoulder, and so forth, and so forth. These inventions, though of little importance, opened all doors for me and made marks that have lasted many years, simply, I suppose, because they were original and promising.

I was looking around in the meantime to find out where I should go to seek my fortune. An inventor at the Fair, by the name of Wiard, was exhibiting an iceboat he had invented to run on the upper Mississippi from Prairie du Chien to St Paul during the winter months, explaining how useful it would be thus to make a highway of the river while it was closed to ordinary navigation by ice. After he saw my inventions he offered me a place in his foundry and machine-shop in Prairie du Chien and promised to assist me all he could. So I made up my mind to accept his offer and rode with him to Prairie du Chien in his iceboat, which was mounted on a flat car. I soon found, however, that he was seldom at home and that I was not likely to learn much at his small shop. I found a place where I could work for my board and devote my spare hours to mechanical drawing, geometry, and physics, making but little headway, however, although the Pelton family, for whom I worked, were very kind. I made up my mind after a few months' stay in Prairie du Chien to return to Madison, hoping that in some way I might be able to gain an education.

At Madison I raised a few dollars by making and selling a few of those bedsteads that set the sleepers on their feet in the morning – inserting in the footboard the works of an ordinary clock that could be bought for a dollar. I also made a few dollars addressing circulars in an insurance office, while at the same time I was paying my board by taking care of a pair of horses and going errands. This is of no great interest except that I was thus winning my bread while hoping that something would turn up that might enable me to make money enough to enter the State University. This was my ambition, and it never wavered no matter what I was doing. No University, it seemed to me, could be more admirably situated, and as I sauntered about it, charmed with its fine lawns and trees and beautiful lakes, and saw the students going and coming with their books, and occasionally practicing with a theodolite in mea-suring distances, I thought that if I could only join them it would be the greatest joy of life. I was desperately hungry and thirsty for knowledge and willing to endure anything to get it.

One day I chanced to meet a student who had noticed my inventions at the Fair and now recognized me. And when I said, 'You are fortunate fellows to be allowed to study in this beautiful place. I wish I could join you.' 'Well, why don't you?' he asked. 'I haven't money enough,' I said. 'Oh, as to money,' he reassuringly explained, 'very little is required. I presume you're able to enter the Freshman class, and you can board yourself as quite a number of us do at a cost of about a dollar a week. The baker and milkman come every day. You can live on bread and milk.' Well, I thought, maybe I have money enough for at least one beginning term. Anyhow I couldn't help trying.

With fear and trembling, overladen with ignorance, I called on Professor Stirling, the Dean of the Faculty, who was then Acting President, presented my case, and told him how far I had got on with my studies at home, and that I hadn't been to school since leaving Scotland at the age of eleven years, excepting one short term of a couple of months at a district school, because I could not be spared from the farm work. After hearing my story, the kind professor welcomed me to the glorious University – next, it seemed to me, to the Kingdom of Heaven. After a few weeks in the preparatory department I entered the Freshman class. In Latin I found that one of the books in use I had already studied in Scotland. So, after an interruption of a dozen years, I began my Latin over again where I had left off; and, strange to say, most of it came back to me, especially the grammar which I had committed to memory at the Dunbar Grammar School.

During the four years that I was in the University, I earned enough in the harvest-fields during the long summer vacations to carry me through the balance of each year, working very hard, cutting with a cradle four acres of wheat a day, and helping to put it in the shock. But, having to buy books and paying, I think, thirty-two dollars a year for instruction, and occasionally buying acids and retorts, glass tubing, bell-glasses, flasks, etc., I had to cut down expenses for board now and then to half a dollar a week.

One winter I taught school ten miles north of Madison, earning much-needed money at the rate of twenty dollars a month, 'boarding round,' and keeping up my University work by studying at night. As I was not then well enough off to own a watch, I used one of my hickory clocks, not only for keeping time, but for starting the school fire in the cold mornings, and regulating class-times. I carried it out on my shoulder to the old log schoolhouse, and set it to work on a little shelf nailed to one of the knotty, bulging logs. The winter was very cold, and I had to go to the schoolhouse and start the fire about eight o'clock to warm it before the arrival of the scholars. This was a rather trying job, and one that my clock might easily be made to do. Therefore, after supper one evening I told the head of the family with whom I was boarding that if he would give me a candle I would go back to the schoolhouse and make arrangements for lighting the fire at eight o'clock, without my having to be present until time to open the school at nine. He said, 'Oh, young man, you have some curious things in the school-room, but I don't think you can do that.' I said, 'Oh, yes! It's easy,' and in hardly more than an hour the simple job was completed. I had only to place a teaspoonful of powdered chlorate of potash and sugar on the stove-hearth near a few shavings and kindling, and at the required time make the clock, through a simple arrangement, touch the inflammable mixture with a drop of sulphuric acid. Every evening after school was dismissed, I shoveled out what was left of the fire into the snow, put in a little kindling, filled up the big box stove with heavy oak wood, placed the lighting arrangement on the hearth, and set the clock to drop the acid at the hour of eight; all this requiring only a few minutes.

The first morning after I had made this simple arrangement I invited the doubting farmer to watch the old squat school-house from a window that overlooked it, to see if a good smoke did not rise from the stovepipe. Sure enough, on the minute, he saw a tall column curling gracefully up through the frosty air, but instead of congratulating me on my success he solemnly shook his head and said in a hollow, lugubrious voice, 'Young man, you will be setting fire to the schoolhouse.' All winter long that faithful clock fire never failed, and by the time I got to the schoolhouse the stove was usually red-hot.

At the beginning of the long summer vacations I returned to the Hickory Hill farm to earn the means in the harvest-fields to continue my University course, walking all the way to save railroad fares. And although I cradled four acres of wheat a day, I made the long, hard, sweaty day's work still longer and harder by keeping up my study of plants. At the noon hour I collected a large handful, put them in water to keep them fresh, and after supper got to work on them and sat up till after midnight, analyzing and classifying, thus leaving only four hours for sleep; and by the end of the last year, after taking up botany, I knew the principal flowering plants of the region.

I received my first lesson in botany from a student by the name of Griswold, who is now County Judge of the County of Waukesha, Wisconsin. In the University he was often laughed at on account of his anxiety to instruct others, and his frequently saying with fine emphasis, 'Imparting instruction is my greatest enjoyment.' One memorable day in June, when I was standing on the stone steps of the north dormitory, Mr Griswold joined me and at once began to teach. He reached up, plucked a flower from an overspreading branch of a locust tree, and, handing it to me, said, 'Muir, do you know what family this tree belongs to?'

'No,' I said, 'I don't know anything about botany.'

'Well, no matter,' said he, 'what is it like?'

'It's like a pea flower,' I replied.

'That's right. You're right,' he said, 'it belongs to the Pea Family.'

'But how can that be,' I objected, 'when the pea is a weak, clinging, straggling herb, and the locust a big, thorny hard-wood tree?'

'Yes, that is true,' he replied, 'as to the difference in size, but it is also true that in all their essential characters they are alike, and therefore they must belong to one and the same family. Just look at the peculiar form of the locust flower; you see that the upper petal, called the banner, is broad and erect, and so is the upper petal of the pea flower; the two lower petals, called the wings, are outspread and wing-shaped; so are those of the pea; and the two petals below the wings are united on their edges, curve upward, and form what is called the keel, and so you see are the corresponding petals of the pea flower. And now look at the stamens and pistils. You see that nine of the ten stamens have their filaments united into a sheath around the pistil, but the tenth stamen has its filament free. These are very marked characters, are they not? And, strange to say, you will find them the same in the tree and in the vine. Now look at the ovules or seeds of the locust, and you will see that they are arranged in a pod or legume like those of the pea. And look at the leaves. You see the leaf of the locust is made up of several leaflets, and so also is the leaf of the pea. Now taste the locust leaf.'

I did so and found that it tasted like the leaf of the pea. Nature has used the same seasoning for both, though one is a straggling one, the other a big tree.

'Now, surely you cannot imagine that all these similar characters are mere coincidences. Do they not rather go to show that the Creator in making the pea vine and locust tree had the same idea in mind, and that plants are not classified arbitrarily? Man has nothing to do with their classification. Nature has attended to all that, giving essential unity with boundless variety, so that the botanist has only to examine plants to learn the harmony of their relations.'

This fine lesson charmed me and sent me flying to the woods and meadows in wild enthusiasm. Like everybody else I was always fond of flowers, attracted by their external beauty and purity. Now my eyes were opened to their inner beauty, all alike revealing glorious traces of the thoughts of God, and leading on and on into the infinite cosmos. I wandered away at every opportunity, making long excursions round the lakes, gathering specimens and keeping them fresh in a bucket in my room to study at night after my regular class tasks were learned; for my eyes never closed on the plant glory I had seen.

Nevertheless, I still indulged my love of mechanical inventions. I invented a desk in which the books I had to study were arranged in order at the beginning of each term. I also made a bed which set me on my feet every morning at the hour determined on, and in dark winter mornings just as the bed set me on the floor it lighted a lamp. Then, after the minutes allowed for dressing had elapsed, a click was heard and the first book to be studied was pushed up from a rack below the top of the desk, thrown open, and allowed to remain there the number of minutes required. Then the machinery closed the book and allowed it to drop back into its stall, then moved the rack forward and threw up the next in order, and so on, all the day being divided according to the times of recitation, and time required and allotted to each study. Besides this, I thought it would be a fine thing in the summertime when the sun rose early, to dispense with the clock-controlled bed machinery, and make use of sunbeams instead. This I did simply by taking a lens out of my small spy-glass, fixing it on a frame on the sill of my bedroom window and pointing it to the sunrise; the sunbeams focused on a thread burned it through, allowing the bed machinery to put me on my feet. When I wished to arise at any given time after sunrise, I had only to turn the pivoted frame that held the lens the requisite number of degrees or minutes. Thus I took Emerson's advice and hitched my dumping-wagon bed to a star.

I also invented a machine to make visible the growth of plants and the action of the sunlight, a very delicate contrivance, enclosed in glass. Besides this I invented a barometer and a lot of novel scientific apparatus. My room was regarded as a sort of show place by the professors, who oftentimes brought visitors to it on Saturdays and holidays. And when, some eighteen years after I had left the University, I was sauntering over the campus in time of vacation, and spoke to a man who seemed to be taking some charge of the grounds, he informed me that he was the janitor; and when I inquired what had become of Pat, the janitor in my time, and a favorite with the students, he replied that Pat was still alive and well, but now too old to do much work. And when I pointed to the dormitory room that I long ago occupied, he said: 'Oh! then I know who you are,' and mentioned my name. 'How comes it that you know my name?' I inquired. He explained that 'Pat always pointed out that room to newcomers and told long stories about the wonders that used to be in it.' So long had the memory of my little inventions survived.

Although I was four years at the University, I did not take the regular course of studies, but instead picked out what I thought would be most useful to me, particularly chemistry, which opened a new world, and mathematics and physics, a little Greek and Latin, botany and geology. I was far from satisfied with what I had learned, and should have stayed longer. Anyhow I wandered away on a glorious botanical and geological excursion, which has lasted nearly fifty years and is not yet completed, always happy and free, poor and rich, without thought of a diploma or of making a name, urged on and on through endless, inspiring, Godful beauty.

From the top of a hill on the north side of Lake Mendota I gained a last wistful, lingering view of the beautiful University grounds and buildings where I had spent so many hungry and happy and hopeful days. There with streaming eyes I bade my blessed Alma Mater farewell. But I was only leaving one University for another, the Wisconsin University for the University of the Wilderness.

MY FIRST SUMMER IN THE SIERRA
(1901)

Chapter 1

THROUGH THE FOOTHILLS WITH A FLOCK OF SHEEP

(1869)

In the great Central Valley of California there are only two seasons – spring and summer. The spring begins with the first rainstorm, which usually falls in November. In a few months the wonderful flowery vegetation is in full bloom, and by the end of May it is dead and dry and crisp, as if every plant had been roasted in an oven.

Then the lolling, panting flocks and herds are driven to the high, cool, green pastures of the Sierra. I was longing for the mountains about this time, but money was scarce and I couldn't see how a bread supply was to be kept up. While I was anxiously brooding on the bread problem, so troublesome to wanderers, and trying to believe that I might learn to live like the wild animals, gleaning nourishment here and there from seeds, berries, etc., sauntering and climbing in joyful independence of money or baggage, Mr Delaney, a sheep-owner, for whom I had worked a few weeks, called on me, and offered to engage me to go with his shepherd and flock to the headwaters of the Merced and Tuolumne rivers – the very region I had most in mind. I was in the mood to accept work of any kind that would take me into the mountains whose treasures I had tasted last summer in the Yosemite region. The flock, he explained, would be moved gradually higher through the successive forest belts as the snow melted, stopping for a few weeks at the best places we came to. These I thought would be good centres of observation from which I might be able to make many telling excursions within a radius of eight or ten miles of the camps to learn something of the plants, animals, and rocks; for he assured me that I should be left perfectly free to follow my studies. I judged, however, that I was in no way the right man for the place, and freely explained my shortcomings, confessing that I was wholly unacquainted with the topography of the upper mountains, the streams that would have to be crossed, and the wild sheep-eating animals, etc.; in short that, what with bears, coyotes, rivers, canyons, and thorny, bewildering chaparral, I feared that half or more of his flock would be lost. Fortunately these shortcomings seemed insignificant to Mr Delaney. The main thing, he said, was to have a man about the camp whom he could trust to see that the shepherd did his duty, and he assured me that the difficulties that seemed so formidable at a distance would vanish as we went on; encouraging me further by saying that the shepherd would do all the herding, that I could study plants and rocks and scenery as much as I liked, and that he would himself accompany us to the first main camp and make occasional visits to our higher ones to replenish our store of provisions and see how we prospered. Therefore I concluded to go, though still fearing, when I saw the silly sheep bouncing one by one through the narrow gate of the home corral to be counted, that of the two thousand and fifty many would never return.

I was fortunate in getting a fine St Bernard dog for a companion. His master, a hunter with whom I was slightly acquainted, came to me as soon as he heard that I was going to spend the summer in the Sierra and begged me to take his favorite dog, Carlo, with me, for he feared that if he were compelled to stay all summer on the plains the fierce heat might be the death of him. 'I think I can trust you to be kind to him,' he said, 'and I am sure he will be good to you. He knows all about the mountain animals, will guard the camp, assist in managing the sheep, and in every way be found able and faithful.' Carlo knew we were talking about him, watched our faces, and listened so attentively that I fancied he understood us. Calling him by name, I asked him if he was willing to go with me. He looked me in the face with eyes expressing wonderful intelligence, then turned to his master, and after permission was given by a wave of the hand toward me and a farewell patting caress, he quietly followed me as if he perfectly understood all that had been said and had known me always.

*

June 3, 1869 – This morning provisions, camp-kettles, blankets, plant-press, etc., were packed on two horses, the flock headed for the tawny foothills, and away we sauntered in a cloud of dust: Mr Delaney, bony and tall, with sharply hacked profile like Don Quixote, leading the pack-horses, Billy, the proud shepherd, a Chinaman and a Digger Indian to assist in driving for the first few days in the brushy foothills, and myself with notebook tied to my belt.

The home ranch from which we set out is on the south side of the Tuolumne River near French Bar, where the foothills of metamorphic gold-bearing slates dip below the stratified deposits of the Central Valley. We had not gone more than a mile before some of the old leaders of the flock showed by the eager, inquiring way they ran and looked ahead that they were thinking of the high pastures they had enjoyed last summer. Soon the whole flock seemed to be hopefully excited, the mothers calling their lambs, the lambs replying in tones wonderfully human, their fondly quavering calls interrupted now and then by hastily snatched mouthfuls of withered grass. Amid all this seeming babel of baas as they streamed over the hills every mother and child recognized each other's voice. In case a tired lamb, half asleep in the smothering dust, should fail to answer, its mother would come running back through the flock toward the spot whence its last response was heard, and refused to be comforted until she found it, the one of a thousand, though to our eyes and ears all seemed alike.

The flock traveled at the rate of about a mile an hour, outspread in the form of an irregular triangle, about a hundred yards wide at the base, and a hundred and fifty yards long, with a crooked, ever-changing point made up of the strongest foragers, called the 'leaders,' which, with the most active of those scattered along the ragged sides of the 'main body,' hastily explored nooks in the rocks and bushes for grass and leaves; the lambs and feeble old mothers dawdling in the rear were called the 'tail end.'

About noon the heat was hard to bear; the poor sheep panted pitifully and tried to stop in the shade of every tree they came to, while we gazed with eager longing through the dim burning glare toward the snowy mountains and streams, though not one was in sight. The landscape is only wavering

foothills roughened here and there with bushes and trees and
out-cropping masses of slate. The trees, mostly the blue oak
(*Quercus Douglasii*), are about thirty to forty feet high, with
pale blue-green leaves and white bark, sparsely planted on the
thinnest soil or in crevices of rocks beyond the reach of grass
fires. The slates in many places rise abruptly through the tawny
grass in sharp lichen covered slabs like tombstones in deserted
burying-grounds. With the exception of the oak and four or
five species of manzanita and ceanothus, the vegetation of the
foothills is mostly the same as that of the plains. I saw this
region in the early spring, when it was a charming landscape
garden full of birds and bees and flowers. Now the scorching
weather makes everything dreary. The ground is full of cracks,
lizards glide about on the rocks, and ants in amazing numbers,
whose tiny sparks of life only burn the brighter with the heat,
fairly quiver with unquenchable energy as they run in long
lines to fight and gather food. How it comes that they do not
dry to a crisp in a few seconds' exposure to such sun-fire is
marvelous. A few rattlesnakes lie coiled in out-of-the-way
places, but are seldom seen. Magpies and crows, usually so
noisy, are silent now, standing in mixed flocks on the ground
beneath the best shade trees, with bills wide open and wings
drooped, too breathless to speak; the quails also are trying to
keep in the shade about the few tepid alkaline water holes;
cottontail rabbits are running from shade to shade among the
ceanothus brush, and occasionally the long-eared hare is seen
cantering gracefully across the wider openings.   •

After a short noon rest in a grove, the poor dust-choked
flock was again driven ahead over the brushy hills, but the dim
roadway we had been following faded away just where it was
most needed, compelling us to stop to look about us and get
our bearings. The Chinaman seemed to think we were lost, and
chattered in pidgin English concerning the abundance of 'litty
stick' (chaparral), while the Indian silently scanned the billowy
ridges and gulches for openings. Pushing through the thorny
jungle, we at length discovered a road trending toward Coulterville, which we followed until an hour before sunset, when
we reached a dry ranch and camped for the night.

Camping in the foothills with a flock of sheep is simple and
easy, but far from pleasant. The sheep were allowed to pick
what they could find in the neighborhood until after sunset,

watched by the shepherd, while the others gathered wood, made a fire, cooked, unpacked and fed the horses, etc. About dusk the weary sheep were gathered on the highest open spot near camp, where they willingly bunched close together, and after each mother had found her lamb and suckled it, all lay down and required no attention until morning.

Supper was announced by the call, 'Grub!' Each with a tin plate helped himself direct from the pots and pans while chatting about such camp studies as sheep feed, mines, coyotes, bears, or adventures during the memorable gold days of paydirt. The Indian kept in the background, saying never a word, as if he belonged to another species. The meal finished, the dogs were fed, the smokers smoked by the fire, and under the influences of fullness and tobacco the calm that settled on their faces seemed almost divine, something like the mellow meditative glow portrayed on the countenances of saints. Then suddenly, as if awakening from a dream, each with a sigh or a grunt knocked the ashes out of his pipe, yawned, gazed at the fire a few moments, said, 'Well, I believe I'll turn in,' and straightway vanished beneath his blankets. The fire smouldered and flickered an hour or two longer; the stars shone brighter; coons, coyotes, and owls stirred the silence here and there, while crickets and hylas made a cheerful, continuous music, so fitting and full that it seemed a part of the very body of the night. The only discordance came from a snoring sleeper, and the coughing sheep with dust in their throats. In the starlight the flock looked like a big gray blanket.

June 4 – The camp was astir at day break; coffee, bacon, and beans formed the breakfast, followed by quick dish-washing and packing. A general bleating began about sunrise. As soon as a mother ewe arose, her lamb came bounding and bunting for its breakfast, and after the thousand youngsters had been suckled the flock began to nibble and spread. The restless wethers with ravenous appetites were the first to move, but dared not go far from the main body. Billy and the Indian and the Chinaman kept them headed along the weary road, and allowed them to pick up what little they could find on a breadth of about a quarter of a mile. But as several flocks had already gone ahead of us, scarce a leaf, green or dry, was left; therefore the starving flock had to be hurried on over the bare, hot hills to the nearest of the green pastures, about twenty or thirty miles from here.

The pack-animals were led by Don Quixote, a heavy rifle over his shoulder intended for bears and wolves. This day has been as hot and dusty as the first, leading over gently sloping brown hills, with mostly the same vegetation, excepting the strange-looking Sabine pine (*Pinus Sabiniana*), which here forms small groves or is scattered among the blue oaks. The trunk divides at a height of fifteen or twenty feet into two or more stems, outleaning or nearly upright, with many straggling branches and long gray needles, casting but little shade. In general appearance this tree looks more like a palm than a pine. The cones are about six or seven inches long, about five in diameter, very heavy, and last long after they fall, so that the ground beneath the trees is covered with them. They make fine resiny, light-giving campfires, next to ears of Indian corn the most beautiful fuel I've ever seen. The nuts, the Don tells me, are gathered in large quantities by the Digger Indians for food. They are about as large and hard-shelled as hazelnuts – food and fire fit for the gods from the same fruit.

June 5 – This morning a few hours after setting out with the crawling sheep-cloud, we gained the summit of the first well-defined bench on the mountain-flank at Pino Blanco. The Sabine pines interest me greatly. They are so airy and strangely palm-like I was eager to sketch them, and was in a fever of excitement without accomplishing much. I managed to halt long enough, however, to make a tolerably fair sketch of Pino Blanco peak from the southwest side, where there is a small field and vineyard irrigated by a stream that makes a pretty fall on its way down a gorge by the roadside.

After gaining the open summit of this first bench, feeling the natural exhilaration due to the slight elevation of a thousand feet or so, and the hopes excited concerning the outlook to be obtained, a magnificent section of the Merced Valley at what is called Horseshoe Bend came full in sight – a glorious wilderness that seemed to be calling with a thousand songful voices. Bold, down-sweeping slopes, feathered with pines and clumps of manzanita with sunny, open spaces between them, make up most of the foreground; the middle and background present fold beyond fold of finely modeled hills and ridges rising into mountain-like masses in the distance, all covered with a shaggy growth of chaparral, mostly adenostoma, planted so marvelously close and even that it looks like soft, rich plush without a single tree or bare spot. As far as the eye can reach it extends, a heaving, swelling sea of green as regular and continuous as that produced by the heaths of Scotland. The sculpture of the landscape is as striking in its main lines as in its lavish richness of detail; a grand congregation of massive heights with the river shining between, each carved into smooth, graceful folds without leaving a single rocky angle exposed, as if the delicate fluting and ridging fashioned out of metamorphic slates had been carefully sandpapered. The whole landscape showed design, like man's noblest sculptures. How wonderful the power of its beauty! Gazing awe-stricken, I might have left everything for it. Glad, endless work would then be mine tracing the forces that have brought forth its features, its rocks and plants and animals and glorious weather. Beauty beyond thought everywhere, beneath, above, made and being made forever. I gazed and gazed and longed and admired until the dusty sheep and packs were far out of sight, made hurried notes and a sketch, though there was no need of either, for the colors and lines and expression of this divine landscape-countenance are so burned into mind and heart they surely can never grow dim.

The evening of this charmed day is cool, calm, cloudless, and full of a kind of lightning I have never seen before – white glowing cloud-shaped masses down among the trees and bushes, like quick-throbbing fire-flies in the Wisconsin meadows rather than the so-called 'wild fire.' The spreading hairs of the horses' tails and sparks from our blankets show how highly charged the air is.

June 6 – We are now on what may be called the second bench or plateau of the Range, after making many small ups and downs over belts of hill-waves, with, of course, corresponding changes in the vegetation. In open spots many of the lowland composit are still to be found, and some of the Mariposa tulips and other conspicuous members of the lily family; but the characteristic blue oak of the foothills is left below, and its place is taken by a fine large species (*Quercus Californica*) with deeply lobed deciduous leaves, picturesquely divided trunk, and broad, massy, finely lobed and modeled head. Here also at a height of about twenty-five hundred feet we come to the edge of the great coniferous forest, made up mostly of yellow pine with just a few sugar pines. We are now in the mountains and they are in us, kindling enthusiasm, making every nerve quiver, filling every pore and cell of us. Our flesh-and-bone tabernacle seems transparent as glass to the beauty about us, as if truly an inseparable part of it, thrilling with the air and trees, streams and rocks, in the waves of the sun – a part of all nature, neither old nor young, sick nor well, but immortal. Just now I can hardly conceive of any bodily condition dependent on food or breath any more than the ground or the sky. How glorious a conversion, so complete and wholesome it is, scarce memory enough of old bondage days left as a standpoint to view it from! In this newness of life we seem to have been so always.

Through a meadow opening in the pine woods I see snowy peaks about the head-waters of the Merced above Yosemite. How near they seem and how clear their outlines on the blue air, or rather *in* the blue air; for they seem to be saturated with it. How consuming strong the invitation they extend! Shall I be allowed to go to them? Night and day I'll pray that I may, but it seems too good to be true. Someone worthy will go, able for the Godful work, yet as far as I can I must drift about these love-monument mountains, glad to be a servant of servants in so holy a wilderness.

Found a lovely lily (*Calochortus albus*) in a shady adenostoma thicket near Coulterville, in company with *Adiantum Chilense*. It is white with a faint purplish tinge inside at the base of the petals, a most impressive plant, pure as a snow crystal, one of the plant saints that all must love and be made so much the purer by it every time it is seen. It puts the roughest mountaineer on his good behavior. With this plant the whole world would seem rich though none other existed. It is not easy to keep on with the camp cloud while such plant people are standing preaching by the wayside.

During the afternoon we passed a fine meadow bounded by stately pines, mostly the arrowy yellow pine, with here and there a noble sugar pine, its feathery arms outspread above the spires of its companion species in marked contrast; a glorious tree, its cones fifteen to twenty inches long, swinging like tassels at the end of the branches with superb ornamental effect. Saw some logs of this species at the Greeley Mill. They are round and regular as if turned in a lathe, excepting the butt cuts, which have a few buttressing projections. The fragrance of the sugary sap is delicious and scents the mill and lumber yard. How beautiful the ground beneath this pine thickly strewn with slender needles and grand cones, and the piles of cone-scales, seed-wings and shells around the instep of each tree where the squirrels have been feasting! They get the seeds by cutting off the scales at the base in regular order, following their spiral arrangement, and the two seeds at the base of each scale, a hundred or two in a cone, must make a good meal. The yellow pine cones and those of most other species and genera are held upside down on the ground by the Douglas squirrel, and turned around gradually until stripped, while he sits usually with his back to a tree, probably for safety. Strange to say, he never seems to get himself smeared with gum, not even his paws or whiskers – and how cleanly and beautiful in color the cone-litter kitchen-middens he makes.

We are now approaching the region of clouds and cool streams. Magnificent white cumuli appeared about noon above the Yosemite region – floating fountains refreshing the glorious wilderness – sky mountains in whose pearly hills and dales the streams take their rise – blessing with cooling shadows and rain. No rock landscape is more varied in sculpture, none more delicately modeled than these landscapes of the sky; domes and peaks rising, swelling, white as finest marble and firmly outlined, a most impressive manifestation of world building. Every rain-cloud, however fleeting, leaves its mark, not only on trees and flowers whose pulses are quickened, and on the replenished streams and lakes, but also on the rocks are its marks engraved whether we can see them or not.

I have been examining the curious and influential shrub *Adenostoma Fascivulata*, first noticed about Horseshoe Bend. It is very abundant on the lower slopes of the second plateau near Coulterville, forming a dense, almost impenetrable growth that looks dark in the distance. It belongs to the rose family, is about six or eight feet high, has small white flowers in racemes eight to twelve inches long, round needle-like leaves, and reddish bark that becomes shreddy when old. It grows on sun-beaten slopes, and like grass is often swept away by running fires, but is quickly renewed from the roots. Any

trees that may have established themselves in its midst are at
length killed by these fires, and this no doubt is the secret of the
unbroken character of its broad belts. A few manzanitas,
which also rise again from the root after consuming fires,
make out to dwell with it, also a few bush composit – baccharis
and linosyris, and some liliaceous plants, mostly calochortus
and brodia, with deepset bulbs safe from fire. A multitude of
birds and 'wee, sleekit, cow'rin', tim'rous beasties' find good
homes in its deepest thickets, and the open bays and lanes that
fringe the margins of its main belts offer shelter and food to the
deer when winter storms drive them down from their high
mountain pastures. A most admirable plant! It is now in
bloom, and I like to wear its pretty fragrant racemes in my
buttonhole.

Azalea occidentalis, another charming shrub, grows beside
cool streams hereabouts and much higher in the Yosemite
region. We found it this evening in bloom a few miles above
Greeley's Mill, where we are camped for the night. It is closely
related to the rhododendrons, is very showy and fragrant, and
everybody must like it not only for itself but for the shady
alders and willows, ferny meadows, and living water associated with it.

Another conifer was met today – incense cedar (*Libocedrus
decurrens*), a large tree with warm yellow-green foliage in flat
plumes like those of arborvit, bark cinnamon-colored, and as
the boles of the old trees are without limbs they make striking
pillars in the woods where the sun chances to shine on them – a
worthy companion of the kingly sugar and yellow pines. I feel
strangely attracted to this tree. The brown close-grained wood,
as well as the small scale-like leaves, is fragrant, and the flat
overlapping plumes make fine beds, and must shed the rain
well. It would be delightful to be storm-bound beneath one of
these noble, hospitable, inviting old trees, its broad sheltering
arms bent down like a tent, incense rising from the fire made
from its dry fallen branches, and a hearty wind chanting
overhead. But the weather is calm tonight, and our camp is
only a sheep camp. We are near the North Fork of the Merced.
The night wind is telling the wonders of the upper mountains,
their snow fountains and gardens, forests and groves; even
their topography is in its tones. And the stars, the everlasting
sky lilies, how bright they are now that we have climbed above

the lowland dust! The horizon is bounded and adorned by a spiry wall of pines, every tree harmoniously related to every other; definite symbols, divine hieroglyphics written with sunbeams. Would I could understand them! The stream flowing past the camp through ferns and lilies and alders makes sweet music to the ear, but the pines marshaled around the edge of the sky make a yet sweeter music to the eye. Divine beauty all. Here I could stay tethered forever with just bread and water, nor would I be lonely; loved friends and neighbors, as love for everything increased, would seem all the nearer however many the miles and mountains between us.

June 7 – The sheep were sick last night, and many of them are still far from well, hardly able to leave camp, coughing, groaning, looking wretched and pitiful, all from eating the leaves of the blessed azalea. So at least say the shepherd and the Don. Having had but little grass since they left the plains, they are starving, and so eat anything green they can get. 'Sheep men' call azalea 'sheep-poison,' and wonder what the Creator was thinking about when he made it – so desperately does sheep business blind and degrade, though supposed to have a refining influence in the good old days we read of. The California sheepowner is in haste to get rich, and often does, now that pasturage costs nothing, while the climate is so favorable that no winter food supply, shelter-pens, or barns are required. Therefore large flocks may be kept at slight expense, and large profits realized, the money invested doubling, it is claimed, every other year. This quickly acquired wealth usually creates desire for more. Then indeed the wool is drawn close down over the poor fellow's eyes, dimming or shutting out almost everything worth seeing.

As for the shepherd, his case is still worse, especially in winter when he lives alone in a cabin. For, though stimulated at times by hopes of one day owning a flock and getting rich like his boss, he at the same time is likely to be degraded by the life he leads, and seldom reaches the dignity or advantage – or disadvantage – of ownership. The degradation in his case has for cause one not far to seek. He is solitary most of the year, and solitude to most people seems hard to bear. He seldom has much good mental work or recreation in the way of books. Coming into his dingy hovel-cabin at night, stupidly weary, he finds nothing to balance and level his life with the universe. No, after his dull drag all day after the sheep, he must get his supper; he is likely to slight this task and try to satisfy his hunger with whatever comes handy. Perhaps no bread is baked; then he just makes a few grimy flapjacks in his unwashed frying-pan, boils a handful of tea, and perhaps fries a few strips of rusty bacon. Usually there are dried peaches or apples in the cabin, but he hates to be bothered with the cooking of them, just swallows the bacon and flapjacks, and depends on the genial stupefaction of tobacco for the rest. Then to bed, often without removing the clothing worn during the day. Of course his health suffers, reacting on his mind; and seeing nobody for weeks or months, he finally becomes semi-insane or wholly so.

The shepherd in Scotland seldom thinks of being anything but a shepherd. He has probably descended from a race of shepherds and inherited a love and aptitude for the business almost as marked as that of his collie. He has but a small flock to look after, sees his family and neighbors, has time for reading in fine weather, and often carries books to the fields with which he may converse with kings. The oriental shepherd, we read, called his sheep by name; they knew his voice and followed him. The flocks must have been small and easily managed, allowing piping on the hills and ample leisure for reading and thinking. But whatever the blessings of sheep-culture in other times and countries, the California shepherd, as far as I've seen or heard, is never quite sane for any considerable time. Of all Nature's voices baa is about all he hears. Even the howls and ki-yis of coyotes might be blessings if well heard, but he hears them only through a blur of mutton and wool, and they do him no good.

The sick sheep are getting well, and the shepherd is discoursing on the various poisons lurking in these high pastures – azalea, kalmia, alkali. After crossing the North Fork of the Merced we turned to the left toward Pilot Peak, and made a considerable ascent on a rocky, brush-covered ridge to Brown's Flat, where for the first time since leaving the plains the flock is enjoying plenty of green grass. Mr Delaney intends to seek a permanent camp somewhere in the neighborhood, to last several weeks.

Before noon we passed Bower Cave, a delightful marble

palace, not dark and dripping, but filled with sunshine, which pours into it through its wide-open mouth facing the south. It has a fine, deep, clear little lake with mossy banks embowered with broad-leaved maples, all under ground, wholly unlike anything I have seen in the cave line even in Kentucky, where a large part of the state is honeycombed with caves. This curious specimen of subterranean scenery is located on a belt of marble that is said to extend from the north end of the Range to the extreme south. Many other caves occur on the belt, but none like this, as far as I have learned, combining as it does sunny outdoor brightness and vegetation with the crystalline beauty of the under-world. It is claimed by a Frenchman, who has fenced and locked it, placed a boat on the lakelet and seats on the mossy bank under the maple trees, and charges a dollar admission fee. Being on one of the ways to the Yosemite Valley, a good many tourists visit it during the travel months of summer, regarding it as an interesting addition to their Yosemite wonders.

Poison oak or poison ivy (*Rhus diversiloba*), both as a bush and a scrambler up trees and rocks, is common throughout the foothill region up to a height of at least three thousand feet above the sea. It is somewhat troublesome to most travelers, inflaming the skin and eyes, but blends harmoniously with its companion plants, and many a charming flower leans confidingly upon it for protection and shade. I have oftentimes found the curious twining lily (*Stropholirion Californicum*) climbing its branches, showing no fear but rather congenial companionship. Sheep eat it without apparent ill effects; so do horses to some extent, though not fond of it, and to many persons it is harmless. Like most other things not apparently useful to man, it has few friends, and the blind question, 'Why was it made?' goes on and on with never a guess that first of all it might have been made for itself.

Brown's Flat is a shallow fertile valley on the top of the divide between the North Fork of the Merced and Bull Creek, commanding magnificent views in every direction. Here the adventurous pioneer David Brown made his headquarters for many years, dividing his time between gold-hunting and bear-hunting. Where could a lonely hunter find a better solitude? Game in the woods, gold in the rocks, health and exhilaration in the air, while the colors and cloud furniture of the sky are ever inspiring through all sorts of weather. Though sternly practical, like most pioneers, old David seems to have been uncommonly fond of scenery. Mr Delaney, who knew him well, tells me that he dearly loved to climb to the summit of a commanding ridge to gaze abroad over the forest to the snow-clad peaks and sources of the rivers, and over the foreground valleys and gulches to note where miners were at work or claims were abandoned, judging by smoke from cabins and campfires, the sounds of axes, etc.; and when a rifle-shot was heard, to guess who was the hunter, whether Indian or some poacher on his wide domain. His dog Sandy accompanied him everywhere, and well the little hairy mountaineer knew and loved his master and his master's aims. In deer-hunting he had but little to do, trotting behind his master as he slowly made his way through the wood, careful not to step heavily on dry twigs, scanning open spots in the chaparral, where the game loves to feed in the early morning and towards sunset; peering cautiously over ridges as new outlooks were reached, and along the meadowy borders of streams. But when bears were hunted, little Sandy became more important, and it was as a bear-hunter that Brown became famous. His hunting method, as described by Mr Delaney, who had passed many a night with him in his lonely cabin and learned his stories, was simply to go slowly and silently through the best bear pastures, with his dog and rifle and a few pounds of flour, until he found a fresh track and then follow it to the death, paying no heed to the time required. Wherever the bear went he followed, led by little Sandy, who had a keen nose and never lost the track, however rocky the ground. When high open points were reached, the likeliest places were carefully scanned. The time of year enabled the hunter to determine approximately where the bear would be found – in the spring and early summer on open spots about the banks of streams and springy places eating grass and clover and lupines, or in dry meadows feasting on strawberries; toward the end of summer, on dry ridges, feasting on manzanita berries, sitting on his haunches, pulling down the laden branches with his paws, and pressing them together so as to get good compact mouthfuls however much mixed with twigs and leaves; in the Indian summer, beneath the pines, chewing the cones cut off by the squirrels, or occasionally climbing a tree to gnaw and break off the fruitful branches. In late autumn, when acorns are ripe, Bruin's favorite feeding-grounds are groves of the California oak in park-like canyon flats. Always the cunning hunter knew where to look, and seldom came upon Bruin unawares. When the hot scent showed the dangerous game was nigh, a long halt was made, and the intricacies of the topography and vegetation leisurely scanned to catch a glimpse of the shaggy wanderer, or to at least determine where he was most likely to be.

'Whenever,' said the hunter, 'I saw a bear before it saw me I had no trouble in killing it. I just studied the lay of the land and got to leeward of it no matter how far around I had to go, and then worked up to within a few hundred yards or so, at the foot of a tree that I could easily climb, but too small for the bear to climb. Then I looked well to the condition of my rifle, took off my boots so as to climb well if necessary, and waited until the bear turned its side in clear view when I could make a sure or at least a good shot. In case it showed fight I climbed out of reach. But bears are slow and awkward with their eyes, and being to leeward of them they could not scent me, and I often got in a second shot before they noticed the smoke. Usually, however, they run when wounded and hide in the brush. I let them run a good safe time before I ventured to follow them, and Sandy was pretty sure to find them dead. If not, he barked and drew their attention, and occasionally rushed in for a distracting bite, so that I was able to get to a safe distance for a final shot. Oh yes, bear-hunting is safe enough when followed in a safe way, though like every other business it has its accidents, and little doggie and I have had some close calls. Bears like to keep out of the way of men as a general thing, but if an old, lean, hungry mother with cubs met a man on her own ground she would, in my opinion, try to catch and eat him. This would be only fair play anyhow, for we eat them, but nobody hereabout has been used for bear grub that I know of.'

Brown had left his mountain home ere we arrived, but a considerable number of Digger Indians still linger in their cedar-bark huts on the edge of the flat. They were attracted in the first place by the white hunter whom they had learned to respect, and to whom they looked for guidance and protection against their enemies the Pah Utes, who sometimes made raids across from the east side of the Range to plunder the stores of the comparatively feeble Diggers and steal their wives.

Chapter 2

IN CAMP ON THE NORTH FORK OF THE MERCED

June 8 – The sheep, now grassy and good natured, slowly nibbled their way down into the valley of the North Fork of the Merced at the foot of Pilot Peak Ridge to the place selected by the Don for our first central camp, a picturesque hopper-shaped hollow formed by converging hill-slopes at a bend of the river. Here racks for dishes and provisions were made in the shade of the river-bank trees, and beds of fern fronds, cedar plumes, and various flowers, each to the taste of its owner, and a corral back on the open flat for the wool.

June 9 – How deep our sleep last night in the mountain's heart, beneath the trees and stars, hushed by solemn-sounding waterfalls and many small soothing voices in sweet accord whispering peace! And our first pure mountain day, warm, calm, cloudless – how immeasurable it seems, how serenely wild! I can scarcely remember its beginning. Along the river, over the hills, in the ground, in the sky, spring work is going on with joyful enthusiasm, new life, new beauty, unfolding, unrolling in glorious exuberant extravagance – new birds in their nests, new winged creatures in the air, and new leaves, new flowers, spreading, shining, rejoicing everywhere.

The trees about the camp stand close, giving ample shade for ferns and lilies, while back from the bank most of the sunshine reaches the ground, calling up the grasses and flowers in glorious array, tall bromus waving like bamboos, starry composit, monardella, Mariposa tulips, lupines, gilias, violets, glad children of light. Soon every fern frond will be unrolled, great beds of common pteris and woodwardia along the river, wreaths and rosettes of pellaea and cheilanthes on sunny rocks. Some of the woodwardia fronds are already six feet high.

A handsome little shrub, *Chamoebatia foliolosa*, belonging to the rose family, spreads a yellow-green mantle beneath the sugar pines for miles without a break, not mixed or roughened with other plants. Only here and there a Washington lily may be seen nodding above its even surface, or a bunch or two of tall bromus as if for ornament. This fine carpet shrub begins to appear at, say, twenty-five hundred or three thousand feet above sea level, is about knee high or less, has brown branches, and the largest stems are only about half an inch in diameter. The leaves, light yellow green, thrice pinnate and finely cut, give them a rich ferny appearance, and they are dotted with minute glands that secrete wax with a peculiar pleasant odor that blends finely with the spicy fragrance of the pines. The flowers are white, five eighths of an inch in diameter, and look like those of the strawberry. Am delighted with this little bush. It is the only true carpet shrub of this part of the Sierra. The manzanita, rhamnus, and most of the species of ceanothus make shaggy rugs and border fringes rather than carpets or mantles.

The sheep do not take kindly to their new pastures, perhaps from being too closely hemmed in by the hills. They are never fully at rest. Last night they were frightened, probably by bears or coyotes prowling and planning for a share of the grand mass of mutton.

June 10 – Very warm. We get water for the camp from a rock basin at the foot of a picturesque cascading reach of the river where it is well stirred and made lively without being beaten into dusty foam. The rock here is black metamorphic slate, worn into smooth knobs in the stream channels, contrasting with the fine gray and white cascading water as it glides and glances and falls in lace-like sheets and braided overfolding currents. Tufts of sedge growing on the rock knobs that rise above the surface produce a charming effect, the long elastic leaves arching over in every direction, the tips of the longest drooping into the current, which dividing against the projecting rocks makes still finer lines, uniting with the sedges to see how beautiful the happy stream can be made. Nor is this all, for the giant saxifrage also is growing on some of the knob rock islets, firmly anchored and displaying their broad round umbrella-like leaves in showy groups by themselves, or above the sedge tufts. The flowers of this species (*Saxifraga peltata*) are purple, and form tall glandular racemes that are in bloom before the appearance of the leaves. The fleshy root-stocks grip the rock in cracks and hollows, and thus enable the plant to hold on against occasional floods – a marked species employed by Nature to make yet more beautiful the most interesting portions of these cool clear streams. Near camp the trees arch over from bank to bank, making a leafy tunnel full of soft subdued light, through which the young river sings and shines like a happy living creature.

Heard a few peals of thunder from the upper Sierra, and saw firm white bossy cumuli rising back of the pines. This was about noon.

June 11 – On one of the eastern branches of the river discovered some charming cascades with a pool at the foot of each of them. White dashing water, a few bushes and tufts of carex on ledges leaning over with fine effect, and large orange lilies assembled in superb groups on fertile soil-beds beside the pools.

There are no large meadows or grassy plains near camp to supply lasting pasture for our thousands of busy nibblers. The main dependence is ceanothus brush on the hills and tufted grass patches here and there, with lupines and pea-vines among the flowers on sunny open spaces. Large areas have already been stripped bare, or nearly so, compelling the poor hungry wool bundles to scatter far and wide, keeping the shepherds and dogs at the top of their speed to hold them within bounds. Mr Delaney has gone back to the plains, taking the Indian and Chinaman with him, leaving instruction to keep the flock here or hereabouts until his return, which he promised would not be long delayed.

How fine the weather is! Nothing more celestial can I conceive. How gently the winds blow! Scarce can these tranquil air-currents be called winds. They seem the very breath of Nature, whispering peace to every living thing. Down in the camp dell there is no swaying of tree-tops; most of the time not a leaf moves. I don't remember having seen a single lily swinging on its stalk, though they are so tall the least breeze would rock them. What grand bells these lilies have! Some of them big enough for children's bonnets. I have been sketching them, and would fain draw every leaf of their wide shining whorls and every curved and spotted petal. More beautiful, better kept gardens cannot be imagined. The species is *Lilium pardalinum*, five to six feet high, leaf-whorls a foot wide, flowers about six inches wide, bright orange, purple spotted in the throat, segments revolute – a majestic plant.

June 12 – A slight sprinkle of rain – large drops far apart, falling with hearty pat and plash on leaves and stones and into the mouths of the flowers. Cumuli rising to the eastward. How beautiful their pearly bosses! How well they harmonize with the upswelling rocks beneath them. Mountains of the sky, solid-looking, finely sculptured, their richly varied topography wonderfully defined. Never before have I seen clouds so substantial looking in form and texture. Nearly every day toward noon they rise with visible swelling motion as if new worlds were being created. And how fondly they brood and hover over the gardens and forests with their cooling shadows and showers, keeping every petal and leaf in glad health and heart. One may fancy the clouds themselves are plants, springing up in the sky-fields at the call of the sun, growing in beauty until they reach their prime, scattering rain and hail like berries and seeds, then wilting and dying.

The mountain live oak, common here and a thousand feet or so higher, is like the live oak of Florida, not only in general appearance, foliage, bark, and wide-branching habit, but in its tough, knotty, unwedgeable wood. Standing alone with plenty of elbow room, the largest trees are about seven to eight feet in diameter near the ground, sixty feet high, and as wide or wider across the head. The leaves are small and undivided, mostly without teeth or wavy edging, though on young shoots some are sharply serrated, both kinds being found on the same tree. The cups of the medium-sized acorns are shallow, thick walled, and covered with a golden dust of minute hairs. Some of the trees have hardly any main trunk, dividing near the ground into large wide-spreading limbs, and these, dividing again and again, terminate in long, drooping, cord-like branchlets, many of which reach nearly to the ground, while a dense canopy of short, shining leafy branchlets forms a round head which looks something like a cumulus cloud when the sunshine is pouring over it.

A marked plant is the bush poppy (*Dendromecon rigidum*), found on the hot hillsides near camp, the only woody member of the order I have yet met in all my walks. Its flowers are bright orange yellow, an inch to two inches wide, fruit-pods three or four inches long, slender and curving – height of bushes about four feet, made up of many slim, straight branches, radiating from the root – a companion of the manzanita and other sun-loving chaparral shrubs.

June 13 – Another glorious Sierra day in which one seems to be dissolved and absorbed and sent pulsing onward we know not where. Life seems neither long nor short, and we take no more heed to save time or make haste than do the trees and stars. This is true freedom, a good practical sort of immortality. Yonder rises another white skyland. How sharply the yellow pine spires and the palm-like crowns of the sugar pines are outlined on its smooth white domes. And hark! the grand thunder billows booming, rolling from ridge to ridge, followed by the faithful shower.

A good many herbaceous plants come thus far up the mountains from the plains, and are now in flower, two months later than their lowland relatives. Saw a few columbines today. Most of the ferns are in their prime – rock ferns on the sunny hillsides, cheilanthes, pellaea, gymnogramme; woodwardia, aspidium, woodsia along the stream banks, and the common *Pteris aquilina* on sandy flats. This last, however common, is here making shows of strong, exuberant, abounding beauty to set the botanist wild with admiration. I measured some scarce full grown that are more than seven feet high. Though the commonest and most widely distributed of all the ferns, I might almost say that I never saw it before. The broad-shouldered fronds held high on smooth stout stalks growing close together, overleaning and overlapping, make a complete ceiling, beneath which one may walk erect over several acres without being seen, as if beneath a roof. And how soft and lovely the light streaming through this living ceiling, revealing the arching branching ribs and veins of the fronds as the framework of countless panes of pale green and yellow plant-glass nicely fitted together – a fairyland created out of the commonest fern-stuff.

The smaller animals wander about as if in a tropical forest. I saw the entire flock of sheep vanish at one side of a patch and reappear a hundred yards farther on at the other, their progress betrayed only by the jerking and trembling of the fronds; and strange to say very few of the stout woody stalks were broken. I sat a long time beneath the tallest fronds, and never enjoyed anything in the way of a bower of wild leaves more strangely impressive. Only spread a fern frond over a man's head and worldly cares are cast out, and freedom and beauty and peace come in. The waving of a pine tree on the top of a mountain – a magic wand in Nature's hand – every devout mountaineer knows its power; but the marvelous beauty value of what the Scotch call a breckan in a still dell, what poet has sung this? It would seem impossible that anyone, however incrusted with care, could escape the Godful influence of these sacred fern forests. Yet this very day I saw a shepherd pass through one of the finest of them without betraying more feeling than his sheep. 'What do you think of these grand ferns?' I asked. 'Oh, they're only d–d big brakes,' he replied.

Lizards of every temper, style, and color dwell here, seemingly as happy and companionable as the birds and squirrels. Lowly, gentle fellow mortals, enjoying God's sunshine, and doing the best they can in getting a living, I like to watch them at their work and play. They bear acquaintance well, and one likes them the better the longer one looks into their beautiful, innocent eyes. They are easily tamed, and one soon learns to love them, as they dart about on the hot rocks, swift as dragonflies. The eye can hardly follow them; but they never make long-sustained runs, usually only about ten or twelve feet, then a sudden stop, and as sudden a start again; going all their journeys by quick, jerking impulses. These many stops I find are necessary as rests, for they are short-winded, and when pursued steadily are soon out of breath, pant pitifully, and are easily caught. Their bodies are more than half tail, but these tails are well managed, never heavily dragged nor curved up as if hard to carry; on the contrary, they seem to follow the body lightly of their own will. Some are colored like the sky, bright as bluebirds, others gray like the lichened rocks on which they hunt and bask. Even the horned toad of the plains is a mild, harmless creature, and so are the snake-like species which glide in curves with true snake motion, while their small, undeve-

loped limbs drag as useless appendages. One specimen fourteen inches long which I observed closely made no use whatever of its tender, sprouting limbs, but glided with all the soft,
sly ease and grace of a snake. Here comes a little, gray, dusty
fellow who seems to know and trust me, running about my
feet, and looking up cunningly into my face. Carlo is watching,
makes a quick pounce on him, for the fun of the thing I
suppose; but Liz has shot away from his paws like an arrow,
and is safe in the recesses of a clump of chaparral. Gentle
saurians, dragons, descendants of an ancient and mighty race,
Heaven bless you all and make your virtues known! For few of
us know as yet that scales may cover fellow creatures as gentle
and lovable as feathers, or hair, or cloth.

Mastodons and elephants used to live here no great geological time ago, as shown by their bones, often discovered by
miners in washing gold-gravel. And bears of at least two
species are here now, besides the California lion or panther,
and wild cats, wolves, foxes, snakes, scorpions, wasps, tar-
antulas; but one is almost tempted at times to regard a small
savage black ant as the master existence of this vast mountain
world. These fearless, restless, wandering imps, though only
about a quarter of an inch long, are fonder of fighting and
biting than any beast I know. They attack every living thing
around their homes, often without cause as far as I can see.
Their bodies are mostly jaws curved like ice-hooks, and to get
work for these weapons seems to be their chief aim and
pleasure. Most of their colonies are established in living oaks
somewhat decayed or hollowed, in which they can conveniently build their cells. These are chosen probably because of
their strength as opposed to the attacks of animals and storms.
They work both day and night, creep into dark caves, climb the
highest trees, wander and hunt through cool ravines as well as
on hot, unshaded ridges, and extend their highways and byways over everything but water and sky. From the foothills to a
mile above the level of the sea nothing can stir without their
knowledge; and alarms are spread in an incredibly short time,
without any howl or cry that we can hear. I can't understand
the need of their ferocious courage; there seems to be no
common sense in it. Sometimes, no doubt, they fight in defense
of their homes, but they fight anywhere and always wherever
they can find anything to bite. As soon as a vulnerable spot is

discovered on man or beast, they stand on their heads and sink their jaws, and though torn limb from limb, they will yet hold on and die biting deeper. When I contemplate this fierce creature so widely distributed and strongly intrenched, I see that much remains to be done ere the world is brought under the rule of universal peace and love.

On my way to camp a few minutes ago, I passed a dead pine nearly ten feet in diameter. It has been enveloped in fire from top to bottom so that now it looks like a grand black pillar set up as a monument. In this noble shaft a colony of large jetblack ants have established themselves, laboriously cutting tunnels and cells through the wood, whether sound or decayed. The entire trunk seems to have been honey-combed, judging by the size of the talus of gnawed chips like sawdust piled up around its base. They are more intelligent looking than their small, belligerent, strong-scented brethren, and have better manners, though quick to fight when required. Their towns are carved in fallen trunks as well as in those left standing, but never in sound, living trees or in the ground. When you happen to sit down to rest or take notes near a colony, some wandering hunter is sure to find you and come cautiously forward to discover the nature of the intruder and what ought to be done. If you are not too near the town and keep perfectly still he may run across your feet a few times, over your legs and hands and face, up your trousers, as if taking your measure and getting comprehensive views, then go in peace without raising an alarm. If, however, a tempting spot is offered or some suspicious movement excites him, a bite follows, and such a bite! I fancy that a bear or wolf bite is not to be compared with it. A quick electric flame of pain flashes along the outraged nerves, and you discover for the first time how great is the capacity for sensation you are possessed of. A shriek, a grab for the animal, and a bewildered stare follow this bite of bites as one comes back to consciousness from sudden eclipse. Fortunately, if careful, one need not be bitten oftener than once or twice in a lifetime. This wonderful electric species is about three fourths of an inch long. Bears are fond of them, and tear and gnaw their home-logs to pieces, and roughly devour the eggs, larvae, parent ants, and the rotten or sound wood of the cells, all in one spicy acid hash. The Digger Indians also are fond of the larvae and even of the perfect ants, so I have been told by old mountaineers. They bite off and reject the head, and eat the tickly acid body with keen relish. Thus are the poor biters bitten, like every other biter, big or little, in the world's great family.

There is also a fine, active, intelligent-looking red species, intermediate in size between the above. They dwell in the ground, and build large piles of seed husks, leaves, straw, etc., over their nests. Their food seems to be mostly insects and plant leaves, seeds and sap. How many mouths Nature has to fill, how many neighbors we have, how little we know about them, and how seldom we get in each other's way! Then to think of the infinite numbers of smaller fellow mortals, invisibly small, compared with which the smallest ants are as mastodons.

June 14 – The pool-basins below the falls and cascades hereabouts, formed by the heavy down-plunging currents, are kept nicely clean and clear of detritus. The heavier parts of the material swept over the falls are heaped up a short distance in front of the basins in the form of a dam, thus tending, together with erosion, to increase their size. Sudden changes, however, are effected during the spring floods, when the snow is melting and the upper tributaries are roaring loud from 'bank to brae.' Then boulders that have fallen into the channels, and which the ordinary summer and winter currents were unable to move, are suddenly swept forward as by a mighty besom, hurled over the falls into these pools, and piled up in a new dam together with part of the old one, while some of the smaller boulders are carried further down stream and variously lodged according to size and shape, all seeking rest where the force of the current is less than the resistance they are able to offer. But the greatest changes made in these relations of fall, pool, and dam are caused, not by the ordinary spring floods, but by extraordinary ones that occur at irregular intervals. The testimony of trees growing on flood boulder deposits shows that a century or more has passed since the last master flood came to awaken everything movable to go swirling and dancing on wonderful journeys. These floods may occur during the summer, when heavy thunder-showers, called 'cloud-bursts,' fall on wide, steeply inclined stream basins furrowed by converging channels, which suddenly gather the waters together into the main trunk in booming torrents of enormous transporting power, though short-lived.

One of these ancient flood boulders stands firm in the middle of the stream channel, just below the lower edge of the pool dam at the foot of the fall nearest our camp. It is a nearly cubical mass of granite about eight feet high, plushed with mosses over the top and down the sides to ordinary high-water mark. When I climbed on top of it today and lay down to rest, it seemed the most romantic spot I had yet found – the one big stone with its mossy level top and smooth sides standing square and firm and solitary, like an altar, the fall in front of it bathing it lightly with the finest of the spray, just enough to keep its moss cover fresh; the clear green pool beneath, with its foam-bells and its half circle of lilies leaning forward like a band of admirers, and flowering dogwood and alder trees leaning over all in sun-sifted arches. How soothingly, restfully cool it is beneath that leafy, translucent ceiling, and how delightful the water music – the deep bass tones of the fall, the clashing, ringing spray, and infinite variety of small low tones of the current gliding past the side of the boulder-island, and glinting against a thousand smaller stones down the ferny channel! All this shut in; every one of these influences acting at short range as if in a quiet room. The place seemed holy, where one might hope to see God.

After dark, when the camp was at rest, I groped my way back to the altar boulder and passed the night on it – above the water, beneath the leaves and stars – everything still more impressive than by day, the fall seen dimly white, singing Nature's old love song with solemn enthusiasm, while the stars peering through the leaf-roof seemed to join in the white water's song. Precious night, precious day to abide in me forever. Thanks be to God for this immortal gift.

June 15 – Another reviving morning. Down the long mountain-slopes the sunbeams pour, gilding the awakening pines, cheering every needle, filling every living thing with joy. Robins are singing in the alder and maple groves, the same old song that has cheered and sweetened countless seasons over almost all of our blessed continent. In this mountain hollow he seems as much at home as in farmers' orchards. Bullock's oriole and the Louisiana tanager are here also, with many warblers and other little mountain troubadours, most of them now busy about their nests.

Discovered another magnificent specimen of the goldcup oak six feet in diameter, a Douglas spruce seven feet, and a twining lily (*Stropholirion*), with stem eight feet long, and sixty rose-colored flowers.

Sugar pine cones are cylindrical, slightly tapered at the end and rounded at the base. Found one today nearly twenty-four inches long and six in diameter, the scales being open. Another specimen nineteen inches long; the average length of full-grown cones on trees favorably situated is nearly eighteen inches. On the lower edge of the belt at a height of about twenty-five hundred feet above the sea they are smaller, say a foot to fifteen inches long, and at a height of seven thousand feet or more near the upper limits of its growth in the Yosemite region they are about the same size. This noble tree is an inexhaustible study and source of pleasure. I never weary of gazing at its grand tassel cones, its perfectly round bole one hundred feet or more without a limb, the fine purplish color of its bark, and its magnificent outsweeping, down-curving feathery arms forming a crown always bold and striking and exhilarating. In habit and general port it looks somewhat like a palm, but no palm that I have yet seen displays such majesty of form and behavior either when poised silent and thoughtful in sunshine, or wide-awake waving in storm winds with every needle quivering. When young it is very straight and regular in form like most other conifers; but at the age of fifty to one hundred years it begins to acquire individuality, so that no two are alike in their prime or old age. Every tree calls for special admiration. I have been making many sketches, and regret that I cannot draw every needle. It is said to reach a height of three hundred feet, though the tallest I have measured falls short of this stature sixty feet or more. The diameter of the largest near the ground is about ten feet, though I've heard of some twelve feet thick or even fifteen. The diameter is held to a great height, the taper being almost imperceptibly gradual. Its companion, the yellow pine, is almost as large. The long silvery foliage of the younger specimens forms magnificent cylindrical brushes on the top shoots and the ends of the upturned branches, and when the wind sways the needles all one way at a certain angle every tree becomes a tower of white quivering sun-fire. Well

may this shining species be called the silver pine. The needles
are sometimes more than a foot long, almost as long as those of
the long-leaf pine of Florida. But though in size the yellow pine
almost equals the sugar pine, and in rugged enduring strength
seems to surpass it, it is far less marked in general habit and
expression, with its regular conventional spire and its comparatively small cones clustered stiffly among the needles.
Were there no sugar pine, then would this be the king of
the world's eighty or ninety species, the brightest of the bright,
waving, worshiping multitude. Were they mere mechanical
sculptures, what noble objects they would still be! How much
more throbbing, thrilling, overflowing, full of life in every fibre
and cell, grand glowing silverrods – the very gods of the plant
kingdom, living their sublime century lives in sight of Heaven,
watched and loved and admired from generation to generation! And how many other radiant resiny sun trees are here
and higher up – libocedrus, Douglas spruce, silver fir, sequoia.
How rich our inheritance in these blessed mountains, the tree
pastures into which our eyes are turned!

Now comes sundown. The west is all a glory of color
transfiguring everything. Far up the Pilot Peak Ridge the
radiant host of trees stand hushed and thoughtful, receiving
the Sun's goodnight, as solemn and impressive a leave-taking
as if sun and trees were to meet no more. The daylight fades,
the color spell is broken, and the forest breathes free in the
night breeze beneath the stars.

June 16 – One of the Indians from Brown's Flat got right into
the middle of the camp this morning, unobserved. I was seated
on a stone, looking over my notes and sketches, and happening
to look up, was startled to see him standing grim and silent
within a few steps of me, as motionless and weather-stained as
an old tree-stump that had stood there for centuries. All
Indians seem to have learned this wonderful way of walking
unseen – making themselves invisible like certain spiders I have
been observing here, which, in case of alarm, caused, for
example, by a bird alighting on the bush their webs are spread
upon, immediately bounce themselves up and down on their
elastic threads so rapidly that only a blur is visible. The wild
Indian power of escaping observation, even where there is little
or no cover to hide in, was probably slowly acquired in hard

hunting and fighting lessons while trying to approach game, take enemies by surprise, or get safely away when compelled to retreat. And this experience transmitted through many generations seems at length to have become what is vaguely called instinct.

How smooth and changeless seems the surface of the mountains about us! Scarce a track is to be found beyond the range of the sheep except on small open spots on the sides of the streams, or where the forest carpets are thin or wanting. On the smoothest of these open strips and patches deer tracks may be seen, and the great suggestive footprints of bears, which, with those of the many small animals, are scarce enough to answer as a kind of light ornamental stitching or embroidery. Along the main ridges and larger branches of the river Indian trails may be traced, but they are not nearly as distinct as one would expect to find them. How many centuries Indians have roamed these woods nobody knows, probably a great many, extending far beyond the time that Columbus touched our shores, and it seems strange that heavier marks have not been made. Indians walk softly and hurt the landscape hardly more than the birds and squirrels, and their brush and bark huts last hardly longer than those of wood rats, while their more enduring monuments, excepting those wrought on the forests by the fires they made to improve their hunting grounds, vanish in a few centuries.

How different are most of those of the white man, especially on the lower gold region – roads blasted in the solid rock, wild streams dammed and tamed and turned out of their channels and led along the sides of canyons and valleys to work in mines like slaves. Crossing from ridge to ridge, high in the air, on long straddling trestles as if flowing on stilts, or down and up across valleys and hills, imprisoned in iron pipes to strike and wash away hills and miles of the skin of the mountain's face, riddling, stripping every gold gully and flat. These are the white man's marks made in a few feverish years, to say nothing of mills, fields, villages, scattered hundreds of miles along the flank of the Range. Long will it be ere these marks are effaced, though Nature is doing what she can, replanting, gardening, sweeping away old dams and flumes, leveling gravel and boulder piles, patiently trying to heal every raw scar. The main gold storm is over. Calm enough are the gray old miners scratching a bare living in waste diggings here and there. Thundering underground blasting is still going on to feed the pounding quartz mills, but their influence on the landscape is light as compared with that of the pick-and-shovel storms waged a few years ago. Fortunately for Sierra scenery the gold-bearing slates are mostly restricted to the foothills. The region about our camp is still wild, and higher lies the snow about as trackless as the sky.

Only a few hills and domes of cloudland were built yesterday and none at all today. The light is peculiarly white and thin, though pleasantly warm. The serenity of this mountain weather in the spring, just when Nature's pulses are beating highest, is one of its greatest charms. There is only a moderate breeze from the summits of the Range at night, and a slight breathing from the sea and the lowland hills and plains during the day, or stillness so complete no leaf stirs. The trees hereabouts have but little wind history to tell.

Sheep, like people, are ungovernable when hungry. Excepting my guarded lily gardens, almost every leaf that these hoofed locusts can reach within a radius of a mile or two from camp has been devoured. Even the bushes are stripped bare, and in spite of dogs and shepherds the sheep scatter to all points of the compass and vanish in dust. I fear some are lost, for one of the sixteen black ones is missing.

June 17 – Counted the wool bundles this morning as they bounced through the narrow corral gate. About three hundred are missing, and as the shepherd could not go to seek them, I had to go. I tied a crust of bread to my belt, and with Carlo set out for the upper slopes of the Pilot Peak Ridge, and had a good day, notwithstanding the care of seeking the silly runaways. I went out for wool, and did not come back shorn. A peculiar light circled around the horizon, white and thin like that often seen over the auroral corona, blending into the blue of the upper sky. The only clouds were a few faint flossy pencilings like combed silk. I pushed direct to the boundary of the usual range of the flock, and around it until I found the outgoing trail of the wanderers. It led far up the ridge into an open place surrounded by a hedge-like growth of ceanothus chaparral. Carlo knew what I was about, and eagerly followed the scent until we came up to them, huddled in a timid, silent bunch. They had evidently been here all night and all the forenoon, afraid to go out to feed. Having escaped restraint, they were, like some people we know of, afraid of their freedom, did not know what to do with it, and seemed glad to get back into the old familiar bondage.

June 18 – Another inspiring morning, nothing better in any world can be conceived. No description of Heaven that I have ever heard or read of seems half so fine. At noon the clouds occupied about .05 of the sky, white filmy touches drawn delicately on the azure.

The high ridges and hilltops beyond the woolly locusts are now gay with monardella, clarkia, coreopsis, and tall tufted grasses, some of them tall enough to wave like pines. The lupines, of which there are many ill-defined species, are now mostly out of flower, and many of the composit are beginning to fade, their radiant corollas vanishing in fluffy pappus like stars in mist.

We had another visitor from Brown's Flat today, an old Indian woman with a basket on her back. Like our first caller from the village, she got fairly into camp and was standing in plain view when discovered. How long she had been quietly looking on, I cannot say. Even the dogs failed to notice her stealthy approach. She was on her way, I suppose, to some wild garden, probably for lupine and starchy saxifrage leaves and rootstocks. Her dress was calico rags, far from clean. In every way she seemed sadly unlike Nature's neat well-dressed animals, though living like them on the bounty of the wilderness. Strange that mankind alone is dirty. Had she been clad in fur, or cloth woven of grass or shreddy bark, like the juniper and libocedrus mats, she might then have seemed a rightful part of the wilderness; like a good wolf at least, or bear. But from no point of view that I have found are such debased fellow beings a whit more natural than the glaring tailored tourists we saw that frightened the birds and squirrels.

June 19 – Pure sunshine all day. How beautiful a rock is made by leaf shadows! Those of the live oak are particularly clear and distinct, and beyond all art in grace and delicacy, now still as if painted on stone, now gliding softly as if afraid of noise, now dancing, waltzing in swift, merry swirls, or jumping on and off sunny rocks in quick dashes like wave embroidery on seashore cliffs. How true and substantial is this shadow beauty, and with what sublime extravagance is beauty thus multiplied! The big orange lilies are now arrayed in all their glory of leaf and flower. Noble plants, in perfect health, Nature's darlings.

June 20 – Some of the silly sheep got caught fast in a tangle of chaparral this morning, like flies in a spider's web, and had to be helped out. Carlo found them and tried to drive them from the trap by the easiest way. How far above sheep are intelligent dogs! No friend and helper can be more affectionate and constant than Carlo. The noble St Bernard is an honor to his race.

The air is distinctly fragrant with balsam and resin and mint – every breath of it a gift we may well thank God for. Who could ever guess that so rough a wilderness should yet be so fine, so full of good things. One seems to be in a majestic domed pavilion in which a grand play is being acted with scenery and music and and incense – all the furniture and action so interesting we are in no danger of being called on to endure one dull moment. God himself seems to be always doing his best here, working like a man in a glow of enthusiasm.

June 21 – Sauntered along the river-bank to my lily gardens. The perfection of beauty in these lilies of the wilderness is a never-ending source of admiration and wonder. Their rhizomes are set in black mould accumulated in hollows of the metamorphic slates beside the pools, where they are well watered without being subjected to flood action. Every leaf in the level whorls around the tall polished stalks is as finely finished as the petals, and the light and heat required are measured for them and tempered in passing through the branches of over-leaning trees. However strong the winds from the noon rain-storms, they are securely sheltered. Beautiful hypnum carpets bordered with ferns are spread beneath them, violets too, and a few daisies. Everything around them sweet and fresh like themselves.

Cloudland today is only a solitary white mountain; but it is so enriched with sunshine and shade, the tones of color on its big domed head and bossy outbulging ridges, and in the hollows and ravines between them, are ineffably fine.

June 22 – Unusually cloudy. Besides the periodical shower-bearing cumuli there is a thin diffused fog-like cloud overhead. About .75 in all.

June 23 – Oh, these vast, calm, measureless mountain days, inciting at once to work and rest! Days in whose light everything seems equally divine, opening a thousand windows to show us God. Nevermore, however weary, should one faint by the way who gains the blessings of one mountain day; whatever his fate, long life, short life, stormy or calm, he is rich forever.

June 24 – Our regular allowance of clouds and thunder. Shepherd Billy is in a peck of trouble about the sheep; he declares that they are possessed with more of the evil one than any other flock from the beginning of the invention of mutton and wool to the last batch of it. No matter how many are missing, he will not, he says, go a step to seek them, because, as he reasons, while getting back one wanderer he would probably lose ten. Therefore runaway hunting must be Carlo's and mine. Billy's little dog Jack is also giving trouble by leaving camp every night to visit his neighbors up the mountain at Brown's Flat. He is a common-looking cur of no particular breed, but tremendously enterprising in love and war. He has cut all the ropes and leather straps he has been tied with, until his master in desperation, after climbing the brushy mountain again and again to drag him back, fastened him with a pole attached to his collar under his chin at one end, and to a stout sapling at the other. But the pole gave good leverage, and by constant twisting during the night, the fastening at the sapling end was chafed off, and he set out on his usual journey, dragging the pole through the brush, and reached the Indian settlement in safety. His master followed, and making no allowance, gave him a beating, and swore in bad terms that next evening he would 'fix that infatuated pup' by anchoring him unmercifully to the heavy cast-iron lid of our Dutch oven, weighing about as much as the dog. It was linked directly to his collar close up under the chin, so that the poor fellow seemed unable to stir. He stood quite discouraged until after dark, unable to look about him, or even to lie down unless he stretched himself out with his front feet across the lid, and his head close down between his paws. Before morning, however, Jack was heard far up the height howling

Excelsior, cast-iron anchor to the contrary notwithstanding. He must have walked, or rather climbed, erect on his hind legs, clasping the heavy lid like a shield against his breast, a formidable iron-clad condition in which to meet his rivals. Next night, dog, pot-lid, and all, were tied up in an old bean-sack, and thus at last angry Billy gained the victory. Just before leaving home, Jack was bitten in the lower jaw by a rattlesnake, and for a week or so his head and neck were swollen to more than double the normal size; nevertheless he ran about as brisk and lively as ever, and is now completely recovered. The only treatment he got was fresh milk – a gallon or two at a time forcibly poured down his sore, poisoned throat.

June 25 – Though only a sheep camp, this grand mountain hollow is home, sweet home, every day growing sweeter, and I shall be sorry to leave it. The lily gardens are safe as yet from the trampling flock. Poor, dusty, raggedy, famishing creatures, I heartily pity them. Many a mile they must go every day to gather their fifteen or twenty tons of chaparral and grass.

June 26 – Nuttall's flowering dogwood makes a fine show when in bloom. The whole tree is then snowy white. The involucres are six to eight inches wide. Along the streams it is a good-sized tree thirty to fifty feet high, with a broad head when not crowded by companions. Its showy involucres attract a crowd of moths, butterflies, and other winged people about it for their own and, I suppose, the tree's advantage. It likes plenty of cool water, and is a great drinker like the alder, willow, and cottonwood, and flourishes best on stream banks, though it often wanders far from streams in damp shady glens beneath the pines, where it is much smaller. When the leaves ripen in the fall, they become more beautiful than the flowers, displaying charming tones of red, purple, and lavender. Another species grows in abundance as a chaparral shrub on the shady sides of the hills, probably *Cornus sessilis*. The leaves are eaten by the sheep. – Heard a few lightning strokes in the distance, with rumbling, mumbling reverberations.

June 27 – The beaked hazel (*Corylus rostrata*, var. *California*) is common on cool slopes up toward the summit of the Pilot Peak Ridge. There is something peculiarly attractive in the hazel, like the oaks and heaths of the cool countries of our forefathers, and through them our love for these plants has, I suppose, been transmitted. This species is four or five feet high, leaves soft and hairy, grateful to the touch, and the delicious nuts are eagerly gathered by Indians and squirrels. The sky as usual adorned with white noon clouds.

June 28 – Warm, mellow summer. The glowing sunbeams make every nerve tingle. The new needles of the pines and firs are nearly full grown and shine gloriously. Lizards are glinting about on the hot rocks; some that live near the camp are more than half tame. They seem attentive to every movement on our part, as if curious to simply look on without suspicion of harm, turning their heads to look back, and making a variety of pretty gestures. Gentle, guileless creatures with beautiful eyes, I shall be sorry to leave them when we leave camp.

June 29 – I have been making the acquaintance of a very interesting little bird that flits about the falls and rapids of the main branches of the river. It is not a water-bird in structure, though it gets its living in the water, and never leaves the streams. It is not web-footed, yet it dives fearlessly into deep swirling rapids, evidently to feed at the bottom, using its wings to swim with under water just as ducks and loons do. Sometimes it wades about in shallow places, thrusting its head under from time to time in a jerking, nodding, frisky way that is sure to attract attention. It is about the size of a robin, has short crisp wings serviceable for flying either in water or air, and a tail of moderate size slanted upward, giving it, with its nodding, bobbing manners, a wrennish look. Its color is plain bluish ash, with a tinge of brown on the head and shoulders. It flies from fall to fall, rapid to rapid, with a solid whir of wingbeats like those of a quail, follows the windings of the stream, and usually alights on some rock jutting up out of the current, or on some stranded snag, or rarely on the dry limb of an overhanging tree, perching like regular tree birds when it suits its convenience. It has the oddest, daintiest mincing manners imaginable; and the little fellow can sing too, a sweet thrushy, fluty song, rather low, not the least boisterous, and much less keen and accentuated than from its vigorous briskness one would be led to look for. What a romantic life this little bird leads on the most beautiful portions of the streams, in a genial climate with shade and cool water and spray to temper the summer heat. No wonder it is a fine singer, considering the stream songs it hears day and night. Every breath the little poet draws is part of a song, for all the air about the rapids and falls is beaten into music, and its first lessons must begin before it is born by the thrilling and quivering of the eggs in unison with the tones of the falls. I have not yet found its nest, but it must be near the streams, for it never leaves them.

June 30 – Half-cloudy, half-sunny, clouds lustrous white. The tall pines crowded along the top of the Pilot Peak Ridge look like six-inch miniatures exquisitely outlined on the satiny sky. Average cloudiness for the day about .25. No rain. And so this memorable month ends, a stream of beauty unmeasured, no more to be sectioned off by almanac arithmetic than sun-radiance or the currents of seas and rivers – a peaceful, joyful stream of beauty. Every morning, arising from the death of sleep, the happy plants and all our fellow animal creatures great and small, and even the rocks, seemed to be shouting, 'Awake, awake, rejoice, rejoice, come love us and join in our song. Come! Come!' Looking back through the stillness and romantic enchanting beauty and peace of the camp grove, this June seems the greatest of all the months of my life, the most truly, divinely free, boundless like eternity, immortal. Everything in it seems equally divine – one smooth, pure, wild glow of Heaven's love, never to be blotted or blurred by anything past or to come.

July 1 – Summer is ripe. Flocks of seeds are already out of their cups and pods seeking their predestined places. Some will strike root and grow up beside their parents, others flying on the wings of the wind far from them, among strangers. Most of the young birds are full feathered and out of their nests, though still looked after by both father and mother, protected and fed and to some extent educated. How beautiful the home life of birds! No wonder we all love them.

I like to watch the squirrels. There are two species here, the large California gray and the Douglas. The latter is the brightest of all the squirrels I have ever seen, a hot spark of life, making every tree tingle with his prickly toes, a condensed

nugget of fresh mountain vigor and valor, as free from disease
as a sunbeam. One cannot think of such an animal ever being
weary or sick. He seems to think the mountains belong to him,
and at first tried to drive away the whole flock of sheep as well
as the shepherd and dogs. How he scolds, and what faces he
makes, all eyes, teeth, and whiskers! If not so comically small,
he would indeed be a dreadful fellow. I should like to know
more about his bringing up, his life in the home knot-hole, as
well as in the tree-tops, throughout all seasons. Strange that I
have not yet found a nest full of young ones. The Douglas is
nearly allied to the red squirrel of the Atlantic slope, and may
have been distributed to this side of the continent by way of the
great unbroken forests of the north.

The California gray is one of the most beautiful, and, next to
the Douglas, the most interesting of our hairy neighbors.
Compared with the Douglas he is twice as large, but far less
lively and influential as a worker in the woods, and he
manages to make his way through leaves and branches with
less stir than his small brother. I have never heard him bark at
anything except our dogs. When in search of food he glides
silently from branch to branch, examining last year's cones, to
see whether some few seeds may not be left between the scales,
or gleans fallen ones among the leaves on the ground, since
none of the present season's crop is yet available. His tail floats
now behind him, now above him, level or gracefully curled like
a wisp of cirrus cloud, every hair in its place, clean and shining
and radiant as thistle-down in spite of rough, gummy work.
His whole body seems about as unsubstantial as his tail. The
little Douglas is fiery, peppery, full of brag and fight and show,
with movements so quick and keen they almost sting the onlooker, and the harlequin gyrating show he makes of himself
turns one giddy to see. The gray is shy, and oftentimes stealthy
in his movements, as if half expecting an enemy in every tree
and bush, and back of every log, wishing only to be let alone
apparently, and manifesting no desire to be seen or admired or
feared. The Indians hunt this species for food, a good cause for
caution, not to mention other enemies – hawks, snakes, wild
cats. In woods where food is abundant they wear paths
through sheltering thickets and over prostrate trees to some
favorite pool where in hot and dry weather they drink at nearly
the same hour every day. These pools are said to be narrowly

watched, especially by the boys, who lie in ambush with bow and arrow, and kill without noise. But, in spite of enemies, squirrels are happy fellows, forest favorites, types of tireless life. Of all Nature's wild beasts, they seem to me the wildest. May we come to know each other better.

The chaparral-covered hill-slope to the south of the camp, besides furnishing nesting-places for countless merry birds, is the home and hiding-place of the curious wood rat (*Neotoma*), a handsome, interesting animal, always attracting attention wherever seen. It is more like a squirrel than a rat, is much larger, has delicate, thick, soft fur of a bluish slate color, white on the belly; ears large, thin, and translucent; eyes soft, full, and liquid; claws slender, sharp as needles; and as his limbs are strong, he can climb about as well as a squirrel. No rat or squirrel has so innocent a look, is so easily approached, or expresses such confidence in one's good intentions. He seems too fine for the thorny thickets he inhabits, and his hut also is as unlike himself as may be, though softly furnished inside. No other animal inhabitant of these mountains builds houses so large and striking in appearance. The traveler coming suddenly upon a group of them for the first time will not be likely to forget them. They are built of all kinds of sticks, old rotten pieces picked up anywhere, and green prickly twigs bitten from the nearest bushes, the whole mixed with miscellaneous odds and ends of everything movable, such as bits of cloddy earth, stones, bones, deerhorn, etc., piled up in a conical mass as if it were got ready for burning. Some of these curious cabins are six feet high and as wide at the base, and a dozen or more of them are occasionally grouped together, less perhaps for the sake of society than for advantages of food and shelter. Coming through the dense shaggy thickets of some lonely hillside, the solitary explorer happening into one of these strange villages is startled at the sight, and may fancy himself in an Indian settlement, and begin to wonder what kind of reception he is likely to get. But no savage face will he see, perhaps not a single inhabitant, or at most two or three seated on top of their wigwams, looking at the stranger with the mildest of wild eyes, and allowing a near approach. In the centre of the rough spiky hut a soft nest is made of the inner fibres of bark chewed to tow, and lined with feathers and the down of various seeds, such as willow and milkweed. The

delicate creature in its prickly, thick-walled home suggests a
tender flower in a thorny involucre. Some of the nests are built
in trees thirty or forty feet from the ground, and even in
garrets, as if seeking the company and protection of man, like
swallows and linnets, though accustomed to the wildest solitude. Among housekeepers Neotoma has the reputation of a
thief, because he carries away everything transportable to his
queer hut – knives, forks, combs, nails, tin cups, spectacles, etc
– merely, however, to stregthen his fortifications, I guess. His
food at home, as far as I have learned, is nearly the same as that
of the squirrels – nuts, berries, seeds, and sometimes the bark
and tender shoots of the various species of *Ceanothus*.

July 2 – Warm, sunny day, thrilling plant and animals and
rocks alike, making sap and blood flow fast, and making every
particle of the crystal mountains throb and swirl and dance in
glad accord like star-dust. No dullness anywhere visible or
thinkable. No stagnation, no death. Everything kept in joyful
rhythmic motion in the pulses of Nature's big heart.

Pearl cumuli over the higher mountains – clouds, not with a
silver lining, but all silver. The brightest, crispest, rockiest-
looking clouds, most varied in features and keenest in outline I
ever saw at any time of year in any country. The daily building
and unbuilding of these snowy cloud-ranges – the highest
Sierra – is a prime marvel to me, and I gaze at the stupendous
white domes, miles high, with ever fresh admiration. But in the
midst of these sky and mountain affairs a change of diet is
pulling us down. We have been out of bread a few days, and
begin to miss it more than seems reasonable, for we have
plenty of meat and sugar and tea. Strange we should feel food-
poor in so rich a wilderness. The Indians put us to shame, so do
the squirrels – starchy roots and seeds and bark in abundance,
yet the failure of the meal sack disturbs our bodily balance, and
threatens our best enjoyments.

July 3 – Warm. Breeze just enough to sift through the woods
and waft fragrance from their thousand fountains. The pine
and fir cones are growing well, resin and balsam dripping from
every tree, and seeds are ripening fast, promising a fine harvest.
The squirrels will have bread. They eat all kinds of nuts long
before they are ripe, and yet never seem to suffer in stomach.

Chapter 3

A BREAD FAMINE

July 4 – The air beyond the flock range, full of the essences of the woods, is growing sweeter and more fragrant from day to day, like ripening fruit.

Mr Delaney is expected to arrive soon from the lowlands with a new stock of provisions, and as the flock is to be moved to fresh pastures we shall all be well fed. In the meantime our stock of beans as well as flour has failed – everything but mutton, sugar, and tea. The shepherd is somewhat demoralized, and seems to care but little what becomes of his flock. He says that since the boss has failed to feed him he is not rightly bound to feed the sheep, and swears that no decent white man can climb these steep mountains on mutton alone. 'It's not fittin' grub for a white man really white. For dogs and coyotes and Indians it's different. Good grub, good sheep. That's what I say.' Such was Billy's Fourth of July oration.

July 5 – The clouds of noon on the high Sierra seem yet more marvelously, indescribably beautiful from day to day as one becomes more wakeful to see them. The smoke of the gunpowder burned yesterday on the lowlands, and the eloquence of the orators has probably settled or been blown away by this time. Here every day is a holiday, a jubilee ever sounding with serene enthusiasm, without wear or waste or cloying weariness. Everything rejoicing. Not a single cell or crystal unvisited or forgotten.

July 6 – Mr Delaney has not arrived, and the bread famine is sore. We must eat mutton a while longer, though it seems hard to get accustomed to it. I have heard of Texas pioneers living without bread or anything made from the cereals for months without suffering, using the breast-meat of wild turkeys for bread. Of this kind they had plenty in the good old days when life, though considered less safe, was fussed over the less. The trappers and fur traders of early days in the Rocky Mountain regions lived on bison and beaver meat for months. Salmon-eaters, too, there are among both Indians and whites who seem to suffer little or not at all from the want of bread. Just at this moment mutton seems the least desirable of food, though of good quality. We pick out the leanest bits, and down they go against heavy disgust, causing nausea and an effort to reject the offensive stuff. Tea makes matters worse, if possible. The stomach begins to assert itself as an independent creature with a will of its own. We should boil lupine leaves, clover, starchy petioles, and saxifrage rootstocks like the Indians. We try to ignore our gastric troubles, rise and gaze about us, turn our eyes to the mountains, and climb doggedly up through brush and rocks into the heart of the scenery. A stifled calm comes on, and the day's duties and even enjoyments are languidly got through with. We chew a few leaves of ceanothus by way of luncheon, and smell or chew the spicy monardella for the dull headache and stomach-ache that now lightens, now comes muffling down upon us and into us like fog. At night more mutton, flesh to flesh, down with it, not too much, and there are the stars shining through the cedar plumes and branches above our beds.

July 7 – Rather weak and sickish this morning, and all about a piece of bread. Can scarce command attention to my best studies, as if one couldn't take a few days' saunter in the Godful woods without maintaining a base on a wheat-field and grist-mill. Like caged parrots we want a cracker, any of the hundred kinds – the remainder biscuit of a voyage around the world would answer well enough, nor would the wholesomeness of saleratus biscuit be questioned. Bread without flesh is a good diet, as on many botanical excursions I have proved. Tea also may easily be ignored. Just bread and water and delightful toil is all I need – not unreasonably much, yet one ought to be trained and tempered to enjoy life in these brave wilds in full independence of any particular kind of nourishment. That this may be accomplished is manifest, as far as bodily welfare is concerned, in the lives of people of other climes. The Eskimo, for example, gets a living far north of the wheat line, from oily seals and whales. Meat, berries, bitter weeds, and blubber, or only the last, for months at a time; and yet these people all around the frozen shores of our continent are said to be hearty, jolly, stout, and brave. We hear, too, of fish-eaters, carnivorous as spiders, yet well enough as far as stomachs are concerned, while we are so ridiculously helpless, making wry faces over our fare, looking sheepish in digestive distress amid rumbling, grumbling sounds that might well pass for smothered baas. We have a large supply of sugar, and this evening it occurred to me that these belligerent stomachs might possibly, like complaining children, be coaxed with candy. Accordingly the frying-pan was cleansed, and a lot of sugar cooked in it to a sort of wax, but this stuff only made matters worse.

Man seems to be the only animal whose food soils him, making necessary much washing and shield-like bibs and napkins. Moles living in the earth and eating slimy worms are yet as clean as seals or fishes, whose lives are one perpetual wash. And, as we have seen, the squirrels in these resiny woods keep themselves clean in some mysterious way; not a hair is sticky, though they handle the gummy cones, and glide about apparently without care. The birds, too, are clean, though they seem to make a good deal of fuss washing and cleaning their feathers. Certain flies and ants I see are in a fix, entangled and sealed up in the sugar-wax we threw away, like some of their ancestors in amber. Our stomachs, like tired muscles, are sore with long squirming. Once I was very hungry in the Bonaventure graveyard near Savannah, Georgia, having fasted for several days; then the empty stomach seemed to chafe in much the same way as now, and a somewhat similar tenderness and aching was produced, hard to bear, though the pain was not acute. We dream of bread, a sure sign we need it. Like the Indians, we ought to know how to get the starch out of fern and saxifrage stalks, lily bulbs, pine bark, etc. Our education has been sadly neglected for many generations. Wild rice would be good. I noticed a leersia in wet meadow edges, but the seeds are small. Acorns are not ripe, nor pine nuts, nor filberts. The inner bark of pine or spruce might be tried. Drank tea until half intoxicated. Man seems to crave a stimulant when anything extraordinary is going on, and this is the only one I use. Billy chews great quantities of tobacco, which I suppose helps to stupefy and moderate his misery. We look and listen for the Don every hour. How beautiful upon the mountains his big feet would be!

In the warm, hospitable Sierra, shepherds and mountain men in general, as far as I have seen, are easily satisfied as to food supplies and bedding. Most of them are heartily content to 'rough it,' ignoring Nature's fineness as bothersome or unmanly. The shepherd's bed is often only the bare ground and a pair of blankets, with a stone, a piece of wood, or a pack-saddle for a pillow. In choosing the spot, he shows less care than the dogs, for they usually deliberate before making up their minds in so important an affair, going from place to place, scraping away loose sticks and pebbles, and trying for comfort by making many changes, while the shepherd casts himself down anywhere, seemingly the least skilled of all rest seekers. His food, too, even when he has all he wants, is usually far from delicate, either in kind or cooking. Beans, bread of any sort, bacon, mutton, dried peaches, and sometimes potatoes and onions, make up his bill-of-fare, the two latter articles being regarded as luxuries on account of their weight as compared with the nourishment they contain; a half-sack or so of each may be put into the pack in setting out from the home ranch and in a few days they are done. Beans are the main standby, portable, wholesome, and capable of going far, besides being easily cooked, although curiously enough a great deal of mystery is supposed to lie about the bean-pot. No two cooks quite agree on the methods of making beans do their best, and, after petting and coaxing and nursing the savory mess – well oiled and mellowed with bacon boiled into the heart of it – the proud cook will ask, after dishing out a quart or two for trial, 'Well, how do you like *my* beans?' as if by no possibility could they be like any other beans cooked in the same way, but must needs possess some special virtue of which he alone is master. Molasses, sugar, or pepper may be used to give desired flavors; or the first water may be poured off and a spoonful or two of ashes or soda added to dissolve or soften the skins more fully, according to various tastes and notions. But, like casks of wine, no two potfuls are exactly alike to every palate. Some are supposed to be spoiled by the moon, by some unlucky day, by the beans having been grown on soil not suitable; or the whole year may be to blame as not favorable for beans.

Coffee, too, has its marvels in the camp kitchen, but not so many, and not so inscrutable as those that beset the bean-pot. A low complacent grunt follows a mouthful drawn in with a gurgle, and the remark cast forth aimlessly, 'That's good coffee.' Then another gurgling sip and repetition of the judgement, '*Yes, sir,* that *is* good coffee.' As to tea, there are but two kinds, weak and strong, the stronger the better. The only remark heard is, 'That tea's weak,' otherwise it is good enough and not worth mentioning. If it has been boiled an hour or two or smoked on a pitchy fire, no matter – who cares for a little tannin or creosote? They make the black beverage all the stronger and more attractive to tobacco-tanned palates.

Sheep-camp bread, like most California camp bread, is baked in Dutch ovens, some of it in the form of yeast powder biscuit, an unwholesome sticky compound leading straight to dyspepsia. The greater part, however, is fermented with sour dough, a handful from each batch being saved and put away in the mouth of the flour sack to inoculate the next. The oven is simply a cast-iron pot, about five inches deep and from twelve to eighteen inches wide. After the batch has been mixed and kneaded in a tin pan, the oven is slightly heated and rubbed with a piece of tallow or pork rind. The dough is then placed in it, pressed out against the sides, and left to rise. When ready for baking a shovelful of coals is spread out by the side of the fire and the oven set upon them, while another shovelful is placed on top of the lid, which is raised from time to time to see that the requisite amount of heat is being kept up. With care good bread may be made in this way, though it is liable to be burned or to be sour, or raised too much, and the weight of the oven is a serious objection.

At last Don Delaney comes doon the lang glen – hunger vanishes, we turn our eyes to the mountains, and tomorrow we go climbing toward cloudland.

Never while anything is left of me shall this first camp be forgotten. It has fairly grown into me, not merely as memory pictures, but as part and parcel of mind and body alike. The deep hopper-like hollow, with its majestic trees through which all the wonderful nights the stars poured their beauty. The flowery wildness of the high steep slope toward Brown's Flat, and its bloom-fragrance descending at the close of the still days. The embowered river-reaches with their multitude of voices making melody, the stately flow and rush and glad exulting onsweeping currents caressing the dipping sedge-leaves and bushes and mossy stones, swirling in pools, dividing against little flowery islands, breaking gray and white here and there, ever rejoicing, yet with deep solemn undertones recalling the ocean – the brave little bird ever beside them, singing with sweet human tones among the waltzing foam-bells, and like a blessed evangel explaining God's love. And the Pilot Peak Ridge, its long withdrawing slopes gracefully modeled and braided, reaching from climate to climate, feathered with trees that are the kings of their race, their ranks nobly marshaled to view, spire above spire, crown above crown, waving their long, leafy arms, tossing their cones like ringing bells – blessed sun-fed mountaineers rejoicing in their strength, every tree tuneful, a harp for the winds and the sun. The hazel and buckthorn pastures of the deer, the sun-beaten brows purple and yellow with mint and golden-rods, carpeted with chambatia, humming with bees.

And the dawns and sunrises and sundowns of these mountain days – the rose light creeping higher among the stars, changing to daffodil yellow, the level beams bursting forth, streaming across the ridges, touching pine after pine, awakening and warming all the mighty host to do gladly their shining day's work. The great sun-gold noons, the alabaster cloud-mountains, the landscape beaming with consciousness like the face of a god. The sunsets, when the trees stood hushed awaiting their goodnight blessings. Divine, enduring, unwastable wealth.

Chapter 4

TO THE HIGH MOUNTAINS

July 8 – Now away we go toward the topmost mountains. Many still, small voices, as well as the noon thunder, are calling, 'Come higher.' Farewell, blessed dell, woods, gardens, streams, birds, squirrels, lizards, and a thousand others. Farewell. Farewell.

Up through the woods the hoofed locusts streamed beneath a cloud of brown dust. Scarcely were they driven a hundred yards from the old corral ere they seemed to know that at last they were going to new pastures, and rushed wildly ahead, crowding through gaps in the brush, jumping, tumbling like exulting, hurrahing flood-waters escaping through a broken dam. A man on each flank kept shouting advice to the leaders, who in their famishing condition were behaving like Gadarene swine; two other drivers were busy with stragglers, helping them out of brush-tangles; the Indian, calm, alert, silently watched for wanderers likely to be over-looked; the two dogs ran here and there, at a loss to know what was best to be done, while the Don, soon far in the rear, was trying to keep in sight of his trouble-some wealth.

As soon as the boundary of the old eaten-out range was passed the hungry horde suddenly became calm, like a mountain stream in a meadow. Thenceforward they were allowed to eat their way as slowly as they wished, care being taken only to keep them headed toward the summit of the Merced and Tuolumne divide. Soon the two thousand flattened paunches were bulged out with sweet-pea vines and grass, and the gaunt, desperate creatures, more like wolves than sheep, became bland and governable, while the howling drivers changed to gentle shepherds, and sauntered in peace.

Toward sundown we reached Hazel Green, a charming spot

on the summit of the dividing ridge between the basins of the
Merced and Tuolumne, where there is a small brook flowing
through hazel and dogwood thickets beneath magnificent
silver firs and pines. Here we are camped for the night, our
big fire, heaped high with rosiny logs and branches, is blazing
like a sunrise, gladly giving back the light slowly sifted from
the sunbeams of centuries of summers; and in the glow of that
old sunlight how impressively surrounding objects are brought
forward in relief against the outer darkness! Grasses, larkspurs, columbines, lilies, hazel bushes, and the great trees form
a circle around the fire like thoughtful spectators, gazing and
listening with human-like enthusiasm. The night breeze is cool,
for all day we have been climbing into the upper sky, the home
of the cloud mountains we so long have admired. How sweet
and keen the air! Every breath a blessing. Here the sugar pine
reaches its fullest development in size and beauty and number
of individuals, filling every swell and hollow and down-plunging ravine almost to the exclusion of other species. A few
yellow pines are still to be found as companions, and in the
coolest places silver firs; but noble as these are, the sugar pine is
king, and spreads long protecting arms above them while they
rock and wave in sign of recognition.

We have now reached a height of six thousand feet. In the
forenoon we passed along a flat part of the dividing ridge that
is planted with manzanita (*Arctostaphylos*), some specimens
the largest I have seen. I measured one, the bole of which is
four feet in diameter and only eighteen inches high from the
ground, where it dissolves into many wide-spreading branches
forming a broad round head about ten or twelve feet high,
covered with clusters of small narrow-throated pink bells. The
leaves are pale green, glandular, and set on edge by a twist of
the petiole. The branches seem naked; for the chocolate-
colored bark is very smooth and thin, and is shed off in flakes
that curl when dry. The wood is red, close-grained, hard, and
heavy. I wonder how old these curious tree-bushes are, probably as old as the great pines. Indians and bears and birds and
fat grubs feast on the berries, which look like small apples,
often rosy on one side, green on the other. The Indians are said
to make a kind of beer or cider out of them. There are many
species. This one, *Arctostaphylos pungens*, is common hereabouts. No need have they to fear the wind, so low they are

and steadfastly rooted. Even the fires that sweep the woods seldom destroy them utterly, for they rise again from the root, and some of the dry ridges they grow on are seldom touched by fire. I must try to know them better.

I miss my river songs tonight. Here Hazel Creek at its topmost springs has a voice like a bird. The wind-tones in the great trees overhead are strangely impressive, all the more because not a leaf stirs below them. But it grows late, and I must to bed. The camp is silent; everybody asleep. It seems extravagant to spend hours so precious in sleep. 'He giveth his beloved sleep.' Pity the poor beloved needs it, weak, weary, forspent; oh, the pity of it, to sleep in the midst of eternal, beautiful motion instead of gazing forever, like the stars.

July 9 – Exhilarated with the mountain air, I feel like shouting this morning with excess of wild animal joy. The Indian lay down away from the fire last night, without blankets, having nothing on, by way of clothing, but a pair of blue overalls and a calico shirt wet with sweat. The night air is chilly at this elevation, and we gave him some horse-blankets, but he didn't seem to care for them. A fine thing to be independent of clothing where it is so hard to carry. When food is scarce, he can live on whatever comes in his way – a few berries, roots, bird eggs, grasshoppers, black ants, fat wasp or bumblebee larvae, without feeling that he is doing anything worth mention, so I have been told.

Our course today was along the broad top of the main ridge to a hollow beyond Crane Flat. It is scarce at all rocky, and is covered with the noblest pines and spruces I have yet seen. Sugar pines from six to eight feet in diameter are not uncommon, with a height of two hundred feet or even more. The silver firs (*Abies concolor* and *A. magnifica*) are exceedingly beautiful, especially the *magnifica*, which becomes more abundant the higher we go. It is of great size, one of the most notable in every way of the giant conifers of the Sierra. I saw specimens that measured seven feet in diameter and over two hundred feet in height, while the average size for what might be called full-grown mature trees can hardly be less than one hundred and eighty or two hundred feet high and five or six feet in diameter; and with these noble dimensions there is a symmetry and perfection of finish not to be seen in any other tree, hereabout at least. The branches are whorled in fives mostly, and stand out from the tall, straight, exquisitely tapered bole in level collars, each branch regularly pinnated like the fronds of ferns, and densely clad with leaves all around the branchlets, thus giving them a singularly rich and sumptuous appearance. The extreme top of the tree is a thick blunt shoot pointing straight to the zenith like an admonishing finger. The cones stand erect like casks on the upper branches. They are about six inches long, three in diameter, blunt, velvety, and cylindrical in form, and very rich and precious looking. The seeds are about three quarters of an inch long, dark reddish brown with brilliant iridescent purple wings, and when ripe, the cone falls to pieces, and the seeds thus set free at a height of one hundred and fifty or two hundred feet have a good send off and may fly considerable distances in a good breeze; and it is when a good breeze is blowing that most of them are shaken free to fly.

The other species, *Abies concolor*, attains nearly as great a height and thickness as the *magnifica*, but the branches do not form such regular whorls, nor are they so exactly pinnated or richly leaf-clad. Instead of growing all around the branchlets, the leaves are mostly arranged in two flat horizontal rows. The cones and seeds are like those of the *magnifica* in form but less than half as large. The bark of the *magnifica* is reddish purple and closely furrowed, that of the *concolor* gray and widely furrowed. A noble pair.

At Crane Flat we climbed a thousand feet or more in a distance of about two miles, the forest growing more dense and the silvery *magnifica* fir forming a still greater portion of the whole. Crane Flat is a meadow with a wide sandy border lying on the top of the divide. It is often visited by blue cranes to rest and feed on their long journeys, hence the name. It is about half a mile long, draining into the Merced, sedgy in the middle, with a margin bright with lilies, columbines, larkspurs, lupines, castilleia, then an outer zone of dry, gently sloping ground starred with a multitude of small flowers – eunanus, mimulus, gilia, with rosettes of spraguea, and tufts of several species of eriogonum and the brilliant zauschneria. The noble forest wall about it is made up of the two silver firs and the yellow and sugar pines, which here seem to reach their highest pitch of beauty and grandeur; for the elevation, six thousand feet or a little more, is not too great for the sugar and yellow pines or too low for the *magnifica* fir, while the *concolor* seems to find this elevation the best possible. About a mile from the north end of the flat there is a grove of *Sequoia gigantea*, the king of all the conifers. Furthermore, the Douglas spruce (*Pseudotsuga Douglasii*) and *Libocedrus decurrens*, and a few two-leaved pines, occur here and there, forming a small part of the forest. Three pines, two silver firs, one Douglas spruce, one sequoia – all of them, except the two-leaved pine, colossal trees – are found here together, an assemblage of conifers unrivaled on the globe.

We passed a number of charming garden-like meadows lying on top of the divide or hanging like ribbons down its sides, imbedded in the glorious forest. Some are taken up chiefly with the tall white-flowered *Veratrum Californicum*, with boat-shaped leaves about a foot long, eight or ten inches wide, and veined like those of cypripedium – a robust, hearty, liliaceous plant, fond of water and determined to be seen. Columbine and larkspur grow on the dryer edges of the meadows, with a tall handsome lupine standing waist-deep in long grasses and sedges. Castilleias, too, of several species make a bright show with beds of violets at their feet. But the glory of these forest meadows is a lily (*L. parvum*). The tallest are from seven to eight feet high with magnificent racemes of ten to twenty or more small orange-colored flowers; they stand out free in open ground, with just enough grass and other companion plants about them to fringe their feet, and show them off to best advantage. This is a grand addition to my lily acquaintances – a true mountaineer, reaching prime vigor and beauty at a height of seven thousand feet or thereabouts. It varies, I find, very much in size even in the same meadow, not only with the soil, but with age. I saw a specimen that had only one flower, and another within a stone's throw had twenty-five. And to think that the sheep should be allowed in these lily meadows! After how many centuries of Nature's care planting and watering them, tucking the bulbs in snugly below winter frost, shading the tender shoots with clouds drawn above them like curtains, pouring refreshing rain, making them perfect in beauty, and keeping them safe by a thousand miracles; yet, strange to say, allowing the trampling of devastating sheep. One might reasonably look for a wall of fire to fence such gardens. So extravagant is Nature with her choicest treasures, spending plant beauty as she spends sunshine, pouring it forth into land and sea, garden and desert. And so the beauty of lilies falls on angels and men, bears and squirrels, wolves and sheep, birds and bees, but as far as I have seen, man alone, and the animals he tames, destroy these gardens. Awkward, lumbering bears, the Don tells me, love to wallow in them in hot weather, and deer with their sharp feet cross them again and again, sauntering and feeding, yet never a lily have I seen spoiled by them. Rather, like gardeners, they seem to cultivate them, pressing and dibbling as required. Anyhow not a leaf or petal seems misplaced.

The trees round about them seem as perfect in beauty and form as the lilies, their boughs whorled like lily leaves in exact order. This evening, as usual, the glow of our campfire is working enchantment on everything within reach of its rays. Lying beneath the firs, it is glorious to see them dipping their spires in the starry sky, the sky like one vast lily meadow in bloom! How can I close my eyes on so precious a night?

July 10 – A Douglas squirrel, peppery, pungent autocrat of the woods, is barking overhead this morning, and the small forest birds, so seldom seen when one travels noisily, are out on sunny branches along the edge of the meadow getting warm, taking a sun bath and dew bath – a fine sight. How charming the sprightly confident looks and ways of these little feathered people of the trees! They seem sure of dainty, wholesome breakfasts, and where are so many breakfasts to come from? How helpless should we find ourselves should we try to set a table for them of such buds, seeds, insects, etc., as would keep them in the pure wild health they enjoy! Not a headache or any other ache amongst them, I guess. As for the irrepressible Douglas squirrels, one never thinks of their breakfasts or the possibility of hunger, sickness, or death; rather they seem like stars above chance or change, even though we may see them at times busy gathering burrs, working hard for a living.

On through the forest ever higher we go, a cloud of dust dimming the way, thousands of feet, trampling leaves and flowers, but in this mighty wilderness they seem but a feeble band, and a thousand gardens will escape their blighting touch. They cannot hurt the trees, though some of the seedlings suffer, and should the woolly locusts be greatly multiplied, as on account of dollar value they are likely to be, then the forests, too, may in time be destroyed. Only the sky will then be safe, though hid from view by dust and smoke, incense of a bad sacrifice. Poor, helpless, hungry sheep, in great part misbegotten, without good right to be, semi-manufactured, made less by God than man, born out of time and place, yet their voices are strangely human and call out one's pity.

Our way is still along the Merced and Tuolumne divide, the streams on our right going to swell the songful Yosemite River, those on our left to the songful Tuolumne, slipping through sunny carex and lily meadows, and breaking into song down a thousand ravines almost as soon as they are born. A more tuneful set of streams surely nowhere exists, or more sparkling crystal pure, now gliding with tinkling whisper, now with merry dimpling rush, in and out through sunshine and shade, shimmering in pools, uniting their currents, bouncing, dancing from form to form over cliffs and inclines, ever more beautiful the farther they go until they pour into the main glacial rivers.

All day I have been gazing in growing admiration at the noble groups of the magnificent silver fir which more and more is taking the ground to itself. The woods above Crane Flat still continue comparatively open, letting in the sunshine on the brown needle-strewn ground. Not only are the individual trees admirable in symmetry and superb in foliage and port, but half a dozen or more often form temple groves in which the trees are so nicely graded in size and position as to seem one. Here, indeed, is the tree-lover's paradise. The dullest eye in the world must surely be quickened by such trees as these.

Fortunately the sheep need little attention, as they are driven slowly and allowed to nip and nibble as they like. Since leaving Hazel Green we have been following the Yosemite trail; visitors to the famous valley coming by way of Coulterville and Chinese Camp pass this way – the two trails uniting at Crane Flat – and enter the valley on the north side. Another trail enters on the south side by way of Mariposa. The tourists we saw were in parties of from three or four to fifteen or twenty, mounted on mules or small mustang ponies. A strange show they made, winding single file through the solemn woods in gaudy attire, scaring the wild creatures, and one might fancy that even the great pines would be disturbed and groan aghast. But what may we say of ourselves and the flock?

We are now camped at Tamarack Flat, within four or five
miles of the lower end of Yosemite. Here is another fine
meadow embosomed in the woods, with a deep, clear stream
gliding through it, its banks rounded and beveled with a thatch
of dipping sedges. The flat is named after the two-leaved pine
(*Pinus contorta*, var. *Murrayana*), common here, especially
around the cool margin of the meadow. On rocky ground it is
a rough, thickset tree, about forty to sixty feet high and one to
three feet in diameter, bark thin and gummy, branches rather
naked, tassels, leaves, and cones small. But in damp, rich soil it
grows close and slender, and reaches a height at times of nearly
a hundred feet. Specimens only six inches in diameter at the
ground are often fifty or sixty feet in height, as slender and
sharp in outline as arrows, like the true tamarack (larch) of the
Eastern States; hence the name, though it is a pine.

July 11 – The Don has gone ahead on one of the pack animals
to spy out the land to the north of Yosemite in search of the
best point for a central camp. Much higher than this we cannot
now go, for the upper pastures, said to be better than any
hereabouts, are still buried in heavy winter snow. Glad I am
that camp is to be fixed in the Yosemite region, for many a
glorious ramble I'll have along the top of the walls, and then
what landscapes I shall find with their new mountains and
canyons, forests and gardens, lakes and streams and falls.

We are now about seven thousand feet above the sea, and the
nights are so cool we have to pile coats and extra clothing on top
of our blankets. Tamarack Creek is icy cold, delicious, exhilarating champagne water. It is flowing bank full in the meadow
with silent speed, but only a few hundred yards below our camp
the ground is bare gray granite strewn with boulders, large
spaces being without a single tree or only a small one here and
there anchored in narrow seams and cracks. The boulders,
many of them very large, are not in piles or scattered like
rubbish among loose crumbling debris as if weathered out of
the solid as boulders of disintegration; they mostly occur singly,
and are lying on a clean pavement on which the sunshine falls in
a glare that contrasts with the shimmer of light and shade we
have been accustomed to in the leafy woods. And, strange to
say, these boulders lying so still and deserted, with no moving
force near them, no boulder carrier anywhere in sight, were

nevertheless brought from a distance, as difference in color and composition shows, quarried and carried and laid down here each in its place; nor have they stirred, most of them, through calm and storm since first they arrived. They look lonely here, strangers in a strange land – huge blocks, angular mountain chips, the largest twenty or thirty feet in diameter, the chips that Nature has made in modeling her landscapes, fashioning the forms of her mountains and valleys. And with what tool were they quarried and carried? On the pavement we find its marks. The most resisting unweathered portion of the surface is scored and striated in a rigidly parallel way, indicating that the region has been overswept by a glacier from the northeastward, grinding down the general mass of the mountains, scoring and polishing, producing a strange, raw, wiped appearance, and dropping whatever boulders it chanced to be carrying at the time it was melted at the close of the Glacial Period. A fine discovery this. As for the forests we have been passing through, they are probably growing on deposits of soil most of which has been laid down by this same ice agent in the form of moraines of different sorts, now in great part disintegrated and out-spread by post-glacial weathering.

Out of the grassy meadow and down over this ice-planed granite runs the glad young Tamarack Creek, rejoicing, exulting, chanting, dancing in white, glowing, irised falls and cascades on its way to the Merced Canyon, a few miles below Yosemite, falling more than three thousand feet in a distance of about two miles.

All the Merced streams are wonderful singers, and Yosemite is the centre where the main tributaries meet. From a point about half a mile from our camp we can see into the lower end of the famous valley, with its wonderful cliffs and groves, a grand page of mountain manuscript that I would gladly give my life to be able to read. How vast it seems, how short human life when we happen to think of it, and how little we may learn, however hard we try! Yet why bewail our poor inevitable ignorance? Some of the external beauty is always in sight, enough to keep every fibre of us tingling, and this we are able to gloriously enjoy though the methods of its creation may lie beyond our ken. Sing on, brave Tamarack Creek, fresh from your snowy fountains, plash and swirl and dance to your fate in the sea; bathing, cheering every living thing along your way.

Have greatly enjoyed all this huge day, sauntering and seeing, steeping in the mountain influences, sketching, noting, pressing flowers, drinking ozone and Tamarack water. Found the white fragrant Washington lily, the finest of all the Sierra lilies. Its bulbs are buried in shaggy chaparral tangles, I suppose for safety from pawing bears; and its magnificent panicles sway and rock over the top of the rough snow-pressed bushes, while big, bold, blunt-nosed bees drone and mumble in its polleny bells. A lovely flower, worth going hungry and footsore endless miles to see. The whole world seems richer now that I have found this plant in so noble a landscape.

A log house serves to mark a claim to the Tamarack meadow, which may become valuable as a station in case travel to Yosemite should greatly increase. Belated parties occasionally stop here. A white man with an Indian woman is holding possession of the place.

Sauntered up the meadow about sundown, out of sight of camp and sheep and all human mark, into the deep peace of the solemn old woods, everything glowing with Heaven's unquenchable enthusiasm.

July 12 – The Don has returned, and again we go on pilgrimage. 'Looking over the Yosemite Creek country,' he said, 'from the tops of the hills you see nothing but rocks and patches of trees; but when you go down into the rocky desert you find no end of small grassy banks and meadows, and so the country is not half so lean as it looks. There we'll go and stay until the snow is melted from the upper country.'

I was glad to hear that the high snow made a stay in the Yosemite region necessary, for I am anxious to see as much of it as possible. What fine times I shall have sketching, studying plants and rocks, and scrambling about the brink of the great valley alone, out of sight and sound of camp!

We saw another party of Yosemite tourists today. Somehow most of these travelers seem to care but little for the glorious objects about them, though enough to spend time and money and endure long rides to see the famous valley. And when they are fairly within the mighty walls of the temple and hear the psalms of the falls, they will forget themselves and become devout. Blessed, indeed, should be every pilgrim in these holy mountains!

We moved slowly eastward along the Mono Trail, and early in the afternoon unpacked and camped on the bank of Cascade Creek. The Mono Trail crosses the range by the Bloody Canyon Pass to gold mines near the north end of Mono Lake. These mines were reported to be rich when first discovered, and a grand rush took place, making a trail necessary. A few small bridges were built over streams where fording was not practicable on account of the softness of the bottom, sections of fallen trees cut out, and lanes made through thickets wide enough to allow the passage of bulky packs; but over the greater part of the way scarce a stone or shovelful of earth has been moved.

The woods we passed through are composed almost wholly of *Abies magnifica*, the companion species, *concolor*, being mostly left behind on account of altitude, while the increasing elevation seems grateful to the charming *magnifica*. No words can do anything like justice to this noble tree. At one place many had fallen during some heavy wind-storm, owing to the loose sandy character of the soil, which offered no secure anchorage. The soil is mostly decomposed and disintegrated moraine material.

The sheep are lying down on a bare rocky spot such as they like, chewing the cud in grassy peace. Cooking is going on, appetites growing keener every day. No lowlander can appreciate the mountain appetite, and the facility with which heavy food called 'grub' is disposed of. Eating, walking, resting, seem alike delightful, and one feels inclined to shout lustily on rising in the morning like a crowing cock. Sleep and digestion as clear as the air. Fine spicy plush boughs for bedding we shall have tonight, and a glorious lullaby from this cascading creek. Never was stream more fittingly named, for as far as I have traced it above and below our camp it is one continuous bouncing, dancing, white bloom of cascades. And at the very last unwearied it finishes its wild course in a grand leap of three hundred feet or more to the bottom of the main Yosemite canyon near the fall of Tamarack Creek, a few miles below the foot of the valley. These falls almost rival some of the far-famed Yosemite falls. Never shall I forget these glad cascade songs, the low booming, the roaring, the keen, silvery clashing of the cool water rushing exulting from form to form beneath irised spray; or in the deep still night seen white in the darkness, and its multitude of voices sounding still more impressively sublime. Here I find the little water ouzel as much at home as any linnet in a leafy grove, seeming to take the greater delight the more boisterous the stream. The dizzy precipices, the swift dashing energy displayed, and the thunder tones of the sheer falls are awe inspiring, but there is nothing awful about this little bird. Its song is sweet and low, and all its gestures, as it flits about amid the loud uproar, bespeak strength and peace and joy. Contemplating these darlings of Nature coming forth from spray-sprinkled nests on the brink of savage streams, Samson's riddle comes to mind, 'Out of the strong cometh forth sweetness.' A yet finer bloom is this little bird than the foam-bells in eddying pools. Gentle bird, a precious message you bring me. We may miss the meaning of the torrent, but thy sweet voice, only love is in it.

July 13 – Our course all day has been eastward over the rim of Yosemite Creek basin and down about halfway to the bottom, where we have encamped on a sheet of glacier-polished granite, a firm foundation for beds. Saw the tracks of a very large bear on the trail, and the Don talked of bears in general. I said I should like to see the maker of these immense tracks as he marched along, and follow him for days, without disturbing him, to learn something of the life of this master beast of the wilderness. Lambs, the Don told me, born in the lowland, that never saw or heard a bear, snort and run in terror when they catch the scent, showing how fully they have inherited a knowledge of their enemy. Hogs, mules, horses, and cattle are afraid of bears, and are seized with ungovernable terror when they approach, particularly hogs and mules. Hogs are frequently driven to pastures in the foothills of the Coast Range and Sierra where acorns are abundant, and are herded in droves of hundreds like sheep. When a bear comes to the range they promptly leave it, emigrating in a body, usually in the night time, the keepers being powerless to prevent; they thus show more sense than sheep, that simply scatter in the rocks and brush and await their fate. Mules flee like the wind with or without riders when they see a bear, and, if picketed, sometimes break their necks in trying to break their ropes, though I have not heard of bears killing mules or horses. Of hogs they are said to be particularly fond, bolting small ones, bones and all, without choice of parts. In particular, Mr Delaney assured me that all kinds of bears in the Sierra are very shy, and that hunters found far greater difficulty in getting within gunshot of them than of deer or indeed any other animal in the Sierra, and if I was anxious to see much of them I should have to wait and watch with endless Indian patience and pay no attention to anything else.

Night is coming on, the gray rock waves are growing dim in the twilight. How raw and young this region appears! Had the ice sheet that swept over it vanished but yesterday, its traces on the more resisting portions about our camp could hardly be more distinct than they now are. The horses and sheep and all of us, indeed, slipped on the smoothest places.

July 14 – How deathlike is sleep in this mountain air, and quick the awakening into newness of life! A calm dawn, yellow and purple, then floods of sun-gold, making everything tingle and glow.

In an hour or two we came to Yosemite Creek, the stream that makes the greatest of all the Yosemite falls. It is about forty feet wide at the Mono Trail crossing, and now about four feet in average depth, flowing about three miles an hour. The distance to the verge of the Yosemite wall, where it makes its tremendous plunge, is only about two miles from here. Calm, beautiful, and nearly silent, it glides with stately gestures, a dense growth of the slender two-leaved pine along its banks, and a fringe of willow, purple spirea, sedges, daisies, lilies, and columbines. Some of the sedges and willow boughs dip into the current, and just outside of the close ranks of trees there is a sunny flat of washed gravelly sand which seems to have been deposited by some ancient flood. It is covered with millions of erethrea, eriogonum, and oxytheca, with more flowers than leaves, forming an even growth, slightly dimpled and ruffled here and there by rosettes of *Spraguea umbellata*. Back of this flowery strip there is a wavy upsloping plain of solid granite, so smoothly ice-polished in many places that it glistens in the sun like glass. In shallow hollows there are patches of trees, mostly the rough form of the two-leaved pine, rather scrawny looking where there is little or no soil. Also a few junipers (*Juniperus occidentalis*), short and stout, with bright cinnamon-colored bark and gray foliage, standing alone mostly, on the sun-beaten pavement, safe from fire, clinging by slight joints – a sturdy storm-enduring mountaineer of a tree, living on sunshine and snow, maintaining tough health on this diet for perhaps more than a thousand years.

Up towards the head of the basin I see groups of domes rising above the wave-like ridges, and some picturesque castellated masses, and dark strips and patches of silver fir, indicating deposits of fertile soil. Would that I could command the time to study them! What rich excursions one could make in this well-defined basin! Its glacial inscriptions and sculptures, how marvelous they seem, how noble the studies they offer! I tremble with excitement in the dawn of these glorious mountain sublimities, but I can only gaze and wonder, and, like a child, gather here and there a lily, half hoping I may be able to study and learn in years to come.

The drivers and dogs had a lively, laborious time getting the sheep across the creek, the second large stream thus far that they have been compelled to cross without a bridge; the first being the North Fork of the Merced near Bower Cave. Men and dogs, shouting and barking, drove the timid, water-fearing creatures in a close crowd against the bank, but not one of the flock would launch away. While thus jammed, the Don and the shepherd rushed through the frightened crowd to stampede those in front, but this would only cause a break backward, and away they would scamper through the stream-bank trees and scatter over the rocky pavement. Then with the aid of the dogs the runaways would again be gathered and made to face the stream, and again the compacted mass would break away, amid wild shouting and barking that might well have disturbed the stream itself and marred the music of its falls, to which visitors no doubt from all quarters of the globe were listening. 'Hold them there! Now hold them there!' shouted the Don; 'the front ranks will soon tire of the pressure, and be glad to take to the water, then all will jump in and cross in a hurry.' But they did nothing of the kind; they only avoided the pressure by breaking back in scores and hundreds, leaving the beauty of the banks sadly trampled.

If only one could be got to cross over, all would make haste to follow; but that one could not be found. A lamb was caught, carried across, and tied to a bush on the opposite bank, where it cried piteously for its mother. But though greatly concerned, the mother only called it back. That play on maternal affection failed, and we began to fear that we should be forced to make a long roundabout drive and cross the wide-spread tributaries of the creek in succession. This would require several days, but it had its advantages, for I was eager to see the sources of so famous a stream. Don Quixote, however, determined that they must ford just here, and immediately began a sort of siege by cutting down slender pines on the bank and building a corral barely large enough to hold the flock when well pressed together. And as the stream would form one side of the corral he believed that they could easily be forced into the water.

In a few hours the inclosure was completed, and the silly animals were driven in and rammed hard against the brink of the ford. Then the Don, forcing a way through the compacted mass, pitched a few of the terrified unfortunates into the stream by main strength; but instead of crossing over, they swam about close to the bank, making desperate attempts to get back into the flock. Then a dozen or more were shoved off, and the Don, tall like a crane and a good natural wader, jumped in after them, seized a struggling wether, and dragged it to the opposite shore. But no sooner did he let it go than it jumped into the stream and swam back to its frightened companions in the corral, thus manifesting sheep-nature as unchangeable as gravitation. Pan with his pipes would have had no better luck, I fear. We were now pretty well baffled. The silly creatures would suffer any sort of death rather than cross that stream. Calling a council, the dripping Don declared that starvation was now the only likely scheme to try, and that we might as well camp here in comfort and let the besieged flock grow hungry and cool, and come to their senses, if they had any. In a few minutes after being thus let alone, an adventurer in the foremost rank plunged in and swam bravely to the farther shore. Then suddenly all rushed in pell-mell together, trampling one another under water, while we vainly tried to hold them back. The Don jumped into the thickest of the gasping, gurgling, drowning mass, and shoved them right and left as if each sheep was a piece of floating timber. The current also served to drift them apart; a long bent column was soon formed, and in a few minutes all were over and began baaing and feeding as if nothing out of the common had happened. That none were drowned seems wonderful. I fully expected that hundreds would gain the romantic fate of being swept into Yosemite over the highest waterfall in the world.

As the day was far spent, we camped a little way back from the ford, and let the dripping flock scatter and feed until sundown. The wool is dry now, and calm, cud-chewing peace has fallen on all the comfortable band, leaving no trace of the watery battle. I have seen fish driven out of the water with less ado than was made in driving these animals into it. Sheep brain must surely be poor stuff. Compare today's exhibition with the performances of deer swimming quietly across broad and rapid rivers, and from island to island in seas and lakes; or with dogs, or even with the squirrels that, as the story goes, cross the Mississippi River on selected chips, with tails for sails comfortably trimmed to the breeze. A sheep can hardly be called an animal; an entire flock is required to make one foolish individual.

Chapter 5

THE YOSEMITE

July 15 – Followed the Mono Trail up the eastern rim of the basin nearly to its summit, then turned off southward to a small shallow valley that extends to the edge of the Yosemite, which we reached about noon, and encamped. After luncheon I made haste to high ground, and from the top of the ridge on the west side of Indian Canyon gained the noblest view of the summit peaks I have ever yet enjoyed. Nearly all the upper basin of the Merced was displayed, with its sublime domes and canyons, dark upsweeping forests, and glorious array of white peaks deep in the sky, every feature glowing, radiating beauty that pours into our flesh and bones like heat rays from fire. Sunshine over all; no breath of wind to stir the brooding calm. Never before had I seen so glorious a landscape, so boundless an affluence of sublime mountain beauty. The most extravagant description I might give of this view to anyone who has not seen similar landscapes with his own eyes would not so much as hint at its grandeur and the spiritual glow that covered it. I shouted and gesticulated in a wild burst of ecstasy, much to the astonishment of St Bernard Carlo, who came running up to me, manifesting in his intelligent eyes a puzzled concern that was very ludicrous, which had the effect of bringing me to my senses. A brown bear, too, it would seem, had been a spectator of the show I had made of myself, for I had gone but a few yards when I started one from a thicket of brush. He evidently considered me dangerous, for he ran away very fast, tumbling over the tops of the tangled manzanita bushes in his haste. Carlo drew back, with his ears depressed as if afraid, and kept looking me in the face, as if expecting me to pursue and shoot, for he had seen many a bear battle in his day.

Following the ridge which made a gradual descent to the

south, I came at length to the brow of that massive cliff that
stands between Indian Canyon and Yosemite Falls, and here
the far-famed valley came suddenly into view throughout
almost its whole extent. The noble walls – sculptured into
endless variety of domes and gables, spires and battlements
and plain mural precipices – all a-tremble with the thunder
tones of the falling water. The level bottom seemed to be
dressed like a garden – sunny meadows here and there, and
groves of pine and oak; the river of Mercy sweeping in majesty
through the midst of them and flashing back the sunbeams.
The great Tissiack, or Half-Dome, rising at the upper end of
the valley to a height of nearly a mile, is nobly proportioned
and life-like, the most impressive of all the rocks, holding the
eye in devout admiration, calling it back again and again from
falls or meadows, or even the mountains beyond – marvelous
cliffs, marvelous in sheer dizzy depth and sculpture, types of
endurance. Thousands of years have they stood in the sky
exposed to rain, snow, frost, earthquake and avalanche, yet
they still wear the bloom of youth.

I rambled along the valley rim to the westward; most of it is
rounded off on the very brink, so that it is not easy to find
places where one may look clear down the face of the wall to
the bottom. When such places were found, and I had cautiously set my feet and drawn my body erect, I could not help
fearing a little that the rock might split off and let me down,
and what a down – more than three thousand feet. Still my
limbs did not tremble, nor did I feel the least uncertainty as to
the reliance to be placed on them. My only fear was that a flake
of the granite, which in some places showed joints more or less
open and running parallel with the face of the cliff, might give
way. After withdrawing from such places, excited with the
view I had got, I would say to myself, 'Now don't go out on the
verge again.' But in the face of Yosemite scenery cautious
remonstrance is vain; under its spell one's body seems to go
where it likes with a will over which we seem to have scarce
any control.

After a mile or so of this memorable cliff work I approached
Yosemite Creek, admiring its easy, graceful, confident gestures
as it comes bravely forward in its narrow channel, singing the
last of its mountain songs on its way to its fate – a few rods
more over the shining granite, then down half a mile in snowy

foam to another world, to be lost in the Merced, where climate, vegetation, inhabitants, all are different. Emerging from its last gorge, it glides in wide lace-like rapids down a smooth incline into a pool where it seems to rest and compose its gray, agitated waters before taking the grand plunge, then slowly slipping over the lip of the pool basin, it descends another glossy slope with rapidly accelerated speed to the brink of the tremendous cliff, and with sublime, fateful confidence springs out free in the air.

I took off my shoes and stockings and worked my way cautiously down alongside the rushing flood, keeping my feet and hands pressed firmly on the polished rock. The booming, roaring water, rushing past close to my head, was very exciting. I had expected that the sloping apron would terminate with the perpendicular wall of the valley, and that from the foot of it, where it is less steeply inclined, I should be able to lean far enough out to see the forms and behavior of the fall all the way down to the bottom. But I found that there was yet another small brow over which I could not see, and which appeared to be too steep for mortal feet. Scanning it keenly, I discovered a narrow shelf about three inches wide on the very brink, just wide enough for a rest for one's heels. But there seemed to be no way of reaching it over so steep a brow. At length, after careful scrutiny of the surface, I found an irregular edge of a flake of the rock some distance back from the margin of the torrent. If I was to get down to the brink at all that rough edge, which might offer slight finger holds, was the only way. But the slope beside it looked dangerously smooth and steep, and the swift roaring flood beneath, overhead, and beside me was very nerve-trying. I therefore concluded not to venture farther, but did nevertheless. Tufts of artemisia were growing in clefts of the rock near by, and I filled my mouth with the bitter leaves, hoping they might help to prevent giddiness. Then, with a caution not known in ordinary circumstances, I crept down safely to the little ledge, got my heels well planted on it, then shuffled in a horizontal direction twenty or thirty feet until close to the outplunging current, which, by the time it had descended thus far, was already white. Here I obtained a perfectly free view down into the heart of the snowy, chanting throng of comet-like streamers, into which the body of the fall soon separates.

While perched on that narrow niche I was not distinctly conscious of danger. The tremendous grandeur of the fall in form and sound and motion, acting at close range, smothered the sense of fear, and in such places one's body takes keen care for safety on its own account. How long I remained down there, or how I returned, I can hardly tell. Anyhow I had a glorious time, and got back to camp about dark, enjoying triumphant exhilaration soon followed by dull weariness. Hereafter I'll try to keep from such extravagant, nerve-straining places. Yet such a day is well worth venturing for. My first view of the High Sierra, first view looking down into Yosemite, the death song of Yosemite Creek, and its flight over the vast cliff, each one of these is of itself enough for a great life-long landscape fortune – a most memorable day of days – enjoyment enough to kill if that were possible.

July 16 – My enjoyments yesterday afternoon, especially at the head of the fall, were too great for good sleep. Kept starting up last night in a nervous tremor, half awake, fancying that the foundation of the mountain we were camped on had given way and was falling into Yosemite Valley. In vain I roused myself to make a new beginning for sound sleep. The nerve strain had been too great, and again and again I dreamed I was rushing through the air above a glorious avalanche of water and rocks. One time, springing to my feet, I said, 'This time it is real – all must die, and where could mountaineer find a more glorious death!'

Left camp soon after sunrise for an all day ramble eastward. Crossed the head of Indian Basin, forested with *Abies magnifica*, underbrush mostly *Ceanothus cordulatus* and manzanita, a mixture not easily trampled over or penetrated, for the ceanothus is thorny and grows in dense snow-pressed masses, and the manzanita has exceedingly crooked, stubborn branches. From the head of the canyon continued on past North Dome into the basin of Dome or Porcupine Creek. Here are many fine meadows imbedded in the woods, gay with *Lilium parvum* and its companions; the elevation, about eight thousand feet, seems to be best suited for it – saw specimens that were a foot or two higher than my head. Had more magnificent views of the upper mountains, and of the great South Dome, said to be the grandest rock in the world. Well it may be, since it is of such noble dimensions and sculpture. A wonderfully impressive monument, its lines exquisite in fineness, and though sublime in size, is finished like the finest work of art, and seems to be alive.

July 17 – A new camp was made today in a magnificent silver fir grove at the head of a small stream that flows into Yosemite by way of Indian Canyon. Here we intend to stay several weeks – a fine location from which to make excursions about the great valley and its fountains. Glorious days I'll have sketching, pressing plants, studying the wonderful topography, and the wild animals, our happy fellow mortals and neighbors. But the vast mountains in the distance, shall I ever know them, shall I be allowed to enter into their midst and dwell with them?

We were pelted about noon by a short, heavy rain-storm, sublime thunder reverberating among the mountains and canyons – some strokes near, crashing, ringing in the tense crisp air with startling keenness, while the distant peaks loomed gloriously through the cloud fringes and sheets of rain. Now the storm is past, and the fresh washed air is full of the essences of the flower gardens and groves. Winter storms in Yosemite must be glorious. May I see them!

Have got my bed made in our new camp – plushy, sumptuous, and deliciously fragrant, most of it *magnifica* fir plumes, of course, with a variety of sweet flowers in the pillow. Hope to sleep tonight without tottering nerve-dreams. Watched a deer eating ceanothus leaves and twigs.

July 18 – Slept pretty well; the valley walls did not seem to fall, though I still fancied myself at the brink, alongside the white, plunging flood, especially when half asleep. Strange the danger of that adventure should be more troublesome now that I am in the bosom of the peaceful woods, a mile or more from the fall, than it was while I was on the brink of it.

Bears seem to be common here, judging by their tracks. About noon we had another rain-storm with keen startling thunder, the metallic, ringing, clashing, clanging notes gradually fading into low bass rolling and muttering in the distance. For a few minutes the rain came in a grand torrent like a waterfall, then hail; some of the hailstones an inch in diameter, hard, icy, and irregular in form, like those oftentimes seen in Wisconsin. Carlo watched them with intelligent astonishment as they came pelting and thrashing through the quivering branches of the trees. The cloud scenery sublime. Afternoon calm, sunful, and clear, with delicious freshness and fragrance from the firs and flowers and steaming ground.

July 19 – Watching the daybreak and sunrise. The pale rose and purple sky changing softly to daffodil yellow and white, sunbeams pouring through the passes between the peaks and over the Yosemite domes, making their edges burn; the silver firs in the middle ground catching the glow on their spiry tops, and our camp grove fills and thrills with the glorious light. Everything awakening alert and joyful; the birds begin to stir and innumerable insect people. Deer quietly withdraw into leafy hiding-places in the chaparral; the dew vanishes, flowers spread their petals, every pulse beats high, every life cell rejoices, the very rocks seem to thrill with life. The whole landscape glows like a human face in a glory of enthusiasm, and the blue sky, pale around the horizon, bends peacefully down over all like one vast flower.

About noon, as usual, big bossy cumuli began to grow above the forest, and the rain storm pouring from them is the most imposing I have yet seen. The silvery zigzag lightning lances are longer than usual, and the thunder gloriously impressive, keen, crashing, intensely concentrated, speaking with such tremendous energy it would seem that an entire mountain is being shattered at every stroke, but probably only a few trees are being shattered, many of which I have seen on my walks hereabouts strewing the ground. At last the clear ringing strokes are succeeded by deep low tones that grow gradually fainter as they roll afar into the recesses of the echoing mountains, where they seem to be welcomed home. Then another and another peal, or rather crashing, splintering stroke, follows in quick succession, perchance splitting some giant pine or fir from top to bottom into long rails and slivers, and scattering them to all points of the compass. Now comes the rain, with corresponding extravagant grandeur, covering the ground high and low with a sheet of flowing water, a transparent film fitted like a skin upon the rugged anatomy of the landscape, making the rocks glitter and glow, gathering in the ravines, flooding the streams, and making them shout and boom in reply to the thunder.

How interesting to trace the history of a single raindrop! It is not long, geologically speaking, as we have seen, since the first raindrops fell on the newborn leafless Sierra landscapes. How different the lot of these falling now! Happy the showers that fall on so fair a wilderness – scarce a single drop can fail to find a beautiful spot – on the tops of the peaks, on the shining glacier pavements, on the great smooth domes, on forests and gardens and brushy moraines, plashing, glinting, pattering, laving. Some go to the high snowy fountains to swell their well-saved stores; some into the lakes, washing the mountain windows, patting their smooth glassy levels, making dimples and bubbles and spray; some into the water-falls and cascades, as if eager to join in their dance and song and beat their foam yet finer; good luck and good work for the happy mountain raindrops, each one of them a high waterfall in itself, descending from the cliffs and hollows of the clouds to the cliffs and hollows of the rocks, out of the sky-thunder into the thunder of the falling rivers. Some, falling on meadows and bogs, creep silently out of sight to the grass roots, hiding softly as in a nest, slipping, oozing hither, thither, seeking and finding their appointed work. Some, descending through the spires of the woods, sift spray through the shining needles, whispering peace and good cheer to each one of them. Some drops with happy aim glint on the sides of crystals – quartz, hornblende, garnet, zircon, tourmaline, feldspar – patter on grains of gold and heavy way-worn nuggets; some, with blunt plap-plap and low bass drumming, fall on the broad leaves of veratrum, saxifrage, cypripedium. Some happy drops fall straight into the cups of flowers, kissing the lips of lilies. How far they have to go, how many cups to fill, great and small, cells too small to be seen, cups holding half a drop as well as lake basins between the hills, each replenished with equal care, every drop in all the blessed throng a silvery newborn star with lake and river, garden and grove, valley and mountain, all that the landscape holds reflected in its crystal depths, God's messenger, angel of love sent on its way with majesty and pomp and display of power that make man's greatest shows ridiculous.

Now the storm is over, the sky is clear, the last rolling thunder-wave is spent on the peaks, and where are the raindrops now – what has become of all the shining throng? In winged vapor rising some are already hastening back to the sky, some have gone into the plants, creeping through invisible doors into the round rooms of cells, some are locked in crystals of ice, some in rock crystals, some in porous moraines to keep their small springs flowing, some have gone journeying on in the rivers to join the larger raindrop of the ocean. From form to form, beauty to beauty, ever changing, never resting, all are speeding on with love's enthusiasm, singing with the stars the eternal song of creation.

July 20 – Fine calm morning; air tense and clear; not the slightest breeze astir; everything shining, the rocks with wet crystals, the plants with dew, each receiving its portion of irised dewdrops and sunshine like living creatures getting their breakfast, their dew manna coming down from the starry sky like swarms of smaller stars. How wondrous fine are the particles in showers of dew, thousands required for a single drop, growing in the dark as silently as the grass! What pains are taken to keep this wilderness in health – showers of snow, showers of rain, showers of dew, floods of light, floods of invisible vapor, clouds, winds, all sorts of weather, interaction of plant on plant, animal on animal, etc., beyond thought! How fine Nature's methods! How deeply with beauty is beauty overlaid! the ground covered with crystals, the crystals with mosses and lichens and low-spreading grasses and flowers, these with larger plants leaf over leaf with ever-changing color and form, the broad palms of the firs outspread over these, the azure dome over all like a bell-flower, and star above star.

Yonder stands the South Dome, its crown high above our camp, though its base is four thousand feet below us; a most noble rock, it seems full of thought, clothed with living light, no sense of dead stone about it, all spiritualized, neither heavy looking nor light, steadfast in serene strength like a god.

Our shepherd is a queer character and hard to place in this wilderness. His bed is a hollow made in red dry-rot punky dust beside a log which forms a portion of the south wall of the corral. Here he lies with his wonderful everlasting clothing on, wrapped in a red blanket, breathing not only the dust of the decayed wood but also that of the corral, as if determined to

take ammoniacal snuff all night after chewing tobacco all day.
Following the sheep he carries a heavy six-shooter swung from
his belt on one side and his luncheon on the other. The ancient
cloth in which the meat, fresh from the frying-pan, is tied
serves as a filter through which the clear fat and gravy juices
drip down on his right hip and leg in clustering stalactites. This
oleaginous formation is soon broken up, however, and diffused and rubbed evenly into his scanty apparel, by sitting
down, rolling over, crossing his legs while resting on logs, etc.,
making shirt and trousers water-tight and shiny. His trousers,
in particular, have become so adhesive with the mixed fat and
resin that pine needles, thin flakes and fibres of bark, hair,
mica scales and minute grains of quartz, hornblende, etc.,
feathers, seed wings, moth and butterfly wings, legs and
antennae of innumerable insects, or even whole insects such
as the small beetles, moths and mosquitoes, with flower petals,
pollen dust and indeed bits of all plants, animals, and minerals
of the region adhere to them and are safely imbedded, so that
though far from being a naturalist he collects fragmentary
specimens of everything and becomes richer than he knows.
His specimens are kept passably fresh, too, by the purity of the
air and the resiny bituminous beds into which they are pressed.
Man is a microcosm, at least our shepherd is, or rather his
trousers. These precious overalls are never taken off, and
nobody knows how old they are, though one may guess by
their thickness and concentric structure. Instead of wearing
thin they wear thick, and in their stratification have no small
geological significance.

Besides herding the sheep, Billy is the butcher, while I have
agreed to wash the few iron and tin utensils and make the
bread. Then, these small duties done, by the time the sun is
fairly above the mountain-tops I am beyond the flock, free to
rove and revel in the wilderness all the big immortal days.

Sketching on the North Dome. It commands views of nearly
all the valley besides a few of the high mountains. I would fain
draw everything in sight – rock, tree, and leaf. But little can I
do beyond mere outlines – marks with meanings like words,
readable only to myself – yet I sharpen my pencils and work on
as if others might possibly be benefited. Whether these picture
sheets are to vanish like fallen leaves or go to friends like
letters, matters not much; for little can they tell to those who

have not themselves seen similar wildness, and like a language have learned it. No pain here, no dull empty hours, no fear of the past, no fear of the future. These blessed mountains are so compactly filled with God's beauty, no petty personal hope or experience has room to be. Drinking this champagne water is pure pleasure, so is breathing the living air, and every movement of limbs is pleasure, while the whole body seems to feel beauty when exposed to it as it feels the campfire or sunshine, entering not by the eyes alone, but equally through all one's flesh like radiant heat, making a passionate ecstatic pleasure glow not explainable. One's body then seems homogeneous throughout, sound as a crystal.

Perched like a fly on this Yosemite dome, I gaze and sketch and bask, oftentimes settling down into dumb admiration without definite hope of ever learning much, yet with the longing, unresting effort that lies at the door of hope, humbly prostrate before the vast display of God's power, and eager to offer self-denial and renunciation with eternal toil to learn any lesson in the divine manuscript.

It is easier to feel than to realize, or in any way explain Yosemite grandeur. The magnitudes of the rocks and trees and streams are so delicately harmonized they are mostly hidden. Sheer precipices three thousand feet high are fringed with tall trees growing close like grass on the brow of a lowland hill, and extending along the feet of these precipices a ribbon of meadow a mile wide and seven or eight long, that seems like a strip a farmer might mow in less than a day. Waterfalls, five hundred to one or two thousand feet high, are so subordinated to the mighty cliffs over which they pour that they seem like wisps of smoke, gentle as floating clouds, though their voices fill the valley and make the rocks tremble. The mountains, too, along the eastern sky, and the domes in front of them, and the succession of smooth rounded waves between, swelling higher, higher, with dark woods in their hollows, serene in massive exuberant bulk and beauty, tend yet more to hide the grandeur of the Yosemite temple and make it appear as a subdued subordinate feature of the vast harmonious landscape. Thus every attempt to appreciate any one feature is beaten down by the overwhelming influence of all the others. And, as if this were not enough, lo! in the sky arises another mountain range with topography as rugged and substantial-looking as the one beneath it – snowy peaks and domes and shadowy Yosemite valleys – another version of the snowy Sierra, a new creation heralded by a thunder-storm. How fiercely, devoutly wild is Nature in the midst of her beauty-loving tenderness! – painting lilies, watering them, caressing them with gentle hand, going from flower to flower like a gardener while building rock mountains and cloud mountains full of lightning and rain. Gladly we run for shelter beneath an overhanging cliff and examine the reassuring ferns and mosses, gentle love tokens growing in cracks and chinks. Daisies, too, and ivesias, confiding wild children of light, too small to fear. To these one's heart goes home, and the voices of the storm become gentle. Now the sun breaks forth and fragrant steam arises. The birds are out singing on the edges of the groves. The west is flaming in gold and purple, ready for the ceremony of the sunset, and back I go to camp with my notes and pictures, the best of them printed in my mind as dreams. A fruitful day, without measured beginning or ending. A terrestrial eternity. A gift of good God.

Wrote to my mother and a few friends, mountain hints to each. They seem as near as if within voice-reach or touch. The deeper the solitude the less the sense of loneliness, and the nearer our friends. Now bread and tea, fir bed and goodnight to Carlo, a look at the sky lilies, and death sleep until the dawn of another Sierra tomorrow.

July 21 – Sketching on the Dome – no rain; clouds at noon about quarter filled the sky, casting shadows with fine effect on the white mountains at the heads of the streams, and a soothing cover over the gardens during the warm hours.

Saw a common house fly and a grasshopper and a brown bear. The fly and grasshopper paid me a merry visit on the top of the Dome, and I paid a visit to the bear in the middle of a small garden meadow between the Dome and the camp where he was standing alert among the flowers as if willing to be seen to advantage. I had not gone more than half a mile from camp this morning, when Carlo, who was trotting on a few yards ahead of me, came to a sudden, cautious standstill. Down went tail and ears, and forward went his knowing nose, while he seemed to be saying 'Ha, what's this? A bear, I guess,' Then a cautious advance of a few steps, setting his feet down softly like a hunting cat, and questioning the air as to the scent he had caught until all doubt vanished. Then he came back to me, looked me in the face, and with his speaking eyes reported a bear near by; then led on softly, careful, like an experienced hunter, not to make the slightest noise, and frequently looking back as if whispering 'Yes, it's a bear, come and I'll show you.' Presently we came to where the sunbeams were streaming through between the purple shafts of the firs, which showed that we were nearing an open spot, and here Carlo came behind me, evidently sure that the bear was very near. So I crept to a low ridge of moraine boulders on the edge of a narrow garden meadow, and in this meadow I felt pretty sure the bear must be. I was anxious to get a good look at the sturdy mountaineer without alarming him; so drawing myself up noiselessly back of one of the largest of the trees I peered past its bulging buttresses, exposing only a part of my head, and there stood neighbor Bruin within a stone's throw, his hips covered by tall grass and flowers, and his front feet on the trunk of a fir that had fallen out into the meadow, which raised his head so high that he seemed to be standing erect. He had not yet seen me, but was looking and listening attentively, showing that in some way he was aware of our approach. I watched his gestures and tried to make the most of my opportunity to learn what I could about him, fearing he would catch sight of me and run away. For I had been told that this sort of bear, the cinnamon, always ran from his bad brother man, never showing fight unless wounded or in defense of young. He made a telling picture standing alert in the sunny forest garden. How well he played his part, harmonizing in bulk and color and shaggy hair with the trunks of the trees and lush vegetation, as natural a feature as any other in the land-scape. After examining at leisure, noting the sharp muzzle thrust inquiringly forward, the long shaggy hair on his broad chest, the stiff erect ears nearly buried in hair, and the slow heavy way he moved his head, I thought I should like to see his gait in running, so I made a sudden rush at him, shouting and swinging my hat to frighten him, expecting to see him make haste to get away. But to my dismay he did not run or show any sign of running. On the contrary, he stood his ground ready to fight and defend himself, lowered his head, thrust it forward, and looked sharply and fiercely at me. Then I suddenly began to fear that upon me would fall the work of running; but I was afraid to run, and therefore, like the bear, held my ground. We stood staring at each other in solemn silence within a dozen yards or thereabouts, while I fervently hoped that the power of the human eye over wild beasts would prove as great as it is said to be. How long our awfully strenuous interview lasted, I don't know; but at length in the slow fullness of time he pulled his huge paws down off the log, and with magnificent deliberation turned and walked leisurely up the meadow, stopping frequently to look back over his shoulder to see whether I was pursuing him, then moving on again, evidently neither fearing me very much nor trusting me. He was probably about five hundred pounds in weight, a broad rusty bundle of ungovernable wildness, a happy fellow whose lines have fallen in pleasant places. The flowery glade in which I saw him so well, framed like a picture, is one of the best of all I have yet discovered, a conservatory of Nature's precious plant people. Tall lilies were swinging their bells over that bear's back, with geraniums, larkspurs, columbines, and daisies brushing against his sides. A place for angels, one would say, instead of bears.

In the great canyons Bruin reigns supreme. Happy fellow, whom no famine can reach while one of his thousand kinds of food is spared him. His bread is sure at all seasons, ranged on the mountain shelves like stores in a pantry. From one to the other, up or down he climbs, tasting and enjoying each in turn in different climates, as if he had journeyed thousands of miles to other countries north or south to enjoy their varied productions. I should like to know my hairy brothers better – though after this particular Yosemite bear, my very neighbor, had sauntered out of sight this morning, I reluctantly went back to camp for the Don's rifle to shoot him, if necessary, in defense of the flock. Fortunately I couldn't find him, and after tracking him a mile or two towards Mt. Hoffman I bade him Godspeed and gladly returned to my work on the Yosemite dome.

The house fly also seemed at home and buzzed about me as I sat sketching, and enjoying my bear interview now it was over. I wonder what draws house flies so far up the mountains, heavy, gross feeders as they are, sensitive to cold, and fond of domestic ease. How have they been distributed from continent to continent, across seas and deserts and mountain chains, usually so influential in determining boundaries of species both of plants and animals. Beetles and butterflies are sometimes restricted to small areas. Each mountain in a range, and even the different zones of a mountain, may have its own peculiar species. But the house fly seems to be everywhere. I wonder if any island in mid-ocean is flyless. The bluebottle is abundant in these Yosemite woods, ever ready with his marvelous store of eggs to make all dead flesh fly. Bumblebees are here, and are well fed on boundless stores of nectar and pollen. The honey-bee, though abundant in the foothills, has not yet got so high. It is only a few years since the first swarm was brought to California.

A queer fellow and a jolly fellow is the grasshopper. Up the mountains he comes on excursions, how high I don't know, but at least as far and high as Yosemite tourists. I was much interested with the hearty enjoyment of the one that danced and sang for me on the Dome this afternoon. He seemed brimful of glad, hilarious energy, manifested by springing into the air to a height of twenty or thirty feet, then diving and springing up again and making a sharp musical rattle just as the lowest point in the descent was reached. Up and down a dozen times or so he danced and sang, then alighted to rest, then up and at it again. The curves he described in the air in diving and rattling resembled those made by cords hanging loosely and attached at the same height at the ends, the loops nearly covering each other. Braver, heartier, keener, carefree enjoyment of life I have never seen or heard in any creature, great or small. The life of this comic redlegs, the mountain's merriest child, seems to be made up of pure, condensed gayety. The Douglas squirrel is the only living creature that I can compare him with in exuberant, rollicking, irrepressible jollity. Wonderful that these sublime mountains are so loudly cheered and brightened by a creature so queer. Nature in him seems to be snapping her fingers in the face of all earthy dejection and melancholy with a boyish hip-hip-hurrah. How the sound is made I do not understand. When he was on the ground he made not the slightest noise, nor when he was simply flying from place to place, but only when diving in curves, the motion seeming to be required for the sound; for the more vigorous the diving the more energetic the corresponding outbursts of jolly rattling. I tried to observe him closely while he was resting in the intervals of his performances; but he would not allow a near approach, always getting his jumping legs ready to spring for immediate flight, and keeping his eyes on me. A fine sermon the little fellow danced for me on the Dome, a likely place to look for sermons in stones, but not for grasshopper sermons. A large and imposing pulpit for so small a preacher. No danger of weakness in the knees of the world while Nature can spring such a rattle as this. Even the bear did not express for me the mountain's wild health and strength and happiness so tellingly as did this comical little hopper. No cloud of care in his day, no winter of discontent in sight. To him every day is a holiday; and when at length his sun sets, I fancy he will cuddle down on the forest floor and die like the leaves and flowers, and like them leave no unsightly remains calling for burial.

Sundown, and I must to camp. Goodnight, friends three – brown bear, rugged boulder of energy in groves and gardens fair as Eden; restless fussy fly with gauzy wings stirring the air around all the world; and grasshopper, crisp electric spark of joy enlivening the massy sublimity of the mountains like the laugh of a child. Thank you, thank you all three for your quickening company. Heaven guide every wing and leg. Goodnight, friends three, goodnight.

July 22 – A fine specimen of the blacktailed deer went bounding past camp this morning. A buck with wide spread of antlers, showing admirable vigor and grace. Wonderful the beauty, strength, and graceful movements of animals in wildernesses, cared for by Nature only, when our experience with domestic animals would lead us to fear that all the so-called neglected wild beasts would degenerate. Yet the upshot of Nature's method of breeding and teaching seems to lead to excellence of every sort. Deer, like all wild animals, are as clean as plants. The beauties of their gestures and attitudes, alert or in repose, surprise yet more than their bounding exuberant strength. Every movement and posture is graceful, the very poetry of manners and motion. Mother Nature is too often spoken of as in reality no mother at all. Yet how wisely, sternly, tenderly she loves and looks after her children in all sorts of weather and wildernesses. The more I see of deer the more I admire them as mountaineers. They make their way into the heart of the roughest solitudes with smooth reserve of strength, through dense belts of brush and forest encumbered with fallen trees and boulder piles, across canyons, roaring streams, and snow-fields, ever showing forth beauty and courage. Over nearly all the continent the deer find homes. In the Florida savannas and hummocks, in the Canada woods, in the far north, roaming over mossy tundras, swimming lakes and rivers and arms of the sea from island to island washed with waves, or climbing rocky mountains, everywhere healthy and able, adding beauty to every landscape – a truly admirable creature and great credit to Nature.

Have been sketching a silver fir that stands on a granite ridge a few hundred yards to the eastward of camp – a fine tree with a particular snow-storm story to tell. It is about one hundred feet high, growing on bare rock, thrusting its roots into a weathered joint less than an inch wide, and bulging out to form a base to bear its weight. The storm came from the north while it was young and broke it down nearly to the ground, as is shown by the old, dead, weather-beaten top leaning out from the living trunk built up from a new shoot below the break. The annual rings of the trunk that have overgrown the dead sapling tell the year of the storm. Wonderful that a side branch forming a portion of one of the level collars that encircle the trunk of this species (*Abies magnifica*) should bend upward, grow erect, and take the place of the lost axis to form a new tree.

Many others, pines as well as firs, bear testimony to the crushing severity of this particular storm. Trees, some of them fifty to seventy-five feet high, were bent to the ground and buried like grass, whole groves vanishing as if the forest had been cleared away, leaving not a branch or needle visible until the spring thaw. Then the more elastic undamaged saplings rose again, aided by the wind, some reaching a nearly erect attitude, others remaining more or less bent, while those with broken backs endeavored to specialize a side branch below the break and make a leader of it to form a new axis of development. It is as if a man, whose back was broken or nearly so and who was compelled to go bent, should find a branch backbone sprouting straight up from below the break and should gradually develop new arms and shoulders and head, while the old damaged portion of his body died.

Grand white cloud mountains and domes created about

noon as usual, ridges and ranges of endless variety, as if Nature dearly loved this sort of work, doing it again and again nearly every day with infinite industry, and producing beauty that never palls. A few zigzags of lightning, five minutes' shower, then a gradual wilting and clearing.

July 23 – Another midday cloudland, displaying power and beauty that one never wearies in beholding, but hopelessly unsketchable and untellable. What can poor mortals say about clouds? While a description of their huge glowing domes and ridges, shadowy gulfs and canyons, and feather-edged ravines is being tried, they vanish, leaving no visible ruins. Nevertheless, these fleeting sky mountains are as substantial and significant as the more lasting upheavals of granite beneath them. Both alike are built up and die, and in God's calendar difference of duration is nothing. We can only dream about them in wondering, worshiping admiration, happier than we dare tell even to friends who see farthest in sympathy, glad to know that not a crystal or vapor particle of them, hard or soft, is lost; that they sink and vanish only to rise again and again in higher and higher beauty. As to our own work, duty, influence, etc., concerning which so much fussy pother is made, it will not fail of its due effect, though, like a lichen on a stone, we keep silent.

July 24 – Clouds at noon occupying about half the sky gave half an hour of heavy rain to wash one of the cleanest landscapes in the world. How well it is washed! The sea is hardly less dusty than the ice-burnished pavements and ridges, domes and canyons, and summit peaks plashed with snow like waves with foam. How fresh the woods are and calm after the last films of clouds have been wiped from the sky! A few minutes ago every tree was excited, bowing to the roaring storm, waving, swirling, tossing their branches in glorious enthusiasm like worship. But though to the outer ear these trees are now silent, their songs never cease. Every hidden cell is throbbing with music and life, every fibre thrilling like harp strings, while incense is ever flowing from the balsam bells and leaves. No wonder the hills and groves were God's first temples, and the more they are cut down and hewn into cathedrals and churches, the farther off and dimmer seems the Lord himself.

The same may be said of stone temples. Yonder, to the eastward of our camp grove, stands one of Nature's cathedrals, hewn from the living rock, almost conventional in form, about two thousand feet high, nobly adorned with spires and pinnacles, thrilling under floods of sunshine as if alive like a grovetemple, and well named 'Cathedral Peak.' Even Shepherd Billy turns at times to this wonderful mountain building, though apparently deaf to all stone sermons. Snow that refused to melt in fire would hardly be more wonderful than unchanging dullness in the rays of God's beauty. I have been trying to get him to walk to the brink of Yosemite for a view, offering to watch the sheep for a day, while he should enjoy what tourists come from all over the world to see. But though within a mile of the famous valley, he will not go to it even out of mere curiosity. 'What,' says he, 'is Yosemite but a canyon – a lot of rocks – a hole in the ground – a place dangerous about falling into – a d–d good place to keep away from.' 'But think of the waterfalls, Billy – just think of that big stream we crossed the other day, falling half a mile through the air – think of that, and the sound it makes. You can hear it now like the roar of the sea.' Thus I pressed Yosemite upon him like a missionary offering the gospel, but he would have none of it. 'I should be afraid to look over so high a wall,' he said. 'It would make my head swim. There is nothing worth seeing anyway, only rocks, and I see plenty of them here. Tourists that spend their money to see rocks and falls are fools, that's all. You can't humbug me. I've been in this country too long for that.' Such souls, I suppose, are asleep, or smothered and befogged beneath mean pleasures and cares.

July 25 – Another cloudland. Some clouds have an over-ripe decaying look, watery and bedraggled and drawn out into wind-torn shreds and patches, giving the sky a littered appearance; not so these Sierra summer midday clouds. All are beautiful with smooth definite outlines and curves like those of glacier-polished domes. They begin to grow about eleven o'clock, and seem so wonderfully near and clear from this high camp one is tempted to try to climb them and trace the streams that pour like cataracts from their shadowy fountains. The rain to which they give birth is often very heavy, a sort of waterfall as imposing as if pouring from rock mountains.

Never in all my travels have I found anything more truly novel and interesting than these midday mountains of the sky, their fine tones of color, majestic visible growth, and everchanging scenery and general effects, though mostly as well let alone as far as description goes. I oftentimes think of Shelley's cloud poem, 'I sift the snow on the mountains below.'

Chapter 6

MOUNT HOFFMAN AND LAKE TENAYA

July 26 – Ramble to the summit of Mt. Hoffman, eleven thousand feet high, the highest point in life's journey my feet have yet touched. And what glorious landscapes are about me, new plants, new animals, new crystals, and multitudes of new mountains far higher than Hoffman, towering in glorious array along the axis of the range, serene, majestic, snow-laden, sundrenched, vast domes and ridges shining below them, forests, lakes, and meadows in the hollows, the pure blue bell-flower sky brooding them all – a glory day of admission into a new realm of wonders as if Nature had wooingly whispered, 'Come higher.' What questions I asked, and how little I know of all the vast show, and how eagerly, tremulously hopeful of some day knowing more, learning the meaning of these divine symbols crowded together on this wondrous page.

Mt. Hoffman is the highest part of a ridge or spur about fourteen miles from the axis of the main range, perhaps a remnant brought into relief and isolated by unequal denudation. The southern slopes shed their waters into Yosemite Valley by Tenaya and Dome Creeks, the northern in part into the Tuolumne River, but mostly into the Merced by Yosemite Creek. The rock is mostly granite, with some small piles and crests rising here and there in picturesque pillared and castellated remnants of red metamorphic slates. Both the granite and slates are divided by joints, making them separable into blocks like the stones of artificial masonry, suggesting the Scripture 'He hath builded the mountains.' Great banks of snow and ice are piled in hollows on the cool precipitous north side forming the highest perennial sources of Yosemite Creek. The southern slopes are much more gradual and accessible. Narrow slot-like gorges extend across the summit at right angles, which look like lanes, formed evidently by the erosion of less resisting beds. They are usually called 'devil's slides,' though they lie far above the region usually haunted by the devil; for though we read that he once climbed an exceeding high mountain, he cannot be much of a mountaineer, for his tracks are seldom seen above the timberline.

The broad gray summit is barren and desolate-looking in general views, wasted by ages of gnawing storms; but looking at the surface in detail, one finds it covered by thousands and millions of charming plants with leaves and flowers so small they form no mass of color visible at a distance of a few hundred yards. Beds of azure daisies smile confidingly in moist hollows, and along the banks of small rills, with several species of eriogonum, silky-leaved ivesia, pentstemon, orthocarpus, and patches of *Primula suffruticosa*, a beautiful shrubby species. Here also I found bryanthus, a charming heathwort covered with purple flowers and dark green foliage like heather, and three trees new to me – a hemlock and two pines. The hemlock (*Tsuga Mertensiana*) is the most beautiful conifer I have ever seen; the branches and also the main axis droop in a singularly graceful way, and the dense foliage covers the delicate, sensitive, swaying branchlets all around. It is now in full bloom, and the flowers, together with thousands of last season's cones still clinging to the drooping sprays, display wonderful wealth of color, brown and purple and blue. Gladly I climbed the first tree I found to revel in the midst of it. How the touch of the flowers makes one's flesh tingle! The pistillate are dark, rich purple, and almost translucent, the staminate blue – a vivid, pure tone of blue like the mountain sky – the most uncommonly beautiful of all the Sierra tree flowers I have seen. How wonderful that, with all its delicate feminine grace and beauty of form and dress and behavior, this lovely tree up here, exposed to the wildest blasts, has already endured the storms of centuries of winters!

The two pines also are brave storm-enduring trees, the mountain pine (*Pinus monticola*) and the dwarf pine (*Pinus albicaulis*). The mountain pine is closely related to the sugar pine, though the cones are only about four to six inches long. The largest trees are from five to six feet in diameter at four feet above the ground, the bark rich brown. Only a few storm-beaten adventurers approach the summit of the mountain. The dwarf or white-bark pine is the species that forms the timber-line, where it is so completely dwarfed that one may walk over the top of a bed of it as over snow-pressed chaparral.

How boundless the day seems as we revel in these storm-beaten sky gardens amid so vast a congregation of onlooking mountains! Strange and admirable it is that the more savage and chilly and storm-chafed the mountains, the finer the glow on their faces and the finer the plants they bear. The myriad flowers tingeing the mountain-top do not seem to have grown out of the dry, rough gravel of disintegration, but rather they appear as visitors, a cloud of witnesses to Nature's love in what we in our timid ignorance and unbelief call howling desert. The surface of the ground, so dull and forbidding at first sight, besides being rich in plants, shines and sparkles with crystals: mica, hornblende, feldspar, quartz, tourmaline. The radiance in some places is so great as to be fairly dazzling, keen lance rays of every color flashing, sparkling in glorious abundance, joining the plants in their fine, brave beauty-work – every crystal, every flower a window opening into heaven, a mirror reflecting the Creator.

From garden to garden, ridge to ridge, I drifted enchanted, now on my knees gazing into the face of a daisy, now climbing again and again among the purple and azure flowers of the hemlocks, now down into the treasuries of the snow, or gazing afar over domes and peaks, lakes and woods, and the billowy glaciated fields of the upper Tuolumne, and trying to sketch them. In the midst of such beauty, pierced with its rays, one's body is all one tingling palate. Who wouldn't be a mountain-eer! Up here all the world's prizes seem nothing.

The largest of the many glacier lakes in sight, and the one with the finest shore scenery, is Tenaya, about a mile long, with an imposing mountain dipping its feet into it on the south side, Cathedral Peak a few miles above its head, many smooth swelling rock-waves and domes on the north, and in the distance southward a multitude of snowy peaks, the foun-tain-heads of rivers. Lake Hoffman lies shimmering beneath my feet, mountain pines around its shining rim. To the north-ward the picturesque basin of Yosemite Creek glitters with lakelets and pools; but the eye is soon drawn away from these bright mirror wells, however attractive, to revel in the glorious congregation of peaks on the axis of the range in their robes of snow and light.

Carlo caught an unfortunate woodchuck when it was running from a grassy spot to its boulder-pile home – one of the hardiest of the mountain animals. I tried hard to save him, but in vain. After telling Carlo that he must be careful not to kill anything, I caught sight, for the first time, of the curious pika, or little chief hare, that cuts large quantities of lupines and other plants and lays them out to dry in the sun for hay, which it stores in underground barns to last through the long, snowy winter. Coming upon these plants freshly cut and lying in handfuls here and there on the rocks has a startling effect of busy life on the lonely mountain-top. These little haymakers, endowed with brain stuff something like our own – God up here looking after them – what lessons they teach, how they widen our sympathy!

An eagle soaring above a sheer cliff, where I suppose its nest is, makes another striking show of life, and helps to bring to mind the other people of the so-called solitude – deer in the forest caring for their young; the strong, well-clad, well-fed bears; the lively throng of squirrels; the blessed birds, great and small, stirring and sweetening the groves; and the clouds of happy insects filling the sky with joyous hum as part and parcel of the down-pouring sunshine. All these come to mind, as well as the plant people, and the glad streams singing their way to the sea. But most impressive of all is the vast glowing countenance of the wilderness in awful, infinite repose.

Toward sunset, enjoyed a fine run to camp, down the long south slopes, across ridges and ravines, gardens and avalanche gaps, through the firs and chaparral, enjoying wild excitement and excess of strength, and so ends a day that will never end.

July 27 – Up and away to Lake Tenaya – another big day, enough for a lifetime. The rocks, the air, everything speaking with audible voice or silent; joyful, wonderful, enchanting, banishing weariness and sense of time. No longing for anything now or hereafter as we go home into the mountain's heart. The level sunbeams are touching the fir-tops, every leaf shining with dew. Am holding an easterly course, the deep canyon of Tenaya Creek on the right hand, Mt. Hoffman on the left, and the lake straight ahead about ten miles distant, the summit of Mt. Hoffman about three thousand feet above me, Tenaya Creek four thousand feet below and separated from the shallow, irregular valley, along which most of the way lies, by smooth domes and wave-ridges. Many mossy emerald bogs, meadows, and gardens in rocky hollows to wade and saunter through – and what fine plants they give me, what joyful streams I have to cross, and how many views are displayed of the Hoffman and Cathedral Peak masonry, and what a wondrous breadth of shining granite pavement to walk over for the first time about the shores of the lake! On I sauntered in freedom complete; body without weight as far as I was aware; now wading through starry parnassia bogs, now through gardens shoulder deep in larkspur and lilies, grasses and rushes, shaking off showers of dew; crossing piles of crystalline moraine boulders, bright mirror pavements, and cool, cheery streams going to Yosemite; crossing bryanthus carpets and the scoured pathways of avalanches, and thickets of snow-pressed ceanothus; then down a broad, majestic stairway into the ice-sculptured lake-basin.

The snow on the high mountains is melting fast, and the streams are singing bankfull, swaying softly through the level meadows and bogs, quivering with sun-spangles, swirling in pot-holes, resting in deep pools, leaping, shouting in wild, exulting energy over rough boulder dams, joyful, beautiful in all their forms. No Sierra landscape that I have seen holds anything truly dead or dull, or any trace of what in manufactories is called rubbish or waste; everything is perfectly clean and pure and full of divine lessons. This quick, inevitable interest attaching to everything seems marvelous until the hand of God becomes visible; then it seems reasonable that what interests Him may well interest us. When we try to pick out anything by itself, we find it hitched to everything else in the universe. One fancies a heart like our own must be beating in every crystal and cell, and we feel like stopping to speak to the plants and animals as friendly fellow-mountaineers. Nature as a poet, an enthusiastic work-ingman, becomes more and more visible the farther and higher we go; for the mountains are fountains – beginning places, however related to sources beyond mortal ken.

I found three kinds of meadows: – (1) Those contained in basins not yet filled with earth enough to make a dry surface. They are planted with several species of carex, and have their margins diversified with robust flowering plants such as ver-atrum, larkspur, lupine, etc. (2) Those contained in the same sort of basins, once lakes like the first, but so situated in relation to the streams that flow through them and beds of transportable sand, gravel, etc., that they are now high and dry and well drained. This dry condition and corresponding dif-ference in their vegetation may be caused by no superiority of position, or power of transporting filling material in the streams that belong to them, but simply by the basin being shallow and therefore sooner filled. They are planted with grasses, mostly fine, silky, and rather short-leaved, *Calama-grostis* and *Agrostis* being the principal genera. They form delightfully smooth, level sods in which one finds two or three species of gentian and as many of purple and yellow ortho-carpus, violet, vaccinium, kalmia, bryanthus, and lonicera. (3) Meadows hanging on ridge and mountain slopes, not in basins at all, but made and held in place by masses of boulders and fallen trees, which, forming dams one above another in close succession on small, outspread, channelless streams, have collected soil enough for the growth of grasses, carices, and many flowering plants, and being kept well watered, without being subject to currents sufficiently strong to carry them away, a hanging or sloping meadow is the result. Their surfaces are seldom so smooth as the others, being roughened more or less by the projecting tops of the dam rocks or logs; but at a little distance this roughness is not noticed, and the effect is very striking – bright green, fluent, down-sweeping flowery ribbons on gray slopes. The broad shallow streams these meadows belong to are mostly derived from banks of snow and because the soil is well drained in some places, while in others the dam rocks are packed close and caulked with bits of wood and leaves, making boggy patches; the vegetation, of course, is correspondingly varied. I saw patches of willow, bryanthus, and a fine show of lilies on some of them, not forming a margin, but scattered about among the carex and grass. Most of these meadows are now in their prime. How wonderful must be the temper of the elastic leaves of grasses and sedges to make curves so perfect and fine. Tempered a little harder, they would stand erect, stiff and bristly, like strips of metal; a little softer, and every leaf would lie flat. And what fine painting and tinting there is on the glumes and pales, stamens and feathery pistils. Butterflies colored like the flowers waver above them in wonderful profusion, and many other beautiful winged people, numbered and known and loved only by the Lord, are waltzing together high over head, seemingly in pure play and hilarious enjoyment of their little sparks of life. How wonderful they are! How do they get a living, and endure the weather? How are their little bodies, with muscles, nerves, organs, kept warm and jolly in such admirable exuberant health? Regarded only as mechanical inventions, how wonderful they are! Compared with these, Godlike man's greatest machines are as nothing.

Most of the sandy gardens on moraines are in prime beauty like the meadows, though some on the north sides of rocks and beneath groves of sapling pines have not yet bloomed. On sunny sheets of crystal soil along the slopes of the Hoffman mountains, I saw extensive patches of ivesia and purple gilia with scarce a green leaf, making fine clouds of color. Ribes bushes, vaccinium, and kalmia, now in flower, make beautiful rugs and borders along the banks of the streams. Shaggy beds of dwarf oak (*Quercus chrysolepis*, var. *vaccinifolia*) over which one may walk are common on rocky moraines, yet this is the same species as the large live oak seen near Brown's Flat. The most beautiful of the shrubs is the purple-flowered bryanthus, here making glorious carpets at an elevation of nine thousand feet.

The principal tree for the first mile or two from camp is the magnificent silver fir, which reaches perfection here both in size and form of individual trees and in the mode of grouping in groves with open spaces between. So trim and tasteful are these silvery, spiry groves one would fancy they must have been placed in position by some master landscape gardener, their regularity seeming almost conventional. But Nature is the only gardener able to do work so fine. A few noble specimens two hundred feet high occupy central positions in the groups with younger trees around them; and outside of these another circle of yet smaller ones, the whole arranged like tastefully symmetrical bouquets, every tree fitting nicely the place assigned to it as if made especially for it; small roses and eriogonums are usually found blooming on the open spaces about the groves, forming charming pleasure grounds. Higher, the firs gradually become smaller and less perfect, many showing double summits, indicating storm stress. Still, where good moraine soil is found, even on the rim of the lake-basin, specimens one hundred and fifty feet in height and five feet in diameter occur nearly nine thousand feet above the sea. The saplings, I find, are mostly bent with the crushing weight of the winter snow, which at this elevation must be at least eight or ten feet deep, judging by marks on the trees; and this depth of compacted snow is heavy enough to bend and bury young trees twenty or thirty feet in height and hold them down for four or five months. Some are broken; the others spring up when the snow melts and at length attain a size that enables them to withstand the snow pressure. Yet even in trees five feet thick the traces of this early discipline are still plainly to be seen in their curved insteps, and frequently in old dried saplings protruding from the trunk, partially overgrown by the new axis developed from a branch below the break. Yet through all this stress the forest is maintained in marvelous beauty.

Beyond the silver firs I find the two-leaved pine (*Pinus contorta*, var. *Murrayana*) forms the bulk of the forest up to an elevation of ten thousand feet or more – the highest timber-belt of the Sierra. I saw a specimen nearly five feet in diameter growing on deep, well-watered soil at an elevation of about nine thousand feet. The form of this species varies very much with position, exposure, soil, etc. On streambanks, where it is closely planted, it is very slender; some specimens seventy-five feet high do not exceed five inches in diameter at the ground, but the ordinary form, as far as I have seen, is well proportioned. The average diameter when full grown at this elevation is about twelve or fourteen inches, height forty or fifty feet, the straggling branches bent up at the end, the bark thin and bedraggled with amber-colored resin. The pistillate flowers form little crimson rosettes a fourth of an inch in diameter on the ends of the branchlets, mostly hidden in the leaf-tassels; the staminate are about three eighths of an inch in diameter, sulphur-yellow, in showy clusters, giving a remarkably rich effect – a brave, hardy mountaineer pine, growing cheerily on rough beds of avalanche boulders and joints of rock pavements, as well as in fertile hollows, standing up to the waist in snow every winter for centuries, facing a thousand storms and blooming every year in colors as bright as those worn by the sun-drenched trees of the tropics.

A still hardier mountaineer is the Sierra juniper (*Juniperus occidentalis*), growing mostly on domes and ridges and glacier pavements. A thickset, sturdy, picturesque highlander, seemingly content to live for more than a score of centuries on sunshine and snow; a truly wonderful fellow, dogged endurance expressed in every feature, lasting about as long as the granite he stands on. Some are nearly as broad as high. I saw one on the shore of the lake nearly ten feet in diameter, and many six to eight feet. The bark, cinnamon-colored, flakes off in long ribbon-like strips with a satiny lustre. Surely the most enduring of all tree mountaineers, it never seems to die a natural death, or even to fall after it has been killed. If protected from accidents, it would perhaps be immortal. I saw some that had withstood an avalanche from snowy Mt. Hoffman cheerily putting out new branches, as if repeating, like Grip, 'Never say die.' Some were simply standing on the pavement where no fissure more than half an inch wide offered a hold for its roots. The common height for these rock-dwellers is from ten to twenty feet; most of the old ones have broken tops, and are mere stumps, with a few tufted branches, forming picturesque brown pillars on bare pavements, with plenty of elbow-room and a clear view in every direction. On good moraine soil it reaches a height of from forty to sixty feet, with dense gray foliage. The rings of the trunk are very thin, eighty to an inch of diameter in some specimens I examined. Those ten feet in diameter must be very old – thousands of years. Wish I could live, like these junipers, on sunshine and snow, and stand beside them on the shore of Lake Tenaya for a thousand years. How much I should see, and how delightful it would be! Everything in the mountains would find me and come to me, and everything from the heavens like light.

The lake was named for one of the chiefs of the Yosemite tribe. Old Tenaya is said to have been a good Indian to his tribe. When a company of soldiers followed his band into Yosemite to punish them for cattle-stealing and other crimes, they fled to this lake by a trail that leads out of the upper end of the valley, early in the spring, while the snow was still deep; but being pursued, they lost heart and surrendered. A fine monument the old man has in this bright lake, and likely to last a long time, though lakes die as well as Indians, being gradually filled with detritus carried in by the feeding streams, and to some extent also by snow avalanches and rain and wind. A considerable portion of the Tenaya basin is already changed into a forested flat and meadow at the upper end, where the main tributary enters from Cathedral Peak. Two other tributaries come from the Hoffman Range. The outlet flows westward through Tenaya Canyon to join the Merced River in Yosemite. Scarce a handful of loose soil is to be seen on the north shore. All is bare, shining granite, suggesting the Indian name of the lake, Pywiack, meaning shining rock. The basin seems to have been slowly excavated by the ancient glaciers, a marvelous work requiring countless thousands of years. On the south side an imposing mountain rises from the water's edge to a height of three thousand feet or more, feathered with hemlock and pine; and huge shining domes on the east, over the tops of which the grinding, wasting, molding glacier must have swept as the wind does today.

July 28 – No cloud mountains, only curly cirrus wisps scarce perceptible, and the want of thunder to strike the noon hour seems strange, as if the Sierra clock had stopped. Have been studying the *magnifica* fir – measured one near two hundred and forty feet high, the tallest I have yet seen. This species is the most symmetrical of all conifers, but though gigantic in size it seldom lives more than four or five hundred years. Most of the trees die from the attacks of a fungus at the age of two or three centuries. This dry-rot fungus perhaps enters the trunk by way of the stumps of limbs broken off by the snow that loads the broad palmate branches. The younger specimens are marvels of symmetry, straight and erect as a plumb-line, their branches in regular level whorls of five mostly, each branch as exact in its divisions as a fern frond, and thickly covered by the leaves, making a rich plush over all the tree, excepting only the trunk and a small portion of the main limbs. The leaves turn upward, especially on the branchlets, and are stiff and sharp, pointed on all the upper portion of the tree. They remain on the tree about eight or ten years, and as the growth is rapid it is not rare to find the leaves still in place on the upper part of the axis where it is three to four inches in diameter, wide apart of course, and their spiral arrangement beautifully displayed. The leaf-scars are conspicuous for twenty years or more, but there is a good deal of variation in different trees as to the thickness and sharpness of the leaves.

After the excursion to Mt. Hoffman I had seen a complete cross-section of the Sierra forest, and I find that *Abies magnifica* is the most symmetrical tree of all the noble coniferous company. The cones are grand affairs, superb in form, size, and color, cylindrical, stand erect on the upper branches like casks, and are from five to eight inches in length by three or four in diameter, greenish gray, and covered with fine down which has a silvery lustre in the sunshine, and their brilliance is augmented by beads of transparent balsam which seems to have been poured over each cone, bringing to mind the old ceremonies of anointing with oil. If possible, the inside of the cone is more beautiful than the outside; the scales, bracts, and seed wings are tinted with the loveliest rosy purple with a bright lustrous iridescence; the seeds, three fourths of an inch long, are dark brown. When the cones are ripe the scales and bracts fall off, setting the seeds free to fly to their predestined places, while the dead spikelike axes are left on the branches for many years to mark the positions of the vanished cones, excepting those cut off when green by the Douglas squirrel. How he gets his teeth under the broad bases of the sessile cones, I don't know. Climbing these trees on a sunny day to visit the growing cones and to gaze over the tops of the forest is one of my best enjoyments.

July 29 – Bright, cool, exhilarating. Clouds about .05. Another glorious day of rambling, sketching, and universal enjoyment.

July 30 – Clouds .20, but the regular shower did not reach us, though thunder was heard a few miles off striking the noon hour. Ants, flies, and mosquitoes seem to enjoy this fine climate. A few house flies have discovered our camp. The Sierra mosquitoes are courageous and of good size, some of them measuring nearly an inch from tip of sting to tip of folded wings. Though less abundant than in most wildernesses, they occasionally make quite a hum and stir, and pay but little attention to time or place. They sting anywhere, any time of day, wherever they can find anything worth while, until they are themselves stung by frost. The large jet-black ants are only ticklish and troublesome when one is lying down under the trees. Noticed a borer drilling a silver fir. Ovipositor about an inch and a half in length, polished and straight like a needle.

When not in use, it is folded back in a sheath, which extends straight behind like the legs of a crane in flying. This drilling, I suppose, is to save nest building, and the aftercare of feeding the young. Who would guess that in the brain of a fly so much knowledge could find lodgment? How do they know that their eggs will hatch in such holes, or, after they hatch, that the soft, helpless grubs will find the right sort of nourishment in silver fir sap? This domestic arrangement calls to mind the curious family of gallflies. Each species seems to know what kind of plant will respond to the irritation or stimulus of the puncture it makes and the eggs it lays, in forming a growth that not only answers for a nest and home but also provides food for the young. Probably these gallflies make mistakes at times, like anybody else; but when they do, there is simply a failure of that particular brood, while enough to perpetuate the species do find the proper plants and nourishment. Many mistakes of this kind might be made without being discovered by us. Once a pair of wrens made the mistake of building a nest in the sleeve of a workman's coat, which was called for at sundown, much to the consternation and discomfiture of the birds. Still the marvel remains that any of the children of such small people as gnats and mosquitoes should escape their own and their parents' mistakes, as well as the vicissitudes of the weather and hosts of enemies, and come forth in full vigor and perfection to enjoy the sunny world. When we think of the small creatures that are visible, we are led to think of many that are smaller still and lead us on and on into infinite mystery.

July 31 – Another glorious day, the air as delicious to the lungs as nectar to the tongue; indeed the body seems one palate, and tingles equally throughout. Cloudiness about .05, but our ordinary shower has not yet reached us, though I hear thunder in the distance.

The cheery little chipmunk, so common about Brown's Flat, is common here also, and perhaps other species. In their light, airy habits they recall the familiar species of the Eastern States, which we admired in the oak openings of Wisconsin as they skimmed along the zigzag rail fences. These Sierra chipmunks are more arboreal and squirrel-like. I first noticed them on the lower edge of the coniferous belt, where the Sabine and yellow pines meet – exceedingly interesting little fellows, full of odd, funny ways, and without being true squirrels, have most of their accomplishments without their aggressive quarrelsomeness. I never weary watching them as they frisk about in the bushes gathering seeds and berries, like song sparrows poising daintily on slender twigs, and making even less stir than most birds of the same size. Few of the Sierra animals interest me more; they are so able, gentle, confiding, and beautiful, they take one's heart, and get themselves adopted as darlings. Though weighing hardly more than field mice, they are laborious collectors of seeds, nuts, and cones, and are therefore well fed, but never in the least swollen with fat or lazily full. On the contrary, of their frisky, birdlike liveliness there is no end. They have a great variety of notes corresponding with their movements, some sweet and liquid like water dripping with tinkling sounds into pools. They seem dearly to love teasing a dog, coming frequently almost within reach, then frisking away with lively chipping, like sparrows, beating time to their music with their tails, which at each chip describe half circles from side to side. Not even the Douglas squirrel is surer-footed or more fearless. I have seen them running about on sheer precipices of the Yosemite walls seemingly holding on with as little effort as flies, and as unconscious of danger, where, if the slightest slip were made, they would have fallen two or three thousand feet. How fine it would be could we mountaineers climb these tremendous cliffs with the same sure grip! The venture I made the other day for a view of the Yosemite Fall, and which tried my nerves so sorely, this little Tamias would have made for an ear of grass.

The woodchuck (*Arctomys monax*) of the bleak mountaintops is a very different sort of mountaineer – the most bovine of rodents, a heavy eater, fat, aldermanic in bulk and fairly bloated, in his high pastures, like a cow in a clover field. One woodchuck would outweigh a hundred chipmunks, and yet he is by no means a dull animal. In the midst of what we regard as storm-beaten desolation he pipes and whistles right cheerily, and enjoys long life in his skyland homes. His burrow is made in disintegrated rocks or beneath large boulders. Coming out of his den in the cold hoarfrost mornings, he takes a sun-bath on some favorite flat-topped rock, then goes to breakfast in garden hollows, eats grass and flowers until comfortably swollen, then goes a-visiting to fight and play.

How long a woodchuck lives in this bracing air I don't know, but some of them are rusty and gray like lichen-covered boulders.

August 1 – A grand cloudland and five-minute shower, refreshing the blessed wilderness, already so fragrant and fresh, steeping the black meadow mold and dead leaves like tea.

The waycup, or flicker, so familiar to every boy in the old Middle West States, is one of the most common of the woodpeckers hereabouts, and makes one feel at home. I can see no difference in plumage or habits from the Eastern species, though the climate here is so different – a fine, brave, confiding, beautiful bird. The robin, too, is here, with all his familiar notes and gestures, tripping daintily on open garden spots and high meadows. Over all America he seems to be at home, moving from the plains to the mountains and from north to south, back and forth, up and down, with the march of the seasons and food supply. How admirable the constitution and temper of this brave singer, keeping in cheery health over so vast and varied a range! Oftentimes, as I wander through these solemn woods, awe-stricken and silent, I hear the reassuring voice of this fellow wanderer ringing out, sweet and clear, 'Fear not! fear not!

The mountain quail (*Oreortyx ricta*) I often meet in my walks – a small brown partridge with a very long, slender, ornamental crest worn jauntily like a feather in a boy's cap, giving it a very marked appearance. This species is considerably larger than the valley quail, so common on the hot foothills. They seldom alight in trees, but love to wander in flocks of from five or six to twenty through the ceanothus and manzanita thickets and over open, dry meadows and rocks of the ridges where the forest is less dense or wanting, uttering a low clucking sound to enable them to keep together. When disturbed they rise with a strong birr of wing-beats, and scatter as if exploded to a distance of a quarter of a mile or so. After the danger is past they call one another together with a louder piping note – Nature's beautiful mountain chickens. I have not yet found their nests. The young of this season are already hatched and away – new broods of happy wanderers half as large as their parents. I wonder how they live through the long winters, when the ground is snow-covered ten feet deep. They must go down towards the lower edge of the forest, like the deer, though I have not heard of them there.

The blue, or dusky, grouse is also common here. They like the deepest and closest fir woods, and when disturbed, burst from the branches of the trees with a strong, loud whir of wing-beats, and vanish in a wavering, silent slide, without moving a feather – a stout, beautiful bird about the size of the prairie chicken of the old west, spending most of the time in the trees, excepting the breeding season, when it keeps to the ground. The young are now able to fly. When scattered by man or dog, they keep still until the danger is supposed to be past, then the mother calls them together. The chicks can hear the call a distance of several hundred yards, though it is not loud. Should the young be unable to fly, the mother feigns desperate lame-ness or death to draw one away, throwing herself at one's feet within two or three yards, rolling over on her back, kicking and gasping, so as to deceive man or beast. They are said to stay all the year in the woods hereabouts, taking shelter in dense tufted branches of fir and yellow pine during snow-storms, and feeding on the young buds of these trees. Their legs are feathered down to their toes, and I have never heard of their suffering in any sort of weather. Able to live on pine and fir buds, they are forever independent in the matter of food, which troubles so many of us and controls our movements. Gladly, if I could, I would live forever on pine buds, however full of turpentine and pitch, for the sake of this grand inde-pendence. Just to think of our sufferings last month merely for grist-mill flour. Man seems to have more difficulty in gaining food than any other of the Lord's creatures. For many in towns it is a consuming, life-long struggle; for others, the danger of coming to want is so great, the deadly habit of endless hoarding for the future is formed, which smothers all real life, and is continued long after every reasonable need has been over-supplied.

On Mt. Hoffman I saw a curious dove-colored bird that seemed half woodpecker, half magpie or crow. It screams something like a crow, but flies like a woodpecker, and has a long, straight bill, with which I saw it opening the cones of the mountain and white-barked pines. It seems to keep to the heights, though no doubt it comes down for shelter during winter, if not for food. So far as food is concerned, these bird-mountaineers, I guess, can glean nuts enough, even in winter, from the different kinds of conifers; for always there are a few that have been unable to fly out of the cones and remain for hungry winter gleaners.

Chapter 7

A STRANGE EXPERIENCE

August 2 – Clouds and showers, about the same as yesterday. Sketching all day on the North Dome until four or five o'clock in the afternoon, when, as I was busily employed thinking only of the glorious Yosemite landscape, trying to draw every tree and every line and feature of the rocks, I was suddenly, and without warning, possessed with the notion that my friend, Professor J. D. Butler, of the State University of Wisconsin, was below me in the valley, and I jumped up full of the idea of meeting him, with almost as much startling excitement as if he had suddenly touched me to make me look up. Leaving my work without the slightest deliberation, I ran down the western slope of the Dome and along the brink of the valley wall, looking for a way to the bottom, until I came to a side canyon, which, judging by its apparently continuous growth of trees and bushes, I thought might afford a practical way into the valley, and immediately began to make the descent, late as it was, as if drawn irresistibly. But after a little, common sense stopped me and explained that it would be long after dark ere I could possibly reach the hotel, that the visitors would be asleep, that nobody would know me, that I had no money in my pockets, and moreover was without a coat. I therefore compelled myself to stop, and finally succeeded in reasoning myself out of the notion of seeking my friend in the dark, whose presence I only felt in a strange, telepathic way. I succeeded in dragging myself back through the woods to camp, never for a moment wavering, however, in my determination to go down to him next morning. This I think is the most unexplainable notion that ever struck me. Had someone whispered in my ear while I sat on the Dome, where I had spent so many days, that Professor Butler was in the valley, I could not have been more surprised and startled. When I was leaving the university he said, 'Now, John, I want to hold you in sight and watch your career. Promise to write me at least once a year.' I received a letter from him in July, at our first camp in the Hollow, written in May, in which he said that he might possibly visit California some time this summer, and therefore hoped to meet me. But inasmuch as he named no meeting-place, and gave no directions as to the course he would probably follow, and as I should be in the wilderness all summer, I had not the slightest hope of seeing him, and all thought of the matter had vanished from my mind until this afternoon, when he seemed to be wafted bodily almost against my face. Well, tomorrow I shall see; for, reasonable or unreasonable, I feel I must go.

August 3 – Had a wonderful day. Found Professor Butler as the compass-needle finds the pole. So last evening's telepathy, transcendental revelation, or whatever else it may be called, was true; for, strange to say, he had just entered the valley by way of the Coulterville Trail and was coming up the valley past El Capitan when his presence struck me. Had he then looked toward the North Dome with a good glass when it first came in sight, he might have seen me jump up from my work and run toward him. This seems the one well-defined marvel of my life of the kind called supernatural; for, absorbed in glad Nature, spirit-rappings, second sight, ghost stories, etc., have never interested me since boyhood, seeming comparatively useless and infinitely less wonderful than Nature's open, harmonious, songful, sunny, every-day beauty.

This morning, when I thought of having to appear among tourists at a hotel, I was troubled because I had no suitable clothes, and at best am desperately bashful and shy. I was determined to go, however, to see my old friend after two years among strangers; got on a clean pair of overalls, a cashmere shirt, and a sort of jacket – the best my camp wardrobe afforded – tied my note-book on my belt, and strode away on my strange journey, followed by Carlo. I made my way through the gap discovered last evening, which proved to be Indian Canyon. There was no trail in it, and the rocks and brush were so rough that Carlo frequently called me back to help him down precipitous places. Emerging from the canyon shadows, I found a man making hay on one of the meadows, and asked him whether Professor Butler was in the valley. 'I don't know,' he replied; 'but you can easily find out at the hotel. There are but few visitors in the valley just now. A small party came in yesterday afternoon, and I heard someone called Professor Butler, or Butterfield, or some name like that.'

In front of the gloomy hotel I found a tourist party adjusting their fishing tackle. They all stared at me in silent wonderment, as if I had been seen dropping down through the trees from the clouds, mostly, I suppose, on account of my strange garb. Inquiring for the office, I was told it was locked, and that the landlord was away, but I might find the landlady, Mrs Hutchings, in the parlor. I entered in a sad state of embarrassment, and after I had waited in the big, empty room and knocked at several doors the landlady at length appeared, and in reply to my question said she rather thought Professor Butler was in the valley, but to make sure, she would bring the register from the office. Among the names of the last arrivals I soon discovered the Professor's familiar handwriting, at the sight of which bashfulness vanished; and having learned that his party had gone up the valley – probably to the Vernal and Nevada Falls – I pushed on in glad pursuit, my heart now sure of its prey. In less than an hour I reached the head of the Nevada Canyon at the Vernal Fall, and just outside of the spray discovered a distinguished-looking gentleman, who, like everybody else I have seen today, regarded me curiously as I approached. When I made bold to inquire if he knew where Professor Butler was, he seemed yet more curious to know what could possibly have happened that required a messenger for the Professor, and instead of answering my question he asked with military sharpness, 'Who wants him?' 'I want him,' I replied with equal sharpness. 'Why? Do *you* know him?' 'Yes,' I said. 'Do *you* know him?' Astonished that anyone in the mountains could possibly know Professor Butler and find him as soon as he had reached the valley, he came down to meet the strange mountaineer on equal terms, and courteously replied, 'Yes, I know Professor Butler very well. I am General Alvord, and we were fellow students in Rutland, Vermont, long ago, when we were both young.' 'But where is he now?' I persisted, cutting short his story. 'He has gone beyond the falls with a companion, to try to climb that big rock, the top of which you see from here.'

His guide now volunteered the information that it was the Liberty Cap Professor Butler and his companion had gone to climb, and that if I waited at the head of the fall I should be sure to find them on their way down. I therefore climbed the ladders alongside the Vernal Fall, and was pushing forward, determined to go to the top of Liberty Cap rock in my hurry, rather than wait, if I should not meet my friend sooner. So heart-hungry at times may one be to see a friend in the flesh, however happily full and carefree one's life may be. I had gone but a short distance, however, above the brow of the Vernal Fall when I caught sight of him in the brush and rocks, half erect, groping his way, his sleeves rolled up, vest open, hat in his hand, evidently very hot and tired. When he saw me coming he sat down on a boulder to wipe the perspiration from his brow and neck, and taking me for one of the valley guides, he inquired the way to the fall ladders. I pointed out the path marked with little piles of stones, on seeing which he called his companion, saying that the way was found; but he did not yet recognize me. Then I stood directly in front of him, looked him in the face, and held out my hand. He thought I was offering to assist him in rising. 'Never mind,' he said. Then I said, 'Professor Butler, don't you know me?' 'I think not,' he replied; but catching my eye, sudden recognition followed, and astonishment that I should have found him just when he was lost in the brush and did not know that I was within hundreds of miles of him. 'John Muir, John Muir, where have you come from?' Then I told him the story of my feeling his presence when he entered the valley last evening, when he was four or five miles distant, as I sat sketching on the North Dome. This, of course, only made him wonder the more. Below the foot of the Vernal Fall the guide was waiting with his saddle-horse, and I walked along the trail, chatting all the way back to the hotel, talking of school days, friends in Madison, of the students, how each had prospered, etc., ever and anon gazing at the stupendous rocks about us, now growing indistinct in the gloaming, and again quoting from the poets – a rare ramble.

It was late ere we reached the hotel, and General Alvord was waiting the Professor's arrival for dinner. When I was introduced he seemed yet more astonished than the Professor at my descent from cloudland and going straight to my friend without knowing in any ordinary way that he was even in California. They had come on direct from the East, had not yet visited any of their friends in the state, and considered themselves undiscoverable. As we sat at dinner, the General leaned back in his chair, and looking down the table, thus introduced me to the dozen guests or so, including the staring fisherman mentioned above: 'This man, you know, came down out of these huge, trackless mountains, you know, to find his friend Professor Butler here, the very day he arrived; and how did he know he was here? He just felt him, he says. This is the queerest case of Scotch farsightedness I ever heard of,' etc., etc. While my friend quoted Shakespeare: 'More things in heaven and earth, Horatio, than are dreamt of in your philosophy,' 'As the sun, ere he has risen, sometimes paints his image in the firmament, e'en so the shadows of events precede the events, and in today already walks tomorrow.'

Had a long conversation, after dinner, over Madison days. The Professor wants me to promise to go with him, sometime, on a camping trip in the Hawaiian Islands, while I tried to get him to go back with me to camp in the high Sierra. But he says, 'Not now.' He must not leave the General; and I was surprised to learn they are to leave the valley tomorrow or next day. I'm glad I'm not great enough to be missed in the busy world.

August 4 – It seemed strange to sleep in a paltry hotel chamber after the spacious magnificence and luxury of the starry sky and silver fir grove. Bade farewell to my friend and the General. The old soldier was very kind, and an interesting talker. He told me long stories of the Florida Seminole war, in which he took part, and invited me to visit him in Omaha. Calling Carlo, I scrambled home through the Indian Canyon gate, rejoicing, pitying the poor Professor and General, bound by clocks, almanacs, orders, duties, etc., and compelled to dwell with lowland care and dust and din, where Nature is covered and her voice smothered, while the poor, insignificant wanderer enjoys the freedom and glory of God's wilderness.

Apart from the human interest of my visit today, I greatly enjoyed Yosemite, which I had visited only once before, having spent eight days last spring in rambling amid its rocks and waters. Wherever we go in the mountains, or indeed in any of God's wild fields, we find more than we seek. Descending four thousand feet in a few hours, we enter a new world – climate, plants, sounds, inhabitants, and scenery all new or changed. Near camp the gold-cup oak forms sheets of chaparral, on top of which we may make our beds. Going down the Indian Canyon we observe this little bush changing by regular grada- tions to a large bush, to a small tree, and then larger, until on the rocky taluses near the bottom of the valley we find it developed into a broad, wide-spreading, gnarled, picturesque tree from four to eight feet in diameter, and forty or fifty feet high. Innumerable are the forms of water displayed. Every gliding reach, cascade, and fall has characters of its own. Had a good view of the Vernal and Nevada, two of the main falls of the valley, less than a mile apart, and offering striking differ- ences in voice, form, color, etc. The Vernal, four hundred feet high and about seventy-five or eighty feet wide, drops smoothly over a round-lipped precipice and forms a superb apron of embroidery, green and white, slightly folded and fluted, maintaining this form nearly to the bottom, where it is suddenly veiled in quick-flying billows of spray and mist, in which the afternoon sunbeams play with ravishing beauty of rainbow colors. The Nevada is white from its first appearance as it leaps out into the freedom of the air. At the head it presents a twisted appearance, by an overfolding of the current from striking on the side of its channel just before the first free outbounding leap is made. About two thirds of the way down, the hurrying throng of comet-shaped masses glance on an inclined part of the face of the precipice and are beaten into yet whiter foam, greatly expanded, and sent bounding outward, making an indescribably glorious show, especially when the afternoon sunshine is pouring into it. In this fall – one of the most wonderful in the world – the water does not seem to be under the dominion of ordinary laws, but rather as if it were a living creature, full of the strength of the mountains and their huge, wild joy.

From beneath heavy throbbing blasts of spray the broken river is seen emerging in ragged boulder-chafed strips. These are speedily gathered into a roaring torrent, showing that the young river is still gloriously alive. On it goes, shouting, roaring, exulting in its strength, passes through a gorge with sublime display of energy, then suddenly expands on a gently inclined pavement, down which it rushes in thin sheets and folds of lace-work into a quiet pool – 'Emerald Pool,' as it is called – a stopping-place, a period separating two grand sentences. Resting here long enough to part with its foam-bells and gray mixtures of air, it glides quietly to the verge of the Vernal precipice in a broad sheet and makes its new display in the Vernal Fall; then more rapids and rock tossings down the canyon, shaded by live oak, Douglas spruce, fir, maple, and dogwood. It receives the Illilouette tributary, and makes a long sweep out into the level, sun-filled valley to join the other streams which, like itself, have danced and sung their way down from snowy heights to form the main Merced – the river of Mercy. But of this there is no end, and life, when one thinks of it, is so short. Never mind, one day in the midst of these divine glories is well worth living and toiling and starving for.

Before parting with Professor Butler he gave me a book, and I gave him one of my pencil sketches for his little son Henry, who is a favorite of mine. He used to make many visits to my room when I was a student. Never shall I forget his patriotic speeches for the Union, mounted on a tall stool, when he was only six years old.

It seems strange that visitors to Yosemite should be so little influenced by its novel grandeur, as if their eyes were bandaged and their ears stopped. Most of those I saw yesterday were looking down as if wholly unconscious of anything going on about them, while the sublime rocks were trembling with the tones of the mighty chanting congregation of waters gathered from all the mountains round about, making music that might draw angels out of heaven. Yet respectable-looking, even wise-looking people were fixing bits of worms on bent pieces of wire to catch trout. Sport they called it. Should church-goers try to pass the time fishing in baptismal fonts while dull sermons were being preached, the so-called sport might not be so bad; but to play in the Yosemite temple, seeking pleasure in the pain of fishes struggling for their lives, while God himself is preaching his sublimest water and stone sermons!

Now I'm back at the campfire, and cannot help thinking about my recognition of my friend's presence in the valley while he was four or five miles away, and while I had no means of knowing that he was not thousands of miles away. It seems supernatural, but only because it is not understood. Anyhow, it seems silly to make so much of it, while the natural and common is more truly marvelous and mysterious than the so-called supernatural. Indeed most of the miracles we hear of are infinitely less wonderful than the commonest of natural phenomena, when fairly seen. Perhaps the invisible rays that struck me while I sat at work on the Dome are something like those which attract and repel people at first sight, concerning which so much nonsense has been written. The worst apparent effect of these mysterious odd things is blindness to all that is divinely common. Hawthorne, I fancy, could weave one of his weird romances out of this little telepathic episode, the one strange marvel of my life, probably replacing my good old Professor by an attractive woman.

August 5 – We were awakened this morning before daybreak by the furious barking of Carlo and Jack and the sound of stampeding sheep. Billy fled from his punk bed to the fire, and refused to stir into the darkness to try to gather the scattered flock, or ascertain the nature of the disturbance. It was a bear attack, as we afterward learned, and I suppose little was gained by attempting to do anything before daylight. Nevertheless, being anxious to know what was up, Carlo and I groped our way through the woods, guided by the rustling sound made by fragments of the flock, not fearing the bear, for I knew that the runaways would go from their enemy as far as possible and Carlo's nose was also to be depended upon. About half a mile east of the corral we overtook twenty or thirty of the flock and succeeded in driving them back; then turning to the westward, we traced another band of fugitives and got them back to the flock. After daybreak I discovered the remains of a sheep carcass, still warm, showing that Bruin must have been enjoying his early mutton breakfast while I was seeking the runaways. He had eaten about half of it. Six dead sheep lay in the corral, evidently smothered by the crowding and piling up of the flock against the side of the corral wall when the bear entered. Making a wide circuit of the camp, Carlo and I discovered a third band of fugitives and drove them back to camp. We also discovered another dead sheep half eaten, showing there had been two of the shaggy free-booters at this early breakfast. They were easily traced. They had each caught a sheep, jumped over the corral fence with them, carrying them as a cat carries a mouse, laid them at the foot of fir trees a

hundred yards or so back from the corral, and eaten their fill.
After breakfast I set out to seek more of the lost, and found
seventy-five at a considerable distance from camp. In the
afternoon I succeeded, with Carlo's help, in getting them back
to the flock. I don't know whether all are together again or not.
I shall make a big fire this evening and keep watch.

When I asked Billy why he made his bed against the corral in
rotten wood, when so many better places offered, he replied
that he 'wished to be as near the sheep as possible in case bears
should attack them.' Now that the bears have come, he has
moved his bed to the far side of the camp, and seems afraid that
he may be mistaken for a sheep.

This has been mostly a sheep day, and of course studies have
been interrupted. Nevertheless, the walk through the gloom of
the woods before the dawn was worth while, and I have
learned something about these noble bears. Their tracks are
very telling, and so are their breakfasts. Scarce a trace of clouds
today, and of course our ordinary mid-day thunder is wanting.

August 6 – Enjoyed the grand illumination of the camp grove,
last night, from the fire we made to frighten the bears –
compensation for loss of sleep and sheep. The noble pillars
of verdure, vividly aglow, seemed to shoot into the sky like the
flames that lighted them. Nevertheless, one of the bears paid us
another visit, as if more attracted than repelled by the fire,
climbed into the corral, killed a sheep and made off with it
without being seen, while still another was lost by trampling
and suffocation against the side of the corral. Now that our
mutton has been tasted, I suppose it will be difficult to put a
stop to the ravages of these freebooters.

The Don arrived today from the lowlands with provisions
and a letter. On learning the losses he had sustained, he
determined to move the flock at once to the upper Tuolumne
region, saying that the bears would be sure to visit the camp
every night as long as we stayed, and that no fire or noise we
might make would avail to frighten them. No clouds save a few
thin, lustrous touches on the eastern horizon. Thunder heard
in the distance.

Chapter 8
THE MONO TRAIL

August 7 – Early this morning bade goodbye to the bears and blessed silver fir camp, and moved slowly eastward along the Mono Trail. At sundown camped for the night on one of the many small flowery meadows so greatly enjoyed on my excursion to Lake Tenaya. The dusty, noisy flock seems outrageously foreign and out of place in these nature gardens, more so than bears among sheep. The harm they do goes to the heart, but glorious hope lifts above all the dust and din and bids me look forward to a good time coming, when money enough will be earned to enable me to go walking where I like in pure wildness, with what I can carry on my back, and when the bread-sack is empty, run down to the nearest point on the bread-line for more. Nor will these run-downs be blanks, for, whether up or down, every step and jump on these blessed mountains is full of fine lessons.

August 8 – Camp at the west end of Lake Tenaya. Arriving early, I took a walk on the glacier-polished pavements along the north shore, and climbed the magnificent mountain rock at the east end of the lake, now shining in the late afternoon light. Almost every yard of its surface shows the scoring and polishing action of a great glacier that enveloped it and swept heavily over its summit, though it is about two thousand feet high above the lake and ten thousand above sea-level. This majestic, ancient ice-flood came from the eastward, as the scoring and crushing of the surface shows. Even below the waters of the lake the rock in some places is still grooved and polished; the lapping of the waves and their disintegrating action have not as yet obliterated even the superficial marks of glaciation. In climbing the steepest polished places I had to take off shoes and stockings. A fine region this for study of glacial action in mountain-making. I found many charming plants: arctic daisies, phlox, white spiraea, bryanthus, and rock-ferns – pellaea, cheilanthes, allosorus – fringing weathered seams all the way up to the summit; and sturdy junipers, grand old gray and brown monuments, stood bravely erect on fissured spots here and there, telling storm and avalanche stories of hundreds of winters. The view of the lake from the top is, I think, the best of all. There is another rock, more striking in form than this, standing isolated at the head of the lake, but it is not more than half as high. It is a knob or knot of burnished granite, perhaps about a thousand feet high, apparently as flawless and strong in structure as a wave-worn pebble, and probably owes its existence to the superior resistance it offered to the action of the overflowing ice-flood.

Made sketch of the lake, and sauntered back to camp, my iron-shod shoes clanking on the pavements disturbing the chipmunks and birds. After dark went out to the shore – not a breath of air astir, the lake a perfect mirror reflecting the sky and mountains with their stars and trees and wonderful sculpture, all their grandeur refined and doubled – a marvelously impressive picture, that seemed to belong more to heaven than earth.

August 9 – I went ahead of the flock, and crossed over the divide between the Merced and Tuolumne basins. The gap between the east end of the Hoffman spur and the mass of mountain rocks about Cathedral Peak, though roughened by ridges and waving folds, seems to be one of the channels of a broad ancient glacier that came from the mountains on the summit of the range. In crossing this divide the ice-river made an ascent of about five hundred feet from the Tuolumne meadows. This entire region must have been overswept by ice.

From the top of the divide, and also from the big Tuolumne Meadows, the wonderful mountain called Cathedral Peak is in sight. From every point of view it shows marked individuality. It is a majestic temple of one stone, hewn from the living rock, and adorned with spires and pinnacles in regular cathedral style. The dwarf pines on the roof look like mosses. I hope some time to climb to it to say my prayers and hear the stone sermons.

The big Tuolumne Meadows are flowery lawns, lying along the south fork of the Tuolumne River at a height of about eighty-five hundred to nine thousand feet above the sea, partially separated by forests and bars of glaciated granite. Here the mountains seem to have been cleared away or set back, so that wide-open views may be had in every direction. The upper end of the series lies at the base of Mt. Lyell, the lower below the east end of the Hoffman Range, so the length must be about ten or twelve miles. They vary in width from a quarter of a mile to perhaps three quarters, and a good many branch meadows put out along the banks of the tributary streams. This is the most spacious and delightful high plea-sure-ground I have yet seen. The air is keen and bracing, yet warm during the day; and though lying high in the sky, the surrounding mountains are so much higher, one feels pro-tected as if in a grand hall. Mts. Dana and Gibbs, massive red mountains, perhaps thirteen thousand feet high or more, bound the view on the east, the Cathedral and Unicorn Peaks, with many nameless peaks, on the south, the Hoffman Range on the west, and a number of peaks unnamed, as far as I know, on the north. One of these last is much like the Cathedral. The grass of the meadows is mostly fine and silky, with exceedingly slender leaves, making a close sod, above which the panicles of minute purple flowers seem to float in airy, misty lightness, while the sod is enriched with at least three species of gentian and as many or more of orthocarpus, potentilla, ivesia, solidago, pentstemon, with their gay colors – purple, blue, yellow, and red – all of which I may know better ere long. A central camp will probably be made in this region, from which I hope to make long excursions into the surrounding mountains.

On the return trip I met the flock about three miles east of Lake Tenaya. Here we camped for the night near a small lake lying on top of the divide in a clump of the two-leaved pine. We are now about nine thousand feet above the sea. Small lakes abound in all sorts of situations – on ridges, along mountain sides, and in piles of moraine boulders, most of them mere pools. Only in those canyons of the larger streams at the foot of declivities, where the down thrust of the glaciers was heaviest, do we find lakes of considerable size and depth. How grateful a task it would be to trace them all and study them! How pure their waters are, clear as crystal in polished stone basins! None of them, so far as I have seen, have fishes, I suppose on account of falls making them inaccessible. Yet one would think their eggs might get into these lakes by some chance or other; on ducks' feet, for example, or in their mouths, or in their crops, as some plant seeds are distributed. Nature has so many ways of doing such things. How did the frogs, found in all the bogs and pools and lakes, however high, manage to get up these mountains? Surely not by jumping. Such excursions through miles of dry brush and boulders would be very hard on frogs. Perhaps their stringy gelatinous spawn is occasionally entangled or glued on the feet of water birds. Anyhow, they are here and in hearty health and voice. I like their cheery tronk and crink. They take the place of songbirds at a pinch.

August 10 – Another of those charming exhilarating days that makes the blood dance and excites nerve currents that render one unweariable and well-nigh immortal. Had another view of the broad ice-ploughed divide, and gazed again and again at the Sierra temple and the great red mountains east of the meadows.

We are camped near the Soda Springs on the north side of the river. A hard time we had getting the sheep across. They were driven into a horseshoe bend and fairly crowded off the bank. They seemed willing to suffer death rather than risk getting wet, though they swim well enough when they have to. Why sheep should be so unreasonably afraid of water, I don't know, but they do fear it as soon as they are born and perhaps before. I once saw a lamb only a few hours old approach a shallow stream about two feet wide and an inch deep, after it had walked only about a hundred yards on its life journey. All the flock to which it belonged had crossed this inch-deep stream, and as the mother and her lamb were the last to cross, I had a good opportunity to observe them. As soon as the flock was out of the way, the anxious mother crossed over and called the youngster. It walked cautiously to the brink, gazed at the water, bleated piteously, and refused to venture. The patient mother went back to it again and again to encourage it, but long without avail. Like the pilgrim on Jordan's stormy bank it feared to launch away. At length gathering its trembling inexperienced legs for the mighty effort, throwing up its head as if it knew all about drowning, and was anxious to keep its nose above water, it made the tremendous leap, and landed in the middle of the inch-deep stream. It seemed astonished to find that, instead of sinking over head and ears, only its toes were wet, gazed at the shining water a few seconds, and then sprang to the shore safe and dry through the dreadful adventure. All kinds of wild sheep are mountain animals, and their descendants' dread of water is not easily accounted for.

August 11 – Fine shining weather, with a ten minutes' noon thunder-storm and rain. Rambling all day getting acquainted with the region north of the river. Found a small lake and many charming glacier meadows embosomed in an extensive forest of the two-leaved pine. The forest is growing on broad, almost continuous deposits of moraine material, is remarkably even in its growth, and the trees are much closer together than in any of the fir or pine woods farther down the range. The evenness of the growth would seem to indicate that the trees are all of the same age or nearly so. This regularity has probably been in great part the result of fire. I saw several large patches and strips of dead bleached spars, the ground beneath them covered with a young even growth. Fire can run in these woods, not only because the thin bark of the trees is dripping with resin, but because the growth is close, and the comparatively rich soil produces good crops of tall broad-leaved grasses on which fire can travel, even when the weather is calm. Besides these fire-killed patches there are a good many fallen uprooted trees here and there, some with the bark and needles still on, as if they had lately been blown down in some thunder-storm blast. Saw a large blacktailed deer, a buck with antlers like the upturned roots of a fallen pine.

After a long ramble through the dense encumbered woods I emerged upon a smooth meadow full of sunshine like a lake of light, about a mile and a half long, a quarter to half a mile wide, and bounded by tall arrowy pines. The sod, like that of all the glacier meadows hereabouts, is made of silky agrostis and calamagrostis chiefly; their panicles of purple flowers and purple stems, exceedingly light and airy, seem to float above the green plush of leaves like a thin misty cloud, while the sod is brightened by several species of gentian, potentilla, ivesia, orthocarpus, and their corresponding bees and butterflies. All

the glacier meadows are beautiful, but few are so perfect as this
one. Compared with it the most carefully leveled, licked,
snipped artificial lawns of pleasure-grounds are coarse things.
I should like to live here always. It is so calm and withdrawn
while open to the universe in full communion with everything
good. To the north of this glorious meadow I discovered the
camp of some Indian hunters. Their fire was still burning, but
they had not yet returned from the chase.

From meadow to meadow, every one beautiful beyond
telling, and from lake to lake through groves and belts of
arrowy trees, I held my way northward toward Mt. Conness,
finding telling beauty everywhere, while the encompassing
mountains were calling 'Come.' Hope I may climb them all.

August 12 – The sky-scenery has changed but little so far
with the change in elevation. Clouds about .05. Glorious
pearly cumulitinted with purple of ineffable fineness of tone.
Moved camp to the side of the glacier meadow mentioned
above. To let sheep trample so divinely fine a place seems
barbarous. Fortunately they prefer the succulent broad-
leaved triticum and other woodland grasses to the silky
species of the meadows, and therefore seldom bite them
or set foot on them.

The shepherd and the Don cannot agree about methods of
herding. Billy sets his dog Jack on the sheep far too often, so
the Don thinks; and after some dispute today, in which the
shepherd loudly claimed the right to dog the sheep as often as
he pleased, he started for the plains. Now I suppose the care of
the sheep will fall on me, though Mr Delaney promises to do
the herding himself for a while, then return to the lowlands and
bring another shepherd, so as to leave me free to rove as I like.

Had another rich ramble. Pushed northward beyond the
forests to the head of the general basin, where traces of glacial
action are strikingly clear and interesting. The recesses among
the peaks look like quarries, so raw and fresh are the moraine
chips and boulders that strew the ground in Nature's glacial
workshops.

Soon after my return to camp we received a visit from an
Indian, probably one of the hunters whose camp I had discovered. He came from Mono, he said, with others of his tribe,
to hunt deer. One that he had killed a short distance from here

he was carrying on his back, its legs tied together in an ornamental bunch on his forehead. Throwing down his burden, he gazed stolidly for a few minutes in silent Indian fashion, then cut off eight or ten pounds of venison for us, and begged a 'lill' (little) of everything he saw or could think of – flour, bread, sugar, tobacco, whiskey, needles, etc. We gave a fair price for the meat in flour and sugar and added a few needles. A strangely dirty and irregular life these dark-eyed, dark-haired, half-happy savages lead in this clean wilderness – starvation and abundance, deathlike calm, indolence, and admirable, indefatigable action succeeding each other in stormy rhythm like winter and summer. Two things they have that civilized toilers might well envy them – pure air and pure water. These go far to cover and cure the grossness of their lives. Their food is mostly good berries, pine nuts, clover, lily bulbs, wild sheep, antelope, deer, grouse, sage hens, and the larvae of ants, wasps, bees, and other insects.

August 13 – Day all sunshine, dawn and evening purple, noon gold, no clouds, air motionless. Mr Delaney arrived with two shepherds, one of them an Indian. On his way up from the plains he left some provisions at the Portuguese camp on Porcupine Creek near our old Yosemite camp, and I set out this morning with one of the pack animals to fetch them. Arrived at the Porcupine camp at noon, and might have returned to the Tuolumne late in the evening, but concluded to stay over night with the Portuguese shepherds at their pressing invitation. They had sad stories to tell of losses from the Yosemite bears, and were so discouraged they seemed on the point of leaving the mountains; for the bears came every night and helped themselves to one or several of the flock in spite of all their efforts to keep them off.

I spent the afternoon in a grand ramble along the Yosemite walls. From the highest of the rocks called the Three Brothers, I enjoyed a magnificent view comprehending all the upper half of the floor of the valley and nearly all the rocks of the walls on both sides and at the head, with snowy peaks in the background. Saw also the Vernal and Nevada Falls, a truly glorious picture – rocky strength and permanence combined with beauty of plants frail and fine and evanescent; water descending in thunder, and the same water gliding through meadows and groves in gentlest beauty. This standpoint is about eight thousand feet above the sea, or four thousand feet above the floor of the valley, and every tree, though looking small and feathery, stands in admirable clearness, and the shadows they cast are as distinct in outline as if seen at a distance of a few yards. They appeared even more so. No words will ever describe the exquisite beauty and charm of this mountain park – Nature's landscape garden at once tenderly beautiful and sublime. No wonder it draws nature-lovers from all over the world.

Glacial action even on this lofty summit is plainly displayed. Not only has all the lovely valley now smiling in sunshine been filled to the brim with ice, but it has been deeply overflowed.

I visited our old Yosemite camp-ground on the head of Indian Creek, and found it fairly patted and smoothed down with beartracks. The bears had eaten all the sheep that were smothered in the corral, and some of the grand animals must have died, for Mr Delaney, before leaving camp, put a large quantity of poison in the carcasses. All sheepmen carry strychnine to kill coyotes, bears, and panthers, though neither coyotes nor panthers are at all numerous in the upper mountains. The little dog-like wolves are far more numerous in the foothill region and on the plains, where they find a better supply of food – saw only one panther-track above eight thousand feet.

On my return after sunset to the Portuguese camp I found the shepherds greatly excited over the behavior of the bears that have learned to like mutton. 'They are getting worse and worse,' they lamented. Not willing to wait decently until after dark for their suppers, they come and kill and eat their fill in broad daylight. The evening before my arrival, when the two shepherds were leisurely driving the flock toward camp half an hour before sunset, a hungry bear came out of the chaparral within a few yards of them and shuffled deliberately toward the flock. 'Portuguese Joe,' who always carried a gun loaded with buckshot, fired excitedly, threw down his gun, fled to the nearest suitable tree, and climbed to a safe height without waiting to see the effect of his shot. His companion also ran, but said that he saw the bear rise on its hind legs and throw out its arms as if feeling for somebody, and then go into the brush as if wounded.

At another of their camps in this neighborhood, a bear with two cubs attacked the flock before sunset, just as they were approaching the corral. Joe promptly climbed a tree out of danger, while Antone, rebuking his companion for cowardice in abandoning his charge, said that he was not going to let bears 'eat up his sheeps' in daylight, and rushed towards the bears, shouting and setting his dog on them. The frightened cubs climbed a tree, but the mother ran to meet the shepherd and seemed anxious to fight. Antone stood astonished for a moment, eyeing the oncoming bear, then turned and fled, closely pursued. Unable to reach a suitable tree for climbing, he ran to the camp and scrambled up to the roof of the little cabin; the bear followed, but did not climb to the roof – only stood glaring up at him for a few minutes, threatening him and holding him in mortal terror, then went to her cubs, called them down, went to the flock, caught a sheep for supper, and vanished in the brush. As soon as the bear left the cabin the trembling Antone begged Joe to show him a good safe tree, up which he climbed like a sailor climbing a mast, and remained as long as he could hold on, the tree being almost branchless. After these disastrous experiences the two shepherds chopped and gathered large piles of dry wood and made a ring of fire around the corral every night, while one with a gun kept watch from a comfortable stage built on a neighboring pine that commanded a view of the corral. This evening the show made by the circle of fire was very fine, bringing out the surrounding trees in most impressive relief, and making the thousands of sheep eyes glow like a glorious bed of diamonds.

August 14 – Up to the time I went to bed last night all was quiet, though we expected the shaggy freebooters every minute. They did not come till near midnight, when a pair walked boldly to the corral between two of the great fires, climbed in, killed two sheep and smothered ten, while the frightened watcher in the tree did not fire a single shot, saying that he was afraid he might kill some of the sheep, for the bears got into the corral before he got a good clear view of them. I told the shepherds they should at once move the flock to another camp. 'Oh, no use, no use,' they lamented; 'where we go, the bears go too. See my poor dead sheeps – soon all dead. No use try another camp. We go down to the plains.' And as I afterwards learned, they were driven out of the mountains a month before the usual time. Were bears much more numerous and destructive, the sheep would be kept away altogether.

It seems strange that bears, so fond of all sorts of flesh, running the risks of guns and fires and poison, should never attack men except in defense of their young. How easily and safely a bear could pick us up as we lie asleep! Only wolves and tigers seem to have learned to hunt man for food, and perhaps sharks and crocodiles. Mosquitoes and other insects would, I suppose, devour a helpless man in some parts of the world, and so might lions, leopards, wolves, hyenas, and panthers at times if pressed by hunger – but under ordinary circumstances, perhaps, only the tiger among land animals may be said to be a man-eater – unless we add man himself.

Clouds as usual about .05. Another glorious Sierra day, warm, crisp, fragrant, and clear. Many of the flowering plants have gone to seed, but many others are unfolding their petals every day, and the firs and pines are more fragrant than ever. Their seeds are nearly ripe, and will soon be flying in the merriest flocks that ever spread a wing.

On the way back to our Tuolumne camp, I enjoyed the scenery if possible more than when it first came to view. Every feature already seems familiar as if I had lived here always. I never weary gazing at the wonderful Cathedral. It has more individual character than any other rock or mountain I ever saw, excepting perhaps the Yosemite South Dome. The forests, too, seem kindly familiar, and the lakes and meadows and glad singing streams. I should like to dwell with them forever. Here with bread and water I should be content. Even if not allowed to roam and climb, tethered to a stake or tree in some meadow or grove, even then I should be content forever. Bathed in such beauty, watching the expressions ever varying on the faces of the mountains, watching the stars, which here have a glory that the lowlander never dreams of, watching the circling seasons, listening to the songs of the waters and winds and birds, would be endless pleasure. And what glorious cloud-lands I should see, storms and calms – a new heaven and a new earth every day, aye and new inhabitants. And how many visitors I should have. I feel sure I should not have one dull moment. And why should this appear extravagant? It is only common sense, a sign of health, genuine, natural, all-awake health. One would be at an endless Godful play, and what speeches and music and acting and scenery and lights! – sun, moon, stars, auroras. Creation just beginning, the morning stars 'still singing together and all the sons of God shouting for joy.'

Selections from

THE MOUNTAINS OF CALIFORNIA

(1894)

Muir's first complete book, published in 1894, was compiled from earlier magazine and newspaper articles, distilled and condensed into this volume of essays. It contains much of his finest mountaineering and nature-writing from the period 1875–82, when he was trying to educate a national audience about the beauty of the High Sierra, and alert people to the need to preserve these wild areas from destruction. In choosing seven of the original sixteen essays I have included: 'The Sierra Nevada'; 'The Glaciers'; 'A Near View of the High Sierra'; 'The Douglas Squirrel'; 'A Wind Storm in the Forests'; 'The Water Ouzel'; and 'The Wild Sheep'.

Each of these is a classic nature essay in its own right and it should be noted that Muir was pioneering a new literary form and setting a standard for popular writing that few have ever surpassed. Following in the footsteps of his own literary heroes, Henry David Thoreau (1817–62) and Ralph Waldo Emerson (1803–82), Muir's style of adventure writing and his nature-philosophy were clearly influenced by Thoreau's 'Walden – Or Life in the Woods' and 'A Week on the Concord and Merrimack Rivers'. His best nature essays resonate with Thoreau's earlier works such as 'The Succession of Trees', 'Autumnal Tints' and 'Wild Apples'. Similarly, there is little doubt that Muir's Christian-Nature-mysticism is suffused with the Transcendentalist poetry and philosophy of Ralph Waldo Emerson's New England school.

However, in recording his expeditions, his first ascents of dangerous peaks and the plants and animals he found there, Muir blazed a trail not only for conservation but for the later development of 'environmental literature'. Many American writers and photographers have followed Muir's trail to bring the beauty of the wild places to a wider audience: the photographs of Ansel Adams, Elliott Porter and Galen Rowell often portray the same territory that Muir first described in words; similarly, the writings of Aldo Leopold (*A Sand County Almanac*), Rachel Carson (*Silent Spring*), Edward Abbey (*Desert Solitaire*), Annie Dillard (*A Pilgrim at Tinker's Creek*), Sigurd Olsen (*The Singing Wilderness*), Barry Lopez (*Arctic Dreams*) – and many other writers, all explore similar territory and conservation themes to John Muir. All of them display a similar scientific curiosity and a profound empathy for wild creatures, and reprise the ethics of Muir's conservation imperative for new generations.

A Near View of the High Sierra is one of the most gripping accounts of a solo mountain climbing experience ever written. In this essay, Muir recalls the historic solo first ascent of Mount Ritter, a dramatic, Matterhorn-like peak in the remote High Sierra, which he made in October 1872. He wrote:

> Mount Ritter is the king of the mountains of the middle portion of the High Sierra, as Shasta is of the North, and Whitney is of the southern sections. Moreoever, as far as I know, it had never been climbed. Its height above sea level is about 13,300ft and it is fenced around by steeply inclined glaciers and canyons of tremendous depth and ruggedness which render it inaccessible. But difficulties of this kind only exhilarate the mountaineer.

Steve Roper, noted American climber and historian of the High Sierra, wrote in his *Climber's Guide to the High Sierra* that:

> While in Tuolumne Meadows in 1869 John Muir made the first ascent of the sharp and beautiful Cathedral Peak . . . while his solo ascents of Mt Ritter, Mt Whitney and many other peaks . . . place him among the first rank of American mountaineers.

Roper's judgement is based on Muir's tally of first ascents, the technical difficulty of his climbs and his solo exploration of vast wilderness territories. Having once hiked the John Muir Trail from Yosemite Valley to the foot of Mt Ritter, I can confirm that Ritter is a mountain of awe-inspiring grandeur; even today, with mobile phones, GPS and modern training and equipment, only a climber of great experience would attempt a solo ascent of Muir's route on Ritter. Back in 1872, there was not the slightest possibility of a rescue if anything had gone wrong.

The three wildlife essays selected here from *The Mountains of California* include: 'The Douglas Squirrel', 'The Water Ouzel' and 'The Wild Sheep'. These intimate animal portraits reveal that Muir was no mere detached scientific observer; following his poetic muse, Robert Burns, he shared a deep empathy with all living creatures, in their struggle for survival. Muir carried the pocket edition of Burns's *Collected Poems* with him on all his expeditions and must often have read 'To a Mouse' or 'To a Mountain Daisy' while musing on humanity's unbridled dominion of nature – and he shared Burns' deep sympathy for all suffering creatures as 'earth-born companions and fellow mortals'. He wrote:

> On my lonely walks I have often thought how wonderful it would be to have the company of Burns. And indeed he was always with me, for I had him by heart. On my first long walk to the Gulf of Mexico I carried a copy of Burns poems and sang them all the way . . . however wild and strange the places I wandered: the Arctic tundras . . . the icy Alps and Himalayas, Manchuria, Siberia, Australia, New Zealand . . . everywhere Burns seemed at home and his poems fitted everybody. Wherever a Scotsman goes, there goes Burns. His grand whole, catholic soul squares with the good of all; therefore we find him in everything, everywhere.

In 'Thoughts on the Birthday of Robert Burns', written for Burns Night 1907, Muir contrasted the one-dimensional, analytic detachment which Science seemed to demand, with the all-embracing empathy of the Poet and Seer:

> The Naturalist too often loses sight of the essential oneness of all living beings, in seeking to classify them in kingdoms, orders, families, genera, species, etc., taking note of the kind and arrangement of limbs, teeth, toes, scales, hair, feathers,

etc., measured and set forth in metres, centimetres, and milli-
metres; while the eye of the Poet, the Seer, never closes on
the kinship of all God's creatures, and his heart ever beats
in sympathy with great and small alike as 'earth-born companions and fellow mortals, equally dependent on Heaven's
eternal love'.

Muir's ethical compulsion to protect these beautiful plants and
animals by conserving their habitat was both scientific and
spiritual; but he knew that the only way to achieve protection
was to recruit concerned citizens who were willing to become
as committed and engaged as Muir himself was to the national
struggle. The campaign for environmental protection which
Muir inspired brought forth the Sierra Club; but the fountainhead which sustained that new movement flowed from Muir's
essays, like those presented here. Undoubtedly, if he had lived
in the era of radio, film or television, Muir would have grasped
all those new media and exploited them to the full, but as it
was, he was restricted to the literary form and the appeal to
Christian ethics.

Chapter 1

THE SIERRA NEVADA

Go where you may within the bounds of California, mountains are ever in sight, charming and glorifying every landscape. Yet so simple and massive is the topography of the State in general views, that the main central portion displays only one valley, and two chains of mountains which seem almost perfectly regular in trend and height: the Coast Range on the west side, the Sierra Nevada on the east. These two ranges coming together in curves on the north and south inclose a magnificent basin, with a level floor more than 400 miles long, and from 35 to 60 miles wide. This is the grand Central Valley of California, the waters of which have only one outlet to the sea through the Golden Gate. But with this general simplicity of features there is great complexity of hidden detail. The Coast Range, rising as a grand green barrier against the ocean, from 2000 to 8000 feet high, is composed of innumerable forest-crowned spurs, ridges, and rolling hill-waves which inclose a multitude of smaller valleys; some looking out through long, forest-lined vistas to the sea; others, with but few trees, to the Central Valley; while a thousand others yet smaller are embosomed and concealed in mild, round-browed hills, each with its own climate, soil, and productions.

Making your way through the mazes of the Coast Range to the summit of any of the inner peaks or passes opposite San Francisco, in the clear springtime, the grandest and most telling of all California landscapes is outspread before you. At your feet lies the great Central Valley glowing golden in the sunshine, extending north and south farther than the eye can reach, one smooth, flowery, lake-like bed of fertile soil. Along its eastern margin rises the mighty Sierra, miles in height, reposing like a smooth, cumulous cloud in the sunny sky, and so gloriously colored, and so luminous, it seems to be not clothed with light, but wholly composed of it, like the wall of some celestial city. Along the top, and extending a good way down, you see a pale, pearl-gray belt of snow; and below it a belt of blue and dark purple, marking the extension of the forests; and along the base of the range a broad belt of rose-purple and yellow, where lie the miner's gold-fields and the foothill gardens. All these colored belts blending smoothly make a wall of light ineffably fine, and as beautiful as a rainbow, yet firm as adamant.

When I first enjoyed this superb view, one glowing April day, from the summit of the Pacheco Pass, the Central Valley, but little trampled or plowed as yet, was one furred, rich sheet of golden compositae, and the luminous wall of the mountains shone in all its glory. Then it seemed to me the Sierra should be called not the Nevada, or Snowy Range, but the Range of Light. And after ten years spent in the heart of it, rejoicing and wondering, bathing in its glorious floods of light, seeing the sunbursts of morning among the icy peaks, the noonday radiance on the trees and rocks and snow, the flush of the alpenglow, and a thousand dashing waterfalls with their marvelous abundance of irised spray, it still seems to me above all others the Range of Light, the most divinely beautiful of all the mountain-chains I have ever seen.

The Sierra is about 500 miles long, 70 miles wide, and from 7000 to nearly 15,000 feet high. In general views no mark of man is visible on it, nor anything to suggest the richness of the life it cherishes, or the depth and grandeur of its sculpture. None of its magnificent forest-crowned ridges rises much above the general level to publish its wealth. No great valley or lake is seen, or river, or group of well-marked features of any kind, standing out in distinct pictures. Even the summit-peaks, so clear and high in the sky, seem comparatively smooth and featureless. Nevertheless, glaciers are still at work in the shadows of the peaks, and thousands of lakes and meadows shine and bloom beneath them, and the whole range is furrowed with canyons to a depth of from 2000 to 5000 feet, in which once flowed majestic glaciers, and in which now flow and sing a band of beautiful rivers.

Though of such stupendous depth, these famous canyons are not raw, gloomy, jagged-walled gorges, savage and inaccessible. With rough passages here and there they still make delightful pathways for the mountaineer, conducting from the fertile lowlands to the highest icy fountains, as a kind of mountain streets full of charming life and light, graded and sculptured by the ancient glaciers, and presenting, throughout all their courses, a rich variety of novel and attractive scenery, the most attractive that has yet been discovered in the mountain-ranges of the world.

In many places, especially in the middle region of the western flank of the range, the main canyons widen into spacious valleys or parks, diversified like artificial landscape-gardens, with charming groves and meadows, and thickets of blooming bushes, while the lofty, retiring walls, infinitely varied in form and sculpture, are fringed with ferns, flowering-plants of many species, oaks, and evergreens, which find anchorage on a thousand narrow steps and benches; while the whole is enlivened and made glorious with rejoicing streams that come dancing and foaming over the sunny brows of the cliffs to join the shining river that flows in tranquil beauty down the middle of each one of them.

The walls of these park valleys of the Yosemite kind are made up of rocks mountains in size, partly separated from each other by narrow gorges and side-canyons; and they are so sheer in front, and so compactly built together on a level floor, that, comprehensively seen, the parks they inclose look like immense halls or temples lighted from above. Every rock seems to glow with life. Some lean back in majestic repose; others, absolutely sheer, or nearly so, for thousands of feet, advance their brows in thoughtful attitudes beyond their companions, giving welcome to storms and calms alike, seemingly conscious yet heedless of everything going on about them, awful in stern majesty, types of permanence, yet associated with beauty of the frailest and most fleeting forms; their feet set in pine-groves and gay emerald meadows, their brows in the sky; bathed in light, bathed in floods of singing water, while snow-clouds, avalanches, and the winds shine and surge and wreathe about them as the years go by, as if into these mountain mansions Nature had taken pains to gather her choicest treasures to draw her lovers into close and confiding communion with her.

Here, too, in the middle region of deepest canyons are the grandest forest-trees, the Sequoia, king of conifers, the noble

Sugar and Yellow Pines, Douglas Spruce, *Libocedrus*, and the Silver Firs, each a giant of its kind, assembled together in one and the same forest, surpassing all other coniferous forests in the world, both in the number of its species and in the size and beauty of its trees. The winds flow in melody through their colossal spires, and they are vocal everywhere with the songs of birds and running water. Miles of fragrant *Ceanothus* and manzanita bushes bloom beneath them, and lily gardens and meadows, and damp, ferny glens in endless variety of fragrance and color, compelling the admiration of every observer. Sweeping on over ridge and valley, these noble trees extend a continuous belt from end to end of the range, only slightly interrupted by sheer-walled canyons at intervals of about fifteen and twenty miles. Here the great burly brown bears delight to roam, harmonizing with the brown boles of the trees beneath which they feed. Deer, also, dwell here, and find food and shelter in the ceanothus tangles, with a multitude of smaller people. Above this region of giants, the trees grow smaller until the utmost limit of the timber line is reached on the stormy mountain-slopes at a height of from ten to twelve thousand feet above the sea, where the Dwarf Pine is so lowly and hard beset by storms and heavy snow, it is pressed into flat tangles, over the tops of which we may easily walk. Below the main forest belt the trees likewise diminish in size, frost and burning drouth repressing and blasting alike.

The rose-purple zone along the base of the range comprehends nearly all the famous gold region of California. And here it was that miners from every country under the sun assembled in a wild, torrent-like rush to seek their fortunes. On the banks of every river, ravine, and gully they have left their marks. Every gravel- and boulder-bed has been desperately riddled over and over again. But in this region the pick and shovel, once wielded with savage enthusiasm, have been laid away, and only quartz-mining is now being carried on to any considerable extent. The zone in general is made up of low, tawny, waving foothills, roughened here and there with brush and trees, and outcropping masses of slate, colored gray and red with lichens. The smaller masses of slate, rising abruptly from the dry, grassy sod in leaning slabs, look like ancient tombstones in a deserted burying-ground. In early spring, say from February to April, the whole of this foothill belt is a paradise of bees and flowers. Refreshing rains then fall freely, birds are busy building their nests, and the sunshine is balmy and delightful. But by the end of May the soil, plants, and sky seem to have been baked in an oven. Most of the plants crumble to dust beneath the foot, and the ground is full of cracks; while the thirsty traveler gazes with eager longing through the burning glare to the snowy summits looming like hazy clouds in the distance.

The trees, mostly *Quercus Douglasii* and *Pinus Sabiniana*, thirty to forty feet high, with thin, pale-green foliage, stand far apart and cast but little shade. Lizards glide about on the rocks enjoying a constitution that no drouth can dry, and ants in amazing numbers, whose tiny sparks of life seem to burn the brighter with the increasing heat, ramble industriously in long trains in search of food. Crows, ravens, magpies – friends in distress – gather on the ground beneath the best shade-trees, panting with drooping wings and bills wide open, scarce a note from any of them during the midday hours. Quails, too, seek the shade during the heat of the day about tepid pools in the channels of the larger mid-river streams. Rabbits scurry from thicket to thicket among the ceanothus bushes, and occasionally a long-eared hare is seen cantering gracefully across the wider openings. The nights are calm and dewless during the summer, and a thousand voices proclaim the abundance of life, notwithstanding the desolating effect of dry sunshine on the plants and larger animals. The hylas make a delightfully pure and tranquil music after sunset; and coyotes, the little, despised dogs of the wilderness, brave, hardy fellows, looking like withered wisps of hay, bark in chorus for hours. Mining-towns, most of them dead, and a few living ones with bright bits of cultivation about them, occur at long intervals along the belt, and cottages covered with climbing roses, in the midst of orange and peach orchards, and sweet-scented hay-fields in fertile flats where water for irrigation may be had. But they are mostly far apart, and make scarce any mark in general views.

Every winter the High Sierra and the middle forest region get snow in glorious abundance, and even the foothills are at times whitened. Then all the range looks like a vast beveled wall of purest marble. The rough places are then made smooth, the death and decay of the year is covered gently and kindly, and the ground seems as clean as the sky. And though silent in its flight from the clouds, and when it is taking its place on rock, or tree, or grassy meadow, how soon the gentle snow finds a voice! Slipping from the heights, gathering in avalanches, it booms and roars like thunder, and makes a glorious show as it sweeps down the mountain-side, arrayed in long, silken streamers and wreathing, swirling films of crystal dust.

The north half of the range is mostly covered with floods of lava, and dotted with volcanoes and craters, some of them recent and perfect in form, others in various stages of decay. The south half is composed of granite nearly from base to summit, while a considerable number of peaks, in the middle of the range, are capped with metamorphic slates, among which are Mounts Dana and Gibbs to the east of Yosemite Valley. Mount Whitney, the culminating point of the range near its southern extremity, lifts its helmet-shaped crest to a height of nearly 14,700 feet. Mount Shasta, a colossal volcanic cone, rises to a height of 14,440 feet at the northern extremity, and forms a noble landmark for all the surrounding region within a radius of a hundred miles. Residual masses of volcanic rocks occur throughout most of the granitic southern portion also, and a considerable number of old volcanoes on the flanks, especially along the eastern base of the range near Mono Lake and southward. But it is only to the northward that the entire range, from base to summit, is covered with lava.

From the summit of Mount Whitney only granite is seen. Innumerable peaks and spires but little lower than its own storm-beaten crags rise in groups like forest-trees, in full view, segregated by canyons of tremendous depth and ruggedness. On Shasta nearly every feature in the vast view speaks of the old volcanic fires. Far to the northward, in Oregon, the icy volcanoes of Mount Pitt and the Three Sisters rise above the dark evergreen woods. Southward innumerable smaller craters and cones are distributed along the axis of the range and on each flank. Of these, Lassen's Butte is the highest, being nearly 11,000 feet above sea-level. Miles of its flanks are reeking and bubbling with hot springs, many of them so boisterous and sulphurous they seem ever ready to become spouting geysers like those of the Yellowstone.

The Cinder Cone nearby marks the most recent volcanic eruption in the Sierra. It is a symmetrical truncated cone about

700 feet high, covered with gray cinders and ashes, and has a regular unchanged crater on its summit, in which a few small Two-leaved Pines are growing. These show that the age of the cone is not less than eighty years. It stands between two lakes, which a short time ago were one. Before the cone was built, a flood of rough vesicular lava was poured into the lake, cutting it in two, and, overflowing its banks, the fiery flood advanced into the pine-woods, overwhelming the trees in its way, the charred ends of some of which may still be seen projecting from beneath the snout of the lava-stream where it came to rest. Later still there was an eruption of ashes and loose obsidian cinders, probably from the same vent, which, besides forming the Cinder Cone, scattered a heavy shower over the surrounding woods for miles to a depth of from six inches to several feet.

The history of this last Sierra eruption is also preserved in the traditions of the Pitt River Indians. They tell of a fearful time of darkness, when the sky was black with ashes and smoke that threatened every living thing with death, and that when at length the sun appeared once more it was red like blood.

Less recent craters in great numbers roughen the adjacent region; some of them with lakes in their throats, others overgrown with trees and flowers, Nature in these old hearths and firesides having literally given beauty for ashes. On the northwest side of Mount Shasta there is a subordinate cone about 3000 feet below the summit, which has been active subsequent to the breaking up of the main ice-cap that once covered the mountain, as is shown by its comparatively unwasted crater and the streams of unglaciated lava radiating from it. The main summit is about a mile and a half in diameter, bounded by small crumbling peaks and ridges, among which we seek in vain for the outlines of the ancient crater.

These ruinous masses, and the deep glacial grooves that flute the sides of the mountain, show that it has been considerably lowered and wasted by ice; how much we have no sure means of knowing. Just below the extreme summit hot sulphurous gases and vapor issue from irregular fissures, mixed with spray derived from melting snow, the last feeble expression of the mighty force that built the mountain. Not in one great convulsion was Shasta given birth. The crags of the summit and the sections exposed by the glaciers down the sides display enough of its internal framework to prove that comparatively long periods of quiescence intervened between many distinct eruptions, during which the cooling lavas ceased to flow, and became permanent additions to the bulk of the growing mountain. With alternate haste and deliberation eruption succeeded eruption till the old volcano surpassed even its present sublime height.

Standing on the icy top of this, the grandest of all the fire-mountains of the Sierra, we can hardly fail to look forward to its next eruption. Gardens, vineyards, homes have been planted confidingly on the flanks of volcanoes which, after remaining steadfast for ages, have suddenly blazed into violent action, and poured forth overwhelming floods of fire. It is known that more than a thousand years of cool calm have intervened between violent eruptions. Like gigantic geysers spouting molten rock instead of water, volcanoes work and rest, and we have no sure means of knowing whether they are dead when still, or only sleeping.

Along the western base of the range a telling series of sedimentary rocks containing the early history of the Sierra are now being studied. But leaving for the present these first chapters, we see that only a very short geological time ago, just before the coming on of that winter of winters called the glacial period, a vast deluge of molten rocks poured from many a chasm and crater on the flanks and summit of the range, filling lake basins and river channels, and obliterating nearly every existing feature on the northern portion. At length these all-destroying floods ceased to flow. But while the great volcanic cones built up along the axis still burned and smoked, the whole Sierra passed under the domain of ice and snow. Then over the bald, featureless, fire-blackened mountains, glaciers began to crawl, covering them from the summits to the sea with a mantle of ice; and then with infinite deliberation the work went on of sculpturing the range anew. These mighty agents of erosion, halting never through unnumbered centuries, crushed and ground the flinty lavas and granites beneath their crystal folds, wasting and building until in the fullness of time the Sierra was born again, brought to light nearly as we behold it today, with glaciers and snow-crushed pines at the top of the range, wheat-fields and orange-groves at the foot of it.

This change from icy darkness and death to life and beauty was slow, as we count time, and is still going on, north and south, over all the world wherever glaciers exist, whether in the form of distinct rivers, as in Switzerland, Norway, the mountains of Asia, and the Pacific Coast; or in continuous mantling folds, as in portions of Alaska, Greenland, Franz-Joseph-Land, Nova Zembla, Spitzbergen, and the lands about the South Pole. But in no country, as far as I know, may these majestic changes be studied to better advantage than in the plains and mountains of California.

Toward the close of the glacial period, when the snow-clouds became less fertile and the melting waste of sunshine became greater, the lower folds of the ice-sheet in California, discharging fleets of icebergs into the sea, began to shallow and recede from the lowlands, and then move slowly up the flanks of the Sierra in compliance with the changes of climate. The great white mantle on the mountains broke up into a series of glaciers more or less distinct and river-like, with many tributaries, and these again were melted and divided into still smaller glaciers, until now only a few of the smallest residual topmost branches of the grand system exist on the cool slopes of the summit peaks.

Plants and animals, biding their time, closely followed the retiring ice, bestowing quick and joyous animation on the newborn landscapes. Pine-trees marched up the sun-warmed moraines in long, hopeful files, taking the ground and establishing themselves as soon as it was ready for them; brown-spiked sedges fringed the shores of the newborn lakes; young rivers roared in the abandoned channels of the glaciers; flowers bloomed around the feet of the great burnished domes – while with quick fertility mellow beds of soil, settling and warming, offered food to multitudes of Nature's waiting children, great and small, animals as well as plants; mice, squirrels, marmots, deer, bears, elephants, etc. The ground burst into bloom with magical rapidity, and the young forests into birdsong: life in every form warming and sweetening and growing richer as the years passed away over the mighty Sierra so lately suggestive of death and consummate desolation only.

It is hard without long and loving study to realize the magnitude of the work done on these mountains during the last glacial period by glaciers, which are only streams of closely compacted snow-crystals. Careful study of the phenomena presented goes to show that the pre-glacial condition of the range was comparatively simple: one vast wave of stone in which a thousand mountains, domes, canyons, ridges, etc., lay concealed. And in the development of these Nature chose for a tool not the earthquake or lightning to rend and split asunder, not the stormy torrent or eroding rain, but the tender snow-flowers noiselessly falling through unnumbered centuries, the offspring of the sun and sea. Laboring harmoniously in united strength they crushed and ground and wore away the rocks in their march, making vast beds of soil, and at the same time developed and fashioned the landscapes into the delightful variety of hill and dale and lordly mountain that mortals call beauty. Perhaps more than a mile in average depth has the range been thus degraded during the last glacial period – a quantity of mechanical work almost inconceivably great. And our admiration must be excited again and again as we toil and study and learn that this vast job of rockwork, so far-reaching in its influences, was done by agents so fragile and small as are these flowers of the mountain clouds. Strong only by force of number, they carried away entire mountains, particle by particle, block by block, and cast them into the sea; sculptured, fashioned, modeled all the range, and developed its predes-tined beauty. All these new Sierra landscapes were evidently predestined, for the physical structure of the rocks on which the features of the scenery depend was acquired while they lay at least a mile deep below the pre-glacial surface. And it was while these features were taking form in the depths of the range, the particles of the rocks marching to their appointed places in the dark with reference to the coming beauty, that the particles of icy vapor in the sky marching to the same music assembled to bring them to the light. Then, after their grand task was done, these bands of snow-flowers, these mighty glaciers, were melted and removed as if of no more importance than dew destined to last but an hour. Few, however, of Nature's agents have left monuments so noble and enduring as they. The great granite domes a mile high, the canyons as deep, the noble peaks, the Yosemite valleys, these, and indeed nearly all other features of the Sierra scenery, are glacier monuments.

Contemplating the works of these flowers of the sky, one

may easily fancy them endowed with life: messengers sent down to work in the mountain mines on errands of divine love. Silently flying through the darkened air, swirling, glinting, to their appointed places, they seem to have taken counsel together, saying, 'Come, we are feeble; let us help one another. We are many, and together we will be strong. Marching in close, deep ranks, let us roll away the stones from these mountain sepulchers, and set the landscapes free. Let us uncover these clustering domes. Here let us carve a lake basin; there, a Yosemite Valley; here, a channel for a river with fluted steps and brows for the plunge of songful cataracts. Yonder let us spread broad sheets of soil, that man and beast may be fed; and here pile trains of boulders for pines and giant Sequoias. Here make ground for a meadow; there, for a garden and grove, making it smooth and fine for small daisies and violets and beds of heathy bryanthus, spicing it well with crystals, garnet feldspar, and zircon.' Thus and so on it has oftentimes seemed to me sang and planned and labored the hearty snow-flower crusaders; and nothing that I can write can possibly exaggerate the grandeur and beauty of their work. Like morning mist they have vanished in sunshine, all save the few small companies that still linger on the coolest mountain-sides, and, as residual glaciers, are still busily at work completing the last of the lake basins, the last beds of soil, and the sculpture of some of the highest peaks.

Chapter 2
THE GLACIERS

Of the small residual glaciers mentioned in the preceding chapter, I have found sixty-five in that portion of the range lying between latitude 36° 30′ and 39°. They occur singly or in small groups on the north sides of the peaks of the High Sierra, sheltered beneath broad frosty shadows, in amphitheaters of their own making, where the snow, shooting down from the surrounding heights in avalanches, is most abundant. Over two thirds of the entire number lie between latitude 37° and 38°, and form the highest fountains of the San Joaquin, Merced, Tuolumne, and Owen's rivers.

The glaciers of Switzerland, like those of the Sierra, are mere wasting remnants of mighty ice-floods that once filled the great valleys and poured into the sea. So, also, are those of Norway, Asia, and South America. Even the grand continuous mantles of ice that still cover Greenland, Spitzbergen, Nova Zembla, Franz-Joseph-Land, parts of Alaska, and the south polar region are shallowing and shrinking. Every glacier in the world is smaller than it once was. All the world is growing warmer, or the crop of snow-flowers is diminishing. But in contemplating the condition of the glaciers of the world, we must bear in mind while trying to account for the changes going on that the same sunshine that wastes them builds them. Every glacier records the expenditure of an enormous amount of sun-heat in lifting the vapor for the snow of which it is made from the ocean to the mountains, as Tyndall strikingly shows.

The number of glaciers in the Alps, according to the Schlagintweit brothers, is 1100, of which 100 may be regarded as primary, and the total area of ice, snow, and *névé* is estimated at 1177 square miles, or an average for each glacier of little more than one square mile. On the same authority, the average height above sea-level at which they melt is about 7414 feet. The Grindelwald glacier descends below 4000 feet, and one of the Mont Blanc glaciers reaches nearly as low a point. One of the largest of the Himalaya glaciers on the head waters of the Ganges does not, according to Captain Hodgson, descend below 12,914 feet. The largest of the Sierra glaciers on Mount Shasta descends to within 9500 feet of the level of the sea, which, as far as I have observed, is the lowest point reached by any glacier within the bounds of California, the average height of all being not far from 11,000 feet.

The changes that have taken place in the glacial conditions of the Sierra from the time of greatest extension is well illustrated by the series of glaciers of every size and form extending along the mountains of the coast to Alaska. A general exploration of this instructive region shows that to the north of California, through Oregon and Washington, groups of active glaciers still exist on all the high volcanic cones of the Cascade Range – Mount Pitt, the Three Sisters, Mounts Jefferson, Hood, St Helens, Adams, Rainier, Baker, and others – some of them of considerable size, though none of them approach the sea. Of these mountains Rainier, in Washington, is the highest and iciest. Its dome-like summit, between 14,000 and 15,000 feet high, is capped with ice, and eight glaciers, seven to twelve miles long, radiate from it as a center, and form the sources of the principal streams of the State. The lowest-descending of this fine group flows through beautiful forests to within 3500 feet of the sea-level, and sends forth a river laden with glacier mud and sand. On through British Columbia and southeastern Alaska the broad, sustained mountain-chain, extending along the coast, is generally glacier-bearing. The upper branches of nearly all the main canyons and fiords are occupied by glaciers, which gradually increase in size, and descend lower until the high region between Mount Fairweather and Mount St Elias is reached, where a considerable number discharge into the waters of the ocean. This is preëminently the ice-land of Alaska and of the entire Pacific Coast.

Northward from here the glaciers gradually diminish in size and thickness, and melt at higher levels. In Prince William Sound and Cook's Inlet many fine glaciers are displayed, pouring from the surrounding mountains; but to the north of latitude 62° few, if any, glaciers remain, the ground being mostly low and the snowfall light. Between latitude 56° and 60° there are probably more than 5000 glaciers, not counting the smallest. Hundreds of the largest size descend through the forests to the level of the sea, or near it, though as far as my own observations have reached, after a pretty thorough examination of the region, not more than twenty-five discharge icebergs into the sea. All the long high-walled fiords into which these great glaciers of the first class flow are of course crowded with icebergs of every conceivable form, which are detached with thundering noise at intervals of a few minutes from an imposing ice-wall that is thrust forward into deep water. But these Pacific Coast icebergs are small as compared with those of Greenland and the Antarctic region, and only a few of them escape from the intricate system of channels, with which this portion of the coast is fringed, into the open sea. Nearly all of them are swashed and drifted by wind and tide back and forth in the fiords until finally melted by the ocean water, the sunshine, the warm winds, and the copious rains of summer. Only one glacier on the coast, observed by Prof. Russell, discharges its bergs directly into the open sea, at Icy Cape, opposite Mount St Elias. The southernmost of the glaciers that reach the sea occupies a narrow, picturesque fiord about twenty miles to the northwest of the mouth of the Stikeen River, in latitude 56° 50′. The fiord is called by the natives 'Hutli,' or Thunder Bay, from the noise made by the discharge of the icebergs. About one degree farther north there are four of these complete glaciers, discharging at the heads of the long arms of Holkam Bay. At the head of the Tahkoo Inlet, still farther north, there is one; and at the head and around the sides of Glacier Bay, trending in a general northerly direction from Cross Sound in latitude 58° to 59°, there are seven of these complete glaciers pouring bergs into the bay and its branches, and keeping up an eternal thundering. The largest of this group, the Muir, has upward of 200 tributaries, and a width below the confluence of the main tributaries of about twenty-five miles. Between the west side of this icy bay and the ocean all the ground, high and low, excepting the peaks of the Fairweather Range, is covered with a mantle of ice from 1000 to probably 3000 feet thick, which discharges by many distinct mouths.

This fragmentary ice-sheet, and the immense glaciers about Mount St Elias, together with the multitude of separate river-like glaciers that load the slopes of the coast mountains, evidently once formed part of a continuous ice-sheet that flowed over all the region hereabouts, and only a comparatively short time ago extended as far southward as the mouth of the Strait of Juan de Fuca, probably farther. All the islands of the Alexander Archipelago, as well as the headlands and promontories of the mainland, display telling traces of this great mantle that are still fresh and unmistakable. They all have the forms of the greatest strength with reference to the action of a vast rigid press of oversweeping ice from the north and northwest, and their surfaces have a smooth, rounded, overrubbed appearance, generally free from angles. The intricate labyrinth of canals, channels, straits, passages, sounds, narrows, etc., between the islands, and extending into the mainland, of course manifest in their forms and trends and general characteristics the same subordination to the grinding action of universal glaciation as to their origin, and differ from the islands and banks of the fiords only in being portions of the pre-glacial margin of the continent more deeply eroded, and therefore covered by the ocean waters which flowed into them as the ice was melted out of them. The formation and extension of fiords in this manner is still going on, and may be witnessed in many places in Glacier Bay, Yakutat Bay, and adjacent regions. That the domain of the sea is being extended over the land by the wearing away of its shores, is well known, but in these icy regions of Alaska, and even as far south as Vancouver Island, the coast rocks have been so short a time exposed to wave-action they are but little wasted as yet. In these regions the extension of the sea effected by its own action in post-glacial time is scarcely appreciable as compared with that effected by ice-action.

Traces of the vanished glaciers made during the period of greater extension abound on the Sierra as far south as latitude 36°. Even the polished rock surfaces, the most evanescent of glacial records, are still found in a wonderfully perfect state of preservation on the upper half of the middle portion of the range, and form the most striking of all the glacial phenomena. They occur in large irregular patches in the summit and middle regions, and though they have been subjected to the action of the weather with its corroding storms for thousands of years, their mechanical excellence is such that they still reflect the sunbeams like glass, and attract the attention of every observer. The attention of the mountaineer is seldom arrested by moraines, however regular and high they may be, or by canyons, however deep, or by rocks, however noble in form and sculpture; but he stoops and rubs his hands admiringly on the shining surfaces and tries hard to account for their mysterious smoothness. He has seen the snow descending in avalanches, but concludes this cannot be the work of snow, for he finds it where no avalanches occur. Nor can water have done it, for he sees this smoothness glowing on the sides and tops of the highest domes. Only the winds of all the agents he knows seem capable of flowing in the directions indicated by the scoring. Indians, usually so little curious about geological phenomena, have come to me occasionally and asked me, 'What makeum the ground so smooth at Lake Tenaya?' Even horses and dogs gaze wonderingly at the strange brightness of the ground, and smell the polished spaces and place their feet cautiously on them when they come to them for the first time, as if afraid of sinking. The most perfect of the polished pavements and walls lie at an elevation of from 7000 to 9000 feet above the sea, where the rock is compact silicious granite. Small dim patches may be found as low as 3000 feet on the driest and most enduring portions of sheer walls with a southern exposure, and on compact swelling bosses partially protected from rain by a covering of large boulders. On the north half of the range the striated and polished surfaces are less common, not only because this part of the chain is lower, but because the surface rocks are chiefly porous lavas subject to comparatively rapid waste. The ancient moraines also, though well preserved on most of the south half of the range, are nearly obliterated to the northward, but their material is found scattered and disintegrated.

A similar blurred condition of the superficial records of glacial action obtains throughout most of Oregon, Washington, British Columbia, and Alaska, due in great part to the action of excessive moisture. Even in southeastern Alaska, where the most extensive glaciers on the continent are, the more evanescent of the traces of their former greater extension, though comparatively recent, are more obscure than those of the ancient California glaciers where the climate is drier and the rocks more resisting.

These general views of the glaciers of the Pacific Coast will enable my readers to see something of the changes that have taken place in California, and will throw light on the residual glaciers of the High Sierra.

Prior to the autumn of 1871 the glaciers of the Sierra were unknown. In October of that year I discovered the Black Mountain Glacier in a shadowy amphitheater between Black and Red Mountains, two of the peaks of the Merced group. This group is the highest portion of a spur that straggles out from the main axis of the range in the direction of Yosemite Valley. At the time of this interesting discovery I was exploring the *névé* amphitheaters of the group, and tracing the courses of the ancient glaciers that once poured from its ample fountains through the Illilouette Basin and the Yosemite Valley, not expecting to find any active glaciers so far south in the land of sunshine.

Beginning on the northwestern extremity of the group, I explored the chief tributary basins in succession, their moraines, *roches moutonnées*, and splendid glacier pavements, taking them in regular succession without any reference to the time consumed in their study. The monuments of the tributary that poured its ice from between Red and Black Mountains I found to be the most interesting of them all; and when I saw its magnificent moraines extending in majestic curves from the spacious amphitheater between the mountains, I was exhilarated with the work that lay before me. It was one of the golden days of the Sierra Indian summer, when the rich sunshine glorifies every landscape however rocky and cold, and suggests anything rather than glaciers. The path of the vanished glacier was warm now, and shone in many places as if washed with silver. The tall pines growing on the moraines stood transfigured in the glowing light, the poplar groves on the levels of the basin were masses of orange-yellow, and the late blooming goldenrods added gold to gold. Pushing on over my rosy glacial highway, I passed lake after lake set in solid basins of granite, and many a thicket and meadow watered by a stream that issues from the amphitheater and links the lakes together; now wading through plushy bogs knee-deep in yellow and purple sphagnum; now passing over bare rock.

The main lateral moraines that bounded the view on either hand are from 100 to nearly 200 feet high, and about as regular as artificial embankments, and covered with a superb growth of Silver Fir and Pine. But this garden and forest luxuriance was speedily left behind. The trees were dwarfed as I ascended; patches of the alpine bryanthus and cassiope began to appear, and arctic willows pressed into flat carpets by the winter snow. The lakelets, which a few miles down the valley were so richly embroidered with flowery meadows, had here, at an elevation of 10,000 feet, only small brown mats of carex, leaving bare rocks around more than half their shores. Yet amid this alpine suppression the Mountain Pine bravely tossed his storm-beaten branches on the ledges and buttresses of Red Mountain, some specimens being over 100 feet high, and 24 feet in circumference, seemingly as fresh and vigorous as the giants of the lower zones.

Evening came on just as I got fairly within the portal of the main amphitheater. It is about a mile wide, and a little less than two miles long. The crumbling spurs and battlements of Red Mountain bound it on the north, the somber, rudely sculptured precipices of Black Mountain on the south, and a hacked, splintery *col*, curving around from mountain to mountain, shuts it in on the east.

I chose a camping-ground on the brink of one of the lakes where a thicket of Hemlock Spruce sheltered me from the night wind. Then, after making a tin-cupful of tea, I sat by my campfire reflecting on the grandeur and significance of the glacial records I had seen. As the night advanced the mighty rock walls of my mountain mansion seemed to come nearer, while the starry sky in glorious brightness stretched across like a ceiling from wall to wall, and fitted closely down into all the spiky irregularities of the summits. Then, after a long fire-side rest and a glance at my note-book, I cut a few leafy branches for a bed, and fell into the clear, death-like sleep of the tired mountaineer.

Early next morning I set out to trace the grand old glacier that had done so much for the beauty of the Yosemite region back to its farthest fountains, enjoying the charm that every explorer feels in Nature's untrodden wildernesses. The voices of the mountains were still asleep. The wind scarce stirred the pine-needles. The sun was up, but it was yet too cold for the birds and the few burrowing animals that dwell here. Only the stream, cascading from pool to pool, seemed to be wholly awake. Yet the spirit of the opening day called to action. The sunbeams came streaming gloriously through the jagged openings of the *col*, glancing on the burnished pavements and lighting the silvery lakes, while every sun-touched rock burned white on its edges like melting iron in a furnace. Passing round the north shore of my camp lake I followed the central stream past many cascades from lakelet to lakelet. The scenery became more rigidly arctic, the Dwarf Pines and Hemlocks disappeared, and the stream was bordered with icicles. As the sun rose higher rocks were loosened on shattered portions of the cliffs, and came down in rattling avalanches, echoing wildly from crag to crag.

The main lateral moraines that extend from the jaws of the amphitheater into the Illilouette Basin are continued in straggling masses along the walls of the amphitheater, while separate boulders, hundreds of tons in weight, are left stranded here and there out in the middle of the channel. Here, also, I observed a series of small terminal moraines ranged along the south wall of the amphitheater, corresponding in size and form with the shadows cast by the highest portions. The meaning of this correspondence between moraines and shadows was afterward made plain. Tracing the stream back to the last of its chain of lakelets, I noticed a deposit of fine gray mud on the bottom except where the force of the entering current had prevented its settling. It looked like the mud worn from a grind stone, and I at once suspected its glacial origin, for the stream that was carrying it came gurgling out of the base of a raw moraine that seemed in process of formation. Not a plant or weather-stain was visible on its rough, unsettled surface. It is from 60 to over 100 feet high, and plunges forward at an angle of 38°. Cautiously picking my way, I gained the top of the moraine and was delighted to see a small but well characterized glacier swooping down from the gloomy precipices of Black Mountain in a finely graduated curve to the moraine on which I stood. The compact ice appeared on all the lower portions of the glacier, though gray with dirt and stones embedded in it. Farther up the ice disappeared beneath coarse granulated snow. The surface of the glacier was further characterized by dirt bands and the outcropping edges of the blue veins, showing the laminated structure of the ice. The upper-most crevasse, or 'bergschrund,' where the *névé* was attached to the mountain, was from 12 to 14 feet wide, and was bridged in a few places by the remains of snow avalanches. Creeping along the edge of the schrund, holding on with benumbed fingers, I discovered clear sections where the bedded structure was beautifully revealed. The surface snow, though sprinkled with stones shot down from the cliffs, was in some places almost pure, gradually becoming crystalline and changing to whitish porous ice of different shades of color, and this again changing at a depth of 20 or 30 feet to blue ice, some of the ribbon-like bands of which were nearly pure, and blended with the paler bands in the most gradual and delicate manner imaginable. A series of rugged zigzags enabled me to make my way down into the weird under-world of the crevasse. Its chambered hollows were hung with a multitude of clustered icicles, amid which pale, subdued light pulsed and shimmered with indescribable loveliness. Water dripped and tinkled over-head, and from far below came strange, solemn murmurings from currents that were feeling their way through veins and fissures in the dark. The chambers of a glacier are perfectly enchanting, notwithstanding one feels out of place in their frosty beauty. I was soon cold in my shirt-sleeves, and the leaning wall threatened to engulf me; yet it was hard to leave the delicious music of the water and the lovely light. Coming again to the surface, I noticed boulders of every size on their journeys to the terminal moraine – journeys of more than a hundred years, without a single stop, night or day, winter or summer.

The sun gave birth to a network of sweet-voiced rills that ran gracefully down the glacier, curling and swirling in their shining channels, and cutting clear sections through the porous surface-ice into the solid blue, where the structure of the glacier was beautifully illustrated.

The series of small terminal moraines which I had observed in the morning, along the south wall of the amphitheater, correspond in every way with the moraine of this glacier, and their distribution with reference to shadows was now under-stood. When the climatic changes came on that caused the melting and retreat of the main glacier that filled the am-phitheater, a series of residual glaciers were left in the cliff shadows, under the protection of which they lingered, until they formed the moraines we are studying. Then, as the snow became still less abundant, all of them vanished in succession, except the one just described; and the cause of its longer life is sufficiently apparent in the greater area of snow-basin it drains, and its more perfect protection from wasting sunshine. How much longer this little glacier will last depends, of course, on the amount of snow it receives from year to year, as compared with melting waste.

After this discovery, I made excursions over all the High Sierra, pushing my explorations summer after summer, and discovered that what at first sight in the distance looked like extensive snow fields, were in great part glaciers, busily at work completing the sculpture of the summit-peaks so grandly blocked out by their giant predecessors.

On August 21, I set a series of stakes in the Maclure Glacier, near Mount Lyell, and found its rate of motion to be little more than an inch a day in the middle, showing a great contrast to the Muir Glacier in Alaska, which, near the front, flows at a rate of from five to ten feet in twenty-four hours.

Mount Shasta has three glaciers, but Mount Whitney, although it is the highest mountain in the range, does not now cherish a single glacier. Small patches of lasting snow and ice occur on its northern slopes, but they are shallow, and present no well marked evidence of glacial motion. Its sides, however, are scored and polished in many places by the action of its ancient glaciers that flowed east and west as tributaries of the great glaciers that once filled the valleys of the Kern and Owen's rivers.

Chapter 4

A NEAR VIEW OF THE HIGH SIERRA

Early one bright morning in the middle of Indian summer, while the glacier meadows were still crisp with frost crystals, I set out from the foot of Mount Lyell, on my way down to Yosemite Valley, to replenish my exhausted store of bread and tea. I had spent the past summer, as many preceding ones, exploring the glaciers that lie on the head waters of the San Joaquin, Tuolumne, Merced, and Owen's rivers; measuring and studying their movements, trends, crevasses, moraines, etc., and the part they had played during the period of their greater extension in the creation and development of the landscapes of this alpine wonderland. The time for this kind of work was nearly over for the year, and I began to look forward with delight to the approaching winter with its wondrous storms, when I would be warmly snow-bound in my Yosemite cabin with plenty of bread and books; but a tinge of regret came on when I considered that possibly I might not see this favorite region again until the next summer, excepting distant views from the heights about the Yosemite walls.

To artists, few portions of the High Sierra are, strictly speaking, picturesque. The whole massive uplift of the range is one great picture, not clearly divisible into smaller ones; differing much in this respect from the older, and what may be called riper, mountains of the Coast Range. All the landscapes of the Sierra, as we have seen, were born again, remodeled from base to summit by the developing icefloods of the last glacial winter. But all these new landscapes were not brought forth simultaneously; some of the highest, where the ice lingered longest, are tens of centuries younger than those of the warmer regions below them. In general, the younger the mountain-landscapes – younger, I mean, with reference to the time of their emergence from the ice of the glacial period – the less separable are they into artistic bits capable of being made into warm, sympathetic, lovable pictures with appreciable humanity in them.

Here, however, on the head waters of the Tuolumne, is a group of wild peaks on which the geologist may say that the sun has but just begun to shine, which is yet in a high degree picturesque, and in its main features so regular and evenly balanced as almost to appear conventional – one somber cluster of snow-laden peaks with gray pinefringed granite bosses braided around its base, the whole surging free into the sky from the head of a magnificent valley, whose lofty walls are beveled away on both sides so as to embrace it all without admitting anything not strictly belonging to it. The foreground was now aflame with autumn colors, brown and purple and gold, ripe in the mellow sunshine; contrasting brightly with the deep, cobalt blue of the sky, and the black and gray, and pure, spiritual white of the rocks and glaciers. Down through the midst, the young Tuolumne was seen pouring from its crystal fountains, now resting in glassy pools as if changing back again into ice, now leaping in white cascades as if turning to snow; gliding right and left between granite bosses, then sweeping on through the smooth, meadowy levels of the valley, swaying pensively from side to side with calm, stately gestures past dipping willows and sedges, and around groves of arrowy pine; and throughout its whole eventful course, whether flowing fast or slow, singing loud or low, ever filling the landscape with spiritual animation, and manifesting the grandeur of its sources in every movement and tone.

Pursuing my lonely way down the valley, I turned again and again to gaze on the glorious picture, throwing up my arms to inclose it as in a frame. After long ages of growth in the darkness beneath the glaciers, through sunshine and storms, it seemed now to be ready and waiting for the elected artist, like yellow wheat for the reaper; and I could not help wishing that I might carry colors and brushes with me on my travels, and learn to paint. In the meantime I had to be content with photographs on my mind and sketches in my note-books. At length, after I had rounded a precipitous headland that puts out from the west wall of the valley, every peak vanished from sight, and I pushed rapidly along the frozen meadows, over the divide between the waters of the Merced and Tuolumne, and down through the forests that clothe the slopes of Cloud's Rest, arriving in Yosemite in due time – which, with me, is *any* time. And, strange to say, among the first people I met here were two artists who, with letters of introduction, were awaiting my return. They inquired whether in the course of my explorations in the adjacent mountains I had ever come upon a landscape suitable for a large painting; whereupon I began a description of the one that had so lately excited my admiration. Then, as I went on further and further into details, their faces began to glow, and I offered to guide them to it, while they declared that they would gladly follow, far or near, whithersoever I could spare the time to lead them.

Since storms might come breaking down through the fine weather at any time, burying the colors in snow, and cutting off the artists' retreat, I advised getting ready at once.

I led them out of the valley by the Vernal and Nevada Falls, thence over the main dividing ridge to the Big Tuolumne Meadows, by the old Mono trail, and thence along the upper Tuolumne River to its head. This was my companions' first excursion into the High Sierra, and as I was almost always alone in my mountaineering, the way that the fresh beauty was reflected in their faces made for me a novel and interesting study. They naturally were affected most of all by the colors – the intense azure of the sky, the purplish grays of the granite, the red and browns of dry meadows, and the translucent purple and crimson of huckleberry bogs; the flaming yellow of aspen groves, the silvery flashing of the streams, and the bright green and blue of the glacier lakes. But the general expression of the scenery – rocky and savage – seemed sadly disappointing; and as they threaded the forest from ridge to ridge, eagerly scanning the landscapes as they were unfolded, they said: 'All this is huge and sublime, but we see nothing as yet at all available for effective pictures. Art is long, and art is limited, you know; and here are foregrounds, middle-grounds, backgrounds, all alike; bare rock-waves, woods, groves, diminutive flecks of meadow, and strips of glittering water.' 'Never mind,' I replied, 'only bide a wee, and I will show you something you will like.'

At length, toward the end of the second day, the Sierra

Crown began to come into view, and when we had fairly rounded the projecting headland before mentioned, the whole picture stood revealed in the flush of the alpenglow. Their enthusiasm was excited beyond bounds, and the more impulsive of the two, a young Scotchman, dashed ahead, shouting and gesticulating and tossing his arms in the air like a madman. Here, at last, was a typical alpine landscape.

After feasting awhile on the view, I proceeded to make camp in a sheltered grove a little way back from the meadow, where pine-boughs could be obtained for beds, and where there was plenty of dry wood for fires, while the artists ran here and there, along the river-bends and up the sides of the canyon, choosing foregrounds for sketches. After dark, when our tea was made and a rousing fire had been built, we began to make our plans. They decided to remain several days, at the least, while I concluded to make an excursion in the meantime to the untouched summit of Ritter.

It was now about the middle of October, the springtime of snow-flowers. The first winter-clouds had already bloomed, and the peaks were strewn with fresh crystals, without, however, affecting the climbing to any dangerous extent. And as the weather was still profoundly calm, and the distance to the foot of the mountain only a little more than a day, I felt that I was running no great risk of being storm-bound.

Mount Ritter is king of the mountains of the middle portion of the High Sierra, as Shasta of the north and Whitney of the south sections. Moreover, as far as I know, it had never been climbed. I had explored the adjacent wilderness summer after summer, but my studies thus far had never drawn me to the top of it. Its height above sea-level is about 13,300 feet, and it is fenced round by steeply inclined glaciers, and canyons of tremendous depth and ruggedness, which render it almost inaccessible. But difficulties of this kind only exhilarate the mountaineer.

Next morning, the artists went heartily to their work and I to mine. Former experiences had given good reason to know that passionate storms, invisible as yet, might be brooding in the calm sun-gold; therefore, before bidding farewell, I warned the artists not to be alarmed should I fail to appear before a week or ten days, and advised them, in case a snow-storm should set in, to keep up big fires and shelter themselves as best they could, and on no account to become frightened and attempt to seek their way back to Yosemite alone through the drifts.

My general plan was simply this: to scale the canyon wall, cross over to the eastern flank of the range, and then make my way southward to the northern spurs of Mount Ritter in compliance with the intervening topography; for to push on directly southward from camp through the innumerable peaks and pinnacles that adorn this portion of the axis of the range, however interesting, would take too much time, besides being extremely difficult and dangerous at this time of year.

All my first day was pure pleasure; simply mountaineering indulgence, crossing the dry pathways of the ancient glaciers, tracing happy streams, and learning the habits of the birds and marmots in the groves and rocks. Before I had gone a mile from camp, I came to the foot of a white cascade that beats its way down a rugged gorge in the canyon wall, from a height of about nine hundred feet, and pours its throbbing waters into the Tuolumne. I was acquainted with its fountains, which, fortunately, lay in my course. What a fine traveling companion it proved to be, what songs it sang, and how passionately it told the mountain's own joy! Gladly I climbed along its dashing border, absorbing its divine music, and bathing from time to time in waftings of irised spray. Climbing higher, higher, new beauty came streaming on the sight: painted meadows, late-blooming gardens, peaks of rare architecture, lakes here and there, shining like silver, and glimpses of the forested middle region and the yellow lowlands far in the west. Beyond the range I saw the so-called Mono Desert, lying dreamily silent in thick purple light – a desert of heavy sun-glare beheld from a desert of ice-burnished granite. Here the waters divide, shouting in glorious enthusiasm, and falling eastward to vanish in the volcanic sands and dry sky of the Great Basin, or westward to the Great Valley of California, and thence through the Bay of San Francisco and the Golden Gate to the sea.

Passing a little way down over the summit until I had reached an elevation of about 10,000 feet, I pushed on southward toward a group of savage peaks that stand guard about Ritter on the north and west, groping my way, and dealing instinctively with every obstacle as it presented itself. Here a huge gorge would be found cutting across my path, along the dizzy edge of which I scrambled until some less precipitous point was discovered where I might safely venture to the bottom and then, selecting some feasible portion of the opposite wall, reascend with the same slow caution. Massive, flat-topped spurs alternate with the gorges, plunging abruptly from the shoulders of the snowy peaks, and planting their feet in the warm desert. These were everywhere marked and adorned with characteristic sculptures of the ancient glaciers that swept over this entire region like one vast ice-wind, and the polished surfaces produced by the ponderous flood are still so perfectly preserved that in many places the sunlight reflected from them is about as trying to the eyes as sheets of snow.

God's glacial-mills grind slowly, but they have been kept in motion long enough in California to grind sufficient soil for a glorious abundance of life, though most of the grist has been carried to the lowlands, leaving these high regions comparatively lean and bare; while the post-glacial agents of erosion have not yet furnished sufficient available food over the general surface for more than a few tufts of the hardiest plants, chiefly carices and eriogonae. And it is interesting to learn in this connection that the sparseness and repressed character of the vegetation at this height is caused more by want of soil than by harshness of climate; for, here and there, in sheltered hollows (countersunk beneath the general surface) into which a few rods of well-ground moraine chips have been dumped, we find groves of spruce and pine thirty to forty feet high, trimmed around the edges with willow and huckleberry bushes, and oftentimes still further by an outer ring of tall grasses, bright with lupines, lark-spurs, and showy columbines, suggesting a climate by no means repressingly severe. All the streams, too, and the pools at this elevation are furnished with little gardens wherever soil can be made to lie, which, though making scarce any show at a distance, constitute charming surprises to the appreciative observer. In these bits of leafiness a few birds find grateful homes. Having no acquaintance with man, they fear no ill, and flock curiously about the stranger, almost allowing themselves to be taken in the hand. In so wild and so beautiful a region was spent my first day, every sight and sound inspiring, leading one far out of himself, yet feeding and building up his individuality.

Now came the solemn, silent evening. Long, blue, spiky shadows crept out across the snow-fields, while a rosy glow, at first scarce discernible, gradually deepened and suffused every mountain-top, flushing the glaciers and the harsh crags above them. This was the alpenglow, to me one of the most impressive of all the terrestrial manifestations of God. At the touch of this divine light, the mountains seemed to kindle to a rapt, religious consciousness, and stood hushed and waiting like devout worshippers. Just before the alpenglow began to fade, two crimson clouds came streaming across the summit like wings of flame, rendering the sublime scene yet more impressive; then came darkness and the stars.

Icy Ritter was still miles away, but I could proceed no farther that night. I found a good camp-ground on the rim of a glacier basin about 11,000 feet above the sea. A small lake nestles in the bottom of it, from which I got water for my tea, and a stormbeaten thicket nearby furnished an abundance of resiny fire-wood. Somber peaks, hacked and shattered, circled halfway around the horizon, wearing a savage aspect in the gloaming, and a waterfall chanted solemnly across the lake on its way down from the foot of a glacier. The fall and the lake and the glacier were almost equally bare; while the scraggy pines anchored in the rock-fissures were so dwarfed and shorn by storm-winds that you might walk over their tops. In tone and aspect the scene was one of the most desolate I ever beheld. But the darkest scriptures of the mountains are illumined with bright passages of love that never fail to make themselves felt when one is alone.

I made my bed in a nook of the pine-thicket, where the branches were pressed and crinkled overhead like a roof, and bent down around the sides. These are the best bedchambers the high mountains afford – snug as squirrel-nests, well ventilated, full of spicy odors, and with plenty of wind-played needles to sing one asleep. I little expected company, but, creeping in through a low side-door, I found five or six birds nestling among the tassels. The night-wind began to blow soon after dark; at first only a gentle breathing, but increasing toward midnight to a rough gale that fell upon my leafy roof in ragged surges like a cascade, bearing wild sounds from the crags overhead. The waterfall sang in chorus, filling the old ice-fountain with its solemn roar, and seeming to increase in power as the night advanced – fit voice for such a landscape. I had to creep out many times to the fire during the night, for it was biting cold and I had no blankets. Gladly I welcomed the morning star.

The dawn in the dry, wavering air of the desert was glorious. Everything encouraged my undertaking and betokened success. There was no cloud in the sky, no storm-tone in the wind. Breakfast of bread and tea was soon made. I fastened a hard, durable crust to my belt by way of provision, in case I should be compelled to pass a night on the mountain-top; then, securing the remainder of my little stock against wolves and wood-rats, I set forth free and hopeful.

How glorious a greeting the sun gives the mountains! To behold this alone is worth the pains of any excursion a thousand times over. The highest peaks burned like islands in a sea of liquid shade. Then the lower peaks and spires caught the glow, and long lances of light, streaming through many a notch and pass, fell thick on the frozen meadows. The majestic form of Ritter was full in sight, and I pushed rapidly on over rounded rock-bosses and pavements, my iron-shod shoes making a clanking sound, suddenly hushed now and then in rugs of bryanthus, and sedgy lake-margins soft as moss. Here, too, in this so-called 'land of desolation,' I met cassiope, growing in fringes among the battered rocks. Her blossoms had faded long ago, but they were still clinging with happy memories to the evergreen sprays, and still so beautiful as to thrill every fiber of one's being. Winter and summer, you may hear her voice, the low, sweet melody of her purple bells. No evangel among all the mountain plants speaks Nature's love more plainly than cassiope. Where she dwells, the redemption of the coldest solitude is complete. The very rocks and glaciers seem to feel her presence, and become imbued with her own fountain sweetness. All things were warming and awakening. Frozen rills began to flow, the marmots came out of their nests in boulder-piles and climbed sunny rocks to bask, and the dun-headed sparrows were flitting about seeking their breakfasts. The lakes seen from every ridge-top were brilliantly rippled and spangled, shimmering like the thickets of the low Dwarf Pines. The rocks, too, seemed responsive to the vital heat – rock-crystals and snow-crystals thrilling alike. I strode on exhilarated, as if never more to feel fatigue, limbs moving of themselves, every sense unfolding like the thawing flowers, to take part in the new day harmony.

All along my course thus far, excepting when down in the canyons, the landscapes were mostly open to me, and expansive, at least on one side. On the left were the purple plains of Mono, reposing dreamily and warm; on the right, the near peaks springing keenly into the thin sky with more and more impressive sublimity. But these larger views were at length lost. Rugged spurs, and moraines, and huge, projecting buttresses began to shut me in. Every feature became more rigidly alpine, without, however, producing any chilling effect; for going to the mountains is like going home. We always find that the strangest objects in these fountain wilds are in some degree familiar, and we look upon them with a vague sense of having seen them before.

On the southern shore of a frozen lake, I encountered an extensive field of hard, granular snow, up which I scampered in fine tone, intending to follow it to its head, and cross the rocky spur against which it leans, hoping thus to come direct upon the base of the main Ritter peak. The surface was pitted with oval hollows, made by stones and drifted pine-needles that had melted themselves into the mass by the radiation of absorbed sun-heat. These afforded good footholds, but the surface curved more and more steeply at the head, and the pits became shallower and less abundant, until I found myself in danger of being shed off like avalanching snow. I persisted, however, creeping on all fours, and shuffling up the smoothest places on my back, as I had often done on burnished granite, until, after slipping several times, I was compelled to retrace my course to the bottom, and make my way around the west end of the lake, and thence up to the summit of the divide between the head waters of Rush Creek and the northernmost tributaries of the San Joaquin.

Arriving on the summit of this dividing crest, one of the most exciting pieces of pure wilderness was disclosed that I ever discovered in all my mountaineering. There, immediately in front, loomed the majestic mass of Mount Ritter, with a glacier swooping down its face nearly to my feet, then curving westward and pouring its frozen flood into a dark blue lake, whose shores were bound with precipices of crystalline snow; while a deep chasm drawn between the divide and the glacier separated the massive picture from everything else. I could see only the one sublime mountain, the one glacier, the one lake; the whole veiled with one blue shadow – rock, ice, and water close together without a single leaf or sign of life. After gazing spellbound, I began instinctively to scrutinize every notch and gorge and weathered buttress of the mountain, with reference to making the ascent. The entire front above the glacier appeared as one tremendous precipice, slightly receding at the top, and bristling with spires and pinnacles set above one another in formidable array. Massive lichen-stained battlements stood forward here and there, hacked at the top with angular notches, and separated by frosty gullies and recesses that have been veiled in shadow ever since their creation; while to right and left, as far as I could see, were huge, crumbling buttresses, offering no hope to the climber. The head of the glacier sends up a few finger-like branches through narrow *couloirs* ; but these seemed too steep and short to be available, especially as I had no axe with which to cut steps, and the numerous narrow-throated gullies down which stones and snow are avalanched seemed hopelessly steep, besides being interrupted by vertical cliffs; while the whole front was rendered still more terribly forbidding by the chill shadow and the gloomy blackness of the rocks.

Descending the divide in a hesitating mood, I picked my way across the yawning chasm at the foot, and climbed out upon the glacier. There were no meadows now to cheer with their brave colors, nor could I hear the dun-headed sparrows, whose cheery notes so often relieve the silence of our highest mountains. The only sounds were the gurgling of small rills down in the veins and crevasses of the glacier, and now and then the rattling report of falling stones, with the echoes they shot out into the crisp air.

I could not distinctly hope to reach the summit from this side, yet I moved on across the glacier as if driven by fate. Contending with myself, the season is too far spent, I said, and even should I be successful, I might be storm-bound on the mountain; and in the cloud-darkness, with the cliffs and crevasses covered with snow, how could I escape? No; I must wait till next summer. I would only approach the mountain now, and inspect it, creep about its flanks, learn what I could of its history, holding myself ready to flee on the approach of

the first storm-cloud. But we little know until tried how much
of the uncontrollable there is in us, urging across glaciers and
torrents, and up dangerous heights, let the judgement forbid as
it may.

I succeeded in gaining the foot of the cliff on the eastern
extremity of the glacier, and there discovered the mouth of a
narrow avalanche gully, through which I began to climb,
intending to follow it as far as possible, and at least obtain
some fine wild views for my pains. Its general course is oblique
to the plane of the mountain-face, and the metamorphic slates
of which the mountain is built are cut by cleavage planes in
such a way that they weather off in angular blocks, giving rise
to irregular steps that greatly facilitate climbing on the sheer
places. I thus made my way into a wilderness of crumbling
spires and battlements, built together in bewildering combinations, and glazed in many places with a thin coating of ice,
which I had to hammer off with stones. The situation was
becoming gradually more perilous; but, having passed several
dangerous spots, I dared not think of descending; for, so steep
was the entire ascent, one would inevitably fall to the glacier in
case a single misstep were made. Knowing, therefore, the tried
danger beneath, I became all the more anxious concerning the
developments to be made above, and began to be conscious of
a vague foreboding of what actually befell; not that I was given
to fear, but rather because my instincts, usually so positive and
true, seemed vitiated in some way, and were leading me astray.
At length, after attaining an elevation of about 12,800 feet, I
found myself at the foot of a sheer drop in the bed of the
avalanche channel I was tracing, which seemed absolutely to
bar further progress. It was only about forty-five or fifty feet
high, and somewhat roughened by fissures and projections;
but these seemed so slight and insecure, as footholds, that I
tried hard to avoid the precipice altogether, by scaling the wall
of the channel on either side. But, though less steep, the walls
were smoother than the obstructing rock, and repeated efforts
only showed that I must either go right ahead or turn back.
The tried dangers beneath seemed even greater than that of the
cliff in front; therefore, after scanning its face again and again,
I began to scale it, picking my holds with intense caution. After
gaining a point about halfway to the top, I was suddenly
brought to a dead stop, with arms outspread, clinging close to

the face of the rock, unable to move hand or foot either up or down. My doom appeared fixed. I *must* fall. There would be a moment of bewilderment, and then a lifeless rumble down the one general precipice to the glacier below.

When this final danger flashed upon me, I became nerve-shaken for the first time since setting foot on the mountains, and my mind seemed to fill with a stifling smoke. But this terrible eclipse lasted only a moment, when life blazed forth again with preternatural clearness. I seemed suddenly to become possessed of a new sense. The other self, bygone experiences, Instinct, or Guardian Angel – call it what you will – came forward and assumed control. Then my trembling muscles became firm again, every rift and flaw in the rock was seen as through a microscope, and my limbs moved with a positiveness and precision with which I seemed to have nothing at all to do. Had I been borne aloft upon wings, my deliverance could not have been more complete.

Above this memorable spot, the face of the mountain is still more savagely hacked and torn. It is a maze of yawning chasms and gullies, in the angles of which rise beetling crags and piles of detached boulders that seem to have been gotten ready to be launched below. But the strange influx of strength I had received seemed inexhaustible. I found a way without effort, and soon stood upon the topmost crag in the blessed light.

How truly glorious the landscape circled around this noble summit! Giant mountains, valleys innumerable, glaciers and meadows, rivers and lakes, with the wide blue sky bent tenderly over them all. But in my first hour of freedom from that terrible shadow, the sunlight in which I was laving seemed all in all.

Looking southward along the axis of the range, the eye is first caught by a row of exceedingly sharp and slender spires, which rise openly to a height of about a thousand feet, above a series of short, residual glaciers that lean back against their bases; their fantastic sculpture and the unrelieved sharpness with which they spring out of the ice rendering them peculiarly wild and striking. These are 'The Minarets.' Beyond them you behold a sublime wilderness of mountains, their snowy summits towering together in crowded abundance, peak beyond peak, swelling higher, higher as they sweep on southward, until the culminating point of the range is reached on Mount

Whitney, near the head of the Kern River, at an elevation of nearly 14,700 feet above the level of the sea.

Westward, the general flank of the range is seen flowing sublimely away from the sharp summits, in smooth undulations; a sea of huge gray granite waves dotted with lakes and meadows, and fluted with stupendous canyons that grow steadily deeper as they recede in the distance. Below this gray region lies the dark forest zone, broken here and there by upswelling ridges and domes; and yet beyond lies a yellow, hazy belt, marking the broad plain of the San Joaquin, bounded on its farther side by the blue mountains of the coast.

Turning now to the northward, there in the immediate foreground is the glorious Sierra Crown, with Cathedral Peak, a temple of marvelous architecture, a few degrees to the left of it; the gray, massive form of Mammoth Mountain to the right; while Mounts Ord, Gibbs, Dana, Conness, Tower Peak, Castle Peak, Silver Mountain, and a host of noble companions, as yet nameless, make a sublime show along the axis of the range.

Eastward, the whole region seems a land of desolation covered with beautiful light. The torrid volcanic basin of Mono, with its one bare lake fourteen miles long; Owen's Valley and the broad lava table-land at its head, dotted with craters, and the massive Inyo Range, rivaling even the Sierra in height; these are spread, map-like, beneath you, with countless ranges beyond, passing and overlapping one another and fading on the glowing horizon.

At a distance of less than 3,000 feet below the summit of Mount Ritter you may find tributaries of the San Joaquin and Owen's rivers, bursting forth from the ice and snow of the glaciers that load its flanks; while a little to the north of here are found the highest affluents of the Tuolumne and Merced. Thus, the fountains of four of the principal rivers of California are within a radius of four or five miles.

Lakes are seen gleaming in all sorts of places – round, or oval, or square, like very mirrors; others narrow and sinuous, drawn close around the peaks like silver zones, the highest reflecting only rocks, snow, and the sky. But neither these nor the glaciers, nor the bits of brown meadow and moorland that occur here and there, are large enough to make any marked impression upon the mighty wilderness of mountains. The eye, rejoicing in its freedom, roves about the vast expanse, yet

returns again and again to the fountain peaks. Perhaps someone of the multitude excites special attention, some gigantic
castle with turret and battlement, or some Gothic cathedral
more abundantly spired than Milan's. But, generally, when
looking for the first time from an all-embracing standpoint like
this, the inexperienced observer is oppressed by the incomprehensible grandeur, variety, and abundance of the mountains rising shoulder to shoulder beyond the reach of vision;
and it is only after they have been studied one by one, long and
lovingly, that their far-reaching harmonies become manifest.
Then, penetrate the wilderness where you may, the main telling
features, to which all the surrounding topography is subordinate, are quickly perceived, and the most complicated clusters
of peaks stand revealed harmoniously correlated and fashioned like works of art – eloquent monuments of the ancient
ice-rivers that brought them into relief from the general mass
of the range. The canyons, too, some of them a mile deep,
mazing wildly through the mighty host of mountains, however
lawless and ungovernable at first sight they appear, are at
length recognized as the necessary effects of causes which
followed each other in harmonious sequence – Nature's poems
carved on tables of stone – the simplest and most emphatic of
her glacial compositions.

Could we have been here to observe during the glacial
period, we should have overlooked a wrinkled ocean of ice
as continuous as that now covering the landscapes of Greenland; filling every valley and canyon with only the tops of the
fountain peaks rising darkly above the rock-encumbered ice-
waves like islets in a stormy sea – those islets the only hints of
the glorious landscapes now smiling in the sun. Standing here
in the deep, brooding silence all the wilderness seems motionless, as if the work of creation were done. But in the midst of
this outer steadfastness we know there is incessant motion and
change. Ever and anon, avalanches are falling from yonder
peaks. These cliff-bound glaciers, seemingly wedged and immovable, are flowing like water and grinding the rocks beneath them. The lakes are lapping their granite shores and
wearing them away, and every one of these rills and young
rivers is fretting the air into music, and carrying the mountains
to the plains. Here are the roots of all the life of the valleys, and
here more simply than elsewhere is the eternal flux of nature

manifested. Ice changing to water, lakes to meadows, and mountains to plains. And while we thus contemplate Nature's methods of landscape creation, and, reading the records she has carved on the rocks, reconstruct, however imperfectly, the landscapes of the past, we also learn that as these we now behold have succeeded those of the preglacial age, so they in turn are withering and vanishing to be succeeded by others yet unborn.

But in the midst of these fine lessons and landscapes, I had to remember that the sun was wheeling far to the west, while a new way down the mountain had to be discovered to some point on the timber line where I could have a fire; for I had not even burdened myself with a coat. I first scanned the western spurs, hoping some way might appear through which I might reach the northern glacier, and cross its snout; or pass around the lake into which it flows, and thus strike my morning track. This route was soon sufficiently unfolded to show that, if practicable at all, it would require so much time that reaching camp that night would be out of the question. I therefore scrambled back eastward, descending the southern slopes obliquely at the same time. Here the crags seemed less formidable, and the head of a glacier that flows northeast came in sight, which I determined to follow as far as possible, hoping thus to make my way to the foot of the peak on the east side, and thence across the intervening canyons and ridges to camp.

The inclination of the glacier is quite moderate at the head, and, as the sun had softened the *névé*, I made safe and rapid progress, running and sliding, and keeping up a sharp outlook for crevasses. About half a mile from the head, there is an ice-cascade, where the glacier pours over a sharp declivity and is shattered into massive blocks separated by deep, blue fissures. To thread my way through the slippery mazes of this crevassed portion seemed impossible, and I endeavored to avoid it by climbing off to the shoulder of the mountain. But the slopes rapidly steepened and at length fell away in sheer precipices, compelling a return to the ice. Fortunately, the day had been warm enough to loosen the ice-crystals so as to admit of hollows being dug in the rotten portions of the blocks, thus enabling me to pick my way with far less difficulty than I had anticipated. Continuing down over the snout, and along the left lateral moraine, was only a confident saunter, showing that the ascent of the mountain by way of this glacier is easy, provided one is armed with an axe to cut steps here and there.

The lower end of the glacier was beautifully waved and barred by the outcropping edges of the bedded ice-layers which represent the annual snowfalls, and to some extent the irregularities of structure caused by the weathering of the walls of crevasses, and by separate snowfalls which have been followed by rain, hail, thawing and freezing, etc. Small rills were gliding and swirling over the melting surface with a smooth, oily appearance, in channels of pure ice – their quick, compliant movements contrasting most impressively with the rigid, invisible flow of the glacier itself, on whose back they all were riding.

Night drew near before I reached the eastern base of the mountain, and my camp lay many a rugged mile to the north; but ultimate success was assured. It was now only a matter of endurance and ordinary mountain-craft. The sunset was, if possible, yet more beautiful than that of the day before. The Mono landscape seemed to be fairly saturated with warm, purple light. The peaks marshaled along the summit were in shadow, but through every notch and pass streamed vivid sunfire, soothing and irradiating their rough, black angles, while companies of small, luminous clouds hovered above them like very angels of light.

Darkness came on, but I found my way by the trends of the canyons and the peaks projected against the sky. All excitement died with the light, and then I was weary. But the joyful sound of the waterfall across the lake was heard at last, and soon the stars were seen reflected in the lake itself. Taking my bearings from these, I discovered the little pine thicket in which my nest was, and then I had a rest such as only a tired mountaineer may enjoy. After lying loose and lost for awhile, I made a sunrise fire, went down to the lake, dashed water on my head, and dipped a cupful for tea. The revival brought about by bread and tea was as complete as the exhaustion from excessive enjoyment and toil. Then I crept beneath the pine-tassels to bed. The wind was frosty and the fire burned low, but my sleep was none the less sound, and the evening constellations had swept far to the west before I awoke.

After thawing and resting in the morning sunshine, I sauntered home – that is, back to the Tuolumne camp – bearing away toward a cluster of peaks that hold the fountain snows of one of the north tributaries of Rush Creek. Here I discovered a group of beautiful glacier lakes, nestled together in a grand amphitheater. Toward evening, I crossed the divide separating the Mono waters from those of the Tuolumne, and entered the glacier basin that now holds the fountain snows of the stream that forms the upper Tuolumne cascades. This stream I traced down through its many dells and gorges, meadows and bogs, reaching the brink of the main Tuolumne at dusk.

A loud whoop for the artists was answered again and again. Their campfire came in sight, and half an hour afterward I was with them. They seemed unreasonably glad to see me. I had been absent only three days; nevertheless, though the weather was fine, they had already been weighing chances as to whether I would ever return, and trying to decide whether they should wait longer or begin to seek their way back to the lowlands. Now their curious troubles were over. They packed their precious sketches, and next morning we set out homeward bound, and in two days entered the Yosemite Valley from the north by way of Indian Canyon.

Chapter 9

THE DOUGLAS SQUIRREL

(Sciurus Douglasii)

The Douglas Squirrel is by far the most interesting and influential of the California sciuridae, surpassing every other species in force of character, numbers, and extent of range, and in the amount of influence he brings to bear upon the health and distribution of the vast forests he inhabits.

Go where you will throughout the noble woods of the Sierra Nevada, among the giant pines and spruces of the lower zones, up through the towering Silver Firs to the storm-bent thickets of the summit peaks, you everywhere find this little squirrel the master-existence. Though only a few inches long, so intense is his fiery vigor and restlessness, he stirs every grove with wild life, and makes himself more important than even the huge bears that shuffle through the tangled underbrush beneath him. Every wind is fretted by his voice, almost every bole and branch feels the sting of his sharp feet. How much the growth of the trees is stimulated by this means it is not easy to learn, but his action in manipulating their seeds is more appreciable. Nature has made him master forester and committed most of her coniferous crops to his paws. Probably over 50 per cent of all the cones ripened on the Sierra are cut off and handled by the Douglas alone, and of those of the Big Trees perhaps 90 per cent pass through his hands: the greater portion is of course stored away for food to last during the winter and spring, but some of them are tucked separately into loosely covered holes, where some of the seeds germinate and become trees. But the Sierra is only one of the many provinces over which he holds sway, for his dominion extends over all the Redwood Belt of the Coast Mountains, and far northward throughout the majestic forests of Oregon, Washington, and British Columbia.

I make haste to mention these facts, to show upon how substantial a foundation the importance I ascribe to him rests.

The Douglas is closely allied to the Red Squirrel or Chickaree of the eastern woods. Ours may be a lineal descendant of this species, distributed westward to the Pacific by way of the Great Lakes and the Rocky Mountains, and thence southward along our forested ranges. This view is suggested by the fact that our species becomes redder and more Chickaree-like in general, the farther it is traced back along the course indicated above. But whatever their relationship, and the evolutionary forces that have acted upon them, the Douglas is now the larger and more beautiful animal.

From the nose to the root of the tail he measures about eight inches; and his tail, which he so effectively uses in interpreting his feelings, is about six inches in length. He wears dark bluish-gray over the back and half-way down the sides, bright buff on the belly, with a stripe of dark gray, nearly black, separating the upper and under colors; this dividing stripe, however, is not very sharply defined. He has long black whiskers, which give him a rather fierce look when observed closely, strong claws, sharp as fish-hooks, and the brightest of bright eyes, full of telling speculation.

A King's River Indian told me that they call him 'Pillil-looeet,' which, rapidly pronounced with the first syllable heavily accented, is not unlike the lusty exclamation he utters on his way up a tree when excited. Most mountaineers in California call him the Pine Squirrel; and when I asked an old trapper whether he knew our little forester, he replied with brightening countenance: 'Oh, yes, of course I know him; everybody knows him. When I'm huntin' in the woods, I often find out where the deer are by his barkin' at 'em. I call 'em Lightnin' Squirrels, because they're so mighty quick and peert.'

All the true squirrels are more or less birdlike in speech and movements; but the Douglas is pre-eminently so, possessing, as he does, every attribute peculiarly squirrelish enthusiastically concentrated. He is the squirrel of squirrels, flashing from branch to branch of his favorite evergreens crisp and glossy and undiseased as a sunbeam. Give him wings and he would outfly any bird in the woods. His big gray cousin is a looser animal, seemingly light enough to float on the wind; yet when leaping from limb to limb, or out of one tree-top to another, he sometimes halts to gather strength, as if making efforts concerning the upshot of which he does not always feel exactly confident. But the Douglas, with his denser body, leaps and glides in hidden strength, seemingly as independent of common muscles as a mountain stream. He threads the tasseled branches of the pines, stirring their needles like a rustling breeze; now shooting across openings in arrowy lines; now launching in curves, glinting deftly from side to side in sudden zigzags, and swirling in giddy loops and spirals around the knotty trunks; getting into what seem to be the most impossible situations without sense of danger; now on his haunches, now on his head; yet ever graceful, and punctuating his most irrepressible outbursts of energy with little dots and dashes of perfect repose. He is, without exception, the wildest animal I ever saw – a fiery, sputtering little bolt of life, luxuriating in quick oxygen and the woods' best juices. One can hardly think of such a creature being dependent, like the rest of us, on climate and food. But, after all, it requires no long acquaintance to learn he is human, for he works for a living. His busiest time is in the Indian summer. Then he gathers burs and hazelnuts like a plodding farmer, working continuously every day for hours; saying not a word; cutting off the ripe cones at the top of his speed, as if employed by the job, and examining every branch in regular order, as if careful that not one should escape him; then, descending, he stores them away beneath logs and stumps, in anticipation of the pinching hunger days of winter. He seems himself a kind of coniferous fruit – both fruit and flower. The resiny essences of the pines pervade every pore of his body, and eating his flesh is like chewing gum.

One never tires of this bright chip of nature – this brave little voice crying in the wilderness – of observing his many works and ways, and listening to his curious language. His musical, piny gossip is as savory to the ear as balsam to the palate; and, though he has not exactly the gift of song, some of his notes are as sweet as those of a linnet – almost flute-like in softness, while others prick and tingle like thistles. He is the mockingbird of squirrels, pouring forth mixed chatter and song like a perennial fountain; barking like a dog, screaming like a hawk, chirping like a blackbird or a sparrow; while in bluff, audacious noisiness he is a very jay.

In descending the trunk of a tree with the intention of

alighting on the ground, he preserves a cautious silence, mindful, perhaps, of foxes and wildcats; but while rocking safely at home in the pine-tops there is no end to his capers and noise; and woe to the gray squirrel or chipmunk that ventures to set foot on his favorite tree! No matter how slyly they trace the furrows of the bark, they are speedily discovered, and kicked down-stairs with comic vehemence, while a torrent of angry notes comes rushing from his whiskered lips that sounds remarkably like swearing. He will even attempt at times to drive away dogs and men, especially if he has had no previous knowledge of them. Seeing a man for the first time, he approaches nearer and nearer, until within a few feet; then, with an angry outburst, he makes a sudden rush, all teeth and eyes, as if about to eat you up. But, finding that the big, forked animal doesn't scare, he prudently beats a retreat, and sets himself up to reconnoiter on some overhanging branch, scrutinizing every movement you make with ludicrous solemnity.

Gathering courage, he ventures down the trunk again, churring and chirping, and jerking nervously up and down in curious loops, eyeing you all the time, as if showing off and demanding your admiration. Finally, growing calmer, he settles down in a comfortable posture on some horizontal branch commanding a good view, and beats time with his tail to a steady 'Chee-up! Chee-up!' or, when somewhat less excited, 'Pee-ah!' with the first syllable keenly accented, and the second drawn out like the scream of a hawk – repeating this slowly and more emphatically at first, then gradually faster, until a rate of about 150 words a minute is reached; usually sitting all the time on his haunches, with paws resting on his breast, which pulses visibly with each word. It is remarkable, too, that, though articulating distinctly, he keeps his mouth shut most of the time, and speaks through his nose. I have occasionally observed him even eating Sequoia seeds and nibbling a troublesome flea, without ceasing or in any way confusing his 'Pee-ah! Pee-ah!' for a single moment.

While ascending trees all his claws come into play, but in descending the weight of his body is sustained chiefly by those of the hind feet; still in neither case do his movements suggest effort, though if you are near enough you may see the bulging strength of his short, bear-like arms, and note his sinewy fists clinched in the bark.

Whether going up or down, he carries his tail extended at full length in line with his body, unless it be required for gestures. But while running along horizontal limbs or fallen trunks, it is frequently folded forward over the back, with the airy tip daintily upcurled. In cool weather it keeps him warm. Then, after he has finished his meal, you may see him crouched close on some level limb with his tail-robe neatly spread and reaching forward to his ears, the electric, outstanding hairs quivering in the breeze like pine-needles. But in wet or very cold weather he stays in his nest, and while curled up there his comforter is long enough to come forward around his nose. It is seldom so cold, however, as to prevent his going out to his stores when hungry.

Once as I lay storm-bound on the upper edge of the timber line on Mount Shasta, the thermometer nearly at zero and the sky thick with driving snow, a Douglas came bravely out several times from one of the lower hollows of a Dwarf Pine near my camp, faced the wind without seeming to feel it much, frisked lightly about over the mealy snow, and dug his way down to some hidden seeds with wonderful precision, as if to his eyes the thick snowcovering were glass.

No other of the Sierra animals of my acquaintance is better fed, not even the deer, amid abundance of sweet herbs and shrubs, or the mountain sheep, or omnivorous bears. His food consists of grass-seeds, berries, hazel-nuts, chinquapins, and the nuts and seeds of all the coniferous trees without exception – Pine, Fir, Spruce, *Libocedrus*, Juniper, and Sequoia – he is fond of them all, and they all agree with him, green or ripe. No cone is too large for him to manage, none so small as to be beneath his notice. The smaller ones, such as those of the Hemlock, and the Douglas Spruce, and the Two-leaved Pine, he cuts off and eats on a branch of the tree, without allowing them to fall; beginning at the bottom of the cone and cutting away the scales to expose the seeds; not gnawing by guess, like a bear, but turning them round and round in regular order, in compliance with their spiral arrangement.

When thus employed, his location in the tree is betrayed by a dribble of scales, shells, and seedwings, and, every few minutes, by the fall of the stripped axis of the cone. Then of course he is ready for another, and if you are watching you may catch a glimpse of him as he glides silently out to the end of a branch and see him examining the cone-clusters until he finds one to his mind; then, leaning over, pull back the springy needles out of his way, grasp the cone with his paws to prevent its falling, snip it off in an incredibly short time, seize it with jaws grotesquely stretched, and return to his chosen seat near the trunk. But the immense size of the cones of the Sugar Pine – from fifteen to twenty inches in length – and those of the Jeffrey variety of the Yellow Pine compel him to adopt a quite different method. He cuts them off without attempting to hold them, then goes down and drags them from where they have chanced to fall up to the bare, swelling ground around the instep of the tree, where he demolishes them in the same methodical way, beginning at the bottom and following the scale-spirals to the top.

From a single Sugar Pine cone he gets from two to four hundred seeds about half the size of a hazelnut, so that in a few minutes he can procure enough to last a week. He seems, however, to prefer those of the two Silver Firs above all others; perhaps because they are most easily obtained, as the scales drop off when ripe without needing to be cut. Both species are filled with an exceedingly pungent, aromatic oil, which spices all his flesh, and is of itself sufficient to account for his lightning energy.

You may easily know this little workman by his chips. On sunny hillsides around the principal trees they lie in big piles – bushels and basketfuls of them, all fresh and clean, making the most beautiful kitchen-middens imaginable. The brown and yellow scales and nut-shells are as abundant and as delicately penciled and tinted as the shells along the sea-shore; while the beautiful red and purple seed-wings mingled with them would lead one to fancy that innumerable butterflies had there met their fate.

He feasts on all the species long before they are ripe, but is wise enough to wait until they are matured before he gathers them into his barns. This is in October and November, which with him are the two busiest months of the year. All kinds of burs, big and little, are now cut off and showered down alike, and the ground is speedily covered with them. A constant thudding and bumping is kept up; some of the larger cones chancing to fall on old logs make the forest re-echo with the sound. Other nut-eaters less industrious know well what is going on, and hasten to carry away the cones as they fall. But however busy the harvester may be, he is not slow to descry the pilferers below, and instantly leaves his work to drive them away. The little striped tamias is a thorn in his flesh, stealing persistently, punish him as he may. The large Gray Squirrel gives trouble also, although the Douglas has been accused of stealing from him. Generally, however, just the opposite is the case.

The excellence of the Sierra evergreens is well known to nurserymen throughout the world, consequently there is considerable demand for the seeds. The greater portion of the supply has hitherto been procured by chopping down the trees in the more accessible sections of the forest alongside of bridle-paths that cross the range. Sequoia seeds at first brought from twenty to thirty dollars per pound, and therefore were eagerly sought after. Some of the smaller fruitful trees were cut down in the groves not protected by government, especially those of Fresno and King's River. Most of the Sequoias, however, are of so gigantic a size that the seedsmen have to look for the greater portion of their supplies to the Douglas, who soon learns he is no match for these freebooters. He is wise enough, however, to cease working the instant he perceives them, and never fails to embrace every opportunity to recover his burs whenever they happen to be stored in any place accessible to him, and the busy seedsman often finds on returning to camp that the little Douglas has exhaustively spoiled the spoiler. I know one seed-gatherer who, whenever he robs the squirrels, scatters wheat or barley beneath the trees as conscience-money.

The want of appreciable life remarked by so many travelers in the Sierra forests is never felt at this time of year. Banish all the humming insects and the birds and quadrupeds, leaving only Sir Douglas, and the most solitary of our so-called solitudes would still throb with ardent life. But if you should go impatiently even into the most populous of the groves on purpose to meet him, and walk about looking up among the branches, you would see very little of him. But lie down at the foot of one of the trees and straightway he will come. For, in the midst of the ordinary forest sounds, the falling of burs, piping of quails, the screaming of the Clark Crow, and the rustling of deer and bears among the chaparral, he is quick to detect your strange footsteps, and will hasten to make a good, close inspection of you as soon as you are still. First, you may hear him sounding a few notes of curious inquiry, but more likely the first intimation of his approach will be the prickly sounds of his feet as he descends the tree overhead, just before he makes his savage onrush to frighten you and proclaim your presence to every squirrel and bird in the neighborhood. If you remain perfectly motionless, he will come nearer and nearer, and probably set your flesh a-tingle by frisking across your body. Once, while I was seated at the foot of a Hemlock Spruce in one of the most inaccessible of the San Joaquin yosemites engaged in sketching, a reckless fellow came up behind me, passed under my bended arm, and jumped on my paper. And one warm afternoon, while an old friend of mine was reading out in the shade of his cabin, one of his Douglas neighbors jumped from the gable upon his head, and then with admirable assurance ran down over his shoulder and on to the book he held in his hand.

Our Douglas enjoys a large social circle; for, besides his numerous relatives, *Sciurus fossor, Tamias quadrivitatus, T. Townsendii, Spermophilus Beecheyi, S. Douglasii*, he maintains intimate relations with the nut-eating birds, particularly the Clark Crow (*Picicorvus columbianus*) and the numerous woodpeckers and jays. The two spermophiles are astonishingly abundant in the lowlands and lower foothills, but more and more sparingly distributed up through the Douglas domains – seldom venturing higher than six or seven thousand feet above the level of the sea. The gray sciurus ranges but little higher than this. The little striped tamias alone is associated with him everywhere. In the lower and middle zones, where they all meet, they are tolerably harmonious – a happy family, though very amusing skirmishes may occasionally be witnessed. Wherever the ancient glaciers have spread forest soil there you find our wee hero, most abundant where depth of soil and genial climate have given rise to a corresponding luxuriance in the trees, but following every kind of growth up the curving moraines to the highest glacial fountains.

Though I cannot of course expect all my readers to sympathize fully in my admiration of this little animal, few, I hope, will think this sketch of his life too long. I cannot begin to tell here how much he has cheered my lonely wanderings during all the years I have been pursuing my studies in these glorious wilds; or how much unmistakable humanity I have found in him. Take this for example: One calm, creamy Indian summer morning, when the nuts were ripe, I was camped in the upper pine-woods of the south fork of the San Joaquin, where the squirrels seemed to be about as plentiful as the ripe burs. They were taking an early breakfast before going to their regular harvest-work. While I was busy with my own breakfast I heard the thudding fall of two or three heavy cones from a Yellow Pine near me. I stole noiselessly forward within about twenty feet of the base of it to observe. In a few moments down came the Douglas. The breakfast-burs he had cut off had rolled on the gently sloping ground into a clump of ceanothus bushes, but he seemed to know exactly where they were, for he found them at once, apparently without searching for them. They were more than twice as heavy as himself, but after turning them into the right position for getting a good hold with his long sickle-teeth he managed to drag them up to the foot of the tree from which he had cut them, moving backward. Then seating himself comfortably, he held them on end, bottom up, and demolished them at his ease. A good deal of nibbling had to be done before he got anything to eat, because the lower scales are barren, but when he had patiently worked his way up to the fertile ones he found two sweet nuts at the base of each, shaped like trimmed hams, and spotted purple like birds' eggs. And notwithstanding these cones were dripping with soft balsam, and covered with prickles, and so strongly put together that a boy would be puzzled to cut them open with a jack-knife, he accomplished his meal with easy dignity and cleanliness, making less effort apparently than a man would in eating soft cookery from a plate.

Breakfast done, I whistled a tune for him before he went to work, curious to see how he would be affected by it. He had not seen me all this while; but the instant I began to whistle he darted up the tree nearest to him, and came out on a small dead limb opposite me, and composed himself to listen. I sang and whistled more than a dozen airs, and as the music changed his eyes sparkled, and he turned his head quickly from side to side, but made no other response. Other squirrels, hearing the strange sounds, came around on all sides, also chipmunks and birds. One of the birds, a handsome, speckle-breasted thrush, seemed even more interested than the squirrels. After listening for awhile on one of the lower dead sprays of a pine, he came swooping forward within a few feet of my face, and remained fluttering in the air for half a minute or so, sustaining himself with whirring wing-beats, like a humming-bird in front of a flower, while I could look into his eyes and see his innocent wonder.

By this time my performance must have lasted nearly half an hour. I sang or whistled 'Bonnie Doon,' 'Lass o' Gowrie,' 'O'er the Water to Charlie,' 'Bonnie Woods o' Cragie Lee,' etc., all of which seemed to be listened to with bright interest, my first Douglas sitting patiently through it all, with his telling eyes fixed upon me until I ventured to give the 'Old Hundredth,' when he screamed his Indian name, Pillillooeet, turned tail, and darted with ludicrous haste up the tree out of sight, his voice and actions in the case leaving a somewhat profane impression, as if he had said, 'I'll be hanged if you get me to hear anything so solemn and unpiny.' This acted as a signal for the general dispersal of the whole hairy tribe, though the birds seemed willing to wait further developments, music being naturally more in their line.

What there can be in that grand old church-tune that is so offensive to birds and squirrels I can't imagine. A year or two after this High Sierra concert, I was sitting one fine day on a hill in the Coast Range where the common Ground Squirrels were abundant. They were very shy on account of being hunted so much; but after I had been silent and motionless for half an hour or so they began to venture out of their holes and to feed on the seeds of the grasses and thistles around me as if I were no more to be feared than a tree-stump. Then it occurred to me that this was a good opportunity to find out whether they also disliked 'Old Hundredth.' Therefore I began to whistle as nearly as I could remember the same familiar airs that had pleased the mountaineers of the Sierra. They at once stopped eating, stood erect, and listened patiently until I came to 'Old Hundredth,' when with ludicrous haste every one of them rushed to their holes and bolted in, their feet twinkling in the air for a moment as they vanished.

No one who makes the acquaintance of our forester will fail to admire him; but he is far too self-reliant and warlike ever to be taken for a darling.

How long the life of a Douglas Squirrel may be, I don't

know. The young seem to sprout from knot-holes, perfect from the first, and as enduring as their own trees. It is difficult, indeed, to realize that so condensed a piece of sun-fire should ever become dim or die at all. He is seldom killed by hunters, for he is too small to encourage much of their attention, and when pursued in settled regions becomes excessively shy, and keeps close in the furrows of the highest trunks, many of which are of the same color as himself. Indian boys, however, lie in wait with unbounded patience to shoot them with arrows. In the lower and middle zones a few fall prey to rattlesnakes. Occasionally he is pursued by hawks and wildcats, etc. But, upon the whole, he dwells safely in the deep bosom of the woods, the most highly favored of all his happy tribe. May his tribe increase!

Chapter 10

A WIND-STORM IN THE FORESTS

The mountain winds, like the dew and rain, sunshine and snow, are measured and bestowed with love on the forests to develop their strength and beauty. However restricted the scope of other forest influences, that of the winds is universal. The snow bends and trims the upper forests every winter, the lightning strikes a single tree here and there, while avalanches mow down thousands at a swoop as a gardener trims out a bed of flowers. But the winds go to every tree, fingering every leaf and branch and furrowed bole; not one is forgotten; the Mountain Pine towering with outstretched arms on the rugged buttresses of the icy peaks, the lowliest and most retiring tenant of the dells; they seek and find them all, caressing them tenderly, bending them in lusty exercise, stimulating their growth, plucking off a leaf or limb as required, or removing an entire tree or grove, now whispering and cooing through the branches like a sleepy child, now roaring like the ocean; the winds blessing the forests, the forests the winds, with ineffable beauty and harmony as the sure result.

After one has seen pines six feet in diameter bending like grasses before a mountain gale, and ever and anon some giant falling with a crash that shakes the hills, it seems astonishing that any, save the lowest thickset trees, could ever have found a period sufficiently stormless to establish themselves; or, once established, that they should not, sooner or later, have been blown down. But when the storm is over, and we behold the same forests tranquil again, towering fresh and unscathed in erect majesty, and consider what centuries of storms have fallen upon them since they were first planted – hail, to break the tender seedlings; lightning, to scorch and shatter; snow, winds, and avalanches, to crush and overwhelm – while the manifest result of all this wild storm-culture is the glorious perfection we behold; then faith in Nature's forestry is established, and we cease to deplore the violence of her most destructive gales, or of any other storm-implement whatsoever.

There are two trees in the Sierra forests that are never blown down, so long as they continue in sound health. These are the Juniper and the Dwarf Pine of the summit peaks. Their stiff, crooked roots grip the storm-beaten ledges like eagles' claws, while their lithe, cord-like branches bend round compliantly, offering but slight holds for winds, however violent. The other alpine conifers – the Needle Pine, Mountain Pine, Two-leaved Pine, and Hemlock Spruce – are never thinned out by this agent to any destructive extent, on account of their admirable toughness and the closeness of their growth. In general the same is true of the giants of the lower zones. The kingly Sugar Pine, towering aloft to a height of more than 200 feet, offers a fine mark to storm-winds; but it is not densely foliaged, and its long, horizontal arms swing round compliantly in the blast, like tresses of green, fluent algae in a brook; while the Silver Firs in most places keep their ranks well together in united strength. The Yellow or Silver Pine is more frequently overturned than any other tree on the Sierra, because its leaves and branches form a larger mass in proportion to its height, while in many places it is planted sparsely, leaving open lanes through which storms may enter with full force. Furthermore, because it is distributed along the lower portion of the range, which was the first to be left bare on the breaking up of the ice-sheet at the close of the glacial winter, the soil it is growing upon has been longer exposed to post-glacial weathering, and consequently is in a more crumbling, decayed condition than the fresher soils farther up the range, and therefore offers a less secure anchorage for the roots.

While exploring the forest zones of Mount Shasta, I discovered the path of a hurricane strewn with thousands of pines of this species. Great and small had been uprooted or wrenched off by sheer force, making a clean gap, like that made by a snow avalanche. But hurricanes capable of doing this class of work are rare in the Sierra, and when we have explored the forests from one extremity of the range to the other, we are compelled to believe that they are the most beautiful on the face of the earth, however we may regard the agents that have made them so.

There is always something deeply exciting, not only in the sounds of winds in the woods, which exert more or less influence over every mind, but in their varied waterlike flow as manifested by the movements of the trees, especially those of the conifers. By no other trees are they rendered so extensively and impressively visible, not even by the lordly tropic palms or tree-ferns responsive to the gentlest breeze. The waving of a forest of the giant Sequoias is indescribably impressive and sublime, but the pines seem to me the best interpreters of winds. They are mighty waving goldenrods, ever in tune, singing and writing wind-music all their long century lives. Little, however, of this noble tree-waving and tree-music will you see or hear in the strictly alpine portion of the forests. The burly Juniper, whose girth sometimes more than equals its height, is about as rigid as the rocks on which it grows. The slender lash-like sprays of the Dwarf Pine stream out in wavering ripples, but the tallest and slenderest are far too unyielding to wave even in the heaviest gales. They only shake in quick, short vibrations. The Hemlock Spruce, however, and the Mountain Pine, and some of the tallest thickets of the Two-leaved species bow in storms with considerable scope and gracefulness. But it is only in the lower and middle zones that the meeting of winds and woods is to be seen in all its grandeur.

One of the most beautiful and exhilarating storms I ever enjoyed in the Sierra occurred in December 1874, when I happened to be exploring one of the tributary valleys of the Yuba River. The sky and the ground and the trees had been thoroughly rain-washed and were dry again. The day was intensely pure, one of those incomparable bits of California winter, warm and balmy and full of white sparkling sunshine, redolent of all the purest influences of the spring, and at the same time enlivened with one of the most bracing wind-storms conceivable. Instead of camping out, as I usually do, I then chanced to be stopping at the house of a friend. But when the storm began to sound, I lost no time in pushing out into the woods to enjoy it. For on such occasions Nature has always something rare to show us, and the danger to life and limb is hardly greater than one would experience crouching deprecatingly beneath a roof.

It was still early morning when I found myself fairly adrift. Delicious sunshine came pouring over the hills, lighting the tops of the pines, and setting free a steam of summery fragrance that contrasted strangely with the wild tones of the storm. The air was mottled with pine-tassels and bright green plumes, that went flashing past in the sunlight like birds pursued. But there was not the slightest dustiness, nothing less pure than leaves, and ripe pollen, and flecks of withered bracken and moss. I heard trees falling for hours at the rate of one every two or three minutes; some uprooted, partly on account of the loose, water-soaked condition of the ground; others broken straight across, where some weakness caused by fire had determined the spot. The gestures of the various trees made a delightful study. Young Sugar Pines, light and feathery as squirrel-tails, were bowing almost to the ground; while the grand old patriarchs, whose massive boles had been tried in a hundred storms, waved solemnly above them, their long, arching branches streaming fluently on the gale, and every needle thrilling and ringing and shedding off keen lances of light like a diamond. The Douglas Spruces, with long sprays drawn out in level tresses, and needles massed in a gray, shimmering glow, presented a most striking appearance as they stood in bold relief along the hilltops. The madronnyos in the dells, with their red bark and large glossy leaves tilted every way, reflected the sunshine in throbbing spangles like those one so often sees on the rippled surface of a glacier lake. But the Silver Pines were now the most impressively beautiful of all. Colossal spires 200 feet in height waved like supple golden-rods chanting and bowing low as if in worship, while the whole mass of their long, tremulous foliage was kindled into one continuous blaze of white sun-fire. The force of the gale was such that the most steadfast monarch of them all rocked down to its roots with a motion plainly perceptible when one leaned against it. Nature was holding high festival, and every fiber of the most rigid giants thrilled with glad excitement.

I drifted on through the midst of this passionate music and motion, across many a glen, from ridge to ridge; often halting in the lee of a rock for shelter, or to gaze and listen. Even when the grand anthem had swelled to its highest pitch, I could distinctly hear the varying tones of individual trees – Spruce, and Fir, and Pine, and leafless Oak – and even the infinitely gentle rustle of the withered grasses at my feet. Each was expressing itself in its own way – singing its own song, and making its own peculiar gestures – manifesting a richness of variety to be found in no other forest I have yet seen. The coniferous woods of Canada, and the Carolinas, and Florida, are made up of trees that resemble one another about as nearly as blades of grass, and grow close together in much the same way. Coniferous trees, in general, seldom possess individual character, such as is manifest among Oaks and Elms. But the California forests are made up of a greater number of distinct species than any other in the world. And in them we find, not only a marked differentiation into special groups, but also a marked individuality in almost every tree, giving rise to storm effects indescribably glorious.

Toward midday, after a long, tingling scramble through copses of hazel and ceanothus, I gained the summit of the highest ridge in the neighborhood; and then it occurred to me that it would be a fine thing to climb one of the trees to obtain a wider outlook and get my ear close to the Aeolian music of its topmost needles. But under the circumstances the choice of a tree was a serious matter. One whose instep was not very strong seemed in danger of being blown down, or of being struck by others in case they should fall; another was branchless to a considerable height above the ground, and at the same time too large to be grasped with arms and legs in climbing; while others were not favorably situated for clear views. After cautiously casting about, I made choice of the tallest of a group of Douglas Spruces that were growing close together like a tuft of grass, no one of which seemed likely to fall unless all the rest fell with it. Though comparatively young, they were about 100 feet high, and their lithe, brushy tops were rocking and swirling in wild ecstasy. Being accustomed to climb trees in making botanical studies, I experienced no difficulty in reaching the top of this one, and never before did I enjoy so noble an exhilaration of motion. The slender tops fairly flapped and swished in the passionate torrent, bending and swirling backward and forward, round and round, tracing indescribable combinations of vertical and horizontal curves, while I clung with muscles firm braced, like a bobo-link on a reed.

In its widest sweeps my tree-top described an arc of from twenty to thirty degrees, but I felt sure of its elastic temper, having seen others of the same species still more severely tried – bent almost to the ground indeed, in heavy snows – without breaking a fiber. I was therefore safe, and free to take the wind into my pulses and enjoy the excited forest from my superb outlook. The view from here must be extremely beautiful in any weather. Now my eye roved over the piny hills and dales as over fields of waving grain, and felt the light running in ripples and broad swelling undulations across the valleys from ridge to ridge, as the shining foliage was stirred by corresponding waves of air. Oftentimes these waves of reflected light would break up suddenly into a kind of beaten foam, and again, after chasing one another in regular order, they would seem to bend forward in concentric curves, and disappear on some hillside, like sea-waves on a shelving shore. The quantity of light reflected from the bent needles was so great as to make whole groves appear as if covered with snow, while the black shadows beneath the trees greatly enhanced the effect of the silvery splendor.

Excepting only the shadows there was nothing somber in all this wild sea of pines. On the contrary, notwithstanding this was the winter season, the colors were remarkably beautiful. The shafts of the pine and *Libocedrus* were brown and purple, and most of the foliage was well tinged with yellow; the laurel groves, with the pale undersides of their leaves turned upward, made masses of gray; and then there was many a dash of chocolate color from clumps of manzanita, and jet of vivid crimson from the bark of the madronyos, while the ground on the hillsides, appearing here and there through openings between the groves, displayed masses of pale purple and brown.

The sounds of the storm corresponded gloriously with this wild exuberance of light and motion. The profound bass of the naked branches and boles booming like waterfalls; the quick, tense vibrations of the pine-needles, now rising to a shrill, whistling hiss, now falling to a silky murmur; the rustling of laurel groves in the dells, and the keen metallic click of leaf on leaf – all this was heard in easy analysis when the attention was calmly bent.

The varied gestures of the multitude were seen to fine advantage, so that one could recognize the different species at a distance of several miles by this means alone, as well as by their forms and colors, and the way they reflected the light. All seemed strong and comfortable, as if really enjoying the storm, while responding to its most enthusiastic greetings. We hear much nowadays concerning the universal struggle for existence, but no struggle in the common meaning of the word was manifest here; no recognition of danger by any tree; no deprecation; but rather an invincible gladness as remote from exultation as from fear.

I kept my lofty perch for hours, frequently closing my eyes to enjoy the music by itself, or to feast quietly on the delicious fragrance that was streaming past. The fragrance of the woods was less marked than that produced during warm rain, when so many balsamic buds and leaves are steeped like tea; but, from the chafing of resiny branches against each other, and the incessant attrition of myriad needles, the gale was spiced to a very tonic degree. And besides the fragrance from these local sources there were traces of scents brought from afar. For this wind came first from the sea, rubbing against its fresh, briny waves, then distilled through the redwoods, threading rich ferny gulches, and spreading itself in broad undulating currents over many a flower-enameled ridge of the coast mountains, then across the golden plains, up the purple foothills, and into these piny woods with the varied incense gathered by the way.

Winds are advertisements of all they touch, however much or little we may be able to read them; telling their wanderings even by their scents alone. Mariners detect the flowery perfume of land-winds far at sea, and sea-winds carry the fragrance of dulse and tangle far inland, where it is quickly recognized, though mingled with the scents of a thousand land-flowers. As an illustration of this, I may tell here that I breathed sea-air on the Firth of Forth, in Scotland, while a boy; then was taken to Wisconsin, where I remained nineteen years; then, without in all this time having breathed one breath of the sea, I walked quietly, alone, from the middle of the Mississippi Valley to the Gulf of Mexico, on a botanical excursion, and while in Florida, far from the coast, my attention wholly bent on the splendid tropical vegetation about me, I suddenly recognized a sea-breeze, as it came sifting through the palmettos and blooming vine-tangles, which at once awakened and set free a thousand dormant associations, and made me a boy again in Scotland, as if all the intervening years had been annihilated.

Most people like to look at mountain rivers, and bear them in mind; but few care to look at the winds, though far more beautiful and sublime, and though they become at times about as visible as flowing water. When the north winds in winter are making upward sweeps over the curving summits of the

High Sierra, the fact is sometimes published with flying snow-banners a mile long. Those portions of the winds thus embodied can scarce be wholly invisible, even to the darkest imagination. And when we look around over an agitated forest, we may see something of the wind that stirs it, by its effects upon the trees. Yonder it descends in a rush of water-like ripples, and sweeps over the bending pines from hill to hill. Nearer, we see detached plumes and leaves, now speeding by on level currents, now whirling in eddies, or, escaping over the edges of the whirls, soaring aloft on grand, upswelling domes of air, or tossing on flame-like crests. Smooth, deep currents, cascades, falls, and swirling eddies, sing around every tree and leaf, and over all the varied topography of the region with telling changes of form, like mountain rivers conforming to the features of their channels.

After tracing the Sierra streams from their fountains to the plains, marking where they bloom white in falls, glide in crystal plumes, surge gray and foam-filled in boulder-choked gorges, and slip through the woods in long, tranquil reaches – after thus learning their language and forms in detail, we may at length hear them chanting all together in one grand anthem, and comprehend them all in clear inner vision, covering the range like lace. But even this spectacle is far less sublime and not a whit more substantial than what we may behold of these storm-streams of air in the mountain woods.

We all travel the milky way together, trees and men; but it never occurred to me until this storm-day, while swinging in the wind, that trees are travelers, in the ordinary sense. They make many journeys, not extensive ones, it is true; but our own little journeys, away and back again, are only little more than tree-wavings – many of them not so much.

When the storm began to abate, I dismounted and sauntered down through the calming woods. The storm-tones died away, and, turning toward the east, I beheld the countless hosts of the forests hushed and tranquil, towering above one another on the slopes of the hills like a devout audience. The setting sun filled them with amber light, and seemed to say, while they listened, 'My peace I give unto you.'

As I gazed on the impressive scene, all the so-called ruin of the storm was forgotten, and never before did these noble woods appear so fresh, so joyous, so immortal.

Chapter 13

THE WATER OUZEL

The waterfalls of the Sierra are frequented by only one bird – the Ouzel or Water Thrush (*Cinclus Mexicanus*, Sw.). He is a singularly joyous and lovable little fellow, about the size of a robin, clad in a plain waterproof suit of bluish gray, with a tinge of chocolate on the head and shoulders. In form he is about as smoothly plump and compact as a pebble that has been whirled in a pot-hole, the flowing contour of his body being interrupted only by his strong feet and bill, the crisp wing-tips, and the up-slanted wren-like tail.

Among all the countless waterfalls I have met in the course of ten years' exploration in the Sierra, whether among the icy peaks, or warm foothills, or in the profound yosemitic canyons of the middle region, not one was found without its Ouzel. No canyon is too cold for this little bird, none too lonely, provided it be rich in falling water. Find a fall, or cascade, or rushing rapid, anywhere upon a clear stream, and there you will surely find its complementary Ouzel, flitting about in the spray, diving in foaming eddies, whirling like a leaf among beaten foam-bells; ever vigorous and enthusiastic, yet self-contained, and neither seeking nor shunning your company.

If disturbed while dipping about in the margin shallows, he either sets off with a rapid whir to some other feeding-ground up or down the stream, or alights on some half-submerged rock or snag out in the current, and immediately begins to nod and curtsey like a wren, turning his head from side to side with many other odd dainty movements that never fail to fix the attention of the observer.

He is the mountain streams' own darling, the humming-bird of blooming waters, loving rocky ripple-slopes and sheets of foam as a bee loves flowers, as a lark loves sunshine and meadows. Among all the mountain birds, none has cheered me so much in my lonely wanderings – none so unfailingly. For both in winter and summer he sings, sweetly, cheerily, independent alike of sunshine and of love, requiring no other inspiration than the stream on which he dwells. While water sings, so must he, in heat or cold, calm or storm, ever attuning his voice in sure accord; low in the drought of summer and the drought of winter, but never silent.

During the golden days of Indian summer, after most of the snow has been melted, and the mountain streams have become feeble – a succession of silent pools, linked together by shallow, transparent currents and strips of silvery lacework – then the song of the Ouzel is at its lowest ebb. But as soon as the winter clouds have bloomed, and the mountain treasuries are once more replenished with snow, the voices of the streams and ouzels increase in strength and richness until the flood season of early summer. Then the torrents chant their noblest anthems, and then is the flood-time of our songster's melody. As for weather, dark days and sun days are the same to him. The voices of most songbirds, however joyous, suffer a long winter eclipse; but the Ouzel sings on through all the seasons and every kind of storm. Indeed no storm can be more violent than those of the waterfalls in the midst of which he delights to dwell. However dark and boisterous the weather, snowing, blowing, or cloudy, all the same he sings, and with never a note of sadness. No need of spring sunshine to thaw *his* song, for it never freezes. Never shall you hear anything wintry from *his* warm breast; no pinched cheeping, no wavering notes between sorrow and joy; his mellow, fluty voice is ever tuned to downright gladness, as free from dejection as cock-crowing.

It is pitiful to see wee frost-pinched sparrows on cold mornings in the mountain groves shaking the snow from their feathers, and hopping about as if anxious to be cheery, then hastening back to their hidings out of the wind, puffing out their breast-feathers over their toes, and subsiding among the leaves, cold and breakfastless, while the snow continues to fall, and there is no sign of clearing. But the Ouzel never calls forth a single touch of pity; not because he is strong to endure, but rather because he seems to live a charmed life beyond the reach of every influence that makes endurance necessary.

One wild winter morning, when Yosemite Valley was swept

its length from west to east by a cordial snow-storm, I sallied forth to see what I might learn and enjoy. A sort of gray, gloaming-like darkness filled the valley, the huge walls were out of sight, all ordinary sounds were smothered, and even the loudest booming of the falls was at times buried beneath the roar of the heavy-laden blast. The loose snow was already over five feet deep on the meadows, making extended walks impossible without the aid of snow-shoes. I found no great difficulty, however, in making my way to a certain ripple on the river where one of my ouzels lived. He was at home, busily gleaning his breakfast among the pebbles of a shallow portion of the margin, apparently unaware of anything extraordinary in the weather. Presently he flew out to a stone against which the icy current was beating, and turning his back to the wind, sang as delightfully as a lark in springtime.

After spending an hour or two with my favorite, I made my way across the valley, boring and wallowing through the drifts, to learn as definitely as possible how the other birds were spending their time. The Yosemite birds are easily found during the winter because all of them excepting the Ouzel are restricted to the sunny north side of the valley, the south side being constantly eclipsed by the great frosty shadow of the wall. And because the Indian Canyon groves, from their peculiar exposure, are the warmest, the birds congregate there, more especially in severe weather.

I found most of the robins cowering on the lee side of the larger branches where the snow could not fall upon them, while two or three of the more enterprising were making desperate efforts to reach the mistletoe berries by clinging nervously to the under side of the snow-crowned masses, back downward, like woodpeckers. Every now and then they would dislodge some of the loose fringes of the snow-crown, which would come sifting down on them and send them screaming back to camp, where they would subside among their companions with a shiver, muttering in low, querulous chatter like hungry children.

Some of the sparrows were busy at the feet of the larger trees gleaning seeds and benumbed insects, joined now and then by a robin weary of his unsuccessful attempts upon the snow-covered berries. The brave woodpeckers were clinging to the snowless sides of the larger boles and overarching branches of the camp trees, making short flights from side to side of the grove, pecking now and then at the acorns they had stored in the bark, and chattering aimlessly as if unable to keep still, yet evidently putting in the time in a very dull way, like storm-bound travelers at a country tavern. The hardy nut-hatches were threading the open furrows of the trunks in their usual industrious manner, and uttering their quaint notes, evidently less distressed than their neighbors. The Steller jays were of course making more noisy stir than all the other birds combined; ever coming and going with loud bluster, screaming as if each had a lump of melting sludge in his throat, and taking good care to improve the favorable opportunity afforded by the storm to steal from the acorn stores of the woodpeckers. I also noticed one solitary gray eagle braving the storm on the top of a tall pine-stump just outside the main grove. He was standing bolt upright with his back to the wind, a tuft of snow piled on his square shoulders, a monument of passive endurance. Thus every snow-bound bird seemed more or less uncomfortable if not in positive distress. The storm was reflected in every gesture, and not one cheerful note, not to say song, came from a single bill; their cowering, joyless endurance offering a striking contrast to the spontaneous, irrepressible gladness of the Ouzel, who could no more help exhaling sweet song than a rose sweet fragrance. He *must* sing though the heavens fall. I remember noticing the distress of a pair of robins during the violent earthquake of the year 1872, when the pines of the Valley, with strange movements, flapped and waved their branches, and beetling rock-brows came thundering down to the meadows in tremendous avalanches. It did not occur to me in the midst of the excitement of other observations to look for the ouzels, but I doubt not they were singing straight on through it all, regarding the terrible rock-thunder as fearlessly as they do the booming of the waterfalls.

What may be regarded as the separate songs of the Ouzel are exceedingly difficult of description, because they are so variable and at the same time so confluent. Though I have been acquainted with my favorite ten years, and during most of this time have heard him sing nearly every day, I still detect notes and strains that seem new to me. Nearly all of his music is sweet and tender, lapsing from his round breast like water over the smooth lip of a pool, then breaking farther on into a sparkling foam of melodious notes, which glow with subdued enthusiasm, yet without expressing much of the strong, gushing ecstasy of the bobolink or skylark.

The more striking strains are perfect arabesques of melody, composed of a few full, round, mellow notes, embroidered with delicate trills which fade and melt in long slender cadences. In a general way his music is that of the streams refined and spiritualized. The deep booming notes of the falls are in it, the trills of rapids, the gurgling of margin eddies, the low whispering of level reaches, and the sweet tinkle of separate drops oozing from the ends of mosses and falling into tranquil pools.

The Ouzel never sings in chorus with other birds, nor with his kind, but only with the streams. And like flowers that bloom beneath the surface of the ground, some of our favorite's best song-blossoms never rise above the surface of the heavier music of the water. I have often observed him singing in the midst of beaten spray, his music completely buried beneath the water's roar; yet I knew he was surely singing by his gestures and the movements of his bill.

His food, as far as I have noticed, consists of all kinds of water insects, which in summer are chiefly procured along shallow margins. Here he wades about ducking his head under water and deftly turning over pebbles and fallen leaves with his bill, seldom choosing to go into deep water where he has to use his wings in diving.

He seems to be especially fond of the larvae of mosquitos, found in abundance attached to the bottom of smooth rock channels where the current is shallow. When feeding in such places he wades up-stream, and often while his head is under water the swift current is deflected upward along the glossy curves of his neck and shoulders, in the form of a clear, crystalline shell, which fairly encloses him like a bell-glass, the shell being broken and re-formed as he lifts and dips his head; while ever and anon he sidles out to where the too powerful current carries him off his feet; then he dexterously rises on the wing and goes gleaning again in shallower places.

But during the winter, when the stream-banks are embossed in snow, and the streams themselves are chilled nearly to the freezing-point, so that the snow falling into them in stormy weather is not wholly dissolved, but forms a thin, blue sludge, thus rendering the current opaque – then he seeks the deeper portions of the main rivers, where he may dive to clear water beneath the sludge. Or he repairs to some open lake or mill-pond, at the bottom of which he feeds in safety.

When thus compelled to betake himself to a lake, he does not plunge into it at once like a duck, but always alights in the first place upon some rock or fallen pine along the shore. Then flying out thirty or forty yards, more or less, according to the character of the bottom, he alights with a dainty glint on the surface, swims about, looks down, finally makes up his mind, and disappears with a sharp stroke of his wings. After feeding for two or three minutes he suddenly reappears, showers the water from his wings with one vigorous shake, and rises abruptly into the air as if pushed up from beneath, comes back to his perch, sings a few minutes, and goes out to dive again; thus coming and going, singing and diving at the same place for hours.

The Ouzel is usually found singly; rarely in pairs, excepting during the breeding season, and *very* rarely in threes or fours. I once observed three thus spending a winter morning in company, upon a small glacier lake, on the Upper Merced, about 7500 feet above the level of the sea. A storm had occurred during the night, but the morning sun shone unclouded, and the shadowy lake, gleaming darkly in its setting of fresh snow, lay smooth and motionless as a mirror. My camp chanced to be within a few feet of the water's edge, opposite a fallen pine, some of the branches of which leaned out over the lake. Here my three dearly welcome visitors took up their station, and at once began to embroider the frosty air with their delicious melody, doubly delightful to me that particular morning, as I had been somewhat apprehensive of danger in breaking my way down through the snow-choked canyons to the lowlands.

The portion of the lake bottom selected for a feeding-ground lies at a depth of fifteen or twenty feet below the surface, and is covered with a short growth of algae and other aquatic plants – facts I had previously determined while sailing over it on a raft. After alighting on the glassy surface, they occasionally indulged in a little play, chasing one another round about in small circles; then all three would suddenly dive together, and then come ashore and sing.

The Ouzel seldom swims more than a few yards on the

surface, for, not being web-footed, he makes rather slow progress, but by means of his strong, crisp wings he swims, or rather flies, with celerity under the surface, often to considerable distances. But it is in withstanding the force of heavy rapids that his strength of wing in this respect is most strikingly manifested. The following may be regarded as a fair illustration of his power of sub-aquatic flight. One stormy morning in winter when the Merced River was blue and green with unmelted snow, I observed one of my ouzels perched on a snag out in the midst of a swift-rushing rapid, singing cheerily, as if everything was just to his mind; and while I stood on the bank admiring him, he suddenly plunged into the sludgy current, leaving his song abruptly broken off. After feeding a minute or two at the bottom, and when one would suppose that he must inevitably be swept far down-stream, he emerged just where he went down, alighted on the same snag, showered the water-beads from his feathers, and continued his unfinished song, seemingly in tranquil ease as if it had suffered no interruption.

The Ouzel alone of all birds dares to enter a white torrent. And though strictly terrestrial in structure, no other is so inseparably related to water, not even the duck, or the bold ocean albatross, or the stormy-petrel. For ducks go ashore as soon as they finish feeding in undisturbed places, and very often make long flights overland from lake to lake or field to field. The same is true of most other aquatic birds. But the Ouzel, born on the brink of a stream, or on a snag or boulder in the midst of it, seldom leaves it for a single moment. For, notwithstanding he is often on the wing, he never flies overland, but whirs with rapid, quail-like beat above the stream, tracing all its windings. Even when the stream is quite small, say from five to ten feet wide, he seldom shortens his flight by crossing a bend, however abrupt it may be; and even when disturbed by meeting someone on the bank, he prefers to fly over one's head, to dodging out over the ground. When, therefore, his flight along a crooked stream is viewed endwise, it appears most strikingly wavered – a description on the air of every curve with lightning-like rapidity.

The vertical curves and angles of the most precipitous torrents he traces with the same rigid fidelity, swooping down the inclines of cascades, dropping sheer over dizzy falls amid the spray, and ascending with the same fearlessness and ease, seldom seeking to lessen the steepness of the acclivity by beginning to ascend before reaching the base of the fall. No matter though it may be several hundred feet in height he holds straight on, as if about to dash headlong into the throng of booming rockets, then darts abruptly upward, and, after alighting at the top of the precipice to rest a moment, proceeds to feed and sing. His flight is solid and impetuous, without any intermission of wing-beats – one homogeneous buzz like that of a laden bee on its way home. And while thus buzzing freely from fall to fall, he is frequently heard giving utterance to a long outdrawn train of unmodulated notes, in no way connected with his song, but corresponding closely with his flight in sustained vigor.

Were the flights of all the ouzels in the Sierra traced on a chart, they would indicate the direction of the flow of the entire system of ancient glaciers, from about the period of the breaking up of the ice-sheet until near the close of the glacial winter; because the streams which the ouzels so rigidly follow are, with the unimportant exceptions of a few side tributaries, all flowing in channels eroded for them out of the solid flank of the range by the vanished glaciers – the streams tracing the ancient glaciers, the ouzels tracing the streams. Nor do we find so complete compliance to glacial conditions in the life of any other mountain bird, or animal of any kind. Bears frequently accept the pathways laid down by glaciers as the easiest to travel; but they often leave them and cross over from canyon to canyon. So also, most of the birds trace the moraines to some extent, because the forests are growing on them. But they wander far, crossing the canyons from grove to grove, and draw exceedingly angular and complicated courses.

The Ouzel's nest is one of the most extraordinary pieces of bird architecture I ever saw, odd and novel in design, perfectly fresh and beautiful, and in every way worthy of the genius of the little builder. It is about a foot in diameter, round and bossy in outline, with a neatly arched opening near the bottom, somewhat like an old-fashioned brick oven, or Hottentot's hut. It is built almost exclusively of green and yellow mosses, chiefly the beautiful fronded hypnum that covers the rocks and old drift-logs in the vicinity of waterfalls. These are deftly interwoven, and felted together into a charming little hut; and so situated that many of the outer mosses continue to flourish as if they had not been plucked. A few fine, silky-stemmed grasses are occasionally found interwoven with the mosses, but, with the exception of a thin layer lining the floor, their presence seems accidental, as they are of a species found growing with the mosses and are probably plucked with them. The site chosen for this curious mansion is usually some little rock-shelf within reach of the lighter particles of the spray of a waterfall, so that its walls are kept green and growing, at least during the time of high water.

No harsh lines are presented by any portion of the nest as seen in place, but when removed from its shelf, the back and bottom, and sometimes a portion of the top, is found quite sharply angular, because it is made to conform to the surface of the rock upon which and against which it is built, the little architect always taking advantage of slight crevices and protuberances that may chance to offer, to render his structure stable by means of a kind of gripping and dovetailing.

In choosing a building-spot, concealment does not seem to be taken into consideration; yet notwithstanding the nest is large and guilelessly exposed to view, it is far from being easily detected, chiefly because it swells forward like any other bulging moss-cushion growing naturally in such situations. This is more especially the case where the nest is kept fresh by being well sprinkled. Sometimes these romantic little huts have their beauty enhanced by rock-ferns and grasses that spring up around the mossy walls, or in front of the door-sill, dripping with crystal beads.

Furthermore, at certain hours of the day, when the sunshine is poured down at the required angle, the whole mass of the spray enveloping the fairy establishment is brilliantly irised; and it is through so glorious a rainbow atmosphere as this that some of our blessed ouzels obtain their first peep at the world.

Ouzels seem so completely part and parcel of the streams they inhabit, they scarce suggest any other origin than the streams themselves; and one might almost be pardoned in fancying they come direct from the living waters, like flowers from the ground. At least, from whatever cause, it never occurred to me to look for their nests until more than a year after I had made the acquaintance of the birds themselves, although I found one the very day on which I began the search.

In making my way from Yosemite to the glaciers at the heads of the Merced and Tuolumne rivers, I camped in a particularly wild and romantic portion of the Nevada canyon where in previous excursions I had never failed to enjoy the company of my favorites, who were attracted here, no doubt, by the safe nesting-places in the shelving rocks, and by the abundance of food and falling water. The river, for miles above and below, consists of a succession of small falls from ten to sixty feet in height, connected by flat, plume-like cascades that go flashing from fall to fall, free and almost channel-less, over waving folds of glacier-polished granite.

On the south side of one of the falls, that portion of the precipice which is bathed by the spray presents a series of little shelves and tablets caused by the development of planes of cleavage in the granite, and by the consequent fall of masses through the action of the water. 'Now here,' said I, 'of all places, is the most charming spot for an Ouzel's nest.' Then carefully scanning the fretted face of the precipice through the spray, I at length noticed a yellowish moss-cushion, growing on the edge of a level tablet within five or six feet of the outer folds of the fall. But apart from the fact of its being situated where one acquainted with the lives of ouzels would fancy an Ouzel's nest ought to be, there was nothing in its appearance visible at first sight, to distinguish it from other bosses of rock-moss similarly situated with reference to perennial spray; and it was not until I had scrutinized it again and again, and had removed my shoes and stockings and crept along the face of the rock within eight or ten feet of it, that I could decide certainly whether it was a nest or a natural growth.

In these moss huts three or four eggs are laid, white like foam-bubbles; and well may the little birds hatched from them sing water songs, for they hear them all their lives, and even before they are born.

I have often observed the young just out of the nest making their odd gestures, and seeming in every way as much at home as their experienced parents, like young bees on their first excursions to the flower fields. No amount of familiarity with people and their ways seems to change them in the least. To all appearance their behavior is just the same on seeing a man for the first time, as when they have seen him frequently.

On the lower reaches of the rivers where mills are built, they sing on through the din of the machinery, and all the noisy confusion of dogs, cattle, and workmen. On one occasion, while a wood-chopper was at work on the river-bank, I observed one cheerily singing within reach of the flying chips. Nor does any kind of unwonted disturbance put him in bad humor, or frighten him out of calm self-possession. In passing through a narrow gorge, I once drove one ahead of me from rapid to rapid, disturbing him four times in quick succession where he could not very well fly past me on account of the narrowness of the channel. Most birds under similar circumstances fancy themselves pursued, and become suspiciously uneasy; but, instead of growing nervous about it, he made his usual dippings, and sang one of his most tranquil strains. When observed within a few yards their eyes are seen to express remarkable gentleness and intelligence; but they seldom allow so near a view unless one wears clothing of about the same color as the rocks and trees, and knows how to sit still. On one occasion, while rambling along the shore of a mountain lake, where the birds, at least those born that season, had never seen a man, I sat down to rest on a large stone close to the water's edge, upon which it seemed the ouzels and sandpipers were in the habit of alighting when they came to feed on that part of the shore, and some of the other birds also, when they came down to wash or drink. In a few minutes, along came a whirring Ouzel and alighted on the stone beside me, within reach of my hand. Then suddenly observing me, he stooped nervously as if about to fly on the instant, but as I remained as motionless as the stone, he gained confidence, and looked me steadily in the face for about a minute, then flew quietly to the outlet and began to sing. Next came a sandpiper and gazed at me with much the same guileless expression of eye as the Ouzel. Lastly, down with a swoop came a Steller's jay out of a fir-tree, probably with the intention of moistening his noisy throat. But instead of sitting confidingly as my other visitors had done, he rushed off at once, nearly tumbling heels over head into the lake in his suspicious confusion, and with loud screams roused the neighborhood.

Love for songbirds, with their sweet human voices, appears to be more common and unfailing than love for flowers. Every one loves flowers to some extent, at least in life's fresh morning, attracted by them as instinctively as humming-birds and bees. Even the young Digger Indians have sufficient love for the brightest of those found growing on the mountains to gather them and braid them as decorations for the hair. And I was glad to discover, through the few Indians that could be induced to talk on the subject, that they have names for the wild rose and the lily, and other conspicuous flowers, whether available as food or otherwise. Most men, however, whether savage or civilized, become apathetic toward all plants that have no other apparent use than the use of beauty. But fortunately one's first instinctive love of songbirds is never wholly obliterated, no matter what the influences upon our lives may be. I have often been delighted to see a pure, spiritual glow come into the countenances of hard business-men and old miners, when a songbird chanced to alight near them. Nevertheless, the little mouthful of meat that swells out the breasts of some songbirds is too often the cause of their death. Larks and robins in particular are brought to market in hundreds. But fortunately the Ouzel has no enemy so eager to eat his little body as to follow him into the mountain solitudes. I never knew him to be chased even by hawks.

An acquaintance of mine, a sort of foothill mountaineer, had a pet cat, a great, dozy, overgrown creature, about as broad-shouldered as a lynx. During the winter, while the snow lay deep, the mountaineer sat in his lonely cabin among the pines smoking his pipe and wearing the dull time away. Tom was his sole companion, sharing his bed, and sitting beside him on a stool with much the same drowsy expression of eye as his master. The good-natured bachelor was content with his hard fare of soda-bread and bacon, but Tom, the only creature in the world acknowledging dependence on him, must needs be provided with fresh meat. Accordingly he bestirred himself to contrive squirrel-traps, and waded the snowy woods with his gun, making sad havoc among the few winter birds, sparing neither robin, sparrow, nor tiny nuthatch, and the pleasure of seeing Tom eat and grow fat was his great reward.

One cold afternoon, while hunting along the river-bank, he noticed a plain-feathered little bird skipping about in the shallows, and immediately raised his gun. But just then the confiding songster began to sing, and after listening to his summery melody the charmed hunter turned away, saying, 'Bless your little heart, I can't shoot you, not even for Tom.'

Even so far north as icy Alaska, I have found my glad singer. When I was exploring the glaciers between Mount Fairweather and the Stikeen River, one cold day in November, after trying in vain to force a way through the innumerable icebergs of Sum Dum Bay to the great glaciers at the head of it, I was weary and baffled and sat resting in my canoe convinced at last that I would have to leave this part of my work for another year. Then I began to plan my escape to open water before the young ice which was beginning to form should shut me in. While I thus lingered drifting with the bergs, in the midst of these gloomy forebodings and all the terrible glacial desolation and grandeur, I suddenly heard the well-known whir of an Ouzel's wings, and, looking up, saw my little comforter coming straight across the ice from the shore. In a second or two he was with me, flying three times round my head with a happy salute, as if saying, 'Cheer up, old friend; you see I'm here, and all's well.' Then he flew back to the shore, alighted on the topmost jag of a stranded iceberg, and began to nod and bow as though he were on one of his favorite boulders in the midst of a sunny Sierra cascade.

The species is distributed all along the mountain-ranges of the Pacific Coast from Alaska to Mexico, and east to the Rocky Mountains. Nevertheless, it is as yet comparatively little known. Audubon and Wilson did not meet it. Swainson was, I believe, the first naturalist to describe a specimen from Mexico. Specimens were shortly afterward procured by Drummond near the sources of the Athabasca River, between the fifty-fourth and fifty-sixth parallels; and it has been collected by nearly all of the numerous exploring expeditions undertaken of late through our Western States and Territories; for it never fails to engage the attention of naturalists in a very particular manner.

Such, then, is our little cinclus, beloved of everyone who is so fortunate as to know him. Tracing on strong wing every curve of the most precipitous torrents from one extremity of the Sierra to the other; not fearing to follow them through their darkest gorges and coldest snow-tunnels; acquainted with every waterfall, echoing their divine music; and throughout the whole of their beautiful lives interpreting all that we in our unbelief call terrible in the utterances of torrents and storms, as only varied expressions of God's eternal love.

Chapter 14

THE WILD SHEEP

(Ovis montana)

The wild sheep ranks highest among the animal mountaineers of the Sierra. Possessed of keen sight and scent, and strong limbs, he dwells secure amid the loftiest summits, leaping unscathed from crag to crag, up and down the fronts of giddy precipices, crossing foaming torrents and slopes of frozen snow, exposed to the wildest storms, yet maintaining a brave, warm life, and developing from generation to generation in perfect strength and beauty.

Nearly all the lofty mountain-chains of the globe are inhabited by wild sheep, most of which, on account of the remote and all but inaccessible regions where they dwell, are imperfectly known as yet. They are classified by different naturalists under from five to ten distinct species or varieties, the best known being the burrhel of the Himalaya (*Ovis burrhel*, Blyth); the argali, the large wild sheep of central and northeastern Asia (*O. ammon*, Linn., or *Caprovis argali*); the Corsican mouflon (*O. musimon*, Pal.); the aoudad of the mountains of northern Africa (*Ammotragus tragelaphus*); and the Rocky Mountain bighorn (*O. montana*, Cuv.). To this last-named species belongs the wild sheep of the Sierra. Its range, according to the late Professor Baird of the Smithsonian Institution, extends 'from the region of the upper Missouri and Yellowstone to the Rocky Mountains and the high grounds adjacent to them on the eastern slope, and as far south as the Rio Grande. Westward it extends to the coast ranges of Washington, Oregon, and California, and follows the highlands some distance into Mexico.' [Pacific Railroad Survey, Vol. VIII, page 678.] Throughout the vast region bounded on the east by the Wahsatch Mountains and on the west by the Sierra there are more than a hundred sub-ordinate ranges and mountain groups, trending north and south, range beyond range, with summits rising from eight to twelve thousand feet above the level of the sea, probably all of which, according to my own observations, is, or has been, inhabited by this species.

Compared with the argali, which, considering its size and the vast extent of its range, is probably the most important of all the wild sheep, our species is about the same size, but the horns are less twisted and less divergent. The more important characteristics are, however, essentially the same, some of the best naturalists maintaining that the two are only varied forms of one species. In accordance with this view, Cuvier conjec-tures that since central Asia seems to be the region where the sheep first appeared, and from which it has been distributed, the argali may have been distributed over this continent from Asia by crossing Bering Strait on ice. This conjecture is not so ill founded as at first sight it would appear; for the Strait is only about fifty miles wide, is interrupted by three islands, and is jammed with ice nearly every winter. Furthermore the argali is abundant on the mountains adjacent to the Strait at East Cape, where it is well known to the Tschuckchi hunters and where I have seen many of their horns.

On account of the extreme variability of the sheep under culture, it is generally supposed that the innumerable domestic breeds have all been derived from the few wild species; but the whole question is involved in obscurity. According to Darwin, sheep have been domesticated from a very ancient period, the remains of a small breed, differing from any now known, having been found in the famous Swiss lake-dwellings.

Compared with the best-known domestic breeds, we find that our wild species is much larger, and, instead of an all-wool garment, wears a thick overcoat of hair like that of the deer, and an undercove ring of fine wool. The hair, though rather coarse, is comfortably soft and spongy, and lies smooth, as if carefully tended with comb and brush. The predominant color during most of the year is brownish-gray, varying to bluish-gray in the autumn; the belly and a large, conspicuous patch on the buttocks are white; and the tail, which is very short, like that of a deer, is black, with a yellowish border. The wool is white, and grows in beautiful spirals down out of sight among the shining hair, like delicate climbing vines among stalks of corn.

The horns of the male are of immense size, measuring in their great diameter from five to six and a half inches, and from two and a half to three feet in length around the curve. They are yelloish-white in color, and ridged transversely, like those of the domestic ram. Their cross-section near the base is somewhat triangular in outline, and flattened toward the tip. Rising boldly from the top of the head, they curve gently backward and outward, then forward and outward, until about three fourths of a circle is described, and until the flattened, blunt tips are about two feet or two and a half feet apart. Those of the female are flattened throughout their entire length, are less curved than those of the male, and much smaller, measuring less than a foot along the curve.

A ram and ewe that I obtained near the Modoc lava-beds, to the northeast of Mount Shasta, measured as follows:

	Ram		Ewe	
	ft.	in.	ft.	in.
Height at shoulders	3	6	3	0
Girth around shoulders	3	11	3	3
Length from nose to root of tail	5	10¼	4	3½
Length of ears	0	4	0	5
Length of tail	0	4½	0	4½
Length of horns around curve	2	9	0	11½
Distance across from tip to tip of horns	2	5		
Circumference of horns at base	1	4	0	6

The measurements of a male obtained in the Rocky Mountains by Audubon vary but little as compared with the above. The weight of his specimen was 344 pounds (Audubon and Bachman's *Quadrupeds of North America*), which is, perhaps, about an average for full-grown males. The females are about a third lighter.

Besides these differences in size, color, hair, etc., as noted above, we may observe that the domestic sheep, in a general way, is expressionless, like a dull bundle of something only half alive, while the wild is as elegant and graceful as a deer, every movement manifesting admirable strength and character. The tame is timid; the wild is bold. The tame is always more or less ruffled and dirty; while the wild is as smooth and clean as the flowers of his mountain pastures.

The earliest mention that I have been able to find of the wild sheep in America is by Father Picolo, a Catholic missionary at Monterey, in the year 1797, who, after describing it, oddly enough, as 'a kind of deer with a sheep-like head, and about as large as a calf one or two years old,' naturally hurries on to remark: 'I have eaten of these beasts; their flesh is very tender and delicious.' Mackenzie, in his northern travels, heard the species spoken of by the Indians as 'white buffaloes.' And Lewis and Clark tell us that, in a time of great scarcity on the head waters of the Missouri, they saw plenty of wild sheep, but they were 'too shy to be shot.'

A few of the more energetic of the Pah Ute Indians hunt the wild sheep every season among the more accessible sections of the High Sierra, in the neighborhood of passes, where, from having been pursued, they have become extremely wary; but in the rugged wilderness of peaks and canyons, where the foaming tributaries of the San Joaquin and King's rivers take their rise, they fear no hunter save the wolf, and are more guileless and approachable than their tame kindred.

While engaged in the work of exploring high regions where they delight to roam I have been greatly interested in studying their habits. In the months of November and December, and probably during a considerable portion of midwinter, they all flock together, male and female, old and young. I once found a complete band of this kind numbering upward of fifty, which, on being alarmed, went bounding away across a jagged lava-bed at admirable speed, led by a majestic old ram, with the lambs safe in the middle of the flock.

In spring and summer, the full-grown rams form separate bands of from three to twenty, and are usually found feeding along the edges of glacier meadows, or resting among the castle-like crags of the high summits; and whether quietly feeding, or scaling the wild cliffs, their noble forms and the power and beauty of their movements never fail to strike the beholder with lively admiration.

Their resting-places seem to be chosen with reference to sunshine and a wide outlook, and most of all to safety. Their feeding-grounds are among the most beautiful of the wild gardens, bright with daisies and gentians and mats of purple bryanthus, lying hidden away on rocky headlands and canyon sides, where sunshine is abundant, or down in the shady glacier valleys, along the banks of the streams and lakes, where the plushy sod is greenest. Here they feast all summer, the happy wanderers, perhaps relishing the beauty as well as the taste of the lovely flora on which they feed.

When the winter storms set in, loading their highland pastures with snow, then, like the birds they gather and go to lower climates, usually descending the eastern flank of the range to the rough, volcanic table-lands and treeless ranges of the Great Basin adjacent to the Sierra. They never make haste, however, and seem to have no dread of storms, many of the strongest only going down leisurely to bare, wind-swept ridges, to feed on bushes and dry bunch-grass, and then returning up into the snow. Once I was snow-bound on Mount Shasta for three days, a little below the timber line. It was a dark and stormy time, well calculated to test the skill and endurance of mountaineers. The snow-laden gale drove on night and day in hissing, blinding floods, and when at length it began to abate, I found that a small band of wild sheep had weathered the storm in the lee of a clump of Dwarf Pines a few yards above my storm-nest, where the snow was eight or ten feet deep. I was warm at the back of a rock, with blankets, bread, and fire. My brave companions lay in the snow, without food, and with only the partial shelter of the short trees, yet they made no sign of suffering or faint-heartedness.

In the months of May and June, the wild sheep bring forth their young in solitary and almost inaccessible crags, far above the nesting-rocks of the eagle. I have frequently come upon the beds of the ewes and lambs at an elevation of from 12,000 to 13,000 feet above sea-level. These beds are simply oval-shaped hollows, pawed out among loose, disintegrating rock-chips and sand, upon some sunny spot commanding a good outlook, and partially sheltered from the winds that sweep those lofty peaks almost without intermission. Such is the cradle of the little mountaineer, aloft in the very sky; rocked in storms, curtained in clouds, sleeping in thin, icy air; but, wrapped in his hairy coat, and nourished by a strong, warm mother, defended from the talons of the eagle and the teeth of the sly coyote, the bonny lamb grows apace. He soon learns to nibble the tufted rock-grasses and leaves of the white spiraea; his horns begin to shoot, and before summer is done he is strong and agile, and goes forth with the flock, watched by the same divine love that tends the more helpless human lamb in its cradle by the fireside.

Nothing is more commonly remarked by noisy, dusty trail-travelers in the Sierra than the want of animal life – no songbirds, no deer, no squirrels, no game of any kind, they say. But if such could only go away quietly into the wilderness, sauntering afoot and alone with natural deliberation, they would soon learn that these mountain mansions are not without inhabitants, many of whom, confiding and gentle, would not try to shun their acquaintance.

In the fall of 1873 I was tracing the South Fork of the San Joaquin up its wild canyon to its farthest glacier fountains. It was the season of alpine Indian summer. The sun beamed lovingly; the squirrels were nutting in the pine-trees, butterflies hovered about the last of the goldenrods, the willow and maple thickets were yellow, the meadows brown, and the whole sunny, mellow landscape glowed like a countenance in the deepest and sweetest repose. On my way over the glacier-polished rocks along the river, I came to an expanded portion of the canyon, about two miles long and half a mile wide, which formed a level park inclosed with picturesque granite walls like those of Yosemite Valley. Down through the middle of it poured the beautiful river shining and spangling in the golden light, yellow groves on its banks, and strips of brown meadow; while the whole park was astir with wild life, some of which even the noisest and least observing of travelers must have seen had they been with me. Deer, with their supple, well-grown fawns, bounded from thicket to thicket as I advanced; grouse kept rising from the brown grass with a great whirring of wings, and, alighting on the lower branches of the pines and poplars, allowed a near approach, as if curious to see me. Farther on, a broad-shouldered wildcat showed himself, coming out of a grove, and crossing the river on a flood-jamb of logs, halting for a moment to look back. The bird-like tamias frisked about my feet everywhere among the pine-needles and seedy grass-tufts; cranes waded the shallows of the river-bends, the kingfisher rattled from perch to perch, and the blessed ouzel sang amid the spray of every cascade. Where may lonely wanderer find a more interesting family of mountain-dwellers, earth-born companions and fellow-mortals? It was afternoon when I joined them, and the glorious landscape began to fade in the gloaming before I awoke from their enchantment. Then I sought a camp-ground on the river-bank, made a cupful of tea, and lay down to sleep on a smooth place among the yellow leaves of an aspen grove. Next day I discovered yet grander landscapes and grander life. Following the river over huge, swelling rock-bosses through a majestic canyon, and past innumerable cascades, the scenery in general became gradually wilder and more alpine. The Sugar Pine and Silver Firs gave place to the hardier Cedar and Hemlock Spruce. The canyon walls became more rugged and bare, and gentians and arctic daisies became more abundant in the gardens and strips of meadow along the streams. Toward the middle of the afternoon I came to another valley, strikingly wild and original in all its features, and perhaps never before touched by human foot. As regards area of level bottom-land, it is one of the very smallest of the Yosemite type, but its walls are sublime, rising to a height of from 2000 to 4000 feet above the river. At the head of the valley the main canyon forks, as is found to be the case in all yosemites. The formation of this one is due chiefly to the action of two great glaciers, whose fountains lay to the eastward, on the flanks of Mounts Humphrey and Emerson and a cluster of nameless peaks farther south.

The gray, boulder-chafed river was singing loudly through the valley, but above its massy roar I heard the booming of a waterfall, which drew me eargerly on; and just as I emerged from the tangled groves and brier-thickets at the head of the valley, the main fork of the river came in sight, falling fresh from its glacier fountains in a snowy cascade, between granite walls 2000 feet high. The steep incline down which the glad waters thundered seemed to bar all farther progress. It was not long, however, before I discovered a crooked seam in the rock, by which I was enabled to climb to the edge of a terrace that crosses the canyon, and divides the cataract nearly in the middle. Here I sat down to take breath and make some entries in my note-book, taking advantage, at the same time, of my elevated position above the trees to gaze back over the valley into the heart of the noble landscape, little knowing the while what neighbors were near.

After spending a few minutes in this way, I chanced to look across the fall, and there stood three sheep quietly observing me. Never did the sudden appearance of a mountain, or fall, or human friend more forcibly seize and rivet my attention. Anxiety to observe accurately held me perfectly still. Eagerly I marked the flowing undulations of their firm, braided muscles, their strong legs, ears, eyes, heads, their graceful rounded necks, the color of their hair, and the bold, upsweeping curves of their noble horns. When they moved I watched every gesture, while they, in no wise disconcerted either by my attention or by the tumultuous roar of the water, advanced deliberately alongside the rapids, between the two divisions of the cataract, turning now and then to look at me. Presently they came to a steep, ice-burnished acclivity, which they ascended by a succession of quick, short, stiff-legged leaps, reaching the top without a struggle. This was the most startling feat of mountaineering I had ever witnessed, and, considering only the mechanics of the thing, my astonishment could hardly have been greater had they displayed wings and taken to flight. 'Surefooted' mules on such ground would have fallen and rolled like loosened boulders. Many a time, where the slopes are far lower, I have been compelled to take off my shoes and stockings, tie them to my belt, and creep barefooted, with the utmost caution. No wonder then, that I watched the progress of these animal mountaineers with keen sympathy, and exulted in the boundless sufficiency of wild nature displayed in their invention, construction, and keeping. A few minutes later I caught sight of a dozen more in one band, near the foot of the upper fall. They were standing on the same side of the river with me, only twenty-five or thirty yards away, looking as unworn and perfect as if created on the spot. It appeared by their tracks, which I had seen in the Little Yosemite, and by their present position, that when I came up the canyon they were all feeding together down in the valley, and in their haste to reach high ground, where they could look about them to ascertain the nature of the strange disturbance, they were divided, three ascending on one side the river, the rest on the other.

The main band, headed by an experienced chief, now began to cross the wild rapids between the two divisions of the cascade. This was another exciting feat; for, among all the varied experiences of mountaineers, the crossing of boisterous, rockdashed torrents is found to be one of the most trying to the nerves. Yet these fine fellows walked fearlessly to the brink, and jumped from boulder to boulder, holding themselves in easy poise above the whirling, confusing current, as if they were doing nothing extraordinary.

In the immediate foreground of this rare picture there was a fold of ice-burnished granite, traversed by a few bold lines in which rock-ferns and tufts of bryanthus were growing, the gray canyon walls on the sides, nobly sculptured and adorned with brown cedars and pines; lofty peaks in the distance, and in the middle ground the snowy fall, the voice and soul of the landscape; fringing bushes beating time to its thunder-tones, the brave sheep in front of it, their gray forms slightly obscured in the spray, yet standing out in good, heavy relief against the close white water, with their huge horns rising like the up-turned roots of dead pine-trees, while the evening sunbeams streaming up the canyon colored all the picture a rosy purple and made it glorious. After crossing the river, the dauntless climbers, led by their chief, at once began to scale the canyon wall, turning now right, now left, in long, single file, keeping well apart out of one another's way, and leaping in regular succession from crag to crag, now ascending slippery dome-curves, now walking leisurely along the edges of precipices, stopping at times to gaze down at me from some flat-topped rock, with heads held aslant, as if curious to learn what I thought about it, or whether I was likely to follow them. After reaching the top of the wall, which, at this place, is somewhere between 1500 and 2000 feet high, they were still visible against the sky as they lingered, looking down in groups of twos or threes.

Throughout the entire ascent they did not make a single awkward step, or an unsuccessful effort of any kind. I have frequently seen tame sheep in mountains jump upon a sloping rock-surface, hold on tremulously a few seconds, and fall back baffled and irresolute. But in the most trying situations, where the slightest want or inaccuracy would have been fatal, these always seemed to move in comfortable reliance on their strength and skill, the limits of which they never appeared to know. Moreover, each one of the flock, while following the guidance of the most experienced, yet climbed with intelligent independence as a perfect individual, capable of separate existence whenever it should wish or be compelled to withdraw from the little clan. The domestic sheep, on the contrary, is only a fraction of an animal, a whole flock being required to form an individual, just as numerous flowerets are required to make one complete sunflower.

Those shepherds who, in summer, drive their flocks to the mountain pastures, and, while watching them night and day, have seen them frightened by bears and storms, and scattered like winddriven chaff, will, in some measure, be able to appreciate the self-reliance and strength and noble individuality of Nature's sheep.

Like the Alp-climbing ibex of Europe, our mountaineer is said to plunge headlong down the faces of sheer precipices, and alight on his big horns. I know only two hunters who claim to have actually witnessed this feat; I never was so fortunate. They describe the act as a diving head-foremost. The horns are so large at the base that they cover the upper portion of the head down nearly to a level with the eyes, and the skull is exceedingly strong. I struck an old, bleached specimen on Mount Ritter a dozen blows with my ice-axe without breaking it. Such skulls would not fracture very readily by the wildest rock-diving, but other bones could hardly be expected to hold together in such a performance; and the mechanical difficulties in the way of controlling their movements, after striking upon an irregular surface, are, in themselves, sufficient to show this boulder-like method of progression to be impossible, even in the absence of all other evidence on the subject; moreover, the ewes follow wherever the rams may lead, although their horns are mere spikes. I have found many pairs of the horns of the old rams considerably battered, doubtless a result of fighting. I was particularly interested in the question, after witnessing the performances of this San Joaquin band upon the glaciated rocks at the foot of the falls; and as soon as I procured specimens and examined their feet, all the mystery disappeared. The secret, considered in connection with exceptionally strong muscles, is simply this: the wide posterior portion of the bottom of the foot, instead of wearing down and becoming flat and hard, like the feet of tame sheep and horses, bulges out in a soft, rubber-like pad or cushion, which not only grips and holds well on smooth rocks, but fits into small cavities, and down upon or against slight protuberances. Even the hardest portions of the edge of the hoof are comparatively soft and elastic; furthermore, the toes admit of an extraordinary amount of both lateral and vertical movement, allowing the foot to accommodate itself still more perfectly to the irregularities of rock surfaces, while at the same time increasing the gripping power.

At the base of Sheep Rock, one of the winter strongholds of the Shasta flocks, there lives a stock-raiser who has had the advantage of observing the movements of wild sheep every winter; and, in the course of a conversation with him on the subject of their diving habits, he pointed to the front of a lava headland about 150 feet high, which is only eight or ten degrees out of the perpendicular. 'There,' said he, 'I followed a band of them fellows to the back of that rock yonder, and expected to capture them all, for I thought I had a dead thing on them. I got behind them on a narrow bench that runs along the face of the wall near the top and comes to an end where they couldn't get away without falling and being killed; but they jumped off, and landed all right, as if that were the regular thing with them.'

'What!' said I, 'jumped 150 feet perpendicular! Did you see them do it?'

'No,' he replied, 'I didn't see them going down, for I was behind them; but I saw them go off over the brink, and then I went below and found their tracks where they struck on the loose rubbish at the bottom. They just *sailed right off*, and landed on their feet right side up. That is the kind of animal *they* is – beats anything else that goes on four legs.'

On another occasion, a flock that was pursued by hunters retreated to another portion of this same cliff where it is still higher, and, on being followed, they were seen jumping down in perfect order, one behind another, by two men who happened to be chopping where they had a fair view of them and could watch their progress from top to bottom of the precipice. Both ewes and rams made the frightful descent without evincing any extraordinary concern, hugging the rock closely, and controlling the velocity of their half falling, half leaping move-

ments by striking at short intervals and holding back with their
cushioned, rubber feet upon small ledges and roughened
inclines until near the bottom, when they 'sailed off' into
the free air and alighted on their feet, but with their bodies
so nearly in a vertical position that they appeared to be diving.

It appears, therefore, that the methods of this wild mountaineering become clearly comprehensible as soon as we make
ourselves acquainted with the rocks, and the kind of feet and
muscles brought to bear upon them.

The Modoc and Pah Ute Indians are, or rather have been,
the most successful hunters of the wild sheep in the regions that
have come under my own observation. I have seen large
numbers of heads and horns in the caves of Mount Shasta
and the Modoc lava-beds, where the Indians had been feasting
in stormy weather; also in the canyons of the Sierra opposite
Owen's Valley; while the heavy obsidian arrow-heads found
on some of the highest peaks show that this warfare has long
been going on.

In the more accessible ranges that stretch across the desert
regions of western Utah and Nevada, considerable numbers of
Indians used to hunt in company like packs of wolves, and
being perfectly acquainted with the topography of their hunt-
ing-grounds, and with the habits and instincts of the game,
they were pretty successful. On the tops of nearly every one of
the Nevada mountains that I have visited, I found small, nest-
like inclosures built of stones, in which, as I afterward learned,
one or more Indians would lie in wait while their companions
scoured the ridges below, knowing that the alarmed sheep
would surely run to the summit, and when they could be made
to approach with the wind they were shot at short range.

Still larger bands of Indians used to make extensive hunts
upon some dominant mountain much frequented by the sheep,
such as Mount Grant on the Wassuck Range to the west of
Walker Lake. On some particular spot, favorably situated with
reference to the well-known trails of the sheep, they built a
high-walled corral, with long guiding wings diverging from the
gateway; and into this inclosure they sometimes succeeded in
driving the noble game. Great numbers of Indians were of
course required, more, indeed, than they could usually muster,
counting in squaws, children, and all; they were compelled,
therefore, to build rows of dummy hunters out of stones, along

the ridge-tops which they wished to prevent the sheep from crossing. And, without discrediting the sagacity of the game, these dummies were found effective; for, with a few live Indians moving about excitedly among them, they could hardly be distinguished at a little distance from men, by anyone not in the secret. The whole ridge-top then seemed to be alive with hunters.

The only animal that may fairly be regarded as a companion or rival of the sheep is the so-called Rocky Mountain goat (*Aplocerus montana*, Rich.), which, as its name indicates, is more antelope than goat. He, too, is a brave and hardy climber, fearlessly crossing the wildest summits, and braving the severest storms, but he is shaggy, short-legged, and much less dignified in demeanor than the sheep. His jet-black horns are only about five or six inches in length, and the long, white hair with which he is covered obscures the expression of his limbs. I have never yet seen a single specimen in the Sierra, though possibly a few flocks may have lived on Mount Shasta a comparatively short time ago.

The ranges of these two mountaineers are pretty distinct, and they see but little of each other; the sheep being restricted mostly to the dry, inland mountains; the goat or chamois to the wet, snowy glacier-laden mountains of the northwest coast of the continent in Oregon, Washington, British Columbia, and Alaska. Probably more than 200 dwell on the icy, volcanic cone of Mount Rainier; and while I was exploring the glaciers of Alaska I saw flocks of these admirable mountaineers nearly every day, and often followed their trails through the mazes of bewildering crevasses, in which they are excellent guides.

Three species of deer are found in California – the black-tailed, white-tailed, and mule deer. The first mentioned (*Cervus Columbianus*) is by far the most abundant, and occasionally meets the sheep during the summer on high glacier meadows, and along the edge of the timber line; but being a forest animal, seeking shelter and rearing its young in dense thickets, it seldom visits the wild sheep in its higher homes. The antelope, though not a mountaineer, is occasionally met in winter by the sheep while feeding along the edges of the sage-plains and bare volcanic hills to the east of the Sierra. So also is the mule deer, which is almost restricted in its range to this eastern region. The white-tailed species belongs to the coast ranges.

Perhaps no wild animal in the world is without enemies, but highlanders, as a class, have fewer than lowlanders. The wily panther, slipping and crouching among long grass and bushes, pounces upon the antelope and deer, but seldom crosses the bald, craggy thresholds of the sheep. Neither can the bears be regarded as enemies; for, though they seek to vary their every-day diet of nuts and berries by an occasional meal of mutton, they prefer to hunt tame and helpless flocks. Eagles and coyotes, no doubt, capture an unprotected lamb at times, or some unfortunate beset in deep, soft snow, but these cases are little more than accidents. So, also, a few perish in long-continued snow-storms, though, in all my mountaineering, I have not found more than five or six that seemed to have met their fate in this way. A little band of three were discovered snow-bound in Bloody Canyon a few years ago, and were killed with an axe by mountaineers, who chanced to be crossing the range in winter.

Man is the most dangerous enemy of all, but even from him our brave mountain-dweller has little to fear in the remote solitudes of the High Sierra. The golden plains of the Sacramento and San Joaquin were lately thronged with bands of elk and antelope, but, being fertile and accessible, they were required for human pastures. So, also, are many of the feeding-grounds of the deer – hill, valley, forest, and meadow – but it will be long before man will care to take the highland castles of the sheep. And when we consider here how rapidly entire species of noble animals, such as the elk, moose, and buffalo, are being pushed to the very verge of extinction, all lovers of wildness will rejoice with me in the rocky security of *Ovis montana*, the bravest of all the Sierra mountaineers.

Selections from

OUR NATIONAL PARKS
(1901)

Muir's second book was compiled and re-edited from ten articles originally published in the *Atlantic Magazine* between 1897 and 1901. They served the national campaign which culminated in Congressional legislation to create a National Park System in 1902. Muir believed that national parks were necessary to protect wilderness from the depredations of the robber-barons, but he also believed that wilderness areas were vital for the health and sanity of the nation. In San Francisco, he observed that 'money-madness' and the obsessive pursuit of wealth, fame and consumerism corrupted people and damaged their lives. The physical pollutions of smoke, noise, poverty and overcrowding brought typhoid, syphilis and tuberculosis, but the mental and spiritual poverty which Muir witnessed in towns and cities was equally damaging. He wrote:

> If the death exhalations which brood our broad towns were made visible, we should flee as from a plague. All are more or less sick; there is not one perfectly sane man in the whole of San Francisco.

> (*Letter, September 1874*)

and that

> Few in these hot, dim, frictiony times are quite sane or free. Choked with cares, like clocks full of dust, laboriously doing so much good, and making so much money . . . they are no longer good for themselves.

> (Atlantic Monthly, *January 1898*)

One wonders what Muir would have written about society today, when mass-media and advertising pervade every aspect of our lives and the tinsel-show of celebrity culture fills the press and television with the voyeurism of *Big Brother*, 'reality television' and the endless vacuity of fictional soap operas.

Muir's prescription for the restoration of physical and mental health was direct contact with Nature:

> Thousands of tired, nerve-shaken people are beginning to find out that going to the mountains is going home; that wildness is a necessity; and that mountain parks and reservations are useful not only as fountains of irrigating rivers, but as fountains of life.

Limited space precludes the inclusion of all ten chapters of this book, but I have selected the central essays on Yellowstone, Yosemite and Sequoia and General Grant National Parks, as being pivotal to the book.

Chapter 2

THE YELLOWSTONE NATIONAL PARK

Of the four national parks of the West, the Yellowstone is far the largest. It is a big, wholesome wilderness on the broad summit of the Rocky Mountains, favored with abundance of rain and snow – a place of fountains where the greatest of the American rivers take their rise. The central portion is a densely forested and comparatively level volcanic plateau with an average elevation of about eight thousand feet above the sea, surrounded by an imposing host of mountains belonging to the subordinate Gallatin, Wind River, Teton, Absaroka, and snowy ranges. Unnumbered lakes shine in it, united by a famous band of streams that rush up out of hot lava beds, or fall from the frosty peaks in channels rocky and bare, mossy and bosky, to the main rivers, singing cheerily on through every difficulty, cunningly dividing and finding their way east and went to the two far-off seas.

Glacier meadows and beaver meadows are out-spread with charming effect along the banks of the streams, parklike expanses in the woods, and innumerable small gardens in rocky recesses of the mountains, some of them containing more petals than leaves, while the whole wilderness is enlivened with happy animals.

Beside the treasures common to most mountain regions that are wild and blessed with a kind climate, the park is full of exciting wonders. The wildest geysers in the world, in bright, triumphant bands, are dancing and singing in it amid thousands of boiling springs, beautiful and awful, their basins arrayed in gorgeous colors like gigantic flowers; and hot paint-pots, mud springs, mud volcanoes, mush and broth caldrons whose contents are of every color and consistency, plash and heave and roar in bewildering abundance. In the adjacent mountains, beneath the living trees the edges of petrified forests are exposed to view, like specimens on the shelves of a museum, standing on ledges tier above tier where they grew, solemnly silent in rigid crystalline beauty after swaying in the winds thousands of centuries ago, opening marvelous views back into the years and climates and life of the past. Here, too, are hills of sparkling crystals, hills of sulphur, hills of glass, hills of cinders and ashes, mountains of every style of architecture, icy or forested, mountains covered with honey-bloom sweet as Hymettus, mountains boiled soft like potatoes and colored like a sunset sky. A that and a that, and twice as muckle's a that, Nature has on show in the Yellowstone Park. Therefore it is called Wonderland, and thousands of tourists and travelers stream into it every summer, and wander about in it enchanted.

Fortunately, almost as soon as it was discovered it was dedicated and set apart for the benefit of the people, a piece of legislation that shines benignly amid the common dust-and-ashes history of the public domain, for which the world must thank Professor Hayden above all others; for he led the first scientific exploring party into it, described it, and with admirable enthusiasm urged Congress to preserve it. As delineated in the year 1872, the park contained about 3344 square miles. On March 30, 1891 it was to all intents and purposes enlarged by the Yellowstone National Park Timber Reserve, and in December, 1897, by the Teton Forest Reserve; thus nearly doubling its original area, and extending the southern boundary far enough to take in the sublime Teton range and the famous pasture-lands of the big Rocky Mountain game animals. The withdrawal of this large tract from the public domain did not harm anyone; for its height, 6000 to over 13,000 feet above the sea, and its thick mantle of volcanic rocks, prevent its ever being available for agriculture or mining, while on the other hand its geographical position, reviving climate, and wonderful scenery combine to make it a grand health, pleasure, and study resort – a gathering-place for travelers from all the world.

The national parks are not only withdrawn from sale and entry like the forest reservations, but are efficiently managed and guarded by small troops of United States cavalry, directed by the Secretary of the Interior. Under this care the forests are flourishing, protected from both axe and fire; and so, of course, are the shaggy beds of underbrush and the herbaceous vegetation. The so-called curiosities, also, are preserved, and the furred and feathered tribes, many of which, in danger of extinction a short time ago, are now increasing in numbers – a refreshing thing to see amid the blind, ruthless destruction that is going on in the adjacent regions. In pleasing contrast to the noisy, ever-changing management, or mismanagement, of blundering, plundering, money-making vote-sellers who receive their places from boss politicians as purchased goods, the soldiers do their duty so quietly that the traveler is scarce aware of their presence.

This is the coolest and highest of the parks. Frosts occur every month of the year. Nevertheless, the tenderest tourist finds it warm enough in summer. The air is electric and full of ozone, healing, reviving, exhilarating, kept pure by frost and fire, while the scenery is wild enough to awaken the dead. It is a glorious place to grow in and rest in; camping on the shores of the lakes, in the warm openings of the woods golden with sunflowers, on the banks of the streams, by the snowy waterfalls, beside the exciting wonders or away from them in the scallops of the mountain walls sheltered from every wind, on smooth silky lawns enameled with gentians, up in the fountain hollows of the ancient glaciers between the peaks, where cool pools and brooks and gardens of precious plants charmingly embowered are never wanting, and good rough rocks with every variety of cliff and scaur are invitingly near for outlooks and exercise.

From these lovely dens you may make excursions whenever you like into the middle of the park, where the geysers and hot springs are reeking and spouting in their beautiful basins, displaying an exuberance of color and strange motion and energy admirably calculated to surprise and frighten, charm and shake up the least sensitive out of apathy into newness of life.

However orderly your excursions or aimless, again and again amid the calmest, stillest scenery you will be brought to a standstill hushed and awe-stricken before phenomena wholly new to you. Boiling springs and huge deep pools of purest green and azure water, thousands of them, are plashing

and heaving in these high, cool mountains as if a fierce furnace
fire were burning beneath each one of them; and a hundred
geysers, white torrents of boiling water and steam, like in-
verted waterfalls, are ever and anon rushing up out of the hot,
black underworld. Some of these ponderous geyser columns
are as large as sequoias – five to sixty feet in diameter, one
hundred and fifty to three hundred feet high – and are
sustained at this great height with tremendous energy for a
few minutes, or perhaps nearly an hour, standing rigid and
erect, hissing, throbbing, booming, as if thunderstorms were
raging beneath their roots, their sides roughened or fluted like
the furrowed boles of trees, their tops dissolving in feathery
branches, while the irised spray, like misty bloom is at times
blown aside, revealing the massive shafts shining against a
background of pine-covered hills. Some of them lean more or
less, as if storm-bent, and instead of being round are flat or fan-
shaped, issuing from irregular slits in silex pavements with
radiate structure, the sunbeams sifting through them in ravishing splendor. Some are broad and round-headed like oaks;
others are low and bunchy, branching near the ground like
bushes; and a few are hollow in the centre like big daisies or
water-lilies. No frost cools them, snow never covers them nor
lodges in their branches; winter and summer they welcome
alike; all of them, of whatever form or size, faithfully rising and
sinking in fairy rhythmic dance night and day, in all sorts of
weather, at varying periods of minutes, hours, or weeks,
growing up rapidly, uncontrollable as fate, tossing their pearly
branches in the wind, bursting into bloom and vanishing like
the frailest flowers – plants of which Nature raises hundreds or
thousands of crops a year with no apparent exhaustion of the
fiery soil.

The so-called geyser basins, in which this rare sort of
vegetation is growing, are mostly open valleys on the central
plateau that were eroded by glaciers after the greater volcanic
fires had ceased to burn. Looking down over the forests as you
approach them from the surrounding heights, you see a multitude of white columns, broad, reeking masses, and irregular
jets and puffs of misty vapor ascending from the bottom of the
valley, or entangled like smoke among the neighboring trees,
suggesting the factories of some busy town or the campfires of
an army. These mark the position of each mush-pot, paint-pot,

hot spring, and geyser, or gusher, as the Icelandic words mean. And when you saunter into the midst of them over the bright sinter pavements, and see how pure and white and pearly gray they are in the shade of the mountains, and how radiant in the sunshine, you are fairly enchanted. So numerous they are and varied, Nature seems to have gathered them from all the world as specimens of her rarest fountains, to show in one place what she can do. Over four thousand hot springs have been counted in the park, and a hundred geysers; how many more there are nobody knows.

These valleys at the heads of the great rivers may be regarded as laboratories and kitchens, in which, amid a thousand retorts and pots, we may see Nature at work as chemist or cook, cunningly compounding an infinite variety of mineral messes; cooking whole mountains; boiling and steaming flinty rocks to smooth paste and mush – yellow, brown, red, pink, lavender, gray, and creamy white – making the most beautiful mud in the world; and distilling the most ethereal essences. Many of these pots and caldrons have been boiling thousands of years. Pots of sulphurous mush, stringy and lumpy, and pots of broth as black as ink, are tossed and stirred with constant care, and thin transparent essences, too pure and fine to be called water, are kept simmering gently in beautiful sinter cups and bowls that grow ever more beautiful the longer they are used. In some of the spring basins, the waters, though still warm, are perfectly calm, and shine blandly in a sod of overleaning grass and flowers, as if they were thoroughly cooked at last, and set aside to settle and cool. Others are wildly boiling over as if running to waste, thousands of tons of the precious liquids being thrown into the air to fall in scalding floods on the clean coral floor of the establishment, keeping onlookers at a distance. Instead of holding limpid pale green or azure water, other pots and craters are filled with scalding mud, which is tossed up from three or four feet to thirty feet, in sticky, rank-smelling masses, with gasping, belching, thudding sounds, plastering the branches of neighboring trees; every flask, retort, hot spring, and geyser has something special in it, no two being the same in temperature, color, or composition.

In these natural laboratories one needs stout faith to feel at ease. The ground sounds hollow underfoot, and the awful subterranean thunder shakes one's mind as the ground is shaken, especially at night in the pale moonlight, or when the sky is overcast with storm-clouds. In the solemn gloom, the geysers, dimly visible, look like monstrous dancing ghosts, and their wild songs and the earthquake thunder replying to the storms overhead seem doubly terrible, as if divine government were at an end. But the trembling hills keep their places. The sky clears, the rosy dawn is reassuring, and up comes the sun like a god, pouring his faithful beams across the mountains and forest, lighting each peak and tree and ghastly geyser alike, and shining into the eyes of the reeking springs, clothing them with rainbow light, and dissolving the seeming chaos of darkness into varied forms of harmony. The ordinary work of the world goes on. Gladly we see the flies dancing in the sun-beams, birds feeding their young, squirrels gathering nuts, and hear the blessed ouzel singing confidingly in the shallows of the river – most faithful evangel, calming every fear, reducing everything to love.

The variously tinted sinter and travertine formations, out-spread like pavements over large areas of the geyser valleys, lining the spring basins and throats of the craters, and forming beautiful coral-like rims and curbs about them, always excite admiring attention; so also does the play of the waters from which they are deposited. The various minerals in them are rich in colors, and these are greatly heightened by a smooth, silky growth of brilliantly colored conferva which lines many of the pools and channels and terraces. No flower-bloom is more exquisite than these myriad minute plants, visible only in mass, growing in the hot waters. Most of the spring borders are low and daintily scalloped, crenelated, and beaded with sinter pearls. Some of the geyser craters are massive and picturesque, like ruined castles or old burned-out sequoia stumps, and are adorned on a grand scale with outbulging, cauliflower-like formations. From these as centres the silex pavements slope gently away in thin, crusty, overlapping layers, slightly interrupted in some places by low terraces. Or, as in the case of the Mammoth Hot Springs, at the north end of the park, where the building waters issue from the side of a steep hill, the deposits form a succession of higher and broader terraces of white travertine tinged with purple, like the famous Pink Terrace at Rotomahana, New Zealand, draped in front with clustering stalactites, each terrace having a pool of indescribably beautiful water upon it in a basin with a raised rim that glistens with conferva, the whole, when viewed at a distance of a mile or two, looking like a broad, massive cascade pouring over shelving rocks in snowy purpled foam.

The stones of this divine masonry, invisible particles of lime or silex, mined in quarries no eye has seen, go to their appointed places in gentle, tinkling, transparent currents or through the dashing turmoil of floods, as surely guided as the sap of plants streaming into bole and branch, leaf and flower. And thus from century to century this beauty-work has gone on and is going on.

Passing through many a mile of pine and spruce woods, toward the centre of the park you come to the famous Yellow-stone Lake. It is about twenty miles long and fifteen wide, and lies at a height of nearly 8000 feet above the level of the sea, amid dense black forests and snowy mountains. Around its winding, wavering shores, closely forested and picturesquely varied with promontories and bays, the distance is more than 100 miles. It is not very deep, only from 200 to 300 feet, and contains less water than the celebrated Lake Tahoe of the California Sierra, which is nearly the same size, lies at a height of 6400 feet, and is over 1600 feet deep. But no other lake in North America of equal area lies so high as the Yellowstone, or gives birth to so noble a river. The terraces around its shores show that at the close of the glacial period its surface was about 160 feet higher than it is now, and its area nearly twice as great.

It is full of trout, and a vast multitude of birds – swans, pelicans, geese, ducks, cranes, herons, curlews, plovers, snipe – feed in it and upon its shores; and many forest animals come out of the woods, and wade a little way in shallow, sandy places to drink and look about them, and cool themselves in the free flowing breezes.

In calm weather it is a magnificent mirror for the woods and mountains and sky, now pattered with hail and rain, now roughened with sudden storms that send waves to fringe the shores and wash its border of gravel and sand. The Absaroka Mountains and the Wind River Plateau on the east and south pour their gathered waters into it, and the river issues from the north side in a broad, smooth, stately current, silently gliding with such serene majesty that one fancies it knows the vast journey of four thousand miles that lies before it, and the work it has to do. For the first twenty miles its course is in a level, sunny valley lightly fringed with trees, through which it flows in silvery reaches stirred into spangles here and there by ducks and leaping trout, making no sound save a low whispering among the pebbles and the dipping willows and sedges of its banks. Then suddenly, as if preparing for hard work; it rushes eagerly, impetuously forward rejoicing in its strength, breaks into foam-bloom, and goes thundering down into the Grand Canyon in two magnificent falls, one hundred and three hundred feet high.

The canyon is so tremendously wild and impressive that even these great falls cannot hold your attention. It is about twenty miles long and a thousand feet deep – a weird, un-earthly-looking gorge of jagged, fantastic architecture, and most brilliantly colored. Here the Washburn range, forming the northern rim of the Yellowstone basin, made up mostly of beds of rhyolite decomposed by the action of thermal waters, has been cut through and laid open to view by the river; and a famous section it has made. It is not the depth or the shape of the canyon nor the waterfall, nor the green and gray river chanting its brave song as it goes foaming on its way, that most impresses the observer, but the colors of the decomposed volcanic rocks. With few exceptions, the traveler in strange lands finds that, however much the scenery and vegetation in different countries may change, Mother Earth is ever familiar and the same. But here the very ground is changed, as if belonging to some other world. The walls of the canyon from top to bottom burn in a perfect glory of color, confounding and dazzling when the sun is shining – white, yellow, green, blue, vermilion, and various other shades of red indefinitely blending. All the earth hereabouts seems to be paint. Millions of tons of it lie in sight, exposed to wind and weather as if of no account, yet marvelously fresh and bright, fast colors not to be washed out or bleached out by either sunshine or storms. The effect is so novel and awful, we imagine that even a river might be afraid to enter such a place. But the rich and gentle beauty of the vegetation is reassuring. The lovely Linna borealis hangs her twin bells over the brink of the cliffs, forests and gardens extend their treasures in smiling confidence on either side, nuts and berries ripen well whatever may be going on below; blind fears varnish, and the grand gorge seems a kindly, beautiful part of the general harmony, full of peace and joy and good will.

The park is easy of access. Locomotives drag you to its northern boundary at Cinnabar, and horses and guides do the rest. From Cinnabar you will be whirled in coaches along the foaming Gardiner River to Mammoth Hot Springs; thence through woods and meadows, gulches and ravines along branches of the Upper Gallatin, Madison, and Firehole rivers to the main geyser basins; thence over the Continental Divide and back again, up and down through dense pine, spruce, and fir woods to the magnificent Yellowstone Lake, along its northern shore to the outlet, down the river to the falls and Grand Canyon, and thence back through the woods to Mammoth Hot Springs and Cinnabar; stopping here and there at the so-called points of interest among the geysers, springs, paint-pots, mud volcanoes, etc., where you will be allowed a few minutes or hours to saunter over the sinter pavements, watch the play of a few of the geysers, and peer into some of the most beautiful and terrible of the craters and pools. These wonders you will enjoy, and also the views of the mountains, especially the Gallatin and Absaroka ranges, the long, willowy glacier and beaver meadows, the beds of violets, gentians, phloxes, asters, phacelias, goldenrods, eriogonums, and many other flowers, some species giving color to whole meadows and hillsides. And you will enjoy your short views of the great lake and river and canyon. No scalping Indians will you see. The Blackfeet and Bannocks that once roamed here are gone; so are the old beaver-catchers, the Coulters and Bridgers, with all their attractive buckskin and romance. There are several bands of buffaloes in the park, but you will not thus cheaply in tourist fashion see them nor many of the other large animals hidden in the wilderness. The songbirds, too, keep mostly out of sight of the rushing tourist, though off the roads thrushes, warblers, orioles, grosbeaks, etc., keep the air sweet and merry. Perhaps in passing rapids and falls you may catch glimpses of the water-ouzel, but in the whirling noise you will not hear his song. Fortunately, no road noise frightens the Douglas squirrel, and his merry play and gossip will amuse you all through the woods. Here and there a deer may be seen crossing the

road, or a bear. Most likely, however, the only bears you will
see are the half tame ones that go to the hotels every night for
dinner-table scraps – yeast-powder biscuit, Chicago canned
stuff, mixed pickles, and beefsteaks that have proved too tough
for the tourists.

Among the gains of a coach trip are the acquaintances made
and the fresh views into human nature; for the wilderness is a
shrewd touchstone, even thus lightly approached, and brings
many a curious trait to view. Setting out, the driver cracks his
whip, and the four horses go off at half gallop, half trot, in
trained, showy style, until out of sight of the hotel. The coach is
crowded, old and young side by side, blooming and fading, full
of hope and fun and care. Some look at the scenery or the
horses, and all ask questions, an odd mixed lot of them:
'Where is the umbrella? What is the name of that blue flower
over there? Are you sure the little bag is aboard? Is that hollow
yonder a crater? How is your throat this morning? How high
did you say the geysers spout? How does the elevation affect
your head? Is that a geyser reeking over there in the rocks, or
only a hot spring?' A long ascent is made, the solemn mountains come to view, small cares are quenched, and all become
natural and silent, save perhaps some unfortunate expounder
who has been reading guidebook geology, and rumbles forth
foggy subsidences and upheavals until he is in danger of being
heaved overboard. The driver will give you the names of the
peaks and meadows and streams as you come to them, call
attention to the glass road, tell how hard it was to build – how
the obsidian cliffs naturally pushed the surveyor's lines to the
right, and the industrious beavers, by flooding the valley in
front of the cliff, pushed them to the left.

Geysers, however, are the main objects, and as soon as they
come in sight other wonders are forgotten. All gather around
the crater of the one that is expected to play first. During the
eruptions of the smaller geysers, such as the Beehive and Old
Faithful, though a little frightened at first, all welcome the
glorious show with enthusiasm, and shout, 'Oh, how wonderful, beautiful, splendid, majestic!' Some venture near enough to
stroke the column with a stick, as if it were a stone pillar or a
tree, so firm and substantial and permanent it seems. While
tourists wait around a large geyser, such as the Castle or the
Giant, there is a chatter of small talk in anything but solemn

mood; and during the intervals between the preliminary splashes and upheavals some adventurer occasionally looks down the throat of the crater, admiring the silex formations and wondering whether Hades is as beautiful. But when, with awful uproar as if avalanches were falling and storms thundering in the depths, the tremendous outburst begins, all run away to a safe distance, and look on, awe-stricken and silent, in devout, worshiping wonder.

The largest and one of the most wonderfully beautiful of the springs is the Prismatic, which the guide will be sure to show you. With a circumference of 300 yards, it is more like a lake than a spring. The water is pure deep blue in the centre, fading to green on the edges, and its basin and the slightly terraced pavement about it are astonishingly bright and varied in color. This one of the multitude of Yellowstone fountains is of itself object enough for a trip across the continent. No wonder that so many fine myths have originated in springs; that so many fountains were held sacred in the youth of the world, and had miraculous virtues ascribed to them. Even in these cold, doubting, questioning, scientific times many of the Yellowstone fountains seem able to work miracles. Near the Prismatic Spring is the great Excelsior Geyser, which is said to throw a column of boiling water 60 to 70 feet in diameter to a height of from 50 to 300 feet, at irregular periods. This is the greatest of all the geysers yet discovered anywhere. The Firehole River, which sweeps past it, is, at ordinary states, a stream about 100 yards wide and 3 feet deep; but when the geyser is in eruption, so great is the quantity of water discharged that the volume of the river is doubled, and it is rendered too hot and rapid to be forded.

Geysers are found in many other volcanic regions – in Iceland, New Zealand, Japan, the Himalayas, the Eastern Archipelago, South America, the Azores, and elsewhere; but only in Iceland, New Zealand, and this Rocky Mountain park do they display their grandest forms, and of these three famous regions the Yellowstone is easily first, both in the number and in the size of its geysers. The greatest height of the column of the Great Geyser of Iceland actually measured was 212 feet, and of the Strokhr 162 feet.

In New Zealand, the Te Pueia at Lake Taupo, the Waikite at Rotorna, and two others are said to lift their waters occasionally to a height of 100 feet, while the celebrated Te Tarata at Rotomahana sometimes lifts a boiling column 20 feet in diameter to a height of 60 feet. But all these are far surpassed by the Excelsior. Few tourists, however, will see the Excelsior in action, or a thousand other interesting features of the park that lie beyond the wagon-roads and the hotels. The regular trips – from three to five days – are too short. Nothing can be done well at a speed of forty miles a day. The multitude of mixed, novel impressions rapidly piled on one another make only a dreamy, bewildering, swirling blur, most of which is unrememberable. Far more time should be taken. Walk away quietly in any direction and taste the freedom of the mountaineer. Camp out among the grass and gentians of glacier meadows, in craggy garden nooks full of Nature's darlings. Climb the mountains and get their good tidings. Nature's peace will flow into you as sunshine flows into trees. The winds will blow their own freshness into you, and the storms their energy, while cares will drop off like autumn leaves. As age comes on, one source of enjoyment after another is closed, but Nature's sources never fail. Like a generous host, she offers here brimming cups in endless variety, served in a grand hall, the sky its ceiling, the mountains its walls, decorated with glorious paintings and enlivened with bands of music ever playing. The petty discomforts that beset the awkward guest, the unskilled camper, are quickly forgotten, while all that is precious remains. Fears vanish as soon as one is fairly free in the wilderness.

Most of the dangers that haunt the unseasoned citizen are imaginary; the real ones are perhaps too few rather than too many for his good. The bears that always seem to spring up thick as trees, in fighting, devouring attitudes before the frightened tourist whenever a camping trip is proposed, are gentle now, finding they are no longer likely to be shot; and rattlesnakes, the other big irrational dread of over-civilized people, are scarce here, for most of the park lies above the snake-line. Poor creatures, loved only by their Maker, they are timid and bashful, as mountaineers know; and though perhaps not possessed of much of that charity that suffers long and is kind, seldom, either by mistake or by mishap, do harm to anyone. Certainly they cause not the hundredth part of the pain and death that follow the footsteps of the admired Rocky

Mountain trapper. Nevertheless, again and again, in season and out of season, the question comes up, 'What are rattle-snakes good for?' As if nothing that does not obviously make for the benefit of man had any right to exist; as if our ways were God's ways. Long ago, an Indian to whom a French traveler put this old question replied that their tails were good for toothache, and their heads for fever. Anyhow, they are all, head and tail, good for themselves, and we need not begrudge them their share of life.

Fear nothing. No town park you have been accustomed to saunter in is so free from danger as the Yellowstone. It is a hard place to leave. Even its names in your guidebook are attractive, and should draw you far from wagon-roads – all save the early ones, derived from the infernal regions: Hell Roaring River, Hell Broth Springs, The Devil's Caldron, etc. Indeed, the whole region was at first called Coulter's Hell, from the fiery brim-stone stories told by trapper Coulter, who left the Lewis and Clark expedition and wandered through the park, in the year 1807, with a bank of Bannock Indians. The later names, many of which we owe to Mr Arnold Hague of the U.S. Geological Survey, are so telling and exhilarating that they set our pulses dancing and make us begin to enjoy the pleasures of excursions ere they are commenced. Three River Peak, Two Ocean Pass, Continental Divide, are capital geographical descriptions, suggesting thousands of miles of rejoicing streams and all that belongs to them. Big Horn Pass, Bison Peak, Big Game Ridge, bring brave mountain animals to mind. Birch Hills, Garnet Hills, Amethyst Mountain, Storm Peak, Electric Peak, Roaring Mountain, are bright, bracing names. Wapiti, Beaver, Tern, and Swan lakes, conjure up fine pictures, and so also do Osprey and Ouzel falls. Antelope Creek, Otter, Mink, and Grayling creeks, Geode, Jasper, Opal, Carnelian, and Chal-cedony creeks, are lively and sparkling names that help the streams to shine; and Azalea, Stellaria, Arnica, Aster, and Phlox creeks, what pictures these bring up! Violet, Morning Mist, Hygeia, Beryl, Vermilion, and Indigo springs, and many beside, give us visions of fountains more beautifully arrayed than Solomon in all his purple and golden glory. All these and a host of others call you to camp. You may be a little cold some nights, on mountain tops above the timber-line, but you will see the stars, and by and by you can sleep enough in your town bed, or at least in your grave. Keep awake while you may in mountain mansions so rare.

If you are not very strong, try to climb Electric Peak when a big bossy, well-charged thunder-cloud is on it, to breathe the ozone set free, and get yourself kindly shaken and shocked. You are sure to be lost in wonder and praise, and every hair of your head will stand up and hum and sing like an enthusiastic congregation.

After this reviving experience, you should take a look into a few of the tertiary volumes of the grand geological library of the park, and see how God writes history. No technical knowledge is required; only a calm day and a calm mind. Perhaps nowhere else in the Rocky Mountains have the volcanic forces been so busy. More than ten thousand square miles hereabouts have been covered to a depth of at least five thousand feet with material spouted from chasms and craters during the tertiary period, forming broad sheets of basalt, andesite, rhyolite, etc., and marvelous masses of ashes, sand, cinders, and stones now consolidated into conglomerates, charged with the remains of plants and animals that lived in the calm, genial periods that separated the volcanic outbursts.

Perhaps the most interesting and telling of these rocks to the hasty tourist, are those that make up the mass of Amethyst Mountain. On its north side it presents a section two thousand feet high of roughly stratified beds of sand, ashes, and conglomerates coarse and fine, forming the untrimmed edges of a wonderful set of volumes lying on their sides – books a million years old, well bound, miles in size, with full-page illustrations. On the ledges of this one section we see trunks and stumps of fifteen or twenty ancient forests ranged one above another, standing where they grew, or prostrate and broken like the pillars of ruined temples in desert sands – a forest fifteen or twenty stories high, the roots of each spread above the tops of the next beneath it, telling wonderful tales of the bygone centuries, with their winters and summers, growth and death, fire, ice, and flood.

There were giants in those days. The largest of the standing opal and agate stumps and prostrate sections of the trunks are from two or three to fifty feet in height or length, and from five to ten feet in diameter; and so perfect is the petrifaction that the annual rings and ducts are clearer and more easily counted than those of living trees, centuries of burial having brightened the records instead of blurring them. They show that the winters of the tertiary period gave as decided a check to vegetable growth as do those of the present time. Some trees favorably located grew rapidly, increasing twenty inches in diameter in as many years, while others of the same species, on poorer soil or overshadowed, increased only two or three inches in the same time.

Among the roots and stumps on the old forest floors we find the remains of ferns and bushes, and the seeds and leaves of trees like those now growing on the southern Alleghanies – such as magnolia, sassafras, laurel, linden, persimmon, ash, alder, dogwood. Studying the lowest of these forests, the soil it grew on and the deposits it is buried in, we see that it was rich in species, and flourished in a genial, sunny climate. When its stately trees were in their glory, volcanic fires broke forth from chasms and craters, like larger geysers, spouting ashes, cinders, stones and mud, which fell on the doomed forest like hail and snow; sifting, hurtling through the leaves and branches, choking the streams, covering the ground, crushing bushes and ferns, rapidly deepening, packing around the trees and breaking them, rising higher until the topmost boughs of the giants were buried, leaving not a leaf or twig in sight, so complete was the desolation. At last the volcanic storm began to abate, the fiery soil settled; mud floods and boulder floods passed over it, enriching it, cooling it; rains fell and mellow sunshine, and it became fertile and ready for another crop. Birds, and the winds, and roaming animals brought seeds from more fortunate woods, and a new forest grew up on the top of the buried one. Centuries of genial growing seasons passed. The seedling trees became giants, and with strong outreaching branches spread a leafy canopy over the gray land.

The sleeping subterranean fires again awake and shake the mountains, and every leaf trembles. The old craters, with perhaps new ones, are opened, and immense quantities of ashes, pumice, and cinders are again thrown into the sky. The sun, and shorn of his beams, glows like a dull red ball, until hidden in sulphurous clouds. Volcanic snow, hail, and floods fall on the new forest, burying it alive, like the one beneath its roots. Then come another noisy band of mud floods and boulder floods, mixing, settling, enriching the new ground, more seeds, quickening sunshine and showers; and a third noble magnolia forest is carefully raised on the top of the second. And so on. Forest was planted above forest and destroyed, as if Nature were ever repenting, undoing the work she had so industriously done, and burying it.

Of course this destruction was creation, progress in the march of beauty through death. How quickly these old monuments excite and hold the imagination! We see the old stone stumps budding and blossoming and waving in the wind as magnificent trees, standing shoulder to shoulder, branches interlacing in grand varied round-headed forests; see the sunshine of morning and evening gilding their mossy trunks, and at high noon spangling on the thick glossy leaves of the magnolia, filtering through translucent canopies of linden and ash, and falling in mellow patches on the ferny floor; see the shining after rain, breathe the exhaling fragrance, and hear the winds and birds and the murmur of brooks and insects. We watch them from season to season; see the swelling buds when the sap begins to flow in the spring, the opening leaves and blossoms, the ripening of summer fruits, the colors of autumn, and the maze of leafless branches and sprays in winter; and we see the sudden oncome of the storms that overwhelmed them.

One calm morning at sunrise I saw the oaks and pines in Yosemite Valley shaken by an earthquake, their tops swishing back and forth, and every branch and needle shuddering as if in distress like the frightened screaming birds. One may imagine the trembling, rocking, tumultuous waving of those ancient Yellowstone woods, and the terror of their inhabitants when the first foreboding shocks were felt, the sky grew dark, and rock-laden floods began to roar. But though they were close pressed and buried, cut off from sun and wind, all their happy leaf-fluttering and waving done, other currents coursed through them, fondling and thrilling every fibre, and beautiful wood was replaced by beautiful stone. Now their rocky sepulchres are partly open, and show forth the natural beauty of death.

After the forest times and fire times had passed away, and the volcanic furnaces were banked and held in abeyance, another great change occurred. The glacial winter came on. The sky was again darkened, not with dust and ashes, but with snow which fell in glorious abundance, piling deeper, deeper, slipping from the overladen heights in booming avalanches, compacting into glaciers, that flowed over all the landscape, wiping off forests, grinding, sculpturing, fashioning the comparatively featureless lava beds into the beautiful rhythm of hill and dale and ranges of mountains we behold today; forming basins for lakes, channels for streams, few soils for forests, gardens, and meadows. While this ice-work was going on, the slumbering volcanic fires were boiling the subterranean waters, and with curious chemistry decomposing the rocks, making beauty in the darkness; these forces, seemingly antagonistic, working harmoniously together. How wild their meetings on the surface were we may imagine. When the glacier period began, geysers and hot springs were playing in grander volume, it may be, than those of today. The glaciers flowed over them while they spouted and thundered, carrying away their fine sinter and travertine structures, and shortening their mysterious channels.

The soils made in the down-grinding required to bring the present features of the landscape into relief are possibly no better than were some of the old volcanic soils that were carried away, and which, as we have seen, nourished magnificent forests, but the glacial landscapes are incomparably more beautiful than the old volcanic ones were. The glacial winter has passed away, like the ancient summers and fire periods, though in the chronology of the geologist all these times are recent. Only small residual glaciers on the cool northern slopes of the highest mountains are left of the vast all-embracing ice-mantle, as solfataras and geysers are all that are left of the ancient volcanoes.

Now the post-glacial agents are at work on the grand old palimpsest of the park region, inscribing new characters; but still in its main telling features it remains distinctly glacial. The moraine soils are being leveled, sorted, refined, re-formed, and covered with vegetation; the polished pavements and scoring and other superficial glacial inscriptions on the crumbling lavas are being rapidly obliterated; gorges are being cut in the decomposed rhyolites and loose conglomerates, and turrets and pinnacles seem to be springing up like growing trees; while the geysers are depositing miles of sinter and travertine. Nevertheless, the ice-work is scarce blurred as yet. These later effects are only spots and wrinkles on the grand glacial countenance of the park.

Perhaps you have already said that you have seen enough for a lifetime. But before you go away you should spend at least one day and a night on a mountain top, for a last general, calming, settling view. Mount Washburn is a good one for the purpose, because it stands in the middle of the park, is unencumbered with other peaks, and is so easy of access that the climb to its summit is only a saunter. First your eye goes roving around the mountain rim amid the hundreds of peaks; some with plain flowing skirts, others abruptly precipitous and defended by sheer battlemented escarpments; flat-topped or round; heaving like sea-waves or spired and turreted like Gothic cathedrals; streaked with snow in the ravines, and darkened with files of adventurous trees climbing the ridges. The nearer peaks are perchance clad in sapphire blue, others far off in creamy white. In the broad glare of noon they seem to shrink and crouch to less than half their real stature, and grow dull and uncommunicative – mere dead, draggled heaps of waste ashes and stone, giving no hint of the multitude of animals enjoying life in their fastnesses, or of the bright bloom-bordered streams and lakes. But when storms blow they awake and arise, wearing robes of cloud and mist in majestic speaking attitudes like gods. In the color glory of morning and evening they become still more impressive; steeped in the divine light of the alpenglow their earthiness disappears, and, blending with the heavens, they seem neither high nor low.

Over all the central plateau, which from here seems level, and over the foothills and lower slopes of the mountains, the forest extends like a black uniform bed of weeds, interrupted only by lakes and meadows and small burned spots called parks – all of them, except the Yellowstone Lake, being mere dots and spangles in general views, made conspicuous by their color and brightness. About 85 per cent of the entire area of the park is covered with trees, mostly the indomitable lodge-pole pine (*Pinus contoria*, var. *Murrayana*), with a few patches and sprinklings of Douglas spruce, Engelmann spruce, silver fir (*Abies lasiocarpa*), Pinus flexilis, and a few alders, aspens, and birches. The Douglas spruce is found only on the lowest portions, the silver fir on the highest, and the Engelmann spruce on the dampest places, best defended from fire. Some fine specimens of the flexilis pine are growing on the margins of openings – wide-branching, sturdy trees, as broad as high, with trunks five feet in diameter, leafy and shady, laden with purple cones and rose-colored flowers. The Engelmann spruce and sub-alpine silver fir are beautiful and notable trees, but as the plateau became drier and fires began to run, they were driven up the mountains, and into the wet spots and islands where we now find them, leaving nearly all the park to the lodge-pole pine, which, though as thin-skinned as they and as easily killed by fire, takes pains to store up its seeds in firmly closed cones, and holds them from three to nine years, so that, let the fire come when it may, it is ready to die and ready to live again in a new generation. For when the killing fires have devoured the leaves and thin resinous bark, many of the cones, only scorched, open as soon as the smoke clears away; the hoarded store of seeds is sown broadcast on the cleared ground, and a new growth immediately springs up triumphant out of the ashes. Therefore, this tree not only holds its ground, but extends its conquests farther after every fire. Thus the evenness and closeness of its growth are accounted for. In one part of the forest that I examined, the growth was about as close as a cane-brake. The trees were from four to eight inches in diameter, one hundred feet high, and one hundred and seventy-five years old. The lower limbs die young and drop off for want of light. Life with these close-planted trees is a race for light, more light, and so they push straight for the sky. Mowing off ten feet from the top of the forest would make it look like a crowded mass of telegraph-poles; for only the sunny tops are leafy. A sapling ten years old, growing in the sunshine, has as many leaves as a crowded tree one or two hundred years old. As fires are multiplied and the mountains become drier, this wonderful lodge-pole pine bids fair to obtain possession of nearly all the forest ground in the West.

How still the woods seem from here, yet how lively a stir the hidden animals are making; digging, gnawing, biting, eyes shining, at work and play, getting food, rearing young, roving through the underbrush, climbing the rocks, wading solitary marshes, tracing the banks of the lakes and streams! Insect swarms are dancing in the sunbeams, burrowing in the ground, diving, swimming – a cloud of witnesses telling Nature's joy. The plants are as busy as the animals, every cell in a swirl of enjoyment, humming like a hive, singing the old new song of creation. A few columns and puffs of steam are seen rising above the treetops, some near, but most of them far off, indicating geysers and hot springs, gentle-looking and noiseless as noiseless as downy clouds, softly hinting the reaction going on between the surface and the hot interior. From here you see them better than when you are standing beside them, frightened and confused, regarding them as lawless cataclysms. The shocks and outbursts of earthquakes, volcanoes, geysers, storms, the pounding of waves, the uprush of sap in plants, each and all tell the orderly love-beats of Nature's heart.

Turning to the eastward, you have the Grand Canyon and reaches of the river in full view; and yonder to the southward lies the great lake, the largest and most important of all the high fountains of the Missouri-Mississippi, and the last to be discovered.

In the year 1541, when De Soto, with a romantic band of adventurers, was seeking gold and glory and the fountain of youth, he found the Mississippi a few hundred miles above its mouth, and made his grave beneath its floods. La Salle, in 1682, after discovering the Ohio, one of the largest and most beautiful branches of the Mississippi, traced the latter to the sea from the mouth of the Illinois, through adventures and privations not easily realized now. About the same time Joliet and Father Marquette reached the 'Father of Waters' by way of the Wisconsin, but more than a century passed ere its highest sources in these mountains were seen. The advancing stream of civilization has ever followed its guidance toward the west, but none of the thousand tribes of Indians living on its banks could tell the explorer whence it came. From those romantic De Soto and La Salle days to these times of locomotives and tourists, how much has the great river seen and done! Great as it now is, and still growing longer through the ground of its delta and the basins of receding glaciers at its head, it was immensely broader toward the close of the glacial period, when the ice-mantle of the mountains was melting: then with its three hundred thousand miles of branches outspread over the plains and valleys of the continent, laden with fertile mud, it made the biggest and most generous bed of soil in the world.

Think of this mighty stream springing in the first place in vapor from the sea, flying on the wind, alighting on the mountains in hail and snow and rain, lingering in many a fountain feeding the trees and grass; then gathering its scattered waters, gliding from its noble lake, and going back home to the sea, singing all the way! On it sweeps, through the gates of the mountains, across the vast prairies and plains, through many a wild, gloomy forest, cane-brake, and sunny savanna; from glaciers and snowbanks and pine woods to warm groves of magnolia and palm; geysers dancing at its head keeping time with the sea-waves at its mouth; roaring and gray in rapids, booming in broad, bossy falls, murmuring, gleaming in long, silvery reaches, swaying now hither, now thither, whirling, bending in huge doubling, eddying folds, serene, majestic, ungovernable, overflowing all its metes and bounds, frightening the dwellers upon its banks; building, wasting, uprooting, planting; engulfing old islands and making new ones, taking away fields and towns as if in sport, carrying canoes and ships of commerce in the midst of its spoils and drift, fertilizing the continent as one vast farm. Then, its work done, it gladly vanishes in its ocean home, welcomed by the waiting waves.

Thus naturally, standing here in the midst of its fountains, we trace the fortunes of the great river. And how much more comes to mind as we overlook this wonderful wilderness! Fountains of the Columbia and Colorado lie before us, interlaced with those of the Yellowstone and Missouri, and fine it would be to go with them to the Pacific; but the sun is already in the west, and soon our day will be done.

Yonder is Amethyst Mountain, and other mountains hardly less rich in old forests, which now seem to spring up again in their glory; and you see the storms that buried them – the ashes and torrents laden with boulders and mud, the centuries of sunshine, and the dark, lurid nights. You see again the vast floods of lava, red-hot and white-hot, pouring out from gigantic geysers, usurping the basins of lakes and streams, absorbing or driving away their hissing, screaming waters, flowing around hills and ridges, submerging every subordinate feature. Then you see the snow and glaciers taking possession of the land, making new landscapes. How admirable it is that, after passing through so many vicissitudes of frost and fire and flood, the physiognomy and even the complexion of the landscape should still be so divinely fine!

Thus reviewing the eventful past, we see Nature working with enthusiasm like a man, blowing her volcanic forges like a blacksmith blowing his smithy fires, shoving glaciers over the landscapes like a carpenter shoving his planes, clearing, ploughing, harrowing, irrigating, planting, and sowing broadcast like a farmer and gardener, doing rough work and fine work, planting sequoias and pines, rosebushes and daisies; working in gems, filling every crack and hollow with them; distilling fine essences; painting plants and shells, clouds, mountains, all the earth and heavens, like an artist – ever working toward beauty higher and higher. Where may the mind find more stimulating, quickening pasturage? A thousand Yellowstone wonders are calling, 'Look up and down and round about you!' And a multitude of still, small voices may be heard directing you to look through all this transient, shifting show of things called 'substantial' into the truly substantial, spiritual world whose forms flesh and wood, rock and water, air and sunshine, only veil and conceal, and to learn that here is heaven and the dwelling-place of the angels.

The sun is setting; long, violet shadows are growing out over the woods from the mountains along the western rim of the park; the Absaroka range is baptized in the divine light of the alpenglow, and its rocks and trees are transfigured. Next to the light of the dawn on high mountain tops, the alpenglow is the most impressive of all the terrestrial manifestations of God.

Now comes the gloaming. The alpenglow is fading into earthy, murky gloom, but do not let your town habits draw you away to the hotel. Stay on this good fire-mountain and spend the night among the stars. Watch their glorious bloom until the dawn, and get one more baptism of light. Then, with fresh heart, go down to your work, and whatever your fate, under whatever ignorance or knowledge you may afterward chance to suffer, you will remember these fine, wild views, and look back with joy to your wanderings in the blessed old Yellowstone Wonderland.

Chapter 3

THE YOSEMITE NATIONAL PARK

Of all the mountain ranges I have climbed, I like the Sierra Nevada the best. Though extremely rugged, with its main features on the grandest scale in height and depth, it is nevertheless easy of access and hospitable; and its marvelous beauty, displayed in striking and alluring forms, wooes the admiring wanderer on and on, higher and higher, charmed and enchanted. Benevolent, solemn, fateful, pervaded with divine light, every landscape glows like a countenance hallowed in eternal repose; and every one of its living creatures, clad in flesh and leaves, and every crystal of its rocks, whether on the surface shining in the sun or buried miles deep in what we call darkness, is throbbing and pulsing with the heartbeats of God. All the world lies warm in one heart, yet the Sierra seems to get more light than other mountains. The weather is mostly sunshine embellished with magnificent storms, and nearly everything shines from base to summit – the rocks, streams, lakes, glaciers, irised falls, and the forests of silver fir and silver pine. And how bright is the shining after summer showers and dewy nights, and after frosty nights in spring and autumn, when the morning sunbeams are pouring through the crystals on the bushes and grass, and in winter through the snow-laden trees!

The average cloudiness for the whole year is perhaps less than ten hundredths. Scarcely a day of all the summer is dark, though there is no lack of magnificent thundering cumuli. They rise in the warm midday hours, mostly over the middle region, in June and July, like new mountain ranges, higher Sierras, mightily augmenting the grandeur of the scenery while giving rain to the forests and gardens and bringing forth their fragrance. The wonderful weather and beauty inspire everybody to be up and doing. Every summer day is a workday to be confidently counted on, the short dashes of rain forming, not interruptions, but rests. The big blessed storm days of winter, when the whole range stands white, are not a whit less inspiring and kind. Well may the Sierra be called the Range of Light, not the Snowy Range; for only in winter is it white; while all the year it is bright.

Of this glorious range the Yosemite National Park is a central section, thirty-six miles in length and forty-eight miles in breadth. The famous Yosemite Valley lies in the heart of it, and it includes the head waters of the Tuolumne and Merced rivers, two of the most songful streams in the world; innumerable lakes and waterfalls and smooth silky lawns; the noblest forests, the loftiest granite domes, the deepest ice-sculptured canons, the brightest crystalline pavements, and snowy mountains soaring into the sky twelve and thirteen thousand feet, arrayed in open ranks and spiry pinnacled groups partially separated by tremendous canyons and amphitheatres; gardens on their sunny brows, avalanches thundering down their long white slopes, cataracts roaring gray and foaming in the crooked rugged gorges, and glaciers in their shadowy recesses working in silence, slowly completing their sculpture; newborn lakes at their feet, blue and green, free or encumbered with drifting icebergs like miniature Arctic Oceans, shining, sparkling, calm as stars.

Nowhere will you see the majestic operations of nature more clearly revealed beside the frailest, most gentle and peaceful things. Nearly all the park is a profound solitude. Yet it is full of charming company, full of God's thoughts, a place of peace and safety amid the most exalted grandeur and eager enthusiastic action, a new song, a place of beginnings abounding in first lessons on life, mountain-building, eternal, invincible, unbreakable order; with sermons in stones, storms, trees, flowers, and animals brimful of humanity. During the last glacial period, just past, the former features of the range were rubbed off as a chalk sketch from a blackboard, and a new beginning was made. Hence the wonderful clearness and freshness of the rocky pages.

But to get all this into words is a hopeless task. The leanest sketch of each feature would need a whole chapter. Nor would any amount of space, however industriously scribbled, be of much avail. To defrauded town toilers, parks in magazine articles are like pictures of bread to the hungry. I can write only hints to incite good wanderers to come to the feast.

While this glorious park embraces big, generous samples of the very best of the Sierra treasure, it is, fortunately, at the same time, the most accessible portion. It lies opposite San Francisco, at a distance of about one hundred and forty miles. Railroads connected with all the continent reach into the foothills, and three good carriage roads, from Big Oak Flat, Coulterville, and Raymond, run into Yosemite Valley. Another, called the Tioga road, runs from Crocker's Station on the Yosemite Big Oak Flat road near the Tuolumne Big Tree Grove, right across the park to the summit of the range by way of Lake Tenaya, the Big Tuolumne Meadows, and Mount Dana. These roads, with many trials that radiate from Yosemite Valley, bring most of the park within reach of everybody, well or half well.

The three main natural divisions of the park, the lower, middle, and alpine regions, are fairly well defined in altitude, topographical features, and vegetation. The lower, with an average elevation of about five thousand feet, is the region of the great forests, made up of sugar pine, the largest and most beautiful of all the pines in the world; the silvery yellow pine, the next in rank; Douglas spruce, libocedrus, the white and red silver firs, and the *Sequoia gigantea*, or 'big tree,' the king of conifers, the noblest of a noble race. On warm slopes next the foothills there are a few Sabine nut pines; oaks make beautiful groves in the canyon valleys; and poplar, alder, maple, laurel, and Nuttall's flowering dogwood shade the banks of the streams. Many of the pines are more than two hundred feet high, but they are not crowded together. The sunbeams streaming through their feathery arches brighten the ground, and you walk beneath the radiant ceiling in devout subdued mood, as if you were in a grand cathedral with mellow light sifting through colored windows, while the flowery pillared aisles open enchanting vistas in every direction. Scarcely a peak or ridge in the whole region rises bare above the forests, though they are thinly planted in some places where the soil is shallow. From the cool breezy heights you look abroad over a boundless waving sea of evergreens, covering hill and ridge and smooth-flowing slope as far as the eye can reach, and filling every hollow and down-plunging ravine in glorious triumphant exuberance.

Perhaps the best general view of the pine forests of the park, and one of the best in the range, is obtained from the top of the Merced and Tuolumne divide near Hazel Green. On the long, smooth, finely folded slopes of the main ridge, at a height of five to six thousand feet above the sea, they reach most perfect development and are marshaled to view in magnificent towering ranks, their colossal spires and domes and broad palmlike crowns, deep in the kind sky, rising above one another – a multitude of giants in perfect health and beauty – sun-fed mountaineers rejoicing in their strength, chanting with the winds, in accord with the falling waters. The ground is mostly open and inviting to walkers. The fragrant chambatia is out-spread in rich carpets miles in extent; the manzanita, in orchard-like groves, covered with pink bell-shaped flowers in the spring, grows in openings facing the sun, hazel and buckthorn in the dells; warm brows are purple with mint, yellow with sunflowers and violets; and tall lilies ring their bells around the borders of meadows and along the ferny, mossy banks of the streams. Never was mountain forest more lavishly furnished.

Hazel Green is a good place quietly to camp and study, to get acquainted with the trees and birds, to drink the reviving water and weather, and to watch the changing lights of the big charmed days. The rose light of the dawn, creeping higher among the stars, changes to daffodil yellow; then come the level enthusiastic sunbeams pouring across the feathery ridges, touching pine after pine, spruce and fir, libocedrus and lordly sequoia, searching every recess, until all are awakened and warmed. In the white noon they shine in silvery splendor, every needle and cell in bole and branch thrilling and tingling with ardent life; and the whole landscape glows with consciousness, like the face of a god. The hours go by uncounted. The evening flames with purple and gold. The breeze that has been blowing from the lowlands dies away, and far and near the mighty host of trees baptized in the purple flood stand hushed and thought-ful, awaiting the sun's blessing and farewell – as impressive a ceremony as if it were never to rise again. When the daylight fades, the night breeze from the snowy summits begins to blow, and the trees, waving and rustling beneath the stars, breathe free again.

It is hard to leave such camps and woods; nevertheless, to

the large majority of travelers the middle region of the park is still more interesting, for it has the most striking features of all the Sierra scenery – the deepest sections of the famous canyons, of which the Yosemite Valley, Hetch Hetchy Valley, and many smaller ones are wider portions, with level parklike floors and walls of immense height and grandeur of sculpture. This middle region holds also the greater number of the beautiful glacier lakes and glacier meadows, the great granite domes, and the most brilliant and most extensive of the glacier pavements. And though in large part it is severely rocky and bare, it is still rich in trees. The magnificent silver fir (*Abies magnifica*), which ranks with the giants, forms a continuous belt across the park above the pines at an elevation of from seven to nine thousand feet, and north and south of the park boundaries to the extremities of the range, only slightly interrupted by the main canyons. The two-leaved or tamarack pine makes another less regular belt along the upper margin of the region, while between these two belts, and mingling with them, in groves or scattered, are the mountain hemlock, the most graceful of evergreens; the noble mountain pine; the Jeffrey form of the yellow pine, with big cones and long needles; and the brown, burly, sturdy Western juniper. All these, except the juniper, which grows on bald rocks, have plenty of flowery brush about them, and gardens in open spaces.

Here, too, lies the broad, shining heavily sculptured region of primeval granite, which best tells the story of the glacial period on the Pacific side of the continent. No other mountain chain on the globe, as far as I know, is so rich as the Sierra in bold, striking, well-preserved glacial monuments, easily understood by anybody capable of patient observation. Every feature is more or less glacial, and this park portion of the range is the brightest and clearest of all. Not a peak, ridge, dome, canon, lake basin, garden, forest, or stream but in some way explains the past existence and modes of action of flowing, grinding, sculpturing, soil-making, scenery-making ice. For, notwithstanding the post-glacial agents – air, rain, frost, rivers, earthquakes, avalanches – have been at work upon the greater part of the range for tens of thousands of stormy years, engraving their own characters over those of the ice, the latter are so heavily emphasized and enduring they still rise in sublime relief, clear and legible through every after inscription.

The streams have traced only shallow wrinkles as yet, and avalanche, wind, rain, and melting snow have made blurs and scars, but the change effected on the face of the landscape is not greater than is made on the face of a mountaineer by a single year of weathering.

Of all the glacial phenomena presented here, the most striking and attractive to travelers are the polished pavements, because they are so beautiful, and their beauty is of so rare a kind – unlike any part of the loose earthy lowlands where people dwell and earn their bread. They are simply flat or gently undulating areas of solid resisting granite, the unchanged surface over which the ancient glaciers flowed. They are found in the most perfect condition at an elevation of from eight to nine thousand feet above sea level. Some are miles in extent, only slightly blurred or scarred by spots that have at last yielded to the weather; while the best preserved portions are brilliantly polished, and reflect the sunbeams as calm water or glass, shining as if rubbed and burnished every day, notwithstanding they have been exposed to plashing, corroding rains, dew, frost, and melting sloppy snows for thousands of years.

The attention of hunters and prospectors, who see so much in their wild journeys, is seldom attracted by moraines, however regular and artificial-looking; or rocks, however boldly sculptured; or canyons, however deep and sheer-walled. But when they come to these pavements, they go down on their knees and rub their hands admiringly on the glistening surface, and try hard to account for its mysterious smoothness and brightness. They may have seen the winter avalanches come down the mountains, through the woods, sweeping away the trees and scouring the ground; but they conclude that this cannot be the work of avalanches, because the stri show that the agent, whatever it was, flowed along the around and over the top of high ridges and domes, and also filled the deep canyons. Neither can they see how water could be the agent, for the strange polish is found thousands of feet above the reach of any conceivable flood. Only the winds seem capable of moving over the face of the country in the directions indicated by the lines and grooves.

The pavements are particularly fine around Lake Tenaya, and have suggested the Indian name Py-we-ack, the Lake of the

Shining Rocks. Indians seldom trouble themselves with geological questions, but a Mono Indian once came to me and asked if I could tell him what made the rocks so smooth at Tenaya. Even dogs and horses, on their first journeys into this region, study geology to the extent of gazing wonderingly at the strange brightness of the ground, and pawing it and smelling it, as if afraid of falling or sinking.

In the production of this admirable hard finish, the glaciers in many places exerted a pressure of more than a hundred tons to the square foot, planing down granite, slate, and quartz alike, showing their structure, and making beautiful mosaics where large feldspar crystals form the greater part of the rock. On such pavements the sunshine is at times dazzling, as if the surface were of burnished silver.

Here, also, are the brightest of the Sierra landscapes in general. The regions lying at the same elevation to the north and south were perhaps subjected to as long and intense a glaciation; but because the rocks are less resisting, their polished surfaces have mostly given way to the weather, leaving here and there only small imperfect patches on the most enduring portions of canyon walls protected from the action of rain and snow, and on hard bosses kept comparatively dry by boulders. The short, steeply inclined canyons of the east flank of the range are in some places brightly polished, but they are far less magnificent than those of the broad west flank.

One of the best general views of the middle region of the park is to be had from the top of a majestic dome which long ago I named the Glacier Monument. It is situated a few miles to the north of Cathedral Peak, and rises to a height of about fifteen hundred feet above its base and ten thousand above the sea. At first sight it seems sternly inaccessible, but a good climber will find that it may be scaled on the south side. Approaching it from this side you pass through a dense bryanthus-fringed grove of mountain hemlock, catching glimpses now and then of the colossal dome towering to an immense height above the dark evergreens; and when at last you have made your way across woods, wading through azalea and ledum thickets, you step abruptly out of the tree shadows and mossy leafy softness upon a bare porphyry pavement, and behold the dome unveiled in all its grandeur. Fancy a nicely proportioned monument, eight or ten feet high, hewn from one stone, standing in a pleasure ground; magnify it to a height of fifteen hundred feet, retaining its simplicity of form and fineness, and cover its surface with crystals; then you may gain an idea of the sublimity and beauty of this ice-burnished dome, one of many adorning this wonderful park.

In making the ascent, one finds that the curve of the base rapidly steepens, until one is in danger of slipping; but feldspar crystals, two or three inches long, that have been weathered into relief, afford slight footholds. The summit is in part burnished, like the sides and base, the stri and scratches indicating that the mighty Tuolumne Glacier, two or three thousand feet deep, overwhelmed it while it stood firm like a boulder at the bottom of a river. The pressure it withstood must have been enormous. Had it been less solidly built, it would have been ground and crushed into moraine fragments, like the general mass of the mountain flank in which at first it lay imbedded; for it is only a hard residual knob or knot with a concentric structure of superior strength, brought into relief by the removal of the less resisting rock about it – an illustration in stone of the survival of the strongest and most favorably situated.

Hardly less wonderful, when we contemplate the storms it has encountered since first it saw the light, is its present unwasted condition. The whole quantity of postglacial wear and tear it has suffered has not diminished its stature a single inch, as may be readily shown by measuring from the level of the unchanged polished portions of the surface. Indeed, the average postglacial denudation of the entire region, measured in the same way, is found to be less than two inches – a mighty contrast to that of the ice; for the glacial denudation here has been not less than a mile; that is, in developing the present landscapes, an amount of rock a mile in average thickness has been silently carried away by flowing ice during the last glacial period.

A few erratic boulders nicely poised on the founded summit of the monument tell an interesting story. They came from a mountain on the crest of the range, about twelve miles to the eastward, floating like chips on the frozen sea, and were stranded here when the top of the monument emerged to the light of day, while the companions of these boulders, whose positions chanced to be over the slopes where they could not find rest, were carried farther on by the shallowing current.

The general view from the summit consists of a sublime assemblage of iceborn mountains and rocks and long wavering ridges, lakes and streams and meadows, moraines in wide-sweeping belts, and beds covered and dotted with forests and groves – hundreds of square miles of them composed in wild harmony. The snowy mountains on the axis of the range, mostly sharp-peaked and crested, rise in a noble array along the sky to the eastward and northward; the gray-pillared Hoffman spur and the Yosemite domes and a countless number of others to the westward; Cathedral Peak with its many spires and companion peaks and domes to the southward; and a smooth billowy multitude of rocks, from fifty feet or less to a thousand feet high, which from their peculiar form seem to be rolling on westward, fill most of the middle ground. Immediately beneath you are the Big Tuolumne Meadows, with an ample swath of dark pine woods on either side, enlivened by the young river, that is seen sparkling and shimmering as it sways from side to side, tracing as best it can its broad glacial channel.

The ancient Tuolumne Glacier, lavishly flooded by many a noble affluent from the snow-laden flanks of Mounts Dana, Gibbs, Lyell, Maclure, and others nameless as yet, poured its majestic overflowing current, four or five miles wide, directly against the high outstanding mass of Mount Hoffman, which divided and deflected it right and left, just as a river is divided against an island that stands in the middle of its channel. Two distinct glaciers were thus formed, one of which flowed through the Big Tuolumne Canyon and Hetch Hetchy Valley, while the other swept upward five hundred feet in a broad current across the divide between the basins of the Tuolumne and Merced into the Tenaya basin, and thence down through the Tenaya Canyon and Yosemite Valley.

The maplike distinctness and freshness of this glacial landscape cannot fail to excite the attention of every observer, no matter how little of its scientific significance he may at first recognize. These bald, glossy, westward-leaning rocks in the open middle ground, with their rounded backs and shoulders toward the glacier fountains of the summit mountains and their split angular fronts looking in the opposite direction, every one of them displaying the form of greatest strength with reference to physical structure and glacial action, show the tremendous force with which through unnumbered centuries the ice flood swept over them, and also the direction of the flow; while the mountains, with their sharp summits and abraded sides, indicate the height to which the glacier rose; and the moraines, curving and swaying in beautiful lines, mark the boundaries of the main trunk and its tributaries as they existed toward the close of the glacial winter. None of the commercial highways of the sea or land, marked with buoys and lamps, fences and guideboards, is so unmistakably indicated as are these channels of the vanished Tuolumne glaciers.

The action of flowing ice, whether in the form of river-like glaciers or broad mantling folds, is but little understood as compared with that of other sculpturing agents. Rivers work openly where people dwell, and so do the rain, and the sea thundering on all the shores of the world; and the universal ocean of air, through unseen, speaks aloud in a thousand voices and explains its modes of working and its power. But glaciers, back in their cold solitudes, work apart from men, exerting their tremendous energies in silence and darkness. Coming in vapor from the sea, flying invisible on the wind, descending in snow, changing to ice, white, spiritlike, they brood outspread over the predestined landscapes, working on unwearied through unmeasured ages, until in the fullness of time the mountains and valleys are brought forth, channels furrowed for the rivers, basins made for meadows and lakes, and soil beds spread for the forests and fields that man and beast may be fed. Then vanishing like clouds, they melt into streams and go singing back home to the sea.

To an observer upon this adamantine old monument in the midst of such scenery, getting glimpses of the thoughts of God, the day seems endless, the sun stands still. Much faithless fuss is made over the passage in the Bible telling of the standing still of the sun for Joshua. Here you may learn that the miracle occurs for every devout mountaineer, for everybody doing anything worth doing, seeing anything worth seeing. One day is as a thousand years, a thousand years as one day, and while yet in the flesh you enjoy immortality.

From the monument you will find an easy way down

through the woods and along the Big Tuolumne Meadows to Mount Dana, the summit of which commands a grand telling view of the alpine region. The scenery all the way is inspiring, and you saunter on without knowing that you are climbing. The spacious sunny meadows, through the midst of which the bright river glides, extend with but little interruption ten miles to the eastward, dark woods rising on either side to the limit of tree growth, and above the woods a picturesque line of gray peaks and spires dotted with snow banks; while, on the axis of the Sierra, Mount Dana and his noble compeers repose in massive sublimity, their vast size and simple flowing contours contrasting in the most striking manner with the clustering spires and thin-pinnacled crests crisply outlined on the horizon to the north and south of them.

Tracing the silky lawns, gradually ascending, gazing at the sublime scenery more and more openly unfolded, noting the avalanche gaps in the upper forests, lingering over beds of blue gentians and purple-flowered bryanthus and cassiope, and dwarf willows an inch high in close-felted gray carpets, brightened here and there with kalmia and soft creeping mats of vaccinium sprinkled with pink bells that seem to have been showered down from the sky like hail – thus beguiled and enchanted, you reach the base of the mountain wholly unconscious of the miles you have walked. And so on to the summit. For all the way up the long red slate slopes, that in the distance seemed barren, you find little garden beds and tufts of dwarf phlox, ivesia, and blue arctic daisies that go straight to your heart, blessed fellow mountaineers kept safe and warm by a thousand miracles. You are now more than thirteen thousand feet above the sea, and to the north and south you behold a sublime wilderness of mountains in glorious array, their snowy summits towering together in crowded, bewildering abundance, shoulder to shoulder, peak beyond peak. To the east lies the Great Basin, barren-looking and silent, apparently a land of pure desolation, rich only in beautiful light. Mono Lake, fourteen miles long, is outspread below you at a depth of nearly seven thousand feet, its shores of volcanic ashes and sand, treeless and sunburned; a group of volcanic cones, with well-formed, unwasted craters rises to the south of the lake; while up from its eastern shore innumerable mountains with soft flowing outlines extend range beyond range, gray, and pale purple, and blue – the farthest gradually fading on the flowing horizon. Westward you look down and over the countless moraines, glacier meadows, and grand sea of domes and rock waves of the upper Tuolumne basin, the Cathedral and Hoffman mountains with their wavering lines and zones of forest, the wonderful region to the north of the Tuolumne Canyon, and across the dark belt of silver firs to the pale mountains of the coast.

In the icy fountains of the Mount Lyell and Ritter groups of peaks, to the south of Dana, three of the most important of the Sierra rivers – the Tuolumne, Merced, and San Joaquin – take their rise, their highest tributaries being within a few miles of one another as they rush forth on their adventurous courses from beneath snow banks and glaciers.

Of the small shrinking glaciers of the Sierra, remnants of the majestic system that sculptured the range, I have seen sixty-five. About twenty-five of them are in the park, and eight are in sight from Mount Dana.

The glacier lakes are sprinkled over all the alpine and subalpine regions, gleaming like eyes beneath heavy rock brows, tree-fringed or bare, embosomed in the woods, or lying in open basins with green and purple meadows around them; but the greater number are in the cool shadowy hollows of the summit mountains not far from the glaciers, the highest lying at an elevation of from eleven to nearly twelve thousand feet above the sea. The whole number in the Sierra, not counting the smallest, can hardly be less than fifteen hundred, of which about two hundred and fifty are in the park. From one standpoint, on Red Mountain, I counted forty-two, most of them within a radius of ten miles. The glacier meadows, which are spread over the filled-up basins of vanished lakes and form one of the most charming features of the scenery, are still more numerous than the lakes.

An observer stationed here, in the glacial period, would have overlooked a wrinkled mantle of ice as continuous as that which now covers the continent of Greenland; and of all the vast landscape now shining in the sun, he would have seen only the tops of the summit peaks, rising darkly like storm-beaten islands, lifeless and hopeless, above rock-encumbered ice waves. If among the agents that nature has employed in making these mountains there be one that above all other deserves the name of Destroyer, it is the glacier. But we quickly learn that destruction is creation. During the dreary centuries through which the Sierra lay in darkness, crushed beneath the ice folds of the glacial winter, there was a steady invincible advance toward the warm life and beauty of today; and it is just where the glaciers crushed most destructively that the greatest amount of beauty is made manifest. But as these landscapes have succeeded the preglacial landscapes, so they in turn are giving place to others already planned and foreseen. The granite domes and pavements, apparently imperishable, we take as symbols of permanence, while these crumbling peaks, down whose frosty gullies avalanches are ever falling, are symbols of change and decay. Yet all alike, fast or slow, are surely vanishing away.

Nature is ever at work building and pulling down, creating and destroying, keeping everything whirling and flowing, allowing no rest but in rhythmical motion, chasing everything in endless song out of one beautiful form into another.

Chapter 9

THE SEQUOIA AND GENERAL GRANT NATIONAL PARKS

The Big Tree (*Sequoia gigantea*) is Nature's forest masterpiece, and, so far as I know, the greatest of living things. It belongs to an ancient stock, as its remains in old rocks show, and has a strange air of other days about it, a thoroughbred look inherited from the long ago – the auld lang syne of trees. Once the genus was common, and with many species flourished in the now desolate Arctic regions, in the interior of North America, and in Europe, but in long, eventful wanderings from climate to climate only two species have survived the hardships they had to encounter, the gigantea and sempervirens, the former now restricted to the western slopes of the Sierra, the other to the Coast Mountains, and both to California, excepting a few groves of Redwood which extend into Oregon. The Pacific Coast in general is the paradise of conifers. Here nearly all of them are giants, and display a beauty and magnificence unknown elsewhere. The climate is mild, the ground never freezes, and moisture and sunshine abound all the year. Nevertheless it is not easy to account for the colossal size of the Sequoias. The largest are about three hundred feet high and thirty feet in diameter. Who of all the dwellers of the plains and prairies and fertile home forests of round-headed oak and maple, hickory and elm, ever dreamed that earth could bear such growths – trees that the familiar pines and firs seem to know nothing about, lonely, silent, serene, with a physiognomy almost godlike; and so old, thousands of them still living had already counted their years by tens of centuries when Columbus set sail from Spain and were in the vigor of youth or middle age when the star led the Chaldean sages to the infant Saviour's cradle! As far as man is concerned they are the same yesterday, today, and forever, emblems of permanence.

No description can give any adequate idea of their singular majesty, much less their beauty. Excepting the sugar-pine, most of their neighbors with pointed tops seem to be forever shouting Excelsior, while the Big Tree, though soaring above them all, seems satisfied, its rounded head, poised lightly as a cloud, giving no impression of trying to go higher. Only in youth does it show like other conifers a heavenward yearning, keenly aspiring with a long quick-growing top. Indeed the whole tree for the first century or two, or until a hundred to a hundred and fifty feet high, is arrowhead in form, and, compared with the solemn rigidity of age, is as sensitive to the wind as a squirrel tail. The lower branches are gradually dropped as it grows older, and the upper ones thinned out until comparatively few are left. These, however, are developed to great size, divide again and again, and terminate in bossy rounded masses of leafy branchlets, while the head becomes dome-shaped. Then poised in fullness of strength and beauty, stern and solemn in mien, it glows with eager, enthusiastic life, quivering to the tip of every leaf and branch and far-reaching root, calm as a granite dome, the first to feel the touch of the rosy beams of the morning, the last to bid the sun goodnight.

Perfect specimens, unhurt by running fires or lightning, are singularly regular and symmetrical in general form, though not at all conventional, showing infinite variety in sure unity and harmony of plan. The immensely strong, stately shafts, with rich purplish brown bark, are free of limbs for a hundred and fifty feet or so, though dense tufts of sprays occur here and there, producing an ornamental effect, while long parallel furrows give a fluted columnar appearance. It shoots forth its limbs with equal boldness in every direction, showing no weather side. On the old trees the main branches are crooked and rugged, and strike rigidly outward mostly at right angles from the trunk, but there is always a certain measured restraint in their reach which keeps them within bounds. No other Sierra tree has foliage so densely massed or outline so finely, firmly drawn and so obediently subordinate to an ideal type. A particularly knotty, angular, ungovernable-looking branch, five to eight feet in diameter and perhaps a thousand years old, may occasionally be seen pushing out from the trunk as if determined to break across the bounds of the regular curve, but like all the others, as soon as the general outline is approached the huge limb dissolves into massy bosses of branchlets and sprays, as if the tree were growing beneath an invisible bell glass against the sides of which the branches were moulded, while many small, varied departures from the ideal form give the impression of freedom to grow as they like.

Except in picturesque old age, after being struck by lightning and broken by a thousand snowstorms, this regularity of form is one of the Big Tree's most distinguishing characteristics. Another is the simple sculptural beauty of the trunk and its great thickness as compared with its height and the width of the branches, many of them being from eight to ten feet in diameter at a height or two hundred feet from the ground, and seeming more like finely modeled and sculptured architectural columns than the stems of trees, while the great strong limbs are like rafters supporting the magnificent dome head.

The root system corresponds in magnitude with the other dimensions of the tree, forming a flat far-reaching spongy network two hundred feet or more in width without any taproot, and the instep is so grand and fine, so suggestive of endless strength, it is long ere the eye is released to look above it. The natural swell of the roots, though at first sight excessive, gives rise to buttresses no greater than are required for beauty as well as strength, as at once appears when you stand back far enough to see the whole tree in its true proportions. The fineness of the taper of the trunk is shown by its thickness at great heights – a diameter of ten feet at a height of two hundred being, as we have seen, not uncommon. Indeed the boles of but few trees hold their thickness as well as Sequoia. Resolute, consummate, determined in form, always beheld with wondering admiration, the Big Tree always seems unfamiliar, standing alone, unrelated, with peculiar physiognomy, awfully solemn and earnest. Nevertheless, there is nothing alien in its looks. The Madrona, clad in thin, smooth, red and yellow bark and big glossy leaves, seems, in the dark coniferous forests of Washington and Vancouver Island, like some lost wanderer from the magnolia groves of the South, while the Sequoia, with all its strangeness, seems more at home than any of its neighbors, holding the best right to the ground as the oldest, strongest inhabitant. One soon becomes acquainted with new species of pine and fir spruce as with friendly people, shaking their outstretched branches like shaking hands, and fondling their beautiful little ones; while the venerable aboriginal Sequoia, ancient of other days, keeps you at a distance, taking no notice of you, speaking only to the winds, thinking only of the sky, looking as strange in aspect and behavior among the neighboring trees as would the mastodon or hairy elephant among the homely bears and deer. Only the Sierra Juniper is at all like it, standing rigid and unconquerable on glacial pavements for thousands of years, grim, rusty, silent, uncommunicative, with an air of antiquity about as pronounced as that so characteristic of Sequoia.

The bark of full grown trees is from one to two feet thick, rich cinnamon brown, purplish on young trees and shady parts of the old, forming magnificent masses of color with the underbrush and beds of flowers. Toward the end of winter the trees themselves bloom while the snow is still eight or ten feet deep. The pistillate flowers are about three eighths of an inch long, pale green, and grow in countless thousands on the ends of the sprays. The staminate are still more abundant, pale yellow, a fourth of an inch long; and when the golden pollen is ripe they color the whole tree and dust the air and the ground far and near.

The cones are bright grass-green in color, about two and a half inches long, one and a half wide, and are made up of thirty or forty strong, closely packed, rhomboidal scales with four to eight seeds at the base of each. The seeds are extremely small and light, being only from an eighth to a fourth of an inch long and wide, including a filmy surrounding wing, which causes them to glint and waver in falling and enables the wind to carry them considerable distances from the tree.

The faint lisp of snowflakes as they alight is one of the smallest sounds mortals can hear. The sound of falling Sequoia seeds, even when they happen to strike on flat leaves or flakes of bark, is about as faint. Very different is the bumping and thudding of the falling cones. Most of them are cut off by the Douglas squirrel and stored for the sake of the seeds, small as they are. In the calm Indian summer these busy harvesters with ivory sickles go to work early in the morning, as soon as breakfast is over, and nearly all day the ripe cones fall in a steady pattering, bumping shower. Unless harvested in this way they discharge their seeds and remain on the trees for many years. In fruitful seasons the trees are fairly laden. On two small specimen branches one and a half and two inches in diameter I counted four hundred and eighty cones. No other California conifer produces nearly so many seeds, excepting perhaps its relative, the Redwood of the Coast Mountains. Millions are ripened annually by a single tree, and the product of one of the main groves in a fruitful year would suffice to plant all the mountain ranges of the world.

The dense tufted sprays make snug nesting places for birds, and in some of the loftiest, leafiest towers of verdure thousands of generations have been reared, the great solemn trees shedding off flocks of merry singers every year from nests, like the flocks of winged seeds from the cones.

The Big Tree keeps its youth far longer than any of its neighbors. Most silver firs are old in their second or third century, pines in their fourth or fifth, while the Big Tree growing beside them is still in the bloom of its youth, juvenile in every feature at the age of old pines, and cannot be said to attain anything like prime size and beauty before its fifteen hundredth year, or under favorable circumstances become old before its three thousandth. Many, no doubt, are much older than this. On one of the Kings River giants, thirty-five feet and eight inches in diameter exclusive of bark, I counted upwards of four thousand annual wood-rings, in which there was no trace of decay after all these centuries of mountain weather. There is no absolute limit to the existence of any tree. Their death is due to accidents, not, as of animals, to the wearing out of organs. Only the leaves die of old age, their fall is foretold in their structure; but the leaves are renewed every year and so also are the other essential organs – wood, roots, bark, buds. Most of the Sierra trees die of disease. Thus the magnificent silver firs are devoured by fungi, and comparatively few of them live to see their three hundredth birth year. But nothing hurts the Big Tree. I never saw one that was sick or showed the slightest sign of decay. It lives on through indefinite thousands of years until burned, blown down, undermined, or shattered by some tremendous lightning stroke. No ordinary bolt ever seriously hurts Sequoia. In all my walks I have seen only one that was thus killed outright. Lightning, though rare in the California lowlands, is common on the Sierra. Almost every day in June and July small thunderstorms refresh the main forest belt. Clouds like snowy mountains of marvelous beauty grow rapidly in the calm sky about midday and cast cooling shadows and showers that seldom last more than an hour. Nevertheless these brief, kind storms wound or kill a good many trees. I have seen silver firs two hundred feet high split into long peeled rails and slivers down to the roots, leaving not even a stump, the rails radiating like the spokes of a wheel from a hole in the ground where the tree stood. But the Sequoia, instead of being split and slivered, usually has forty or fifty feet of its brash knotty top smashed off in short chunks about the size of cord-wood, the beautiful rosy red ruins covering the ground in a circle a hundred feet wide or more. I never saw any that had been cut down to the ground or even to below the branches except one in the Stanislaus Grove, about twelve feet in diameter, the greater part of which was smashed to fragments, leaving only a leafless stump about seventy-five feet high. It is a curious fact that all the very old Sequoias have lost their heads by lightning. 'All things come to him who waits.' But of all living things Sequoia is perhaps the only one able to wait long enough to make sure of being struck by lightning. Thousands of years it stands ready and waiting, offering its head to every passing cloud as if inviting its fate, praying for heaven's fire as a blessing; and when at last the old head is off, another of the same shape immediately begins to grow on. Every bud and branch seems excited, like bees that have lost their queen, and tries hard to repair the damage. Branches that for many centuries have been growing out horizontally at once turn upward and all their branchlets arrange themselves with reference to a new top of the same peculiar curve as the old one. Even the small subordinate branches halfway down the trunk do their best to push up to the top and help in this curious head-making.

The great age of these noble trees is even more wonderful than their huge size, standing bravely up, millennium in, millennium out, to all that fortune may bring them, triumphant over tempest and fire and time, fruitful and beautiful, giving food and shelter to multitudes of small fleeting creatures dependent on their bounty. Other trees may claim to be about as large or as old: Australian Gums, Senegal Baobabs, Mexican Taxodiums, English Yews, and venerable Lebanon Cedars, trees of renown, some of which are from ten to thirty feet in diameter. We read of oaks that are supposed to have existed ever since the creation, but strange to say I can find no definite accounts of the age of any of these trees, but only estimates based on tradition and assumed average rates of growth. No other known tree approaches the Sequoia in grandeur, height and thickness being considered, and none as far as I know has looked down on so many centuries or opens such impressive and suggestive views into history. The majestic monument of the Kings River Forest is, as we have seen, fully four thousand years old, and measuring the rings of annual growth we find it was no less than twenty-seven feet in diameter at the beginning of the Christian era, while many observations lead me to expect the discovery of others ten or twenty centuries older. As to those of moderate age, there are thousands, mere youth as yet, that –

> Saw the light that shone
> On Mahomet's uplifted crescent,
> On many a royal gilded throne
> And deed forgotten in the present,
> . . . saw the age of sacred trees
> And Druid groves and mystic larches,
> And saw from forest domes like these
> The builder bring his Gothic arches.

Great trees and groves used to be venerated as sacred monuments and halls of council and worship. But soon after the discovery of the Calaveras Grove one of the grandest trees was cut down for the sake of a stump! The laborious vandals had seen 'the biggest tree in the world,' then, forsooth, they must try to see the biggest stump and dance on it.

The growth in height for the first two centuries is usually at the rate of eight to ten inches a year. Of course all very large trees are old, but those equal in size may vary greatly in age on account of variations in soil, closeness or openness of growth, etc. Thus a tree about ten feet in diameter that grew on the side of a meadow was, according to my own count of the wood-rings, only two hundred and fifty-nine years old at the time it was felled, while another in the same grove, of almost exactly the same size but less favorably situated, was fourteen hundred and forty years old. The Calaveras tree cut for a dance floor was twenty-four feet in diameter and only thirteen hundred years old, another about the same size was a thousand years older.

The following Sequoia notes and measurements are copied from my notebooks:

Diameter. Feet.	Inches.	Height in Feet.	Age. Years.
0	1	10	7
0	5	24	20
0	5	25	41
0	6	25	66
0	6	28 ½	39
0	8	25	29
0	11	45	71
1	0	60	71
3	2	156	260
6	0	192	240
7	3	195	339
7	3	255	506
7	6	240	493
7	7	207	424
9	0	243	259
9	3	222	280
10	6		1440
12			1825
15			2150
24			1300
25			2300
35	8 inside bark.		over 4000

Little, however, is to be learned in confused, hurried tourist trips, spending only a poor noisy hour in a branded grove with a guide. You should go looking and listening alone on long walks through the wild forests and groves in all the seasons of the year. In the spring the winds are balmy and sweet, blowing up and down over great beds of chaparral and through the woods now rich in softening balsam and rosin and the scent of steaming earth. The sky is mostly sunshine, oftentimes tempered by magnificent clouds, the breath of the sea built up into new mountain ranges, warm during the day, cool at night, good flower-opening weather. The young cones of the Big Trees are showing in clusters, their flower time already past, and here and there you may see the sprouting of their tiny seeds of the previous autumn, taking their first feeble hold of the ground and unpacking their tender whorls of cotyledon leaves. Then you will naturally be led on to consider their wonderful growth up and up through the mountain weather, now buried in snow bent and crinkled, now straightening in summer sunshine like uncoiling ferns, shooting eagerly aloft in youth's joyful prime, and towering serene and satisfied through countless years of calm and storm, the greatest of plants and all but immortal.

Under the huge trees up come the small plant people, putting forth fresh leaves and blossoming in such profusion that the hills and valleys would still seem gloriously rich and glad were all the grand trees away. By the side of melting snowbanks rise the crimson sarcodes, round-topped and massive as the Sequoias themselves, and beds of blue violets and larger yellow one with leaves curiously lobed; azalea and saxifrage, daisies and lilies on the mossy banks of the streams; and a little way back of them, beneath the trees and on sunny spots on the hills around the groves, wild rose and rubus, spira and ribes, mitella, tiarella, campanula, monardella, forget-me-not, etc., many of them as worthy of lore immortality as the famous Scotch daisy, wanting only a Burns to sing them home to all hearts.

In the midst of this glad plant work the birds are busy nesting, some singing at their work, some silent, others, especially the big pileated woodpeckers, about as noisy as backwoodsmen building their cabins. Then every bower in the groves is a bridal bower, the winds murmur softly overhead, the streams sing with the birds, while from far-off waterfalls and thunder-clouds come deep rolling organ notes.

In summer the days go by in almost constant brightness, cloudless sunshine pouring over the forest roof, while in the shady depths there is the subdued light of perpetual morning.

The new leaves and cones are growing fast and make a grand show, seeds are ripening, young birds learning to fly, and with myriad insects glad as birds keep the air whirling, joy in every wingbeat, their humming and singing blending with the gentle ah-ing of the winds; while at evening every thicket and grove is enchanted by the tranquil chirping of the blessed hylas, the sweetest and most peaceful of sounds, telling the very heart-joy of earth as it rolls through the heavens.

In the autumn the sighing of the winds is softer than ever, the gentle ah-ah-ing filling the sky with a fine universal mist of music, the birds have little to say, and there is no appreciable stir or rustling among the trees save that caused by the harvesting squirrels. Most of the seeds are ripe and away, those of the trees mottling the sunny air, glinting, glancing through the midst of the merry insect people, rocks and trees, everything alike drenched in gold light, heaven's colors coming down to the meadows and groves, making every leaf a romance, air, earth, and water in peace beyond thought, the great brooding days opening and closing in divine psalms of color.

Winter comes suddenly, arrayed in storms, though to mountaineers silky streamers on the peaks and the tones of the wind give sufficient warning. You hear strange whisperings among the tree-tops, as if the giants were taking counsel together. One after another, nodding and swaying, calling and replying, spreads the news, until at with one accord break forth into glorious song, welcoming the first grand snowstorm of the year, and looming up in the dim clouds and snowdrifts like lighthouse towers in flying scud and spray. Studying the behavior of the giants from some friendly shelter, you will see that even in the glow of their wildest enthusiasm, when the storm roars loudest, they never lose their god-like composure, never toss their arms or bow or wave like the pines, but only slowly, solemnly nod and sway, standing erect, making no sign of strife, none of rest, neither in alliance nor at war with the winds, too calmly, unconsciously noble and strong to strive with or bid defiance to anything. Owing to the density of the leafy branchlets and great breadth of head the Big Tree carries a much heavier load of snow than any of its neighbors, and after a storm, when the sky clears, the laden trees are a glorious spectacle, worth any amount of cold camping to see. Every bossy limb and crown is solid white, and the immense height of the giants becomes visible as the eye travels the white steps of the colossal tower, each relieved by a mass of blue shadow.

In midwinter the forest depths are as fresh and pure as the crevasses and caves of glaciers. Grouse, nuthatches, a few woodpeckers, and other hardy birds dwell in the groves all winter, and the squirrels may be seen every clear day frisking about, lively as ever, tunneling to their stores, never coming up empty-mouthed, dividing in the loose snow about as quickly as ducks in water, while storms and sunshine sing to each other.

One of the noblest and most beautiful of the late winter sights is the blossoming of the Big Tree-like gigantic gold-enrods and the sowing of their pollen over all the forest and the snow-covered ground-a most glorious view of Nature's immortal virility and flower-love.

One of my own best excursions among the Sequoias was made in the autumn of 1875, when I explored the then unknown or little known Sequoia region south of the Mariposa Grove for comprehensive views of the belt, and to learn what I could of the peculiar distribution of the species and its history in general. In particular I was anxious to try to find out whether it had ever been more widely distributed since the glacial period; what conditions favorable or otherwise were affecting it; what were its relations to climate, topography, soil, and the other trees growing with it, etc.; and whether, as was generally supposed, the species was nearing extinction. I was already acquainted in a general way with the northern groves, but excepting some passing glimpses gained on excursions into the high Sierra about the head-waters of Kings and Kern rivers I had seen nothing of the south end of the belt.

Nearly all my mountaineering has been done on foot, carrying as little as possible, depending on campfires for warmth, that so I might be light and free to go wherever my studies might lead. On this Sequoia trip, which promised to be long, I was persuaded to take a small wild mule with me to carry provisions and a pair of blankets. The friendly owner of the animal, having noticed that I sometimes looked tired when I came down from the peaks to replenish my bread sack, assured me that his 'little Brownie mule' was just what I wanted, tough as a knot, perfectly untirable, low and narrow, just right for squeezing through brush, able to climb like a chipmunk, jump from boulder to boulder like a wild sheep, and go anywhere a man could go. But tough as he was and accomplished as a climber, many a time in the course of our journey when he was jaded and hungry, wedged fast in rocks or struggling in chaparral like a fly in a spiderweb, his troubles were sad to see, and I wished he would leave me and find his way home alone.

We set out from Yosemite about the end of August, and our first camp was made in the well-known Mariposa Grove. Here and in the adjacent pine woods I spent nearly a week, carefully examining the boundaries of the grove for traces of its greater extension without finding any. Then I struck out into the majestic trackless forest to the southeastward, hoping to find new groves or traces of old ones in the dense silver fir and pine woods about the head of Big Creek, where soil and climate seemed most favorable to their growth, but not a single tree or old monument of any sort came to light until I climbed the high rock called Wamellow by the Indians. Here I obtained telling views of the fertile forest-filled basin of the upper Fresno. Innumerable spires of the noble yellow pine were displayed rising above one another on the braided slopes, and yet nobler sugar pines with superb arms outstretched in the rich autumn light, while away toward the southwest, on the verge of the glowing horizon, I discovered the majestic dome-like crowns of Big Trees towering high over all, singly and in close grove congregations. There is something wonderfully attractive in this king tree, even when beheld from afar, that draws us to it with indescribable enthusiasm; its superior height and massive smoothly rounded outlines proclaiming its character in any company; and when one of the oldest attains full stature on some commanding ridge it seems the very god of the woods. I ran back to camp, packed Brownie, steered over the divide and down into the heart of the Fresno Grove. Then choosing a camp on the side of a brook where the grass was good, I made a cup of tea, and set off free among the brown giants, glorying in the abundance of new work about me. One of the first special things that caught my attention was an extensive landslip. The ground on the side of a stream had given way to a depth of about fifty feet and with all its trees had been launched into the bottom of the stream ravine. Most of the trees – pines, firs, incense cedar, and Sequoia – were still standing erect and uninjured, as if unconscious that anything out of the common had happened. Tracing the ravine alongside the avalanche, I saw many trees whose roots had been laid bare, and in one instance discovered a Sequoia about fifteen feet in diameter growing above an old prostrate trunk that seemed to belong to a former generation. This slip had occurred seven or eight years ago, and I was glad to find that not only were most of the Big Trees uninjured, but that many companies of hopeful seedlings and saplings were growing confidently on the fresh soil along the broken front of the avalanche. These young trees were already eight or ten feet high, and were shooting up vigorously, as if sure of eternal life, though young pines, firs, and libocedrus were runing a race with them for the sunshine with an even start. Farther down the ravine I counted five hundred and thirty-six promising young Sequoias on a bed of rough bouldery soil not exceeding two acres in extent.

The Fresno Big Trees covered an area of about four square miles, and while wandering about surveying the boundaries of the grove, anxious to see every tree, I came suddenly on a handsome log cabin, richly embowered and so fresh and unweathered it was still redolent of gum and balsam like a newly felled tree. Strolling forward, wondering who could have built it, I found an old, weary-eyed, speculative, gray-haired man on a bark stool by the door, reading a book. The discovery of his hermitage by a stranger seemed to surprise him, but when I explained that I was only a tree-lover saunter-ing along the mountains to study Sequoia, he bade me wel-come, made me bring my mule down to a little slanting meadow before his door and camp with him, promising to show me his pet trees and many curious things bearing on my studies.

After supper, as the evening shadows were falling, the good hermit sketched his life in the mines, which in the main was like that of most other pioneer gold-hunters – a succession of intense experiences full of big ups and downs like the mountain topography. Since ' '49' he had wandered over most of the Sierra, sinking innumerable prospect holes like a sailor making soundings, digging new channels for streams, sifting gold-sprinkled boulder and gravel beds with unquenchable energy, life's noon the mean-while passing unnoticed into late after-noon shadows. Then, health and gold gone, the game played and lost, like a wounded deer creeping into this forest solitude, he awaits the sundown call. How sad the undertones of many a life here, now the noise of the first big gold battles has died away! How many interesting wrecks lie drifted and stranded in hidden nooks of the gold region! Perhaps no other range contains the remains of so many rare and interesting men. The name of my hermit friend is John A. Nelder, a fine kind man, who in going into the woods has at last gone home; for he loves nature truly, and realizes that these last shadowy days with scarce a glint of gold in them are the best of all. Birds, squirrels, plants get loving, natural recognition, and delightful it was to see how sensitively he responds to the silent influences of the woods. His eyes brightened as he gazed on the trees that stand guard around his little home; squirrels and mountain quail came to his call to be fed, and he tenderly stroked the little snowbent sapling Sequoias, hoping they yet might grow straight to the sky and rule the grove. One of the greatest of his trees stands a little way back of his cabin, and he proudly led me to it, bidding me admire its colossal proportions and measure it to see if in all the forest there could be another so grand. It proved to be only twenty-six feet in diameter, and he seemed distressed to learn that the Mariposa Grizzly Giant was larger. I tried to comfort him by observing that his was the taller, finer formed, and perhaps the more favorably situated. Then he led me to some noble ruins, remnants of gigantic trunks of trees that he supposed must have been larger than any now standing, and though they had lain on the damp ground exposed to fire and the weather for centuries, the wood was perfectly sound. Sequoia timber is not only beautiful in color, rose red when fresh, and as easily worked as pine, but it is almost absolutely unperishable. Build a house of Big Tree logs on granite and that house will last about as long as its foundation. Indeed fire seems to be the only agent that has any appreciable effect on it. From one of these ancient trunk remnants I cut a specimen of the wood, which neither in color, strength, nor soundness could be distinguished from specimens cut from living trees, although it had certainly lain on the damp forest floor for more than three hundred and eighty years, probably more than thrice as long. The time in this instance was determined as follows: When the tree from which the specimen was derived fell it sunk itself into the ground, making a ditch about two hundred feet long and five or six feet deep; and in the middle of this ditch, where a part of the fallen trunk had been burned, a silver fir four feet in diameter and three hundred and eighty years old was growing, showing that the Sequoia trunk had lain on the ground three hundred and eighty years plus the unknown time that it lay before the part whose place had been taken by the fir was burned out of the way, and that which had elapsed ere the seed from which the monumental fir sprang fell into the prepared soil and took root. Now because Sequoia trunks are never wholly consumed in one forest fire and these fires recur only at considerable intervals, and because Sequoia ditches, after being cleared, are often left unplanted for centuries, it becomes evident that the trunk remnant in question may have been on the ground a thousand years or more. Similar vestiges are common, and together with the root-bowls and long straight ditches of the fallen monarchs, throw a sure light back on the post-glacial history of the species, bearing on its distribution. One of the most interesting features of this grove is the apparent ease and strength and comfortable independence in which the trees occupy their place in the general forest. Seedlings, saplings, young and middle-aged trees are grouped promisingly around the old patriarchs, betraying no sign of approach to extinction. On the contrary, all seem to be saying, 'Everything is to our mind and we mean to live forever.' But, sad to tell, a lumber company was building a large mill and flume near by, assuring widespread destruction.

In the cones and sometimes in the lower portion of the trunk and roots there is a dark gritty substance which dissolves readily in water and yields a magnificent purple color. It is a strong astringent, and is said to be used by the Indians as a big medicine. Mr Nelder showed me specimens of ink he had made from it, which I tried and found good, flowing freely and holding its color well. Indeed everything about the tree seems constant. With these interesting trees, forming the largest of the northern groves, I stopped only a week, for I had far to go before the fall of the snow. The hermit seemed to cling to me and tried to make me promise to winter with him after the season's work was done. Brownie had to be got home, however, and other work awaited me, therefore I could only promise to stop a day or two on my way back to Yosemite and give him the forest news.

The next two weeks were spent in the wide basin of the San Joaquin, climbing innumerable ridges and surveying the far-extending sea of pines and firs. But not a single Sequoia crown appeared among them all, nor any trace of a fallen trunk, until I had crossed the south divide of the basin, opposite Dinky Creek, one of the northmost tributaries of Kings River. On this stream there is a small grove, said to have been discovered a few years before my visit by two hunters in pursuit of a wounded bear. Just as I was fording one of the branches of Dinky Creek I met a shepherd, and when I asked him whether he knew anything about the Big Trees of the neighborhood he replied, 'I know all about them, for I visited them only a few days ago and pastured my sheep in the grove.' He was fresh from the East, and as this was his first summer in the Sierra I was curious to learn what impression the Sequoias had made on him. When I asked whether it was true that the Big Trees were really so big as people say, he warmly replied, 'Oh, yes sir, you bet. They're whales. I never used to believe half I heard about the awful size of California trees, but they're monsters and no mistake. One of them over here, they tell me, is the biggest tree in the whole world, and I guess it is, for it's forty foot through and as many good long paces around.' He was very earnest, and in fullness of faith offered to guide me to the grove that I might not miss seeing this biggest tree. A fair measurement four feet from the ground, above the main swell of the roots, showed a diameter of only thirty-two feet, much to the young man's disgust. 'Only thirty-two feet,' he lamented, 'only thirty-two, and I always thought it was forty!' Then with a sigh of relief, 'No matter, that's a big tree, anyway; no fool of a tree, sir, that you can cut a plank out of thirty feet broad, straight-edged, no bark, all good wood, sound and solid. It would make the brag white pine planks from old Maine look like laths.' A good many other fine specimens are distributed along three small branches of the creek, and I noticed several thrifty moderate-sized Sequoias growing on a granite ledge, apparently as independent of deep soil as the pines and firs, clinging to seams and fissures and sending their roots far abroad in search of moisture.

The creek is very clear and beautiful, gliding through tangles of shrubs and flower beds, gay bee and butterfly pastures, the grove's own stream, pure Sequoia water, flowing all the year, every drop filtered through moss and leaves and the myriad spongy rootlets of the giant trees. One of the most interesting features of the grove is a small waterfall with a flowery, ferny, clear brimming pool at the foot of it. How cheerily it sings the songs of the wilderness, and how sweet it tones! You seem to taste as well as hear them, while only the subdued roar of the river in the deep canyon reaches up into the grove, sounding like the sea and the winds. So charming a fall and pool in the heart of so glorious a forest food pagans would have consecrated to some lovely nymph.

Hence down into the main Kings River canyon, a mile deep, I led and dragged and shoved my patient, much-enduring mule through miles and miles and gardens and brush, fording innumerable streams, crossing savage rock slopes and taluses, scrambling, sliding through gulches and gorges, then up into the grand Sequoia forests of the south side, cheered by the royal crowns displayed on the narrow horizon. In a day and a half we reached the Sequoia woods in the neighborhood of the old Thomas Mill Flat. Thence striking off northeastward I found a magnificent forest nearly six miles long by two in width, composed mostly of Big Trees, with outlying groves as far east as Boulder Creek. Here five or six days were spent, and it was delightful to learn from countless trees, old and young, how comfortably they were settled down in concordance with climate and soil and their noble neighbors.

Imbedded in these majestic woods there are numerous meadows, around the sides of which the Big Trees press close together in beautiful lines, showing their grandeur openly from the ground to their domed heads in the sky. The young trees are still more numerous and exuberant than in the Fresno and Dinky groves, standing apart in beautiful family groups, or crowding around the old giants. For every venerable lightning-stricken tree, there is one or more in all the glory of prime, and for each of these, many young trees and crowds of saplings. The young trees express the grandeur of their race in a way indefinable by any words at my command. When they are five or six feet in diameter and a hundred and fifty feet high, they seem like mere baby saplings as many inches in diameter, their juvenile habit and gestures completely veiling their real size, even to those who, from long experience, are able to make fair approximation in their measurements of common trees. One morning I noticed three airy, spiry, quick-growing babies on the side of a meadow, the largest of which I took to be about eight inches in diameter. On measuring it, I found to my astonishment it was five feet six inches in diameter, and about a hundred and forty feet high.

On a bed of sandy ground fifteen yards square, which had been occupied by four sugar pines, I counted ninety-four promising seedlings, an instance of Sequoia gaining ground from its neighbors. Here also I noted eighty-six young Sequoias from one to fifty feet high on less than half an acre of ground that had been cleared and prepared for their reception by fire. This was a small bay burned into dense chaparral, showing that fire, the great destroyer of tree life, is sometimes followed by conditions favorable for new growths. Sufficient fresh soil, however, is furnished for the constant renewal of the forest by the fall of old trees without the help of any other agent – burrowing animals, fire, flood, landslip, etc – for the ground is thus turned and stirred as well as cleared, and in every roomy, shady hollow beside the walls of upturned roots many hopeful seedlings spring up.

The largest, and as far as I know the oldest, of all the Kings River trees that I saw is the majestic stump, already referred to, about a hundred and forty feet high, which above the swell of the roots is thirty-five feet and eight inches inside the bark, and over four thousand years old. It was burned nearly half through at the base, and I spent a day in chopping off the charred surface, cutting into the heart, and counting the wood-rings with the aid of a lens. I made out a little over four thousand without difficulty or doubt, but I was unable to get a complete count, owing to confusion in the rings where wounds had been healed over. Judging by what is left of it, this was a fine, tall, symmetrical tree nearly forty feet in diameter before it lost its bark. In the last sixteen hundred and seventy-two years the increase in diameter was ten feet. A short distance south of this forest lies a beautiful grove, now mostly included in the General Grant National Park. I found many shake-makers at work in it, access to these magnificent woods having been made easy by the old mill wagon road. The Park is only two miles square, and the largest of its many fine trees is the General Grant, so named before the date of my first visit, twenty-eight years ago, and said to be the largest tree in the world, though above the craggy bulging base the diameter is less than thirty feet. The Sanger Lumber Company owns nearly all the Kings River groves outside the Park, and for many years the mills have been spreading desolation without any advantage.

One of the shake-makers directed me to an 'old snag biggeren Grant.' It proved to be a huge black charred stump thirty-two feet in diameter, the next in size to the grand monument, mentioned above.

I found a scattered growth of Big Trees extending across the main divide to within a short distance of Hyde's Mill, on a tributary of Dry Creek. The mountain ridge on the south side of the stream was covered from base to summit with a most superb growth of Big Trees. What a picture it made! In all my wide forest wanderings I had seen none so sublime. Every tree of all the mighty host seemed perfect in beauty and strength, and their majestic domed heads, rising above one another on the mountain slope, were most imposingly displayed, like a range of bossy upswelling cumulus clouds on a calm sky.

In this glorious forest the mill was busy, forming a sore, sad centre of destruction, though small as yet, so immensely heavy was the growth. Only the smaller and most accessible of the trees were being cut. The logs, from three to ten or twelve feet in diameter, were dragged or rolled with long strings of oxen into a chute and sent flying down the steep mountain side to the mill flat, where the largest of them were blasted into manageable dimensions for the saws. And as the timber is very brash, by this blasting and careless felling on uneven ground, half or three fourths of the timber was wasted.

I spent several days exploring the ridge and counting the annual wood rings on a large number of stumps in the clearings, then replenished my bread sack and pushed on southward. All the way across the broad rough basins of the Kaweah and Tule rivers Sequoia ruled supreme, forming an almost continuous belt for sixty or seventy miles, waving up and down in huge massy mountain billows in compliance with the grand glacier-ploughed topography.

Day after day, from grove to grove, canyon to canyon, I made a long, wavering way, terribly rough in some places for Brownie, but cheery for me, for Big Trees were seldom out of sight. We crossed the rugged, picturesque basins of Redwood

Creek, the North Fork of the Kaweah, and Marble Fork gloriously forested, and full of beautiful cascades and falls, sheer and slanting, infinitely varied with broad curly foam fleeces and strips of embroidery in which the sunbeams revel. Thence we climbed into the noble forest on the Marble and Middle Fork Divide. After a general exploration of the Kaweah basin, this part of the Sequoia belt seemed to me the finest, and I then named it 'the Giant Forest.' It extends, a magnificent growth of giants grouped in pure temple groves, ranged in colonnades along the sides of meadows, or scattered among the other trees, from the granite headlands overlooking the hot foothills and plains of the San Joaquin back to within a few miles of the old glacier fountains at an elevation of 5000 to 8400 feet above the sea.

When I entered this sublime wilderness the day was nearly done, the trees with rosy, glowing countenances seemed to be hushed and thoughtful, as if waiting in conscious religious dependence on the sun, and one naturally walked softly and give-stricken among them. I wandered on, meeting nobler trees where all are noble, subdued in the general calm, as if in some vast hall pervaded by the deepest sanctities and solemnities that away human souls. At sundown the trees seemed to cease their worship and breathe free. I heard the birds going home. I too sought a home for the night on the edge of a level meadow where there is a long, open view between the evenly ranked trees standing guard along its sides. Then after a good place was found for poor Brownie, who had had a hard, weary day sliding and scrambling across the Marble Canyon, I made my bed and supper and lay on my back looking up to the stars through pillared arches finer far than the pious heart of man, telling its love, ever reared. Then I took a walk up the meadow to see the trees in the pale light. They seemed still more marvelously massive and tall than by day, heaving their colossal heads into the depths of the sky, among the stars, some of which appeared to be sparkling on their branches like flowers. I built a big fire that vividly illumined the huge brown boles of the nearest trees and the little plants and cones and fallen leaves at their feet, keeping up the show until I fell asleep to dream of boundless forests and trail-building for Brownie.

Joyous birds welcomed the dawn; and the squirrels, now their food cones were ripe and had to be quickly gathered and stored for winter, began their work before sunrise. My tea-and-breadcrumb breakfast was soon done, and leaving jaded Brownie to feed and rest I sauntered forth to my studies. In every direction Sequoia ruled the woods. Most of the other big conifers were present here and there, but not as rivals or companions. They only served to thicken and enrich the general wilderness. Trees of every age cover craggy ridges as well as the deep moraine-soiled slopes, and plant their magnificent shafts along every brookside and meadow. Bogs and meadows are rare or entirely wanting in the isolated groves north of Kings River; here there is a beautiful series of them lying on the broad top of the main dividing ridge, imbedded in the very heart of the mammoth woods as if for ornament, their smooth, plushy bosoms kept bright and fertile by streams and sunshine.

Resting awhile on one of the most beautiful of them when the sun was high, it seemed impossible that any other forest picture in the world could rival it. There lay the grassy, flowery lawn, three fourths of a mile long, smoothly outspread, basking in mellow autumn light, colored brown and yellow and purple, streaked with lines of green along the streams, and ruffled here and there with patches of ledum and scarlet vaccinium. Around the margin there is first a fringe of azalea and willow bushes, colored orange-yellow, enlivened with vivid dashes of red cornel, as if painted. Then up spring the mighty walls of verdure three hundred feet high, the brown fluted pillars so thick and tall and strong they seem fit to uphold the sky; the dense foliage, swelling forward in rounded bosses on the upper half, variously shaded and tinted, that of the young trees dark green, of the old yellowish. An aged lightning-smitten patriarch standing a little forward beyond the general line with knotty arms outspread was covered with gray and yellow lichens and surrounded by a group of saplings whose slender spires seemed to lack not a single leaf or spray in their wondrous perfection. Such was the Kaweah meadow picture that golden afternoon, and as I gazed every color seemed to deepen and glow as if the progress of the fresh sun-work were visible from hour to hour, while every tree seemed religious and conscious of the presence of God. A free man revels in a scene like this and time goes by unmeasured. I stood fixed in silent wonder or sauntered about shifting my points of view, studying the physiognomy of separate trees, and going out to the different color patches to see how they were put on and what they were made of, giving free expression to my joy, exulting in Nature's wild immortal vigor and beauty, never dreaming any other human being was near. Suddenly the spell was broken by dull bumping, thudding sounds, and a man and horse came in sight at the farther end of the meadow, where they seemed sadly out of place. A good big bear or mastodon or megatherium would have been more in keeping with the old mammoth forest. Nevertheless, it is always pleasant to meet one of our own species after solitary rambles, and I stepped out where I could be seen and shouted, when the rider reined in his galloping mustang and waited my approach. He seemed too much surprised to speak until, laughing in his puzzled face, I said I was glad to meet a fellow mountaineer in so lonely a place. Then he abruptly asked, 'What are you doing? How did you get here?' I explained that I came across the canyons from Yosemite and was only looking at the trees. 'Oh then, I know,' he said, greatly to my surprise, 'you must be John Muir.' He was herding a band of horses that had been driven up a rough trail from the lowlands to feed on these forest meadows. A few handfuls of crumb detritus was all that was left in my bread sack, so I told him that I was nearly out of provision and asked whether he could spare me a little flour. 'Oh yes, of course you can have anything I've got,' he said. 'Just take my track and it will lead you to my camp in a big hollow log on the side of a meadow two or three miles from here. I must ride after some strayed horses, but I'll be back before night; in the meantime make yourself at home.' He galloped away to the northward, I returned to my own camp, saddled Brownie, and by the middle of the afternoon discovered his noble den in a fallen Sequoia hollowed by fire – a spacious loghouse of one log, carbon-lined, centuries old yet sweet and fresh, weather proof, earthquake proof, likely to outlast the most durable stone castle, and commanding views of garden and grove grander far than the richest king ever enjoyed. Brownie found plenty of grass and I found bread, which I ate with views from the big round, ever-open door. Soon the good Samaritan mountaineer came in, and I enjoyed a famous rest listening to his observations on trees, animals, adventures, etc., while he was busily preparing supper. In

answer to inquiries concerning the distribution of the Big Trees
he gave a good deal of particular information of the forest we
were in, and he had heard that the species extended a long way
south, he knew not how far. I wandered about for several days
within a radius of six or seven miles of the camp, surveying
boundaries, measuring trees, and climbing the highest points
for general views. From the south side of the divide I saw
telling ranks of Sequoia-crowned headlands stretching far into
the hazy distance, and plunging vaguely down into profound
canyon depths foreshadowing weeks of good work. I had now
been out on the trip more than a month, and I began to fear my
studies would be interrupted by snow, for winter was drawing
nigh. 'Where there isn't a way make a way,' is easily said when
no way at the time is needed, but to the Sierra explorer with a
mule traveling across the canyon lines of drainage the brave
old phrase becomes heavy with meaning. There are ways
across the Sierra graded by glaciers, well marked, and followed
by men and beasts and birds, and one of them even by
locomotives; but none natural or artificial along the range,
and the explorer who would thus travel at right angles to the
glacial ways must traverse canyons and ridges extending side
by side in endless succession, roughened by side gorges and
gulches and stubborn chaparral, and defended by innumerable
sheer-fronted precipices. My own ways are easily made in any
direction, but Brownie, though one of the toughest and most
skillful of his race, was oftentimes discouraged for want of
hands, and caused endless work. Wild at first, he was tame
enough now; and when turned loose he not only refused to run
away, but as his troubles increased came to depend on me in
such a pitiful, touching way, I became attached to him and
helped him as if he were a good-natured boy in distress, and
then the labor grew lighter. Bidding goodbye to the kind
Sequoia cave-dweller, we vanished again in the wilderness,
drifting slowly southward, Sequoias on every ridge-top beck-
oning and pointing the way.

In the forest between the Middle and East forks of the
Kaweah, I met a great fire, and as fire is the master scourge
and controller of the distribution of trees, I stopped to watch it
and learn what I could of its works and ways with the giants. It
came racing up the steep chaparral-covered slopes of the East
Fork canyon with passionate enthusiasm in a broad cataract of

flames, now bending down low to feed on the green bushes, devouring acres of them at a breath, now towering high in the air as if looking abroad to choose a way, then stooping to feed again, the lurid flapping surges and the smoke and terrible rushing and roaring hiding all that is gentle and orderly in the work. But as soon as the deep forest was reached the ungovernable flood became calm like a torrent entering a lake, creeping and spreading beneath the trees where the ground was level or sloped gently, slowly nibbling the cake of compressed needles and scales with flames an inch high, rising here and there to a foot or two on dry twigs and clumps of small bushes and brome grass. Only at considerable intervals were fierce bonfires lighted, where heavy branches broken off by snow had accumulated, or around some venerable giant whose head had been stricken off by lightning.

I tethered Brownie on the edge of a little meadow beside a stream a good safe way off, and then cautiously chose a camp for myself in a big stout hollow trunk not likely to be crushed by the fall of burning trees, and made a bed of ferns and boughs in it. The night, however, and the strange wild fireworks were too beautiful and exciting to allow much sleep. There was no danger of being chased and hemmed in, for in the main forest belt of the Sierra, even when swift winds are blowing, fires seldom or never sweep over the trees in broad all-embracing sheets as they do in the dense Rocky Mountain woods and in those of the Cascade Mountains of Oregon and Washington. Here they creep from tree to tree with tranquil deliberation, allowing close observation, though caution is required in venturing around the burning giants to avoid falling limbs and knots and fragments from dead shattered tops. Though the day was best for study, I sauntered about night after night, learning what I could and admiring the wonderful show vividly displayed in the lonely darkness, the ground-fire advancing in long crooked lines gently grazing and smoking on the close-pressed leaves, springing up in thousands of little jets of pure flame on dry tassels and twigs, and tall spires and flat sheets with jagged flapping edges dancing here and there on grass tufts and bushes, big bonfires blazing in perfect storms of energy where heavy branches mixed with small ones lay smashed together in hundred cord piles, big red arches between spreading root-swells and trees growing close together, huge-fire-mantled trunks on the hill slopes glowing like bars of hot iron, violet-colored fire running up the tall trees, tracing the furrows of the bark in quick quivering rills, and lighting magnificent torches on dry shattered tops, and ever and anon, with a tremendous roar and burst of light, young trees clad in low-descending feathery branches vanishing in one flame two or three hundred feet high.

One of the most impressive and beautiful sights was made by the great fallen trunks lying on the hillsides all red and glowing like colossal iron bars fresh from a furnace, two hundred feet long some of them, and ten to twenty feet thick. After repeated burnings have consumed the bark and sapwood, the sound charred surface, being full of cracks and sprinkled with leaves, is quickly overspread with a pure, rich, furred, ruby glow almost flameless and smokeless, producing a marvelous effect in the night. Another grand and interesting sight are the fires on the tops of the largest living trees flaming above the green branches at a height of perhaps two hundred feet, entirely cut off from the ground-fires, and looking like signal beacons on watch towers. From one standpoint I sometimes saw a dozen or more, those in the distance looking like great stars above the forest roof. At first I could not imagine how these Sequoia lamps were lighted, but the very first night, strolling about waiting and watching, I saw the thing done again and again. The thick, fibrous bark of old trees is divided by deep, nearly continuous furrows, the sides of which are bearded with the bristling ends of fibres broken by the growth swelling of the trunk, and when the fire comes creeping around the feet of the trees, it runs up these bristly furrows in lovely pale blue quivering, bickering rills of flame with a low, earnest whispering sound to the lightning-shattered top of the trunk, which, in the dry Indian summer, with perhaps leaves and twigs and squirrel-gnawed cone-scales and seed-wings lodged in it, is readily ignited. These lamp-lighting rills, the most beautiful fire streams I ever saw, last only a minute or two, but the big lamps burn with varying brightness for days and weeks, throwing off sparks like the spray of a fountain, while ever and anon a shower of red coals comes sifting down through the branches, followed at times with startling effect by a big burned-off chunk weighing perhaps half a ton.

The immense bonfires where fifty or a hundred cords of peeled, split, smashed wood has been piled around some old giant by a single stroke of lightning is another grand sight in the night. The light is so great I found I could read common print three hundred yards from them, and the illumination of the circle of onlooking trees is indescribably impressive. Other big fires, roaring and booming like waterfalls, were blazing on the upper sides of trees on hillslopes, against which limbs broken off by heavy snow had rolled, while branches high overhead, tossed and shaken by the ascending air current, seemed to be writhing in pain. Perhaps the most startling phenomenon of all was the quick death of childlike Sequoias only a century or two of age. In the midst of the other comparatively slow and steady fire work one of these tall, beautiful saplings, leafy and branchy, would be seen blazing up suddenly, all in one heaving, booming, passionate flame reaching from the ground to the top of the tree and fifty to a hundred feet or more above it, with a smoke column bending forward and streaming away on the upper, free-flowing wind. To burn these green trees a strong fire of dry wood beneath them is required, to send up a current of air hot enough to distill inflammable gases from the leaves and sprays; then instead of the lower limbs gradually catching fire and igniting the next and next in succession, the whole tree seems to explode almost simultaneously, and with awful roaring and throbbing a round, tapering flame shoots up two or three hundred feet, and in a second or two is quenched, leaving the green spire a black, dead mast, bristled and roughened with down-curling boughs. Nearly all the trees that have been burned down are lying with their heads uphill, because they are burned far more deeply on the upper side, on account of broken limbs rolling down against them to make hot fires, while only leaves and twigs accumulate on the lower side and are quickly consumed without injury to the tree. But green, resinless Sequoia wood burns very slowly, and many successive fires are required to burn down a large tree. Fires can run only at intervals of several years, and when the ordinary amount of firewood that has rolled against the gigantic trunk is consumed, only a shallow scar is made, which is slowly deepened by recurring fires until far beyond the centre of gravity, and when at last the tree falls, it of course falls uphill. The healing folds of wood

layers on some of the deeply burned trees show that centuries
have elapsed since the last wounds were made.

When a great Sequoia falls, its head is smashed into fragments about as small as those made by lightning, which are
mostly devoured by the first running, hunting fire that finds
them, while the trunk is slowly wasted away by centuries of
fire and weather. One of the most interesting fire actions on the
trunk is the boring of those great tunnel-like hollows through
which horsemen may gallop. All of these famous hollows are
burned out of the solid wood, for no Sequoia is ever hollowed
by decay. When the tree falls the brash trunk is often broken
straight across into sections as if sawed; into these joints the
fire creeps, and, on account of the great size of the broken ends,
burns for weeks or even months without being much influenced by the weather. After the great glowing ends fronting
each other have burned so far apart that their rims cease to
burn, the fire continues to work on in the centres, and the ends
become deeply concave. Then heat being radiated from side to
side, the burning goes on in each section of the trunk independent of the other, until the diameter of the bore is so great
that the heat radiated across from side to side is not sufficient
to keep them burning. It appears, therefore, that only very
large trees can receive the fire-auger and have any shell rim left.

Fire attacks the large trees only at the ground, consuming
the fallen leaves and humus at their feet, doing them but little
harm unless considerable quantities of fallen limbs happen to
be piled about them, their thick mail of spongy, unpitchy,
almost unburnable bark affording strong protection. Therefore the oldest and most perfect unscarred trees are found on
ground that is nearly level, while those growing on hillsides,
against which falling branches roll, are always deeply scarred
on the upper side, and as we have seen are sometimes burned
down. The saddest thing of all was to see the hopeful seedlings,
many of them crinkled and bent with the pressure of winter
snow, yet bravely aspiring at the top, helplessly perishing, and
young trees, perfect spires of verdure and naturally immortal,
suddenly changed to dead masts. Yet the sun looked cheerily
down the openings in the forest roof, turning the black smoke
to a beautiful brown, as if all was for the best.

Beneath the smoke-clouds of the suffering forest we again
pushed southward, descending a side-gorge of the East Fork

canyon and climbing another into new forests and groves not a whit less noble. Brownie, meanwhile, had been resting, while I was weary and sleepy with almost ceaseless wanderings, giving only an hour or two each night or day to sleep in my log home. Way-making here seemed to become more and more difficult, 'impossible,' in common phrase, for four-legged travelers. Two or three miles was all the day's work as far as distance was concerned. Nevertheless, just before sundown we found a charming camp ground with plenty of grass, and a forest to study that had felt no fire for many a year. The camp hollow was evidently a favorite home of bears. On many of the trees, at a height of six or eight feet, their autographs were inscribed in strong, free, flowing strokes on the soft bark where they had stood up like cats to stretch their limbs. Using both hands, every claw a pen, the handsome curved lines of their writing take the form of remarkably regular interlacing pointed arches, producing a truly ornamental effect. I looked and listened, half expecting to see some of the writers alarmed and withdrawing from the unwonted disturbance. Brownie also looked and listened, for mules fear bears instinctively and have a very keen nose for them. When I turned him loose, instead of going to the best grass, he kept cautiously near the campfire for protection, but was careful not to step on me. The great starry night passed away in deep peace and the rosy morning sunbeams were searching the grove ere I woke from a long, blessed sleep.

The breadth of the Sequoia belt here is about the same as on the north side of the river, extending, rather thin and scattered in some places, among the noble pines from near the mains forest belt of the range well back towards the frosty peaks, where most of the trees are growing on moraines but little changed as yet.

Two days' scramble above Bear Hollow I enjoyed an interesting interview with deer. Soon after sunrise a little company of four came to my camp in a wild garden imbedded in chaparral, and after much cautious observation quietly began to eat breakfast with me. Keeping perfectly still, I soon had their confidence, and they came so near I found no difficulty, while admiring their graceful manners and gestures, in determining what plants they were eating, thus gaining a far finer knowledge and sympathy than comes by killing and hunting.

Indian summer gold with scarce a whisper of winter in it was painting the glad wilderness in richer and yet richer colors as we scrambled across the South canyon into the basin of the Tule. Here the Big Tree forests are still more extensive, and furnished abundance of work in tracing boundaries and gloriously crowned ridges up and down, back and forth, exploring, studying, admiring, while the great measureless days passed on and away uncounted. But in the calm of the campfire the end of the season seemed near. Brownie too often brought snowstorms to mind. He became doubly jaded, though I never rode him, and always left him in camp to feed and rest while I explored. The invincible bread business also troubled me again; the last mealy crumbs were consumed, and grass was becoming scarce even in the roughest rock-piles naturally inaccessible to sheep. One afternoon, as I gazed over the rolling bossy Sequoia billows stretching interminably southward, seeking a way and counting how far I might go without food, a rifle shot rang out sharp and clear. Marking the direction I pushed gladly on, hoping to find some hunter who could spare a little food. Within a few hundred rods I struck the track of a shod horse, which led to the camp of two Indian shepherds. One of them was cooking supper when I arrived. Glancing curiously at me he saw that I was hungry, and gave me some mutton and bread, and said encouragingly as he pointed to the west, 'Putty soon Indian come, heap speak English.' Toward sundown two thousand sheep beneath a cloud of dust came streaming through the grand Sequoias to a meadow below the camp, and presently the English-speaking shepherd came in, to whom I explained my wants and what I was doing. Like most white men, he could not conceive how anything other than gold could be the object of such rambles as mine, and asked repeatedly whether I had discovered any mines. I tried to make him talk about trees and the wild animals, but unfortunately he proved to be a tame Indian from the Tule Reservation, had been to school, claimed to be civilized, and spoke contemptuously of 'wild Indians,' and so of course his inherited instincts were blurred or lost. The Big Trees, he said, grew far south, for he had seen them in crossing the mountains from Porterville to Lone Pine. In the morning he kindly gave me a few pounds of flour, and assured me that I would get plenty more at a sawmill on the South Fork if I reached it before it was shut down for the season.

Of all the Tule basin forest the section on the North Fork seemed the finest, surpassing, I think, even the Giant Forest of the Kaweah. Southward from here, though the width and general continuity of the belt is well sustained, I thought I could detect a slight falling off in the height of the trees and in closeness of growth. All the basin was swept by swarms of hoofed locusts, the southern part over and over again, until not a leaf within the reach was left on the wettest bogs, the outer edges of the thorniest chaparral beds, or even on the young conifers, which unless under the stress of dire famine, sheep never touch. Of course Brownie suffered, though I made diligent search for grassy sheep-proof spots. Turning him loose one evening on the side of a carex bog, he dolefully prospected the desolate neighborhood without finding anything that even a starving mule could eat. Then, utterly discouraged, he stole up behind me while I was bent over on my knees making a fire for tea, and in a pitiful mixture of bray and neigh, begged for help. It was a mighty touching prayer, and I answered it as well as I could with half of what was left of a cake made from the last of the flour given me by the Indians, hastily passing it over my shoulder, and saying, 'Yes, poor fellow, I know, but soon you'll have plenty. Tomorrow down we go to alfalfa and barley,' speaking to him as if he were human, as through stress of trouble plainly he was. After eating his portion of bread he seemed content, for he said no more, but patiently turned away to gnaw leafless ceanothus stubs. Such clinging, confiding dependence after all our scrambles and adventures together was very touching, and I felt conscience-stricken for having led him so far in so rough and desolate a country. 'Man,' says Lord Bacon, 'is the god of the dog.' So, also, he is of the mule and many other dependent fellow mortals.

Next morning I turned westward, determined to force a way straight to pasture, letting Sequoia wait. Fortunately ere we had struggled down through half a mile of chaparral we heard a mill whistle, for which we gladly made a bee line. At the sawmill we both got a good meal, then taking the dusty lumber road pursued our way to the lowlands. The nearest good pasture I counted might be thirty or forty miles away. But scarcely had we gone ten when I noticed a little log cabin a hundred yards or so back from the road, and a tall man straight as a pine standing in front of it observing us as we came plodding down through the dust. Seeing no sign of grass or hay, I was going past without stopping, when he shouted, 'Travelin'?' Then drawing nearer, 'Where have you come from? I didn't notice you go up.' I replied I had come through the woods from the north, looking at the trees. 'Oh, then, you must be John Muir. Halt, you're tired; come and rest and I'll cook for you.' Then I explained that I was tracing the Sequoia belt, that on account of sheep my mule was starving, and therefore must push on to the lowlands. 'No, no,' he said, 'that corral over there is full of hay and grain. Turn your mule into it. I don't own it, but the fellow who does is hauling lumber, and it will be all right. He's a white man. Come and rest. How tired you must be! The Big Trees don't go much farther south, nohow. I know the country up there, have hunted all over it. Come and rest, and let your little doggone rat of a mule rest. How in heavens did you get him across the canyons – roll him? Or carry him? He's poor, but he'll get fat, and I'll give you a horse and go with you up the mountains, and while you're looking at the trees I'll go hunting. It will be a short job, for the end of the Big Trees is not far.' Of course I stopped. No true invitation is ever declined. He had been hungry and tired himself many a time in the Rocky Mountains as well as in the Sierra. Now he owned a band of cattle and lived alone. His cabin was about eight by ten feet, the door at one end, a fireplace at the other, and a bed on one side fastened to the logs. Leading me in without a word of mean apology, he made me lie down on the bed, then reached under it, brought forth a sack of apple and advised me to keep 'chawing' at them until he got supper ready. Finer, braver hospitality I never found in all this good world so often called selfish.

Next day with hearty, easy alacrity the mountaineer procured horses, prepared and packed provisions, and got everything ready for an early start the following morning. Well mounted, we pushed rapidly upon the South Fork of the river and soon after noon were among the giants once more. On the divide between the Tule and Deer Creek a central camp was made, and the mountaineer spent his time in deer-hunting, while with provisions for two or three days I explored the woods, and in accordance with what I had been told soon reached the southern extremity of the belt on the South Fork of Deer Creek. To make sure, I searched the woods a considerable distance south of the last Deer Creek grove, passed over into the basin of the Kern, and climbed several high points commanding extensive views over the sugar-pine woods, without seeing a single Sequoia crown in all the wide expanse to the southward. On the way back to camp, however, I was greatly interested in a grove I discovered on the east side of the Kern River divide, opposite the North Fork of Deer Creek. The height of the pass where the species crossed over is about 7000 feet, and I heard of still another grove whose waters drain into the upper Kern opposite the Middle Fork of the Tule.

It appears, therefore, that though the Sequoia belt is two hundred and sixty miles long, most of the trees are on a section to the south of Kings River only about seventy miles in length. But though the area occupied by the species increases so much to the southward, there is but little difference in the size of the trees. A diameter of twenty feet and height of two hundred and seventy-five is perhaps about the average for anything like mature and favorably situated trees. Specimens twenty-five feet in diameter are not rare, and a good many approach a height of three hundred feet. Occasionally one meets a specimen thirty feet in diameter, and rarely one that is larger. The majestic stump on Kings River is the largest I saw and measured on the entire trip. Careful search around the boundaries of the forests and groves and in the gaps of the belt failed to discover any trace of the former existence of the species beyond its present limits. On the contrary, it seems to be slightly extending its boundaries; for the outstanding stragglers, occasionally met a mile or two from the main bodies, are young instead of old monumental trees. Ancient ruins and the ditches and root-bowls the big trunks make in falling were found in all the groves, but none outside of them. We may therefore conclude that the area covered by the species has not been diminished during the last eight or ten thousand years, and probably not at all in post-glacial times. For admitting that upon those areas supposed to have been once covered by Sequoia every tree may have fallen, and that fire and the weather had left not a vestige of them, many of the ditches made by the fall of the ponderous trunks, weighing five hundred to nearly a thousand tons, and the bowls made by their up-turned roots would remain visible for thousands of years after the last remnants of the trees had vanished. Some of these records would doubtless be effaced in a comparatively short time by the inwashing of sediments, but no inconsiderable part of them would remain enduringly engraved on flat ridge tops, almost wholly free from such action.

In the northern groves, the only ones that at first came under the observation of students, there are but few seedlings and young trees to take the places of the old ones. Therefore the species was regarded as doomed to speedy extinction, as being only an expiring remnant vanquished in the so-called struggle for life, and shoved into its last strongholds in moist glens where conditions are exceptionally favorable. But the majestic continuous forests of the south end of the belt create a very different impression. Here, as we have seen, no tree in the forest is more enduringly established. Nevertheless it is oftentimes vaguely said that the Sierra climate is drying out, and that this oncoming, constantly increasing drought will of itself surely extinguish King Sequoia, though sections of wood-rings show that there has been no appreciable change of climate during the last forty centuries. Furthermore, that Sequoia can grow and is growing on as dry ground as any of its neighbors or rivals, we have seen proved over and over again. 'Why, then,' it will be asked, 'are the Big Tree groves always found on well-watered spots?' Simply because Big Trees give rise to streams. It is a mistake to suppose that the water is the cause of the groves being there. On the contrary, the groves are the cause of the water being there. The roots of this immense tree fill the ground, forming a sponge which hoards the bounty of the clouds and sends it forth in clear perennial streams instead of allowing it to rush headlong in short-lived destructive floods. Evaporation is also checked, and the air kept still in the shady Sequoia depths, while thirsty robber winds are shut out.

Since, then, it appears that Sequoia can and does grow on as dry ground as its neighbors and that the greater moisture found with it is an effect rather than a cause of its presence, the notions as to the former greater extension of the species and its near approach to extinction, based on its supposed dependence on greater moisture, are seen to be erroneous. Indeed, all my observations go to show that in case of prolonged drought the sugar pines and firs would die before Sequoia. Again, if the restricted and irregular distribution of the species be interpreted as the result of the desiccation of the range, then, instead of increasing in individuals toward the south, where the rainfall is less, it should diminish.

If, then, its peculiar distribution has not been governed by superior conditions of soil and moisture, by what has it been governed? Several years before I made this trip, I noticed that the northern groves were located on those parts of the Sierra soil-belt that were first laid bare and opened to premption when the ice-sheet began to break up into individual glaciers. And when I was examining the basin of the San Joaquin and trying to account for the absence of Sequoia, when every condition seemed favorable for its growth, it occurred to me that this remarkable gap in the belt is located in the channel of the great ancient glacier of the San Joaquin and Kings River basins, which poured its frozen floods to the plain, fed by the snows that fell on more than fifty miles of the Summit peaks of the range. Constantly brooding on the question, I next perceived that the great gap in the belt to the northward, forty miles wide, between the Stanislaus and Tuolumne groves, occurs in the channel of the great Stanislaus and Tuolumne glacier, and that the smaller gap between the Merced and Mariposa groves occurs in the channel of the smaller Merced glacier. The wider the ancient glacier, the wider the gap in the Sequoia belt, while the groves and forests attain their greatest development in the Kaweah and Tule River basins, just where, owing to topographical conditions, the region was first cleared and warmed, while protected from the main ice-rivers, that flowed past to right and left down the Kings and Kern valleys. In general, where the ground on the belt was first cleared of ice, there the Sequoia now is, and where at the same elevation and time the ancient glaciers lingered, there the Sequoia is not. What the other conditions may have been which enabled the Sequoia to establish itself upon these oldest and warmest parts of the main soil-belt I cannot say. I might venture to state, however, that since the Sequoia forests present a more and more ancient and long established aspect to the southward, the species was probably distributed from the south toward the close of the glacial period, before the arrival of other trees. About this branch of the question, however, there is at present much fog, but the general relationship we have pointed out between the distribution of the Big Tree and the ancient glacial

424   *Journeys in the Wilderness*

system is clear. And when we bear in mind that all the existing forests of the Sierra are growing on comparatively fresh moraine soil, and that the range itself has been recently sculptured and brought to light from beneath the ice-mantle of the glacial winter, then many lawless mysteries vanish, and harmonies take their places.

But notwithstanding all the observed phenomena bearing on the post-glacial history of this colossal tree, point to the conclusion that it never was more widely distributed on the Sierra since the close of the glacial epoch; that its present forests are scarcely past prime; if, indeed, they have reached prime; that the post-glacial day of the species is probably not half done; yet, when from a wider outlook the vast antiquity of the genus is considered, and its ancient richness in species and individuals, comparing our Sierra giant and Sequoia semper-virens of the coast, the only other living species, with the many fossil species already discovered, and described by the Heer and Lesquereux, some of which flourished over large areas around the Arctic Circle, and in Europe and our own terri-tories, during tertiary and cretaceous times – then, indeed, it becomes plain that our two surviving species, restricted to narrow belts within the limits of California, are mere remnants of the genus both as to species and individuals, and that they probably are verging on extinction. But the verge of a period beginning in cretaceous times may have a breadth of tens of thousands of years, not to mention the possible existence of conditions calculated to multiply and re-extend both species and individuals. No unfavorable change of climate, so far as I can see, no disease, but only fire and the axe and the ravages of flocks and herds threaten the existence of these noblest of God's trees. In Nature's keeping they are safe, but through man's agency destruction is making rapid progress, while in the work of protection only a beginning has been made. The Mariposa Grove belongs to and is guarded by the State; the General Grant and Sequoia National Parks, established ten years ago, are efficiently guarded by a troop of cavalry under the direction of the Secretary of the Interior; so also are the small Tuolumne and Merced groves, which are included in the Yosemite National Park, while a few scattered patches and fringes, scarce at all protected, though belonging to the na-tional government, are in the Sierra Forest Reservation.

Perhaps more than half of all the Big Trees have been sold, and are now in the hands of speculators and mill men. Even the beautiful little Calaveras Grove of ninety trees, so historically interesting from its being the first discovered, is now owned, together with the much larger South or Stanislaus Grove, by a lumber company.

Far the largest and most important section of protected Big Trees is in the grand Sequoia National Park, now easily accessible by stage from Visalia. It contains seven townships and extends across the whole breadth of the magnificent Kaweah basin. But large as it is, it should be made much larger. Its natural eastern boundary is the high Sierra, and the northern and southern boundaries, and the Kings and Kern rivers, and thus including the sublime scenery on the headwaters of these rivers and perhaps nine tenths of all the Big Trees in existence. Private claims cut and blotch both of the Sequoia parks as well as all the best of the forests, every one of which the government should gradually extinguish by purchase, as it readily may, for none of these holdings are of much value to their owners. Thus as far as possible the grand blunder of selling would be corrected. The value of these forests in storing and dispensing the bounty of the mountain clouds is infinitely greater than lumber or sheep. To the dwellers of the plain, dependent on irrigation, the Big Tree, leaving all its higher uses out of the count, is a tree of life, a never-failing spring, sending living water to the lowlands all through the hot, rainless summer. For every grove cut down a stream is dried up. Therefore, all California is crying, 'Save the trees of the fountains,' nor, judging by the signs of the times, it is likely that the cry will cease until the salvation of all that is left of *Sequoia gigantea* is sure.

Selections from
THE YOSEMITE

John Muir lived in and around Yosemite Valley from 1868 until 1874 and witnessed the destruction wrought by uncontrolled logging and sheep-grazing, as well as the detrimental impacts of the early tourist industry. In 1902 Muir's friend and publisher, Robert Underwood Johnson of *Century Magazine*, was urging Muir to write a tourist guidebook for the increasing tide of nature lovers who came to the valley, but *The Yosemite* was largely compiled from articles published twenty years earlier, during the campaign to establish the national park. While camping in Yosemite with Muir in 1889, Johnson had been equally appalled by the destruction of Tuolumne Meadows by vast flocks of sheep; he encouraged Muir to campaign for the creation of a wider Yosemite National Park and their friendship was largely born out of that successful struggle; Yosemite National Park came into being on 1 October 1890 as America's second national park. Earlier in this campaign Muir wrote in the California press:

At present the valley is like a grand hall, its walls covered with fine paintings and perfect in every way, and the floor covered with a beautiful carpet, but torn and dusty in some spots, and strewn with unsightly litter. The stench of a certain pigsty rises to the top of the domes at least, and a train of cars might be loaded with tin cans and other kitchen-midden rubbish, lying exposed in this pleasure ground of the world, where everyone may see it, as if like precious silverware it were exposed for sale.

('Yosemite Valley', *San Francisco Daily Evening Bulletin*,
21 June 1889)

His outrage at the rapacious exploitation of all and any resources to be found in the high country is clear in this similar article:

> If possible, and profitable, every tree, bush and leaf, with the soil they are growing on, and the whole solid uplift of the mountains would be cut, blasted, scraped, shoveled and shipped away to any market, home or foreign. Everything, without exception, even to souls and geography, would be sold for money could a market be found for such articles.
>
> ('Forests of the Sierra',
> *San Francisco Daily Evening Bulletin*,
> 29 June 1889)

That first campaign culminated in Johnson's publication of Muir's 'The Treasures of the Yosemite' in *Century Magazine* in August 1890, and his 'Features of the Proposed Yosemite National Park' in September 1890. Muir dedicated *The Yosemite* to Johnson in recognition of his leadership and support in the successful creation of Yosemite National Park. Muir procrastinated over the production of the book, compiled from dozens of earlier magazine articles, but he was given new impetus to complete it by the threatened destruction of Hetch Hetchy Valley, a neighbouring canyon to Yosemite within the national park.

This remote canyon, equally as beautiful as Yosemite Valley, was targeted by the city authorities of San Francisco as a potential water reservoir, following the great fire of 1906. Muir fought a long battle against the construction of the O'Shaughnessy dam which eventually drowned the valley; it is often said that the bitterness and stress which ensued hastened Muir's death in 1914. Nevertheless, although Muir lost this last and fiercest battle, the Hetch Hetchy campaign marked a sea-change in American society as the first great legal struggle between the developers and the conservationists, which continues to this day. Muir wrote:

> In these ravaging, money-mad days, San Francisco capitalists are now doing their best to destroy Yosemite Park, the most wonderful of all our mountain National Parks . . . These temple-destroyers, devotees of ravaging commercialism, seem

to have a perfect contempt for Nature, and instead of lifting their eyes to the God of the mountains, lift them to the almighty dollar. Dam Hetch Hetchy! As well dam for water tanks the people's churches and cathedrals, for no holier temple has ever been consecrated by the heart of man.

(John Muir, Sierra Club Bulletin, January 1908)

The selections from *The Yosemite* presented here include: 'The Approach to the Valley', 'Snow Banners', 'The Big Trees', 'The South Dome', 'Glaciers – How the Valley Was Formed' and finally 'Hetch Hetchy Valley'. Taken together, these still constitute a superb introduction for any visitor to Yosemite National Park, from the pen of a writer who knew every rock, tree and stream in the area from first-hand study.

Chapter 1

THE APPROACH TO THE VALLEY

When I set out on the long excursion that finally led to California I wandered afoot and alone, from Indiana to the Gulf of Mexico, with a plant-press on my back, holding a generally southward course, like the birds when they are going from summer to winter. From the west coast of Florida I crossed the gulf to Cuba, enjoyed the rich tropical flora there for a few months, intending to go thence to the north end of South America, make my way through the woods to the headwaters of the Amazon, and float down that grand river to the ocean. But I was unable to find a ship bound for South America – fortunately perhaps, for I had incredibly little money for so long a trip and had not yet fully recovered from a fever caught in the Florida swamps. Therefore I decided to visit California for a year or two to see its wonderful flora and the famous Yosemite Valley. All the world was before me and every day was a holiday, so it did not seem important to which one of the world's wildernesses I first should wander.

Arriving by the Panama steamer, I stopped one day in San Francisco and then inquired for the nearest way out of town. 'But where do you want to go?' asked the man to whom I had applied for this important information. 'To any place that is wild,' I said. This reply startled him. He seemed to fear I might be crazy and therefore the sooner I was out of town the better, so he directed me to the Oakland ferry.

So on the first of April, 1868, I set out afoot for Yosemite. It was the bloom-time of the year over the lowlands and coast ranges the landscapes of the Santa Clara Valley were fairly drenched with sunshine, all the air was quivering with the songs of the meadow-larks, and the hills were so covered with flowers that they seemed to be painted. Slow indeed was my progress through these glorious gardens, the first of the California flora I had seen. Cattle and cultivation were making few scars as yet, and I wandered enchanted in long wavering curves, knowing by my pocket map that Yosemite Valley lay to the east and that I should surely find it.

THE SIERRA FROM THE WEST

Looking eastward from the summit of the Pacheco Pass one shining morning, a landscape was displayed that after all my wanderings still appears as the most beautiful I have ever beheld. At my feet lay the Great Central Valley of California, level and flowery, like a lake of pure sunshine, forty or fifty miles wide, five hundred miles long, one rich furred garden of yellow *Compositae*. And from the eastern boundary of this vast golden flower-bed rose the mighty Sierra, miles in height, and so gloriously colored and so radiant, it seemed not clothed with light, but wholly composed of it, like the wall of some celestial city. Along the top and extending a good way down, was a rich pearl-gray belt of snow; below it a belt of blue and lark purple, marking the extension of the forests; and stretching along the base of the range a broad belt of rose-purple; all these colors, from the blue sky to the yellow valley smoothly blending as they do in a rainbow, making a wall of light ineffably fine. Then it seemed to me that the Sierra should be called, not the Nevada or Snowy Range, but the Range of Light. And after ten years of wandering and wondering in the heart of it, rejoicing in its glorious floods of light, the white beams of the morning streaming through the passes, the noonday radiance on the crystal rocks, the flush of the alpenglow, and the irised spray of countless waterfalls, it still seems above all others the Range of Light.

In general views no mark of man is visible upon it, nor any thing to suggest the wonderful depth and grandeur of its sculpture. None of its magnificent forest-crowned ridges seems to rise mud above the general level to publish its wealth. No great valley or river is seen, or group of well-marked features of any kind standing out as distinct pictures. Even the summit peaks, marshaled in glorious array so high in the sky, seem comparatively regular in form. Nevertheless the whole range five hundred miles long is furrowed with canyons 2000 to 5000 feet deep, in which once flowed majestic glaciers, and in which now flow and sing the bright rejoicing rivers.

CHARACTERISTICS OF THE CANYONS

Though of such stupendous depth, these canyons are not gloom gorges, savage and inaccessible. With rough passages here and there they are flowery pathways conducting to the snowy, icy fountains; mountain streets full of life and light, graded and sculptured by the ancient glaciers, and presenting throughout all their course a rich variety of novel and attractive scenery – the most attractive that has yet been discovered in the mountain ranges of the world. In many places, especially in the middle region of the western flank, the main canyons widen into spacious valleys or parks diversified like landscape gardens with meadows and groves and thickets of blooming bushes, while the lofty walls, infinitely varied in form, are fringed with ferns, flowering plants, shrubs of many species and tall evergreens and oaks that find footholds on small benches and tables, all enlivened and made glorious with rejoicing stream that come chanting in chorus over the cliffs and through side canyons in falls of every conceivable form, to join the river that flows in tranquil, shining beauty down the middle of each one of them.

THE INCOMPARABLE YOSEMITE

The most famous and accessible of these canyon valleys, and also the one that presents their most striking and sublime features on the grandest scale, is the Yosemite, situated in the basin of the Merced River at an elevation of 4000 feet above the level of the sea. It is about seven miles long, half a mile to a mile wide, and nearly a mile deep in the solid granite flank of the range. The walls are made up of rocks, mountains in size, partly separated from each other by side canyons, and they are so sheer in front, and so compactly and harmoniously arranged on a level floor, that the Valley, comprehensively seen, looks like an immense hall or temple lighted from above.

But no temple made with hands can compare with Yosemite. Every rock in its walls seems to glow with life. Some lean back in majestic repose; others, absolutely sheer or nearly so for thousands of feet, advance beyond their companions in thoughtful attitudes, giving welcome to storms and calms alike, seemingly aware, yet heedless, of everything going on about them. Awful in stern, immovable majesty, how softly these rocks are adorned, and how fine and reassuring the company they keep: their feet among beautiful groves and meadows, their brows in the sky, a thousand flowers leaning confidingly against their feet, bathed in floods of water, floods of light, while the snow and waterfalls, the winds and avalanches and clouds shine and sing and wreathe about them as the years go by, and myriad small winged creatures – birds, bees, butterflies – give glad animation and help to make all the air into music. Down through the middle of the Valley flows the crystal Merced, River of Mercy, peacefully quiet, reflecting lilies and trees and the onlooking rocks; things frail and fleeting and types of endurance meeting here and blending in countless forms, as if into this one mountain mansion Nature had gathered her choicest treasures, to draw her lovers into close and confiding communion with her.

THE APPROACH TO THE VALLEY

Sauntering up the foothills to Yosemite by any of the old trails or roads in use before the railway was built from the town of Merced up the river to the boundary of Yosemite Park, richer and wilder become the forests and streams. At an elevation of 6000 feet above the level of the sea the silver firs are 200 feet high, with branches whorled around the colossal shafts in regular order, and every branch beautifully pinnate like a fern frond. The Douglas spruce, the yellow and sugar pines and brown-barked libocedrus here reach their finest developments of beauty and grandeur. The majestic Sequoia is here, too, the king of conifers, the noblest of all the noble race. These colossal trees are as wonderful in fineness of beauty and proportion as in stature – an assemblage of conifers surpassing all that have ever yet been discovered in the forests of the world. Here indeed is the tree-lover's paradise; the woods, dry and wholesome, letting in the light in shimmering masses of half sunshine, half shade; the night air as well as the day air indescribably spicy and exhilarating; plushy fir-boughs for campers' beds and cascades to sing us to sleep. On the highest ridges, over which these old Yosemite ways passed, the silver fir (*Abies magnifica*) forms the bulk of the woods, pressing forward in glorious array to the very brink of the Valley walls on both sides, and beyond the Valley to a height of from 8000 to 9000 feet above the level of the sea. Thus it appears that Yosemite, presenting such stupendous faces of bare granite, is nevertheless imbedded in magnificent forests, and the main species of pine, fir, spruce and libocedrus are also found in the Valley itself, but there are no 'big trees' (*Sequoia gigantea*) in the Valley or about the rim of it. The nearest are about ten and twenty miles beyond the lower end of the valley on small tributaries of the Merced and Tuolumne Rivers.

THE FIRST VIEW: THE BRIDAL VEIL

From the margin of these glorious forests the first general view of the Valley used to be gained – a revelation in landscape affairs that enriches one's life forever. Entering the Valley, gazing overwhelmed with the multitude of grand objects about us, perhaps the first to fix our attention will be the Bridal Veil, a beautiful waterfall on our right. Its brow, where it first leaps free from the cliff, is about 900 feet above us; and as it sways and sings in the wind, clad in gauzy, sun-sifted spray, half falling, half floating, it seems infinitely gentle and fine; but the hymns it sings tell the solemn fateful power hidden beneath its soft clothing.

The Bridal Veil shoots free from the upper edge of the cliff by the velocity the stream has acquired in descending a long slope above the head of the fall. Looking from the top of the rock-avalanche talus on the west side, about one hundred feet above the foot of the fall, the under surface of the water arch is seen to be finely grooved and striated; and the sky is seen through the arch between rock and water, making a novel and beautiful effect.

Under ordinary weather conditions the fall strikes on flat-topped slabs, forming a kind of ledge about two-thirds of the way down from the top, and as the fall sways back and forth with great variety of motions among these flat-topped pillars, kissing and plashing notes as well as thunder-like detonations are produced, like those of the Yosemite Fall, though on a smaller scale.

The rainbows of the Veil, or rather the spray- and foam-bows, are superb, because the waters are dashed among angular blocks of granite at the foot, producing abundance of spray of the best quality for iris effects, and also for a luxuriant growth of grass and maiden-hair on the side of the talus, which lower down is planted with oak, laurel and willows.

GENERAL FEATURES OF THE VALLEY

On the other side of the Valley, almost immediately opposite the Bridal Veil, there is another fine fall, considerably wider than the Veil when the snow is melting fast and more than 1000 feet in height, measured from the brow of the cliff where it first springs out into the air to the head of the rocky talus on which it strikes and is broken up into ragged cascades. It is called the Ribbon Fall or Virgin's Tears. During the spring floods it is a magnificent object, but the suffocating blasts of spray that fill the recess in the wall which it occupies prevent a near approach. In autumn, however when its feeble current falls in a shower, it may then pass for tear with the sentimental onlooker fresh from a visit to the Bridal Veil.

Just beyond this glorious flood the El Capitan Rock, regarded by many as the most sublime feature of the Valley, is seen through the pine groves, standing forward beyond the general line of the wall in most imposing grandeur, a type of permanence. It is 3300 feet high, a plain, severely simple, glacier-sculptured face of granite, the end of one of the most compact and enduring of the mountain ridges, unrivaled in height and breadth and flawless strength.

Across the Valley from here, next to the Bridal Veil, are the picturesque Cathedral Rocks, nearly 2700 feet high, making a noble display of fine yet massive sculpture. They are closely related to El Capitan, having been eroded from the same mountain ridge by the great Yosemite Glacier when the Valley was in process of formation.

Next to the Cathedral Rocks on the south side towers the Sentinel Rock to a height of more than 3000 feet, a telling monument of the glacial period.

Almost immediately opposite the Sentinel are the Three Brothers, an immense mountain mass with three gables fronting the Valley, one above another, the topmost gable nearly 4000 feet high. They were named for three brothers, sons of old Tenaya, the Yosemite chief, captured here during the Indian War, at the time of the discovery of the Valley in 1852.

Sauntering up the Valley through meadow and grove, in the company of these majestic rocks, which seem to follow us as we advance, gazing, admiring, looking for new wonders ahead where all about us is so wonderful, the thunder of the Yosemite Fall is heard, and when we arrive in front of the Sentinel Rock it is revealed in all its glory from base to summit, half a mile in height, and seeming to spring out into the Valley sunshine direct from the sky. But even this fall, perhaps the most wonderful of its kind in the world, cannot at first hold our attention, for now the wide upper portion of the Valley is displayed to view, with the finely modeled North Dome, the Royal Arches and Washington Column on our left; Glacier Point, with its massive, magnificent sculpture on the right; and in the middle, directly in front, looms Tissiack or Half Dome, the most beautiful and most sublime of all the wonderful Yosemite rocks, rising in serene majesty from flowery groves and meadows to a height of 4750 feet.

THE UPPER CANYONS

Here the Valley divides into three branches, the Tenaya, Nevada, and Illilouette Canyons, extending back into the fountains of the High Sierra, with scenery every way worthy the relation they bear to Yosemite.

In the south branch, a mile or two from the main Valley, is the Illilouette Fall, 600 feet high, one of the most beautiful of all the Yosemite choir, but to most people inaccessible as yet on account of its rough, steep, boulder-choked canyon. Its principal fountains of ice and snow lie in the beautiful and interesting mountains of the Merced group, while its broad open basin between its fountain mountains and canyon is noted for the beauty of its lakes and forests and magnificent moraines.

Returning to the Valley, and going up the north branch of Tenaya Canyon, we pass between the North Dome and Half Dome, and in less than an hour come to Mirror Lake, the Dome Cascade and Tenaya Fall. Beyond the Fall, on the north side of the canyon is the sublime Ed Capitan-like rock called Mount Watkins; on the south the vast granite wave of Clouds' Rest, a mile in height; and between them the fine Tenaya Cascade with silvery plumes outspread on smooth glacier-polished folds of granite, making a vertical descent in all of about 700 feet.

Just beyond the Dome Cascades, on the shoulder of Mount Watkins, there is an old trail once used by Indians on their way across the range to Mono, but in the canyon above this point there is no trail of any sort. Between Mount Watkins and

Clouds' Rest the canyon is accessible only to mountaineers, and it is so dangerous that I hesitate to advise even good climbers, anxious to test their nerve and skill, to attempt to pass through it. Beyond the Cascades no great difficulty will be encountered. A succession of charming lily gardens and meadows occurs in filled-up lake basins among the rock-waves in the bottom of the canyon, and everywhere the surface of the granite has a smooth-wiped appearance, and in many places reflects the sunbeams like glass, a phenomenon due to glacial action, the canyon having been the channel of one of the main tributaries of the ancient Yosemite Glacier.

About ten miles above the Valley we come to the beautiful Tenaya Lake, and here the canyon terminates. A mile or two above the lake stands the grand Sierra Cathedral, a building of one stone, sewn from the living rock, with sides, roof, gable, spire and ornamental pinnacles, fashioned and finished symmetrically like a work of art, and set on a well-graded plateau about 9000 feet high, as if Nature in making so fine a building had also been careful that it should be finely seen. From every direction its peculiar form and graceful, majestic beauty of expression never fail to charm. Its height from its base to the ridge of the roof is about 2500 feet, and among the pinnacles that adorn the front grand views may be gained of the upper basins of the Merced and Tuolumne Rivers.

Passing the Cathedral we descend into the delightful, spacious Tuolumne Valley, from which excursions may be made to Mounts Dana, Lyell, Ritter, Conness, and Mono Lake, and to the many curious peaks that rise above the meadows on the south, and to the Big Tuolumne Canyon, with its glorious abundance of rock and falling, gliding, tossing water. For all these the beautiful meadows near the Soda Springs form a delightful center.

NATURAL FEATURES NEAR THE VALLEY

Returning now to Yosemite and ascending the middle or Nevada branch of the Valley, occupied by the main Merced River, we come within a few miles to the Vernal and Nevada Falls, 400 and 600 feet high, pouring their white, rejoicing waters in the midst of the most novel and sublime rock scenery to be found in all the World. Tracing the river beyond the head of the Nevada Fall we are lead into the Little Yosemite, a valley like the great Yosemite in form, sculpture and vegetation. It is about three miles long, with walls 1500 to 2000 feet high, cascades coming over them, and the ever flowing through the meadows and groves of the level bottom in tranquil, richly embowered reaches.

Beyond this Little Yosemite in the main canyon, there are three other little yosemites, the highest situated a few miles below the base of Mount Lyell, at an elevation of about 7800 feet above the sea. To describe these, with all their wealth of Yosemite furniture, and the wilderness of lofty peaks above them, the home of the avalanche and treasury of the fountain snow, would take us far beyond the bounds of a single book. Nor can we here consider the formation of these mountain landscapes – how the crystal rock were brought to light by glaciers made up of crystal snow, making beauty whose influence is so mysterious on every one who sees it.

Of the small glacier lakes so characteristic of these upper regions, there are no fewer than sixty-seven in the basin of the main middle branch, besides countless smaller pools. In the basin of the Illilouette there are sixteen, in the Tenaya basin and its branches thirteen, in the Yosemite Creek basin fourteen, and in the Pohono or Bridal Veil one, making a grand total of one hundred and eleven lakes whose waters come to sing at Yosemite. So glorious is the background of the great Valley, so harmonious its relations to its widespreading fountains.

The same harmony prevails in all the other features of the adjacent landscapes. Climbing out of the Valley by the subordinate canyons, we find the ground rising from the brink of the walls: on the south side to the fountains of the Bridal Veil Creek, the basin of which is noted for the beauty of its meadows and its superb forests of silver fir; on the north side through the basin of the Yosemite Creek to the dividing ridge along the Tuolumne Canyon and the fountains of the Hoffman Range.

DOWN THE YOSEMITE CREEK

In general views the Yosemite Creek basin seems to be paved with domes and smooth, whaleback masses of granite in every stage of development – some showing only their crowns; others rising high and free above the girdling forests, singly or in groups. Others are developed only on one side, forming bold outstanding bosses usually well fringed with shrubs and trees, and presenting the polished surfaces given them by the glacier that brought them into relief. On the upper portion of the basin broad moraine beds have been deposited and on these fine, thrifty forests are growing. Lakes and meadows and small spongy bogs may be found hiding here and there in the woods or back in the fountain recesses of Mount Hoffman, while a thousand gardens are planted along the banks of the streams.

All the wide, fan-shaped upper portion of the basin is covered with a network of small rills that go cheerily on their way to their grand fall in the Valley, now flowing on smooth pavements in sheets thin as glass, now diving under willows and laving their red roots, oozing through green, plushy bogs, plashing over small falls and dancing down slanting cascades, calming again, gliding through patches of smooth glacier meadows with sod of alpine agrostis mixed with blue and white violets and daisies, breaking, tossing among rough boulders and fallen trees, resting in calm pools, flowing together until, all united, they go to their fate with stately, tranquil gestures like a full-grown river. At the crossing of the Mono Trail, about two miles above the head of the Yosemite Fall, the stream is nearly forty feet wide, and when the snow is melting rapidly in the spring it is about four feet deep, with a current of two and a half miles an hour. This is about the volume of water that forms the Fall in May and June when there had been much snow the preceding winter; but it varies greatly from month to month. The snow rapidly vanishes from the open portion of the basin, which faces southward, and only a few of the tributaries reach back to perennial snow and ice fountains in the shadowy amphitheaters on the precipitous northern slopes of Mount Hoffman. The total descent made by the stream from its highest sources to its confluence with the Merced in the Valley is about 6000 feet, while the distance is only about ten miles, an average fall of 600 feet per mile. The last mile of its course lies between the sides of sunken domes and swelling folds of the granite that are clustered and pressed together like a mass of bossy cumulus clouds. Through this shining way Yosemite Creek goes to its fate, swaying and swirling with easy, graceful gestures and singing the last of its mountain songs before it reaches the dizzy edge of Yosemite to fall 2600 feet into another world, where climate, vegetation, inhabitants, all are different. Emerging from this last canyon the stream glides, in flat lace-like folds, down a smooth incline into a small pool where it seems to rest and compose itself before taking the grand plunge. Then calmly, as if leaving a lake, it slips over the polished lip of the pool down another incline and out over the brow of the precipice in a magnificent curve thick-sown with rainbow spray.

THE YOSEMITE FALL

Long ago before I had traced this fine stream to its head back of Mount Hoffman, I was eager to reach the extreme verge to see how it behaved in flying so far through the air; but after enjoying this view and getting safely away I have never advised anyone to follow my steps. The last incline down which the stream journeys so gracefully is so steep and smooth one must slip cautiously forward on hands and feet alongside the rushing water, which so near one's head is very exciting. But to gain a perfect view one must go yet farther, over a curving brow to a slight shelf on the extreme brink. This shelf, formed by the flaking off of a fold of granite, is about three inches wide, just wide enough for a safe rest for one's heels. To me it seemed nerve-trying to slip to this narrow foothold and poise on the edge of such precipice so close to the confusing whirl of the waters; and after casting longing glances over the shining brow of the fall and listening to its sublime psalm, I concluded not to attempt to go nearer, but, nevertheless, against reasonable judgement, I did. Noticing some tufts of artemisia in a cleft of rock, I filled my mouth with the leaves, hoping their bitter taste might help to keep caution keen and prevent giddiness. In spite of myself I reached the little ledge, got my heels well set, and worked sidewise twenty or thirty feet to a point close to the out-plunging current. Here the view is perfectly free down into the heart of the bright irised throng of comet-like streamers into which the whole ponderous volume of the fall separates, two or three hundred feet below the brow. So glorious a display of pure wildness, acting at close range while cut off from all the world beside, is terribly impressive. A less nerve-trying view may be obtained from a fissured portion of the edge of the cliff about forty yards to the eastward of the fall. Seen from this point towards noon, in the spring, the rainbow on its brow seems to be broken up and mingled with the rushing comets until all the fall is stained with iris colors, leaving no white water visible. This is the best of the safe views from above, the huge steadfast rocks, the flying waters, and the rainbow light forming one of the most glorious pictures conceivable.

The Yosemite Fall is separated into an upper and a lower fall with a series of falls and cascades between them, but when viewed in front from the bottom of the Valley they all appear as one.

So grandly does this magnificent fall display itself from the floor of the Valley, few visitors take the trouble to climb the walls to gain nearer views, unable to realize how vastly more impressive it is nearby than at a distance of one or two miles.

A WONDERFUL ASCENT

The views developed in a walk up the zigzags of the trail leading to the foot of the Upper Fall are about as varied and impressive as those displayed along the favorite Glacier Point Trail. One rises as if on wings. The groves, meadows, fern-flats and reaches of the river gain new interest, as if never seen before; all the views changing in a most striking manner as we go higher from point to point. The foreground also changes every few rods in the most surprising manner, although the earthquake talus and the level bench on the face of the wall over which the trail passes seem monotonous and common-place as seen from the bottom of the Valley. Up we climb with glad exhilaration, through shaggy fringes of laurel, ceanothus, glossy-leaved manzanita and live-oak, from shadow to shadow across bars and patches of sunshine, the leafy openings making charming frames for the Valley pictures beheld through gem, and for the glimpses of the high peaks that appear in the distance. The higher we go the farther we seem to be from the summit of the vast granite wall. Here we pass a projecting buttress whose grooved and rounded surface tells a plain story of the time when the Valley, now filled with sunshine, was filled with ice, when the grand old Yosemite Glacier, flowing river-like from its distant fountains, swept through it, crushing, grinding, wearing its way ever deeper, developing and fashioning these sublime rocks. Again we cross a white, battered gully,

the pathway of rock avalanches or snow avalanches. Farther
on we come to a gentle stream slipping down the face of the
cliff in lace-like strips, and dropping from ledge to ledge – too
small to be called a fall – trickling, dripping, oozing, a pathless
wanderer from one of the upland meadow lying a little way
back of the Valley rim, seeking a way century after century to
the depths of the Valley without any appreciable channel.
Every morning after a cool night, evaporation being checked, it
gathers strength and sings like a bird, but as the day advances
and the sun strikes its thin currents outspread on the heated
precipices, most of its waters vanish ere the bottom of
the Valley is reached. Many a fine, hanging-garden aloft on
breezy inaccessible heights awes to it its freshness and fullness
of beauty; ferneries in shady nooks, filled with *Adiantum*,
Woodwardia, *Woodsia*, *Aspidium*, *Pellaea*, and *Cheilanthes*,
rosetted and tufted and ranged in lines, daintily overlapping,
thatching the stupendous cliffs with softest beauty, some of the
delicate fronds seeming to float on the warm moist air, without
any connection with rock or stream. Nor is there any lack of
colored plants wherever they can find a place to cling to; lilies
and mints, the showy cardinal mimulus, and glowing cushions
of the golden bahia, enlivened with butterflies and bees and all
the other small, happy humming creatures that belong to them.

After the highest point on the lower division of the trail is
gained it leads up into the deep recess occupied by the great
fall, the noblest display of falling water to be found in the
Valley, or perhaps in the world. When it first comes in sight it
seems almost within reach of one's hand, so great in the spring
is its volume and velocity, yet it is still nearly a third of a mile
away and appears to recede as we advance. The sculpture of
the walls about it is on a scale of grandeur, according nobly
with the fall plain and massive, though elaborately finished,
like all the other cliffs about the Valley.

In the afternoon an immense shadow is cast athwart the
plateau in front of the fall, and over the chaparral bushes that
clothe the slopes and benches of the walls to the eastward,
creeping upward until the fall is wholly overcast, the contrast
between the shaded and illumined sections being very striking
in these near views.

Under this shadow, during the cool centuries immediately
following the breaking-up of the Glacial Period, dwelt a small

residual glacier, one of the few that lingered on this sun-beaten side of the Valley after the main trunk glacier had vanished. It sent down a long winding current through the narrow canyon on the west side of the fall, and must have formed a striking feature of the ancient scenery of the Valley; the lofty fall of ice and fall of water side by side, yet separate and distinct.

The coolness of the afternoon shadow and the abundant dewy spray make a fine climate for the plateau ferns and grasses, and for the beautiful azalea bushes that grow here in profusion and bloom in September, long after the warmer thickets down on the floor of the Valley have withered and gone to seed. Even close to the fall, and behind it at the base of the cliff, a few venturesome plants may be found undisturbed by the rock-shaking torrent.

The basin at the foot of the fall into which the current directly pours, when it is not swayed by the wind, is about ten feet deep and fifteen to twenty feet in diameter. That it is not much deeper is surprising, when the great height and force of the fall is considered. But the rock where the water strikes probably suffers less erosion than it would were the descent less than half as great, since the current is outspread, and much of its force is spent ere it reaches the bottom – being received on the air as upon an elastic cushion, and borne outward and dissipated over a surface more than fifty yards wide.

This surface, easily examined when the water is low, is in tensely clean and fresh looking. It is the raw, quick flesh of then mountain wholly untouched by the weather. In summer droughts when the snowfall of the preceding winter has been light, the fall is reduced to a mere shower of separate drops without any obscuring spray. Then we may safely go back of it and view the crystal shower from beneath, each drop wavering and pulsing as it makes its way through the air, and flashing off jets of colored light of ravishing beauty. But all this is invisible from the bottom of the Valley, like a thousand other interesting things. One must labor for beauty as for bread, here as elsewhere.

THE GRANDEUR OF THE YOSEMITE FALL

During the time of the spring floods the best near view of the fall is obtained from Fern Ledge on the east side above the blinding spray at a height of about 400 feet above the base of the fall. A climb of about 1400 feet from the Valley has to be made, and there is no trail, but to anyone fond of climbing this will make the ascent all the more delightful. A narrow part of the ledge extends to the side of the fall and back of it, enabling us to approach it as closely as we wish. When the afternoon sunshine is streaming through the throng of comets, ever wasting, ever renewed, fineness, firmness and variety of their forms are beautifully revealed. At the top of the fall they seem to burst forth in irregular spurts from some grand, throbbing mountain heart. Now and then one mighty throb sends forth a mass of solid water into the free air far beyond the others which rushes alone to the bottom of the fall with long stream-ing tail, like combed silk, while the others, descending in clusters, gradually mingle and lose their identity. But they all rush past us with amazing velocity and display of power though apparently drowsy and deliberate in their movements when observed from a distance of a mile or two. The heads of these comet-like masses are composed of nearly solid water, and are dense white in color like pressed snow, from the friction they suffer in rushing through the air, the portion worn off forming the tail between the white lustrous threads and films of which faint, grayish pencilings appear, while the outer, finer sprays of water-dust, whirling in sunny eddies, are pearly gray throughout. At the bottom of the fall there is but little distinction of form visible. It is mostly a hissing, clashing, seething, upwhirling mass of scud and spray, through which the light sifts in gray and purple tones while at times when the sun strikes at the required angle, the whole wild and appar-ently lawless, stormy, striving mass is changed to brilliant rainbow hues, manifesting finest harmony. The middle portion of the fall is the most openly beautiful; lower, the various forms into which the waters are wrought are more closely and voluminously veiled, while higher, towards the head, the current is comparatively simple and undivided. But even at the bottom, in the boiling clouds of spray, there is no confu-sion, while the rainbow light makes all divine, adding glorious beauty and peace to glorious power. This noble fall has far the richest, as well as the most powerful, voice of all the falls of the Valley, its tones varying from the sharp hiss and rustle of the wind in the glossy leaves of the live-oak and the soft, sifting, hushing tones of the pines, to the loudest rush and roar of storm winds and thunder among the crags of the summit peaks. The low bass, booming, reverberating tones, heard under favorable circumstances five or six miles away are formed by the dashing and exploding of heavy masses mixed with air upon two projecting ledges on the face of the cliff, the one on which we are standing and another about 200 feet above it. The torrent of massive comets is continuous at time of high water, while the explosive, booming notes are wildly intermittent, because, unless influenced by the wind, most of the heavier masses shoot out from the face of the precipice, and pass the ledges upon which at other times they are exploded. Occasionally the whole fall is swayed away from the front of the cliff, then suddenly dashed flat against it, or vibrated from side to side like a pendulum, giving rise to endless variety of forms and sounds.

THE NEVADA FALL

The Nevada Fall is 600 feet high and is usually ranked next to the Yosemite in general interest among the five main falls of the Valley. Coming through the Little Yosemite in tranquil reaches, the river is first broken into rapids on a moraine boulder-bar that crosses the lower end of the Valley. Thence it pursues its way to the head of the fall in a rough, solid rock channel, dashing on side angles, heaving in heavy surging masses against elbow knobs, and swirling and swashing in pot-holes without a moment's rest. Thus, already chafed and dashed to foam, overfolded and twisted, it plunges over the brink of the precipice as if glad to escape into the open air. But before it reaches the bottom it is pulverized yet finer by impinging upon a sloping portion of the cliff about half-way down, thus making it the whitest of all the falls of the Valley, and altogether one of the most wonderful in the world.

On the north side, close to its head, a slab of granite projects over the brink, forming a fine point for a view, over its throng of streamers and wild plunging, into its intensely white bosom, and through the broad drifts of spray, to the river far below, gathering its spent waters and rushing on again down the canyon in glad exultation into Emerald Pool, where at length it grows calm and gets rest for what still lies before it. All the features of the view correspond with the waters in grandeur and wildness. The glacier sculptured walls of the canyon on either hand, with the sublime mass of the Glacier Point Ridge in front, form a huge triangular pit-like basin, which, filled with the roaring of the falling river seems as if it might be the hopper of one of the mills of the gods in which the mountains were being ground.

THE VERNAL FALL

The Vernal, about a mile below the Nevada, is 400 feet high, a staid, orderly, graceful, easy-going fall, proper and exact in every movement and gesture, with scarce a hint of the passionate enthusiasm of the Yosemite or of the impetuous Nevada, whose chafed and twisted waters hurrying over the cliff seem glad to escape into the open air, while its deep, booming, thunder-tones reverberate over the listening landscape. Nevertheless it is a favorite with most visitors, doubtless because it is more accessible than any other, more closely approached and better seen and heard. A good stairway ascends the cliff beside it and the level plateau at the head enables one to saunter safely along the edge of the river as it comes from Emerald Pool and to watch its waters, calmly bending over the brow of the precipice, in a sheet eighty feet wide, changing in color from green to purplish gray and white until dashed on a boulder talus. Thence issuing from beneath its fine broad spray-clouds we see the tremendously adventurous river still unspent, beating its way down the wildest and deepest of all its canyons in gray roaring rapids, dear to the ouzel, and below the confluence of the Illilouette, sweeping around the shoulder of the Half Dome on its approach to the head of the tranquil levels of the Valley.

THE ILLILOUETTE FALL

The Illilouette in general appearance most resembles the Nevada. The volume of water is less than half as great, but it is about the same height (600 feet) and its waters receive the same kind of preliminary tossing in a rocky, irregular channel. Therefore it is a very white and fine-grained fall. When it is in full springtime bloom it is partly divided by rocks that roughen the lip of the precipice, but this division amounts only to a kind of fluting and grooving of the column, which has a beautiful effect. It is not nearly so grand a fall as the upper Yosemite, or so symmetrical as the Vernal, or so airily graceful and simple as the Bridal Veil, nor does it ever display so tremendous an outgush of snowy magnificence as the Nevada; but in the exquisite fineness and richness of texture of its flowing folds it surpasses them all.

One of the finest effects of sunlight on falling water I ever saw in Yosemite or elsewhere I found on the brow of this beautiful fall. It was in the Indian summer, when the leaf colors were ripe and the great cliffs and domes were transfigured in the hazy golden air. I had scrambled up its rugged talus-dammed canyon, oftentimes stopping to take breath and look back to admire the wonderful views to be had there of the great Half Dome, and to enjoy the extreme purity of the water, which in the motionless pools on this stream is almost perfectly invisible; the colored foliage of the maples, dogwoods, *Rubus* tangles, etc., and the late goldenrods and asters. The voice of the fall was now low, and the grand spring and summer floods had waned to sifting, drifting gauze and thin-broidered folds of linked and arrowy lace-work. When I reached the foot of the fall sunbeams were glinting across its head, leaving all the rest of it in shadow; and on its illumined brow a group of yellow spangles of singular form and beauty were playing, flashing up and dancing in large flame-shaped masses, wavering at times, then steadying, rising and falling in accord with the shifting forms of the water. But the color of the dancing spangles changed not at all. Nothing in clouds or flowers, on bird-wings or the lips of shells, could rival it in fineness. It was the most divinely beautiful mass of rejoicing yellow light I ever beheld – one of Nature's precious gifts that perchance may come to us but once in a lifetime.

THE MINOR FALLS
There are many other comparatively small falls and cascades in the Valley. The most notable are the Yosemite Gorge Fall and Cascades, Tenaya Fall and Cascades, Royal Arch Falls, the two Sentinel Cascades and the falls of Cascade and Tamarack Creeks, a mile or two below the lower end of the Valley. These last are often visited. The others are seldom noticed or mentioned; although in almost any other country they would be visited and described as wonders.

The six intermediate falls in the gorge between the head of the Lower and the base of the Upper Yosemite Falls, separated by a few deep pools and strips of rapids, and three slender, tributary cascades on the west side form a series more strikingly varied and combined than any other in the Valley, yet very few of all the Valley visitors ever see them or hear of them. No available standpoint commands a view of them all. The best general view is obtained from the mouth of the gorge near the head of the Lower Fall. The two lowest of the series, together with one of the three tributary cascades, are visible from this standpoint, but in reaching it the last twenty or thirty feet of the descent is rather dangerous in time of high water, the shelving rocks being then slippery on account of spray, but if one should chance to slip when the water is low, only a bump or two and a harmless plash would be the penalty. No part of the gorge, however, is safe to any but cautious climbers.

Though the dark gorge hall of these rejoicing waters is never flushed by the purple light of morning or evening, it is warmed and cheered by the white light of noonday, which, falling into so much foam and spray of varying degrees of fineness, makes marvelous displays of rainbow colors. So filled, indeed, is it with this precious light, at favorable times it seems to take the place of common air. Laurel bushes shed fragrance into it from above and live-oaks, those fearless mountaineers, hold fast to angular seams and lean out over it with their fringing sprays and bright mirror leaves.

One bird, the ouzel, loves this gorge and flies through it merrily, or cheerily, rather, stopping to sing on foam-washed bosses where other birds could find no rest for their feet. I have even seen a gray squirrel down in the heart of it beside the wild rejoicing water.

One of my favorite night walks was along the rim of this wild gorge in times of high water when the moon was full, to see the lunar bows in the spray.

For about a mile above Mirror Lake the Tenaya Canyon is level, and richly planted with fir, Douglas spruce and libocedrus, forming a remarkably fine grove, at the head of which is the Tenaya Fall. Though seldom seen or described, this is, I think, the most picturesque of all the small falls. A considerable distance above it, Tenaya Creek comes hurrying down, white and foamy, over a flat pavement inclined at an angle of about eighteen degrees. In time of high water this sheet of rapids is nearly seventy feet wide, and is varied in a very striking way by three parallel furrows that extend in the direction of its flow. These furrows, worn by the action of the stream upon cleavage joints, vary in width, are slightly sinuous, and have large boulders firmly wedged in them here and there in narrow places, giving rise, of course, to a complicated series of wild dashes, doublings, and upleaping arches in the swift torrent. Just before it reaches the head of the fall the current is divided, the left division making a vertical drop of about eighty feet in a romantic, leafy, flowery, mossy nook, while the other forms a rugged cascade.

The Royal Arch Fall in time of high water is a magnificent object, forming a broad ornamental sheet in front of the arches. The two Sentinel Cascades, 3000 feet high, are also grand spectacles when the snow is melting fast in the spring, but by the middle of summer they have diminished to mere streaks scarce noticeable amid their sublime surroundings.

THE BEAUTY OF THE RAINBOWS

The Bridal Veil and Vernal Falls are famous for their rainbows; and special visits to them are often made when the sun shines into the spray at the most favorable angle. But amid the spray and foam and fine-ground mist ever rising from the various falls and cataracts there is an affluence and variety of iris bows scarcely known to visitors who stay only a day or two. Both day and night, winter and summer, this divine light may be seen wherever water is falling, dancing, singing; telling the heart-peace of Nature amid the wildest displays of her power. In the bright spring mornings the black-walled recess at the foot of the Lower Yosemite Fall is lavishly fine with irised spray; and not simply does this span the dashing foam, but the foam itself, the whole mass of it, beheld at a certain distance, seems to be colored, and drips and wavers from color to color, mingling with the foliage of the adjacent trees, without suggesting any relationship to the ordinary rainbow. This is perhaps the largest and most reservoir-like fountain of iris colors to be found in the Valley.

Lunar rainbows or spray-bows also abound in the glorious affluence of dashing, rejoicing, hurrahing, enthusiastic spring floods, their colors as distinct as those of the sun and regularly and obviously banded, though less vivid. Fine specimens may be found any night at the foot of the Upper Yosemite Fall, glowing gloriously amid the gloomy shadows and thundering waters, whenever there is plenty of moonlight and spray. Even the secondary bow is at times distinctly visible.

The best point from which to observe them is on Fern Ledge. For some time after moonrise, at time of high water, the arc has a span of about five hundred feet, and is set upright; one end planted in the boiling spray at the bottom, the other in the edge of the fall, creeping lower, of course, and becoming less upright as the moon rises higher. This grand arc of color, glowing in mild, shapely beauty in so weird and huge a chamber of night shadows, and amid the rush and roar and tumultuous dashing of this thunder-voiced fall, is one of the most impressive and most cheering of all the blessed mountain evangels.

Smaller bows may be seen in the gorge on the plateau between the Upper and Lower Falls. Once toward midnight, after spending a few hours with the wild beauty of the Upper Fall, I sauntered along the edge of the gorge, looking in here and there, wherever the footing felt safe, to see what I could learn of the night aspects of the smaller falls that dwell there. And down in an exceedingly black, pit-like portion of the gorge, at the foot of the highest of the intermediate falls, into which the moonbeams were pouring through a narrow opening, I saw a well-defined spray-bow, beautifully distinct in colors, spanning the pit from side to side, while pure white foam-waves beneath the beautiful bow were constantly springing up out of the dark into the moonlight like dancing ghosts.

AN UNEXPECTED ADVENTURE

A wild scene, but not a safe one, is made by the moon as it appears through the edge of the Yosemite Fall when one is behind it. Once, after enjoying the night-song of the waters and watching the formation of the colored bow as the moon came round the domes and sent her beams into the wild uproar, I ventured out on the narrow bench that extends back of the fall from Fern Ledge and began to admire the dim-veiled grandeur of the view. I could see the fine gauzy threads of the fall's filmy border by having the light in front; and wishing to look at the moon through the meshes of some of the denser portions of the fall, I ventured to creep farther behind it while it was gently wind-swayed, without taking sufficient thought about the consequences of its swaying back to its natural position after the wind-pressure should be removed. The effect was enchanting: fine, savage music sounding above, beneath, around me; while the moon, apparently in the very midst of the rushing waters, seemed to be struggling to keep her place, on account of the ever-varying form and density of the water masses through which she was seen, now darkly veiled or eclipsed by a rush of thick-headed comets, now flashing out through openings between their tails. I was in fairyland between the dark wall and the wild throng of illumined waters, but suffered sudden disenchantment; for, like the witch-scene in Alloway Kirk, 'in an instant all was dark'. Down came a dash of spent comets, thin and harmless-looking in the distance, but they felt desperately solid and stony when they struck my shoulders, like a mixture of choking spray and gravel and big hailstones. Instinctively dropping on my knees, I gripped an angle of the rock, curled up like a young fern frond with my face pressed against my breast, and in this attitude submitted as best I could to my thundering bath. The heavier masses seemed to strike like cobblestones, and there was a confused noise of many waters about my ears – hissing, gurgling, clashing sounds that were not heard as music. The situation was quickly realized. How fast one's thoughts burn in such times of stress! I was weighing chances of escape. Would the column be swayed a few inches away from the wall, or would it come yet closer? The fall was in flood and not so lightly would its ponderous mass be swayed. My fate seemed to depend on a breath of the 'idle wind.' It was moved gently forward, the pounding ceased, and I was once more visited by glimpses of the moon. But fearing I might be caught at a disadvantage in making too hasty a retreat, I moved only a few feet along the bench to where a block of ice lay. I wedged myself between the ice and the wall and lay face downwards, until the steadiness of the light gave encouragement to rise and get away. Somewhat nerve-shaken, drenched, and benumbed, I made out to build a fire, warmed myself, ran home, reached my cabin before daylight, got an hour or two of sleep, and awoke sound and comfortable, better, not worse for my hard midnight bath.

CLIMATE AND WEATHER
Owing to the westerly trend of the Valley and its vast depth there is a great difference between the climates of the north and

south sides – greater than between many countries far apart; for the south wall is in shadow during the winter months, while the north is bathed in sunshine every clear day. Thus there is mild spring weather on one side of the Valley while winter rules the other. Far up the north-side cliffs many a nook may be found closely embraced by sun-beaten rock-bosses in which flowers bloom every month of the year. Even butterflies may be seen in these high winter gardens except when snow-storms are falling and a few days after they have ceased. Near the head of the lower Yosemite Fall in January I found the ant lions lying in wait in their warm sand-cups, rock ferns being unrolled, club mosses covered with fresh-growing plants, the flowers of the laurel nearly open, and the honeysuckle rosetted with bright young leaves; every plant seemed to be thinking about summer. Even on the shadow-side of the Valley the frost is never very sharp. The lowest temperature I ever observed during four winters was 7° Fahrenheit. The first twenty-four days of January had an average temperature at 9 a.m. of 32°, minimum 22°; at 3 p.m. the average was 40° 30′, the minimum 32°. Along the top of the walls, 7000 and 8000 feet high, the temperature was, of course, much lower. But the difference in temperature between the north and south sides is due not so much to the winter sunshine as to the heat of the preceding summer, stored up in the rocks, which rapidly melts the snow in contact with them. For though summer sun-heat is stored in the rocks of the south side also, the amount is much less because the rays fall obliquely on the south wall even in summer and almost vertically on the north.

The upper branches of the Yosemite streams are buried every winter beneath a heavy mantle of snow, and set free in the spring in magnificent floods. Then, all the fountains, full and overflowing, every living thing breaks forth into singing, and the glad exulting streams shining and falling in the warm sunny weather, shake everything into music making all the mountain-world a song.

The great annual spring thaw usually begins in May in the forest region, and in June and July on the high Sierra, varying somewhat both in time and fullness with the weather and the depth of the snow. Toward the end of summer the streams are at their lowest ebb, few even of the strongest singing much above a whisper they slip and ripple through gravel and boulder-beds from pool to pool in the hollows of their channels, and drop in pattering showers like rain, and slip down precipices and fall in sheets of embroidery, fold over fold. But, however low their singing, it is always ineffably fine in tone, in harmony with the restful time of the year.

The first snow of the season that comes to the help of the streams usually falls in September or October, sometimes even in the latter part of August, in the midst of yellow Indian summer when the goldenrods and gentians of the glacier meadows are in their prime. This Indian-summer snow, however, soon melts, the chilled flowers spread their petals to the sun, and the gardens as well as the streams are refreshed as if only a warm shower had fallen. The snow-storms that load the mountains to form the main fountain supply for the year seldom set in before the middle or end of November.

WINTER BEAUTY OF THE VALLEY

When the first heavy storms stopped work on the high mountains, I made haste down to my Yosemite den, not to 'hole up' and sleep the white months away; I was out every day, and often all night, sleeping but little, studying the so-called wonders and common things ever on show, wading, climbing, sauntering among the blessed storms and calms, rejoicing in almost everything alike that I could see or hear: the glorious brightness of frosty mornings; the sunbeams pouring over the white domes and crags into the groves and waterfalls, kindling marvelous iris fires in the hoarfrost and spray; the great forests and mountains in their deep noon sleep; the goodnight alpenglow; the stars; the solemn gazing moon, drawing the huge domes and headlands one by one glowing white out of the shadows hushed and breathless like an audience in awful enthusiasm, while the meadows at their feet sparkle with frost-stars like the sky; the sublime darkness of storm-nights, when all the lights are out; the clouds in whose depths the frail snow-flowers grow; the behavior and many voices of the different kinds of storms, trees, birds, waterfalls, and snow-avalanches in the ever-changing weather.

Every clear, frosty morning loud sounds are heard booming and reverberating from side to side of the Valley at intervals of a few minutes, beginning soon after sunrise and continuing an hour or two like a thunder-storm. In my first winter in the

Valley I could not make out the source of this noise. I thought of falling boulders, rock-blasting, etc. Not till I saw what looked like hoarfrost dropping from the side of the Fall was the problem explained. The strange thunder is made by the fall of sections of ice formed of spray that is frozen on the face of the cliff along the sides of the Upper Yosemite Fan – a sort of crystal plaster, a foot or two thick, racked off by the sunbeams, awakening all the Valley like cock-crowing, announcing the finest weather, shouting aloud Nature's infinite industry and love of hard work in creating beauty.

EXPLORING AN ICE CONE

This frozen spray gives rise to one of the most interesting winter features of the Valley – a cone of ice at the foot of the fall, four or five hundred feet high. From the Fern Ledge standpoint its crater-like throat is seen, down which the fall plunges with deep, gasping explosions of compressed air, and, after being well churned in the wormy interior, the water bursts forth through arched openings at its base, apparently scourged and weary and glad to escape, while belching spray, spouted up out of the throat past the descending current, is wafted away in irised drifts to the adjacent rocks and groves. It is built during the night and early hours of the morning; only in spells of exceptionally cold and cloudy weather is the work continued through the day. The greater part of the spray material falls in crystalline showers direct to its place, something like a small local snow-storm; but a considerable portion is first frozen on the face of the cliff along the sides of the fall and stays there until expanded and cracked off in irregular masses, some of them tons in weight, to be built into the walls of the cone; while in windy, frosty weather, when the fall is swayed from side to side, the cone is well drenched and the loose ice masses and spray-dust are all firmly welded and frozen together. Thus the finest of the downy wafts and curls of spray-dust, which in mild nights fall about as silently as dew, are held back until sunrise to make a store of heavy ice to reinforce the waterfall's thunder-tones.

While the cone is in process of formation, growing higher and wider in the frosty weather, it looks like a beautiful smooth, pure-white hill; but when it is wasting and breaking up in the spring its surface is strewn with leaves, pine branches, stones, sand, etc., that have been brought over the fall, making it look like a heap of avalanche detritus.

Anxious to learn what I could about the structure of this curious hill I often approached it in calm weather and tried to climb it, carrying an axe to cut steps. Once I nearly succeeded in gaining the summit. At the base I was met by a current of spray and wind that made seeing and breathing difficult. I pushed on backward however, and soon gained the slope of the hill, where by creeping close to the surface most of the choking blast passed over me and I managed to crawl up with but little difficulty. Thus I made my way nearly to the summit, halting at times to peer up through the wild whirls of spray at the veiled grandeur of the fall, or to listen to the thunder beneath me; the whole hill was sounding as if it were a huge, bellowing drum. I hoped that by waiting until the fall was blown aslant I should be able to climb to the lip of the crater and get a view of the interior; but a suffocating blast, half air, half water, followed by the fall of an enormous mass of frozen spray from a spot high up on the wall, quickly discouraged me. The whole cone was jarred by the blow and some fragments of the mass sped past me dangerously near; so I beat a hasty retreat, chilled and drenched, and lay down on a sunny rock to dry.

Once during a wind-storm when I saw that the fall was frequently blown westward, leaving the cone dry, I ran up to Fern Ledge hoping to gain a clear view of the interior. I set out at noon. All the way up the storm notes were so loud about me that the voice of the fall was almost drowned by them. Notwithstanding the rocks and bushes everywhere were drenched by the wind-driven spray, I approached the brink of the precipice overlooking the mouth of the ice cone, but I was almost suffocated by the drenching, gusty spray, and was compelled to seek shelter. I searched for some hiding-place in the wall from whence I might run out at some opportune moment when the fall with its whirling spray and torn shreds of comet tails and trailing, tattered skirts was borne westward, as I had seen it carried several times before, leaving the cliffs on the east side and the ice hill bare in the sunlight. I had not long to wait, for, as if ordered so for my special accommodation, the mighty downrush of comets with their whirling drapery swung westward and remained aslant for nearly half an hour.

The cone was admirably lighted and deserted by the water, which fell most of the time on the rocky western slopes mostly outside of the cone. The mouth into which the fall pours was, as near as I could guess, about one hundred feet in diameter north and south and about two hundred feet east and west, which is about the shape and size of the fall at its best in its normal condition at this season.

The crater-like opening was not a true oval, but more like a huge coarse mouth. I could see down the throat about one hundred feet or perhaps farther.

The fall precipice overhangs from a height of 400 feet above the base; therefore the water strikes some distance from the base off the cliff, allowing space for the accumulation of a considerable mass of ice between the fall and the wall.

Chapter 4

SNOW BANNERS

But it is on the mountain tops, when they are laden with loose, dry snow and swept by a gale from the north, that the most magnificent storm scenery is displayed. The peaks along the axis of the Range are then decorated with resplendent banners, some of them more than a mile long, shining, streaming, waving with solemn exuberant enthusiasm as if celebrating some surpassingly glorious event.

The snow of which these banners are made falls on the high Sierra in most extravagant abundance, sometimes to a depth of fifteen or twenty feet, coming from the fertile clouds not in large angled flakes such as one oftentimes sees in Yosemite, seldom even in complete crystals, for many of the starry blossoms fall before they are ripe, while most of those that attain perfect development as six-petaled flowers are more or less broken by glinting and chafing against one another on the way down to their work. This dry frosty snow is prepared for the grand banner-waving celebrations by the action of the wind. Instead of at once finding rest like that which falls into the tranquil depths of the forest, it is shoved and rolled and beaten against boulders and out-jutting rocks, swirled in pits and hollows like sand in river pot-holes, and ground into sparkling dust. And when storm winds find this snow-dust in a loose condition on the slopes above the timber-line they toss it flack into the sky and sweep it onward from peak to peak in the form of smooth regular banners, or in cloudy drifts, according to the velocity and direction of the wind, and the conformation of the slopes over which it is driven. While thus flying through the air a small portion escapes from the mountains to the sky as vapor; but far the greater part is at length locked fast in bossy overcurling cornices along the ridges, or in stratified sheets in the glacier cirques, some of it to replenish the small residual glaciers and remain silent and rigid for centuries before it is finally melted and sent singing down home to the sea.

But, though snow-dust and storm-winds abound on the mountains, regular shapely banners are, for causes we shall presently see, seldom produced. During the five winters that I spent in Yosemite I made many excursions to high points above the walls in all kinds of weather to see what was going on outside; from all my lofty outlooks I saw only one banner-storm that seemed in every way perfect. This was in the winter of 1873, when the snow-laden peaks were swept by a powerful norther. I was awakened early in the morning by a wild storm-wind and of course I had to make haste to the middle of the Valley to enjoy it. Rugged torrents and avalanches from the main wind-flood overhead were roaring down the side canyons and over the cliffs, arousing the rocks and the trees and the streams alike into glorious hurrahing enthusiasm, shaking the whole Valley into one huge song. Yet inconceivable as it must seem even to those who love all Nature's wildness, the storm was telling its story on the mountains in still grander characters.

A WONDERFUL WINTER SCENE

I had long been anxious to study some points in the structure of the ice-hill at the foot of the Upper Yosemite Fall, but, as I have already explained, blinding spray had hitherto prevented me from getting sufficiently near it. This morning the entire body of the Fall was oftentimes torn into gauzy strips and blown horizontally along the face of the cliff, leaving the ice-hill dry; and while making my way to the top of Fern Ledge to seize so favorable an opportunity to look down its throat, the peaks of the Merced group came in sight over the shoulder of the South Dome, each waving a white glowing banner against the dark blue sky, as regular in form and firm and fine in texture as if it were made of silk. So rare and splendid a picture, of course, smothered everything else and I at once began to scramble and wallow up the snow-choked Indian Canyon to a ridge about 8000 feet high, commanding a general view of the main summits along the axis of the Range, feeling assured I should find them bannered still more gloriously; nor was I in the least disappointed. I reached the top of the ridge in four or five hours, and through an opening in the woods the most imposing wind-storm effect I ever beheld came full in sight; unnumbered mountains rising sharply into the cloudless sky, their bases solid white, their sides plashed with snow, like ocean rocks with foam, and on every summit a magnificent silvery banner, from two thousand to six thousand feet in length, slender at the point of attachment, and widening gradually until about a thousand or fifteen hundred feet in breadth, and as shapely and as substantial looking in texture as the banners of the finest silk, all streaming and waving free and clear in the sun-glow with nothing to blur the sublime picture they made.

Fancy yourself standing beside me on this Yosemite Ridge. There is a strange garish glitter in the air and the gale drives wildly overhead, but you feel nothing of its violence, for you are looking out through a sheltered opening in the woods, as through a window. In the immediate foreground there is a forest of silver fir their foliage warm yellow-green, and the snow beneath them strewn with their plumes, plucked off by the storm; and beyond broad, ridgy, canyon-furrowed, dome-dotted middle ground, darkened here and there with belts of pines, you behold the lofty snow laden mountains in glorious array, waving their banners with jubilant enthusiasm as if shouting aloud for joy. They are twenty miles away, but you would not wish them nearer, for every feature is distinct and the whole wonderful show is seen in its right proportions, like a painting on the sky.

And now after this general view, mark how sharply the ribs and buttresses and summits of the mountains are defined, excepting the portions veiled by the banners; how gracefully and nobly the banners are waving in accord with the throbbing of the wind flood; how trimly each is attached to the very summit of its peak like a streamer at a mast-head; how bright and glowing white they are, and how finely their fading fringes are penciled on the sky! See how solid white and opaque they are at the point of attachment and how filmy and translucent toward the end, so that the parts of the peaks past which they are streaming look dim as if seen through a veil of ground glass. And see how some of the longest of the banners on the highest peaks are streaming perfectly free from peak to peak across intervening notches or passes, while others overlap and partly hide one another.

As to their formation, we find that the main causes of the wondrous beauty and perfection of those we are looking at are the favorable direction and force of the wind, the abundance of snow-dust, and the form of the north sides of the peaks. In general, the north sides are concave in both their horizontal and vertical sections, having been sculptured into this shape by the residual glaciers that lingered in the protecting northern shadows, while the sun-beaten south sides, having never been subjected to this kind of glaciation, are convex or irregular. It is essential, therefore, not only that the wind should move with great velocity and steadiness to supply a sufficiently copious and continuous stream of snow-dust, but that it should come from the north. No perfect banner is ever hung on the Sierra peaks by the south wind. Had the gale today blown from the south, leaving the other conditions unchanged, only swirling, interfering, cloudy drifts would have been produced; for the snow, instead of being spouted straight up and over the tops of the peaks in condensed currents to be drawn out as streamers, would have been driven over the convex southern slopes from peak to peak like white pearly fog.

It appears, therefore, that shadows in great part determine not only the forms of lofty ice mountains, but also those of the snow banners that the wild winds hang upon them.

EARTHQUAKE STORMS

The avalanche taluses, leaning against the walls at intervals of a mile or two, are among the most striking and interesting of the secondary features of the Valley. They are from about three to five hundred feet high, made up of huge, angular, well-preserved, unshifting boulders, and instead of being slowly weathered from the cliffs like ordinary taluses, they were all formed suddenly and simultaneously by a great earthquake that occurred at least three centuries ago. And though thus hurled into existence in a few seconds or minutes, they are the least changeable of all the Sierra soil-beds. Excepting those which were launched directly into the channels of swift rivers, scarcely one of their wedged and interlacing boulders has moved since the day of their creation; and though mostly made up of huge blocks of granite, many of them from ten to fifty feet cube, weighing thousands of tons with only a few small chips, trees and shrubs make out to live and thrive on them and even delicate herbaceous plants – *Draperia*, *Collomia*, *Zauschneria*, etc., soothing and coloring their wild rugged slopes with gardens and groves.

I was long in doubt on some points concerning the origin of those taluses. Plainly enough they were derived from the cliffs above them, because they are of the size of scars on the wall, the rough angular surface of which contrasts with the rounded, glaciated, unfractured parts. It was plain, too, that instead of being made up of material slowly and gradually weathered from the cliffs like ordinary taluses, almost every one of them had been formed suddenly in a single avalanche, and had not been increased in size during the last three or four centuries, for trees three or four hundred years old are growing on them, some standing at the top close to the wall without a bruise or broken branch, showing that scarcely a single boulder had ever fallen among them. Furthermore, all these taluses throughout the Range seemed by the trees and lichens growing on them to be of the same age. All the phenomena thus pointed straight to a grand ancient earthquake. But for years I left the question open, and went on from canyon to canyon, observing again and again; measuring the heights of taluses throughout the Range on both flanks, and the variations in the angles of their surface slopes; studying the way their boulders had been assorted and related and brought to rest, and their correspondence in size with the cleavage joints of the cliffs from whence they were derived, cautious about making up my mind. But at last all doubt as to their formation vanished.

At half-past two o'clock of a moonlit morning in March, I was awakened by a tremendous earthquake, and though I had never before enjoyed a storm of this sort, the strange thrilling motion could not be mistaken, and I ran out of my cabin, both glad and frightened, shouting, 'A noble earthquake! A noble earthquake!' feeling sure I was going to learn something. The shocks were so violent and varied, and succeeded one another so closely, that I had to balance myself carefully in walking as if on the deck of a ship among waves, and it seemed impossible that the high cliffs of the Valley could escape being shattered. In particular, I feared that the sheer-fronted Sentinel Rock, towering above my cabin, would be shaken down, and I took shelter back of a large yellow pine, hoping that it might protect me from at least the smaller outbounding boulders. For a minute or two the shocks became more and more violent – flashing horizontal thrusts mixed with a few twists and battering, explosive, upheaving jolts – as if Nature were wrecking her Yosemite temple, and getting ready to build a still better one.

I was now convinced before a single boulder had fallen that earthquakes were the talus-makers and positive proof soon came. It was a calm moonlight night, and no sound was heard for the first minute or so, save low, muffled, underground, bubbling rumblings, and the whispering and rustling of the agitated trees, as if Nature were holding her breath. Then, suddenly, out of the strange silence and strange motion there came a tremendous roar. The Eagle Rock on the south wall, about half a mile up the Valley, gave way and I saw it falling in thousands of the great boulders I had so long been studying, pouring to the Valley floor in a free curve luminous from friction, making a terribly sublime spectacle – an arc of glowing, passionate fire, fifteen hundred feet span, as true in form and as serene in beauty as a rainbow in the midst of the stupendous, roaring rock-storm. The sound was so tremendously deep and broad and earnest, the whole earth like a living creature seemed to have at last found a voice and to be calling to her sister planets. In trying to tell something of the size of this awful sound it seems to me that if all the thunder of all the storms had ever heard were condensed into one roar it would not equal this rock-roar at the birth of a mountain talus. Think, then, of the roar that arose to heaven at the simultaneous birth of all the thousands of ancient canyon-taluses throughout the length and breadth of the Range!

The first severe shocks were soon over, and eager to examine the new-born talus I ran up the Valley in the moonlight and climbed upon it before the huge blocks, after their fiery flight, had come to complete rest. They were slowly settling into their places, chafing, grating against one another, groaning, and whispering; but no motion was visible except in a stream of small fragments pattering down the face of the cliff. A cloud of dust particles, lighted by the moon, floated out across the whole breadth of the Valley, forming a ceiling that lasted until after sunrise, and the air was filled with the odor of crushed Douglas spruces from a grove that had been mowed down and mashed like weeds.

After the ground began to calm I ran across the meadow to the river to see in what direction it was flowing and was glad to find that *down* the Valley was still down. Its waters were muddy from portions of its banks having given way, but it was flowing around its curves and over its ripples and shallows with ordinary tones and gestures. The mud would soon be cleared away and the raw slips on the banks would be the only visible record of the shaking it suffered.

The Upper Yosemite Fall, glowing white in the moonlight, seemed to know nothing of the earthquake, manifesting no change in form or voice, as far as I could see or hear.

After a second startling shock, about half-past three o'clock, the ground continued to tremble gently, and smooth, hollow rumbling sounds, not always distinguishable from the rounded, bumping, explosive tones of the falls, came from deep in the mountains in a northern direction.

The few Indians fled from their huts to the middle of the Valley, fearing that angry spirits were trying to kill them; and, as I afterward learned, most of the Yosemite tribe, who were spending the winter at their village on Bull Creek forty miles away, were so terrified that they ran into the river and washed themselves – getting themselves clean enough to say their prayers, I suppose, or to die. I asked Dick, one of the Indians with whom I was acquainted, 'What made the ground shake and jump so much?' He only shook his head and said, 'No good. No good,' and looked appealingly to me to give him hope that his life was to be spared.

In the morning I found the few white settlers assembled in front of the old Hutchings Hotel comparing notes and meditating light to the lowlands, seemingly as sorely frightened as the Indians. Shortly after sunrise a low, blunt, muffled rumbling, like distant thunder, was followed by another series of shocks, which, though not nearly so severe as the first, made the cliffs and domes tremble like jelly, and the big pines and oaks thrill and swish and wave their branches with startling effect. Then the talkers were suddenly hushed, and the solemnity on their faces was sublime. One in particular of these winter neighbors, a somewhat speculative thinker with whom I had openly conversed, was a firm believer in the cataclysmic origin of the Valley; and I now jokingly remarked that his wild tumble-down-and-engulfment hypothesis might soon be proved, since these underground rumblings and shakings might be the forerunners of another Yosemite-making cataclysm, which would perhaps double the depth of the Valley by swallowing the floor, leaving the ends of the roads and trails dangling three or four thousand feet in the air. Just then came the third series of shocks, and it was fine to see how awfully silent and solemn he became. His belief in the existence of a mysterious abyss, into which the suspended floor of the Valley and all the domes and battlements of the walls might at any moment go roaring down, mightily troubled him. To diminish his fears and laugh him into something like reasonable faith, I said, 'Come, cheer up; smile a little and clap your hands, now that kind Mother Earth is trotting us on her knee to amuse us and make us good.' But the well-meant joke seemed irreverent and utterly failed, as if only prayerful terror could rightly belong to the wild beauty-making business. Even after all the heavier shocks were over I could do nothing to reassure him, on the contrary, he handed me the keys of his little store to keep, saying that with a companion of like mind he was going to the lowlands to stay until the fate of poor, trembling Yosemite was settled. In vain I rallied them on their fears, calling attention to the strength of the granite walls of our Valley home, the very best and solidest masonry in the world, and less likely to collapse and sink than the sedimentary lowlands to which they were looking for safety; and saying that in any case they sometime would have to die, and so grand a burial was not to be slighted. But they were too seriously panic-stricken to get comfort from anything I could say.

During the third severe shock the trees were so violently shaken that the birds flew out with frightened cries. In particular, I noticed two robins flying in terror from a leafless oak, the branches of which swished and quivered as if struck by a heavy battering-ram. Exceedingly interesting were the flashing and quivering of the elastic needles of the pines in the sunlight and the waving up and down of the branches while the trunks stood rigid. There was no swaying, waving or swirling as in wind-storms, but quick, quivering jerks, and at times the heavy tasseled branches moved as if they had all been pressed down against the trunk and suddenly let go, to spring up and vibrate until they came to rest again. Only the owls seemed to be undisturbed. Before the rumbling echoes had died away a hollow-voiced owl began to hoot in philosophical tranquility from near the edge of the new talus as if nothing extraordinary had occurred, although, perhaps, he was curious to know what all the noise was about. His 'hoot-too-hoot-too-whoo' might have meant, 'what's a' the steer, kimmer?'

It was long before the Valley found perfect rest. The rocks trembled more or less every day for over two months, and I kept a bucket of water on my table to learn what I could of the movements. The blunt thunder in the depths of the mountains was usually followed by sudden jarring, horizontal thrusts from the northward, often succeeded by twisting, upjolting movements. More than a month after the first great shock, when I was standing on a fallen tree up the Valley near Lamon's winter cabin, I heard a distinct bubbling thunder from the direction of Tenaya Canyon Carlo, a large intelligent St Bernard dog standing beside me seemed greatly astonished, and looked intently in that direction with mouth open and uttered a low *Wouf!* as if saying, 'What's that?' He must have known that it was not thunder, though like it. The air was perfectly still, not the faintest breath of wind perceptible, and a fine, mellow, sunny hush pervaded everything, in the midst of which came that subterranean thunder. Then, while we gazed and listened, came the corresponding shocks, distinct as if some mighty hand had shaken the ground. After the sharp horizontal jars died away, they were followed by a gentle rocking and undulating of the ground so distinct that Carlo looked at the log on which he was standing to see who was shaking it. It was the season of flooded meadows and the pools about me, calm as sheets of glass, were suddenly thrown into low ruffling waves.

Judging by its effects, this Yosemite, or Inyo earthquake, as it is sometimes called, was gentle as compared with the one that gave rise to the grand talus system of the Range and did so much for the canyon scenery. Nature, usually so deliberate in her operations, then created, as we have seen, a new set of features, simply by giving the mountains a shake – changing not only the high peaks and cliffs, but the streams. As soon as these rock avalanches fell the streams began to sing new songs; for in many places thousands of boulders were hurled into their channels, roughening and half-damming them, compelling the waters to surge and roar in rapids where before they glided smoothly. Some of the streams were completely dammed; driftwood, leaves, etc., gradually filling the interstices between the boulders, thus giving rise to lakes and level reaches; and these again, after being gradually filled in, were changed to meadows, through which the streams are now silently meandering; while at the same time some of the taluses took the places of old meadows and groves. Thus rough places were made smooth, and smooth places rough. But, on the whole, by what at first sight seemed pure confounded confusion and ruin, the landscapes were enriched; for gradually every talus was covered with groves and gardens, and made a finely proportioned and ornamental base for the cliffs. In this work of beauty, every boulder is prepared and measured and put in its place more thoughtfully than are the stones of temples. If for a moment you are inclined to regard these taluses as mere draggled, chaotic dumps, climb to the top of one of them, and run down without any haggling, puttering hesitation, boldly jumping from boulder to boulder with even speed. You will then find your feet playing a tune, and quickly discover the music and poetry of these magnificent rock piles – a fine lesson; and all Nature's wildness tells the same story – the shocks and outbursts of earthquakes, volcanoes, geysers, roaring, thundering waves and floods, the silent uprush of sap in plants, storms of every sort – each and all are the orderly beauty-making love-beats of Nature's heart.

Chapter 7
THE BIG TREES

Between the heavy pine and silver fir zones towers the Big Tree (*Sequoia gigantea*), the king of all the conifers in the world, 'the noblest of the noble race.' The groves nearest Yosemite Valley are about twenty miles to the westward and southward and are called the Tuolumne, Merced and Mariposa groves. It extends, a widely interrupted belt, from a very small grove on the middle fork of the American River to the head of Deer Creek, a distance of about 260 miles, its northern limit being near the thirty-ninth parallel, the southern a little below the thirty-sixth. The elevation of the belt above the sea varies from about 5000 to 8000 feet. From the American River to Kings River the species occurs only in small isolated groups so sparsely distributed along the belt that three of the gaps in it are from forty to sixty miles wide. But from Kings River south-ward the sequoia is not restricted to mere groves but extends across the wide rugged basins of the Kaweah and Tule Rivers in noble forests, a distance of nearly seventy miles, the continuity of this part of the belt being broken only by the main canyons. The Fresno, the largest of the northern groves, has an area of three or four square miles, a short distance to the southward of the famous Mariposa grove. Along the south rim of the canyon of the south fork of Kings River there is a majestic sequoia forest about six miles long by two wide. This is the northernmost group that may fairly be called a forest. Descending the divide between the Kings and Kaweah Rivers you come to the grand forests that form the main continuous portion of the belt. Southward the giants become more and more irrepressibly exuberant, heaving their massive crowns into the sky from every ridge and slope, waving onward in graceful compliance with the complicated topography of the region. The finest of the Kaweah section of the belt is on the broad ridge between Marble Creek and the middle fork, and is called the Giant Forest. It extends from the granite headlands, overlooking the hot San Joaquin plains, to within a few miles of the cool glacial fountains of the summit peaks. The extreme upper limit of the belt is reached between the middle and south forks of the Kaweah at a height of 8400 feet, but the finest block of big tree forests in the entire belt is on the north fork of Tule River, and is included in the Sequoia National Park.

In the northern groves there are comparatively few young trees or saplings. But here for every old storm-beaten giant there are many in their prime and for each of these a crowd of hopeful young trees and saplings, growing vigorously on moraines, rocky edges, along water courses and meadows. But though the area occupied by the big tree increases so greatly from north to south, there is no marked increase in the size of the trees. The height of 275 feet or thereabouts and a diameter of about twenty feet, four feet from the ground is, perhaps, about the average size of what may be called full-grown trees, where they are favorably located. The specimens twenty-five feet in diameter are not very rare and a few are nearly three hundred feet high. In the Calaveras grove there are four trees over 300 feet in height, the tallest of which as measured by the Geological Survey is 325 feet. The very largest that I have yet met in the course of my explorations is a majestic old fire-scarred monument in the Kings River forest. It is thirty-five feet and eight inches in diameter inside the bark, four feet above the ground. It is burned half through, and I spent a day in clearing away the charred surface with a sharp axe and counting the annual wood-rings with the aid of a pocket lens. I succeeded in laying bare a section all the way from the outside to the heart and counted a little over four thousand rings, showing that this tree was in its prime about twenty-seven feet in diameter at the beginning of the Christian era. No other tree in the world, as far as I know, has looked down on so many centuries as the sequoia or opens so many impressive and suggestive views into history. Under the most favorable conditions these giants probably live 5000 years or more though few of even the larger trees are half as old. The age of one that was felled in Calaveras grove, for the sake of having its stump for a dancing-floor, was about 1300 years, and its diameter measured across the stump twenty-four feet inside the bark. Another that was felled in the Kings River forest was about the same size but nearly a thousand years older (2200 years), though not a very old-looking tree.

So harmonious and finely balanced are even the mightiest of these monarchs in all their proportions that there is never anything overgrown or monstrous about them. Seeing them for the first time you are more impressed with their beauty than their size, their grandeur being in great part invisible; but sooner or later it becomes manifest to the loving eye, stealing slowly on the senses like the grandeur of Niagara or of the Yosemite Domes. When you approach them and walk around them you begin to wonder at their colossal size and try to measure them. They bulge considerably at the base, but not more than is required for beauty and safety and the only reason that this bulging seems in some cases excessive is that only a comparatively small section is seen in near views. One that I measured in the Kings River forest was twenty-five feet in diameter at the ground and ten feet in diameter 220 feet above the ground showing the fineness of the taper of the trunk as a whole. No description can give anything like an adequate idea of their singular majesty, much less of their beauty. Except the sugar pine, most of their neighbors with pointed tops seem ever trying to go higher, while the big tree, soaring above them all, seems satisfied. Its grand domed head seems to be poised about as lightly as a cloud, giving no impression of seeking to rise higher. Only when it is young does it show like other conifers a heavenward yearning, sharply aspiring with a long quick-growing top. Indeed, the whole tree for the first century or two, or until it is a hundred or one hundred and fifty feet high, is arrowhead in form, and, compared with the solemn rigidity of age, seems as sensitive to the wind as a squirrel's tail. As it grows older, the lower branches are gradually dropped and the upper ones thinned out until comparatively few are left. These, however, are developed to a great size, divide again and again and terminate in bossy, rounded masses of leafy branch-lets, while the head becomes dome-shaped, and is the first to feel the touch of the rosy beams of the morning, the last to bid the sun good night. Perfect specimens, unhurt by running fires or lightning, are singularly regular and symmetrical in general form though not in the least conventionalized, for they show extraordinary variety in the unity and harmony of their general outline. The immensely strong, stately shafts are free of limbs for one hundred end fifty feet or so. The large limbs reach out with equal boldness a every direction, showing no weather side, and no other tree has foliage so densely massed, so finely molded in outline and so perfectly subordinate to an ideal type. A particularly knotty, angular, ungovernable-looking branch, from five to seven or eight feet in diameter and perhaps a thousand years old, may occasionally be seen pushing out from the trunk as if determined to break across the bounds of the regular curve, but like all the others it dissolves in bosses of branchlets and sprays as soon as the general outline is approached. Except in picturesque old age, after being struck by lightning or broken by thousands of snow-storms, the regularity of forms is one of their most distinguishing characteristics. Another is the simple beauty of the trunk and its great thickness as compared with its height and the width of the branches, which makes them look more like finely modeled and sculptured architectural columns than the stems of trees, while the great limbs look like rafters, supporting the magnificent dome-head. But though so consummately beautiful, the big tree always seems unfamiliar, with peculiar physiognomy, awfully solemn and earnest; yet with all its strangeness it impresses us as being more at home than any of its neighbors, holding the best right to the ground as the oldest strongest inhabitant. One soon becomes acquainted with new species of pine and fir and spruce as with friendly people, shaking their outstretched branches like shaking hands and fondling their little ones, while the venerable aboriginal sequoia, ancient of other days, keeps you at a distance, looking as strange in aspect and behavior among its neighbor trees as would the mastodon among the homely bears and deers. Only the Sierra juniper is at all like it, standing rigid and unconquerable on glacier pavements for thousands of years, grim and silent, with an air of antiquity about as pronounced as that of the sequoia.

The bark of the largest trees is from one to two feet thick, rich cinnamon brown, purplish on young trees, forming magnificent masses of color with the underbrush. Toward the end of winter the trees are in bloom, while the snow is still eight or ten feet deep. The female flowers are about three-eighths of an inch long, pale green, and grow in countless thousands on the ends of sprays. The male are still more abundant, pale yellow, a fourth of an inch long and when the pollen is ripe they color the whole tree and dust the sir and the ground. The cones are bright grass-green in color, about two and a half inches long, one and a half wide, made up of thirty or forty strong, closely packed, rhomboidal scales, with four to eight seeds at the base of each. The seeds are wonderfully small and light, being only from an eighth to a fourth of an inch long and wide, including a filmy surrounding wing, which causes them to glint and waver in falling and enables the wind to carry them considerable distances. Unless harvested by the squirrels, the cones discharge their seed and remain on the tree for many years. In fruitful seasons the trees are fairly laden. On two small branches one and a half and two inches in diameter I counted 480 cones. No other California conifer produces nearly so many seeds, except, perhaps, the other sequoia, the Redwood of the Coast Mountains. Millions are ripened annually by a single tree, and in a fruitful year the product of one of the northern groves would be enough to plant all the mountain ranges in the world.

As soon as any accident happens to the crown, such as being smashed off by lightning, the branches beneath the wound, no matter how situated, seem to be excited, like a colony of bees that have lost their queen, and become anxious to repair the damage. Limbs that have grown outward for centuries at right angles to the trunk begin to turn upward to assist in making a new crown, each speedily assuming the special form of true summits. Even in the case of mere stumps, burned half through, some mere ornamental tuft will try to go aloft and do its best as a leader in forming a new head. Groups of two or three are often found standing close together, the seeds from which they sprang having probably grown on ground cleared for their reception by the fall of a large tree of a former generation. They are called 'loving couples,' 'three graces,' etc. When these trees are young they are seen to stand twenty or thirty feet apart, by the time they are full-grown their trunks will touch and crowd against each other and in some cases even appear as one.

It is generally believed that the sequoia was once far more widely distributed over the Sierra; but after long and careful study I have come to the conclusion that it never was, at least since the close of the glacial period, because a diligent search along the margins of the groves, and in the gaps between fails to reveal a single trace of its previous existence beyond its present bounds. Notwithstanding, I feel confident that if every sequoia in the Range were to die today, numerous monuments of their existence would remain, of so imperishable a nature as to be available for the student more than ten thousand years hence.

In the first place, no species of coniferous tree in the Range keeps its members so well together as the sequoia; a mile is, perhaps, the greatest distance of any straggler from the main body, and all of those stragglers that have come under my observation are young, instead of old monumental trees, relics of a more extended growth.

Again, the great trunks of the sequoia last for centuries after they fall. I have a specimen block of sequoia wood, cut from a fallen tree, which is hardly distinguishable from a similar section cut from a living tree, although the one cut from the fallen trunk has certainly lain on the damp forest floor more than 380 years, probably thrice as long. The time-measure in the case is simply this: When the ponderous trunk to which the old vestige belonged fell, it sunk itself into the ground, thus making a long, straight ditch, and in the middle of this ditch a silver fir four feet in diameter and 380 years old was growing, as I determined by cutting it half through and counting the rings, thus demonstrating that the remnant of the trunk that made the ditch has lain on the ground *more* than 380 years. For it is evident that, to find the whole time, we must add to the 380 years the time that the vanished portion of the trunk lay in the ditch before being burned out of the way, plus the time that passed before the seed from which the monumental fir sprang fell into the prepared soil and took root. Now, because sequoia trunks are never wholly consumed in one forest fire, and those fires recur only at considerable intervals, and because sequoia ditches after being cleared are often left unplanted for centuries, it becomes evident that the trunk-remnant in question may probably have lain a thousand years or more. And this instance is by no means a late one.

Again, admitting that upon those areas supposed to have been once covered with sequoia forests, every tree may have fallen, and every trunk may have been burned or buried, leaving not a remnant, many of the ditches made by the fall of the ponderous trunks, and the bowls made by their upturning roots, would remain patent for thousands of years after the last vestige of the trunks that made them had vanished. Much of this ditch-writing would no doubt be quickly effaced by the flood-action of overflowing streams and rain-washing; but no inconsiderable portion would remain enduringly engraved on ridge-tops beyond such destructive action; for, where all the conditions are favorable, it is almost imperishable. Now these historic ditches and root-bowls occur in all the present sequoia groves and forests, but, as far as I have observed, not the faintest vestige of one presents itself outside of them.

We therefore conclude that the area covered by sequoia has not been diminished during the last eight or ten thousand years, and probably not at all in post-glacial time. Nevertheless, the questions may be asked: Is the species verging toward extinction? What are its relations to climate, soil, and associated trees?

All the phenomena bearing on these questions also throw light, as we shall endeavor to show, upon the peculiar distribution of the species, and sustain the conclusion already arrived at as to the question of former extension. In the northern groups, as we have seen, there are few young trees or saplings growing up around the old ones to perpetuate the race, and inasmuch as those aged sequoias, so nearly childless, are the only ones commonly known the species, to most observers, seems doomed to speedy extinction, as being nothing more than an expiring remnant, vanquished in the so-called struggle for life by pines and firs that have driven it into its last strongholds in moist glens where the climate is supposed to be exceptionally favorable. But the story told by the majestic continuous forests of the south creates a very different impression. No tree in the forest is more enduringly established in concordance with both climate and soil. It grows heartily everywhere – on moraines, rocky ledges, along watercourses, and in the deep, moist alluvium of meadows with, as we have seen, a multitude of seedlings and saplings crowding up around the aged, abundantly able to maintain the forest in prime vigor. So that if all the trees of any section of the main sequoia forest were ranged together according to age, a very promising curve would be presented, all the way up from last year's seedlings to giants, and with the young and middle-aged portion of the curve many times longer than the old portion. Even as far north as the Fresno, I counted 536 saplings and seedlings, growing promisingly upon a landslip not exceeding two acres in area. This soil-bed was about seven years old, and had been seeded almost simultaneously by pines, firs, libocedrus, and sequoia, presenting a simple and instructive illustration of the struggle for life among the rival species; and it was interesting to note that the conditions thus far affecting them have enabled the young sequoias to gain a marked advantage. Toward the south where the sequoia becomes most exuberant and numerous, the rival trees become less so; and where they mix with sequoias they grow up beneath them like slender grasses among stalks of Indian corn. Upon a bed of sandy floodsoil I counted ninety-four sequoias, from one to twelve feet high, on a patch of ground once occupied by four large sugar pines which lay crumbling beneath them – an instance of conditions which have enabled sequoias to crowd out the pines. I also noted eighty-six vigorous saplings upon a piece of fresh ground prepared for their reception by fire. Thus fire, the great destroyer of the sequoia, also furnishes the bare ground required for its growth from the seed. Fresh ground is, however, furnished in sufficient quantities for the renewal of the forests without the aid of fire – by the fall of old trees. The soil is thus upturned and mellowed, and many trees are planted for every one that falls.

It is constantly asserted in a vague way that the Sierra was vastly wetter than now, and that the increasing drought will of itself extinguish the sequoia, leaving its ground to other trees supposed capable of flourishing in a drier climate. But that the sequoia can and does grow on as dry ground as any of its present rivals is manifest in a thousand places. 'Why, then,' it will be asked, 'are sequoias always found only in well-watered places?' Simply because a growth of sequoias creates those streams. The thirsty mountaineer knows well that in every sequoia grove he will find running water, but it is a mistake to suppose that the water is the cause of the grove being there; on the contrary, the grove is the cause of the water being there. Drain off the water and the trees will remain, but cut off the trees, and the streams will vanish. Never was cause more completely mistaken for effect than in the case of these related phenomena of sequoia woods and perennial streams.

When attention is called to the method of sequoia stream-making, it will be apprehended at once. The roots of this immense tree fill the ground, forming a thick sponge that absorbs and holds back the rain and melting snow, only allowing it to ooze and flow gently. Indeed, every fallen leaf and rootlet, as well as long clasping root, and prostrate trunk, may be regarded as a dam hoarding the bounty of storm-clouds, and dispensing it as blessings all through the summer, instead of allowing it to go headlong in short-lived floods.

Since, then, it is a fact that thousands of sequoias are growing thriftily on what is termed dry ground, and even clinging like mountain pines to rifts in granite precipices, and since it has also been shown that the extra moisture found in connection with the denser growths is an effect of their presence, instead of a cause of their presence, then the notions as to the former extension of the species and its near approach to extinction, based upon its supposed dependence on greater moisture, are seen to be erroneous.

The decrease in rain and snowfall since the close of the glacial period in the Sierra is much less than is commonly guessed. The highest post-glacial water-marks are well pre-served in all the upper river channels, and they are not greatly higher than the spring flood-marks of the present; showing conclusively that no extraordinary decrease has taken place in the volume of the upper tributaries of post-glacial Sierra streams since they came into existence. But, in the meantime, eliminating all this complicated question of climatic change, the plain fact remains that the present rain and snowfall is abundantly sufficient for the luxuriant growth of sequoia forests. Indeed, all my observations tend to show that in a prolonged drought the sugar pines and firs would perish before the sequoia, not alone because of the greater longevity of individual trees, but because the species can endure more drought, and make the most of whatever moisture falls.

Again, if the restriction and irregular distribution of the species be interpreted as a result of the desiccation of the Range, then instead of increasing as it does in individuals toward the south where the rainfall is less, it should diminish. If, then, the peculiar distribution of sequoia has not been governed by superior conditions of soil as to fertility or moisture, by what has it been governed?

In the course of my studies I observed that the northern groves, the only ones I was at first acquainted with, were located on just those portions of the general forest soil-belt that were first laid bare toward the close of the glacial period when the ice-sheet began to break up into individual glaciers. And while searching the wide basin of the San Joaquin, and trying to account for the absence of sequoia where every condition seemed favorable for its growth, it occurred to me that this remarkable gap in the sequoia belt fifty miles wide is located exactly in the basin of the vast, ancient *mer de glace* of the San Joaquin and Kings River basins which poured its frozen floods to the plain through this gap as its channel. I then perceived that the next great gap in the belt to the northward, forty miles wide, extending between the Calaveras and Tuolumne groves, occurs in the basin of the great ancient mer de glace of the Tuolumne and Stanislaus basins; and that the smaller gap between the Merced and Mariposa groves occurs in the basin of the smaller glacier of the Merced. The wider the ancient glacier, the wider the corresponding gap in the sequoia belt.

Finally, pursuing my investigations across the basins of the Kaweah and Tule, I discovered that the sequoia belt attained its greatest development just where, owing to the topographical peculiarities of the region, the ground had been best protected from the main ice-rivers that continued to pour past from the summit fountains long after the smaller local glaciers had been melted.

Taking now a general view of the belt, beginning at the south we see that the majestic ancient glaciers were shed off right and left down the valleys of Kern and Kings Rivers by the lofty protective spurs outspread embracingly above the warm sequoia-filled basins of the Kaweah and Tule. Then, next northward, occurs the wide sequoia-less channel, or basin of the ancient San Joaquin and sings River mer de glace; then the warm, protected spots of Fresno and Mariposa groves; then the sequoia-less channel of the ancient Merced glacier; next the warm, sheltered ground of the Merced and Tuolumne groves; then the sequoia-less channel of the grand ancient mer de glace of the Tuolumne and Stanislaus; then the warm old ground of the Calaveras and Stanislaus groves. It appears, therefore, that just where, at a certain period in the history of the Sierra, the glaciers were not, there the sequoia is, and just where the glaciers were, there the sequoia is not.

But although all the observed phenomena bearing on the post-glacial history of this colossal tree point to the conclusion that it never was more widely distributed on the Sierra since the close of the glacial epoch; that its present forests are scarcely past prime, if, indeed, they have reached prime; that the post-glacial day of the species is probably not half done; yet, when from a wider outlook the vast antiquity of the genus is considered, and its ancient richness in species and individuals – comparing our Sierra Giant and *Sequoia sempervirens* of the Coast Range, the only other living species of sequoia, with the twelve fossil species already discovered and described by Heer and Lesquereux, some of which flourished over vast areas in the Arctic regions and in Europe and our own territories, during tertiary and cretaceous times – then, indeed, it becomes plain that our two surviving species, restricted to narrow belts within the limits of California, are mere remnants of the genus, both as to species and individuals, and that they may be verging to extinction. But the verge of a period beginning in cretaceous times may have a breadth of tens of thousands of years, not to mention the possible existence of conditions calculated to multiply and re-extend both species and individuals.

There is no absolute limit to the existence of any tree. Death is due to accidents, not, as that of animals, to the wearing out of organs. Only the leaves die of old age. Their fall is foretold in their structure; but the leaves are renewed every year, and so also are the essential organs wood, roots, bark, buds. Most of the Sierra trees die of disease, insects, fungi, etc., but nothing hurts the big tree. I never saw one that was sick or showed the slightest sign of decay. Barring accidents, it seems to be immortal. It is a curious fact that all the very old sequoias had lost their heads by lightning strokes. 'All things come to him who waits.' But of all living things, sequoia is perhaps the only one able to wait long enough to make sure of being struck by lightning.

So far as I am able to see at present only fire and the axe threaten the existence of these noblest of God's trees. In Nature's keeping they are safe, but through the agency of man destruction is making rapid progress, while in the work of protection only a good beginning has been made. The Fresno grove, the Tuolumne, Merced and Mariposa groves are under the protection of the Federal Government in the Yosemite National Park. So are the General Grant and Sequoia National Parks; the latter, established twenty-one years ago, has an area of 240 square miles and is efficiently guarded by a troop of cavalry under the direction of the Secretary of the Interior; so also are the small General Grant National Park, established at the same time with an area of four square miles, and the Mariposa grove, about the same size and the small Merced and Tuolumne group. Perhaps more than half of all the big trees have been thoughtlessly sold and are now in the hands of speculators and mill men. It appears, therefore, that far the largest and important section of protected big trees is in the great Sequoia National Park, now easily accessible by rail to Lemon Cove and thence by a good stage road into the giant forest of the Kaweah and thence by rail to other parts of the park; but large as it is it should be made much larger. Its natural eastern boundary is the High Sierra and the northern and southern boundaries are the Kings and Kern Rivers. Thus could be included the sublime scenery on the headwaters of these rivers and perhaps nine-tenths of all the big trees in existence. All private claims within these bounds should be gradually extinguished by purchase by the Government. The big tree, leaving all its higher uses out of the count, is a tree of life to the dwellers of the plain dependent on irrigation, a never-failing spring, sending living waters to the lowland. For every grove cut down a stream is dried up. Therefore all California is crying, 'Save the trees of the fountains.' Nor, judging by the signs of the times, is it likely that the cry will cease until the salvation of all that is left of *Sequoia gigantea* is made sure.

Chapter 10
THE SOUTH DOME

With the exception of a few spires and pinnacles, the South Dome is the only rock about the Valley that is strictly inaccessible without artificial means, and its inaccessibility is expressed in severe terms. Nevertheless many a mountaineer, gazing admiringly, tried hard to invent a way to the top of its noble crown – all in vain, until in the year 1875, George Anderson, an indomitable Scotchman, undertook the adventure. The side facing Tenaya Canyon is an absolutely vertical precipice from the summit to a depth of about 1600 feet, and on the opposite side it is nearly vertical for about as great a depth. The southwest side presents a very steep and finely drawn curve from the top down a thousand feet or more, while on the northeast, where it is united with the Clouds' Rest Ridge, one may easily reach a point called the Saddle, about seven hundred feet below the summit. From the Saddle the Dome rises in a graceful curve a few degrees too steep for unaided climbing, besides being defended by overleaning ends of the concentric dome layers of the granite.

A year or two before Anderson gained the summit, John Conway, the master trail-builder of the Valley, and his little sons, who climbed smooth rocks like lizards, made a bold effort to reach the top by climbing barefooted up the grand curve with a rope which they fastened at irregular intervals by means of eye-bolts driven into joints of the rock. But finding that the upper part would require laborious drilling, they abandoned the attempt, glad to escape from the dangerous position they had reached, some 300 feet above the Saddle. Anderson began with Conway's old rope, which had been left in place, and resolutely drilled his way to the top, inserting eye-bolts five to six feet apart, and making his rope fast to each in succession, resting his feet on the last bolt while he drilled a hole for the next above. Occasionally some irregularity in the curve, or slight foothold, would enable him to climb a few feet without a rope, which he would pass and begin drilling again, and thus the whole work was accomplished in a few days. From this slender beginning he proposed to construct a substantial stairway which he hoped to complete in time for the next year's travel, but while busy getting out timber for his stairway and dreaming of the wealth he hoped to gain from tolls, he was taken sick and died all alone in his little cabin.

On the 10th of November, after returning from a visit to Mount Shasta, a month or two after Anderson had gained the summit, I made haste to the Dome, not only for the pleasure of climbing, but to see what I might learn. The first winter storm-clouds had blossomed and the mountains and all the high points about the Valley were mantled in fresh snow. I was, therefore, a little apprehensive of danger from the slipperiness of the rope and the rock. Anderson himself tried to prevent me from making the attempt, refusing to believe that anyone could climb his rope in the now-muffled condition in which it then was. Moreover, the sky was overcast and solemn snow-clouds began to curl around the summit, and my late experiences on icy Shasta came to mind. But reflecting that I had matches in my pocket, and that a little firewood might be found, I concluded that in case of a storm the night could be spent on the Dome without suffering anything worth minding, no matter what the clouds might bring forth. I therefore pushed on and gained the top.

It was one of those brooding, changeful days that come between Indian summer and winter, when the leaf colors have grown dim and the clouds come and go among the cliffs like living creatures looking for work: now hovering aloft, now caressing rugged rock-brows with great gentleness, or, wandering afar over the tops of the forests, touching the spires of fir and pine with their soft silken fringes as if trying to tell the glad news of the coming of snow.

The first view was perfectly glorious. A massive cloud of pure pearl luster, apparently as fixed and calm as the meadows and groves in the shadow beneath it, was arched across the Valley from wall to wall, one end resting on the grand abutment of El Capitan, the other on Cathedral Rock. A little later, as I stood on the tremendous verge overlooking Mirror Lake, a flock of smaller clouds, white as snow, came from the north, trailing their downy skirts over the dark forests, and entered the Valley with solemn god-like gestures through Indian Canyon and over the North Dome and Royal Arches, moving swiftly, yet with majestic deliberation. On they came, nearer and nearer, gathering and massing beneath my feet and filling the Tenaya Canyon. Then the sun shone free, lighting the pearly gray surface of the cloud-like sea and making it glow. Gazing, admiring, I was startled to see for the first time the rare optical phenomenon of the 'Specter of the Brocken.' My shadow, clearly outlined, about half a mile long, lay upon this glorious white surface with startling effect. I walked back and forth, waved my arms and struck all sorts of attitudes, to see every slightest movement enormously exaggerated. Considering that I have looked down so many times from mountain tops on seas of all sorts of clouds, it seems strange that I should have seen the 'Brocken Specter' only this once. A grander surface and a grander stand-point, however, could hardly have been found in all the Sierra.

After this grand show the cloud-sea rose higher, wreathing the Dome, and for a short time submerging it, making darkness like night, and I began to think of looking for a camp ground in a cluster of dwarf pines. But soon the sun shone free again, the clouds, sinking lower and lower, gradually vanished, leaving the Valley with its Indian-summer colors apparently refreshed, while to the eastward the summit-peaks, clad in new snow, towered along the horizon in glorious array.

Though apparently it is perfectly bald, there are four clumps of pines growing on the summit, representing three species, *Pinus albicaulis*, *P. contorta* and *P. ponderosa*, var. *Jeffreyi* – all three, of course, repressed and storm-beaten. The alpine spiraea grows here also and blossoms profusely with potentilla, erigeron, eriogonum, pentstemon, solidago, and an interesting species of onion, and four or five species of grasses and sedges. None of these differs in any respect from those of other summits of the same height, excepting the curious little narrow-leaved, waxen-bulbed onion, which I had not seen elsewhere.

Notwithstanding the enthusiastic eagerness of tourists to reach the crown of the Dome the views of the Valley from this lofty standpoint are less striking than from many other points comparatively low, chiefly on account of the foreshortening effect produced by looking down from so great a height. The North Dome is dwarfed almost beyond recognition, the grand sculpture of the Royal Arches is scarcely noticeable, and the whole range of walls on both sides seem comparatively low, especially when the Valley is flooded with noon sunshine; while the Dome itself, the most sublime feature of all the Yosemite views, is out of sight beneath one's feet. The view of Little Yosemite Valley is very fine, though inferior to one obtained from the base of the Starr King Cone, but the summit landscapes towards Mounts Ritter, Lyell, Dana, Conness, and the Merced Group, are very effective and complete.

No one has attempted to carry out Anderson's plan of making the Dome accessible. For my part I should prefer leaving it in pure wildness, though, after all, no great damage could be done by tramping over it. The surface would be strewn with tin cans and bottles, but the winter gales would blow the rubbish away. Avalanches might strip off any sort of stairway or ladder that might be built. Blue jays and Clark's crows have trodden the Dome for many a day, and so have beetles and chipmunks, and Tissiack would hardly be more 'conquered' or spoiled should man be added to her list of visitors. His louder scream and heavier scrambling would not stir a line of her countenance.

When the sublime ice-floods of the glacial period poured down the flank of the Range over what is now Yosemite Valley, they were compelled to break through a dam of domes extending across from Mount Starr King to North Dome; and as the period began to draw near a close the shallowing ice-currents were divided and the South Dome was, perhaps, the first to emerge, burnished and shining like a mirror above the surface of the icy sea; and though it has sustained the wear and tear of the elements tens of thousands of years, it yet remains a telling monument of the action of the great glaciers that brought it to light. Its entire surface is still covered with glacial hieroglyphics whose interpretation is the reward of all who devoutly study them.

Chapter 11

THE ANCIENT YOSEMITE GLACIERS: HOW THE VALLEY WAS FORMED

All California has been glaciated, the low plains and valleys as well as the mountains. Traces of an ice-sheet, thousands of feet in thickness, beneath whose heavy folds the present landscapes have been molded, may be found everywhere, though glaciers now exist only among the peaks of the High Sierra. No other mountain chain on this or any other of the continents that I have seen is so rich as the Sierra in bold, striking, well-preserved glacial monuments. Indeed, every feature is more or less tellingly glacial. Not a peak, ridge, dome, canyon, yosemite, lake-basin, stream or forest will you see that does not in some way explain the past existence and modes of action of flowing, grinding, sculpturing, soil-making, scenery-making ice. For, notwithstanding the post-glacial agents – the air, rain, snow, frost, river, avalanche, etc – have been at work upon the greater portion of the Range for tens of thousands of stormy years, each engraving its own characters more and more deeply over those of the ice, the latter are so enduring and so heavily emphasized, they still rise in sublime relief, clear and legible, through every after-inscription. The landscapes of North Greenland, Antarctica, and some of those of our own Alaska, are still being fashioned beneath a slow-crawling mantle of ice, from a quarter of a mile to probably more than a mile in thickness, presenting noble illustrations of the ancient condition of California, when its sublime scenery lay hidden in process of formation. On the Himalaya, the mountains of Norway and Switzerland, the Caucasus, and on most of those of Alaska, their ice-mantle has been melted down into separate glaciers that flow river-like through the valleys, illustrating a similar past condition in the Sierra, when every canyon and valley was the channel of an ice-stream, all of which may be easily traced back to their fountains, where some sixty-five or seventy of their topmost residual branches still linger beneath protecting mountain shadows.

The change from one to another of those glacial conditions was slow as we count time. When the great cycle of snow years, called the Glacial Period, was nearly complete in California, the ice-mantle, wasting from season to season faster than it was renewed, began to withdraw from the lowlands and gradually became shallower everywhere. Then the highest of the Sierra domes and dividing ridges, containing distinct glaciers between them, began to appear above the icy sea. These first river-like glaciers remained united in one continuous sheet toward the summit of the Range for many centuries. But as the snow-fall diminished, and the climate became milder, this upper part of the ice-sheet was also in turn separated into smaller distinct glaciers, and these again into still smaller ones, while at the same time all were growing shorter and shallower, though fluctuations of the climate now and then occurred that brought their receding ends to a standstill, or even enabled them to advance for a few tens or hundreds of years.

Meanwhile, hardy, home-seeking plants and animals, after long waiting, flocked to their appointed places, pushing bravely on higher and higher, along every sun-warmed slope, closely following the retreating ice, which, like shreds of summer clouds, at length vanished from the new-born mountains, leaving them in all their main, telling features nearly as we find them now.

Tracing the ways of glaciers, learning how Nature sculptures mountain-waves in making scenery-beauty that so mysteriously influences every human being, is glorious work.

The most striking and attractive of the glacial phenomena in the upper Yosemite region are the polished glacier pavements, because they are so beautiful, and their beauty is of so rare a kind, so unlike any portion of the loose, deeply weathered lowlands where people make homes and earn their bread. They are simply flat or gently undulating areas of hard resisting granite, which present the unchanged surface upon which with enormous pressure the ancient glaciers flowed. They are found in most perfect condition in the subalpine region, at an elevation of from eight thousand to nine thousand feet. Some are miles in extent, only slightly interrupted by spots that have given way to the weather, while the best preserved portions reflect the sunbeams like calm water or glass, and shine as if polished afresh every day, notwithstanding they have been exposed to corroding rains, dew, frost, and snow measureless thousands of years.

The attention of wandering hunters and prospectors, who see so many mountain wonders, is seldom commanded by other glacial phenomena, moraines however regular and arti-ficial-looking, canyons however deep or strangely modeled, rocks however high; but when they come to these shining pavements they stop and stare in wondering admiration, kneel again and again to examine the brightest spots, and try hard to account for their mysterious shining smoothness. They may have seen the winter avalanches of snow descending in awful majesty through the woods, scouring the rocks and sweeping away like weeds the trees that stood in their way, but conclude that this cannot be the work of avalanches, because the scratches and fine polished strife show that the agent, whatever it was, moved along the sides of high rocks and ridges and up over the tops of them as well as down their slopes. Neither can they see how water may possibly have been the agent, for they find the same strange polish upon ridges and domes thousands of feet above the reach of any conceivable flood. Of all the agents of whose work they know anything, only the wind seems capable of moving across the face of the country in the directions indicated by the scratches and grooves. The Indian name of Lake Tenaya is 'Pyweak' – the lake of shining rocks. One of the Yosemite tribe, Indian Tom, came to me and asked if I could tell him what had made the Tenaya rocks so smooth. Even dogs and horses, when first led up the mountains, study geology to this extent that they gaze wonderingly at the strange brightness of the ground and smell it, and place their feet cautiously upon it as if afraid of falling or sinking.

In the production of this admirable hard finish, the glaciers in many places flowed with a pressure of more than a thousand tons to the square yard, planing down granite, slate, and quartz alike, and bringing out the veins and crystals of the rocks with beautiful distinctness. Over large areas below the sources of the Tuolumne and Merced the granite is porphyritic;

feldspar crystals in inch or two in length in many places form the greater part of the rock, and these, when planed off level with the general surface, give rise to a beautiful mosaic on which the happy sunbeams plash and glow in passionate enthusiasm. Here lie the brightest of all the Sierra landscapes. The Range both to the north and south of this region was, perhaps, glaciated about as heavily, but because the rocks are less resisting, their polished surfaces have mostly given way to the weather, leaving only small imperfect patches. The lower remnants of the old glacial surface occur at an elevation of from 3000 to 5000 feet above the sea level, and twenty to thirty miles below the axis of the Range. The short, steeply inclined canyons of the eastern flank also contain enduring, brilliantly striated and polished rocks, but these are less magnificent than those of the broad western flank.

One of the best general views of the brightest and best of the Yosemite park landscapes that every Yosemite tourist should see, is to be had from the top of Fairview Dome, a lofty conoidal rock near Cathedral Peak that long ago I named the Tuolumne Glacier Monument, one of the most striking and best preserved of the domes. Its burnished crown is about 1500 feet above the Tuolumne Meadows and 10,000 above the sea. At first sight it seems inaccessible, though a good climber will find it may be scaled on the south side. About half-way up you will find it so steep that there is danger of slipping, but feldspar crystals, two or three inches long, of which the rock is full, having offered greater resistance to atmospheric erosion than the mass of the rock in which they are imbedded, have been brought into slight relief in some places, roughening the surface here and there, and affording helping footholds.

The summit is burnished and scored like the sides and base, the scratches and strife indicating that the mighty Tuolumne Glacier swept over it as if it were only a mere boulder in the bottom of its channel. The pressure it withstood must have been enormous. Had it been less solidly built it would have been carried away, ground into moraine fragments, like the adjacent rock in which it lay imbedded; for, great as it is, it is only a hard residual knot like the Yosemite domes, brought into relief by the removal of less resisting rock about it; an illustration of the survival of the strongest and most favorably situated.

Hardly less wonderful is the resistance it has offered to the trying mountain weather since first its crown rose above the icy sea. The whole quantity of post-glacial wear and tear it has suffered has not degraded it a hundredth of an inch, as may readily be shown by the polished portions of the surface. A few erratic boulders, nicely poised on its crown, tell an interesting story. They came from the summit-peaks twelve miles away, drifting like chips on the frozen sea, and were stranded here when the top of the monument merged from the ice, while their companions, whose positions chanced to be above the slopes of the sides where they could not find rest, were carried farther on by falling back on the shallowing ice current.

The general view from the summit consists of a sublime assemblage of ice-born rocks and mountains, long wavering ridges, meadows, lakes, and forest-covered moraines, hundreds of square miles of them. The lofty summit-peaks rise grandly along the sky to the east, the gray pillared slopes of the Hoffman Range toward the west, and a billowy sea of shining rocks like the Monument, some of them almost as high and which from their peculiar sculpture seem to be rolling westward in the middle ground, something like breaking waves. Immediately beneath you are the Big Tuolumne Meadows, smooth lawns with large breadths of woods on either side, and watered by the young Tuolumne River, rushing cool and clear from its many snow- and ice-fountains. Nearly all the upper part of the basin of the Tuolumne Glacier is in sight, one of the greatest and most influential of all the Sierra ice-rivers. Lavishly flooded by many a noble affluent from the ice-laden flanks of Mounts Dana, Lyell, McClure, Gibbs, Conness, it poured its majestic outflowing current full against the end of the Hoffman Range, which divided and deflected it to right and left, just as a river of water is divided against an island in the middle of its channel. Two distinct glaciers were thus formed, one of which flowed through the great Tuolumne Canyon and Hetch Hetchy Valley, while the other swept upward in a deep current two miles wide across the divide, five hundred feet high between the basins of the Tuolumne and Merced, into the Tenaya Basin, and thence down through the Tenaya Canyon and Yosemite.

The map-like distinctness and freshness of this glacial landscape cannot fail to excite the attention of every beholder, no matter how little of its scientific significance may be recognized. These bald, westward-leaning rocks, with their rounded backs and shoulders toward the glacier fountains of the summit-mountains, and their split, angular fronts looking in the opposite direction, explain the tremendous grinding force with which the ice-flood passed over them, and also the direction of its flow. And the mountain peaks around the sides of the upper general Tuolumne Basin, with their sharp unglaciated summits and polished rounded sides, indicate the height to which the glaciers rose; while the numerous moraines, curving and swaying in beautiful lines, mark the boundaries of the main trunk and its tributaries as they existed toward the close of the glacial winter. None of the commerical highways of the land or sea, marked with buoys and lamps, fences, and guide-boards, is so unmistakably indicated as are these broad, shining trails of the vanished Tuolumne Glacier and its far-reaching tributaries.

I should like now to offer some nearer views of a few characteristic specimens of these wonderful old ice-streams, though it is not easy to make a selection from so vast a system intimately inter-blended. The main branches of the Merced Glacier are, perhaps, best suited to our purpose, because their basins, full of telling inscriptions, are the ones most attractive and accessible to the Yosemite visitors who like to look beyond the valley walls. They number five, and may well be called Yosemite glaciers, since they were the agents Nature used in developing and fashioning the grand Valley. The names I have given them are, beginning with the northern-most, Yosemite Creek, Hoffman, Tenaya, South Lyell, and Illilouette Glaciers. These all converged in admirable poise around from northeast to southeast, welded themselves together into the main Yosemite Glacier, which, grinding gradually deeper, swept down through the Valley, receiving small tributaries on its way from the Indian, Sentinel, and Pohono Canyons; and at length flowed out of the Valley, and on down the Range in a general westerly direction. At the time that the tributaries mentioned above were well defined as to their boundaries, the upper portion of the valley walls, and the highest rocks about them, such as the Domes, the uppermost of the Three Brothers and the Sentinel, rose above the surface of the ice. But during the Valley's earlier history, all its rocks, however lofty, were buried beneath a continuous sheet, which swept on above and about them like the wind, the upper portion of the current flowing steadily, while the lower portion went mazing and swedging down in the crooked and dome-blocked canyons toward the head of the Valley.

Every glacier of the Sierra fluctuated in width and depth and length, and consequently in degree of individuality, down to the latest glacial days. It must, therefore, be borne in mind that the following description of the Yosemite glaciers applies only to their separate condition, and to that phase of their separate condition that they presented toward the close of the glacial period after most of their work was finished, and all the more telling features of the Valley and the adjacent region were brought into relief.

The comparatively level, many-fountained Yosemite Creek Glacier was about fourteen miles in length by four or five in width, and from five hundred to a thousand feet deep. Its principal tributaries, drawing their sources from the northern spurs of the Hoffman Range, at first pursued a westerly course; then, uniting with each other, and a series of short affluents from the western rim of the basin, the trunk thus formed swept around to the southward in a magnificent curve, and poured its ice over the north wall of Yosemite in cascades about two miles wide. This broad and comparatively shallow glacier formed a sort of crawling, wrinkled ice-cloud, that gradually became more regular in shape and river-like as it grew older. Encircling peaks began to overshadow its highest fountains, rock islets rose here and there amid its ebbing currents, and its picturesque banks, adorned with domes and round-backed ridges, extended in massive grandeur down to the brink of the Yosemite walls.

In the meantime the chief Hoffman tributaries, slowly receding to the shelter of the shadows covering their fountains, continued to live and work independently, spreading soil, deepening lake-basins and giving finishing touches to the sculpture in general. At length these also vanished, and the whole basin is now full of light. Forests flourish luxuriantly upon its ample moraines, lakes and meadows shine and bloom amid its polished domes, and a thousand gardens adorn the banks of its streams.

It is to the great width and even slope of the Yosemite Creek

Glacier that we owe the unrivaled height and sheerness of the Yosemite Falls. For had the positions of the ice-fountains and the structure of the rocks been such as to cause down-thrusting concentration of the Glacier as it approached the Valley, then, instead of a high vertical fall we should have had a long slanting cascade, which after all would perhaps have been as beautiful and interesting, if we only had a mind to see it so.

The short, comparatively swift-flowing Hoffman Glacier, whose fountains extend along the south slopes of the Hoffman Range, offered a striking contrast to the one just described. The erosive energy of the latter was diffused over a wide field of sunken, boulder-like domes and ridges. The Hoffman Glacier, on the contrary moved right ahead on a comparatively even surface, making a descent of nearly five thousand feet in five miles, steadily contracting and deepening its current, and finally united with the Tenaya Glacier as one of its most influential tributaries in the development and sculpture of the great Half Dome, North Dome and the rocks adjacent to them about the head of the Valley.

The story of its death is not unlike that of its companion already described, though the declivity of its channel, and its uniform exposure to sun-heat prevented any considerable portion of its current from becoming torpid, lingering only well up on the Mountain slopes to finish their sculpture and encircle them with a zone of moraine soil for forests and gardens. Nowhere in all this wonderful region will you find more beautiful trees and shrubs and flowers covering the traces of ice.

The rugged Tenaya Glacier wildly crevassed here and there above the ridges it had to cross, instead of drawing its sources direct from the summit of the Range, formed, as we have seen, one of the outlets of the great Tuolumne Glacier, issuing from this noble fountain like a river from a lake, two miles wide, about fourteen miles long, and from 1500 to 2000 feet deep.

In leaving the Tuolumne region it crossed over the divide, as mentioned above, between the Tuolumne and Tenaya basins, making an ascent of five hundred feet. Hence, after contracting its wide current and receiving a strong affluent from the fountains about Cathedral Peak, it poured its massive flood over the northeastern rim of its basin in splendid cascades. Then, crushing heavily against the Clouds' Rest Ridge, it bore down upon the Yosemite domes with concentrated energy.

Toward the end of the ice period, while its Hoffman companion continued to grind rock-meal for coming plants, the main trunk became torpid, and vanished, exposing wide areas of rolling rock-waves and glistening pavements, on whose channelless surface water ran wild and free. And because the trunk vanished almost simultaneously throughout its whole extent, no terminal moraines are found in its canyon channel; nor, since its walls are, in most places, too steeply inclined to admit of the deposition of moraine matter, do we find much of the two main laterals. The lowest of its residual glaciers lingered beneath the shadow of the Yosemite Half Dome; others along the base of Coliseum Peak above Lake Tenaya and along the precipitous wall extending from the lake to the Big Tuolumne Meadows. The latter, on account of the uniformity and continuity of their protecting shadows, formed moraines of considerable length and regularity that are liable to be mistaken for portions of the left lateral of the Tuolumne tributary glacier.

Spend all the time you can spare or steal on the tracks of this grand old glacier, charmed and enchanted by its magnificent canyon, lakes and cascades and resplendent glacier pavements.

The Nevada Glacier was longer and more symmetrical than the last, and the only one of the Merced system whose sources extended directly back to the main summits on the axis of the Range. Its numerous fountains were ranged side by side in three series, at an elevation of from 10,000 to 12,000 feet above the sea. The first, on the right side of the basin, extended from the Matterhorn to Cathedral Peak; that on the left through the Merced group, and these two parallel series were united by a third that extended around the head of the basin in a direction at right angles to the others.

The three ranges of high peaks and ridges that supplied the snow for these fountains, together with the Clouds' Rest Ridge, nearly inclose a rectangular basin, that was filled with a massive sea of ice, leaving an outlet toward the west through which flowed the main trunk glacier, three-fourths of a mile to a mile and a half wide, fifteen miles long, and from 1000 to 1500 feet deep, and entered Yosemite between the Half Dome and Mount Starr King.

Could we have visited Yosemite Valley at this period of its history, we should have found its ice cascades vastly more glorious than their tiny water representatives of the present day. One of the grandest of these was formed by that portion of the Nevada Glacier that poured over the shoulder of the Half Dome.

This glacier, as a whole, resembled an oak, with a gnarled swelling base and wide-spreading branches. Picturesque rocks of every conceivable form adorned its banks, among which glided the numerous tributaries, mottled with black and red and gray boulders, from the fountain peaks, while ever and anon, as the deliberate centuries passed away, dome after dome raised its burnished crown above the ice-flood to enrich the slowly opening landscapes.

The principal moraines occur in short irregular sections along the sides of the canyons, their fragmentary condition being due to interruptions caused by portions of the sides of the canyon walls being too steep for moraine matter to lie on, and to down-sweeping torrents and avalanches. The left lateral of the trunk may be traced about five miles from the mouth of the first main tributary to the Illilouette Canyon. The corresponding section of the right lateral, extending from Cathedral tributary to the Half Dome, is more complete because of the more favorable character of the north side of the canyon. A short side-glacier came in against it from the slopes of Clouds' Rest; but being fully exposed to the sun, it was melted long before the main trunk, allowing the latter to deposit this portion of its moraine undisturbed. Some conception of the size and appearance of this fine moraine may be gained by following the Clouds' Rest trail from Yosemite, which crosses it obliquely and conducts past several sections made by streams. Slate boulders may be seen that must have come from the Lyell group, twelve miles distant. But the bulk of the moraine is composed of porphyritic granite derived from Feldspar and Cathedral Valleys.

On the sides of the moraines we find a series of terraces, indicating fluctuations in the level of the glacier, caused by variations of snow-fall, temperature, etc., showing that the climate of the glacial period was diversified by cycles of milder or stormier seasons similar to those of post-glacial time.

After the depth of the main trunk diminished to about five hundred feet, the greater portion became torpid, as is shown by the moraines, and lay dying in its crooked channel like a wounded snake, maintaining for a time a feeble squirming motion in places of exceptional depth, or where the bottom of the canyon was more steeply inclined. The numerous fountain-wombs, however, continued fruitful long after the trunk had vanished, giving rise to an imposing array of short residual glaciers, extending around the rim of the general basin a distance of nearly twenty-four miles. Most of these have but recently succumbed to the new climate, dying in turn as determined by elevation, size, and exposure, leaving only a few feeble survivors beneath the coolest shadows, which are now slowly completing the sculpture of one of the noblest of the Yosemite basins.

The comparatively shallow glacier that at this time filled the Illilouette Basin, though once far from shallow, more resembled a lake than a river of ice, being nearly half as wide as it was long. Its greatest length was about ten miles, and its depth perhaps nowhere much exceeded 1000 feet. Its chief fountains, ranged along the west side of the Merced group, at an elevation of about 10,000 meet, gave birth to fine tributaries that flowed in a westerly direction, and united in the center of the basin. The broad trunk at first poured north-westward, then curved to the northward, deflected by the lofty wall forming its western bank, and finally united with the grand Yosemite trunk, opposite Glacier Point.

All the phenomena relating to glacial action in this basin are remarkably simple and orderly, on account of the sheltered positions occupied by its ice-fountains, with reference to the disturbing effects of larger glaciers from the axis of the main Range earlier in the period. From the eastern base of the Starr King cone you may obtain a fine view of the principal moraines sweeping grandly out into the middle of the basin from the shoulders of the peaks, between which the ice-fountains lay. The right lateral of the tributary, which took its rise between Red and Merced Mountains, measures 250 feet in height at its upper extremity, and displays three well-defined terraces, similar to those of the south Lyell Glacier. The comparative smoothness of the upper-most terrace shows that it is considerably more ancient than the others, many of the boulders of which it is composed having crumbled. A few miles to the westward, this moraine has an average slope of twenty-seven degrees, and an elevation above the bottom of the channel of six hundred and sixty feet. Near the middle of the main basin, just where the regularly formed medial and lateral moraines flatten out and disappear, there is a remarkably smooth field of gravel, planted with arctostaphylos, that looks at the distance of a mile like a delightful meadow. Stream sections show the gravel deposit to be composed of the same material as the moraines, but finer, and more water-worn from the action of converging torrents issuing from the tributary glaciers after the trunk was melted. The southern boundary of the basin is a strikingly perfect wall, gray on the top, and white down the sides and at the base with snow, in which many a crystal brook takes rise. The northern boundary is made up of smooth undulating masses of gray granite, that lift here and there into beautiful domes of which the Starr King cluster is the finest, while on the east tower of the majestic fountain-peaks with wide canyons and neve amphitheaters between them, whose variegated rocks show out gloriously against the sky.

The ice-plows of this charming basin, ranged side by side in orderly gangs, furrowed the rocks with admirable uniformity, producing irrigating channels for a brood of wild streams, and abundance of rich soil adapted to every requirement of garden and grove. No other section of the Yosemite uplands is in so perfect a state of glacial cultivation. Its domes and peaks, and swelling rock-waves, however majestic in themselves, and yet submissively subordinate to the garden center. The other basins we have been describing are combinations of sculptured rocks, embellished with gardens and groves; the Illilouette is one grand garden and forest, embellished with rocks, each of the five beautiful in its own way, and all as harmoniously related as are the five petals of a flower. After uniting in the Yosemite Valley, and expending the down-thrusting energy derived from their combined weight and the declivity of their channels, the grand trunk flowed on through and out of the Valley. In effecting its exit a considerable ascent was made, traces of which may still be seen on the abraded rocks at the lower end of the Valley, while the direction pursued after leaving the Valley is surely indicated by the immense lateral moraines extending from the ends of the walls at an elevation of from 1500 to 1800 feet. The right lateral moraine was disturbed by a large tributary glacier that occupied the basin of Cascade Creek, causing considerable complication in its structure. The left is simple in form for several miles of its length, or to the point where a tributary came in from the southeast. But both are greatly obscured by the forests and underbrush growing upon them, and by the denuding action of rains and melting snows, etc. It is, therefore, the less to be wondered at that these moraines, made up of material derived from the distant fountain-mountains, and from the Valley itself, were not sooner recognized.

The ancient glacier systems of the Tuolumne, San Joaquin, Kern, and Kings River Basins were developed on a still grander scale and are so replete with interest that the most sketchy outline descriptions of each, with the works they have accomplished would fill many a volume. Therefore I can do but little more than invite everybody who is free to go and see for himself.

The action of flowing ice, whether in the form of river-like glaciers or broad mantles, especially the part it played in sculpturing the earth, is as yet but little understood. Water rivers work openly where people dwell, and so does the rain, and the sea, thundering on all the shores of the world; and the universal ocean of air, though invisible, speaks aloud in a thousand voices, and explains its modes of working and its power. But glaciers, back in their white solitudes, work apart from men, exerting their tremendous energies in silence and darkness. Outspread, spirit-like, they brood above the pre-destined landscapes, work on unwearied through immeasurable ages, until, in the fullness of time, the mountains and valleys are brought forth, channels furrowed for rivers, basins made for lakes and meadows, and arms of the sea, soils spread for forests and fields; then they shrink and vanish like summer clouds.

Chapter 16

HETCH HETCHY VALLEY

Yosemite is so wonderful that we are apt to regard it as an exceptional creation, the only valley of its kind in the world; but Nature is not so poor as to have only one of anything. Several other Yosemites have been discovered in the Sierra that occupy the same relative positions on the Range and were formed by the same forces in the same kind of granite. One of these, the Hetch Hetchy Valley, is in the Yosemite National Park about twenty miles from Yosemite and is easily accessible to all sorts of travelers by a road and trail that leaves the Big Oak Flat road at Bronson Meadows a few miles below Crane Flat, and to mountaineers by way of Yosemite Creek basin and the head of the middle fork of the Tuolumne.

It is said to have been discovered by Joseph Screech, a hunter, in 1850, a year before the discovery of the great Yosemite. After my first visit to it in the autumn of 1871, I have always called it the 'Tuolumne Yosemite,' for it is a wonderfully exact counterpart of the Merced Yosemite, not only in its sublime rocks and waterfalls but in the gardens, groves and meadows of its flowery park-like floor. The floor of Yosemite is about 4000 feet above the sea; the Hetch Hetchy floor about 3700 feet. And as the Merced River flows through Yosemite, so does the Tuolumne through Hetch Hetchy. The walls of both are of gray granite, rise abruptly from the floor, are sculptured in the same style and in both every rock is a glacier monument.

Standing boldly out from the south wall is a strikingly picturesque rock called by the Indians, Kolana, the outermost of a group 2300 feet high, corresponding with the Cathedral Rocks of Yosemite both in relative position and form. On the opposite side of the Valley, facing Kolana, there is a counterpart of the El Capitan that rises sheer and plain to a height of 1800 feet, and over its massive brow flows a stream which makes the most graceful fall I have ever seen. From the edge of the cliff to the top of an earthquake talus it is perfectly free in the air for a thousand feet before it is broken into cascades among talus boulders. It is in all its glory in June, when the snow is melting fast, but fades and vanishes toward the end of summer. The only fall I know with which it may fairly be compared is the Yosemite Bridal Veil; but it excels even that favorite fall both in height and airy-fairy beauty and behavior. Lowlanders are apt to suppose that mountain streams in their wild career over cliffs lose control of themselves and tumble in a noisy chaos of mist and spray. On the contrary, on no part of their travels are they more harmonious and self-controlled. Imagine yourself in Hetch Hetchy on a sunny day in June, standing waist-deep in grass and flowers (as I have often stood), while the great pines sway dreamily with scarcely perceptible motion. Looking northward across the Valley you see a plain, gray granite cliff rising abruptly out of the gardens and groves to a height of 1800 feet, and in front of it Tueeulala's silvery scarf burning with irised sun-fire. In the first white outburst at the head there is abundance of visible energy, but it is speedily hushed and concealed in divine repose, and its tranquil progress to the base of the cliff is like that of a downy feather in a still room. Now observe the fineness and marvelous distinctness of the various sun-illumined fabrics into which the water is woven; they sift and float from form to form down the face of that grand gray rock in so leisurely and unconfused a manner that you can examine their texture, and patterns and tones of color as you would a piece of embroidery held in the hand. Toward the top of the fall you see groups of booming, comet-like masses, their solid, white heads separate, their tails like combed silk interlacing among delicate gray and purple shadows, ever forming and dissolving, worn out by friction in their rush through the air. Most of these vanish a few hundred feet below the summit, changing to varied forms of cloud-like drapery. Near the bottom the width of the fall has increased from about twenty-five feet to a hundred feet. Here it is composed of yet finer tissues, and is still without a trace of disorder – air, water and sunlight woven into stuff that spirits might wear.

So fine a fall might well seem sufficient to glorify any valley; but here, as in Yosemite, Nature seems in no-wise moderate, for a short distance to the eastward of Tueeulala booms and thunders the great Hetch Hetchy Fall, Wapama, so near that you have both of them in full view from the same standpoint. It is the counterpart of the Yosemite Fall, but has a much greater volume of water, is about 1700 feet in height, and appears to be nearly vertical, though considerably inclined, and is dashed into huge outbounding bosses of foam on projecting shelves and knobs. No two falls could be more unlike – Tueeulala out in the open sunshine descending like thistledown; Wapama in a jagged, shadowy gorge roaring and thundering, pounding its way like an earthquake avalanche.

Besides this glorious pair there is a broad, massive fall on the main river a short distance above the head of the Valley. Its position is something like that of the Vernal in Yosemite, and its roar as it plunges into a surging trout-pool may be heard a long way, though it is only about twenty feet high. On Rancheria Creek, a large stream, corresponding in position with the Yosemite Tenaya Creek, there is a chain of cascades joined here and there with swift flashing plumes like the one between the Vernal and Nevada Falls, making magnificent shows as they go their glacier-sculptured way, sliding, leaping, hurrahing, covered with crisp clashing spray made glorious with sifting sunshine. And besides all these a few small streams come over the walls at wide intervals, leaping from ledge to ledge with birdlike song and watering many a hidden cliff-garden and fernery, but they are too unshowy to be noticed in so grand a place.

The correspondence between the Hetch Hetchy walls in their trends, sculpture, physical structure, and general arrangement of the main rock-masses and those of the Yosemite Valley has excited the wondering admiration of every observer. We have seen that the El Capitan and Cathedral rocks occupy the same relative positions in both valleys; so also do their Yosemite points and North Domes. Again, that part of the Yosemite north wall immediately to the east of the Yosemite Fall has two horizontal benches, about 500 and 1500 feet above the floor, timbered with golden-cup oak. Two benches similarly situated and timbered occur on the same relative portion of the Hetch Hetchy north wall, to the east of Wapama

Fall, and on no other. The Yosemite is bounded at the head by the great Half Dome. Hetch Hetchy is bounded in the same way though its head rock is incomparably less wonderful and sublime in form.

The floor of the Valley is about three and a half miles long, and from a fourth to half a mile wide. The lower portion is mostly a level meadow about a mile long, with the trees restricted to the sides and the river banks, and partially separated from the main, upper, forested portion by a low bar of glacier-polished granite across which the river breaks in rapids.

The principal trees are the yellow and sugar pines, digger pine, incense cedar, Douglas spruce, silver fir, the California and golden-cup oaks, balsam cottonwood, Nuttall's flowering dogwood, alder, maple, laurel, tumion, etc. The most abundant and influential are the great yellow or silver pines like those of Yosemite, the tallest over two hundred feet in height, and the oaks assembled in magnificent groves with massive rugged trunks four to six feet in diameter, and broad, shady, wide-spreading heads. The shrubs forming conspicuous flowery clumps and tangles are manzanita, azalea, spiraea, brierrose, several species of ceanothus, calycanthus, philadelphus, wild cherry, etc.; with abundance of showy and fragrant herbaceous plants growing about them or out in the open in beds by themselves – lilies, Mariposa tulips, brodiaeas, orchids, iris, spraguea, draperia, collomia, collinsia, castilleja, nemophila, larkspur, columbine, goldenrods, sunflowers, mints of many species, honeysuckle, etc. Many fine ferns dwell here also, especially the beautiful and interesting rock-ferns – pellaea, and cheilanthes of several species – fringing and rosetting dry rock-piles and ledges; woodwardia and asplenium on damp spots with fronds six or seven feet high; the delicate maiden-hair in mossy nooks by the falls, and the sturdy, broad-shouldered pteris covering nearly all the dry ground beneath the oaks and pines.

It appears, therefore, that Hetch Hetchy Valley, far from being a plain, common, rock-bound meadow, as many who have not seen it seem to suppose, is a grand landscape garden, one of Nature's rarest and most precious mountain temples. As in Yosemite, the sublime rocks of its walls seem to glow with life, whether leaning back in repose or standing erect in thoughtful attitudes, giving welcome to storms and calms alike, their brows in the sky, their feet set in the groves and gay flowery meadows, while birds, bees, and butterflies help the river and waterfalls to stir all the air into music – things frail and fleeting and types of permanence meeting here and blending, just as they do in Yosemite, to draw her lovers into close and confiding communion with her.

Sad to say, this most precious and sublime feature of the Yosemite National Park, one of the greatest of all our natural resources for the uplifting joy and peace and health of the people, is in danger of being dammed and made into a reservoir to help supply San Francisco with water and light, thus flooding it from wall to wall and burying its gardens and groves one or two hundred feet deep. This grossly destructive commercial scheme has long been planned and urged (though water as pure and abundant can be got from outside of the people's park, in a dozen different places), because of the comparative cheapness of the dam and of the territory which it is sought to divert from the great uses to which it was dedicated in the Act of 1890 establishing the Yosemite National Park.

The making of gardens and parks goes on with civilization all over the world, and they increase both in size and number as their value is recognized. Everybody needs beauty as well as bread, places to play in and pray in, where Nature may heal and cheer and give strength to body and soul alike. This natural beauty-hunger is made manifest in the little window-sill gardens of the poor, though perhaps only a geranium slip in a broken cup, as well as in the carefully tended rose and lily gardens of the rich, the thousands of spacious city parks and botanical gardens, and in our magnificent National parks – the Yellowstone, Yosemite, Sequoia, etc. – Nature's sublime wonderlands, the admiration and joy of the world. Nevertheless, like anything else worth while, from the very beginning, however well guarded, they have always been subject to attack by despoiling gainseekers and mischief-makers of every degree from Satan to Senators, eagerly trying to make everything immediately and selfishly commercial, with schemes disguised in smug-smiling philanthropy, industriously, shampiously crying, 'Conservation, conservation, panutilization,' that man and beast may be fed and the dear Nation made

great. Thus long ago a few enterprising merchants utilized the
Jerusalem temple as a place of business instead of a place of
prayer, changing money, buying and selling cattle and sheep
and doves; and earlier still, the first forest reservation, including only one tree, was likewise despoiled. Ever since the
establishment of the Yosemite National Park, strife has been
going on around its borders and I suppose this will go on as
part of the universal battle between right and wrong, however
much its boundaries may be shorn, or its wild beauty destroyed.

The first application to the Government by the San Francisco Supervisors for the commercial use of Lake Eleanor and
the Hetch Hetchy Valley was made in 1903, and on December
22nd of that year it was denied by the Secretary of the Interior,
Mr Hitchcock, who truthfully said:

> Presumably the Yosemite National Park was created such by
> law because within its boundaries, inclusive alike of its beau-
> tiful small lakes, like Eleanor, and its majestic wonders, like
> Hetch Hetchy and Yosemite Valley. It is the aggregation of
> such natural scenic features that makes the Yosemite Park a
> wonderland which the Congress of the United States sought
> by law to reserve for all coming time as nearly as practicable
> in the condition fashioned by the hand of the Creator – a
> worthy object of national pride and a source of healthful
> pleasure and rest for the thousands of people who may an-
> nually sojourn there during the heated months.

In 1907 when Mr Garfield became Secretary of the Interior the
application was renewed and granted; but under his successor,
Mr Fisher, the matter has been referred to a Commission,
which as this volume goes to press still has it under consideration.

The most delightful and wonderful camp grounds in the
Park are its three great valleys – Yosemite, Hetch Hetchy, and
Upper Tuolumne; and they are also the most important places
with reference to their positions relative to the other great
features – the Merced and Tuolumne Canyons, and the High
Sierra peaks and glaciers, etc., at the head of the rivers. The
main part of the Tuolumne Valley is a spacious flowery lawn
four or five miles long, surrounded by magnificent snowy

mountains, slightly separated from other beautiful meadows, which together make a series about twelve miles in length, the highest reaching to the feet of Mount Dana, Mount Gibbs, Mount Lyell and Mount McClure. It is about 8500 feet above the sea, and forms the grand central High Sierra camp ground from which excursions are made to the noble mountains, domes, glaciers, etc.; across the Range to the Mono Lake and volcanoes and down the Tuolumne Canyon to Hetch Hetchy. Should Hetch Hetchy be submerged for a reservoir, as proposed, not only would it be utterly destroyed, but the sublime canyon way to the heart of the High Sierra would be hopelessly blocked and the great camping ground, as the watershed of a city drinking system, virtually would be closed to the public. So far as I have learned, few of all the thousands who have seen the park and seek rest and peace in it are in favor of this outrageous scheme.

One of my later visits to the Valley was made in the autumn of 1907 with the late William Keith, the artist. The leaf-colors were then ripe, and the great godlike rocks in repose seemed to glow with life. The artist, under their spell, wandered day after day along the river and through the groves and gardens, studying the wonderful scenery; and, after making about forty sketches, declared with enthusiasm that although its walls were less sublime in height, in picturesque beauty and charm Hetch Hetchy surpassed even Yosemite.

That anyone would try to destroy such a place seems incredible; but sad experience shows that there are people good enough and bad enough for anything. The proponents of the dam scheme bring forward a lot of bad arguments to prove that the only righteous thing to do with the people's parks is to destroy them bit by bit as they are able. Their arguments are curiously like those of the devil, devised for the destruction of the first garden – so much of the very best Eden fruit going to waste; so much of the best Tuolumne water and Tuolumne scenery going to waste. Few of their statements are even partly true, and all are misleading.

Thus, Hetch Hetchy, they say, is a 'low-lying meadow.' On the contrary, it is a high-lying natural landscape garden, as the photographic illustrations show.

'It is a common minor feature, like thousands of others.' On the contrary it is a very uncommon feature; after Yosemite, the rarest and in many ways the most important in the National Park.

'Damming and submerging it 175 feet deep would enhance its beauty by forming a crystal-clear lake.' Landscape gardens, places of recreation and worship, are never made beautiful by destroying and burying them. The beautiful sham lake, forsooth, should be only an eyesore, a dismal blot on the landscape, like many others to be seen in the Sierra. For, instead of keeping it at the same level all the year, allowing Nature centuries of time to make new shores, it would, of course, be full only a month or two in the spring, when the snow is melting fast; then it would be gradually drained, exposing the slimy sides of the basin and shallower parts of the bottom, with the gathered drift and waste, death and decay of the upper basins, caught here instead of being swept on to decent natural burial along the banks of the river or in the sea. Thus the Hetch Hetchy dam-lake would be only a rough imitation of a natural lake for a few of the spring months, an open sepulcher for the others.

'Hetch Hetchy water is the purest of all to be found in the Sierra, unpolluted, and forever unpollutable.' On the contrary, excepting that of the Merced below Yosemite, it is less pure than that of most of the other Sierra streams, because of the sewerage of camp grounds draining into it, especially of the Big Tuolumne Meadows camp ground, occupied by hundreds of tourists and mountaineers, with their animals, for months every summer, soon to be followed by thousands from all the world.

These temple destroyers, devotees of ravaging commercialism, seem to have a perfect contempt for Nature, and, instead of lifting their eyes to the God of the mountains, lift them to the Almighty Dollar.

Dam Hetch Hetchy! As well dam for water-tanks the people's cathedrals and churches, for no holier temple has ever been consecrated by the heart of man.

STICKEEN

(1909)

During the 1880s, Muir made seven lengthy expeditions to the wildest parts of Alaska, during which he spent months living with the indigenous Chilcat, Sitka and Stickeen tribes, who enabled him to explore the coasts and rivers in their large sea-going canoes.

Muir was the first white European to 'discover' Glacier Bay in the Klondyke territory, and his exploration of the islands, rivers and glaciers of the remote Wrangell area laid the groundwork for the eventual creation of the national parks in this region. While at Glacier Bay he named glaciers in honour of two Scottish geology heroes: Hugh Miller and Archibald Geikie; the largest glacier here is of course Muir Glacier.

Later, as geological and botanical adviser to the Corwin and Harriman expeditions, Muir sailed over a thousand miles further north, to the Bering Straits and the coast of Siberia, and was present when Wrangell Land was annexed for the United States.

During his 500-mile canoe trip to Glacier Bay with the Stickeen Indians, Muir was made an honorary chief and they gifted his companion, Samuel Hall Young, a pet dog which he named 'Stickeen' after the river of that name and of their tribal territory.

Stickeen is a much-loved story derived from an incident in which Muir almost lost his life in a desperate attempt to bridge a crevasse on a glacier above Taylor Bay in 1880. This was first published as 'An Adventure with a Dog and a Glacier' in the *Century Magazine* of September 1897, but it was told and retold in various forms until this definitive version was published as a book in 1909.

Stickeen reveals an interesting side of Muir's adherence to

Burns' natural philosophy, and his deep empathy for all living things. In the 1890s many scientific-materialists declared that laboratory animals such as dogs, cats, monkeys and rats, were mere 'animated machines', devoid of soul, mind, intellect or feeling. This perverse philosophy was used to justify vivisection and appalling experiments on animals without anaesthesia of any kind; their screamings under the knife were mere 'nervous reactions'. This view was gaining acceptance among the scientific experimentalists of the day but Muir retorted that the little dog Stickeen, which had shared his perilous adventure on the glacier, was living proof that even a dog had a mind, emotional feelings and a soul. Muir's experience with the dog confirmed his Burnsian vision of all living beings as manifestations of a common Divinity; it is a deeply affectionate tale, written as a kind of moral fable for Muir's daughter Helen, but it remains relevant to today's debates.

STICKEEN

In the summer of 1880 I set out from Fort Wrangell in a canoe to continue the exploration of the icy region of southeastern Alaska, begun in the fall of 1879. After the necessary provisions, blankets, etc., had been collected and stowed away, and my Indian crew were in their places ready to start, while a crowd of their relatives and friends on the wharf were bidding them goodbye and good luck, my companion, the Rev. S. H. Young, for whom we were waiting, at last came aboard, followed by a little black dog, that immediately made himself at home by curling up in a hollow among the baggage. I like dogs, but this one seemed so small and worthless that I objected to his going, and asked the missionary why he was taking him.

'Such a little helpless creature will only be in the way,' I said; 'you had better pass him up to the Indian boys on the wharf, to be taken home to play with the children. This trip is not likely to be good for toy-dogs. The poor silly thing will be in rain and snow for weeks or months, and will require care like a baby.' But his master assured me that he would be no trouble at all; that he was a perfect wonder of a dog, could endure cold and hunger like a bear, swim like a seal, and was wondrous wise and cunning, etc., making out a list of virtues to show he might be the most interesting member of the party.

Nobody could hope to unravel the lines of his ancestry. In all the wonderfully mixed and varied dog-tribe I never saw any creature very much like him, though in some of his sly, soft, gliding motions and gestures he brought the fox to mind. He was short-legged and bunch-bodied, and his hair, though smooth, was long and silky and slightly waved, so that when the wind was at his back it ruffled, making him look shaggy. At first sight his only noticeable feature was his fine tail, which was about as airy and shady as a squirrel's, and was carried curling forward almost to his nose. On closer inspection you might notice his thin sensitive ears, and sharp eyes with cunning tan-spots above them. Mr Young told me that when the little fellow was a pup about the size of a woodrat he was presented to his wife by an Irish prospector at Sitka, and that on his arrival at Fort Wrangell he was adopted with enthusiasm by the Stickeen Indians as a sort of new good-luck totem, was named 'Stickeen' for the tribe, and became a universal favorite; petted, protected, and admired wherever he went, and regarded as a mysterious fountain of wisdom.

On our trip he soon proved himself a queer character – odd, concealed, independent, keeping invincibly quiet, and doing many little puzzling things that piqued my curiosity. As we sailed week after week through the long intricate channels and inlets among the innumerable islands and mountains of the coast, he spent most of the dull days in sluggish ease, motionless, and apparently as unobserving as if in deep sleep. But I discovered that somehow he always knew what was going on. When the Indians were about to shoot at ducks or seals, or when anything along the shore was exciting our attention, he would rest his chin on the edge of the canoe and calmly look out like a dreamy-eyed tourist. And when he heard us talking about making a landing, he immediately roused himself to see what sort of a place we were coming to, and made ready to jump overboard and swim ashore as soon as the canoe neared the bench. Then, with a vigorous shake to get rid of the brine in his hair, he ran into the woods to hunt small game. But though always the first out of the canoe, he was always the last to get into it. When we were ready to start he could never be found, and refused to come to our call. We soon found out, however, that though we could not see him at such times, he saw us, and from the cover of the briers and huckleberry bushes in the fringe of the woods was watching the canoe with wary eye. For as soon as we were fairly off he came trotting down the beach, plunged into the surf, and swam after us, knowing well that we would cease rowing and take him in. When the contrary little vagabond came alongside, he was lifted by the neck, held at arm's length a moment to drip, and dropped aboard. We tried to cure him of this trick by compelling him to swim a long way, as if we had a mind to abandon him; but this did no good; the longer the swim the better he seemed to like it.

Though capable of great idleness, he never failed to be ready for all sorts of adventures and excursions. One pitch-dark rainy night we landed about ten o'clock at the mouth of a salmon stream when the water was phosphorescent. The salmon were running, and the myriad fins of the onrushing multitude were churning all the stream into a silvery glow, wonderfully beautiful and impressive in the ebon darkness. To get a good view of the show I set out with one of the Indians and sailed up through the midst of it to the foot of a rapid about half a mile from camp, where the swift current dashing over rocks made the luminous glow most glorious. Happening to look back down the stream, while the Indian was catching a few of the struggling fish, I saw a long spreading fan of light like the tail of a comet, which we thought must be made by some big strange animal that was pursuing us. On it came with its magnificent train, until we imagined we could see the monster's head and eyes; but it was only Stickeen, who, finding I had left the camp, came swimming after me to see what was up.

When we camped early, the best hunter of the crew usually went to the woods for a deer, and Stickeen was sure to be at his heels, provided I had not gone out. For, strange to say, though I never carried a gun, he always followed me, forsaking the hunter and even his master to share my wanderings. The days that were too stormy for sailing I spent in the woods, or on the adjacent mountains, wherever my studies called me; and Stickeen always insisted on going with me, however wild the weather, gliding like a fox through dripping huckleberry bushes and thorny tangles of panax and rubus, scarce stirring their rain-laden leaves; wading and wallowing through snow, swimming icy streams, skipping over logs and rocks and the crevasses of glaciers with the patience and endurance of a determined mountaineer, never tiring or getting discouraged. Once he followed me over a glacier the surface of which was so crusty and rough that it cut his feet until every step was marked with blood; but he trotted on with Indian fortitude until I noticed his red track, and, taking pity on him, made him a set of moccasins out of a handkerchief. However great his troubles he never asked help or made any complaint, as if, like a philosopher, he had learned that without hard work and suffering there could be no pleasure worth having.

Yet none of us was able to make out what Stickeen was really good for. He seemed to meet danger and hardships without anything like reason, insisted on having his own way, never obeyed an order, and the hunter could never set him on anything, or make him fetch the birds he shot. His equanimity was so steady it seemed due to want of feeling; ordinary storms were pleasures to him, and as for mere rain, he flourished in it like a vegetable. No matter what advances you might make, scarce a glance or a tail-wag would you get for your pains. But though he was apparently as cold as a glacier and about as impervious to fun, I tried hard to make his acquaintance, guessing there must be something worth while hidden beneath so much courage, endurance, and love of wild-weathery adventure. No superannuated mastiff or bulldog grown old in office surpassed this fluffy midget in stoic dignity. He sometimes reminded me of a small, squat, unshakable desert cactus. For he never displayed a single trace of the merry, tricksy, elfish fun of the terriers and collies that we all know, nor of their touching affection and devotion. Like children, most small dogs beg to be loved and allowed to love; but Stickeen seemed a very Diogenes, asking only to be let alone: a true child of the wilderness, holding the even tenor of his hidden life with the silence and serenity of nature. His strength of character lay in his eyes. They looked as old as the hills, and as young, and as wild. I never tired of looking into them: it was like looking into a landscape; but they were small and rather deep-set, and had no explaining lines around them to give out particulars. I was accustomed to look into the faces of plants and animals, and I watched the little sphinx more and more keenly as an interesting study. But there is no estimating the wit and wisdom concealed and latent in our lower fellow mortals until made manifest by profound experiences; for it is through suffering that dogs as well as saints are developed and made perfect.

After exploring the Sum Dum and Tahkoo fiords and their glaciers, we sailed through Stephen's Passage into Lynn Canal and thence through Icy Strait into Cross Sound, searching for unexplored inlets leading toward the great fountain ice-fields of the Fairweather Range. Here, while the tide was in our favor, we were accompanied by a fleet of icebergs drifting out to the ocean from Glacier Bay. Slowly we paddled around Vancouver's Point, Wimbledon, our frail canoe tossed like a feather on the massive heaving swells coming in past Cape Spenser. For miles the sound is bounded by precipitous mural cliffs, which, lashed with wave-spray and their heads hidden in clouds, looked terribly threatening and stern. Had our canoe been crushed or upset we could have made no landing here, for the cliffs, as high as those of Yosemite, sink sheer into deep water. Eagerly we scanned the wall on the north side for the first sign of an opening fiord or harbor, all of us anxious except Stickeen, who dozed in peace or gazed dreamily at the tremendous precipices when he heard us talking about them. At length we made the joyful discovery of the mouth of the inlet now called 'Taylor Bay,' and about five o'clock reached the head of it and encamped in a Spruce grove near the front of a large glacier.

While camp was being made, Joe the hunter climbed the mountain wall on the east side of the fiord in pursuit of wild goats, while Mr Young and I went to the glacier. We found that it is separated from the waters of the inlet by a tide-washed moraine, and extends, an abrupt barrier, all the way across from wall to wall of the inlet, a distance of about three miles. But our most interesting discovery was that it had recently advanced, though again slightly receding. A portion of the terminal moraine had been plowed up and shoved forward, uprooting and overwhelming the woods on the east side. Many of the trees were down and buried, or nearly so, others were leaning away from the ice-cliffs, ready to fall, and some stood erect, with the bottom of the ice plow still beneath their roots and its lofty crystal spires towering huge above their tops. The spectacle presented by these century-old trees standing close beside a spiry wall of ice, with their branches almost touching it, was most novel and striking. And when I climbed around the front, and a little way up the west side of the glacier, I found that it had swelled and increased in height and width in accordance with its advance, and carried away the outer ranks of trees on its bank.

On our way back to camp after these first observations I planned a far-and-wide excursion for the morrow. I awoke early, called not only by the glacier, which had been on my mind all night, but by a grand flood-storm. The wind was blowing a gale from the north and the rain was flying with the clouds in a wide passionate horizontal flood, as if it were all passing over the country instead of falling on it. The main perennial streams were booming high above their banks, and hundreds of new ones, roaring like the sea, almost covered the lofty gray walls of the inlet with white cascades and falls. I had intended making a cup of coffee and getting something like a breakfast before starting, but when I heard the storm and looked out I made haste to join it; for many of Nature's finest lessons are to be found in her storms, and if careful to keep in right relations with them, we may go safely abroad with them, rejoicing in the grandeur and beauty of their works and ways, and chanting with the old Norsemen, 'The blast of the tempest aids our oars, the hurricane is our servant and drives us whither we wish to go.' So, omitting breakfast, I put a piece of bread in my pocket and hurried away.

Mr Young and the Indian were asleep, and so, I hoped, was Stickeen; but I had not gone a dozen rods before he left his bed in the tent and came boring through the blast after me. That a man should welcome storms for their exhilarating music and motion, and go forth to see God making landscapes, is reasonable enough; but what fascination could there be in such tremendous weather for a dog? Surely nothing akin to human enthusiasm for scenery or geology. Anyhow, on he came, breakfastless, through the choking blast. I stopped and did my best to turn him back. 'Now don't,' I said, shouting to make myself heard in the storm. 'Now don't, Stickeen. What has got into your queer noddle now? You must be daft. This wild day has nothing for you. There is no game abroad, nothing but weather. Go back to camp and keep warm, get a good breakfast with your master, and be sensible for once. I can't carry you all day or feed you, and this storm will kill you.'

But Nature, it seems, was at the bottom of the affair, and she gains her ends with dogs as well as with men, making us do as she likes, shoving and pulling us along her ways, however rough, all but killing us at times in getting her lessons driven hard home. After I had stopped again and again, shouting good warning advice, I saw that he was not to be shaken off; as well might the earth try to shake off the moon. I had once led his master into trouble, when he fell on one of the topmost jags of a mountain and dislocated his arm; now the turn of his humble companion was coming. The pitiful wanderer just stood there in the wind, drenched and blinking, saying doggedly, 'Where thou goest I will go.' So at last I told him to come on if he must, and gave him a piece of the bread I had in my pocket; then we struggled on together, and thus began the most memorable of all my wild days.

The level flood, driving hard in our faces, thrashed and washed us wildly until we got into the shelter of a grove on the east side of the glacier near the front, where we stopped awhile for breath and to listen and look out. The exploration of the glacier was my main object, but the wind was too high to allow excursions over its open surface, where one might be dangerously shoved while balancing for a jump on the brink of a crevasse. In the meantime the storm was a fine study. There the end of the glacier, descending an abrupt swell of resisting rock about five hundred feet high, leans forward and falls in ice-cascades. And as the storm came down the glacier from the north, Stickeen and I were beneath the main current of the blast, while favorably located to see and hear it. What a psalm the storm was singing, and how fresh the smell of the washed earth and leaves, and how sweet the still small voices of the storm! Detached wafts and swirls were coming through the woods, with music from the leaves and branches and furrowed boles, and even from the splintered rocks and ice-crags overhead, many of the tones soft and low and flute-like, as if each leaf and tree, crag and spire were a tuned reed. A broad torrent, draining the side of the glacier, now swollen by scores of new streams from the mountains, was rolling boulders along its rocky channel, with thudding, bumping, muffled sounds, rushing toward the bay with tremendous energy, as if in haste to get out of the mountains; the winters above and beneath calling to each other, and all to the ocean, their home.

Looking southward from our shelter, we had this great torrent and the forested mountain wall above it on our left, the spiry ice-crags on our right, and smooth gray gloom ahead. I tried to draw the marvelous scene in my note-book, but the rain blurred the page in spite of all my pains to shelter it, and the sketch was almost worthless. When the wind began to abate, I traced the east side of the glacier. All the trees standing on the edge of the woods were barked and bruised, showing high-ice mark in a very telling way, while tens of thousands of those that had stood for centuries on the bank of the glacier farther out lay crushed and being crushed. In many places I could see down fifty feet or so beneath the margin of the glacier-mill, where trunks from one to two feet in diameter were being ground to pulp against outstanding rock-ribs and bosses of the bank.

About three miles above the front of the glacier I climbed to the surface of it by means of axe-steps made easy for Stickeen. As far as the eye could reach, the level, or nearly level, glacier stretched away indefinitely beneath the gray sky, a seemingly boundless prairie of ice. The rain continued, and grew colder, which I did not mind, but a dim snowy look in the drooping clouds made me hesitate about venturing far from land. No trace of the west shore was visible, and in case the clouds would settle and give snow, or the wind again become violent. I feared getting caught in a tangle of crevasses. Snow-crystals, the flowers of the mountain clouds, are frail, beautiful things, but terrible then flying on storm-winds in darkening, benumbing swarms or when welded together into glaciers full of deadly crevasses. Watching the weather, I sauntered about on the crystal sea. For a mile or so out I found the ice remarkably safe. The marginal crevasses mere mostly narrow, while the few wider ones were easily avoided by passing around them, and the clouds began to open here and there.

Thus encouraged, I at last pushed out for the other side; for Nature can make us do anything she likes. At first we made rapid progress, and the sky was not very threatening, while I took bearings occasionally with a pocket compass to enable me to find my way back more surely in case the storm should become blinding; but the structure lines of the glacier were my main guide. Toward the west side we came to a closely crevassed section in which we had to make long, narrow tacks and doublings, tracing the edges of tremendous traverse and longitudinal crevasses, many of which were from twenty to thirty feet wide, and perhaps a thousand feet deep – beautiful and awful. In working a way through them I was severely cautious, but Stickeen came on as unhesitating as the flying clouds. The widest crevasse that I could jump he would leap without so much as halting to take a look at it. The weather was now making quick changes, scattering bits of dazzling brightness through the wintry gloom at rare intervals, when the sun broke forth wholly free, the glacier was seen from shore to shore with a bright array of encompassing mountains partly revealed, wearing the clouds as garments, while the prairie bloomed and sparkled with irised light from myriad washed crystals. Then suddenly all the glorious show would be darkened and blotted out.

Stickeen seemed to care for none of these things, bright or dark, nor for the crevasses, wells, moulins, or swift flashing streams into which he might fall. The little adventurer was only about two years old, yet nothing seemed novel to him. Nothing daunted him. He showed neither caution nor curiosity, wonder nor fear, but bravely trotted on as if glaciers were playgrounds. His stout, muffled body seemed all one skipping muscle, and it was truly wonderful to see how swiftly and to all appearance heedlessly he flashed across nerve-trying chasms six or eight feet wide. His courage was so unwavering that it seemed to be due to dullness of perception, as if he were only blindly bold; and I kept warning him to be careful. For we had been close companions on so many wilderness trips that I had formed the habit of talking to him as if he were a boy and understood every word.

We gained the west shore in about three hours; the width of the glacier here being about seven miles. Then I pushed northward in order to see as far back as possible into the fountains of the Fairweather Mountains, in case the clouds should rise. The walking was easy along the margin of the forest, which, of course, like that on the other side, had been invaded and crushed by the swollen, overflowing glacier. In an hour or so, after passing a massive headland, we came suddenly on a branch of the glacier, which, in the form of a magnificent ice-cascade two miles wide, was pouring over the rim of the main basin in a westerly direction, its surface broken into wave-shaped blades and shattered blocks, suggesting the wildest updashing, heaving, plunging motion of a great river cataract. Tracing it down three or four miles, I found that it discharged into a lake, filling it with icebergs.

I would gladly have followed the lake outlet to tide-water, but the day was already far spent, and the threatening sky called for haste on the return trip to get off the ice before dark. I decided therefore to go no farther and, after taking a general view of the wonderful region, turned back, hoping to see it again under more favorable auspices. We made good speed up the canyon of the great ice-torrent, and out on the main glacier until we had left the west shore about two miles behind us. Here we got into a difficult network of crevasses, the gathering clouds began to drop misty fringes, and soon the dreaded snow came flying thick and fast. I now began to feel anxious about finding a way in the blurring storm. Stickeen showed no trace of fear. He was still the same silent, able little hero. I noticed, however, that after the storm-darkness came on he kept close up behind me. The snow urged us to make still greater haste, but at the same time hid our way. I pushed on as best I could, jumping innumerable crevasses, and for every hundred rods or so of direct advance traveling a mile in doubling up and down in the turmoil of chasms and dislocated ice-blocks. After an hour or two of this work we came to a series of longitudinal crevasses of appalling width, and almost straight and regular in trend, like immense furrows. These I traced with firm nerve, excited and strengthened by the danger, making wide jumps, poising cautiously on their dizzy edges after cutting hollows for my feet before making the spring, to avoid possible slipping or any uncertainty on the farther sides, where only one trial is granted – exercise at once frightful and inspiring. Stickeen followed seemingly without effort.

Many a mile we thus traveled, mostly up and down, making but little real headway in crossing, running instead of walking most of the time as the danger of being compelled to spend the night on the glacier became threatening. Stickeen seemed able for anything. Doubtless we could have weathered the storm for one night, dancing on a flat spot to keep from freezing, and I faced the threat without feeling anything like despair; but we were hungry and wet, and the wind from the mountains was still thick with snow and bitterly cold, so of course that night would have seemed a very long one. I could not see far enough through the blurring snow to judge in which general direction the least dangerous route lay, while the few dim, momentary glimpses I caught of mountains through rifts in the flying clouds were far from encouraging either as weather signs or as guides. I had simply to grope my way from crevasse to crevasse, holding a general direction by the ice-structure, which was not to be seen everywhere, and partly by the wind.

Again and again I was put to my mettle, but Stickeen followed easily, his nerve apparently growing more unflinching as the danger increased. So it always is with mountaineers when hard beset. Running hard and jumping, holding every minute of the remaining daylight, poor as it was, precious, we doggedly persevered and tried to hope that every difficult crevasse we overcame would prove to be the last of its kind. But on the contrary, as we advanced they became more deadly trying.

At length our way was barred by a very wide and straight crevasse, which I traced rapidly northward a mile or so without finding a crossing or hope of one; then down the glacier about as far, to where it united with another uncrossable crevasse. In all this distance of perhaps two miles there was only one place where I could possibly jump it, but the width of this jump was the utmost I dared attempt, while the danger of slipping on the farther side was so great that I was loath to try it. Furthermore, the side I was on was about a foot higher than the other, and even with this advantage the crevasse seemed dangerously wide. One is liable to underestimate the width of crevasses where the magnitudes in general are great. I therefore stared at this one mighty keenly, estimating its width and the shape of the edge on the farther side, until I thought that I could jump it if necessary, but that in case I should be compelled to jump back from the lower side I might fail. Now, a cautious mountaineer seldom takes a step on unknown ground which seems at all dangerous that he cannot retrace in case he should be stopped by unseen obstacles ahead. This is the rule of mountaineers who live long, and, though in haste, I compelled myself to sit down and calmly deliberate before I broke it.

Retracing my devious path in imagination as if it were drawn on a chart, I saw that I was recrossing the glacier a mile or two farther up stream than the course pursued in the morning, and that I was now entangled in a section I had not before seen. Should I risk this dangerous jump, or try to regain the woods on the west shore, make a fire, and have only hunger to endure while waiting for a new day! I had already crossed so broad a stretch of dangerous ice that I saw it would be difficult to get back to the woods through the storm, before dark, and the attempt would most likely result in a dismal night-dance on the glacier; while just beyond the present barrier the surface seemed more promising, and the east shore was now perhaps about as near as the west. I was therefore eager to go on. But this wide jump was a dreadful obstacle.

At length, because of the dangers already behind me, I determined to venture against those that might be ahead, jumped and landed well, but with so little to spare that I more than ever dreaded being compelled to take that jump back from the lower side. Stickeen followed, making nothing of it, and we ran eagerly forward, hoping we were leaving all our troubles behind. But within the distance of a few hundred yards we were stopped by the widest crevasse yet encountered. Of course I made haste to explore it, hoping all might yet be remedied by finding a bridge or a way around either end. About three fourths of a mile up stream I found that it united with the one we had just crossed, as I feared it would. Then, tracing it down, I found it joined the same crevasse at the lower end also, maintaining throughout its whole course a width of forty to fifty feet. Thus to my dismay I discovered that we were on a narrow island about two miles long, with two barely possible ways to escape: one back by the way we came, the other ahead by an almost inaccessible sliver-bridge that crossed the great crevasse from near the middle of it!

After this nerve-trying discovery I ran back to the sliver-bridge and cautiously examined it. Crevasses, caused by strains from variations in the rate of motion of different parts of the glacier and convexities in the channel, are mere cracks when they first open, so narrow as hardly to admit the blade of a pocket-knife, and gradually widen according to the extent of the strain and the depth of the glacier. Now some of these cracks are interrupted, like the cracks in wood, and in the opening the strip of ice between overlapping ends is dragged out, and may maintain a continuous connection between the side, just as the two sides of a slivered crack in wood that is being split are connected. Some crevasses remain open for months or even years, and by the melting of their sides continue to increase in width long after the opening strain has ceased; while the sliver-bridges, level on top at first and perfectly safe, are at length melted to thin, vertical, knife-edged blades, the upper portion being most exposed to the weather; and since the exposure is greatest in the middle, they at length curve downward like the cables of suspension bridges. This one was evidently very old, for it had been weathered and wasted until it was the most dangerous and inaccessible that ever lay in my way. The width of the crevasse was here about fifty feet, and the sliver crossing diagonally was about seventy feet long; its thin knife-edge near the middle was depressed twenty-five or thirty feet below the level of the glacier, and the up-curving ends were attached to the sides eight or ten feet below the brink. Getting down the nearly vertical wall to the end of the sliver and up the other side were the main difficulties, and they seemed all but insurmountable. Of the many perils encountered in my years of wandering on mountains and glaciers none seemed so plain and stern and merciless as this. And it was presented when we were wet to the skin and hungry, the sky dark with quick driving snow, and the night near. But we were forced to face it. It was a tremendous necessity.

Beginning, not immediately above the sunken end of the bridge, but a little to one side, I cut a deep hollow on the brink for my knees to rest in. Then, leaning over, with my short-handled axe I cut a step sixteen or eighteen inches below, which on account of the sheerness of the wall was necessarily shallow. That step, however, was well made; its floor sloped slightly inward and formed a good hold for my heels. Then, slipping cautiously upon it, and crouching as low as possible, with my left side toward the wall, I steadied myself against the wind with my left hand in a slight notch, while with the right I cut other similar steps and notches in succession, guarding against losing balance by glinting of the axe, or by wind-gusts, for life and death were in every stroke and in the niceness of finish of every foothold.

After the end of the bridge was reached I chipped it down until I had made a level platform six or eight inches wide, and it was a trying thing to poise on this little slippery platform while bending over to get safely astride of the sliver. Crossing was then comparatively easy by chipping off the sharp edge with short, careful strokes, and hitching forward an inch or two at a time, keeping my balance with my knees pressed against the sides. The tremendous abyss on either hand I studiously ignored. To me the edge of that blue sliver was then all the world. But the most trying part of the adventure, after working my way across inch by inch and chipping another small platform, was to rise from the safe position astride and to cut a step-ladder in the nearly vertical face of the wall – chipping, climbing, holding on with feet and fingers in mere notches. At such times one's whole body is eye, and common skill and fortitude are replaced by power beyond our call or knowledge. Never before had I been so long under deadly strain. How I got up that cliff I never could tell. The thing seemed to have been done by somebody else. I never have held death in contempt, though in the course of my explorations I have oftentimes felt that to meet one's fate on a noble mountain, or in the heart of a glacier, would be blessed as compared with death from disease, or from some shabby lowland accident. But the best death, quick and crystal-pure, set so glaringly open before us, is hard enough to face, even though we feel gratefully sure that we have already had happiness enough for a dozen lives.

But poor Stickeen, the wee, hairy, sleekit beastie, think of him! When I had decided to dare the bridge, and while I was on my knees chipping a hollow on the rounded brow above it, he came behind me, pushed his head past my shoulder, looked down and across, scanned the sliver and its approaches with his mysterious eyes, then looked me in the face with a startled air of surprise and concern, and began to mutter and whine; saying as plainly as if speaking with words, 'Surely, you are not going into that awful place.' This was the first time I had seen him gaze deliberately into a crevasse, or into my face with an eager, speaking, troubled look. That he should have recognized and appreciated the danger at the first glance showed wonderful sagacity. Never before had the daring midget seemed to know that ice was slippery or that there was any such thing as danger anywhere. His looks and tones of voice when he began to complain and speak his fears were so human that I unconsciously talked to him in sympathy as I would to a frightened boy, and in trying to calm his fears perhaps in some measure moderated my own. 'Hush your fears, my boy,' I said, 'we will get across safe, though it is not going to be easy. No right way is easy in this rough world. We must risk our lives to save them. At the worst we can only slip, and then how grand a grave we will have, and by and by our nice bones will do good in the terminal moraine.'

But my sermon was far from reassuring him: he began to cry, and after taking another piercing look at the tremendous gulf, ran away in desperate excitement, seeking some other crossing. By the time he got back, baffled of course, I had made a step or two. I dared not look back, but he made himself heard; and when he saw that I was certainly bent on crossing he cried aloud in despair. The danger was enough to haunt anybody, but it seems wonderful that he should have been able to weight and appreciate it so justly. No mountaineer could have seen it more quickly or judged it more wisely, discriminating between real and apparent peril.

When I gained the other side, he screamed louder than ever, and after running back and forth in vain search for a way of escape, he would return to the brink of the crevasse above the bridge, moaning and wailing as if in the bitterness of death. Could this be the silent, philosophic Stickeen? I shouted encouragement, telling him the bridge was not so bad as it looked, that I had left it flat and safe for his feet, and he could walk it easily. But he was afraid to try. Strange so small an animal should be capable of such big, wise fears. I called again and again in a reassuring tone to come on and fear nothing; that he could come if he would only try. He would hush for a moment, look down again at the bridge, and shout his unshakable conviction that he could never, never come that way; then lie back in despair, as if howling, 'O-o-oh! what a place! No-o-o, I can never go-o-o down there!' His natural composure and courage had vanished utterly in a tumultuous storm of fear. Had the danger been less, his distress would have seemed ridiculous. But in this dismal, merciless abyss lay the shadow of death, and his heart-rending cries might well have called Heaven to his help. Perhaps they did. So hidden before, he was now transparent, and one could see the workings of his heart and mind like the movements of a clock out of its case. His voice and gestures, hopes and fears, were so perfectly human that none could mistake them; while he seemed to understand every word of mine. I was troubled at the thought of having to leave him out all night, and of the danger of not finding him in the morning. It seemed impossible to get him to venture. To compel him to try through fear of being abandoned, I started off as if leaving him to his fate, and disappeared back of a hummock; but this did no good; he only lay down and moaned in utter hopeless misery. So, after hiding a few minutes, I went back to the brink of the crevasse and in a severe tone of voice shouted across to him that now I must certainly leave him, I could wait no longer, and that, if he would not come, all I could promise was that I would return to seek him next day. I warned him that if he went back to the woods the wolves would kill him, and finished by urging him once more by words and gestures to come on, come on.

He knew very well what I meant, and at last, with the courage of despair, hushed and breathless, he crouched down on the brink in the hollow I had made for my knees, pressed his body against the ice as if trying to get the advantage of the friction of every hair, gazed into the first step, put his little feet together and slid them slowly, slowly over the edge and down into it, bunching all four in it and almost standing on his head. Then, without lifting his feet, as well as I could see through the snow, he slowly worked them over the edge of the step and down into the next and the next in succession in the same way, and gained the end of the bridge. Then, lifting his feet with the regularity and slowness of the vibrations of a seconds pendulum, as if counting and measuring *one-two-three,* holding himself steady against the gusty wind, and giving separate attention to each little step, he gained the foot of the cliff, while I was on my knees leaning over to give him a lift should he succeed in getting within reach of my arm. Here he halted in dead silence, and it was here I feared he might fail, for dogs are poor climbers. I had no cord. If I had had one, I would have dropped a noose over his head and hauled him up. But while I was thinking whether an available cord might be made out of clothing, he was looking keenly into the series of notched steps and finger-holds I had made, as if counting them, and fixing the position of each one of them in his mind. Then suddenly up he came in a springy rush, hooking his paws into the steps and notches so quickly that I could not see how it was done, and whizzed past my head, safe at last!

And now came a scene! 'Well done, well done, little boy! Brave boy!' I cried, trying to catch and caress him; but he would not be caught. Never before or since have I seen anything like so passionate a revulsion from the depths of despair to exultant, triumphant, uncontrollable joy. He flashed and darted hither and thither as if fairly demented, screaming and shouting, swirling round and round in giddy loops and circles like a leaf in a whirlwind, lying down, and rolling over and over, sidewise and heels over head, and pouring forth a tumultuous flood of hysterical cries and sobs and gasping mutterings. When I ran up to him to shake him, fearing he might die of joy, he flashed off two or three hundred yards, his feet in a mist of motion; then, turning suddenly, came back in a wild rush and launched himself at my face, almost knocking me down, all the while screeching and screaming and shouting as if saying, 'Saved! saved! saved!' Then away again, dropping suddenly at times with his feet in the air, trembling and fairly sobbing. Such passionate emotion was enough to kill him. Moses' stately song of triumph after escaping the Egyptians and the Red Sea was nothing to it. Who could have guessed the capacity of the dull, enduring little fellow for all that most stirs this mortal frame? Nobody could have helped crying with him!

But there is nothing like work for toning down excessive fear or joy. So I ran ahead, calling him in as gruff a voice as I could command to come on and stop his nonsense, for we had far to go and it would soon he dark. Neither of us feared another trial like this. Heaven would surely count one enough for a lifetime. The ice ahead was gashed by thousands of crevasses, but they were common ones. The joy of deliverance burned in us like fire, and we ran without fatigue, every muscle with immense rebound glorying in its strength. Stickeen flew across everything in his way, and not till dark did he settle into his normal fox-like trot. At last the cloudy mountains came in sight, and we soon felt the solid rock beneath our feet, and were safe. Then came weakness. Danger had vanished, and so had our strength. We tottered down the lateral moraine in the dark, over boulders and tree trunks, through the bushes and devil-club thickets of the grove where we had sheltered ourselves in the morning, and across the level mudslope of the terminal moraine. We reached camp about ten o'clock, and found a big fire and a big supper. A party of Hoona Indians had visited Mr Young, bringing a gift of porpoise meat and wild strawberries, and Hunter Joe had brought in a wild goat. But we lay down, too tired to eat much, and soon fell into a troubled sleep. The man who said, 'The harder the toil, the sweeter the rest,' never was profoundly tired. Stickeen kept springing up and muttering in his sleep, no doubt dreaming that he was still on the brink of the crevasse; and so did I, that night and many others long afterward, when I was over-tired.

Thereafter Stickeen was a changed dog. During the rest of the trip, instead of holding aloof, he always lay by my side, tried to keep me constantly in sight, and would hardly accept a morsel of food, however tempting, from any hand but mine. At night, when all was quiet about the campfire, he would come to me and rest his head on my knee with a look of devotion as if I were his god. And often as he caught my eye he seemed to be trying to say, 'Wasn't that an awful time we had together on the glacier?'

Nothing in after years has dimmed that Alaska storm-day. As I write it all comes rushing and roaring to mind as if I were again in the heart of it. Again I see the gray flying clouds with their rain-floods and snow, the ice-cliffs towering above the shrinking forest, the majestic ice-cascade, the vast glacier outspread before its white mountain-fountains, and in the heart of it the tremendous crevasse – emblem of the valley of the shadow of death – low clouds trailing over it, the snow falling into it; and on its brink I see little Stickeen, and I hear his cries for help and his shouts of joy. I have known many dogs, and many a story I could tell of their wisdom and devotion; but to none do I owe so much as to Stickeen. At first the least promising and least known of my dog-friends, he suddenly became the best known of them all. Our storm-battle for life brought him to light, and through him as through a window I have ever since been looking with deeper sympathy into all my fellow mortals.

None of Stickeen's friends knows what finally became of him. After my work for the season was done I departed for California, and I never saw the dear little fellow again. In reply to anxious inquiries his master wrote me that in the summer of 1883 he was stolen by a tourist at Fort Wrangell and taken away on a steamer. His fate is wrapped in mystery. Doubtless he has left this world – crossed the last crevasse – and gone to another. But he will not be forgotten. To me Stickeen is immortal.

Selections from

STEEP TRAILS

(1918)

This posthumous book was originally derived from a collection of Muir's magazine articles and essays, originally published in *Picturesque California* between 1873 and 1902. They were compiled after Muir's death by William Frederick Bade, his literary executor. The quality of these essays varies considerably and there is simply not space here to include the twenty-four original chapters. Three outstanding examples of Muir's adventure writing are selected here, namely: 'A Geologist's Winter Walk' (1873); 'A Perilous Night on Shasta's Summit' (1888) and 'An Ascent of Mt Rainier' (1888). In addition I have included Muir's essay 'The Grand Canyon of the Colorado', published in *Century Magazine* in 1902, which prepared the way for the creation of the later national park in 1908.

'A Geologist's Winter Walk' is an excerpt from a letter Muir wrote to his mentor Jeanne Carr describing his exploration of the remote Tenaya Canyon and the high country around Lake Tenaya in Yosemite. Carr found Muir's letter so compelling that she sent it to the *Overland Monthly Magazine* without his knowledge. It is the story of a remarkable winter adventure in the High Sierra during which Muir slipped on the edge of a precipice, was knocked unconscious, and survived only by sheer chance. It gives an insight into the level of risk which Muir took in venturing into mountain wildernesses, at all seasons, alone, with no earthly hope of rescue. The activity of 'mountaineering' was in its infancy in America at this time and equipment, techniques and knowledge were largely matters of improvisation and personal invention. Muir had no tent, sleeping bag, crampons, mobile phone, GPS or freeze-dried foods when he ventured into the mountains. His equipment consisted of an old tweed jacket and a pair of leather boots; his tent was normally a Juniper thicket and his food consisted of bricks of dried bread, which sustained him on week-long climbs above 10,000 feet.

'A Perilous Night on Shasta's Summit' merges two of Muir's Mount Shasta adventures into one narrative. His first solo exploration of this 14,400-foot snow-capped volcano in northern California took place on 2 November 1874. This story is fused with the account of his near-death experience with Jerome Fay on his third climb of Shasta on 30 April 1875. On this epic ice-climb they became trapped by hurricane-force winds and a violent lightning storm near the summit of the giant volcano. Muir was confident that he could descend the perilous cornices to safety in the woods 10,000 feet below, but his fellow-climber was utterly terrified and unable to carry on. Faced with abandoning his companion to save his own life, Muir opted to stay with his weaker friend, but the only way to survive the raging blizzard and deep, sub-zero cold on the open slopes was to bury themselves in the scalding volcanic mud beneath the snow. For more than twelve hours they had to lie beneath the snow: their flesh scalded by boiling mud; hands and feet blackened by frostbite; lungs burned by sulphuric-acid vapour. They survived a night of unimaginable torture, arguably among the most memorable ever recorded in mountaineering literature. When dawn finally came, Muir dragged and carried his friend for thousands of feet down the mountain through the deep snowdrifts until they finally collapsed into the arms of rescuers who had set out to find them. They were put to bed for many days and recovery was slow and painful. Muir later wrote that his lungs and his limbs never truly recovered from this appalling experience and he remained susceptible to attacks of pleurisy and pneumonia for the rest of his life; it was a sudden attack of pneumonia which killed him in Los Angeles in 1914. The essay was first published in 1888 as part of *Picturesque California* and was later included in *Steep Trails*. It is an epic of mountaineering which stands comparison with any modern account.

*

'An Ascent of Mount Rainier' is Muir's account of the ascent of 14,411 ft Rainier, on 14 August 1888, the seventh recorded ascent of this giant snow-capped volcano which overlooks modern Seattle. Muir wrote to his wife that he had not intended to climb this mountain – just to visit the area; but then he 'got excited' and climbed it anyway. The ascent of Mt Rainier is a daunting proposition even today, with the benefits of modern equipment and clothing, and the guarantee of helicopter mountain rescue; Muir's equipment consisted of a wood-axe and a length of washing-line, and he wore his old tweed jacket. The account is one of the finest of Muir's mountaineering tales; his ecstatic descriptions of the unspoiled alpine wilderness that girdles the mountain were later published as a series of articles campaigning for the establishment of Mount Rainier National Park, which eventually came in 1899.

'The Grand Canyon of the Colorado' was originally published in *Century Magazine* in 1902 and served as a vehicle to support the campaign to have the area designated as a National Park, which ensued in 1908. Even today, it would be hard to find a better introductory guide to the glories of this natural wonder.

Chapter 2

A GEOLOGIST'S WINTER WALK

After reaching Turlock, I sped afoot over the stubble fields and through miles of brown hemizonia and purple erigeron, to Hopeton, conscious of little more than that the town was behind and beneath me, and the mountains above and before me; on through the oaks and chaparral of the foothills to Coulterville; and then ascended the first great mountain step upon which grows the sugar pine. Here I slackened pace, for I drank the spicy, resiny wind, and beneath the arms of this noble tree I felt that I was safely home. Never did pine trees seem so dear. How sweet was their breath and their song, and how grandly they winnowed the sky! I tingled my fingers among their tassels, and rustled my feet among their brown needles and burrs, and was exhilarated and joyful beyond all I can write.

When I reached Yosemite, all the rocks seemed talkative, and more telling and lovable than ever. They are dear friends, and seemed to have warm blood gushing through their granite flesh; and I love them with a love intensified by long and close companionship. After I had bathed in the bright river, sauntered over the meadows, conversed with the domes, and played with the pines, I still felt blurred and weary, as if tainted in some way with the sky of your streets. I determined, therefore, to run out for a while to say my prayers in the higher mountain temples. 'The days are sunful,' I said, 'and, though now winter, no great danger need be encountered, and no sudden storm will block my return, if I am watchful.'

The morning after this decision, I started up the canyon of Tenaya, caring little about the quantity of bread I carried; for, I thought, a fast and a storm and a difficult canyon were just the medicine I needed. When I passed Mirror Lake, I scarcely noticed it, for I was absorbed in the great Tissiack – her crown a mile away in the hushed azure; her purple granite drapery flowing in soft and graceful folds down to my feet, embroidered gloriously around with deep, shadowy forest. I have gazed on Tissiack a thousand times – in days of solemn storms, and when her form shone divine with the jewelry of winter, or was veiled in living clouds; and I have heard her voice of winds, and snowy, tuneful waters when floods were falling; yet never did her soul reveal itself more impressively than now. I hung about her skirts, lingering timidly, until the higher mountains and glaciers compelled me to push up the canyon.

This canyon is accessible only to mountaineers, and I was anxious to carry my barometer and clinometer through it, to obtain sections and altitudes, so I chose it as the most attractive highway. After I had passed the tall groves that stretch a mile above Mirror Lake, and scrambled around the Tenaya Fall, which is just at the head of the lake groves, I crept through the dense and spiny chaparral that plushes the roots of the mountains here for miles in warm green, and was ascending a precipitous rock front, smoothed by glacial action, when I suddenly fell – for the first time since I touched foot to Sierra rocks. After several somersaults, I became insensible from the shock, and when consciousness returned I found myself wedged among short, stiff bushes, trembling as if cold, not injured in the slightest.

Judging by the sun, I could not have been insensible very long; probably not a minute, possibly an hour; and I could not remember what made me fall, or where I had fallen from; but I saw that if I had rolled a little further, my mountain climbing would have been finished, for just beyond the bushes the canyon wall steepened and I might have fallen to the bottom. 'There,' said I, addressing my feet, to whose separate skill I had learned to trust night and day on any mountain, 'that is what you get by intercourse with stupid town stairs, and dead pavements.' I felt degraded and worthless. I had not yet reached the most difficult portion of the canyon, but I determined to guide my humbled body over the most nerve-trying places I could find; for I was now awake, and felt confident that the last of the town fog had been shaken from both head and feet.

I camped at the mouth of a narrow gorge which is cut into

the bottom of the main canyon, determined to take earnest exercise next day. No plushy boughs did my ill-behaved bones enjoy that night, nor did my bumped head get a spicy cedar plume pillow mixed with flowers. I slept on a naked boulder, and when I awoke all my nervous trembling was gone.

The gorged portion of the canyon, in which I spent all the next day, is about a mile and a half in length; and I passed the time in tracing the action of the forces that determined this peculiar bottom gorge, which is an abrupt, ragged-walled, narrow-throated canyon, formed in the bottom of the wide-mouthed, smooth, and beveled main canyon. I will not stop now to tell you more; some day you may see it, like a shadowy line, from Cloud's Rest. In high water, the stream occupies all the bottom of the gorge, surging and chafing in glorious power from wall to wall. But the sound of the grinding was low as I entered the gorge, scarcely hoping to be able to pass through its entire length. By cool efforts, along glassy, ice-worn slopes, I reached the upper end in a little over a day, but was compelled to pass the second night in the gorge, and in the moonlight I wrote you this short pencil-letter in my notebook: –

The moon is looking down into the canyon, and how marvelously the great rocks kindle to her light! Every dome, and brow, and swelling boss touched by her white rays, glows as if lighted with snow. I am now only a mile from last night's camp; and have been climbing and sketching all day in this difficult but instructive gorge. It is formed in the bottom of the main canyon, among the roots of Cloud's Rest. It begins at the filled-up lake basin where I camped last night, and ends a few hundred yards above, in another basin of the same kind. The walls everywhere are craggy and vertical, and in some places they overlean. It is only from twenty to sixty feet wide, and not, though black and broken enough, the thin, crooked mouth of some mysterious abyss; but it was eroded, for in many places I saw its solid, seamless floor.

I am sitting on a big stone, against which the stream divides, and goes brawling by in rapids on both sides; half of my rock is white in the light, half in shadow. As I look from the opening jaws of this shadowy gorge, South Dome is immediately in front – high in the stars, her face turned from the moon, with the rest of her body gloriously muffled in waved folds of granite. On the left, sculptured from the main Cloud's Rest ridge, are three magnificent rocks, sisters of the great South Dome. On the right is the massive, moonlit front of Mount Watkins, and between, low down in the furthest distance, is Sentinel Dome, girdled and darkened with forest. In the near foreground Tenaya Creek is singing against boulders that are white with snow and moonbeams. Now look back twenty yards, and you will see a waterfall fair as a spirit; the moonlight just touches it, bringing it into relief against a dark background of shadow. A little to the left, and a dozen steps this side of the fall, a flickering light marks my camp – and a precious camp it is. A huge, glacier-polished slab, falling from the smooth, glossy flank of Cloud's Rest, happened to settle on edge against the wall of the gorge. I did not know that this slab was glacier-polished until I lighted my fire. Judge of my delight. I think it was sent here by an earthquake. It is about twelve feet square. I wish I could take it home for a hearthstone. Beneath this slab is the only place in this torrent-swept gorge where I could find sand sufficient for a bed.

I expected to sleep on the boulders, for I spent most of the afternoon on the slippery wall of the canyon, endeavoring to get around this difficult part of the gorge, and was compelled to hasten down here for water before dark. I shall sleep soundly on this sand; half of it is mica. Here, wonderful to behold, are a few green stems of prickly rubus, and a tiny grass. They are here to meet us. Ay, even here in this darksome gorge, 'frightened and tormented' with raging torrents and choking avalanches of snow. Can it be? As if rubus and the grass leaf were not enough of God's tender prattle words of love, which we so much need in these mighty temples of power, yonder in the 'benmost bore' are two blessed adiantums. Listen to them! How wholly infused with God is this one big word of love that we call the world! Goodnight. Do you see the fire-glow on my ice-smoothed slab, and on my two ferns and the rubus and grass panicles? And do you hear how sweet a sleep-song the fall and cascades are singing?

The water-ground chips and knots that I found fastened between the rocks kept my fire alive all through the night. Next morning I rose nerved and ready for another day of sketching and noting, and any form of climbing. I escaped from the gorge about noon, after accomplishing some of the most delicate feats of mountaineering I ever attempted; and here the canyon is all broadly open again – the floor luxuriantly forested with pine, and spruce, and silver fir, and brown-trunked *Libocedrus*. The walls rise in Yosemite forms, and Tenaya Creek comes down seven hundred feet in a white brush of foam. This is a little Yosemite valley. It is about two thousand feet above the level of the main Yosemite, and about twenty-four hundred below Lake Tenaya.

I found the lake frozen, and the ice was so clear and unruffled that the surrounding mountains and the groves that look down upon it were reflected almost as perfectly as I ever beheld them in the calm evening mirrors of summer. At a little distance, it was difficult to believe the lake frozen at all; and when I walked out on it, cautiously stamping at short intervals to test the strength of the ice, I seemed to walk mysteriously, without adequate faith, on the surface of the water. The ice was so transparent that I could see through it the beautifully wave-rippled, sandy bottom, and the scales of mica glinting back the down-pouring light. When I knelt down with my face close to the ice, through which the sunbeams were pouring, I was delighted to discover myriad Tyndall's six-rayed water flowers, magnificently colored.

A grand old mountain mansion is this Tenaya region! In the glacier period it was a mer de glace, far grander than the mer de glace of Switzerland, which is only about half a mile broad. The Tenaya mer de glace was not less than two miles broad, late in the glacier epoch, when all the principal dividing crests were bare; and its depth was not less than fifteen hundred feet. Ice streams from Mounts Lyell and Dana, and all the mountains between, and from the nearer Cathedral Peak, flowed hither, welded into one, and worked together. After eroding this Tanaya Lake basin, and all the splendidly sculptured rocks and mountains that surround and adorn it, and the great Tenaya Canyon, with its wealth of all that makes mountains sublime, they were welded with the vast South, Lyell, and Illilouette glaciers on one side, and with those of Hoffman on the other – thus forming a portion of a yet grander mer de glace in Yosemite Valley.

I reached the Tenaya Canyon, on my way home, by coming in from the northeast, rambling down over the shoulders of Mount Watkins, touching bottom a mile above Mirror Lake. From thence home was but a saunter in the moonlight.

After resting one day, and the weather continuing calm, I ran up over the left shoulder of South Dome and down in front of its grand split face to make some measurements, completed my work, climbed to the right shoulder, struck off along the ridge for Cloud's Rest, and reached the topmost heave of her sunny wave in ample time to see the sunset.

Cloud's Rest is a thousand feet higher than Tissiack. It is a wavelike crest upon a ridge, which begins at Yosemite with Tissiack, and runs continuously eastward to the thicket of peaks and crests around Lake Tenaya. This lofty granite wall is bent this way and that by the restless and weariless action of glaciers just as if it had been made of dough. But the grand circumference of mountains and forests are coming from far and near, densing into one close assemblage; for the sun, their god and father, with love ineffable, is glowing a sunset farewell. Not one of all the assembled rocks or trees seemed remote. How impressively their faces shone with responsive love!

I ran home in the moonlight with firm strides; for the sun-love made me strong. Down through the junipers; down through the firs; now in jet shadows, now in white light; over sandy moraines and bare, clanking rocks; past the huge ghost of South Dome rising weird through the firs; past the glorious fall of Nevada, the groves of Illilouette; through the pines of the valley; beneath the bright crystal sky blazing with stars. All of this mountain wealth in one day! – one of the rich ripe days that enlarge one's life; so much of the sun upon one side of it, so much of the moon and stars on the other.

Chapter 4

A PERILOUS NIGHT ON SHASTA'S SUMMIT

Toward the end of summer, after a light, open winter, one may reach the summit of Mount Shasta without passing over much snow, by keeping on the crest of a long narrow ridge, mostly bare, that extends from near the camp-ground at the timberline. But on my first excursion to the summit the whole mountain, down to its low swelling base, was smoothly laden with loose fresh snow, presenting a most glorious mass of winter mountain scenery, in the midst of which I scrambled and reveled or lay snugly snowbound, enjoying the fertile clouds and the snow-bloom in all their growing, drifting grandeur.

I had walked from Redding, sauntering leisurely from station to station along the old Oregon stage road, the better to see the rocks and plants, birds and people, by the way, tracing the rushing Sacramento to its fountains around icy Shasta. The first rains had fallen on the lowlands, and the first snows on the mountains, and everything was fresh and bracing, while an abundance of balmy sunshine filled all the noonday hours. It was the calm afterglow that usually succeeds the first storm of the winter. I met many of the birds that had reared their young and spent their summer in the Shasta woods and chaparral. They were then on their way south to their winter homes, leading their young full-fledged and about as large and strong as the parents. Squirrels, dry and elastic after the storms, were busy about their stores of pine nuts, and the latest goldenrods were still in bloom, though it was now past the middle of October. The grand color glow – the autumnal jubilee of ripe leaves – was past prime, but, freshened by the rain, was still making a fine show along the banks of the river and in the ravines and the dells of the smaller streams.

At the salmon-hatching establishment on the McCloud River I halted a week to examine the limestone belt, grandly developed there, to learn what I could of the inhabitants of the river and its banks, and to give time for the fresh snow that I knew had fallen on the mountain to settle somewhat, with a view to making the ascent. A pedestrian on these mountain roads, especially so late in the year, is sure to excite curiosity, and many were the interrogations concerning my ramble. When I said that I was simply taking a walk, and that icy Shasta was my mark, I was invariably admonished that I had come on a dangerous quest. The time was far too late, the snow was too loose and deep to climb, and I should be lost in drifts and slides. When I hinted that new snow was beautiful and storms not so bad as they were called, my advisers shook their heads in token of superior knowledge and declared the ascent of 'Shasta Butte' through loose snow impossible. Nevertheless, before noon of the second of November I was in the frosty azure of the utmost summit.

When I arrived at Sisson's everything was quiet. The last of the summer visitors had flitted long before, and the deer and bears also were beginning to seek their winter homes. My barometer and the sighing winds and filmy half-transparent clouds that dimmed the sunshine gave notice of the approach of another storm, and I was in haste to be off and get myself established somewhere in the midst of it, whether the summit was to be attained or not. Sisson, who is a mountaineer, speedily fitted me out for storm or calm as only a mountaineer could, with warm blankets and a week's provisions so generous in quantity and kind that they easily might have been made to last a month in case of my being closely snowbound. Well I knew the weariness of snow-climbing, and the frosts, and the dangers of mountaineering so late in the year; therefore I could not ask a guide to go with me, even had one been willing. All I wanted was to have blankets and provisions deposited as far up in the timber as the snow would permit a pack animal to go. There I could build a storm nest and lie warm, and make raids up and around the mountain in accordance with the weather.

Setting out on the afternoon of November first, with Jerome Fay, mountaineer and guide, in charge of the animals, I was soon plodding wearily upward through the muffled winter woods, the snow of course growing steadily deeper and looser, so that we had to break a trail. The animals began to get discouraged, and after night and darkness came on they became entangled in a bed of rough lava, where, breaking through four or five feet of mealy snow, their feet were caught between angular boulders. Here they were in danger of being lost, but after we had removed packs and saddles and assisted their efforts with ropes, they all escaped to the side of a ridge about a thousand feet below the timberline.

To go farther was out of the question, so we were compelled to camp as best we could. A pitch pine fire speedily changed the temperature and shed a blaze of light on the wild lava-slope and the straggling storm-bent pines around us. Melted snow answered for coffee, and we had plenty of venison to roast. Toward midnight I rolled myself in my blankets, slept an hour and a half, arose and ate more venison, tied two days' provisions to my belt, and set out for the summit, hoping to reach it ere the coming storm should fall. Jerome accompanied me a little distance above camp and indicated the way as well as he could in the darkness. He seemed loath to leave me, but, being reassured that I was at home and required no care, he bade me goodbye and returned to camp, ready to lead his animals down the mountain at daybreak.

After I was above the dwarf pines, it was fine practice pushing up the broad unbroken slopes of snow, alone in the solemn silence of the night. Half the sky was clouded; in the other half the stars sparkled icily in the keen, frosty air; while everywhere the glorious wealth of snow fell away from the summit of the cone in flowing folds, more extensive and continuous than any I had ever seen before. When day dawned the clouds were crawling slowly and becoming more massive, but gave no intimation of immediate danger, and I pushed on faithfully, though holding myself well in hand, ready to return to the timber; for it was easy to see that the storm was not far off. The mountain rises ten thousand feet above the general level of the country, in blank exposure to the deep upper currents of the sky, and no labyrinth of peaks and canyons I had ever been in seemed to me so dangerous as these immense slopes, bare against the sky.

The frost was intense, and drifting snow dust made breathing at times rather difficult. The snow was as dry as meal, and the finer particles drifted freely, rising high in the air, while the larger portions of the crystals rolled like sand. I frequently sank to my armpits between buried blocks of loose lava, but generally only to my knees. When tired with walking I still wallowed slowly upward on all fours. The steepness of the slope – thirty-five degrees in some places – made any kind of progress fatiguing, while small avalanches were being constantly set in motion in the steepest places. But the bracing air and the sublime beauty of the snowy expanse thrilled every nerve and made absolute exhaustion impossible. I seemed to be walking and wallowing in a cloud; but, holding steadily onward, by half-past ten o'clock I had gained the highest summit.

I held my commanding foothold in the sky for two hours, gazing on the glorious landscapes spread maplike around the immense horizon, and tracing the outlines of the ancient lava-streams extending far into the surrounding plains, and the pathways of vanished glaciers of which Shasta had been the center. But, as I had left my coat in camp for the sake of having my limbs free in climbing, I soon was cold. The wind increased in violence, raising the snow in magnificent drifts that were drawn out in the form of wavering banners blowing in the sun. Toward the end of my stay a succession of small clouds struck against the summit rocks like drifting icebergs, darkening the air as they passed, and producing a chill as definite and sudden as if ice-water had been dashed in my face. This is the kind of cloud in which snow-flowers grow, and I turned and fled.

Finding that I was not closely pursued, I ventured to take time on the way down for a visit to the head of the Whitney Glacier and the 'Crater Butte.' After I had reached the end of the main summit ridge the descent was but little more than one continuous soft, mealy, muffled slide, most luxurious and rapid, though the hissing, swishing speed attained was obscured in great part by flying snow dust – a marked contrast to the boring seal-wallowing upward struggle. I reached camp about an hour before dusk, hollowed a strip of loose ground in the lee of a large block of red lava, where firewood was abundant, rolled myself in my blankets, and went to sleep.

Next morning, having slept little the night before the ascent and being weary with climbing after the excitement was over, I slept late. Then, awaking suddenly, my eyes opened on one of the most beautiful and sublime scenes I ever enjoyed. A boundless wilderness of storm clouds of different degrees of ripeness were congregated over all the lower landscape for thousands of square miles, colored gray, and purple, and pearl, and deep-glowing white, amid which I seemed to be floating; while the great white cone of the mountain above was all aglow in the free, blazing sunshine. It seemed not so much an ocean as a land of clouds – undulating hill and dale, smooth purple plains, and silvery mountains of cumuli, range over range, diversified with peak and dome and hollow fully brought out in light and shade.

I gazed enchanted, but cold gray masses, drifting like dust on a wind-swept plain, began to shut out the light, forerunners of the coming storm I had been so anxiously watching. I made haste to gather as much wood as possible, snugging it as a shelter around my bed. The storm side of my blankets was fastened down with stakes to reduce as much as possible the sifting-in of drift and the danger of being blown away. The precious bread sack was placed safely as a pillow, and when at length the first flakes fell I was exultingly ready to welcome them. Most of my firewood was more than half rosin and would blaze in the face of the fiercest drifting; the winds could not demolish my bed, and my bread could be made to last indefinitely; while in case of need I had the means of making snowshoes and could retreat or hold my ground as I pleased.

Presently the storm broke forth into full snowy bloom, and the thronging crystals darkened the air. The wind swept past in hissing floods, grinding the snow into meal and sweeping down into the hollows in enormous drifts all the heavier particles, while the finer dust was sifted through the sky, increasing the icy gloom. But my fire glowed bravely as if in glad defiance of the drift to quench it, and, notwithstanding but little trace of my nest could be seen after the snow had leveled and buried it, I was snug and warm, and the passionate uproar produced a glad excitement.

Day after day the storm continued, piling snow on snow in weariless abundance. There were short periods of quiet, when the sun would seem to look eagerly down through rents in the clouds, as if to know how the work was advancing. During these calm intervals I replenished my fire – sometimes without leaving the nest, for fire and woodpile were so near this could easily be done – or busied myself with my notebook, watching the gestures of the trees in taking the snow, examining separate crystals under a lens, and learning the methods of their deposition as an enduring fountain for the streams. Several times, when the storm ceased for a few minutes, a Douglas squirrel came frisking from the foot of a clump of dwarf pines, moving in sudden interrupted spurts over the bossy snow; then, without any apparent guidance, he would dig rapidly into the drift where were buried some grains of barley that the horses had left. The Douglas squirrel does not strictly belong to these upper woods, and I was surprised to see him out in such weather. The mountain sheep also, quite a large flock of them, came to my camp and took shelter beside a clump of matted dwarf pines a little above my nest.

The storm lasted about a week, but before it was ended Sisson became alarmed and sent up the guide with animals to see what had become of me and recover the camp outfit. The news spread that 'there was a man on the mountain,' and he must surely have perished, and Sisson was blamed for allowing anyone to attempt climbing in such weather; while I was as safe as anybody in the lowlands, lying like a squirrel in a warm, fluffy nest, busied about my own affairs and wishing only to be let alone. Later, however, a trail could not have been broken for a horse, and some of the camp furniture would have had to be abandoned. On the fifth day I returned to Sisson's, and from that comfortable base made excursions, as the weather permitted, to the Black Butte, to the foot of the Whitney Glacier, around the base of the mountain, to Rhett and Klamath Lakes, to the Modoc region and elsewhere, developing many interesting scenes and experiences.

But the next spring, on the other side of this eventful winter, I saw and felt still more of the Shasta snow. For then it was my fortune to get into the very heart of a storm, and to be held in it for a long time.

On the 28th of April [1875] I led a party up the mountain for the purpose of making a survey of the summit with reference to the location of the Geodetic monument. On the 30th, accompanied by Jerome Fay, I made another ascent to make some barometrical observations, the day intervening between the two ascents being devoted to establishing a camp on the extreme edge of the timberline. Here, on our red trachyte bed, we obtained two hours of shallow sleep broken for occasional glimpses of the keen, starry night. At two o'clock we rose, breakfasted on a warmed tin-cupful of coffee and a piece of frozen venison broiled on the coals, and started for the summit. Up to this time there was nothing in sight that betokened the approach of a storm; but on gaining the summit, we saw toward Lassen's Butte hundreds of square miles of white cumuli boiling dreamily in the sunshine far beneath us, and causing no alarm.

The slight weariness of the ascent was soon rested away, and our glorious morning in the sky promised nothing but enjoyment. At 9 a.m. the dry thermometer stood at 34 degrees in the shade and rose steadily until at 1 p.m. it stood at 50 degrees, probably influenced somewhat by radiation from the sun-warmed cliffs. A common bumblebee, not at all benumbed, zigzagged vigorously about our heads for a few moments, as if unconscious of the fact that the nearest honey flower was a mile beneath him.

In the meantime clouds were growing down in Shasta Valley – massive swelling cumuli, displaying delicious tones of purple and gray in the hollows of their sun-beaten bosses. Extending gradually southward around on both sides of Shasta, these at length united with the older field towards Lassen's Butte, thus encircling Mount Shasta in one continuous cloud zone. Rhett and Klamath Lakes were eclipsed beneath clouds scarcely less brilliant than their own silvery disks. The Modoc Lava Beds, many a snow-laden peak far north in Oregon, the Scott and Trinity and Siskiyou Mountains, the peaks of the Sierra, the blue Coast Range, Shasta Valley, the dark forests filling the valley of the Sacramento, all in turn were obscured or buried, leaving the lofty cone on which we stood solitary in the sunshine between two skies – a sky of spotless blue above, a sky of glittering cloud beneath. The creative sun shone glorious on the vast expanse of cloudland; hill and dale, mountain and valley springing into existence responsive to his rays and steadily developing in beauty and individuality. One huge mountain-cone of cloud, corresponding to Mount Shasta in these newborn cloud ranges, rose close alongside with a visible motion, its firm, polished bosses seeming so near and substantial that we almost fancied that we might leap down upon them from where we stood and make our way to the lowlands. No hint was given, by anything in their appearance, of the fleeting character of these most sublime and beautiful cloud mountains. On the contrary they impressed one as being lasting additions to the landscape.

The weather of the springtime and summer, throughout the Sierra in general, is usually varied by slight local rains and dustings of snow, most of which are obviously far too joyous and life-giving to be regarded as storms – single clouds growing in the sunny sky, ripening in an hour, showering the heated landscape, and passing away like a thought, leaving no visible bodily remains to stain the sky. Snowstorms of the same gentle kind abound among the high peaks, but in spring they not unfrequently attain larger proportions, assuming a violence and energy of expression scarcely surpassed by those bred in the depths of winter. Such was the storm now gathering about us.

It began to declare itself shortly after noon, suggesting to us the idea of at once seeking our safe camp in the timber and abandoning the purpose of making an observation of the barometer at 3 p.m – two having already been made, at 9 a.m., and 12 m, while simultaneous observations were made at Strawberry Valley. Jerome peered at short intervals over the ridge, contemplating the rising clouds with anxious gestures in the rough wind, and at length declared that if we did not make a speedy escape we should be compelled to pass the rest of the day and night on the summit. But anxiety to complete my observations stifled my own instinctive promptings to retreat, and held me to my work. No inexperienced person was depending on me, and I told Jerome that we two mountaineers should be able to make our way down through any storm likely to fall.

Presently thin, fibrous films of cloud began to blow directly over the summit from north to south, drawn out in long fairy webs like carded wool, forming and dissolving as if by magic. The wind twisted them into ringlets and whirled them in a succession of graceful convolutions like the outside sprays of Yosemite Falls in flood time; then, sailing out into the thin azure over the precipitous brink of the ridge they were drifted together like wreaths of foam on a river. These higher and finer cloud fabrics were evidently produced by the chilling of the air from its own expansion caused by the upward deflection of the wind against the slopes of the mountain. They steadily increased on the north rim of the cone, forming at length a thick, opaque, ill-defined embankment from the icy meshes of which snow-flowers began to fall, alternating with hail. The sky speedily darkened, and just as I had completed my last observation and boxed my instruments ready for the descent, the storm began in serious earnest. At first the cliffs were beaten with hail, every stone of which, as far as I could see, was regular in form, six-sided pyramids with rounded base, rich and sumptuous-looking, and fashioned with loving care, yet seemingly thrown away on those desolate crags down which they went rolling, falling, sliding in a network of curious streams.

After we had forced our way down the ridge and past the group of hissing fumaroles, the storm became inconceivably violent. The thermometer fell 22 degrees in a few minutes, and soon dropped below zero. The hail gave place to snow, and darkness came on like night. The wind, rising to the highest pitch of violence, boomed and surged amid the desolate crags; lightning flashes in quick succession cut the gloomy darkness; and the thunders, the most tremendously loud and appalling I ever heard, made an almost continuous roar, stroke following stroke in quick, passionate succession, as though the mountain were being rent to its foundations and the fires of the old volcano were breaking forth again.

Could we at once have begun to descend the snow slopes leading to the timber, we might have made good our escape, however dark and wild the storm. As it was, we had first to make our way along a dangerous ridge nearly a mile and a half long, flanked in many places by steep ice-slopes at the head of the Whitney Glacier on one side and by shattered precipices on the other. Apprehensive of this coming darkness, I had taken the precaution, when the storm began, to make the most dangerous points clear to my mind, and to mark their relations with reference to the direction of the wind. When, therefore, the darkness came on, and the bewildering drift, I felt confident that we could force our way through it with no other guidance. After passing the 'Hot Springs' I halted in the lee of a lava-block to let Jerome, who had fallen a little behind, come up. Here he opened a council in which, under circumstances sufficiently exciting but without evincing any bewilderment, he maintained, in opposition to my views, that it was impossible to proceed. He firmly refused to make the venture to find the camp, while I, aware of the dangers that would necessarily attend our efforts, and conscious of being the cause of his present peril, decided not to leave him.

Our discussions ended, Jerome made a dash from the shelter of the lava-block and began forcing his way back against the wind to the 'Hot Springs,' wavering and struggling to resist being carried away, as if he were fording a rapid stream. After waiting and watching in vain for some flaw in the storm that might be urged as a new argument in favor of attempting the descent, I was compelled to follow. 'Here,' said Jerome, as we shivered in the midst of the hissing, sputtering fumaroles, 'we shall be safe from frost.' 'Yes,' said I, 'we can lie in this mud and steam and sludge, warm at least on one side; but how can we protect our lungs from the acid gases, and how, after our clothing is saturated, shall we be able to reach camp without freezing, even after the storm is over? We shall have to wait for sunshine, and when will it come?'

The tempered area to which we had committed ourselves extended over about one fourth of an acre; but it was only about an eighth of an inch in thickness, for the scalding gas jets were shorn off close to the ground by the oversweeping flood of frosty wind. And how lavishly the snow fell only mountaineers may know. The crisp crystal flowers seemed to touch one another and fairly to thicken the tremendous blast that carried them. This was the bloom-time, the summer of the cloud, and never before have I seen even a mountain cloud flowering so profusely.

When the bloom of the Shasta chaparral is falling, the ground is sometimes covered for hundreds of square miles to a depth of half an inch. But the bloom of this fertile snow cloud grew and matured and fell to a depth of two feet in a few hours. Some crystals landed with their rays almost perfect, but most of them were worn and broken by striking against one another, or by rolling on the ground. The touch of these snow-flowers in calm weather is infinitely gentle – glinting, swaying, settling silently in the dry mountain air, or massed in flakes soft and downy. To lie out alone in the mountains of a still night and be touched by the first of these small silent messengers from the sky is a memorable experience, and the fineness of that touch none will forget. But the storm-blast laden with crisp, sharp snow seems to crush and bruise and stupefy with its multitude of stings, and compels the bravest to turn and flee.

The snow fell without abatement until an hour or two after what seemed to be the natural darkness of the night. Up to the time the storm first broke on the summit its development was remarkably gentle. There was a deliberate growth of clouds, a weaving of translucent tissue above, then the roar of the wind and the thunder, and the darkening flight of snow. Its subsidence was not less sudden. The clouds broke and vanished, not a crystal was left in the sky, and the stars shone out with pure and tranquil radiance.

During the storm we lay on our backs so as to present as little surface as possible to the wind, and to let the drift pass over us. The mealy snow sifted into the folds of our clothing and in many places reached the skin. We were glad at first to see the snow packing about us, hoping it would deaden the force of the wind, but it soon froze into a stiff, crusty heap as the temperature fell, rather augmenting our novel misery.

When the heat became unendurable, on some spot where steam was escaping through the sludge, we tried to stop it with snow and mud, or shifted a little at a time by shoving with our heels; for to stand in blank exposure to the fearful wind in our frozen-and-broiled condition seemed certain death. The acrid incrustations sublimed from the escaping gases frequently gave way, opening new vents to scald us; and, fearing that if at any time the wind should fall, carbonic acid, which often formed a considerable portion of the gaseous exhalations of volcanoes, might collect in sufficient quantities to cause sleep and death, I warned Jerome against forgetting himself for a single moment, even should his sufferings admit of such a thing.

Accordingly, when during the long, dreary watches of the night we roused from a state of half-consciousness, we called each other by name in a frightened, startled way, each fearing the other might be benumbed or dead. The ordinary sensations of cold give but a faint conception of that which comes on after hard climbing with want of food and sleep in such exposure as this. Life is then seen to be a fire, that now smoulders, now brightens, and may be easily quenched. The weary hours wore away like dim half-forgotten years, so long and eventful they seemed, though we did nothing but suffer. Still the pain was not always of that bitter, intense kind that precludes thought and takes away all capacity for enjoyment. A sort of dreamy stupor came on at times in which we fancied we saw dry, resinous logs suitable for campfires, just as after going days without food men fancy they see bread.

Frozen, blistered, famished, benumbed, our bodies seemed lost to us at times – all dead but the eyes. For the duller and fainter we became the clearer was our vision, though only in momentary glimpses. Then, after the sky cleared, we gazed at the stars, blessed immortals of light, shining with marvelous brightness with long lance rays, near-looking and new-looking, as if never seen before. Again they would look familiar and remind us of stargazing at home. Oftentimes imagination coming into play would present charming pictures of the warm zone below, mingled with others near and far. Then the bitter wind and the drift would break the blissful vision and dreary pains cover us like clouds. 'Are you suffering much?' Jerome would inquire with pitiful faintness. 'Yes,' I would say, striving to keep my voice brave, 'frozen and burned; but never mind, Jerome, the night will wear away at last, and tomorrow we go a-Maying, and what campfires we will make, and what sun-baths we will take!'

The frost grew more and more intense, and we became icy and covered over with a crust of frozen snow, as if we had lain cast away in the drift all winter. In about thirteen hours – every hour like a year – day began to dawn, but it was long ere the summit's rocks were touched by the sun. No clouds were visible from where we lay, yet the morning was dull and blue, and bitterly frosty; and hour after hour passed by while we eagerly watched the pale light stealing down the ridge to the hollow where we lay. But there was not a trace of that warm, flushing sunrise splendor we so long had hoped for.

As the time drew near to make an effort to reach camp, we became concerned to know what strength was left us, and whether or no we could walk; for we had lain flat all this time without once rising to our feet. Mountaineers, however, always find in themselves a reserve of power after great exhaustion. It is a kind of second life, available only in emergencies like this; and, having proved its existence, I had no great fear that either of us would fail, though one of my arms was already benumbed and hung powerless.

At length, after the temperature was somewhat mitigated on this memorable first of May, we arose and began to struggle homeward. Our frozen trousers could scarcely be made to bend at the knee, and we waded the snow with difficulty. The summit ridge was fortunately wind-swept and nearly bare, so we were not compelled to lift our feet high, and on reaching the long home slopes laden with loose snow we made rapid progress, sliding and shuffling and pitching headlong, our feebleness accelerating rather than diminishing our speed. When we had descended some three thousand feet the sunshine warmed our backs and we began to revive. At 10 a.m. we reached the timber and were safe.

Half an hour later we heard Sisson shouting down among the firs, coming with horses to take us to the hotel. After breaking a trail through the snow as far as possible he had tied his animals and walked up. We had been so long without food that we cared but little about eating, but we eagerly drank the coffee he prepared for us. Our feet were frozen, and thawing them was painful, and had to be done very slowly by keeping them buried in soft snow for several hours, which avoided permanent damage. Five thousand feet below the summit we found only three inches of new snow, and at the base of the mountain only a slight shower of rain had fallen, showing how local our storm had been, notwithstanding its terrific fury. Our feet were wrapped in sacking, and we were soon mounted and on our way down into the thick sunshine – 'God's Country', as Sisson calls the Chaparral Zone. In two hours' ride the last snowbank was left behind. Violets appeared along the edges of the trail, and the chaparral was coming into bloom, with young lilies and larkspurs about the open places in rich profusion. How beautiful seemed the golden sunbeams streaming through the woods between the warm brown boles of the cedars and pines! All my friends among the birds and plants seemed like OLD friends, and we felt like speaking to every one of them as we passed, as if we had been a long time away in some far, strange country.

In the afternoon we reached Strawberry Valley and fell asleep. Next morning we seemed to have risen from the dead. My bedroom was flooded with sunshine, and from the window I saw the great white Shasta cone clad in forests and clouds and bearing them loftily in the sky. Everything seemed full and radiant with the freshness and beauty and enthusiasm of youth. Sisson's children came in with flowers and covered my bed, and the storm on the mountaintop banished like a dream.

Chapter 20

AN ASCENT OF MOUNT RAINIER

Ambitious climbers, seeking adventures and opportunities to test their strength and skill, occasionally attempt to penetrate the wilderness on the west side of the Sound, and push on to the summit of Mount Olympus. But the grandest excursion of all to be made hereabouts is to Mount Rainier, to climb to the top of its icy crown. The mountain is very high, 14,400 feet, and laden with glaciers that are terribly roughened and interrupted by crevasses and ice cliffs. Only good climbers should attempt to gain the summit, led by a guide of proved nerve and endurance. A good trail has been cut through the woods to the base of the mountain on the north; but the summit of the mountain never has been reached from this side, though many brave attempts have been made upon it.

Last summer I gained the summit from the south side, in a day and a half from the timberline, without encountering any desperate obstacles that could not in some way be passed in good weather. I was accompanied by Keith, the artist, Professor Ingraham, and five ambitious young climbers from Seattle. We were led by the veteran mountaineer and guide Van Trump, of Yelm, who many years before guided General Stevens in his memorable ascent, and later Mr Bailey, of Oakland. With a cumbersome abundance of campstools and blankets we set out from Seattle, traveling by rail as far as Yelm Prairie, on the Tacoma and Oregon road. Here we made our first camp and arranged with Mr Longmire, a farmer in the neighborhood, for pack and saddle animals. The noble King Mountain was in full view from here, glorifying the bright, sunny day with his presence, rising in godlike majesty over the woods, with the magnificent prairie as a foreground.

The distance to the mountain from Yelm in a straight line is perhaps fifty miles; but by the mule and yellowjacket trail we had to follow it is a hundred miles. For, notwithstanding a portion of this trail runs in the air, where the wasps work hardest, it is far from being an air line as commonly understood.

By night of the third day we reached the Soda Springs on the right bank of the Nisqually, which goes roaring by, gray with mud, gravel, and boulders from the caves of the glaciers of Rainier, now close at hand. The distance from the Soda Springs to the Camp of the Clouds is about ten miles. The first part of the way lies up the Nisqually Canyon, the bottom of which is flat in some places and the walls very high and precipitous, like those of the Yosemite Valley. The upper part of the canyon is still occupied by one of the Nisqually glaciers, from which this branch of the river draws its source, issuing from a cave in the gray, rock-strewn snout. About a mile below the glacier we had to ford the river, which caused some anxiety, for the current is very rapid and carried forward large boulders as well as lighter material, while its savage roar is bewildering.

At this point we left the canyon, climbing out of it by a steep zigzag up the old lateral moraine of the glacier, which was deposited when the present glacier flowed past at this height, and is about eight hundred feet high. It is now covered with a superb growth of *Picea amabilis*; so also is the corresponding portion of the right lateral. From the top of the moraine, still ascending, we passed for a mile or two through a forest of mixed growth, mainly silver fir, Patton spruce, and mountain pine, and then came to the charming park region, at an elevation of about five thousand feet above sea level. Here the vast continuous woods at length begin to give way under the dominion of climate, though still at this height retaining their beauty and giving no sign of stress of storm, sweeping upward in belts of varying width, composed mainly of one species of fir, sharp and spiry in form, leaving smooth, spacious parks, with here and there separate groups of trees standing out in the midst of the openings like islands in a lake. Every one of these parks, great and small, is a garden filled knee-deep with fresh, lovely flowers of every hue, the most luxuriant and the most extravagantly beautiful of all the alpine gardens I ever beheld in all my mountain-top wanderings.

We arrived at the Cloud Camp at noon, but no clouds were in sight, save a few gauzy ornamental wreaths adrift in the sunshine. Out of the forest at last there stood the mountain, wholly unveiled, awful in bulk and majesty, filling all the view like a separate, new-born world, yet withal so fine and so beautiful it might well fire the dullest observer to desperate enthusiasm. Long we gazed in silent admiration, buried in tall daisies and anemones by the side of a snowbank. Higher we could not go with the animals and find food for them and wood for our own campfires, for just beyond this lies the region of ice, with only here and there an open spot on the ridges in the midst of the ice, with dwarf alpine plants, such as saxifrages and drabas, which reach far up between the glaciers, and low mats of the beautiful bryanthus, while back of us were the gardens and abundance of everything that heart could wish. Here we lay all the afternoon, considering the lilies and the lines of the mountains with reference to a way to the summit.

At noon next day we left camp and began our long climb. We were in light marching order, save one who pluckily determined to carry his camera to the summit. At night, after a long easy climb over wide and smooth fields of ice, we reached a narrow ridge, at an elevation of about ten thousand feet above the sea, on the divide between the glaciers of the Nisqually and the Cowlitz. Here we lay as best we could, waiting for another day, without fire of course, as we were now many miles beyond the timberline and without much to cover us. After eating a little hardtack, each of us leveled a spot to lie on among lava-blocks and cinders. The night was cold, and the wind coming down upon us in stormy surges drove gritty ashes and fragments of pumice about our ears while chilling to the bone. Very short and shallow was our sleep that night; but day dawned at last, early rising was easy, and there was nothing about breakfast to cause any delay. About four o'clock we were off, and climbing began in earnest. We followed up the ridge on which we had spent the night, now along its crest, now on either side, or on the ice leaning against it, until we came to where it becomes massive and precipitous. Then we were compelled to crawl along a seam or narrow shelf, on its face, which we traced to its termination in the base of the great ice cap. From this point all the climbing was over ice, which was here desperately steep but fortunately was at the same time carved into innumerable spikes and pillars which afforded good footholds, and we crawled cautiously on, warm with ambition and exercise.

At length, after gaining the upper extreme of our guiding ridge, we found a good place to rest and prepare ourselves to scale the dangerous upper curves of the dome. The surface almost everywhere was bare, hard, snowless ice, extremely slippery; and, though smooth in general, it was interrupted by a network of yawning crevasses, outspread like lines of defense against any attempt to win the summit. Here every one of the party took off his shoes and drove stout steel caulks about half an inch long into them, having brought tools along for the purpose, and not having made use of them until now so that the points might not get dulled on the rocks ere the smooth, dangerous ice was reached. Besides being well shod each carried an alpenstock, and for special difficulties we had a hundred feet of rope and an axe.

Thus prepared, we stepped forth afresh, slowly groping our way through tangled lines of crevasses, crossing on snow bridges here and there after cautiously testing them, jumping at narrow places, or crawling around the ends of the largest, bracing well at every point with our alpenstocks and setting our spiked shoes squarely down on the dangerous slopes. It was nerve-trying work, most of it, but we made good speed nevertheless, and by noon all stood together on the utmost summit, save one who, his strength failing for a time, came up later.

We remained on the summit nearly two hours, looking about us at the vast maplike views, comprehending hundreds of miles of the Cascade Range, with their black interminable forests and white volcanic cones in glorious array reaching far into Oregon; the Sound region also, and the great plains of eastern Washington, hazy and vague in the distance. Clouds began to gather. Soon of all the land only the summits of the mountains, St Helen's, Adams, and Hood, were left in sight, forming islands in the sky. We found two well-formed and well-preserved craters on the summit, lying close together like two plates on a table with their rims touching. The highest point of the mountain is located between the craters, where their edges come in contact. Sulphurous fumes and steam issue from several vents, giving out a sickening smell that can be detected at a considerable distance. The unwasted condition of these craters, and, indeed, to a great extent, of the entire mountain, would tend to show that Rainier is still a comparatively young mountain. With the exception of the projecting lips of the craters and the top of a subordinate summit a short distance to the northward, the mountains is solidly capped with ice all around; and it is this ice cap which forms the grand central fountain whence all the twenty glaciers of Rainier flow, radiating in every direction.

The descent was accomplished without disaster, though several of the party had narrow escapes. One slipped and fell, and as he shot past me seemed to be going to certain death. So steep was the ice slope no one could move to help him, but fortunately, keeping his presence of mind, he threw himself on his face and digging his alpenstock into the ice, gradually retarded his motion until he came to rest. Another broke through a slim bridge over a crevasse, but his momentum at the time carried him against the lower edge and only his alpenstock was lost in the abyss. Thus crippled by the loss of his staff, we had to lower him the rest of the way down the dome by means of the rope we carried. Falling rocks from the upper precipitous part of the ridge were also a source of danger, as they came whizzing past in successive volleys; but none told on us, and when we at length gained the gentle slopes of the lower ice fields, we ran and slid at our ease, making fast, glad time, all care and danger past, and arrived at our beloved Cloud Camp before sundown.

We were rather weak from want of nourishment, and some suffered from sunburn, notwithstanding the partial protection of glasses and veils; otherwise, all were unscathed and well. The view we enjoyed from the summit could hardly be surpassed in sublimity and grandeur; but one feels far from home so high in the sky, so much so that one is inclined to guess that, apart from the acquisition of knowledge and the exhilaration of climbing, more pleasure is to be found at the foot of the mountains than on their tops. Doubly happy, however, is the man to whom lofty mountain tops are within reach, for the lights that shine there illumine all that lies below.

Chapter 24
THE GRAND CANYON OF THE COLORADO

Happy nowadays is the tourist, with earth's wonders, new and old, spread invitingly open before him, and a host of able workers as his slaves making everything easy, padding plush about him, grading roads for him, boring tunnels, moving hills out of his way, eager, like the Devil, to show him all the kingdoms of the world and their glory and foolishness, spiritualizing travel for him with lightning and steam, abolishing space and time and almost everything else. Little children and tender, pulpy people, as well as storm-seasoned explorers, may now go almost everywhere in smooth comfort, cross oceans and deserts scarce accessible to fishes and birds, and, dragged by steel horses, go up high mountains, riding gloriously beneath starry showers of sparks, ascending like Elijah in a whirlwind and chariot of fire.

First of the wonders of the great West to be brought within reach of the tourist were the Yosemite and the Big Trees, on the completion of the first transcontinental railway; next came the Yellowstone and icy Alaska, by the northern roads; and last the Grand Canyon of the Colorado, which, naturally the hardest to reach, has now become, by a branch of the Santa Fe, the most accessible of all.

Of course, with this wonderful extension of steel ways through our wildness there is loss as well as gain. Nearly all railroads are bordered by belts of desolation. The finest wilderness perishes as if stricken with pestilence. Bird and beast people, if not the dryads, are frightened from the groves. Too often the groves also vanish, leaving nothing but ashes. Fortunately, nature has a few big places beyond man's power to spoil – the ocean, the two icy ends of the globe, and the Grand Canyon.

When I first heard of the Santa Fe trains running to the edge of the Grand Canyon of Arizona, I was troubled with thoughts of the disenchantment likely to follow. But last winter, when I saw those trains crawling along through the pines of the Coconino Forest and close up to the brink of the chasm at Bright Angel, I was glad to discover that in the presence of such stupendous scenery they are nothing. The locomotives and trains are mere beetles and caterpillars, and the noise they make is as little disturbing as the hooting of an owl in the lonely woods.

In a dry, hot, monotonous forested plateau, seemingly boundless, you come suddenly and without warning upon the abrupt edge of a gigantic sunken landscape of the wildest, most multitudinous features, and those features, sharp and angular, are made out of flat beds of limestone and sandstone forming a spiry, jagged, gloriously colored mountain range countersunk in a level gray plain. It is a hard job to sketch it even in scrawniest outline; and, try as I may, not in the least sparing myself, I cannot tell the hundredth part of the wonders of its features – the side canyons, gorges, alcoves, cloisters, and amphitheaters of vast sweep and depth, carved in its magnificent walls; the throng of great architectural rocks it contains resembling castles, cathedrals, temples, and palaces, towered and spired and painted, some of them nearly a mile high, yet beneath one's feet. All this, however, is less difficult than to give any idea of the impression of wild, primeval beauty and power one receives in merely gazing from its brink. The view down the gulf of color and over the rim of its wonderful wall, more than any other view I know, leads us to think of our earth as a star with stars swimming in light, every radiant spire pointing the way to the heavens.

But it is impossible to conceive what the canyon is, or what impression it makes, from descriptions or pictures, however good. Naturally it is untellable even to those who have seen something perhaps a little like it on a small scale in this same plateau region. One's most extravagant expectations are indefinitely surpassed, though one expects much from what is said of it as 'the biggest chasm on earth' – 'so big is it that all other big things – Yosemite, the Yellowstone, the Pyramids, Chicago – all would be lost if tumbled into it.' Naturally enough, illustrations as to size are sought for among other canyons like or unlike it, with the common result of worse confounding confusion. The prudent keep silence. It was once said that the 'Grand Canyon could put a dozen Yosemites in its vest pocket.'

The justly famous Grand Canyon of the Yellowstone is, like the Colorado, gorgeously colored and abruptly countersunk in a plateau, and both are mainly the work of water. But the Colorado's canyon is more than a thousand times larger, and as a score or two of new buildings of ordinary size would not appreciably change the general view of a great city, so hundreds of Yellowstones might be eroded in the sides of the Colorado Canyon without noticeably augmenting its size or the richness of its sculpture.

But it is not true that the great Yosemite rocks would be thus lost or hidden. Nothing of their kind in the world, so far as I know, rivals El Capitan and Tissiack, much less dwarfs or in any way belittles them. None of the sandstone or limestone precipices of the canyon that I have seen or heard of approaches in smooth, flawless strength and grandeur the granite face of El Capitan or the Tenaya side of Cloud's Rest. These colossal cliffs, types of permanence, are about three thousand and six thousand feet high; those of the canyon that are sheer are about half as high, and are types of fleeting change; while glorious-domed Tissiack, noblest of mountain buildings, far from being overshadowed or lost in this rosy, spiry canyon company, would draw every eye, and, in serene majesty, 'aboon them a'' she would take her place – castle, temple, palace, or tower. Nevertheless a noted writer, comparing the Grand Canyon in a general way with the glacial Yosemite, says: 'And the Yosemite – ah, the lovely Yosemite! Dumped down into the wilderness of gorges and mountains, it would take a guide who knew of its existence a long time to find it.' This is striking, and shows up well above the levels of commonplace description, but it is confusing, and has the fatal fault of not being true. As well try to describe an eagle by putting a lark in it. 'And the lark – ah, the lovely lark! Dumped down the red, royal gorge of the eagle, it would be hard to find.' Each in its own place is better, singing at heaven's gate, and sailing the sky with the clouds.

Every feature of Nature's big face is beautiful – height and hollow, wrinkle, furrow, and line – and this is the main master-furrow of its kind on our continent, incomparably greater and more impressive than any other yet discovered, or likely to be discovered, now that all the great rivers have been traced to their heads.

The Colorado River rises in the heart of the continent on the dividing ranges and ridges between the two oceans, drains thousands of snowy mountains through narrow or spacious valleys, and thence through canyons of every color, sheer-walled and deep, all of which seem to be represented in this one grand canyon of canyons.

It is very hard to give anything like an adequate conception of its size; much more of its color, its vast wall-sculpture, the wealth of ornate architectural buildings that fill it, or, most of all, the tremendous impression it makes. According to Major Powell, it is about two hundred and seventeen miles long, from five to fifteen miles wide from rim to rim, and from about five thousand to six thousand feet deep. So tremendous a chasm would be one of the world's greatest wonders even if, like ordinary canyons cut in sedimentary rocks, it were empty and its walls were simple. But instead of being plain, the walls are so deeply and elaborately carved into all sorts of recesses – alcoves, cirques, amphitheaters, and side canyons – that, were you to trace the rim closely around on both sides, your journey would be nearly a thousand miles long. Into all these recesses the level, continuous beds of rock in ledges and benches, with their various colors, run like broad ribbons, marvelously beautiful and effective even at a distance of ten or twelve miles. And the vast space these glorious walls inclose, instead of being empty, is crowded with gigantic architectural rock forms gorgeously colored and adorned with towers and spires like works of art.

Looking down from this level plateau, we are more impressed with a feeling of being on the top of everything than when looking from the summit of a mountain. From side to side of the vast gulf, temples, palaces, towers, and spires come soaring up in thick array half a mile or nearly a mile above their sunken, hidden bases, some to a level with our standpoint, but none higher. And in the inspiring morning light all are so fresh and rosy-looking that they seem new-born; as if, like the quick-growing crimson snowplants of the California woods, they had just sprung up, hatched by the warm, brooding, motherly weather.

In trying to describe the great pines and sequoias of the Sierra, I have often thought that if one of these trees could be set by itself in some city park, its grandeur might there be impressively realized; while in its home forests, where all magnitudes are great, the weary, satiated traveler sees none of them truly. It is so with these majestic rock structures.

Though mere residual masses of the plateau, they are dowered with the grandeur and repose of mountains, together with the finely chiseled carving and modeling of man's temples and palaces, and often, to a considerable extent, with their symmetry. Some, closely observed, look like ruins; but even these stand plumb and true, and show architectural forms loaded with lines strictly regular and decorative, and all are arrayed in colors that storms and time seem only to brighten. They are not placed in regular rows in line with the river, but 'a' through ither,' as the Scotch say, in lavish, exuberant crowds, as if nature in wildest extravagance held her bravest structures as common as gravel-piles. Yonder stands a spiry cathedral nearly five thousand feet in height, nobly symmetrical, with sheer buttressed walls and arched doors and windows, as richly finished and decorated with sculptures as the great rock temples of India or Egypt. Beside it rises a huge castle with arched gateway, turrets, watch-towers, ramparts, etc., and to right and left palaces, obelisks, and pyramids fairly fill the gulf, all colossal and all lavishly painted and carved. Here and there a flat-topped structure may be seen, or one imperfectly domed; but the prevailing style is ornate Gothic, with many hints of Egyptian and Indian.

Throughout this vast extent of wild architecture – nature's own capital city – there seem to be no ordinary dwellings. All look like grand and important public structures, except perhaps some of the lower pyramids, broad-based and sharp-pointed, covered with down-flowing talus like loosely set tents with hollow, sagging sides. The roofs often have disintegrated rocks heaped and draggled over them, but in the main the masonry is firm and laid in regular courses, as if done by square and rule.

Nevertheless they are ever changing; their tops are now a dome, now a flat table or a spire, as harder or softer strata are reached in their slow degradation, while the sides, with all their fine moldings, are being steadily undermined and eaten away.

But no essential change in style or color is thus effected. From century to century they stand the same. What seems confusion among the rough earthquake-shaken crags nearest one comes to order as soon as the main plan of the various structures appears. Every building, however complicated and laden with ornamental lines, is at one with itself and every one of its neighbors, for the same characteristic controlling belts of color and solid strata extend with wonderful constancy for very great distances, and pass through and give style to thousands of separate structures, however their smaller characters may vary.

Of all the various kinds of ornamental work displayed – carving, tracery on cliff faces, moldings, arches, pinnacles – none is more admirably effective or charms more than the webs of rain-channeled taluses. Marvelously extensive, without the slightest appearance of waste or excess, they cover roofs and dome tops and the base of every cliff, belt each spire and pyramid and massy, towering temple, and in beautiful continuous lines go sweeping along the great walls in and out around all the intricate system of side canyons, amphitheaters, cirques, and scallops into which they are sculptured. From one point hundreds of miles of the fairy embroidery may be traced. It is all so fine and orderly that it would seem that not only had the clouds and streams been kept harmoniously busy in the making of it, but that every raindrop sent like a bullet to a mark had been the subject of a separate thought, so sure is the outcome of beauty through the stormy centuries. Surely nowhere else are there illustrations so striking of the natural beauty of desolation and death, so many of nature's own mountain buildings wasting in glory of high desert air – going to dust. See how steadfast in beauty they all are in their going. Look again and again how the rough, dusty boulders and sand of disintegration from the upper ledges wreathe in beauty for ashes – as in the flowers of a prairie after fires – but here the very dust and ashes are beautiful.

Gazing across the mighty chasm, we at last discover that it is not its great depth nor length, nor yet these wonderful buildings, that most impresses us. It is its immense width, sharply defined by precipitous walls plunging suddenly down from a flat plain, declaring in terms instantly apprehended that the vast gulf is a gash in the once unbroken plateau, made by slow, orderly erosion and removal of huge beds of rocks. Other valleys of erosion are as great – in all their dimensions some are greater – but none of these produces an effect on the imagination at once so quick and profound, coming without study, given at a glance. Therefore by far the greatest and most influential feature of this view from Bright Angel or any other of the canyon views is the opposite wall. Of the one beneath our feet we see only fragmentary sections in cirques and amphitheaters and on the sides of the out-jutting promontories between them, while the other, though far distant, is beheld in all its glory of color and noble proportions – the one supreme beauty and wonder to which the eye is ever turning. For while charming with its beauty it tells the story of the stupendous erosion of the canyon – the foundation of the unspeakable impression made on everybody. It seems a gigantic statement for even nature to make, all in one mighty stone word, apprehended at once like a burst of light, celestial color its natural vesture, coming in glory to mind and heart as to a home prepared for it from the very beginning. Wildness so godful, cosmic, primeval, bestows a new sense of earth's beauty and size. Not even from high mountains does the world seem so wide, so like a star in glory of light on its way through the heavens.

I have observed scenery-hunters of all sorts getting first views of yosemites, glaciers, White Mountain ranges, etc. Mixed with the enthusiasm which such scenery naturally excites, there is often weak gushing, and many splutter aloud like little waterfalls. Here, for a few moments at least, there is silence, and all are in dead earnest, as if awed and hushed by an earthquake – perhaps until the cook cries 'Breakfast!' or the stable-boy 'Horses are ready!' Then the poor unfortunates, slaves of regular habits, turn quickly away, gasping and muttering as if wondering where they had been and what had enchanted them.

Roads have been made from Bright Angel Hotel through the Coconino Forest to the ends of outstanding promontories, commanding extensive views up and down the canyon. The nearest of them, three or four miles east and west, are O'Neill's Point and Rowe's Point; the latter, besides commanding the eternally interesting canyon, gives wide-sweeping views southeast and west over the dark forest roof to the San Francisco and Mount Trumbull volcanoes – the bluest of mountains over the blackest of level woods.

Instead of thus riding in dust with the crowd, more will be gained by going quietly afoot along the rim at different times of day and night, free to observe the vegetation, the fossils in the rocks, the seams beneath overhanging ledges once inhabited by Indians, and to watch the stupendous scenery in the changing lights and shadows, clouds, showers, and storms. One need not go hunting the so-called 'points of interest.' The verge anywhere, everywhere, is a point of interest beyond one's wildest dreams.

As yet, few of the promontories or throng of mountain buildings in the canyon are named. Nor among such exuberance of forms are names thought of by the bewildered, hurried tourist. He would be as likely to think of names for waves in a storm. The Eastern and Western Cloisters, Hindu Amphitheater, Cape Royal, Powell's Plateau, Grand View Point, Point Sublime, Bissell and Moran Points, the Temple of Set, Vishnu's Temple, Shiva's Temple, Twin Temples, Tower of Babel, Hance's Column – these fairly good names given by Dutton, Holmes, Moran, and others are scattered over a large stretch of the canyon wilderness.

All the canyon rock-beds are lavishly painted, except a few neutral bars and the granite notch at the bottom occupied by the river, which makes but little sign. It is a vast wilderness of rocks in a sea of light, colored and glowing like oak and maple woods in autumn, when the sun-gold is richest. I have just said that it is impossible to learn what the canyon is like from descriptions and pictures. Powell's and Dutton's descriptions present magnificent views not only of the canyon but of all the grand region round about it; and Holmes's drawings, accompanying Dutton's report, are wonderfully good. Surely faithful and loving skill can go no farther in putting the multitudinous decorated forms on paper. But the COLORS, the living rejoicing COLORS, chanting morning and evening in chorus to heaven! Whose brush or pencil, however lovingly inspired, can give us these? And if paint is of no effect, what hope lies in pen-work? Only this: some may be incited by it to go and see for themselves.

No other range of mountainous rock-work of anything like the same extent have I seen that is so strangely, boldly, lavishly colored. The famous Yellowstone Canyon below the falls comes to mind; but, wonderful as it is, and well deserved as is its fame, compared with this it is only a bright rainbow ribbon at the roots of the pines. Each of the series of level, continuous beds of carboniferous rocks of the canyon has, as we have seen, its own characteristic color. The summit limestone beds are pale yellow; next below these are the beautiful rose-colored cross-bedded sandstones; next there are a thousand feet of brilliant red sandstones; and below these the red wall limestones, over two thousand feet thick, rich massy red, the greatest and most influential of the series, and forming the main color-fountain. Between these are many neutral-tinted beds. The prevailing colors are wonderfully deep and clear, changing and blending with varying intensity from hour to hour, day to day, season to season; throbbing, wavering, glowing, responding to every passing cloud or storm, a world of color in itself, now burning in separate rainbow bars streaked and blotched with shade, now glowing in one smooth, all-pervading ethereal radiance like the alpenglow, uniting the rocky world with the heavens.

The dawn, as in all the pure, dry desert country is ineffably beautiful; and when the first level sunbeams sting the domes and spires, with what a burst of power the big, wild days begin! The dead and the living, rocks and hears alike, awake and sing the new-old song of creation. All the massy headlands and salient angles of the walls, and the multitudinous temples and palaces, seem to catch the light at once, and cast thick black shadows athwart hollow and gorge, bringing out details as well as the main massive features of the architecture; while all the rocks, as if wild with life, throb and quiver and glow in the glorious sunburst, rejoicing. Every rock temple then becomes a temple of music; every spire and pinnacle an angel of light and song, shouting color hallelujahs.

As the day draws to a close, shadows, wondrous, black, and thick, like those of the morning, fill up the wall hollows, while the glowing rocks, their rough angles burned off, seem soft and hot to the heart as they stand submerged in purple haze, which now fills the canyon like a sea. Still deeper, richer, more divine grow the great walls and temples, until in the supreme flaming glory of sunset the whole canyon is transfigured, as if all the life and light of centuries of sunshine stored up and condensed in the rocks was now being poured forth as from one glorious fountain, flooding both earth and sky.

Strange to say, in the full white effulgence of the midday hours the bright colors grow dim and terrestrial in common gray haze; and the rocks, after the manner of mountains, seem to crouch and drowse and shrink to less than half their real stature, and have nothing to say to one, as if not at home. But it is fine to see how quickly they come to life and grow radiant and communicative as soon as a band of white clouds come floating by. As if shouting for joy, they seem to spring up to meet them in hearty salutation, eager to touch them and beg their blessings. It is just in the midst of these dull midday hours that the canyon clouds are born.

A good storm cloud full of lightning and rain on its way to its work on a sunny desert day is a glorious object. Across the canyon, opposite the hotel, is a little tributary of the Colorado called Bright Angel Creek. A fountain-cloud still better deserves the name 'Angel of the Desert Wells' – clad in bright plumage, carrying cool shade and living water to countless animals and plants ready to perish, noble in form and gesture, seeming able for anything, pouring life-giving, wonder-working floods from its alabaster fountains, as if some sky-lake had broken. To every gulch and gorge on its favorite ground is given a passionate torrent, roaring, replying to the rejoicing lightning – stones, tons in weight, hurrying away as if frightened, showing something of the way Grand Canyon work is done. Most of the fertile summer clouds of the canyon are of this sort, massive, swelling cumuli, growing rapidly, displaying delicious tones of purple and gray in the hollows of their sun-beaten houses, showering favored areas of the heated landscape, and vanishing in an hour or two. Some, busy and thoughtful-looking, glide with beautiful motion along the middle of the canyon in flocks, turning aside here and there, lingering as if studying the needs of particular spots, exploring side canyons, peering into hollows like birds seeding nest-places, or hovering aloft on outspread wings. They scan all the red wilderness, dispensing their blessings of cool shadows and rain where the need is the greatest, refreshing the rocks, their offspring as well as the vegetation, continuing their sculpture, deepening gorges and sharpening peaks. Sometimes, blending all together, they weave a ceiling from rim to rim, perhaps opening a window here and there for sunshine to stream through, suddenly lighting some palace or temple and making it flare in the rain as if on fire.

Sometimes, as one sits gazing from a high, jutting promontory, the sky all clear, showing not the slightest wisp or penciling, a bright band of cumuli will appear suddenly, coming up the canyon in single file, as if tracing a well-known trail, passing in review, each in turn darting its lances and dropping its shower, making a row of little vertical rivers in the air above the big brown one. Others seem to grow from mere points, and fly high above the canyon, yet following its course for a long time, noiseless, as if hunting, then suddenly darting lightning at unseen marks, and hurrying on. Or they loiter here and there as if idle, like laborers out of work, waiting to be hired.

Half a dozen or more showers may oftentimes be seen falling at once, while far the greater part of the sky is in sunshine, and not a raindrop comes nigh one. These thundershowers from as many separate clouds, looking like wisps of long hair, may vary greatly in effects. The pale, faint streaks are showers that fail to reach the ground, being evaporated on the way down through the dry, thirsty air, like streams in deserts. Many, on the other hand, which in the distance seem insignificant, are really heavy rain, however local; these are the gray wisps well zigzagged with lightning. The darker ones are torrent rain, which on broad, steep slopes of favorable conformation give rise to so-called 'cloudbursts'; and wonderful is the commotion they cause. The gorges and gulches below them, usually dry, break out in loud uproar, with a sudden downrush of muddy, boulder-laden floods. Down they all go in one simultaneous gush, roaring like lions rudely awakened, each of the tawny brood actually kicking up a dust at the first onset.

During the winter months snow falls over all the high plateau, usually to a considerable depth, whitening the rim and the roofs of the canyon buildings. But last winter, when I arrived at Bright Angel in the middle of January, there was no snow in sight, and the ground was dry, greatly to my disappointment, for I had made the trip mainly to see the canyon in its winter garb. Soothingly I was informed that this was an exceptional season, and that the good snow might arrive at any time. After waiting a few days, I gladly hailed a broad-browed cloud coming grandly on from the west in big promising blackness, very unlike the white sailors of the summer skies. Under the lee of a rim-ledge, with another snow-lover, I watched its movements as it took possession of the canyon and all the adjacent region in sight. Trailing its gray fringes over the spiry tops of the great temples and towers, it gradually settled lower, embracing them all with ineffable kindness and gentleness of touch, and fondled the little cedars and pines as they quivered eagerly in the wind like young birds begging their mothers to feed them. The first flakes and crystals began to fly about noon, sweeping straight up the middle of the canyon, and swirling in magnificent eddies along the sides. Gradually the hearty swarms closed their ranks, and all the canyon was lost in gray bloom except a short section of the wall and a few trees beside us, which looked glad with snow in their needles and about their feet as they leaned out over the gulf. Suddenly the storm opened with magical effect to the north over the canyon of Bright Angel Creek, inclosing a sunlit mass of the canyon architecture, spanned by great white concentric arches of cloud like the bows of a silvery aurora. Above these and a little back of them was a series of upboiling purple clouds, and high above all, in the background, a range of noble cumuli towered aloft like snow-laden mountains, their pure pearl bosses flooded with sunshine. The whole noble picture, calmly glowing, was framed in thick gray gloom, which soon closed over it; and the storm went on, opening and closing until night covered all.

Two days later, when we were on a jutting point about eighteen miles east of Bright Angel and one thousand feet higher, we enjoyed another storm of equal glory as to cloud effects, though only a few inches of snow fell. Before the storm began we had a magnificent view of this grander upper part of the canyon and also of the Coconino Forest and the Painted Desert. The march of the clouds with their storm banners flying over this sublime landscape was unspeakable glorious, and so also was the breaking up of the storm next morning – the mingling of silver-capped rock, sunshine, and cloud.

Most tourists make out to be in a hurry even here; therefore their days or hours would be best spent on the promontories nearest the hotel. Yet a surprising number go down the Bright Angel Trail to the brink of the inner gloomy granite gorge overlooking the river. Deep canyons attract like high mountains; the deeper they are, the more surely are we drawn into them. On foot, of course, there is no danger whatever, and, with ordinary precautions, but little on animals. In comfortable tourist faith, unthinking, unfearing, down go men, women, and children on whatever is offered, horse, mule, or burro, as if saying with Jean Paul, 'fear nothing but fear' – not without reason, for these canyon trails down the stairways of the gods are less dangerous than they seem, less dangerous than home stairs. The guides are cautious, and so are the experienced, much-enduring beasts. The scrawniest Rosinantes and wizened-rat mules cling hard to the rocks endwise or sidewise, like lizards or ants. From terrace to terrace, climate to climate, down one creeps in sun and shade, through gorge and gully and grassy ravine, and, after a long scramble on foot, at last beneath the mighty cliffs one comes to the grand, roaring river.

To the mountaineer the depth of the canyon, from five thousand to six thousand feet, will not seem so very wonderful, for he has often explored others that are about as deep. But the most experienced will be awestruck by the vast extent of huge rock monuments of pointed masonry built up in regular courses towering above, beneath, and round about him. By the Bright Angel Trail the last fifteen hundred feet of the descent to the river has to be made afoot down the gorge of Indian Garden Creek. Most of the visitors do not like this part, and are content to stop at the end of the horse trail and look down on the dull-brown flood from the edge of the Indian Garden Plateau. By the new Hance Trail, excepting a few daringly steep spots, you can ride all the way to the river, where there is a good spacious camp-ground in a mesquite grove. This trail, built by brave Hance, begins on the highest part of the rim, eight thousand feet above the sea, a thousand feet higher than the head of Bright Angel Trail, and the descent is a little over six thousand feet, through a wonderful variety of climate and life. Often late in the fall, when frosty winds are blowing and snow is flying at one end of the trail, tender plants are blooming in balmy summer weather at the other. The trip down and up can be made afoot easily in a day. In this way one is free to observe the scenery and vegetation, instead of merely clinging to his animal and watching its steps. But all who have time should go prepared to camp awhile on the riverbank, to rest and learn something about the plants and animals and the mighty flood roaring past. In cool, shady amphitheaters at the head of the trail there are groves of white silver fir and Douglas spruce, with ferns and saxifrages that recall snowy mountains; below these, yellow pine, nut pine, juniper, hop-hornbeam, ash, maple, holly-leaved berberis, cowania, spiraea, dwarf oak, and other small shrubs and trees. In dry gulches and on taluses and sun-beaten crags are sparsely scattered yuccas, cactuses, agave, etc. Where springs gush from the rocks there are willow thickets, grassy flats, and bright, flowery gardens, and in the hottest recesses the delicate abronia, mesquite, woody compositae, and arborescent cactuses.

The most striking and characteristic part of this widely varied vegetation are the cactaceae – strange, leafless, old-fashioned plants with beautiful flowers and fruit, in every way able and admirable. While grimly defending themselves with innumerable barbed spears, they offer both food and drink to man and beast. Their juicy globes and disks and fluted cylindrical columns are almost the only desert wells that never go dry, and they always seem to rejoice the more and grow plumper and juicier the hotter the sunshine and sand. Some are spherical, like rolled-up porcupines, crouching in rock-hollows beneath a mist of gray lances, unmoved by the wildest winds. Others, standing as erect as bushes and trees or tall branchless pillars crowned with magnificent flowers, their prickly armor sparkling, look boldly abroad over the glaring desert, making the strangest forests ever seen or dreamed of. *Cereus giganteus*, the grim chief of the desert tribe, is often thirty or forty feet high in southern Arizona. Several species of tree yuccas in the same desert, laden in early spring with superb white lilies, form forests hardly less wonderful, though here they grow singly or in small lonely groves. The low, almost stemless *Yucca baccata*, with beautiful lily flowers and sweet banana-like fruit, prized by the Indians, is common along the canyon rim, growing on lean, rocky soil beneath mountain mahogany, nut pines, and junipers, beside dense flowery mats of *Spiraea caespitosa* and the beautiful pinnate-leaved *Spiraea millefolia*. The nut pine (*Pinus edulis*) scattered along the upper slopes and roofs of the canyon buildings, is the principal tree of the strange dwarf Coconino Forest. It is a picturesque stub of a pine about twenty-five feet high, usually with dead, lichened limbs thrust through its rounded head, and grows on crags and fissured rock tables, braving heat and frost, snow and drought, and continuing patiently, faithfully fruitful for centuries. Indians and insects and almost every desert bird and beast come to it to be fed.

To civilized people from corn and cattle and wheat-field countries the canyon at first sight seems as uninhabitable as a glacier crevasse, utterly silent and barren. Nevertheless it is the home of the multitude of our fellow-mortals, men as well as animals and plants. Centuries ago it was inhabited by tribes of Indians, who, long before Columbus saw America, built thousands of stone houses in its crags, and large ones, some of them several stories high, with hundreds of rooms, on the mesas of the adjacent regions. Their cliff-dwellings, almost numberless, are still to be seen in the canyon, scattered along both sides from top to bottom and throughout its entire length, built of stone and mortar in seams and fissures like swallows' nests, or on isolated ridges and peaks. The ruins of larger buildings are found on open spots by the river, but most of them aloft on the brink of the wildest, giddiest precipices, sites evidently chosen for safety from enemies, and seemingly accessible only to the birds of the air. Many caves were also used as dwelling-places, as were mere seams on cliff-fronts formed by unequal weathering and with or without outer or side walls; and some of them were covered with colored pictures of animals. The most interesting of these cliff-dwellings had pathetic little ribbon-like strips of garden on narrow terraces, where irrigating water could be carried to them – most romantic of sky-gardens, but eloquent of hard times.

In recesses along the river and on the first plateau flats above its gorge were fields and gardens of considerable size, where irrigating ditches may still be traced. Some of these ancient gardens are still cultivated by Indians, descendants of cliff-dwellers, who raise corn, squashes, melons, potatoes, etc., to reinforce the produce of the many wild food-furnishing plants – nuts, beans, berries, yucca and cactus fruits, grass and sunflower seeds, etc – and the flesh of animals – deer, rabbits, lizards, etc. The canyon Indians I have met here seem to be living much as did their ancestors, though not now driven into rock-dens. They are able, erect men, with commanding eyes, which nothing that they wish to see can escape. They are never in a hurry, have a strikingly measured, deliberate, bearish manner of moving the limbs and turning the head, are capable of enduring weather, thirst, hunger, and over-abundance, and are blessed with stomachs which triumph over everything the wilderness may offer. Evidently their lives are not bitter.

The largest of the canyon animals one is likely to see is the wild sheep, or Rocky Mountain bighorn, a most admirable beast, with limbs that never fail, at home on the most nerve-trying precipices, acquainted with all the springs and passes and broken-down jumpable places in the sheer ribbon cliffs, bounding from crag to crag in easy grace and confidence of strength, his great horns held high above his shoulders, wild red blood beating and hissing through every fiber of him like the wind through a quivering mountain pine.

Deer also are occasionally met in the canyon, making their way to the river when the wells of the plateau are dry. Along the short spring streams beavers are still busy, as is shown by the cottonwood and willow timber they have cut and peeled, found in all the river drift-heaps. In the most barren cliffs and gulches there dwell a multitude of lesser animals, well-dressed, clear-eyed, happy little beasts – wood rats, kangaroo rats, gophers, wood mice, skunks, rabbits, bobcats, and many others, gathering food, or dozing in their sun-warmed dens. Lizards, too, of every kind and color are here enjoying life on the hot cliffs, and making the brightest of them brighter.

Nor is there any lack of feathered people. The golden eagle may be seen, and the osprey, hawks, jays, hummingbirds, the mourning dove, and cheery familiar singers – the black-headed grosbeak, robin, bluebird, Townsend's thrush, and many warblers, sailing the sky and enlivening the rocks and bushes through all the canyon wilderness.

Here at Hance's river camp or a few miles above it brave Powell and his brave men passed their first night in the canyon on the adventurous voyage of discovery thirty-three years ago. They faced a thousand dangers, open or hidden, now in their boats gladly sliding down swift, smooth reaches, now rolled over and over in back-combing surges of rough, roaring cataracts, sucked under in eddies, swimming like beavers, tossed and beaten like castaway drift – stout-hearted, undaunted, doing their work through it all. After a month of this they floated smoothly out of the dark, gloomy, roaring abyss into light and safety two hundred miles below. As the flood rushes past us, heavy-laden with desert mud, we naturally think of its sources, its countless silvery branches outspread on thousands of snowy mountains along the crest of the continent, and the life of them, the beauty of them, their history and romance. Its topmost springs are far north and east in Wyoming and Colorado, on the snowy Wind River, Front, Park, and Sawatch Ranges, dividing the two ocean waters, and the Elk, Wahsatch, Uinta, and innumerable spurs streaked with streams, made famous by early explorers and hunters. It is a river of rivers – the Du Chesne, San Rafael, Yampa, Dolores, Gunnison, Cochetopa, Uncompahgre, Eagle, and Roaring Rivers, the Green and the Grand, and scores of others with branches innumerable, as mad and glad a band as ever sang on mountains, descending in glory of foam and spray from snow-banks and glaciers through their rocky moraine-dammed, beaver-dammed channels. Then, all emerging from dark balsam and pine woods and coming together, they meander through wide, sunny park valleys, and at length enter the great plateau and flow in deep canyons, the beginning of the system culminating in this grand canyon of canyons.

Our warm canyon camp is also a good place to give a thought to the glaciers which still exist at the heads of the highest tributaries. Some of them are of considerable size, especially those on the Wind River and Sawatch ranges in Wyoming and Colorado. They are remnants of a vast system of glaciers which recently covered the upper part of the Colorado basin, sculptured its peaks, ridges, and valleys to their present forms, and extended far out over the plateau region – how far I cannot now say. It appears, therefore, that, however old the main trunk of the Colorado may be, all its widespread upper branches and the landscapes they flow through are new-born, scarce at all changed as yet in any important feature since they first came to light at the close of the Glacial Period.

The so-called Grand Colorado Plateau, of which the Grand Canyon is only one of the well-proportioned features, extends with a breadth of hundreds of miles from the flanks of the Wahsatch and Park Mountains to the south of the San Francisco Peaks. Immediately to the north of the deepest part of the canyon it rises in a series of subordinate plateaus, diversified with green meadows, marshes, bogs, ponds, forests, and grovy park valleys, a favorite Indian hunting ground, inhabited by elk, deer, beaver, etc. But far the greater part of the plateau is good sound desert, rocky, sandy, or fluffy with loose ashes and dust, dissected in some places into a labyrinth of stream-channel chasms like cracks in a dry clay-bed, or the narrow slit crevasses of glaciers – blackened with lava flows, dotted with volcanoes and beautiful buttes, and lined with long continuous escarpments – a vast bed of sediments of an ancient sea-bottom, still nearly as level as when first laid down after being heaved into the sky a mile or two high.

Walking quietly about in the alleys and byways of the Grand Canyon city, we learn something of the way it was made; and all must admire effects so great from means apparently so simple; rain striking light hammer blows or heavier in streams, with many rest Sundays; soft air and light, gentle sappers and miners, toiling forever; the big river sawing the plateau asunder, carrying away the eroded and ground waste, and exposing the edges of the strata to the weather; rain torrents sawing cross-streets and alleys, exposing the strata in the same way in hundreds of sections, the softer, less resisting beds weathering and receding faster, thus undermining the harder beds, which fall, not only in small weathered particles, but in heavy sheer-cleaving masses, assisted down from time to time by kindly earthquakes, rain torrents rushing the fallen material to the river, keeping the wall rocks constantly exposed. Thus the canyon grows wider and deeper. So also do the side canyons and amphitheaters, while secondary gorges and cirques gradually isolate masses of the promontories, forming new buildings, all of which are being weathered and pulled and shaken down while being built, showing destruction and creation as one. We see the proudest temples and palaces in stateliest attitudes, wearing their sheets of detritus as royal robes, shedding off showers of red and yellow stones like trees in autumn shedding their leaves, going to dust like beautiful days to night, proclaiming as with the tongues of angels the natural beauty of death.

Every building is seen to be a remnant of once continuous beds of sediments – sand and slime on the floor of an ancient sea, and filled with the remains of animals – and every particle of the sandstones and limestones of these wonderful structures to be derived from other landscapes, weathered and rolled and ground in the storms and streams of other ages. And when we examine the escarpments, hills, buttes, and other monumental masses of the plateau on either side of the canyon, we discover that an amount of material has been carried off in the general denudation of the region compared with which even that carried away in the making of the Grand Canyon is as nothing. Thus each wonder in sight becomes a window through which other wonders come to view. In no other part of this continent are the wonders of geology, the records of the world's auld lang syne, more widely opened, or displayed in higher piles. The whole canyon is a mine of fossils, in which five thousand feet of horizontal strata are exposed in regular succession over more than a thousand square miles of wall-space, and on the adjacent plateau region there is another series of beds twice as thick, forming a grand geological library – a collection of stone books covering thousands of miles of shelving, tier on tier, conveniently arranged for the student. And with what wonderful scriptures are their pages filled – myriad forms of successive floras and faunas, lavishly illustrated with colored drawings, carrying us back into the midst of the life of a past infinitely remote. And as we go on and on, studying this old, old life in the light of the life beating warmly about us, we enrich and lengthen our own.